KU-740-468

Avizandum Statutes on

Scots Commercial
and Consumer Law
2006–2007

4th edition

Avizandum Statutes on

Scots Commercial and Consumer Law
2006–2007

Fourth edition

Editor

J A Hamilton LLB, LLM
Barrister and Solicitor (Aust)
Professor of law, University of Strathclyde

Avizandum Publishing Ltd
Edinburgh
2006

Published by
Avizandum Publishing Ltd
58 Candlemaker Row
Edinburgh EH1 2QE

First published   2003
2nd edition   2004
3rd edition   2005
4th edition   2006

ISBN 1-904968-16-3
    978-1-904968-16-0

© Avizandum Publishing Ltd 2006

Crown copyright material is reproduced with the permission of the Controller
of HMSO and the Queen's Printer for Scotland.

European material in the work which has been reproduced from EUR-lex, the
official European Communities website, is European Communities copyright.

British Library Cataloguing in Publication Data
A catalogue record for this book is available from the British Library

All rights reserved. No part of this publication may be reproduced, stored in a
retrieval system, or transmitted in any form or by any means, electronic,
mechanical, photocopying, recording or otherwise, without the written
permission of the copyright owner. Applications for the copyright owner's
permission to reproduce any part of this publication should be addressed to the
publisher.

Typeset by AFS Image Setters Ltd, Glasgow
Printed and bound by Bell & Bain Ltd, Glasgow

PREFACE

While there have been other collections of statutes aimed at students of commercial and consumer law, these collections have generally not included those provisions applicable only to Scotland. This is the only volume designed specifically to meet the needs of students studying commercial and consumer law in the Scottish context, either as part of a law degree or as part of other undergraduate programmes offering components in commercial and consumer law.

Inevitably, because of the broad sweep of the concept of 'commercial and consumer law' decisions have had to be made about what materials to include, include in part, or omit altogether. The desire to be as inclusive as possible has had to be balanced against issues of length and cost, bearing in mind that this collection is aimed primarily at undergraduate students. For this reason the decision was taken in the first edition to omit company law, partnership and financial services statutes in favour of a broader range of shorter, but equally important, commercial and consumer legislation which, until now, has been more difficult for students to access readily. However, as the result of feedback, some materials on partnership and on agency were added in the second edition. Again for reasons of length and cost, where European directives have been implemented the directives have not been included, reasoning that the primary focus of most undergraduate courses will be on the implementing legislation.

The most important changes for this edition are the incorporation of amendments made by the Consumer Credit Act 2006 into the Consumer Credit Act 1974. The 2006 Act provides for the regulation of consumer credit and consumer hire agreements; makes provision for the licensing of providers of consumer credit, consumer hire and ancillary credit services; enables debtors to challenge unfair relationships with creditors; and provides for an Ombudsman scheme to hear complaints in relation to businesses licensed under the 1974 Act. It also amends the Bankruptcy (Scotland) Act 1985 as a consequence of the provisions dealing with unfair relationships.

All amendments to legislation appear in square brackets. Where part of a statutory provision has been repealed this is indicated by [. . .]. This edition has been updated to July 2006.

As with the previous editions, the editor and publishers would welcome any feedback on material that users consider should or should not have been included.

August 2006

CONTENTS

PART I
STATUTES

BILLS OF EXCHANGE ACT 1882
(45 & 46 Vict, c 61)

PART I
PRELIMINARY

1   Short title
This Act may be cited as the Bills of Exchange Act, 1882.

2   Interpretation of terms
In this Act, unless the context otherwise requires,—

'Acceptance' means an acceptance completed by delivery or notification.

'Action' includes a counter claim and set off.

'Banker' includes a body of persons whether incorporated or not who carry on the business of banking.

'Bankrupt' includes any person whose estate is vested in a trustee or assignee under the law for the time being in force relating to bankruptcy.

'Bearer' means the person in possession of a bill or note which is payable to bearer.

'Bill' means bill of exchange, and 'note' means promissory note.

'Delivery' means transfer of possession, actual or constructive, from one person to another.

'Holder' means the payee or indorsee of a bill or note who is in possession of it, or the bearer thereof.

'Indorsement' means an indorsement completed by delivery.

'Issue' means the first delivery of a bill or note, complete in form to a person who takes it as a holder.

'Person' includes a body of persons whether incorporated or not.

['Postal operator' has the meaning given by section 125(1) of the Postal Services Act 2000.]

'Value' means valuable consideration.

'Written' includes printed, and 'writing' includes print.

PART II
BILLS OF EXCHANGE

Form and interpretation

3   Bill of exchange defined
(1)   A bill of exchange is an unconditional order in writing, addressed by one person to another, signed by the person giving it, requiring the person to whom it is addressed to pay on demand or at a fixed or determinable future time a sum certain in money to or to the order of a specified person, or to bearer.

(2)   An instrument which does not comply with these conditions, or which orders any act to be done in addition to the payment of money, is not a bill of exchange.

(3)   An order to pay out of a particular fund is not unconditional within the meaning of this section; but an unqualified order to pay, coupled with (a) an indication of a particular fund out of which the drawee is to reimburse himself or a particular account to be debited with the amount, or (b) a statement of the transaction which gives rise to the bill, is unconditional.

(4)   A bill is not invalid by reason—

(a)   That it is not dated;

(b)   That it does not specify the value given, or that any value has been given therefor;

(c)   That it does not specify the place where it is drawn or the place where it is payable.

4   Inland and foreign bills

(1)   An inland bill is a bill which is or on the face of it purports to be (a) both drawn and payable within the British Islands, or (b) drawn within the British Islands upon some person resident therein. Any other bill is a foreign bill.

For the purposes of this Act 'British Islands' means any part of the United Kingdom of Great Britain and Ireland, the islands of Man, Guernsey, Jersey, Alderney, and Sark, and the islands adjacent to any of them being part of the dominions of Her Majesty.

(2)   Unless the contrary appear on the face of the bill the holder may treat it as an inland bill.

5   Effect where different parties to bill are the same person

(1)   A bill may be drawn payable to, or to the order of, the drawer; or it may be drawn payable to, or to the order of, the drawee.

(2)   Where in a bill drawer and drawee are the same person, or where the drawee is a fictitious person or a person not having capacity to contract, the holder may treat the instrument, at his option, either as a bill of exchange or as a promissory note.

6   Address to drawee

(1)   The drawee must be named or otherwise indicated in a bill with reasonable certainty.

(2)   A bill may be addressed to two or more drawees whether they are partners or not, but an order addressed to two drawees in the alternative or to two or more drawees in succession is not a bill of exchange.

7   Certainty required as to payee

(1)   Where a bill is not payable to bearer, the payee must be named or otherwise indicated therein with reasonable certainty.

(2)   A bill may be made payable to two or more payees jointly, or it may be made payable in the alternative to one of two, or one or some of several payees. A bill may also be made payable to the holder of an office for the time being.

(3)   Where the payee is a fictitious or non-existing person the bill may be treated as payable to bearer.

8   What bills are negotiable?

(1)   When a bill contains words prohibiting transfer, or indicating an intention that it should not be transferable, it is valid as between the parties thereto, but is not negotiable.

(2)   A negotiable bill may be payable either to order or to bearer.

(3)   A bill is payable to bearer which is expressed to be so payable, or on which the only or last indorsement is an indorsement in blank.

(4)   A bill is payable to order which is expressed to be so payable, or which is expressed to be payable to a particular person, and does not contain words prohibiting transfer or indicating an intention that it should not be transferable.

(5)   Where a bill, either originally or by indorsement, is expressed to be payable

to the order of a specified person, and not to him or his order, it is nevertheless payable to him or his order at his option.

9   Sum payable
(1)   The sum payable by a bill is a sum certain within the meaning of this Act, although it is required to be paid—
   (a)   With interest.
   (b)   By stated instalments.
   (c)   By stated instalments, with a provision that upon default in payment of any instalment the whole shall become due.
   (d)   According to an indicated rate of exchange or according to a rate of exchange to be ascertained as directed by the bill.
(2)   Where the sum payable is expressed in words and also in figures, and there is a discrepancy between the two, the sum denoted by the words is the amount payable.
(3)   Where a bill is expressed to be payable with interest, unless the instrument otherwise provides, interest runs from the date of the bill, and if the bill is undated from the issue thereof.

10   Bill payable on demand
(1)   A bill is payable on demand—
   (a)   Which is expressed to be payable on demand, or at sight, or on presentation; or
   (b)   In which no time for payment is expressed.
(2)   Where a bill is accepted or indorsed when it is overdue, it shall, as regards the acceptor who so accepts, or any indorser who so indorses it, be deemed a bill payable on demand.

11   Bill payable at a future time
A bill is payable at a determinable future time within the meaning of this Act which is expressed to be payable—
(1)   At a fixed period after date or sight.
(2)   On or at a fixed period after the occurrence of a specified event which is certain to happen, though the time of happening may be uncertain.
An instrument expressed to be payable on a contingency is not a bill, and the happening of the event does not cure the defect.

12   Omission of date in bill payable after date
Where a bill expressed to be payable at a fixed period after date is issued undated, or where the acceptance of a bill payable at a fixed period after sight is undated, any holder may insert therein the true date of issue or acceptance, and the bill shall be payable accordingly.
Provided that (1) where the holder in good faith and by mistake inserts a wrong date, and (2) in every case where a wrong date is inserted, if the bill subsequently comes into the hands of a holder in due course the bill shall not be avoided thereby, but shall operate and be payable as if the date so inserted had been the true date.

13   Ante-dating and post-dating
(1)   Where a bill or an acceptance or any indorsement on a bill is dated, the date shall, unless the contrary be proved, be deemed to be the true date of the drawing, acceptance, or indorsement, as the case may be.
(2)   A bill is not invalid by reason only that it is ante-dated or post-dated, or that it bears date on a Sunday.

14   Computation of time of payment
Where a bill is not payable on demand the day on which it falls due is determined as follows:
   [(1)   The bill is due and payable in all cases on the last day of the time of pay-

ment as fixed by the bill or, if that is a non-business day, on the succeeding business day.]

(2)   Where a bill is payable at a fixed period after date, after sight, or after the happening of a specified event, the time of payment is determined by excluding the day from which the time is to begin to run and by including the day of payment.

(3)   Where a bill is payable at a fixed period after sight, the time begins to run from the date of the acceptance if the bill be accepted, and from the date of noting or protest if the bill be noted or protested for non-acceptance, or for non-delivery.

15   Case of need

The drawer of a bill and any indorser may insert therein the name of a person to whom the holder may resort in case of need, that is to say, in case the bill is dishonoured by non-acceptance or non-payment. Such person is called the referee in case of need. It is in the option of the holder to resort to the referee in case of need or not as he may think fit.

16   Optional stipulations by drawer or indorser

The drawer of a bill, and any indorser, may insert therein an express stipulation—

(1)   Negativing or limiting his own liability to the holder;

(2)   Waiving as regards himself some or all of the holder's duties.

17   Definition and requisites of acceptance

(1)   The acceptance of a bill is the signification by the drawee of his assent to the order of the drawer.

(2)   An acceptance is invalid unless it complies with the following conditions, namely:

(a)   It must be written on the bill and be signed by the drawee. The mere signature of the drawee without additional words is sufficient.

(b)   It must not express that the drawee will perform his promise by any other means than the payment of money.

18   Time for acceptance

A bill may be accepted—

(1)   Before it has been signed by the drawer, or while otherwise incomplete;

(2)   When it is overdue, or after it has been dishonoured by a previous refusal to accept, or by non-payment;

(3)   When a bill payable after sight is dishonoured by non-acceptance, and the drawee subsequently accepts it, the holder, in the absence of any different agreement, is entitled to have the bill accepted as of the date of first presentment to the drawee for acceptance.

19   General and qualified acceptance

(1)   An acceptance is either (a) general, or (b) qualified.

(2)   A general acceptance assents without qualification to the order of the drawer. A qualified acceptance in express terms varies the effect of the bill as drawn.

In particular an acceptance is qualified which is—

(a)   conditional, that is to say, which makes payment by the acceptor dependent on the fulfilment of a condition therein stated;

(b)   partial, that is to say, an acceptance to pay part only of the amount for which the bill is drawn;

(c)   local, that is to say, an acceptance to pay only at a particular specified place;

An acceptance to pay at a particular place is a general acceptance, unless it expressly states that the bill is to be paid there only and not elsewhere:

(d)   qualified as to time;

(e)   the acceptance of some one or more of the drawees, but not of all.

20 Inchoate instruments

(1) Where a simple signature on a blank paper is delivered by the signer in order that it may be converted into a bill, it operates as a prima facie authority to fill it up as a complete bill for any amount [. . .] using the signature for that of the drawer, or the acceptor, or an indorser; and, in like manner, when a bill is wanting in any material particular, the person in possession of it has a prima facie authority to fill up the omission in any way he thinks fit.

(2) In order that any such instrument when completed may be enforceable against any person who became a party thereto prior to its completion, it must be filled up within a reasonable time, and strictly in accordance with the authority given. Reasonable time for this purpose is a question of fact.

Provided that if any such instrument after completion is negotiated to a holder in due course it shall be valid and effectual for all purposes in his hands and he may enforce it as if it had been filled up within a reasonable time and strictly in accordance with the authority given.

21 Delivery

(1) Every contract on a bill, whether it be the drawer's, the acceptor's, or an indorser's is incomplete and revocable, until delivery of the instrument in order to give effect thereto.

Provided that where an acceptance is written on a bill, and the drawee gives notice to or according to the directions of the person entitled to the bill that he has accepted it, the acceptance then becomes complete and irrevocable.

(2) As between immediate parties, and as regards a remote party other than a holder in due course, the delivery—

(a) in order to be effectual must be made either by or under the authority of the party drawing, accepting, or indorsing, as the case may be:

(b) may be shown to have been conditional or for a special purpose only, and not for the purpose of transferring the property in the bill.

But if the bill be in the hands of a holder in due course a valid delivery of the bill by all parties prior to him so as to make them liable to him is conclusively presumed.

(3) Where a bill is no longer in the possession of a party who has signed it as drawer, acceptor, or indorser, a valid and unconditional delivery by him is presumed until the contrary is proved.

Capacity and authority of parties

22 Capacity of parties

(1) Capacity to incur liability as a party to a bill is co-extensive with capacity to contract.

Provided that nothing in this section shall enable a corporation to make itself liable as drawer, acceptor, or indorser of a bill unless it is competent to do so under the law for the time being in force relating to corporations.

(2) Where a bill is drawn or indorsed by an infant, minor, or corporation having no capacity or power to incur liability on a bill, the drawing or indorsement entitles the holder to receive payment of the bill, and to enforce it against any other party thereto.

23 Signature essential to liability

No person is liable as drawer, indorser, or acceptor of a bill who has not signed it as such: Provided that

(1) Where a person signs a bill in a trade or assumed name, he is liable thereon as if he had signed it in his own name:

(2) The signature of the name of a firm is equivalent to the signature by the person so signing of the names of all persons liable as partners in that firm.

24 Forged or unauthorised signature

Subject to the provisions of this Act, where a signature on a bill is forged or placed thereon without the authority of the person whose signature it purports to be, the forged or unauthorised signature is wholly inoperative, and no right to retain the bill or to give a discharge therefor or to enforce payment thereof against any party thereto can be acquired through or under that signature, unless the party against whom it is sought to retain or enforce payment of the bill is precluded from setting up the forgery or want of authority.

Provided that nothing in this section shall affect the ratification of an unauthorised signature not amounting to a forgery.

25 Procuration signatures

A signature by procuration operates as notice that the agent has but a limited authority to sign, and the principal is only bound by such signature if the agent in so signing was acting within the actual limits of his authority.

26 Person signing as agent or in representative capacity

(1)   Where a person signs a bill as drawer, indorser, or acceptor, and adds words to his signature, indicating that he signs for or on behalf of a principal, or in a representative character, he is not personally liable thereon; but the mere addition to his signature of words describing him as an agent, or as filling a representative character, does not exempt him from personal liability.

(2)   In determining whether a signature on a bill is that of the principal or that of the agent by whose hand it is written, the construction most favourable to the validity of the instrument shall be adopted.

The consideration for a bill

27 Value and holder for value

(1)   Valuable consideration for a bill may be constituted by,—
  (a)   Any consideration sufficient to support a simple contract;
  (b)   An antecedent debt or liability. Such a debt or liability is deemed valuable consideration whether the bill is payable on demand or at a future time.

(2)   Where value has at any time been given for a bill the holder is deemed to be a holder for value as regards the acceptor and all parties to the bill who became parties prior to such time.

(3)   Where the holder of a bill has a lien on it, arising either from contract or by implication of law, he is deemed to be a holder for value to the extent of the sum for which he has a lien.

28 Accommodation bill or party

(1)   An accommodation party to a bill is a person who has signed a bill as drawer, acceptor, or indorser, without receiving value therefor, and for the purpose of lending his name to some other person.

(2)   An accommodation party is liable on the bill to a holder for value; and it is immaterial whether, when such holder took the bill, he knew such party to be an accommodation party or not.

29 Holder in due course

(1)   A holder in due course is a holder who has taken a bill, complete and regular on the face of it, under the following conditions, namely,
  (a)   That he became the holder of it before it was overdue, and without notice that it had been previously dishonoured, if such was the fact;
  (b)   That he took the bill in good faith and for value, and that at the time the bill was negotiated to him he had no notice of any defect in the title of the person who negotiated it.

(2)   In particular the title of a person who negotiates a bill is defective within

the meaning of this Act when he obtained the bill, or the acceptance thereof, by fraud, duress or force and fear, or other unlawful means, or for an illegal consideration, or when he negotiates it in breach of faith, or under such circumstances as amount to a fraud.

(3) A holder (whether for value or not), who derives his title to a bill through a holder in due course, and who is not himself a party to any fraud or illegality affecting it, has all the rights of that holder in due course as regards the acceptor and all parties to the bill prior to that holder.

30 Presumption of value and good faith

(1) Every party whose signature appears on a bill is prima facie deemed to have become a party thereto for value.

(2) Every holder of a bill is prima facie deemed to be a holder in due course; but if in an action on a bill it is admitted or proved that the acceptance, issue, or subsequent negotiation of the bill is affected with fraud, duress, or force and fear, or illegality, the burden of proof is shifted, unless and until the holder proves that, subsequent to the alleged fraud or illegality, value has in good faith been given for the bill.

Negotiation of bills

31 Negotiation of bill

(1) A bill is negotiated when it is transferred from one person to another in such a manner as to constitute the transferee the holder of the bill.

(2) A bill payable to bearer is negotiated by delivery.

(3) A bill payable to order is negotiated by the indorsement of the holder completed by delivery.

(4) Where the holder of a bill payable to his order transfers it for value without indorsing it, the transfer gives the transferee such title as the transferor had in the bill, and the transferee in addition acquires the right to have the indorsement of the transferor.

(5) Where any person is under obligation to indorse a bill in a representative capacity, he may indorse a bill in such terms as to negative personal liability.

32 Requisites of a valid indorsement

An indorsement in order to operate as a negotiation must comply with the following conditions, namely:—

(1) It must be written on the bill itself and signed by the indorser. The simple signature of the indorser on the bill, without additional words, is sufficient.

An indorsement written on an allonge, or a 'copy' of a bill issued or negotiated in a country where 'copies' are recognised, is deemed to have been written on the bill itself.

(2) It must be an indorsement of the entire bill. A partial indorsement, that is to say, an indorsement which purports to transfer to the indorsee a part only of the amount payable, or which purports to transfer the bill to two or more indorsees severally, does not operate as a negotiation of the bill.

(3) Where a bill is payable to the order of two or more payees or indorsees who are not partners all must indorse, unless the one indorsing has authority to indorse for the others.

(4) Where, in a bill payable to order, the payee or indorsee is wrongly designated, or his name is mis-spelt, he may indorse the bill as therein described, adding, if he think fit, his proper signature.

(5) Where there are two or more indorsements on a bill, each indorsement is deemed to have been made in the order in which it appears on the bill, until the contrary is proved.

(6) An indorsement may be made in blank or special. It may also contain terms making it restrictive.

33   Conditional indorsement

Where a bill purports to be indorsed conditionally the condition may be disregarded by the payer, and payment to the indorsee is valid whether the condition has been fulfilled or not.

34   Indorsement in blank and special indorsement

(1)   An indorsement in blank specifies no indorsee, and a bill so indorsed becomes payable to bearer.

(2)   A special indorsement specifies the person to whom, or to whose order, the bill is to be payable.

(3)   The provisions of this Act relating to a payee apply with the necessary modifications to an indorsee under a special indorsement.

(4)   When a bill has been indorsed in blank, any holder may convert the blank indorsement into a special indorsement by writing above the indorser's signature a direction to pay the bill to or to the order of himself or some other person.

35   Restrictive indorsement

(1)   An indorsement is restrictive which prohibits the further negotiation of the bill or which expresses that it is a mere authority to deal with the bill as thereby directed and not a transfer of ownership thereof, as, for example, if a bill be indorsed 'Pay D. only', or 'Pay D. for the account of X.,' or 'Pay D. or order for collection.'

(2)   A restrictive indorsement gives the indorsee the right to receive payment of the bill and to sue any party thereto that his indorser could have sued, but gives him no power to transfer his rights as indorsee unless it expressly authorises him to do so.

(3)   Where a restrictive indorsement authorises further transfer, all subsequent indorsees take the bill with the same rights and subject to the same liabilities as the first indorsee under the restrictive indorsement.

36   Negotiation of overdue or dishonoured bills

(1)   Where a bill is negotiable in its origin it continues to be negotiable until it has been (a) restrictively indorsed or (b) discharged by payment or otherwise.

(2)   Where an overdue bill is negotiated, it can only be negotiated subject to any defect of title affecting it at its maturity, and thenceforward no person who takes it can acquire or give a better title than that which the person from whom he took it had.

(3)   A bill payable on demand is deemed to be overdue within the meaning and for the purposes of this section, when it appears on the face of it to have been in circulation for an unreasonable length of time. What is an unreasonable length of time for this purpose is a question of fact.

(4)   Except where an indorsement bears date after the maturity of the bill, every negotiation is prima facie deemed to have been effected before the bill was overdue.

(5)   Where a bill which is not overdue has been dishonoured any person who takes it with notice of the dishonour takes it subject to any defect of title attaching thereto at the time of dishonour, but nothing in this sub-section shall affect the rights of a holder in due course.

37   Negotiation of bill to party already liable thereon

Where a bill is negotiated back to the drawer, or to a prior indorser or to the acceptor, such party may, subject to the provisions of this Act, reissue and further negotiate the bill, but he is not entitled to enforce payment of the bill against any intervening party to whom he was previously liable.

38   Rights of the holder

The rights and powers of the holder of a bill are as follows:

(1)   He may sue on the bill in his own name:

(2)   Where he is a holder in due course, he holds the bill free from any defect of title of prior parties, as well as from mere personal defences available to prior parties among themselves, and may enforce payment against all parties liable on the bill:

(3)   Where his title is defective (a) if he negotiates the bill to a holder in due course, that holder obtains a good and complete title to the bill, and (b) if he obtains payment of the bill the person who pays him in due course gets a valid discharge for the bill.

General duties of the holder

39   When presentment for acceptance is necessary

(1)   Where a bill is payable after sight, presentment for acceptance is necessary in order to fix the maturity of the instrument.

(2)   Where a bill expressly stipulates that it shall be presented for acceptance, or where a bill is drawn payable elsewhere than at the residence or place of business of the drawee, it must be presented for acceptance before it can be presented for payment.

(3)   In no other case is presentment for acceptance necessary in order to render liable any party to the bill.

(4)   Where the holder of a bill, drawn payable elsewhere than at the place of business or residence of the drawee, has not time, with the exercise of reasonable diligence, to present the bill for acceptance before presenting it for payment on the day that it falls due, the delay caused by presenting the bill for acceptance before presenting it for payment is excused, and does not discharge the drawer and the indorsers.

40   Time for presenting bill payable after sight

(1)   Subject to the provisions of this Act, when a bill payable after sight is negotiated, the holder must either present it for acceptance or negotiate it within a reasonable time.

(2)   If he do not do so, the drawer and all indorsers prior to that holder are discharged.

(3)   In determining what is a reasonable time within the meaning of this section, regard shall be had to the nature of the bill, the usage of trade with respect to similar bills, and the facts of the particular case.

41   Rules as to presentment for acceptance and excuses for non-presentment

(1)   A bill is duly presented for acceptance which is presented in accordance with the following rules:

(a)   The presentment must be made by or on behalf of the holder to the drawee or to some person authorised to accept or refuse acceptance on his behalf at a reasonable hour on a business day and before the bill is overdue:

(b)   Where a bill is addressed to two or more drawees, who are not partners, presentment must be made to them all, unless one has authority to accept for them all, then presentment must be made to him only:

(c)   Where the drawee is dead, presentment may be made to his personal representative:

(d)   Where the drawee is bankrupt, presentment may be made to him or to his trustee:

(e)   Where authorised by agreement or usage, a presentment through [a postal operator] is sufficient.

(2)   Presentment in accordance with these rules is excused, and a bill may be treated as dishonoured by non-acceptance—

(a)   Where the drawee is dead or bankrupt, or is a fictitious person or a person not having capacity to contract by bill:

(b)   Where, after the exercise of reasonable diligence, such presentment cannot be effected:

(c)   Where although the presentment has been irregular, acceptance has been refused on some other ground.

(3)   The fact that the holder has reason to believe that the bill, on presentment, will be dishonoured does not excuse presentment.

42   Non-acceptance

(1)   When a bill is duly presented for acceptance and is not accepted within the customary time, the person presenting it must treat it as dishonoured by non-acceptance. If he does not, the holder shall lose his right of recourse against the drawer and indorsers.

43   Dishonour by non-acceptance and its consequences

(1)   A bill is dishonoured by non-acceptance—

(a)   when it is duly presented for acceptance, and such an acceptance as is prescribed by this Act is refused or cannot be obtained; or

(b)   when presentment for acceptance is excused and the bill is not accepted.

(2)   Subject to the provisions of this Act when a bill is dishonoured by non-acceptance an immediate right of recourse against the drawer and indorsers accrues to the holder, and no presentment for payment is necessary.

44   Duties as to qualified acceptances

(1)   The holder of a bill may refuse to take a qualified acceptance, and if he does not obtain an unqualified acceptance may treat the bill as dishonoured by non-acceptance.

(2)   Where a qualified acceptance is taken, and the drawer or an indorser has not expressly or impliedly authorised the holder to take a qualified acceptance, or does not subsequently assent thereto, such drawer or indorser is discharged from his liability on the bill.

The provisions of this sub-section do not apply to a partial acceptance, whereof due notice has been given. Where a foreign bill has been accepted as to part, it must be protested as to the balance.

(3)   When the drawer or indorser of a bill receives notice of a qualified acceptance, and does not within a reasonable time express his dissent to the holder he shall be deemed to have assented thereto.

45   Rules as to presentment for payment

Subject to the provisions of this Act a bill must be duly presented for payment. If it be not so presented the drawer and indorsers shall be discharged.

A bill is duly presented for payment which is presented in accordance with the following rules:—

(1)   Where the bill is not payable on demand, presentment must be made on the day it falls due.

(2)   Where the bill is payable on demand then, subject to the provisions of this Act, presentment must be made within a reasonable time after its issue in order to render the drawer liable, and within a reasonable time after the indorsement, in order to render the indorser liable.

In determining what is a reasonable time, regard shall be had to the nature of the bill, the usage of trade with regard to similar bills, and the facts of the particular case.

(3)   Presentment must be made by the holder or by some person authorised to receive payment on his behalf at a reasonable hour on a business day, at the proper place as hereinafter defined, either to the person designated by the bill as payer, or to some person authorised to pay or refuse payment on his behalf if with the exercise of reasonable diligence such person can there be found.

(4)   A bill is presented at the proper place:—

(a)   Where a place of payment is specified in the bill and the bill is there presented.

(b)   Where no place of payment is specified, but the address of the drawee or acceptor is given in the bill, and the bill is there presented.

(c)   Where no place of payment is specified and no address given, and the bill is presented at the drawee's or acceptor's place of business if known, and if not, at his ordinary residence if known.

(d)   In any other case if presented to the drawer or acceptor wherever he can be found, or if presented at his last known place of business or residence.

(5)   Where a bill is presented at the proper place, and after the exercise of reasonable diligence no person authorised to pay or refuse payment can be found there, no further presentment to the drawee or acceptor is required.

(6)   Where a bill is drawn upon, or accepted by two or more persons who are not partners, and no place of payment is specified, presentment must be made to them all.

(7)   Where the drawee or acceptor of a bill is dead, and no place of payment is specified, presentment must be made to a personal representative, if such there be, and with the exercise of reasonable diligence he can be found.

(8)   Where authorised by agreement or usage a presentment through [a postal operator] is sufficient.

46   Excuses for delay or non-presentment for payment

(1)   Delay in making presentment for payment is excused when the delay is caused by circumstances beyond the control of the holder, and not imputable to his default, misconduct, or negligence. When the cause of delay ceases to operate presentment must be made with reasonable diligence.

(2)   Presentment for payment is dispensed with,—

(a)   Where, after the exercise of reasonable diligence presentment, as required by this Act, cannot be effected.

The fact that the holder has reason to believe that the bill will, on presentment, be dishonoured, does not dispense with the necessity for presentment.

(b)   Where the drawee is a fictitious person.

(c)   As regards the drawer where the drawee or acceptor is not bound, as between himself and the drawee, to accept or pay the bill, and the drawer has no reason to believe that the bill would be paid if presented.

(d)   As regards an indorser, where the bill was accepted or made for the accommodation of the indorser, and he has no reason to expect that the bill would be paid if presented.

(e)   By waiver of presentment, express or implied.

47   Dishonour by non-payment

(1)   A bill is dishonoured by non-payment (a) when it is duly presented for payment and payment is refused or cannot be obtained, or (b) when presentment is excused and the bill is overdue and unpaid.

(2)   Subject to the provisions of this Act, when a bill is dishonoured by non-payment, an immediate right of recourse against the drawer and indorsers accrues to the holder.

48   Notice of dishonour and effect of non-notice

Subject to the provisions of this Act, when a bill has been dishonoured by non-acceptance or by non-payment, notice of dishonour must be given to the drawer and each indorser, and any drawer or indorser to whom such notice is not given is discharged; Provided that—

(1)   Where a bill is dishonoured by non-acceptance, and notice of dishonour is not given, the rights of the holder in due course subsequent to the omission, shall not be prejudiced by the omission.

(2)   Where a bill is dishonoured by non-acceptance and due notice of dishonour

is given, it shall not be necessary to give notice of a subsequent dishonour by non-payment unless the bill shall in the meantime have been accepted.

49   Rules as to notice of dishonour
Notice of dishonour in order to be valid and effectual must be given in accordance with the following rules:—

(1)   The notice must be given by or on behalf of the holder, or by or on behalf of an indorser who, at the time of giving it, is himself liable on the bill.

(2)   Notice of dishonour may be given by an agent either in his own name, or in the name of any party entitled to give notice whether that party be his principal or not.

(3)   Where the notice is given by or on behalf of the holder, it enures for the benefit of all subsequent holders and all prior indorsers who have a right of recourse against the party to whom it is given.

(4)   Where notice is given by or on behalf of an indorser entitled to give notice as herein-before provided, it enures for the benefit of the holder and all indorsers subsequent to the party to whom notice is given.

(5)   The notice may be given in writing or by personal communication, and may be given in any terms which sufficiently identify the bill, and intimate that the bill has been dishonoured by non-acceptance or non-payment.

(6)   The return of a dishonoured bill to the drawer or an indorser is, in point of form, deemed a sufficient notice of dishonour.

(7)   A written notice need not be signed, and an insufficient written notice may be supplemented and validated by verbal communication. A misdescription of the bill shall not vitiate the notice unless the party to whom the notice is given is in fact misled thereby.

(8)   Where notice of dishonour is required to be given to any person, it may be given either to the party himself, or to his agent in that behalf.

(9)   Where the drawer or indorser is dead, and the party giving notice knows it, the notice must be given to a personal representative if such there be, and with the exercise of reasonable diligence he can be found.

(10)   Where the drawer or indorser is bankrupt, notice may be given either to the party himself or to the trustee.

(11)   Where there are two or more drawers or indorsers who are not partners, notice must be given to each of them, unless one of them has authority to receive such notice for the others.

(12)   The notice may be given as soon as the bill is dishonoured and must be given within a reasonable time thereafter.

In the absence of special circumstances notice is not deemed to have been given within a reasonable time, unless—

(a)   where the person giving and the person to receive notice reside in the same place, the notice is given or sent off in time to reach the latter on the day after the dishonour of the bill.

(b)   where the person giving and the person to receive notice reside in different places, the notice is sent off on the day after the dishonour of the bill, if there be a post at a convenient hour on that day, and if there be no such post on that day then by the next post thereafter.

(13)   Where a bill when dishonoured is in the hands of an agent, he may either himself give notice to the parties liable on the bill, or he may give notice to his principal. If he gives notice to his principal, he must do so within the same time as if he were the holder, and the principal upon receipt of such notice has himself the same time for giving notice as if the agent had been an independent holder.

(14)   Where a party to a bill receives due notice of dishonour, he has after the receipt of such notice the same period of time for giving notice to antecedent parties that the holder has after the dishonour.

(15)   Where a notice of dishonour is duly addressed and posted, the sender is

deemed to have given due notice of dishonour, notwithstanding any miscarriage by the [postal operator concerned].

50 Excuses for non-notice and delay

(1)   Delay in giving notice of dishonour is excused where the delay is caused by circumstances beyond the control of the party giving notice, and not imputable to his default, misconduct, or negligence. When the cause of delay ceases to operate the notice must be given with reasonable diligence.

(2)   Notice of dishonour is dispensed with—

(a)   When, after the exercise of reasonable diligence, notice as required by this Act cannot be given to or does not reach the drawer or indorser sought to be charged:

(b)   By waiver express or implied. Notice of dishonour may be waived before the time of giving notice has arrived, or after the omission to give due notice:

(c)   As regards the drawer in the following cases, namely, (1) where drawer and drawee are the same person, (2) where the drawee is a fictitious person or a person not having capacity to contract, (3) where the drawer is the person to whom the bill is presented for payment, (4) where the drawee or acceptor is as between himself and the drawer under no obligation to accept or pay the bill, (5) where the drawer has countermanded payment:

(d)   As regards the indorser in the following cases, namely, (1) where the drawee is a fictitious person or a person not having the capacity to contract and the indorser was aware of the fact at the time he indorsed the bill, (2) where the indorser is the person to whom the bill is presented for payment, (3) where the bill was accepted or made for his accommodation.

51 Noting or protest of bill

(1)   Where an inland bill has been dishonoured it may, if the holder think fit, be noted for non-acceptance or non-payment, as the case may be; but it shall not be necessary to note or protest any such bill in order to preserve the recourse against the drawer or indorser.

(2)   Where a foreign bill, appearing on the face of it to be such, has been dishonoured by non-acceptance it must be duly protested for non-acceptance and where such a bill, which has not been previously dishonoured by non-acceptance, is dishonoured by non-payment it must be duly protested for non-payment. If it be not so protested the drawer and indorsers are discharged. Where a bill does not appear on the face of it to be a foreign bill, protest thereof in the case of dishonour is unnecessary.

(3)   A bill which has been protested for non-acceptance may be subsequently protested for non-payment.

(4)   Subject to the provisions of this Act, when a bill is noted or protested, [it may be noted on the day of its dishonour and must be noted not later than the next succeeding business day]. When a bill has been duly noted, the protest may be subsequently extended as of the date of the noting.

(5)   Where the acceptor of the bill becomes bankrupt or insolvent or suspends payment before it matures, the holder may cause the bill to be protested for better security against the drawer and indorsers.

(6)   A bill must be protested at the place where it is dishonoured: Provided that—

(a)   When a bill is presented through [a postal operator], and returned by post dishonoured, it may be protested at the place to which it is returned and on the day of its return if received during business hours, and if not received during business hours, then not later than the next business day:

(b)   When a bill drawn payable at the place of business or residence of some person other than the drawee, has been dishonoured by non-acceptance, it must be protested for non-payment at the place where it is expressed to be payable, and no further presentment for payment to, or demand on, the drawee is necessary.

(7)   A protest must contain a copy of the bill, and must be signed by the notary making it, and must specify—

(a)   The person at whose request the bill is protested:

(b)   The place and date of protest, the cause or reason for protesting the bill, the demand made, and the answer given, if any, or the fact that the drawee or acceptor could not be found.

(8)   Where a bill is lost or destroyed, or is wrongly detained from the person entitled to hold it, protest may be made on a copy or written particulars thereof.

(9)   Protest is dispensed with by any circumstance which would dispense with notice of dishonour. Delay in noting or protesting is excused when the delay is caused by circumstances beyond the control of the holder, and not imputable to his default, misconduct, or negligence. When the cause of delay ceases to operate the bill must be noted or protested with reasonable diligence.

52   Duties of holder as regards drawee or acceptor

(1)   When a bill is accepted generally presentment for payment is not necessary in order to render the acceptor liable.

(2)   When by the terms of a qualified acceptance presentment for payment is required, the acceptor, in the absence of an express stipulation to that effect, is not discharged by the omission to present the bill for payment on the day that it matures.

(3)   In order to render the acceptor of a bill liable it is not necessary to protest it, or that notice of dishonour should be given to him.

(4)   Where the holder of a bill presents it for payment, he shall exhibit the bill to the person from whom he demands payment, and when a bill is paid the holder shall forthwith deliver it up to the party paying it.

Liabilities of parties

53   Funds in hands of drawee

(1)   [*Does not apply to Scotland.*]

(2)   In Scotland, where the drawee of a bill has in his hands funds available for the payment thereof, the bill operates as an assignment of the sum for which it is drawn in favour of the holder, from the time when the bill is presented to the drawee.

54   Liability of acceptor

The acceptor of a bill, by accepting it—

(1)   Engages that he will pay it according to the tenour of his acceptance:

(2)   Is precluded from denying to a holder in due course:

(a)   The existence of the drawer, the genuineness of his signature, and his capacity and authority to draw the bill;

(b)   In the case of a bill payable to drawer's order, the then capacity of the drawer to indorse, but not the genuineness or validity of his indorsement;

(c)   In the case of a bill payable to the order of a third person, the existence of the payee and his then capacity to indorse, but not the genuineness or validity of his indorsement.

55   Liability of drawer or indorser

(1)   The drawer of a bill by drawing it—

(a)   Engages that on due presentment it shall be accepted and paid according to its tenour, and that if it be dishonoured he will compensate the holder or any indorser who is compelled to pay it, provided that the requisite proceedings on dishonour be duly taken;

(b)   Is precluded from denying to a holder in due course the existence of the payee and his then capacity to indorse.

(2)   The indorser of a bill by indorsing it—

(a)   Engages that on due presentment it shall be accepted and paid according to its tenour, and that if it be dishonoured he will compensate the holder or a subsequent indorser who is compelled to pay it, provided that the requisite proceedings on dishonour be duly taken;

(b)   Is precluded from denying to a holder in due course the genuineness and regularity in all respects of the drawer's signature and all previous indorsements;

(c)   Is precluded from denying to his immediate or a subsequent indorsee that the bill was at the time of his indorsement a valid and subsisting bill, and that he had then a good title thereto.

56   Stranger signing bill liable as indorser

Where a person signs a bill otherwise than as drawer or acceptor, he thereby incurs the liabilities of an indorser to a holder in due course.

57   Measure of damages against parties to dishonoured bill

Where a bill is dishonoured, the measure of damages, which shall be deemed to be liquidated damages, shall be as follows:

(1)   The holder may recover from any party liable on the bill, and the drawer who has been compelled to pay the bill may recover from the acceptor, and an indorser who has been compelled to pay the bill may recover from the acceptor or from the drawer, or from a prior indorser—

(a)   The amount of the bill:

(b)   Interest thereon from the time of presentment for payment if the bill is payable on demand, and from the maturity of the bill in any other case:

(c)   The expenses of noting, or, when protest is necessary, and the protest has been extended, the expenses of protest.

[. . .]

(3)   Where by this Act interest may be recovered as damages, such interest may, if justice require it, be withheld wholly or in part, and where a bill is expressed to be payable with interest at a given rate, interest as damages may or may not be given at the same rate as interest proper.

58   Transferor by delivery and transferee

(1)   Where the holder of a bill payable to bearer negotiates it by delivery without indorsing it, he is called a 'transferor by delivery'.

(2)   A transferor by delivery is not liable on the instrument.

(3)   A transferor by delivery who negotiates a bill thereby warrants to his immediate transferee being a holder for value that the bill is what it purports to be, that he has a right to transfer it, and that at the time of the transfer he is not aware of any fact which renders it valueless.

Discharge of bill

59   Payment in due course

(1)   A bill is discharged by payment in due course by or on behalf of the drawee or acceptor.

'Payment in due course' means payment made at or after the maturity of the bill to the holder thereof in good faith and without notice that his title to the bill is defective.

(2)   Subject to the provisions herein-after contained, when a bill is paid by the drawer or an indorser it is not discharged; but

(a)   Where a bill payable to, or to the order of, a third party is paid by the drawer, the drawer may enforce payment thereof against the acceptor, but may not re-issue the bill.

(b)   Where a bill is paid by an indorser, or where a bill payable to drawer's order is paid by the drawer, the party paying it is remitted to his former rights as regards the acceptor or antecedent parties, and he may, if he thinks fit, strike out his own and subsequent indorsements, and again negotiate the bill.

(3)   Where an accommodation bill is paid in due course by the party accommodated the bill is discharged.

60   Banker paying demand draft whereon indorsement is forged

When a bill payable to order on demand is drawn on a banker, and the banker on whom it is drawn pays the bill in good faith and in the ordinary course of business, it is not incumbent on the banker to show that the indorsement of the payee or any subsequent indorsement was made by or under the authority of the person whose indorsement it purports to be, and the banker is deemed to have paid the bill in due course, although such indorsement has been forged or made without authority.

61   Acceptor the holder at maturity

When the acceptor of a bill is or becomes the holder of it at or after its maturity, in his own right, the bill is discharged.

62   Express waiver

(1)   When the holder of a bill at or after its maturity absolutely and unconditionally renounces his rights against the acceptor the bill is discharged.

The renunciation must be in writing, unless the bill is delivered up to the acceptor.

(2)   The liabilities of any party to a bill may in like manner be renounced by the holder before, at, or after its maturity; but nothing in this section shall affect the rights of a holder in due course without notice of the renunciation.

63   Cancellation

(1)   Where a bill is intentionally cancelled by the holder or his agent, and the cancellation is apparent thereon, the bill is discharged.

(2)   In like manner any party liable on a bill may be discharged by the intentional cancellation of his signature by the holder or his agent. In such case any indorser who would have had a right of recourse against the party whose signature is cancelled, is also discharged.

(3)   A cancellation made unintentionally, or under a mistake, or without the authority of the holder is inoperative; but where a bill or any signature thereon appears to have been cancelled the burden of proof lies on the party who alleges that the cancellation was made unintentionally, or under a mistake, or without authority.

64   Alteration of bill

(1)   Where a bill or acceptance is materially altered without the assent of all parties liable on the bill, the bill is avoided except as against a party who has himself made, authorised, or assented to the alteration, and subsequent indorsers.

Provided that,

Where a bill has been materially altered, but the alteration is not apparent, and the bill is in the hands of a holder in due course, such holder may avail himself of the bill as if it had not been altered, and may enforce payment of it according to its original tenour.

(2)   In particular the following alterations are material, namely, any alteration of the date, the sum payable, the time of payment, the place of payment, and where a bill has been accepted generally, the addition of a place of payment without the acceptor's assent.

Acceptance and payment for honour

65   Acceptance for honour supra protest

(1)   Where a bill of exchange has been protested for dishonour by non-acceptance, or protested for better security, and is not overdue, any person, not

being a party already liable thereon, may, with the consent of the holder, intervene and accept the bill supra protest, for the honour of any party liable thereon, or for the honour of the person for whose account the bill is drawn.

(2)   A bill may be accepted for honour for part only of the sum for which it is drawn.

(3)   An acceptance for honour supra protest in order to be valid must—

   (a)   be written on the bill, and indicate that it is an acceptance for honour;

   (b)   be signed by the acceptor for honour.

(4)   Where an acceptance for honour does not expressly state for whose honour it is made, it is deemed to be an acceptance for the honour of the drawer.

(5)   Where a bill payable after sight is accepted for honour, its maturity is calculated from the date of the noting for non-acceptance, and not from the date of the acceptance for honour.

66   Liability of acceptor for honour

(1)   The acceptor for honour of a bill by accepting it engages that he will, on due presentment, pay the bill according to the tenour of his acceptance, if it is not paid by the drawee, provided it has been duly presented for payment, and protested for non-payment, and that he receives notice of these facts.

(2)   The acceptor for honour is liable to the holder and to all parties to the bill subsequent to the party for whose honour he has accepted.

67   Presentment to acceptor for honour

(1)   Where a dishonoured bill has been accepted for honour supra protest, or contains a reference in case of need, it must be protested for non-payment before it is presented for payment to the acceptor for honour, or referee in case of need.

(2)   Where the address of the acceptor for honour is in the same place where the bill is protested for non-payment, the bill must be presented to him not later than the day following its maturity; and where the address of the acceptor for honour is in some place other than the place where it was protested for non-payment, the bill must be forwarded not later than the day following its maturity for presentment to him.

(3)   Delay in presentment or non-presentment is excused by any circumstances which would excuse delay in presentment for payment or non-presentment for payment.

(4)   When a bill of exchange is dishonoured by the acceptor for honour it must be protested for non-payment by him.

68   Payment for honour supra protest

(1)   Where a bill has been protested for non-payment any person may intervene and pay it supra protest for the honour of any party liable thereon, or for the honour of the person for whose account the bill is drawn.

(2)   Where two or more persons offer to pay a bill for the honour of different parties, the person whose payment will discharge most parties to the bill shall have the preference.

(3)   Payment for honour supra protest, in order to operate as such and not as a mere voluntary payment, must be attested by a notarial act of honour which may be appended to the protest or form an extension of it.

(4)   The notarial act of honour must be founded on a declaration made by the payer for honour, or his agent in that behalf, declaring his intention to pay the bill for honour, and for whose honour he pays.

(5)   Where a bill has been paid for honour, all parties subsequent to the party for whose honour it is paid are discharged, but the payer for honour is subrogated for, and succeeds to both the rights and duties of, the holder as regards the party for whose honour he pays, and all parties liable to that party.

(6)   The payer for honour on paying to the holder the amount of the bill and the notarial expenses incidental to its dishonour is entitled to receive both the bill

itself and the protest. If the holder do not on demand deliver them up he shall be liable to the payer for honour in damages.

(7)   Where the holder of a bill refuses to receive payment supra protest he shall lose his right of recourse against any party who would have been discharged by such payment.

Lost instruments

69   Holder's right to duplicate of lost bill
Where a bill has been lost before it is overdue, the person who was the holder of it may apply to the drawer to give him another bill of the same tenour, giving security to the drawer if required to indemnify him against all persons whatever in case the bill alleged to have been lost shall be found again.

If the drawer on request as aforesaid refuses to give such duplicate bill, he may be compelled to do so.

70   Action on lost bill
In any action or proceeding upon a bill, the court or a judge may order that the loss of the instrument shall not be set up, provided an indemnity be given to the satisfaction of the court or judge against the claims of any other person upon the instrument in question.

Bill in a set

71   Rules as to sets
(1)   Where a bill is drawn in a set, each part of the set being numbered and containing a reference to the other parts, the whole of the parts constitute one bill.

(2)   Where the holder of a set indorses two or more parts to different persons, he is liable to every such part, and every indorser subsequent to him is liable on the part he has himself indorsed as if the said parts were separate bills.

(3)   Where two or more parts of a set are negotiated to different holders in due course, the holder whose title first accrues is as between such holders deemed the true owner of the bill; but nothing in this sub-section shall affect the rights of a person who in due course accepts or pays the part first presented to him.

(4)   The acceptance may be written on any part, and it must be written on one part only.

If the drawee accepts more than one part, and such accepted parts get into the hands of different holders in due course, he is liable on every such part as if it were a separate bill.

(5)   When the acceptor of a bill drawn in a set pays it without requiring the part bearing the acceptance to be delivered up to him, and that part at maturity is outstanding in the hands of a holder in due course, he is liable to the holder thereof.

(6)   Subject to the preceding rules, where any one part of a bill drawn in a set is discharged by payment or otherwise, the whole bill is discharged.

Conflict of laws

72   Rules where laws conflict
Where a bill drawn in one country is negotiated, accepted, or payable in another, the rights, duties, and liabilities of the parties thereto are determined as follows:

(1)   The validity of a bill as regards requisites in form is determined by the law of the place of issue, and the validity as regards requisites in form of the supervening contracts, such as acceptance, or indorsement, or acceptance supra protest, is determined by the law of the place where such contract was made.

Provided that—

(a)   Where a bill is issued out of the United Kingdom it is not invalid by reason only that it is not stamped in accordance with the law of the place of issue:

(b) Where a bill, issued out of the United Kingdom, conforms, as regards requisites in form, to the law of the United Kingdom, it may, for the purpose of enforcing payment thereof, be treated as valid as between all persons who negotiate, hold, or become parties to it in the United Kingdom.

(2) Subject to the provisions of this Act, the interpretation of the drawing, indorsement, acceptance, or acceptance supra protest of a bill, is determined by the law of the place where such contract is made.

Provided that where an inland bill is indorsed in a foreign country the indorsement shall as regards the payer be interpreted according to the law of the United Kingdom.

(3) The duties of the holder with respect to presentment for acceptance or payment and the necessity for or sufficiency of a protest or notice of dishonour, or otherwise, are determined by the law of the place where the act is done or the bill is dishonoured.

[. . .]

(5) Where a bill is drawn in one country and is payable in another, the due date thereof is determined according to the law of the place where it is payable.

PART III
CHEQUES ON A BANKER

73 Cheque defined

A cheque is a bill of exchange drawn on a banker payable on demand. Except as otherwise provided in this Part, the provisions of this Act applicable to a bill of exchange payable on demand apply to a cheque.

74 Presentment of cheque for payment

Subject to the provisions of this Act—

(1) Where a cheque is not presented for payment within a reasonable time of its issue, and the drawer or the person on whose account it is drawn had the right at the time of such presentment as between him and the banker to have the cheque paid and suffers actual damage through the delay, he is discharged to the extent of such damage, that is to say, to the extent to which such drawer or person is a creditor of such banker to a larger amount than he would have been had such cheque been paid.

(2) In determining what is a reasonable time regard shall be had to the nature of the instrument, the usage of trade and of bankers, and the facts of the particular case.

(3) The holder of such cheque as to which such drawer or person is discharged shall be a creditor, in lieu of such drawer or person, of such banker to the extent of such discharge, and entitled to recover the amount from him.

[74A Presentment of cheque for payment: alternative place of presentment

Where the banker on whom a cheque is drawn—

(a) has by notice published in the London, Edinburgh and Belfast Gazettes specified an address at which cheques drawn on him may be presented, and

(b) has not by notice so published cancelled the specification of that address,

the cheque is also presented at the proper place if it is presented there.]

[74B Presentment of cheque for payment: alternative means of presentment by banker

(1) A banker may present a cheque for payment to the banker on whom it is drawn by notifying him of its essential features by electronic means or otherwise, instead of by presenting the cheque itself.

(2) If a cheque is presented for payment under this section, presentment need not be made at the proper place or at a reasonable hour on a business day.

(3) If, before the close of business on the next business day following presentment of a cheque under this section, the banker on whom the cheque is drawn

requests the banker by whom the cheque was presented to present the cheque itself—

    (a)   the presentment under this section shall be disregarded, and

    (b)   this section shall not apply in relation to the subsequent presentment of the cheque.

    (4)   A request under subsection (3) above for the presentment of a cheque shall not constitute dishonour of the cheque by non-payment.

    (5)   Where presentment of a cheque is made under this section, the banker who presented the cheque and the banker on whom it is drawn shall be subject to the same duties in relation to the collection and payment of the cheque as if the cheque itself had been presented for payment.

    (6)   For the purposes of this section, the essential features of a cheque are—

    (a)   the serial number of the cheque,

    (b)   the code which identifies the banker on whom the cheque is drawn,

    (c)   the account number of the drawer of the cheque, and

    (d)   the amount of the cheque is entered by the drawer of the cheque.]

[74C   Cheques presented for payment under section 74B: disapplication of section 52(4)

Section 52(4) above—

    (a)   so far as relating to presenting a bill for payment, shall not apply to presenting a cheque for payment under section 74B above, and

    (b)   so far as relating to a bill which is paid, shall not apply to a cheque which is paid following presentment under that section.]

75   Revocation of banker's authority

The duty and authority of a banker to pay a cheque drawn on him by his customer are determined by—

    (1)   Countermand of payment:

    (2)   Notice of the customer's death.

[75A

    (1)   On the countermand of payment of a cheque, the banker shall be treated as having no funds available for the payment of the cheque.

    (2)   This section applies to Scotland only.]

Crossed cheques

76   General and special crossings defined

    (1)   Where a cheque bears across its face an addition of—

    (a)   The words 'and company' or any abbreviation thereof between two parallel transverse lines either with or without the words 'not negotiable'; or

    (b)   Two parallel transverse lines simply, either with or without the words 'not negotiable';

that addition constitutes a crossing, and the cheque is crossed generally.

    (2)   Where a cheque bears across its face an addition of the name of a banker, either with or without the words 'not negotiable', that addition constitutes a crossing, and the cheque is crossed specially and to that banker.

77   Crossing by drawer or after issue

    (1)   A cheque may be crossed generally or specially by the drawer.

    (2)   Where a cheque is uncrossed, the holder may cross it generally or specially.

    (3)   Where a cheque is crossed generally, the holder may cross it specially.

    (4)   Where a cheque is crossed generally or specially, the holder may add the words 'not negotiable'.

    (5)   Where a cheque is crossed specially, the banker to whom it is crossed may again cross it specially to another banker for collection.

(6)   Where an uncrossed cheque, or a cheque crossed generally is sent to a banker for collection, he may cross it specially to himself.

78   Crossing a material part of cheque

A crossing authorised by this Act is a material part of the cheque; it shall not be lawful for any person to obliterate or, except as authorised by this Act, to add to or alter the crossing.

79   Duties of banker as to crossed cheques

(1)   Where a cheque is crossed specially to more than one banker except when crossed to an agent for collection being a banker, the banker on whom it is drawn shall refuse payment thereof.

(2)   Where the banker on whom a cheque is drawn which is so crossed nevertheless pays the same, or pays a cheque crossed generally otherwise than to a banker, or if crossed specially otherwise than to the banker to whom it is crossed, or his agent for collection being a banker, he is liable to the true owner of the cheque for any loss he may sustain owing to the cheque having been so paid.

Provided that where a cheque is presented for payment which does not at the time of presentment appear to be crossed, or to have had a crossing which had been obliterated, or to have been added to or altered otherwise than as authorised by this Act, the banker paying the cheque in good faith and without negligence shall not be responsible or incur any liability, nor shall the payment be questioned by reason of the cheque having been crossed, or of the crossing having been obliterated on having been added to or altered otherwise than as authorised by this Act, and of payment having been made otherwise than to a banker or to the banker to whom the cheque is or was crossed, or to his agent for collection being a banker as the case may be.

80   Protection to banker and drawer where cheque is crossed

Where the banker, on whom a crossed cheque [(including a cheque which under section 81A below or otherwise is not transferable)] is drawn in good faith and without negligence pays it, if crossed generally to a banker, and if crossed specially, to the banker to whom it is crossed, or his agent for collection being a banker, the banker paying the cheque, and, if the cheque has come into the hands of the payee, the drawer, shall respectively be entitled to the same rights and be placed in the same position as if payment of the cheque had been made to the true owner thereof.

81   Effect of crossing on holder

Where a person takes a crossed cheque which bears on it the words 'not negotiable', he shall not have and shall not be capable of giving a better title to the cheque than that which the person from whom he took it had.

[81A   Non-transferable cheques

(1)   Where a cheque is crossed and bears across its face the words 'account payee' or 'a/c payee', either with or without the words 'only', the cheque shall not be transferable, but shall only be valid as between the parties thereto.

(2)   A banker is not to be treated for the purposes of section 80 above as having been negligent by reason only of his failure to concern himself with any purported indorsement of a cheque which under subsection (1) above or otherwise is not transferable.]

[. . .]

PART IV

PROMISSORY NOTES

83   Promissory note defined

(1)   A promissory note is an unconditional promise in writing made by one person to another signed by the maker, engaging to pay, on demand or at a fixed

or determinable future time, a sum certain in money, to, or to the order of, a specified person or to bearer.

(2)   An instrument in the form of a note payable to maker's order is not a note within the meaning of this section unless and until it is indorsed by the maker.

(3)   A note is not invalid by reason only that it contains also a pledge of collateral security with authority to sell or dispose thereof.

(4)   A note which is, or on the face of it purports to be, both made and payable within the British Islands is an inland note. Any other note is a foreign note.

84   Delivery necessary
A promissory note is inchoate and incomplete until delivery thereof to the payee or bearer.

85   Joint and several notes
(1)   A promissory note may be made by two or more makers, and they may be liable thereon jointly, or jointly and severally according to its tenour.

(2)   Where a note runs 'I promise to pay' and is signed by two or more persons it is deemed to be their joint and several note.

86   Note payable on demand
(1)   Where a note payable on demand has been indorsed, it must be presented for payment within a reasonable time of the indorsement. If it be not so presented the indorser is discharged.

(2)   In determining what is a reasonable time, regard shall be had to the nature of the instrument, the usage of trade, and the facts of the particular case.

(3)   Where a note payable on demand is negotiated, it is not deemed to be overdue for the purpose of affecting the holder with defects of title of which he had no notice, by reason that it appears that a reasonable time for presenting it for payment has elapsed since its issue.

87   Presentment of note for payment
(1)   Where a promissory note is in the body of it made payable at a particular place, it must be presented for payment at that place in order to render the maker liable. In any other case, presentment for payment is not necessary to render the maker liable.

(2)   Presentment for payment is necessary in order to render the indorser of a note liable.

(3)   Where a note is in the body of it made payable at a particular place, presentment at that place is necessary in order to render an indorser liable; but when a place of payment is indicated by way of memorandum only, presentment at that place is sufficient to render the indorser liable, but a presentment to the maker elsewhere, if sufficient in other respects, shall also suffice.

88   Liability of maker
The maker of a promissory note by making it—

(1)   Engages that he will pay it according to its tenour;

(2)   Is precluded from denying to a holder in due course the existence of the payee and his then capacity to indorse.

89   Application of Part II to notes
(1)   Subject to the provisions in this part and, except as by this section provided, the provisions of this Act relating to bills of exchange apply, with the necessary modifications, to promissory notes.

(2)   In applying those provisions the maker of a note shall be deemed to correspond with the acceptor of a bill, and the first indorser of a note shall be deemed to correspond with the drawer of an accepted bill payable to drawer's order.

(3)   The following provisions as to bills do not apply to notes; namely, provisions relating to—

(a)   Presentment for acceptance;

(b)   Acceptance;
(c)   Acceptance supra protest;
(d)   Bills in a set.
(4)   Where a foreign note is dishonoured, protest thereof is unnecessary.

PART V
SUPPLEMENTARY

90   Good faith

A thing is deemed to be done in good faith, within the meaning of this Act, where it is in fact done honestly, whether it is done negligently or not.

91   Signature

(1)   Where, by this Act, any instrument or writing is required to be signed by any person, it is not necessary that he should sign it with his own hand, but it is sufficient if his signature is written thereon by some other person by or under his authority.

(2)   In the case of a corporation, where, by this Act, any instrument or writing is required to be signed, it is sufficient if the instrument or writing be sealed with the corporate seal.

But nothing in this section shall be construed as requiring the bill or note of a corporation to be under seal.

92   Computation of time

Where, by this Act, the time limited for doing any act or thing is less than three days, in reckoning time, non-business days are excluded.

'Non-business days' for the purposes of this Act mean—
(a)   [Saturday,] Sunday, Good Friday, Christmas Day;
(b)   A bank holiday under [the Banking and Financial Dealings Act 1971];
(c)   A day appointed by Royal proclamation as a public fast or thanksgiving day;
[(d)   A day declared by an order under section 2 of the Banking and Financial Dealings Act 1971 to be a non-business day.]

Any other day is a business day.

93   When noting equivalent to protest

For the purposes of this Act, where a bill or note is required to be protested within a specified time or before some further proceeding is taken, it is sufficient that the bill has been noted for protest before the expiration of the specified time or the taking of the proceeding; and the formal protest may be extended at any time thereafter as of the date of the noting.

94   Protest when notary not accessible

Where a dishonoured bill or note is authorised or required to be protested, and the services of a notary cannot be obtained at the place where the bill is dishonoured, any householder, or substantial resident of the place may, in the presence of two witnesses, give a certificate, signed by them, attesting to the dishonour of the bill, and the certificate shall in all respects operate as if it were a formal protest of the bill.

The form given in Schedule I to this Act may be used with necessary modifications, and if used shall be sufficient.

95   Dividend warrants may be crossed

The provisions of this Act as to crossed cheques shall apply to a warrant for payment of dividend.

[. . .]

97   Savings

(1)   The rules in bankruptcy relating to bills of exchange, promissory notes, and

cheques, shall continue to apply thereto notwithstanding anything in this Act contained.

(2)   The rules of common law including the law merchant, save in so far as they are inconsistent with the express provisions of this Act, shall continue to apply to bills of exchange, promissory notes, and cheques.

(3)   Nothing in this Act or in any repeal effected thereby shall affect—

(a)   [. . .] any law or enactment for the time being in force relating to the revenue:

(b)   The provisions of the Companies Act, 1862, or Acts amending it, or any Act relating to joint stock banks or companies:

(c)   The provisions of any Act relating to or confirming the privileges of the Bank of England or the Bank of Ireland respectively:

(d)   The validity of any usage relating to dividend warrants, or the indorsements thereof.

98   Saving of summary diligence in Scotland
Nothing in this Act or in any repeal effected thereby shall extend or restrict, or in any way alter the law and practice in Scotland in regard to summary diligence.

99   Construction with other Acts, etc
Where any Act or document refers to any enactment repealed by this Act, the Act or document shall be construed, and shall operate as if it referred to the corresponding provisions of this Act.

100   Parole evidence allowed in certain judicial proceedings in Scotland
In any judicial proceeding in Scotland, any fact relating to a bill of exchange, bank cheque, or promissory note, which is relevant to any question of liability thereon, may be proved by parole evidence: Provided that this enactment shall not in any way affect the existing law and practice whereby the party who is, according to the tenour of any bill of exchange, bank cheque, or promissory note, debtor to the holder in the amount thereof, may be required, as a condition of obtaining a sist of diligence, or suspension of a charge, or threatened charge, to make such consignation, or to find such caution as the court or judge before whom the cause is depending may require. [. . .]

SCHEDULES

FIRST SCHEDULE
Section 94

Form of protest which may be used when the services of a notary cannot be obtained

Know all men that I, *A. B.* [householder], of   in the county of   in the United Kingdom, at the request of *C. D.*, there being no notary public available, did on the   day of   188   at_____
demand payment [*or* acceptance] of the bill of exchange hereunder written, from *E. F.*, to which demand he made answer [state answer, if any] wherefore I now, in the presence of *G. H.* and *J. K.* do protest the said bill of exchange.

(Signed)   A. B.
             G. H. } *Witnesses*
             J. K.

N.B.—The bill itself should be annexed, or a copy of the bill and all that is written thereon should be underwritten.

FACTORS ACT 1889
(52 & 53 Vict, c 45)

Preliminary

1 Definitions
For the purposes of this Act—

(1)   The expression 'mercantile agent' shall mean a mercantile agent having in the customary course of his business as such agent authority either to sell goods or to consign goods for the purpose of sale, or to buy goods, or to raise money on the security of goods:

(2)   A person shall be deemed to be in possession of goods or of the documents of title to goods, where the goods or documents are in the actual custody or are held by any other person subject to his control or for him or on his behalf:

(3)   The expression 'goods' shall include wares and merchandise:

(4)   The expression 'document of title' shall include any bill of lading, dock warrant, warehouse-keeper's certificate, and warrant or order for the delivery of goods, and any other document used in the ordinary course of business as proof of the possession or control of goods, or authorising or purporting to authorise, either by endorsement or by delivery, the possessor of the document to transfer or receive goods thereby represented:

(5)   The expression 'pledge' shall include any contract pledging, or giving a lien or security on, goods, whether in consideration of an original advance or of any further or continuing advance or of any pecuniary liability:

(6)   The expression 'person' shall include any body of persons corporate or unincorporated.

Dispositions by mercantile agents

2 Powers of mercantile agent with respect to disposition of goods

(1)   Where a mercantile agent is, with the consent of the owner, in possession of goods or of the documents of title to goods, any sale, pledge, or other disposition of the goods, made by him when acting in the ordinary course of business of a mercantile agent, shall, subject to the provisions of this Act, be as valid as if he were expressly authorised by the owner of the goods to make the same; provided that the person taking under the disposition acts in good faith, and has not at the time of the disposition notice that the person making the disposition has not authority to make the same.

(2)   Where a mercantile agent has, with the consent of the owner, been in possession of goods or of the documents of title to goods, any sale, pledge, or other disposition, which would have been valid if the consent had continued, shall be valid notwithstanding the determination of the consent; provided that the person taking under the disposition has not at the time thereof notice that the consent has been determined.

(3)   Where a mercantile agent has obtained possession of any documents of title to goods by reason of his being or having been, with the consent of the owner, in possession of the goods represented thereby, or of any other documents of title to the goods, his possession of the first-mentioned documents shall, for the purposes of this Act, be deemed to be with the consent of the owner.

(4)   For the purposes of this Act the consent of the owner shall be presumed in the absence of evidence to the contrary.

Dispositions by sellers and buyers of goods

8 Disposition by seller remaining in possession
Where a person, having sold goods, continues, or is, in possession of the goods or of the documents of title to the goods, the delivery or transfer by that person, or by

a mercantile agent acting for him, of the goods or documents of title under any sale, pledge, or other disposition thereof, or under any agreement for sale, pledge, or other disposition thereof, to any person receiving the same in good faith and without notice of the previous sale, shall have the same effect as if the person making the delivery or transfer were expressly authorised by the owner of the goods to make the same.

9 Disposition by buyer obtaining possession
Where a person, having bought or agreed to buy goods, obtains with the consent of the seller possession of the goods or the documents of title to the goods, the delivery or transfer, by that person or by a mercantile agent acting for him, of the goods or documents of title under any sale, pledge, or other disposition thereof, or under any agreement for sale, pledge, or other disposition thereof, to any person receiving the same in good faith and without notice of any lien or other right of the original seller in respect of the goods, shall have the same effect as if the person making the delivery or transfer were a mercantile agent in possession of the goods or documents of title with the consent of the owner.

[For the purposes of this section—
(i) the buyer under a conditional sale agreement shall be deemed not to be a person who has bought or agreed to buy goods, and
(ii) 'conditional sale agreement' means an agreement for the sale of goods which is a consumer credit agreement within the meaning of the Consumer Credit Act 1974 under which the purchase price or part of it is payable in instalments, and the property in the goods is to remain in the seller (notwithstanding that the buyer is to be in possession of the goods) until such conditions as to the payment of instalments or otherwise as may be specified in the agreement are fulfilled.]

PARTNERSHIP ACT 1890
(53 & 54 Vict, c 39)

Nature of partnership

1 Definition of partnership
(1) Partnership is the relation which subsists between persons carrying on a business in common with a view of profit.
(2) But the relation between members of any company or association which is—
(a) Registered as a company under the Companies Act, 1862, or any other Act of Parliament for the time being in force and relating to the registration of joint stock companies; or
(b) Formed or incorporated by or in pursuance of any other Act of Parliament or letters patent, or Royal Charter
[. . .]
is not a partnership within the meaning of this Act.

2 Rules for determining existence of partnership
In determining whether a partnership does or does not exist, regard shall be had to the following rules:
(1) joint tenancy, tenancy in common, joint property, common property, or part ownership does not of itself create a partnership as to anything so held or owned, whether the tenants or owners do or do not share any profits made by the use thereof.
(2) The sharing of gross returns does not of itself create a partnership, whether the persons sharing such returns have or have not a joint or common right or interest in any property from which or from the use of which the returns are derived.
(3) The receipt by a person of a share of the profits of a business is prima facie

evidence that he is a partner in the business, but the receipt of such a share, or of a payment contingent on or varying with the profits of a business, does not of itself make him a partner in the business; and in particular—

(a)   The receipt by a person of a debt or other liquidated amount by instalments, or otherwise out of the accruing profits of a business does not of itself make him a partner in the business or liable as such:

(b)   A contract for the remuneration of a servant or agent of a person engaged in a business by a share of the profits of the business does not of itself make the servant or agent a partner in the business or liable as such:

(c)   A person being the widow [, widower, surviving civil partner] or child of a deceased partner, and receiving by way of annuity a portion of the profits made in the business in which the deceased person was a partner, is not by reason only of such receipt a partner in the business or liable as such:

(d)   The advance of money by way of loan to a person engaged or about to engage in any business on a contract with that person that the lender shall receive a rate of interest varying with the profits, or shall receive a share of the profits arising from carrying on the business, does not of itself make the lender a partner with the person or persons carrying on the business or liable as such. Provided that the contract is in writing, and signed by or on behalf of all the parties thereto:

(e)   A person receiving by way of annuity or otherwise a portion of the profits of a business in consideration of the sale by him of the goodwill of the business is not by reason only of such receipt a partner in the business or liable as such.

3   Postponement of rights of person lending or selling in consideration of share of profits in case of insolvency

In the event of any person to whom money has been advanced by way of loan upon such a contract as is mentioned in the last foregoing section, or of any buyer of a goodwill in consideration of a share of the profits of the business, being adjudged a bankrupt, entering into an arrangement to pay his creditors less than [100p] in the pound, or dying in insolvent circumstances, the lender of the loan shall not be entitled to recover anything in respect of the loan, and the seller of the goodwill shall not be entitled to recover anything in respect of the share of profits contracted for, until the claims of the other creditors of the borrower or buyer for valuable consideration in money or money's worth have been satisfied.

4   Meaning of firm

(1)   Persons who have entered into partnership with one another are for the purposes of this Act called collectively a firm, and the name under which their business is carried on is called the firm-name.

(2)   In Scotland a firm is a legal person distinct from the partners of whom it is composed, but an individual partner may be charged on a decree or diligence directed against the firm, and on payment of the debts is entitled to relief pro rata from the firm and its other members.

Relations of partners to persons dealing with them

5   Power of partner to bind the firm

Every partner is an agent of the firm and his other partners for the purpose of the business of the partnership; and the acts of every partner who does any act for carrying on in the usual way business of the kind carried on by the firm of which he is a member bind the firm and his partners, unless the partner so acting has in fact no authority to act for the firm in the particular matter, and the person with whom he is dealing either knows that he has no authority, or does not know or believe him to be a partner.

6 Partners bound by acts on behalf of firm

An act or instrument relating to the business of the firm and done or executed in the firm-name, or in any other manner showing an intention to bind the firm, by any person thereto authorised, whether a partner or not, is binding on the firm and all the partners.

Provided that this section shall not affect any general rule of law relating to the execution of deeds or negotiable instruments.

7 Partner using credit of firm for private purposes

Where one partner pledges the credit of the firm for a purpose apparently not connected with the firm's ordinary course of business, the firm is not bound, unless he is in fact specially authorised by the other partners; but this section does not affect any personal liability incurred by an individual partner.

8 Effect of notice that firm will not be bound by acts of partner

If it has been agreed between the partners that any restriction shall be placed on the power of any one or more of them to bind the firm, no act done in contravention of the agreement is binding on the firm with respect to persons having notice of the agreement.

9 Liability of partners

Every partner in a firm is liable jointly with the other partners, and in Scotland severally also, for all debts and obligations of the firm incurred while he is a partner; and after his death his estate is also severally liable in a due course of administration for such debts and obligations, so far as they remain unsatisfied, but subject in England or Ireland to the prior payment of his separate debts.

10 Liability of the firm for wrongs

Where, by any wrongful act or omission of any partner acting in the ordinary course of the business of the firm, or with the authority of his co-partners, loss or injury is caused to any person not being a partner in the firm, or any penalty is incurred, the firm is liable therefor to the same extent as the partner so acting or omitting to act.

11 Misapplication of money or property received for or in custody of the firm

In the following cases; namely—

(a) Where one partner acting within the scope of his apparent authority receives the money or property of a third person and misapplies it; and

(b) Where a firm in the course of its business receives money or property of a third person, and the money or property so received is misapplied by one or more of the partners while it is in the custody of the firm;

the firm is liable to make good the loss.

12 Liability for wrongs joint and several

Every partner is liable jointly with his co-partners and also severally for everything for which the firm while he is a partner therein becomes liable under either of the two last preceding sections.

13 Improper employment of trust-property for partnership purposes

If a partner, being a trustee, improperly employs trust property in the business or on the account of the partnership, no other partner is liable for the trust-property to the persons beneficially interested therein.

Provided as follows:—

(1) This section shall not affect any liability incurred by any partner by reason of his having notice of a breach of trust; and

(2) Nothing in this section shall prevent trust money from being followed and recovered from the firm if still in its possession or under its control.

14   Persons liable by 'holding out'
(1)   Every one who by words spoken or written or by conduct represents himself, or who knowingly suffers himself to be represented, as a partner in a particular firm, is liable as a partner to one who has on the faith of any such representation given credit to the firm, whether the representation has or has not been made or communicated to the person so giving credit by or with the knowledge of the apparent partner making the representation or suffering it to be made.
(2)   Provided that where after a partner's death the partnership business is continued in the old firm-name, the continued use of that name or of the deceased partner's name as part thereof shall not of itself make his executors' or administrators' estate or effects liable for any partnership debts contracted after his death.

15   Admissions and representations of partners
An admission or representation made by any partner concerning the partnership affairs, and in the ordinary course of its business, is evidence against the firm.

16   Notice to acting partner to be notice to the firm
Notice to any partner who habitually acts in the partnership business of any matter relating to partnership affairs operates as a notice to the firm, except in the case of a fraud on the firm committed by or with the consent of that partner.

17   Liabilities of incoming and outgoing partners
(1)   A person who is admitted as a partner into an existing firm does not thereby become liable to the creditors of the firm for anything done before he became a partner.
(2)   A partner who retires from a firm does not thereby cease to be liable for partnership debts or obligations incurred before his retirement.
(3)   A retiring partner may be discharged from any existing liabilities, by an agreement to that effect between himself and the members of the firm as newly constituted and the creditors, and this agreement may be either express or inferred, as a fact from the course of dealing between the creditors and the firm as newly constituted.

18   Revocation of continuing guaranty by change in firm
A continuing guaranty or cautionary obligation given either to a firm or to a third person in respect of the transactions of a firm is, in the absence of agreement to the contrary, revoked as to future transactions by any change in the constitution of the firm to which, or of the firm in respect of the transactions of which, the guaranty or obligation was given.

Relations of partners to one another

19   Variation by consent of terms of partnership
The mutual rights and duties of partners, whether ascertained by agreement or defined by this Act, may be varied by the consent of all the partners, and such consent may be either express or inferred from a course of dealing.

20   Partnership property
(1)   All property and rights and interests in property originally brought into the partnership stock or acquired, whether by purchase or otherwise, on account of the firm or for the purposes and in the course of the partnership business, are called in this Act partnership property, and must be held and applied by the partners exclusively for the purposes of the partnership and in accordance with the partnership agreement.
(2)   Provided that the legal estate or interest in any land, or in Scotland the title to and interest in any heritable estate, which belongs to the partnership shall devolve according to the nature and tenure thereof, and the general rules of law thereto applicable, but in trust, so far as necessary, for the persons beneficially interested in the land under this section.

(3)   Where co-owners of an estate or interest in any land, or in Scotland of any heritable estate, not being itself partnership property, are partners as to profits made by the use of that land or estate, and purchase other land or estate out of the profits to be used in like manner, the land or estate so purchased belongs to them, in the absence of an agreement to the contrary, not as partners but as co-owners for the same respective estates and interests as are held by them in the land or estate first mentioned at the date of the purchase.

21   Property bought with partnership money
Unless the contrary intention appears, property bought with money belonging to the firm is deemed to have been bought on account of the firm.

[. . .]

23   *[Does not apply to Scotland]*

24   Rules as to interests and duties of partners subject to special agreement
The interests of partners in the partnership property and their rights and duties in relation to the partnership shall be determined, subject to any agreement express or implied between the partners, by the following rules:

(1)   All the partners are entitled to share equally in the capital and profits of the business, and must contribute equally towards the losses whether of capital or otherwise sustained by the firm.

(2)   The firm must indemnify every partner in respect of payments made and personal liabilities incurred by him—

(a)   In the ordinary and proper conduct of the business of the firm-, or,

(b)   In or about anything necessarily done for the preservation of the business or property of the firm.

(3)   A partner making, for the purpose of the partnership, any actual payment or advance beyond the amount of capital which he has agreed to subscribe, is entitled to interest at the rate of five per cent. per annum from the date of the payment or advance.

(4)   A partner is not entitled, before the ascertainment of profits, to interest on the capital subscribed by him.

(5)   Every partner may take part in the management of the partnership business.

(6)   No partner shall be entitled to remuneration for acting in the partnership business.

(7)   No person may be introduced as a partner without the consent of all existing partners.

(8)   Any difference arising as to ordinary matters connected with the partnership business may be decided by a majority of the partners, but no change may be made in the nature of the partnership business without the consent of all existing partners.

(9)   The partnership books are to be kept at the place of business of the partnership (or the principal place, if there is more than one), and every partner may, when he thinks fit, have access to and inspect and copy any of them.

25   Expulsion of partner
No majority of the partners can expel any partner unless a power to do so has been conferred by express agreement between the partners.

26   Retirement from partnership at will
(1)   Where no fixed term has been agreed upon for the duration of the partnership, any partner may determine the partnership at any time on giving notice of his intention so to do to all the other partners.

(2)   Where the partnership has originally been constituted by deed, a notice in writing, signed by the partner giving it, shall be sufficient for this purpose.

27   Where partnership for term is continued over, continuance on old terms presumed

(1)   Where a partnership entered into for a fixed term is continued after the term has expired, and without any express new agreement, the rights and duties of the partners remain the same as they were at the expiration of the term, so far as is consistent with the incidents of a partnership at will.

(2)   A continuance of the business by the partners or such of them as habitually acted therein during the term, without any settlement or liquidation of the partnership affairs, is presumed to be a continuance of the partnership.

28   Duty of partners to render accounts, &c

Partners are bound to render true accounts and full information of all things affecting the partnership to any partner or his legal representatives.

29   Accountability of partners for private profits

(1)   Every partner must account to the firm for any benefit derived by him without the consent of the other partners from any transaction concerning the partnership, or from any use by him of the partnership property name or business connexion.

(2)   This section applies also to transactions undertaken after a partnership has been dissolved by the death of a partner, and before the affairs thereof have been completely wound up, either by any surviving partner or by the representatives of the deceased partner.

30   Duty of partner not to compete with firm

If a partner, without the consent of the other partners, carries on any business of the same nature as and competing with that of the firm, he must account for and pay over to the firm all profits made by him in that business.

31   Rights of assignee of share in partnership

(1)   An assignment by any partner of his share in the partnership, either absolute or by way of mortgage or redeemable charge, does not, as against the other partners, entitle the assignee, during the continuance of the partnership, to interfere in the management or administration of the partnership business or affairs, or to require any accounts of the partnership transactions, or to inspect the partnership books, but entitles the assignee only to receive the share of profits to which the assigning partner would otherwise be entitled, and the assignee must accept the account of profits agreed to by the partners.

(2)   In the case of a dissolution of the partnership, whether as respects all the partners or as respects the assigning partner, the assignee is entitled to receive the share of the partnership assets to which the assigning partner is entitled as between himself and the other partners, and, for the purpose of ascertaining that share, to an account as from the date of the dissolution.

Dissolution of partnership, and its consequences

32   Dissolution by expiration or notice

Subject to any agreement between the partners a partnership is dissolved—

(a)   If entered into for a fixed term, by the expiration of that term:

(b)   If entered into for a single adventure or undertaking, by the termination of that adventure or undertaking:

(c)   If entered into for an undefined time, by any partner giving notice to the other or others of his intention to dissolve the partnership.

In the last-mentioned case the partnership is dissolved as from the date mentioned in the notice as the date of dissolution, or, if no date is so mentioned, as from the date of the communication of the notice.

33   Dissolution by bankruptcy, death, or charge

(1)   Subject to any agreement between the partners, every partnership is dissolved as regards all partners by the death or bankruptcy of any partner.

(2)   A partnership may, at the option of the other partners, be dissolved if any partner suffers his share of the partnership property to be charged under this Act for his separate debt.

34   Dissolution by illegality of partnership

A partnership is in every case dissolved by the happening of any event which makes it unlawful for the business of the firm to be carried on or for the members of the firm to carry it on in partnership.

35   Dissolution by the Court

On application by a partner the Court may decree a dissolution of the partnership in any of the following cases:

[. . .]

(b)   When a partner, other than the partner suing, becomes in any other way permanently incapable of performing his part of the partnership contract:

(c)   When a partner, other than the partner suing, has been guilty of such conduct as, in the opinion of the Court, regard being had to the nature of the business, is calculated to prejudicially affect the carrying on of the business:

(d)   When a partner, other than the partner suing, wilfully or persistently commits a breach of the partnership agreement, or otherwise so conducts himself in matters relating to the partnership business that it is not reasonably practicable for the other partner or partners to carry on the business in partnership with him:

(e)   When the business of the partnership can only be carried on at a loss:

(f)   Whenever in any case circumstances have arisen which, in the opinion of the Court, render it just and equitable that the partnership be dissolved.

36   Rights of persons dealing with firm against apparent members of firm

(1)   Where a person deals with a firm after a change in its constitution he is entitled to treat all apparent members of the old firm as still being members of the firm until he has notice of the change.

(2)   An advertisement in the London Gazette as to a firm whose principal place of business is in England or Wales, in the Edinburgh Gazette as to a firm whose principal place of business is in Scotland, and in the Dublin Gazette as to a firm whose principal place of business is in Ireland, shall be notice as to persons who had not dealings with the firm before the date of the dissolution or change so advertised.

(3)   The estate of a partner who dies, or who becomes bankrupt, or of a partner who, not having been known to the person dealing with the firm to be a partner, retires from the firm, is not liable for partnership debts contracted after the date of the death, bankruptcy, or retirement respectively.

37   Right of partners to notify dissolution

On dissolution of a partnership or retirement of a partner any partner may publicly notify the same, and may require the other partner or partners to concur for that purpose in all necessary or proper acts, if any, which cannot be done without his or their concurrence.

38   Continuing authority of partners for purposes of winding up

After the dissolution of a partnership the authority of each partner to bind the firm, and the other rights and obligations of the partners, continue notwithstanding the dissolution so far as may be necessary to wind up the affairs of the partnership, and to complete transactions begun but unfinished at the time of the dissolution, but not otherwise.

Provided that the firm is in no case bound by the acts of a partner who has become bankrupt; but this proviso does not affect the liability of any person who has after the bankruptcy represented himself or knowingly suffered himself to be represented as a partner of the bankrupt.

39 Rights of partners as to application of partnership property
On the dissolution of a partnership every partner is entitled, as against the other partners in the firm, and all persons claiming through them in respect of their interests as partners, to have the property of the partnership applied in payment of the debts and liabilities of the firm, and to have the surplus assets after such payment applied in payment of what may be due to the partners respectively after deducting what may be due from them as partners to the firm; and for that purpose any partner or his representatives may on the termination of the partnership apply to the Court to wind up the business and affairs of the firm.

40 Apportionment of premium where partnership prematurely dissolved
Where one partner has paid a premium to another on entering into a partnership for a fixed term, and the partnership is dissolved before the expiration of that term otherwise than by the death of a partner, the Court may order the repayment of the premium, or of such part thereof as it thinks just, having regard to the terms of the partnership contract and to the length of time during which the partnership has continued; unless

(a)   the dissolution is, in the judgment of the Court, wholly or chiefly due to the misconduct of the partner who paid the premium, or

(b)   the partnership has been dissolved by an agreement containing no provision for a return of any part of the premium.

41 Rights where partnership dissolved for fraud or misrepresentation
Where a partnership contract is rescinded on the ground of fraud or misrepresentation of one of the parties thereto, the party entitled to rescind is, without prejudice to any other right, entitled—

(a)   to a lien on, or right of retention of, the surplus of the partnership assets, after satisfying the partnership liabilities, for any sum of money paid by him for the purchase of a share in the partnership and for any capital contributed by him, and is

(b)   to stand in the place of the creditors of the firm for any payments made by him in respect of the partnership liabilities, and

(c)   to be indemnified by the person guilty of the fraud or making the representation against all the debts and liabilities of the firm.

42 Right of outgoing partner in certain cases to share in profits made after dissolution
(1)   Where any member of a firm has died or otherwise ceased to be a partner, and the surviving or continuing partners carry on the business of the firm with its capital or assets without any final settlement of accounts as between the firm and the outgoing partner or his estate, then, in the absence of any agreement to the contrary, the outgoing partner or his estate is entitled at the option of himself or his representatives to such share of the profits made since the dissolution as the Court may find to be attributable to the use of his share of the partnership assets, or to interest at the rate of five per cent. per annum on the amount of his share of the partnership assets.

(2)   Provided that where by the partnership contract an option is given to surviving or continuing partners to purchase the interest of a deceased or outgoing partner, and that option is duly exercised, the estate of the deceased partner, or the outgoing partner or his estate, as the case may be, is not entitled to any further or other share of profits; but if any partner assuming to act in exercise of the option does not in all material respects comply with the terms thereof, he is liable to account under the foregoing provisions of this section.

43   Retiring or deceased partner's share to be a debt
Subject to any agreement between the partners, the amount due from surviving or
continuing partners to an outgoing partner or the representatives of a deceased
partner in respect of the outgoing or deceased partner's share is a debt accruing at
the date of the dissolution or death.

44   Rule for distribution of assets on final settlement of accounts
In settling accounts between the partners after a dissolution of partnership, the following rules shall, subject to any agreement, be observed:
    (a)   Losses, including losses and deficiencies of capital, shall be paid first out
of profits, next out of capital, and lastly, if necessary, by the partners
individually in the proportion in which they were entitled to share profits:
    (b)   The assets of the firm including the sums, if any, contributed by the
partners to make up losses or deficiencies of capital, shall be applied in the
following manner and order:
    1   In paying the debts and liabilities of the firm to persons who are not
partners therein:
    2   In paying to each partner rateably what is due from the firm to him
for advances as distinguished from capital:
    3   In paying to each partner rateably what is due from the firm to him in
respect of capital:
    4   The ultimate residue, if any, shall be divided among the partners in
the proportion in which the profits are divisible.

Supplemental

45   Definitions of 'court' and 'business'
In this Act, unless the contrary intention appears—
    The expression 'court' includes every court and judge having jurisdiction in the
case:
    The expression 'business' includes every trade, occupation or profession.

46   Saving for rules of equity and common law
The rules of equity and of common law applicable to partnership shall continue in
force except so far as they are inconsistent with the express provisions of this Act.

47   Provision as to bankruptcy in Scotland
    (1)   In the application of this Act to Scotland the bankruptcy of a firm or of an
individual shall mean sequestration under the Bankruptcy (Scotland) Acts, and
also in the case of an individual the issue against him of a decree of cessio
bonorum.
    (2)   Nothing in this Act shall alter the rules of the law of Scotland relating to
the bankruptcy of a firm or of the individual partners thereof.

[. . .]

50   Short title
This Act may be cited as the Partnership Act, 1890.

FACTORS (SCOTLAND) ACT 1890
(53 & 54 Vict, c 40)

1   Application of 52 & 53 Vict c 45 to Scotland
Subject to the following provisions, the Factors Act, 1889, shall apply to Scotland—
    (1)   The expression 'lien' shall mean and include right of retention; the expres-
sion 'vendor's lien' shall mean and include any right of retention competent to the
original owner or vendor; and the expression 'set off' shall mean and include
compensation.

(2)   In the application of section five of the recited Act, a sale, pledge, or other disposition of goods shall not be valid unless made for valuable consideration.

MARINE INSURANCE ACT 1906
(6 Edw 7, c 41)

Marine insurance

1   Marine insurance defined
A contract of marine insurance is a contract whereby the insurer undertakes to indemnify the assured, in manner and to the extent thereby agreed, against marine losses, that is to say, the losses incident to marine adventure.

2   Mixed sea and land risks
(1)   A contract of marine insurance may, by its express terms, or by usage of trade, be extended so as to protect the assured against losses on inland waters or on any land risk which may be incidental to any sea voyage.

(2)   Where a ship in course of building, or the launch of a ship, or any adventure analogous to marine adventure, is covered by a policy in the form of a marine policy, the provisions of this Act, in so far as applicable, shall apply thereto; but, except as by this section provided, nothing in this Act shall alter or affect any rule of law applicable to any contract of insurance other than a contract of marine insurance as by this Act defined.

3   Marine adventure and maritime perils defined
(1)   Subject to the provisions of this Act, every lawful marine adventure may be the subject of marine insurance.

(2)   In particular there is a marine adventure where—

(a)   Any ship goods or other moveables are exposed to maritime perils. Such property is in this Act referred to as 'insurable property';

(b)   The earning or acquisition of any freight, passage money, commission, profit, or other pecuniary benefit, or the security for any advances, loan or disbursements, is endangered by the exposure of insurable property to maritime perils;

(c)   Any liability to a third party may be incurred by the owner of, or other person interested in or responsible for, insurable property, by reason of maritime perils.

'Maritime perils' means the perils consequent on, or incidental to, the navigation of the sea, that is to say, perils of the seas, fire, war perils, pirates, rovers, thieves, captures, seizures, restraints, and detainments of princes and peoples, jettisons, barratry, and any other perils, either of the like kind or which may be designated by the policy.

Insurable interest

4   Avoidance of wagering or gaming contracts
(1)   Every contract of marine insurance by way of gaming or wagering is void.

(2)   A contract of marine insurance is deemed to be a gaming or wagering contract—

(a)   Where the assured has not an insurable interest as defined by this Act, and the contract is entered into with no expectation of acquiring such an interest; or

(b)   Where the policy is made 'interest or no interest', or 'without further proof of interest than the policy itself', or 'without benefit of salvage to the insurer', or subject to any other like term:

Provided that, where there is no possibility of salvage, a policy may be effected without benefit of salvage to the insurer.

5   Insurable interest defined
(1)   Subject to the provisions of this Act, every person has an insurable interest who is interested in a marine adventure.

(2)   In particular a person is interested in a marine adventure where he stands in any legal or equitable relation to the adventure or to any insurable property at risk therein, in consequence of which he may benefit by the safety or due arrival of insurable property, or may be prejudiced by its loss, or damage thereto, or by the detention thereof, or may incur liability in respect thereof.

6   When interest must attach
(1)   The assured must be interested in the subject-matter insured at the time of the loss though he need not be interested when the insurance is effected:

Provided that where the subject-matter is insured 'lost or not lost', the assured may recover although he may not have acquired his interest until after the loss, unless at the time of effecting the contract of insurance the assured was aware of the loss, and the insurer was not.

(2)   Where the assured has no interest at the time of the loss, he cannot acquire interest by any act or election after he is aware of the loss.

7   Defeasible or contingent interest
(1)   A defeasible interest is insurable, as also is a contingent interest.

(2)   In particular, where the buyer of goods has insured them, he has an insurable interest, notwithstanding that he might, at his election, have rejected the goods, or have treated them as at the seller's risk, by reason of the latter's delay in making delivery or otherwise.

8   Partial interest
A partial interest of any nature is insurable.

9   Re-insurance
(1)   The insurer under a contract of marine insurance has an insurable interest in his risk, and may re-insure in respect of it.

(2)   Unless the policy otherwise provides, the original assured has no right or interest in respect of such re-insurance.

10   Bottomry
The lender of money on bottomry or respondentia has an insurable interest in respect of the loan.

11   Master's and seamen's wages
The master or any member of the crew of a ship has an insurable interest in respect of his wages.

12   Advance freight
In the case of advance freight, the person advancing the freight has an insurable interest, in so far as such freight is not repayable in case of loss.

13   Charges of insurance
The assured has an insurable interest in the charges of any insurance which he may effect.

14   Quantum of interest
(1)   Where the subject-matter insured is mortgaged, the mortgagor has an insurable interest in the full value thereof, and the mortgagee has an insurable interest in respect of any sum due or to become due under the mortgage.

(2)   A mortgagee, consignee, or other person having an interest in the subject-matter insured may insure on his own behalf and for the benefit of other persons interested as well as for his own benefit.

(3)   The owner of insurable property has an insurable interest in respect of the

full value thereof, notwithstanding that some third person may have agreed, or be liable, to indemnify him in case of loss.

15   Assignment of interest

Where the assured assigns or otherwise parts with his interest in the subject-matter insured, he does not thereby transfer to the assignee his rights under the contract of insurance, unless there be an express or implied agreement with the assignee to that effect.

But the provisions of this section do not affect a transmission of interest by operation of law.

Insurable value

16   Measure of insurable value

Subject to any express provision or valuation in the policy, the insurable value of the subject-matter insured must be ascertained as follows:—

(1)   In insurance on ship, the insurable value is the value, at the commencement of the risk, of the ship, including her outfit, provisions and stores for the officers and crew, money advanced for seamen's wages, and other disbursements (if any) incurred to make the ship fit for the voyage or adventure contemplated by the policy, plus the charges of insurance upon the whole.

The insurable value, in the case of a steamship, includes also the machinery, boilers, and coals and engine stores if owned by the assured, and, in the case of a ship engaged in a special trade, the ordinary fittings requisite for that trade.

(2)   In insurance on freight, whether paid in advance or otherwise, the insurable value is the gross amount of freight at the risk of the assured, plus the charges of insurance.

(3)   In insurance on goods or merchandise, the insurable value is the prime cost of the property insured, plus the expenses of and incidental to shipping and the charges of insurance upon the whole.

(4)   In insurance on any other subject-matter, the insurable value is the amount at the risk of the assured when the policy attaches, plus the charges of insurance.

Disclosure and representations

17   Insurance is uberrimae fidei

A contract of marine insurance is a contract based upon the utmost good faith, and, if the utmost good faith is not observed by either party, the contract may be avoided by the other party.

18   Disclosure by assured

(1)   Subject to the provisions of this section, the assured must disclose to the insurer, before the contract is concluded, every material circumstance which is known to the assured, and the assured is deemed to know every circumstance which, in the ordinary course of business, ought to be known by him. If the assured fails to make such disclosure, the insurer may avoid the contract.

(2)   Every circumstance is material which would influence the judgment of a prudent insurer in fixing the premium, or determining whether he will take the risk.

(3)   In the absence of inquiry the following circumstances need not be disclosed, namely:—

(a)   Any circumstance which diminishes the risk;

(b)   Any circumstance which is known or presumed to be known to the insurer. The insurer is presumed to know matters of common notoriety or knowledge, and matters which an insurer in the ordinary course of his business, as such, ought to know;

(c)   Any circumstance as to which information is waived by the insurer;

(d)   Any circumstance which it is superfluous to disclose by reason of any express or implied warranty.

(4)   Whether any particular circumstance, which is not disclosed, be material or not is, in each case, a question of fact.

(5)   The term 'circumstance' includes any communication made to, or information received by, the assured.

19   Disclosure by agent effecting insurance

Subject to the provisions of the preceding section as to circumstances which need not be disclosed, where an insurance is effected for the assured by an agent, the agent must disclose to the insurer—

(a)   Every material circumstance which is known to himself, and an agent to insure is deemed to know every circumstance which, in the ordinary course of business, ought to be known by, or to have been communicated to, him; and

(b)   Every material circumstance which the assured is bound to disclose, unless it come to his knowledge too late to communicate it to the agent.

20   Representations pending negotiation of contract

(1)   Every material representation made by the assured or his agent to the insurer during the negotiations for contract, and before the contract is concluded, must be true. If it be untrue the insurer may avoid the contract.

(2)   A representation is material which would influence the judgment of a prudent insurer in fixing the premium, or determining whether he will take the risk.

(3)   A representation may be either a representation as to a matter of fact, or as to a matter of expectation or belief.

(4)   A representation as to matter of fact is true, if it be substantially correct, that is to say, if the difference between what is represented and what is actually correct would not be considered material by a prudent insurer.

(5)   A representation as to a matter of expectation or belief is true if it be made in good faith.

(6)   A representation may be withdrawn or corrected before the contract is concluded.

(7)   Whether a particular representation be material or not is, in each case, a question of fact.

21   When contract is deemed to be concluded

A contract of marine insurance is deemed to be concluded when the proposal of the assured is accepted by the insurer, whether the policy be then issued or not; and, for the purpose of showing when the proposal was accepted, reference may be made to the slip or covering note or other customary memorandum of the contract. [. . .]

The policy

22   Contract must be embedded in policy

Subject to the provisions of any statute, a contract of marine insurance is inadmissible in evidence unless it is embodied in a marine policy in accordance with this Act. The policy may be executed and issued either at the time when the contract is concluded or afterwards.

23   What policy must specify

A marine policy must specify—

(1)   The name of the assured, or of some person who effects the insurance on his behalf.

[. . .]

24   Signature of insurer

(1)   A marine policy must be signed by or on behalf of the insurer, provided

that in the case of a corporation the corporate seal may be sufficient, but nothing in this section shall be construed as requiring the subscription of a corporation to be under seal.

(2)   Where a policy is subscribed by or on behalf of two or more insurers, each subscription, unless the contrary be expressed, constitutes a distinct contract with the assured.

25 Voyage and time policies

(1)   Where the contract is to insure the subject-matter 'at and from', or from one place to another or others, the policy is called a 'voyage policy', and where the contract is to insure the subject-matter for a definite period of time the policy is called a 'time policy'. A contract for both voyage and time may be included in the same policy.

  [. . .]

26 Designation of subject-matter

(1)   The subject-matter insured must be designated in a marine policy with reasonable certainty.

(2)   The nature and extent of the interest of the assured in the subject-matter insured need not be specified in the policy.

(3)   Where the policy designates the subject-matter insured in general terms, it shall be construed to apply to the interest intended by the assured to be covered.

(4)   In the application of this section regard shall be had to any usage regulating the designation of the subject-matter insured.

27 Valued policy

(1)   A policy may be either valued or unvalued.

(2)   A valued policy is a policy which specifies the agreed value of the subject-matter insured.

(3)   Subject to the provisions of this Act, and in the absence of fraud, the value fixed by the policy is, as between the insurer and the assured, conclusive of the insurable value of the subject intended to be insured, whether the loss be total or partial.

(4)   Unless the policy otherwise provides, the value fixed by the policy is not conclusive for the purpose of determining whether there has been a constructive total loss.

28 Unvalued policy

An unvalued policy is a policy which does not specify the value of the subject-matter insured, but, subject to the limit of the sum insured, leaves the insurable value to be subsequently ascertained, in the manner herein-before specified.

29 Floating policy by ship or ships

(1)   A floating policy is a policy which describes the insurance in general terms, and leaves the name of the ship or ships and other particulars to be defined by subsequent declaration.

(2)   The subsequent declaration or declarations may be made by indorsement on the policy, or in other customary manner.

(3)   Unless the policy otherwise provides, the declarations must be made in the order of dispatch or shipment. They must, in the case of goods, comprise all consignments within the terms of the policy, and the value of the goods or other property must be honestly stated, but an omission or erroneous declaration may be rectified even after loss or arrival, provided the omission or declaration was made in good faith.

(4)   Unless the policy otherwise provides, where a declaration of value is not made until after notice of loss or arrival, the policy must be treated as an unvalued policy as regards the subject-matter of that declaration.

30   Construction of terms in policy

(1)   A policy may be in the form in the First Schedule to this Act.

(2)   Subject to the provisions of this Act, and unless the context of the policy otherwise requires, the terms and expressions mentioned in the First Schedule to this Act shall be construed as having the scope and meaning in that schedule assigned to them.

31   Premium to be arranged

(1)   Where an insurance is effected at a premium to be arranged, and no arrangement is made, a reasonable premium is payable.

(2)   Where an insurance is effected on the terms that an additional premium is to be arranged in a given event, and that event happens but no arrangement is made, then a reasonable additional premium is payable.

Double insurance

32   Double insurance

(1)   Where two or more policies are effected by or on behalf of the assured on the same adventure and interest or any part thereof, and the sums insured exceed the indemnity allowed by this Act, the assured is said to be over-insured by double insurance.

(2)   Where the assured is over-insured by double insurance—

(a)   The assured, unless the policy otherwise provides, may claim payment from the insurers in such order as he may think fit, provided that he is not entitled to receive any sum in excess of the indemnity allowed by this Act;

(b)   Where the policy under which the assured claims is a valued policy, the assured must give credit as against the valuation for any sum received by him under any other policy without regard to the actual value of the subject-matter insured;

(c)   Where the policy under which the assured claims is an unvalued policy he must give credit, as against the full insurable value, for any sum received by him under any other policy.

(d)   Where the assured receives any sum in excess of the indemnity allowed by this Act, he is deemed to hold such sum in trust for the insurers, according to their right of contribution among themselves.

Warranties, etc

33   Nature of warranty

(1)   A warranty, in the following sections relating to warranties, means a promissory warranty, that is to say, a warranty by which the assured undertakes that some particular thing shall or shall not be done, or that some condition shall be fulfilled, or whereby he affirms or negatives the existence of a particular state of facts.

(2)   A warranty may be express or implied.

(3)   A warranty, as above defined, is a condition which must be exactly complied with, whether it be material to the risk or not. If it be not so complied with, then, subject to any express provision in the policy, the insurer is discharged from liability as from the date of the breach of warranty, but without prejudice to any liability incurred by him before that date.

34   When breach of warranty excused

(1)   Non-compliance with a warranty is excused when, by reason of a change of circumstances, the warranty ceases to be applicable to the circumstances of the contract, or when compliance with the warranty is rendered unlawful by any subsequent law.

(2)   Where a warranty is broken, the assured cannot avail himself of the defence that the breach has been remedied, and the warranty complied with, before loss.

(3)   A breach of warranty may be waived by the insurer.

35   Express warranties
(1)   An express warranty may be in any form of words from which the intention to warrant is to be inferred.

(2)   An express warranty must be included in, or written upon, the policy, or must be contained in some document incorporated by reference into the policy.

(3)   An express warranty does not exclude an implied warranty, unless it be inconsistent therewith.

36   Warranty of neutrality
(1)   Where insurable property, whether ship or goods, is expressly warranted neutral, there is an implied condition that the property shall have a neutral character at the commencement of the risk, and that, so far as the assured can control the matter, its neutral character shall be preserved during the risk.

(2)   Where a ship is expressly warranted 'neutral' there is also an implied condition that, so far as the assured can control the matter, she shall be properly documented, that is to say, that she shall carry the necessary papers to establish her neutrality, and that she shall not falsify or suppress her papers, or use simulated papers. If any loss occurs through breach of this condition, the insurer may avoid the contract.

37   No implied warranty of nationality
There is no implied warranty as to the nationality of a ship, or that her nationality shall not be changed during the risk.

38   Warranty of good safety
Where the subject-matter insured is warranted 'well' or 'in good safety' on a particular day, it is sufficient if it be safe at any time during that day.

39   Warranty of seaworthiness of ship
(1)   In a voyage policy there is an implied warranty that at the commencement of the voyage the ship shall be seaworthy for the purpose of the particular adventure insured.

(2)   Where the policy attaches while the ship is in port, there is also an implied warranty that she shall, at the commencement of the risk, be reasonably fit to encounter the ordinary perils of the port.

(3)   Where the policy relates to a voyage which is performed in different stages, during which the ship requires different kinds of or further preparation or equipment, there is an implied warranty that at the commencement of each stage the ship is seaworthy in respect of such preparation or equipment for the purposes of that stage.

(4)   A ship is deemed to be seaworthy when she is reasonably fit in all respects to encounter the ordinary perils of the seas of the adventure insured.

(5)   In a time policy there is no implied warranty that the ship shall be seaworthy at any stage of the adventure, but where, with the privity of the assured, the ship is sent to sea in an unseaworthy state, the insurer is not liable for any loss attributable to unseaworthiness.

40   No implied warranty that goods are seaworthy
(1)   In a policy on goods or other moveables there is no implied warranty that the goods or moveables are seaworthy.

(2)   In a voyage policy on goods or other moveables there is an implied warranty that at the commencement of the voyage the ship is not only seaworthy as a ship, but also that she is reasonably fit to carry the goods or other moveables to the destination contemplated by the policy.

41   Warranty of legality
There is an implied warranty that the adventure insured is a lawful one, and that,

so far as the assured can control the matter, the adventure shall be carried out in a lawful manner.

The voyage

42 Implied condition as to commencement of risk

(1) Where the subject-matter is insured by a voyage policy 'at and from' or 'from' a particular place, it is not necessary that the ship should be at that place when the contract is concluded, but there is an implied condition that the adventure shall be commenced within a reasonable time, and that if the adventure be not so commenced the insurer may avoid the contract.

(2) The implied condition may be negatived by showing that the delay was caused by circumstances known to the insurer before the contract was concluded, or by showing that he waived the condition.

43 Alteration of port of departure

Where the place of departure is specified by the policy, and the ship instead of sailing from that place sails from any other place, the risk does not attach.

44 Sailing for different destination

Where the destination is specified in the policy, and the ship, instead of sailing for that destination, sails for any other destination, the risk does not attach.

45 Change of voyage

(1) Where, after the commencement of the risk, the destination of the ship is voluntarily changed from the destination contemplated by the policy, there is said to be a change of voyage.

(2) Unless the policy otherwise provides, where there is a change of voyage, the insurer is discharged from liability as from the time of the change, that is to say, as from the time when the determination to change it is manifested; and it is immaterial that the ship may not have left the course of voyage contemplated by the policy when the loss occurs.

46 Deviation

(1) Where a ship, without lawful excuse, deviates from the voyage contemplated by the policy, the insurer is discharged from liability as from the time of deviation, and it is immaterial that the ship may have regained her route before any loss occurs.

(2) There is a deviation from the voyage contemplated by the policy—

   (a) Where the course of the voyage is specifically designated by the policy, and that course is departed from; or

   (b) Where the course of the voyage is not specifically designated by the policy, but the usual and customary course is departed from.

(3) The intention to deviate is immaterial; there must be a deviation in fact to discharge the insurer from his liability under the contract.

47 Several ports of discharge

(1) Where several ports of discharge are specified by the policy, the ship may proceed to all or any of them, but, in the absence of any usage or sufficient cause to the contrary, she must proceed to them, or such of them as she goes to, in the order designated by the policy. If she does not there is a deviation.

(2) Where the policy is to 'ports of discharge', within a given area, which are not named, the ship must, in the absence of any usage or sufficient cause to the contrary, proceed to them, or such of them as she goes to, in their geographical order. If she does not there is a deviation.

48 Delay in voyage

In the case of a voyage policy, the adventure insured must be prosecuted throughout its course with reasonable dispatch, and, if without lawful excuse it is not so prosecuted, the insurer is discharged from liability as from the time when the delay becomes unreasonable.

49 Excuses for deviation or delay
(1)   Deviation or delay in prosecuting the voyage contemplated by the policy is excused—
(a)   Where authorised by any special term in the policy; or
(b)   Where caused by circumstances beyond the control of the master and his employer; or
(c)   Where reasonably necessary in order to comply with an express or implied warranty; or
(d)   Where reasonably necessary for the safety of the ship or subject-matter insured; or
(e)   For the purpose of saving human life, or aiding a ship in distress where human life may be in danger; or
(f)   Where reasonably necessary for the purpose of obtaining medical or surgical aid for any person on board the ship; or
(g)   Where caused by the barratrous conduct of the master or crew, if barratry be one of the perils insured against.
(2)   When the cause excusing the deviation or delay ceases to operate, the ship must resume her course, and prosecute her voyage, with reasonable dispatch.

Assignment of policy

50 When and how policy is assignable
(1)   A marine policy is assignable unless it contains terms expressly prohibiting assignment. It may be assigned either before or after loss.
(2)   Where a marine policy has been assigned so as to pass the beneficial interest in such policy, the assignee of the policy is entitled to sue thereon in his own name; and the defendant is entitled to make any defence arising out of the contract which he would have been entitled to make if the action had been brought in the name of the person by or on behalf of whom the policy was effected.
(3)   A marine policy may be assigned by indorsement thereon or in other customary manner.

51 Assured who has no interest cannot assign
Where the assured has parted with or lost his interest in the subject-matter insured, and has not, before or at the time of so doing, expressly or impliedly agreed to assign the policy, any subsequent assignment of the policy is inoperative:
Provided that nothing in this section affects the assignment of a policy after loss.

The premium

52 When premium payable
Unless otherwise agreed, the duty of the assured or his agent to pay the premium, and the duty of the insurer to issue the policy to the assured or his agent, are concurrent conditions, and the insurer is not bound to issue the policy until payment or tender of the premium.

53 Policy effected through broker
(1)   Unless otherwise agreed, where a marine policy is effected on behalf of the assured by a broker, the broker is directly responsible to the insurer for the premium, and the insurer is directly responsible to the assured for the amount which may be payable in respect of losses, or in respect of returnable premium.
(2)   Unless otherwise agreed, the broker has, as against the assured, a lien upon the policy for the amount of the premium and his charges in respect of effecting the policy; and, where he has dealt with the person who employs him as a principal, he has also a lien on the policy in respect of any balance on any insurance

account which may be due to him from such person, unless when the debt was incurred he had reason to believe that such person was only an agent.

54   Effect of receipt on policy
Where a marine policy effected on behalf of the assured by a broker acknowledges the receipt of the premium, such acknowledgement is, in the absence of fraud, conclusive as between the insurer and the assured, but not as between the insurer and broker.

Loss and abandonment

55   Included and excluded losses
(1)   Subject to the provisions of this Act, and unless the policy otherwise provides, the insurer is liable for any loss proximately caused by a peril insured against, but, subject as aforesaid, he is not liable for any loss which is not proximately caused by a peril insured against.

(2)   In particular,—

(a)   The insurer is not liable for any loss attributable to the wilful misconduct of the assured, but, unless the policy otherwise provides, he is liable for any loss proximately caused by a peril insured against, even though the loss would not have happened but for the misconduct or negligence of the master or crew;

(b)   Unless the policy otherwise provides, the insurer on ship or goods is not liable for any loss proximately caused by delay, although the delay be caused by a peril insured against.

(c)   Unless the policy otherwise provides, the insurer is not liable for ordinary wear and tear, ordinary leakage and breakage, inherent vice or nature of the subject-matter insured, or for any loss proximately caused by rats or vermin, or for any injury to machinery not proximately caused by maritime perils.

56   Partial and total loss
(1)   A loss may be either total or partial. Any loss other than a total loss, as herein-after defined, is a partial loss.

(2)   A total loss may be either an actual total loss, or a constructive total loss.

(3)   Unless a different intention appears from the terms of the policy, an insurance against total loss includes a constructive, as well as an actual, total loss.

(4)   Where the assured brings an action for a total loss and the evidence proves only a partial loss, he may, unless the policy otherwise provides, recover for a partial loss.

(5)   Where goods reach their destination in specie, but by reason of obliteration of marks, or otherwise, they are incapable of identification, the loss, if any, is partial, and not total.

57   Actual total loss
(1)   Where the subject-matter insured is destroyed, or so damaged as to cease to be a thing of the kind insured, or where the assured is irretrievably deprived thereof, there is an actual total loss.

(2)   In the case of an actual total loss no notice of abandonment need be given.

58   Missing ship
Where the ship concerned in the adventure is missing, and after the lapse of a reasonable time no news of her has been received, an actual total loss may be presumed.

59   Effect of transhipment, etc
Where, by a peril insured against, the voyage is interrupted at any intermediate port or place, under such circumstances as apart from any special stipulation in the contract of affreightment, to justify the master in landing and re-shipping the goods or other moveables, or in transhipping them, and sending them on to their

destination, the liability of the insurer continues, notwithstanding the landing or transhipment.

60 Constructive total loss defined

(1) Subject to any express provision in the policy, there is a constructive total loss where the subject-matter insured is reasonably abandoned on account of its total loss appearing to be unavoidable, or because it could not be preserved from the actual total loss without an expenditure which would exceed its value when the expenditure had been incurred.

(2) In particular, there is a constructive total loss—

(i) Where the assured is deprived of the possession of his ship or goods by a peril insured against, and (a) it is unlikely that he can recover the ship or goods, as the case may be, or (b) the cost of recovering the ship or goods, as the case may be, would exceed their value when recovered; or

(ii) In the case of damage to a ship, where she is so damaged by a peril insured against that the cost of repairing the damage would exceed the value of the ship when repaired.

In estimating the cost of repairs, no deduction is to be made in respect of general average contributions to those repairs payable by other interests, but account is to be taken of the expense of future salvage operations and of any future general average contributions to which the ship would be liable if repaired; or

(iii) In the case of damage to goods, where the cost of repairing the damage and forwarding the goods to their destination would exceed their value on arrival.

61 Effect of constructive total loss

Where there is a constructive total loss the assured may either treat the loss as a partial loss, or abandon the subject-matter insured to the insurer and treat the loss as if it were an actual total loss.

62 Notice of abandonment

(1) Subject to the provisions of this section, where the assured elects to abandon the subject-matter insured to the insurer, he must give notice of the abandonment. If he fails to do so the loss can only be treated as a partial loss.

(2) Notice of abandonment may be given in writing, or by word of mouth, or partly in writing and partly by word of mouth, and may be given in terms which indicate the intention of the assured to abandon his insured interest in the subject-matter insured unconditionally to the insurer.

(3) Notice of abandonment must be given with reasonable diligence after the receipt of reliable information of the loss, but where the information is of a doubtful character the assured is entitled to a reasonable time to make inquiry.

(4) Where notice of abandonment is properly given, the rights of the assured are not prejudiced by the fact that the insurer refuses to accept the abandonment.

(5) The acceptance of an abandonment may be either express or implied from the conduct of the insurer. The mere silence of the insurer after notice is not an acceptance.

(6) Where a notice of abandonment is accepted the abandonment is irrevocable. The acceptance of the notice conclusively admits liability for the loss and the sufficiency of the notice.

(7) Notice of abandonment is unnecessary where, at the time when the assured receives information of the loss, there would be no possibility of benefit to the insurer if notice were given to him.

(8) Notice of abandonment may be waived by the insurer.

(9) Where an insurer has re-insured his risk, no notice of abandonment need be given by him.

63   Effect of abandonment

(1)   Where there is a valid abandonment the insurer is entitled to take over the interest of the assured in whatever may remain of the subject-matter insured, and all proprietary rights incidental thereto.

(2)   Upon the abandonment of a ship, the insurer thereof is entitled to any freight in course of being earned, and which is earned by her subsequent to the casualty causing the loss, less the expenses of earning it incurred after the casualty; and, where a ship is carrying the owner's goods, the insurer is entitled to a reasonable remuneration for the carriage of them subsequent to the casualty causing the loss.

Partial losses (including salvage and general average and particular charges)

64   Particular average loss

(1)   A particular average loss is a partial loss of the subject-matter insured, caused by a peril insured against, and which is not a general average loss.

(2)   Expenses incurred by or on behalf of the assured for the safety or preservation of the subject-matter insured, other than general average and salvage charges, are called particular charges. Particular charges are not included in particular average.

65   Salvage charges

(1)   Subject to any express provision in the policy, salvage charges incurred in preventing a loss by perils insured against may be recovered as a loss by those perils.

(2)   'Salvage charges' means the charges recoverable under maritime law by a salvor independently of contract. They do not include the expenses of services in the nature of salvage rendered by the assured or his agents, or any person employed for hire by them, for the purpose of averting a peril insured against. Such expenses, where properly incurred, may be recovered as particular charges or as a general average loss, according to the circumstances under which they were incurred.

66   General average loss

(1)   A general average loss is a loss caused by or directly consequential on a general average act. It includes a general average expenditure as well as a general average sacrifice.

(2)   There is a general average act where any extraordinary sacrifice or expenditure is voluntarily and reasonably made or incurred in the time of peril for the purpose of preserving the property imperilled in the common adventure.

(3)   Where there is a general average loss, the party on whom it falls is entitled, subject to the conditions imposed by maritime law, to a rateable contribution from the other parties interested, and such contribution is called a general average contribution.

(4)   Subject to any express provision in the policy, where the assured has incurred a general average expenditure, he may recover from the insurer in respect of the proportion of the loss which falls upon him; and, in the case of a general average sacrifice, he may recover from the insurer in respect of the whole loss without having enforced his right of contribution from the other parties liable to contribute.

(5)   Subject to any express provision in the policy, where the assured has paid, or is liable to pay, a general average contribution in respect of the subject insured, he may recover therefor from the insurer.

(6)   In the absence of express stipulation, the insurer is not liable for any general average loss or contribution where the loss was not incurred for the purpose of avoiding, or in connexion with the avoidance of, a peril insured against.

(7)   Where ship, freight, and cargo, or any two of those interests, are owned by

the same assured, the liability of the insurer in respect of general average losses or contributions is to be determined as if those subjects were owned by different persons.

Measure of indemnity

67 Extent of liability of insurer for loss
(1) The sum which the assured can recover in respect of a loss on a policy by which he is insured, in the case of an unvalued policy to the full extent of the insurable value, or in the case of a valued policy to the full extent of the value fixed by the policy, is called the measure of indemnity.

(2) Where there is a loss recoverable under the policy, the insurer, or each insurer if there be more than one, is liable for such proportion of the measure of indemnity as the amount of his subscription bears to the value fixed by the policy in the case of a valued policy, or to the insurable value in the case of an unvalued policy.

68 Total loss
Subject to the provisions of this Act and to any express provision in the policy, where there is a total loss of the subject-matter insured,—

(1) If the policy be a valued policy, the measure of indemnity is the sum fixed by the policy.

(2) If the policy be an unvalued policy, the measure of indemnity is the insurable value of the subject-matter insured.

69 Partial loss of ship
Where a ship is damaged, but not totally lost, the measure of indemnity, subject to any express provision in the policy, is as follows:—

(1) Where the ship has been repaired, the assured is entitled to the reasonable cost of the repairs, less the customary deductions, but not exceeding the sum insured in respect of any one casualty.

(2) Where the ship has been only partially repaired, the assured is entitled to the reasonable cost of such repairs, computed as above, and also to be indemnified for the reasonable depreciation, if any, arising from the unrepaired damage, provided that the aggregate amount shall not exceed the cost of repairing the whole damage, computed as above.

(3) Where the ship has not been repaired, and has not been sold in her damaged state during the risk, the assured is entitled to be indemnified for the reasonable depreciation arising from the unrepaired damage, but not exceeding the reasonable cost of repairing such damage, computed as above.

70 Partial loss of freight
Subject to any express provision in the policy, where there is a partial loss of freight, the measure of indemnity is such proportion of the sum fixed by the policy in the case of a valued policy, or of the insurable value in the case of an unvalued policy, as the proportion of freight lost by the assured bears to the whole freight at the risk of the assured under the policy.

71 Partial loss of goods, merchandise, etc
Where there is a partial loss of goods, merchandise, or other moveables, the measure of indemnity, subject to any express provision in the policy, is as follows:—

(1) Where part of the goods, merchandise, or other moveables insured by a valued policy is totally lost, the measure of indemnity is such proportion of the sum fixed by the policy as the insurable value of the part lost bears to the insurable value of the whole, ascertained as in the case of an unvalued policy.

(2) Where part of the goods, merchandise, or other moveables insured by an

unvalued policy is totally lost, the measure of indemnity is the insurable value of the part lost, ascertained as in the case of total loss.

(3)   Where the whole or any part of the goods or merchandise insured has been delivered damaged at its destination, the measure of indemnity is such proportion of the sum fixed by the policy in the case of a valued policy, or of the insurable value in the case of an unvalued policy, as the difference between the gross sound and damaged values at the place of arrival bears to the gross sound value.

(4)   'Gross value' means the wholesale price or, if there be no such price, the estimated value, with, in either case, freight, landing charges, and duty paid beforehand; provided that, in the case of goods or merchandise customarily sold in bond, the bonded price is deemed to be the gross value. 'Gross proceeds' means the actual price obtained at a sale where all charges on sale are paid by the sellers.

72   Apportionment of valuation

Where different species of property are insured under a single valuation, the valuation must be apportioned over the different species in proportion to their respective insurable values, as in the case of an unvalued policy. The insured value of any part of a species is such proportion of the total insured value of the same as the insurable value of the part bears to the insurable value of the whole, ascertained in both cases as provided by this Act.

(2)   Where a valuation has to be apportioned, and particulars of the prime cost of each separate species, quality, or description of goods cannot be ascertained, the division of the valuation may be made over the net arrived sound values of the different species, qualities, or descriptions of goods.

73   General average contributions and salvage charges

(1)   Subject to any express provision in the policy, where the assured has paid, or is liable for, any general average contribution, the measure of indemnity is the full amount of such contribution, if the subject-matter liable to contribution is insured for its full contributory value; but, if such subject-matter be not insured for its full contributory value, or if only part of it be insured, the indemnity payable by the insurer must be reduced in proportion to the under insurance, and where there has been a particular average loss which constitutes a deduction from the contributory value, and for which the insurer is liable, that amount must be deducted from the insured value in order to ascertain what the insurer is liable to contribute.

(2)   Where the insurer is liable for salvage charges the extent of his liability must be determined on the like principle.

74   Liabilities to third parties

Where the assured has effected an insurance in express terms against any liability to a third party, the measure of indemnity, subject to any express provision in the policy, is the amount paid or payable by him to such third party in respect of such liability.

75   General provisions as to measure of indemnity

(1)   Where there has been a loss in respect of any subject-matter not expressly provided for in the foregoing provisions of this Act, the measure of indemnity shall be ascertained, as nearly as may be, in accordance with those provisions, in so far as applicable to the particular case.

(2)   Nothing in the provisions of this Act relating to the measure of indemnity shall affect the rules relating to double insurance, or prohibit the insurer from disproving interest wholly or in part, or from showing that at the time of the loss the whole or any part of the subject-matter insured was not at risk under the policy.

76   Particular average warranties

(1)   Where the subject-matter insured is warranted free from particular average, the assured cannot recover for a loss of part, other than a loss incurred by a

general average sacrifice, unless the contract contained in the policy be apportionable; but, if the contract be apportionable, the assured may recover for a total loss of any apportionable part.

(2)   Where the subject-matter insured is warranted free from particular average, either wholly or under a certain percentage, the insurer is nevertheless liable for salvage charges, and for particular charges and other expenses properly incurred pursuant to the provisions of the suing and labouring clause in order to avert a loss insured against.

(3)   Unless the policy otherwise provides, where the subject-matter is warranted free from particular average under a specified percentage, a general average loss cannot be added to a particular average loss to make up the specified percentage.

(4)   For the purpose of ascertaining whether the specified percentage has been reached, regard shall be had only to the actual loss suffered by the subject-matter insured. Particular charges and the expenses of and incidental to ascertaining and proving the loss must be excluded.

77   Successive losses

(1)   Unless the policy otherwise provides, and subject to the provisions of this Act, the insurer is liable for successive losses, even though the total amount of such losses may exceed the sum insured.

(2)   Where, under the same policy, a partial loss, which has not been repaired or otherwise made good, is followed by a total loss, the assured can only recover in respect of the total loss:

Provided that nothing in this section shall affect the liability of the insurer under the suing and labouring clause.

78   Suing and labouring clause

(1)   Where the policy contains a suing and labouring clause, the engagement thereby entered into is deemed to be supplementary to the contract of insurance, and the assured may recover from the insurer any expenses properly incurred pursuant to the clause, notwithstanding that the insurer may have paid for a total loss, or that the subject-matter may have been warranted free from particular average, either wholly or under a certain percentage.

(2)   General average losses and contributions and salvage charges, as defined by this Act, are not recoverable under the suing and labouring clause.

(3)   Expenses incurred for the purpose of averting or diminishing any loss not covered by the policy are not recoverable under the suing and labouring clause.

(4)   It is the duty of the assured and his agents, in all cases, to take such measures as may be reasonable for the purpose of averting or minimising a loss.

Rights of insurer on payment

79   Right of subrogation

(1)   Where the insurer pays for a total loss, either of the whole, or in the case of goods of any apportionable part, of the subject-matter insured, he thereupon becomes entitled to take over the interest of the assured in whatever may remain of the subject-matter so paid for, and he is thereby subrogated to all the rights and remedies of the assured in and in respect of that subject-matter as from the time of the casualty causing the loss.

(2)   Subject to the foregoing provisions, where the insurer pays for a partial loss, he acquires no title to the subject-matter insured, or such part of it as may remain, but he is thereupon subrogated to all rights and remedies of the assured in and in respect of the subject-matter insured as from the time of the casualty causing the loss, in so far as the assured has been indemnified, according to this Act, by such payment for the loss.

80   Right of contribution

(1)   Where the assured is over-insured by double insurance, each insurer is

bound, as between himself and the other insurers, to contribute rateably to the loss in proportion to the amount for which he is liable under his contract.

(2)   If any insurer pays more than his proportion of the loss, he is entitled to maintain an action for contribution against the other insurers, and is entitled to the like remedies as a surety who has paid more than his proportion of the debt.

81   Effect of under insurance

Where the assured is insured for an amount less than the insurable value or, in the case of a valued policy, for an amount less than the policy valuation, he is deemed to be his own insurer in respect of the uninsured balance.

Return of premium

82   Enforcement of return

Where the premium or a proportionate part thereof is, by this Act, declared to be returnable,—

   (a)   If already paid, it may be recovered by the assured from the insurer; and

   (b)   If unpaid, it may be retained by the assured or his agent.

83   Return by agreement

Where the policy contains a stipulation for the return of the premium, or a proportionate part thereof, on the happening of a certain event, and that event happens, the premium, or, as the case may be, the proportionate part thereof, is thereupon returnable to the assured.

84   Return for failure of consideration

(1)   Where the consideration for the payment of the premium totally fails, and there has been no fraud or illegality on the part of the assured or his agents, the premium is thereupon returnable to the assured.

(2)   Where the consideration for the payment of the premium is apportionable and there is a total failure of any apportionable part of the consideration, a proportionate part of the premium is, under the like conditions, thereupon returnable to the assured.

(3)   In particular—

   (a)   Where the policy is void, or is avoided by the insurer as from the commencement of the risk, the premium is returnable, provided that there has been no fraud or illegality on the part of the assured; but if the risk is not apportionable, and has once attached, the premium is not returnable;

   (b)   Where the subject-matter insured, or part thereof, has never been imperilled, the premium, or, as the case may be, a proportionate part thereof, is returnable:

   Provided that where the subject-matter has been insured 'lost or not lost' and has arrived in safety at the time when the contract is concluded, the premium is not returnable unless, at such time, the insurer knew of the safe arrival.

   (c)   Where the assured has no insurable interest throughout the currency of the risk, the premium is returnable, provided that this rule does not apply to a policy effected by way of gaming or wagering;

   (d)   Where the assured has a defeasible interest which is terminated during the currency of the risk, the premium is not returnable;

   (e)   Where the assured has over-insured under an unvalued policy, a proportionate part of the premium is returnable;

   (f)   Subject to the foregoing provisions, where the assured has over-insured by double insurance, a proportionate part of the several premiums is returnable:

   Provided that, if the policies are effected at different times, and any earlier policy has at any time borne the entire risk, or if a claim has been paid on the policy in respect of the full sum insured thereby, no premium is returnable in respect of that policy, and when the double insurance is effected knowingly by the assured no premium is returnable.

Mutual insurance

85 Modification of Act in case of mutual insurance

(1) Where two or more persons mutually agree to insure each other against marine losses there is said to be a mutual insurance.

(2) The provisions of this Act relating to the premium do not apply to mutual insurance, but a guarantee, or such other arrangement as may be agreed upon, may be substituted for the premium.

(3) The provisions of this Act, in so far as they may be modified by the agreement of the parties, may in the case of mutual insurance be modified by the terms of the policies issued by the association, or by the rules and regulations of the association.

(4) Subject to the expectations mentioned in this section, the provisions of this Act apply to a mutual insurance.

Supplemental

86 Ratification by assured

Where a contract of marine insurance is in good faith effected by one person on behalf of another, the person on whose behalf it is effected may ratify the contract even after he is aware of a loss.

87 Implied obligations varied by agreement or usage

(1) Where any right, duty, or liability would arise under a contract of marine insurance by implication of law, it may be negatived or varied by express agreement or by usage, if the usage be such as to bind both parties to the contract.

(2) The provisions of this section extend to any right, duty, or liability declared by this Act which may be lawfully modified by agreement.

88 Reasonable time, etc, a question of fact

Where by this Act any reference is made to reasonable time, reasonable premium, or reasonable diligence, the question what is reasonable is a question of fact.

89 Slip as evidence

Where there is a duly stamped policy, reference may be made, as heretofore, to the slip or covering note, in any legal proceeding.

90 Interpretation of terms

In this Act, unless the context or subject-matter otherwise requires,—

'Action' includes counter-claim and set off:

'Freight' includes the profit derivable by a shipowner from the employment of his ship to carry his own goods or moveables, as well as freight payable by a third party, but does not include passage money:

'Moveables' means any moveable tangible property, other than the ship, and includes money, valuable securities, and other documents:

'Policy' means a marine policy.

91 Savings

(1) Nothing in this Act, or in any repeal effected thereby, shall affect—

(a) The provisions of the Stamp Act 1891, or any enactment for the time being in force relating to the revenue;

(b) The provisions of the Companies Act 1862, or any enactment amending or substituted for the same;

(c) The provisions of any statute not expressly repealed by this Act.

(2) The rules of the common law including the law merchant, save in so far as they are inconsistent with the express provisions of this Act, shall continue to apply to contracts of marine insurance.

94 Short title

This Act may be cited as the Marine Insurance Act 1906.

SCHEDULES

SCHEDULE 1
FORM OF POLICY
Section 30

BE IT KNOWN THAT .. .. .. as well in .. .. own name as for and in the name and
names of all and every other person or persons to whom the same doth, may, or
shall appertain, in part or in all doth make assurance and cause .. .. and them,
and every of them, to be insured lost or not lost, at and from .. ..

Upon any kind of goods and merchandise, and also upon the body, tackle,
apparel, ordnance, munition, artillery, boat, and other furniture, of and in the good
ship or vessel called the .. .. whereof is master under God, for this present
voyage, ... or whosoever else shall go for master in the said ship, or by whatsoever other name or names the said ship, or the master thereof, is or shall be
named or called; beginning the adventure upon the said goods and merchandises
from the loading thereof aboard the said ship, ... upon the said ship, ... etc
and so shall continue and endure, during her abode there, upon the said ship, etc.
And further, until the said ship, with all her ordnance, tackle, apparel, etc, and
goods and merchandises whatsoever shall be arrived at .. .. upon the said ship,
etc, until she hath moored at anchor for twenty-four hours in good safety; and
upon the goods and merchandises, until the same be there discharged and safely
landed. And it shall be lawful for the said ship, etc, in this voyage, to proceed and
sail to and touch and stay at any ports or places whatsoever without prejudice to
this insurance. The said ship, etc, goods and merchandises, etc, for so much as
concerns the assured by agreement between the assured and assurers in this
policy, are and shall be valued at .. ..

Touching the adventures and perils which we the assurers are contented to bear
and do take upon us in this voyage: they are of the seas, men of war, fire, enemies,
pirates, rovers, thieves, jettisons, letters of mart and countermart, surprisals,
takings at sea, arrests, restraints, and detainments of all kings, princes, and people,
of what nation, condition, or quality soever, barratry of the master and mariners,
and of all other perils, losses, and misfortunes, that have or shall come to the hurt,
detriment, or damage of the said goods and merchandises, and ship, etc, or any
part thereof. And in case of any loss or misfortune it shall be lawful to the assured,
their factors, servants and assigns, to sue, labour, and travel for, in and about the
defence, safeguards, and recovery of the said goods and merchandises, and ship,
etc, or any part thereof, without prejudice to this insurance; to the charges whereof
we, the assurers, will contribute each one according to the rate and quantity of his
sum herein assured. And it is especially declared and agreed that no acts of the
insurer or insured in recovering, saving, or preserving the property insured shall
be considered as a waiver, or acceptance of abandonment. And it is agreed by us,
the insurers, that this writing or policy of assurance shall be of as much force and
effect as the surest writing or policy of assurance heretofore made in Lombard
Street, or in the Royal Exchange, or elsewhere in London. And so we, the assurers,
are contented, and do hereby promise and bind ourselves, each one for his own
part, our heirs, executors, and goods to the assured, their executors, administrators, and assigns, for the true performance of the premises, confessing ourselves
paid the consideration due unto us for this assurance by the assured, at and after
the rate of .. ..

IN WITNESS whereof we, the assurers, have subscribed our names and sums
assured in London.

N.B.—Corn, fish, salt, fruit, flour, and seed are warranted free from average,
unless general, or the ship be stranded—sugar, tobacco, hemp, flax, hides and
skins are warranted free from average, under five pounds per cent, and all other

goods, also the ship and freight, are warranted free from average, under three pounds per cent unless general, or the ship be stranded.

Rules for construction of policy

The following are the rules referred to by this Act for the construction of a policy in the above or other like form, where the context does not otherwise require:—

1   Where the subject-matter is insured 'lost or not lost', and the loss has occurred before the contract is concluded, the risk attaches, unless at such time the assured was aware of the loss, and the insurer was not.

2   Where the subject-matter is insured 'from' a particular place, the risk does not attach until the ship starts on the voyage insured.

3   (a)   Where a ship is insured 'at and from' a particular place, and she is at that place in good safety when the contract is concluded, the risk attaches immediately.

(b)   If she be not at that place when the contract is concluded, the risk attaches as soon as she arrives there in good safety, and, unless the policy otherwise provides, it is immaterial that she is covered by another policy for a specified time after arrival.

(c)   Where chartered freight is insured 'at and from' a particular place, and the ship is at that place in good safety when the contract is concluded the risk attaches immediately. If she be not there when the contract is concluded, the risk attaches as soon as she arrives there in good safety.

(d)   Where freight, other than chartered freight, is payable without special conditions and is insured 'at and from' a particular place, the risk attaches pro rata as the goods or merchandise are shipped; provided that if there be cargo in readiness which belongs to the shipowner, or which some other person has contracted with him to ship, the risk attaches as soon as the ship is ready to receive such cargo.

4   Where goods or other moveables are insured 'from the loading thereof', the risk does not attach until such goods or moveables are actually on board, and the insurer is not liable for them while in transit from shore to ship.

5   Where the risk on goods or other moveables continues until they are 'safely landed', they must be landed in the customary manner and within a reasonable time after arrival at the port of discharge, and if they are not so landed the risk ceases.

6   In the absence of any further license or usage, the liberty to touch and stay 'at any port or place whatsoever' does not authorise the ship to depart from the course of her voyage from the port of departure to the port of destination.

7   The term 'perils of the seas' refers only to fortuitous accidents or casualties of the seas. It does not include the ordinary action of the winds and waves.

8   The term 'pirates' includes passengers who mutiny and rioters who attack the ship from the shore.

9   The term 'thieves' does not cover clandestine theft or a theft committed by anyone of the ship's company, whether crew or passengers.

10   The term 'arrests, etc, of kings, princes, and people' refers to political or executive acts, and does not include a loss caused by riot or by ordinary judicial process.

11   The term 'barratry' includes every wrongful act wilfully committed by the master or crew to the prejudice of the owner, or, as the case may be, the charterer.

12   The term 'all other perils' includes only perils similar in kind to the perils specifically mentioned in the policy.

13   The term 'average unless general' means a partial loss of the subject-matter insured other than a general average loss, and does not include 'particular charges'.

14   Where the ship has stranded, the insurer is liable for the excepted losses,

although the loss is not attributable to the stranding, provided that when the stranding takes place the risk has attached and, if the policy be on goods, that the damaged goods are on board.

15   The term 'ship' includes the hull, materials and outfit, stores and provisions for the officers and crew, and, in the case of vessels engaged in a special trade, the ordinary fittings requisite for the trade, and also, in the case of a steamship, the machinery, boilers, and coals and engine stores, if owned by the assured.

16   The term 'freight' includes the profit derivable by a shipowner from the employment of his ship to carry his own goods or moveables, as well as freight payable by a third party, but does not include passage money.

17   The term 'goods' means goods in the nature of merchandise, and does not include personal effects or provisions and stores for use on board.

In the absence of any usage to the contrary, deck cargo and living animals must be insured specifically, and not under the general denomination of goods.

CHEQUES ACT 1957
(5 & 6 Eliz 2, c 36)

1   Protection of bankers paying unindorsed or irregularly indorsed cheques, etc

(1)   Where a banker in good faith and in the ordinary course of business pays a cheque drawn on him which is not indorsed or is irregularly indorsed, he does not in doing so, incur any liability by reason only of the absence of, or irregularly in indorsement, and he is deemed to have paid it in due course.

(2)   Where a banker in good faith and in the ordinary course of business pays any such instrument as the following namely—

(a)   a document issued by a customer of his which, though not a bill of exchange, is intended to enable a person to obtain payment from him of the sum mentioned in the document;

(b)   a draft payable on demand drawn by him upon himself, whether payable at the head office or some other office of his bank; he does not, in so doing, incur any liability by reason only of the absence of, or irregularity in, indorsement, and the payment discharges the instrument.

2   Rights of bankers collecting cheques not indorsed by holders

A banker who gives value for, or has a lien on, a cheque payable to order which the holder delivers to him for collection without indorsing it, has such (if any) rights as he would have had if, upon delivery, the holder had indorsed it in blank.

3   Unindorsed cheques as evidence of payment

[(1)]   An unindorsed cheque which appears to have been paid by the banker on whom it is drawn is evidence of the receipt by the payee of the sum payable by the cheque.

[(2)   For the purposes of subsection (1) above, a copy of a cheque to which that subsection applies is evidence of the cheque if—

(a)   the copy is made by the banker in whose possession the cheque is after presentment and,

(b)   it is certified by him to be a true copy of the original.]

4   Protection of bankers collecting payment of cheques, etc

(1)   Where a banker, in good faith and without negligence—

(a)   receives payment for a customer of an instrument to which this section applies; or

(b)   having credited a customer's account with the amount of such an instrument, receives payment thereof for himself;

and the customer has no title, or a defective title, to the instrument, the banker does not incur any liability to the true owner of the instrument by reason only of having received payment thereof.

(2) This section applies to the following instruments, namely:—

(a) cheques [(including cheques which under section 81A(1) of the Bills of Exchange Act 1882 or otherwise are not transferable)];

(b) any document issued by a customer of a banker which, though not a bill of exchange, is intended to enable a person to obtain payment from that banker of the sum mentioned in the document;

(c) any document issued by a public officer is intended to enable a person to obtain payment from the Paymaster General or the Queen's and Lord Treasurer's Remembrancer of the sum mentioned in the document but is not a bill of exchange;

(d) any draft payable on demand drawn by a banker upon himself whether payable at the head office or some other office of his bank.

(3) A banker is not to be treated for the purposes of this section as having been negligent by reason only of his failure to concern himself with absence of, or irregularity in, indorsement of an instrument.

5 Application of certain provisions of Bills of Exchange Act, 1882, to instruments not being bills of exchange

The provisions of the Bills of Exchange Act, 1882, relating to crossed cheques shall, so far as applicable, have effect in relation to instruments (other than cheques) to which the last foregoing section applies as they have effect in relation to cheques.

6 Construction, saving and repeal

(1) This Act shall be construed as one with the Bills of Exchange Act, 1882.

(2) The foregoing provisions of this Act do not make negotiable any instrument which, apart from them, is not negotiable.

[. . .]

HIRE-PURCHASE ACT 1964
(1964, c 53)

[PART III
TITLE TO MOTOR VEHICLES ON HIRE-PURCHASE OR CONDITIONAL SALE

27 Protection of purchasers of motor vehicles

(1) This section applies where a motor vehicle has been bailed or (in Scotland) hired under a hire-purchase agreement, or has been agreed to be sold under a conditional sale agreement, and, before the property in the vehicle has become vested in the debtor, he disposes of the vehicle to another person.

(2) Where the disposition referred to in subsection (1) above is to a private purchaser, and he is a purchaser of the motor vehicle in good faith without notice of the hire-purchase or conditional sale agreement (the 'relevant agreement') that disposition shall have effect as if the creditor's title to the vehicle has been vested in the debtor immediately before that disposition.

(3) Where the person to whom the disposition referred to in subsection (1) above is made (the 'original purchaser') is a trade or finance purchaser, then if the person who is the first private purchaser of the motor vehicle after that disposition (the 'first private purchaser') is a purchaser of the vehicle in good faith without notice of the relevant agreement, the disposition of the vehicle to the first private purchaser shall have effect as if the title of the creditor to the vehicle had been vested in the debtor immediately before he disposed of it to the original purchaser.

(4) Where, in a case within subsection (3) above—

(a) the disposition by which the first private purchaser becomes a purchaser of the motor vehicle in good faith without notice of the relevant agreement is itself a bailment or hiring under a hire-purchase agreement, and

(b)   the person who is the creditor in relation to that agreement disposes of the vehicle to the first private purchaser, or a person claiming under him, by transferring to him the property in the vehicle in pursuance of a provision in the agreement in that behalf, the disposition referred to in paragraph (b) above (whether or not the person to whom it is made is a purchaser in good faith without notice of the relevant agreement) shall as well as the disposition referred to in paragraph (a) above, have effect as mentioned in subsection (3) above.

(5)   The preceding provisions of this section apply—

(a)   notwithstanding anything in [section 21 of the Sale of Goods Act 1979] (sale of goods by a person not the owner), but

(b)   without prejudice to the provisions of the Factors Acts (as defined by [section 61(1) of the said Act of 1979]) or any other enactment enabling the apparent owner of goods to dispose of them as if he were the true owner.

(6)   Nothing in this section shall exonerate the debtor from any liability (whether criminal or civil) to which he would be subject apart from this section; and, in a case where the debtor disposes of the motor vehicle to a trade or finance purchaser, nothing in this section shall exonerate—

(a)   that trade or finance purchaser, or

(b)   any other trade or finance purchaser who becomes a purchaser of the vehicle and is not a person claiming under the first private purchaser,

from any liability (whether criminal or civil) to which he would be subject apart from this section.

28   Presumptions relating to dealings with motor vehicles

(1)   Where in any proceedings (whether criminal or civil) relating to a motor vehicle it is proved—

(a)   that the vehicle was bailed or (in Scotland) hired under a hire-purchase agreement, or was agreed to be sold under a conditional sale agreement, and

(b)   that a person (whether a party to the proceedings or not) became a private purchaser of the vehicle in good faith without notice of the hire-purchase or conditional sale agreement (the 'relevant agreement'), this section shall have effect for the purposes of the operation of section 27 of this Act in relation to those proceedings.

(2)   It shall be presumed for those purposes unless the contrary is proved, that the disposition of the vehicle to the person referred to in subsection (1)(b) above (the 'relevant purchaser') was made by the debtor.

(3)   If it is proved that that disposition was not made by the debtor, then it shall be presumed for those purposes, unless the contrary is proved—

(a)   that the debtor disposed of the vehicle to a private purchaser purchasing in good faith without notice of the relevant agreement, and

(b)   that the relevant purchaser is or was a person claiming under the person to whom the debtor so disposed of the vehicle.

(4)   If it is proved that the disposition of the vehicle to the relevant purchaser was not made by the debtor, and that the person to whom the debtor disposed of the vehicle (the 'original purchaser') was a trade or finance purchaser, then it shall be presumed for those purposes, unless the contrary is proved—

(a)   that the person who, after the disposition of the vehicle to the original purchaser, first became a private purchaser of the vehicle was a purchaser in good faith without notice of the relevant agreement, and

(b)   that the relevant purchaser is or was a person claiming under the original purchaser.

(5)   Without prejudice to any other method of proof, where in any proceedings a party thereto admits a fact, that fact shall, for the purposes of this section, be taken as against him to be proved in relation to those proceedings.

29   Interpretation of Part III

(1)   In this Part of this Act—

'conditional sale agreement' means an agreement for the sale of goods under which the purchase price or part of it is payable by instalments, and the property in the goods is to remain in the seller (notwithstanding that the buyer is to be in possession of the goods) until such conditions as to the payment of instalments or otherwise as may be specified in the agreement are fulfilled;

'creditor' means the person by whom goods are bailed or (in Scotland) hired under a hire-purchase agreement or as the case may be, the seller under a conditional sale agreement, or the person to whom his rights and duties have passed by assignment or operation of law;

'disposition' means any sale or contract of sale (including a conditional sale agreement), any bailment or (in Scotland) hiring under a hire-purchase agreement and any transfer of the property of goods in pursuance of a provision in that behalf contained in a hire-purchase agreement, and includes any transaction purporting to be a disposition (as so defined), and 'dispose of' shall be construed accordingly;

'hire-purchase agreement' means an agreement, other than a conditional sale agreement, under which—

(a)   goods are bailed or (in Scotland) hired in return for periodical payments by the person to whom they are bailed or hired, and

(b)   the property in the goods will pass to that person if the terms of the agreement are complied with and one or more of the following occurs—

(i)   the exercise of an option to purchase by that person,

(ii)   the doing of any other specified act by any party to the agreement,

(iii)   the happening of any other specified events; and

'motor vehicle' means a mechanically propelled vehicle intended or adapted for use on roads to which the public has access.

(2)   In this Part of this Act 'trade or finance purchaser' means a purchaser who, at the time of the disposition made to him, carries on a business which consists, wholly or partly—

(a)   of purchasing motor vehicles for the purpose of offering or exposing them for sale, or

(b)   of providing finance by purchasing motor vehicles for the purpose of bailing or (in Scotland) hiring them under hire-purchase agreements or agreeing to sell them under conditional sale agreements,

and 'private purchaser' means a purchaser who, at the time of the disposition made to him, does not carry on any such business.

(3)   For the purposes of this Part of this Act a person becomes a purchaser of a motor vehicle if, and at the time when, a disposition of the vehicle is made to him; and a person shall be taken to be a purchaser of a motor vehicle without notice of a hire-purchase agreement or conditional sale agreement if, at the time of the disposition made to him, he has no actual notice that the vehicle is or was the subject of any such agreement.

(4)   In this Part of this Act the 'debtor' in relation to a motor vehicle which has been bailed or hired under a hire-purchase agreement, or, as the case may be, agreed to be sold under a conditional sale agreement, means the person who at the material time (whether the agreement has before that time been terminated or not) either—

(a)   is the person to whom the vehicle is bailed or hired under that agreement, or

(b)   is, in relation to the agreement, the buyer,

including a person who at that time is, by virtue of section 130(4) of the Consumer Credit Act 1974 treated as a bailee or (in Scotland) a custodier of the vehicle.

(5)   In this Part of this Act any reference to the title of the creditor to a motor vehicle which has been bailed or (in Scotland) hired under a hire-purchase agreement or agreed to be sold under a conditional sale agreement, and is disposed of

by the debtor, is a reference to such title (if any) to the vehicle as, immediately before that disposition, was vested in the person who then was the creditor in relation to the agreement.]

CARRIAGE OF GOODS BY ROAD ACT 1965
(1965, c 37)

1   Convention to have force of law
Subject to the following provisions of this Act, the provisions of the Convention on the Contract for the International Carriage of Goods by Road (in this Act referred to as 'the Convention'), as set out in the Schedule to this Act, shall have the force of law in the United Kingdom so far as they relate to the rights and liabilities of persons concerned in the carriage of goods by road under a contract to which the Convention applies.

2   Designation of High Contracting Parties
(1)   Her Majesty may by Order in Council from time to time certify who are the High Contracting Parties to the Convention and in respect of what territories they are respectively parties.

(2)   An Order in Council under this section shall, except so far as it has been superseded by a subsequent Order, be conclusive evidence of the matters so certified.

3   Power of court to take account of other proceedings
(1)   A court before which proceedings are brought to enforce a liability which is limited by article 23 in the Schedule to this Act may at any stage of the proceedings make any such order as appears to the court to be just and equitable in view of the provisions of the said article 23 and of any other proceedings which have been, or are likely to be, commenced in the United Kingdom or elsewhere to enforce the liability in whole or in part.

(2)   Without prejudice to the preceding subsection, a court before which proceedings are brought to enforce a liability which is limited by the said article 23 shall, where the liability is, or may be, partly enforceable in other proceedings in the United Kingdom or elsewhere, have jurisdiction to award an amount less than the court would have awarded if the limitation applied solely to the proceedings before the court, or to make any part of its award conditional on the result of any other proceedings.

4   Registration of foreign judgments
(1)   Subject to the next following subsection, Part I of the Foreign Judgments (Reciprocal Enforcement) Act 1933 (in this section referred to as 'the Act of 1933') shall apply whether or not it would otherwise have so applied, to any judgment which—

(a)   has been given in any such action as is referred to in paragraph 1 of article 31 in the Schedule to this Act, and

(b)   has been so given by any court or tribunal of a territory in respect of which one of the High Contracting Parties other than the United Kingdom, is a party to the Convention, and

(c)   has become enforceable in that territory.

(2)   In the application of Part I of the Act of 1933 in relation to any such judgment as is referred to in the preceding subsection, section 4 of that Act shall have effect with the omission of subsections (2) and (3).

(3)   The registration, in accordance with Part I of the Act of 1933, of any such judgment as is referred to in subsection (1) of this section shall constitute, in relation to that judgment compliance with the formalities for the purposes of paragraph 3 of article 31 in the Schedule to this Act.

5 Contribution between carriers

(1) Where a carrier under a contract to which the Convention applies is liable in respect of any loss or damage for which compensation is payable under the Convention, nothing in [section 1 of the Civil Liability (Contribution) Act 1978] or section 3(2) of the Law Reform (Miscellaneous Provisions) (Scotland) Act 1940 shall confer on him any right to recover contribution in respect of that loss or damage from any other carrier who, in accordance with article 34 in the Schedule to this Act, is a party to the contract of carriage.

(2) The preceding subsection shall be without prejudice to the operation of article 37 in the Schedule to this Act.

6 Actions against High Contracting Parties

Every High Contracting Party to the Convention shall, for the purpose of any proceedings brought in a court in the United Kingdom in accordance with the provisions of article 31 in the Schedule to this Act to enforce a claim in respect of carriage undertaken by that Party, be deemed to have submitted to the jurisdiction of that court, and accordingly rules of court may provide for the manner in which any such action is to be commenced and carried on; but nothing in this section shall authorise the issue of execution, or in Scotland the execution of diligence, against the property of any High Contracting Party.

7 Arbitrations

(1) Any reference in the preceding provisions of this Act to a court includes a reference to an arbitration tribunal acting by virtue of article 33 in the Schedule to this Act.

(2) For the purposes of article 32 in the Schedule to this Act, as it has effect (by virtue of the said article 33) in relation to arbitrations,—

[(a) as respects England and Wales and Northern Ireland, the provisions of section 14(3) to (5) of the Arbitration Act 1996 (which determine the time at which an arbitration is commenced) apply;]

(c) as respects Scotland, an arbitration shall be deemed to be commenced when one party to the arbitration serves on the other party or parties a notice requiring him or them to appoint an arbiter or to agree to the appointment of an arbiter or, where the arbitration agreement provides that the reference shall be to a person named or designated in the agreement, requiring him or them to submit the dispute to the person so named or designated.

8 Resolution of conflicts between Conventions on carriage of goods

(1) If it appears to Her Majesty in Council that there is any conflict between the provisions of this Act (including the provisions of the Convention as set out in the Schedule to this Act) and any provisions relating to the carriage of goods for reward by land, sea or air contained in—

(a) any other Convention which has been signed or ratified by or on behalf of Her Majesty's Government in the United Kingdom before the passing of this Act, or

(b) any enactment of the Parliament of the United Kingdom giving effect to such a Convention,

Her Majesty may by Order in Council make such provision as may seem to her to be appropriate for resolving that conflict by amending or modifying this Act or any such enactment.

(2) Any statutory instrument made by virtue of this section shall be subject to annulment in pursuance of a resolution of either House of Parliament.

[8A Amendments consequential on revision of Convention

(1) If at any time it appears to Her Majesty in Council that Her Majesty's Government in the United Kingdom have agreed to any revision of the Convention, Her Majesty may by Order in Council make such amendment of—

[(a)   this Act; and]
    (c)   section 5(1) of the Carriage by Air and Road Act 1979,
as appear to Her to be appropriate in consequence of the revision.
    (2)   In the preceding subsection 'revision' means an omission from, addition to
or alteration of the Convention and includes replacement of the Convention or
part of it by another Convention.
    (3)   An Order in Council under this section shall not be made unless a draft of
the Order has been laid before Parliament and approved by a resolution of each
House of Parliament. [. . .]

9   Application to British possessions, etc
Her Majesty may by Order in Council direct that this Act shall extend, subject to
such exceptions, adaptations and modifications as may be specified in the Order,
to—
    (a)   the Isle of Man;
    (b)   any of the Channel Islands;
    (c)   any colony.

10   Application to Scotland
In its application to Scotland, the Schedule to this Act shall have effect as if—
    (a)   any reference therein to a plaintiff included a reference to a pursuer;
    (b)   any reference therein to a defendant included a defender; and
    (c)   any reference to security for costs included a reference to caution for
expenses.

11   [*Applies to Northern Ireland*]

12   Orders in Council
An Order in Council made under any of the preceding provisions of this Act may
contain such transitional and supplementary provisions as appear to Her Majesty
to be expedient and may be varied or revoked by a subsequent Order in Council
made under that provision.

13   Application to Crown
This Act shall bind the Crown.

14   Short title, interpretation and commencement
    (1)   This Act may be cited as the Carriage of Goods by Road Act 1965.
    (2)   The persons who, for the purposes of this Act, are persons concerned in
the carriage of goods by road under a contract to which the Convention applies
are—
    (a)   the sender,
    (b)   the consignee,
    (c)   any carrier who, in accordance with article 34 in the Schedule to this Act
or otherwise, is a party to the contract of carriage,
    (d)   any person for whom such a carrier is responsible by virtue of article 3 in
the Schedule to this Act,
    (e)   any person to whom the rights and liabilities of any of the persons
referred to in paragraphs (a) to (d) of this subsection have passed (whether by
assignment or assignation or by operation of law).
    (3)   Except in so far as the context otherwise requires, any reference in this Act
to an enactment shall be construed as a reference to that enactment as amended or
extended by or under any other enactment.
    (4)   This Act shall come into operation on such day as Her Majesty may by
Order in Council appoint; but nothing in this Act shall apply in relation to any
contract for the carriage of goods by road made before the day so appointed.

SCHEDULE
CONVENTION ON THE CONTRACT FOR THE INTERNATIONAL CARRIAGE
OF GOODS BY ROAD (CMR)
Section 1

CHAPTER I
Scope of application

Article 1

1   This Convention shall apply to every contract for the carriage of goods by road in vehicles for reward, when the place of taking over of the goods and the place designated for delivery, as specified in the contract, are situated in two different countries, of which at least one is a contracting country, irrespective of the place of residence and the nationality of the parties.

2   For the purposes of this Convention, 'vehicles' means motor vehicles, articulated vehicles, trailers and semi-trailers as defined in article 4 of the Convention on Road Traffic dated 19th September 1949.

3   This Convention shall apply also where carriage coming within its scope is carried out by States or by governmental institutions or organisations.

4   This Convention shall not apply:
   (a)   to carriage performed under the terms of any international postal convention;
   (b)   to funeral consignments;
   (c)   to furniture removal.

5   The Contracting Parties agree not to vary any of the provisions of this Convention by special agreements between two or more of them, except to make it inapplicable to their frontier traffic or to authorise the use in transport operations entirely confined to their territory of consignment notes representing a title to the goods.

Article 2

1   Where the vehicle containing the goods is carried over part of the journey by sea, rail, inland waterways or air, and except where the provisions of article 14 are applicable, the goods are not unloaded from the vehicle, this Convention shall nevertheless apply to the whole of the carriage. Provided that to the extent that it is proved that any loss, damage or delay in delivery of the goods which occurs during the carriage by the other means of transport was not caused by an act or omission of the carrier by road, but by some event which could only have occurred in the course of and by reason of the carriage by that other means of transport, the liability of the carrier by road shall be determined not by this Convention but in the manner in which the liability of the carrier by the other means of transport would have been determined if a contract for the carriage of the goods alone had been made by the sender with the carrier by the other means of transport in accordance with the conditions prescribed by law for the carriage of goods by that means of transport. If, however, there be no such prescribed conditions, the liability of the carrier by road shall be determined by this Convention.

2   If the carrier by road is also himself the carrier by the other means of transport, his liability shall also be determined in accordance with the provisions of paragraph 1 of this article, but as if, in his capacities as carrier by road and as carrier by the other means of transport, he were two separate persons.

CHAPTER II
Persons for whom the carrier is responsible

Article 3

For the purposes of this Convention the carrier shall be responsible for the acts and omissions of his agents and servants and of any other persons of whose services he makes use for the performance of the carriage, when such agents, servants or other persons are acting within the scope of their employment, as if such acts or omissions were his own.

CHAPTER III

Conclusion and performance of the contract of carriage

Article 4
The contract of carriage shall be confirmed by the making out of a consignment note. The absence, irregularity or loss of the consignment note shall not affect the existence or the validity of the contract of carriage which shall remain subject to the provisions of this Convention.

Article 5
  1   The consignment note shall be made out in three original copies signed by the sender and by the carrier. These signatures may be printed or replaced by the stamps of the sender and the carrier if the law of the country in which the consign-ment note has been made out so permits. The first copy shall be handed to the sender, the second shall accompany the goods and the third shall be retained by the carrier.
  2   When the goods which are to be carried have to be loaded in different vehicles, or are of different kinds or are divided into different lots, the sender or the carrier shall have the right to require a separate consignment note to be made out for each vehicle used, or for each kind or lot of goods.

Article 6
  1   The consignment note shall contain the following particulars:
      (a)   the date of the consignment note and the place at which it is made out;
      (b)   the name and address of the sender;
      (c)   the name and address of the carrier;
      (d)   the place and the date of taking over of the goods and the place designated for delivery;
      (e)   the name and address of the consignee;
      (f)   the description in common use of the nature of the goods and the method of packing, and, in the case of dangerous goods, their generally recognised description;
      (g)   the number of packages and their special marks and numbers;
      (h)   the gross weight of the goods or their quantity otherwise expressed;
      (i)   charges relating to the carriage (carriage charges, supplementary charges, customs duties and other charges incurred from the making of the contract to the time of delivery);
      (j)   the requisite instructions for Customs and other formalities;
      (k)   a statement that the carriage is subject, notwithstanding any clause to the contrary, to the provisions of this Convention.
  2   Where applicable, the consignment note shall also contain the following particulars:
      (a)   a statement that transhipment is not allowed;
      (b)   the charges which the sender undertakes to pay;
      (c)   the amount of 'cash on delivery' charges;
      (d)   a declaration of the value of the goods and the amount representing special interest on delivery;
      (e)   the sender's instructions to the carrier regarding insurance of the goods;
      (f)   the agreed time-limit within which the carriage is to be carried out;
      (g)   a list of documents handed to the carrier.
  3   The parties may enter in the consignment note any other particulars which they deem useful.

Article 7

1 The sender shall be responsible for all expenses, loss and damage sustained by the carrier by reason of the inaccuracy or inadequacy of:

(a) the particulars specified in article 6, paragraph 1, (b), (d), (e), (f), (g), (h) and (j);

(b) the particulars specified in article 6, paragraph 2;

(c) any other particulars or instructions given by him to enable the consignment note to be made out or for the purpose of their being entered therein.

2 If, at the request of the sender, the carrier enters in the consignment note the particulars referred to in paragraph 1 of this article, he shall be deemed, unless the contrary is proved to have done so on behalf of the sender.

3 If the consignment note does not contain the statement specified in article 6, paragraph 1(k), the carrier shall be liable for all expenses, loss and damage sustained through such omission by the person entitled to dispose of the goods.

Article 8

1 On taking over the goods, the carrier shall check:

(a) the accuracy of the statements in the consignment note as to the number of packages and their marks and numbers, and

(b) the apparent condition of the goods and their packaging.

2 Where the carrier has no reasonable means of checking the accuracy of the statements referred to in paragraph 1(a) of this article, he shall enter his reservations in the consignment note together with the grounds on which they are based. He shall likewise specify the grounds for any reservations which he makes with regard to the apparent condition of the goods and their packaging. Such reservations shall not bind the sender unless he has expressly agreed to be bound by them in the consignment note.

3 The sender shall be entitled to require the carrier to check the gross weight of the goods or their quantity otherwise expressed. He may also require the contents of the packages to be checked. The carrier shall be entitled to claim the cost of such checking. The result of the checks shall be entered in the consignment note.

Article 9

1 The consignment note shall be prima facie evidence of the making of the contract of carriage, the conditions of the contract and the receipt of the goods by the carrier.

2 If the consignment note contains no specific reservations by the carrier, it shall be presumed, unless the contrary is proved, that the goods and their packaging appeared to be in good condition when the carrier took them over and that the number of packages, their marks and numbers corresponded with the statements in the consignment note.

Article 10

The sender shall be liable to the carrier for damage to persons, equipment or other goods, and for any expenses due to defective packing of the goods, unless the defect was apparent or known to the carrier at the time when he took over the goods and he made no reservations concerning it.

Article 11

1 For the purposes of the Customs or other formalities which have to be completed before delivery of the goods, the sender shall attach the necessary documents to the consignment note or place them at the disposal of the carrier and shall furnish him with all the information which he requires.

2 The carrier shall not be under any duty to enquire into either the accuracy or the adequacy of such documents and information. The sender shall be liable to the carrier for any damage caused by the absence, inadequacy or irregularity of such

documents and information, except in the case of some wrongful act or neglect on the part of the carrier.

3   The liability of the carrier for the consequences arising from the loss or incorrect use of the documents specified in and accompanying the consignment note or deposited with the carrier shall be that of an agent, provided that the compensation payable by the carrier shall not exceed that payable in the event of loss of the goods.

Article 12

1   The sender has a right to dispose of the goods, in particular by asking the carrier to stop the goods in transit, to change the place at which delivery is to take place or to deliver the goods to a consignee other than the consignee indicated in the consignment note.

2   This right shall cease to exist when the second copy of the consignment note is handed to the consignee or when the consignee exercises his right under article 13, paragraph 1; from that time onwards the carrier shall obey the orders of the consignee.

3   The consignee shall, however, have the right of disposal from the time when the consignment note is drawn up, if the sender makes an entry to that effect in the consignment note.

4   If in exercising his right of disposal the consignee has ordered the delivery of the goods to another person, that other person shall not be entitled to name other consignees.

5   The exercise of the right of disposal shall be subject to the following conditions:

(a)   that the sender or, in the case referred to in paragraph 3 of this article, the consignee who wishes to exercise the right produces the first copy of the consignment note on which the new instructions to the carrier have been entered and indemnifies the carrier against all expenses, loss and damage involved in carrying out such instructions;

(b)   that the carrying out of such instructions is possible at the time when the instructions reach the person who is to carry them out and does not either interfere with the normal working of the carrier's undertaking or prejudice the senders or consignees of other consignments;

(c)   that the instructions do not result in a division of the consignment.

6   When, by reason of the provisions of paragraph 5(b) of this article, the carrier cannot carry out the instructions which he receives he shall immediately notify the person who gave him such instructions.

7   A carrier who has not carried out the instructions given under the conditions provided for in this article, or who has carried them out without requiring the first copy of the consignment note to be produced, shall be liable to the person entitled to make a claim for any loss or damage caused thereby.

Article 13

1   After arrival of the goods at the place designated for delivery, the consignee shall be entitled to require the carrier to deliver to him, against a receipt, the second copy of the consignment note and the goods. If the loss of the goods is established or if the goods have not arrived after the expiry of the period provided for in article 19, the consignee shall be entitled to enforce in his own name against the carrier any rights arising from the contract of carriage.

2   The consignee who avails himself of the rights granted to him under paragraph 1 of this article shall pay the charges shown to be due on the consignment note, but in the event of dispute on this matter the carrier shall not be required to deliver the goods unless security has been furnished by the consignee.

Article 14

1   If for any reason it is or becomes impossible to carry out the contract in accordance with the terms laid down in the consignment note before the goods

reach the place designated for delivery, the carrier shall ask for instructions from the person entitled to dispose of the goods in accordance with the provisions of article 12.

2   Nevertheless, if circumstances are such as to allow the carriage to be carried out under conditions differing from those laid down in the consignment note and if the carrier has been unable to obtain instructions in reasonable time from the person entitled to dispose of the goods in accordance with the provisions of article 12, he shall take such steps as seem to him to be in the best interests of the person entitled to dispose of the goods.

Article 15

1   Where circumstances prevent delivery of the goods after their arrival at the place designated for delivery, the carrier shall ask the sender for his instructions. If the consignee refuses the goods the sender shall be entitled to dispose of them without being obliged to produce the first copy of the consignment note.

2   Even if he has refused the goods, the consignee may nevertheless require delivery so long as the carrier has not received instructions to the contrary from the sender.

3   When circumstances preventing delivery of the goods arise after the consignee, in exercise of his rights under article 12, paragraph 3, has given an order for the goods to be delivered to another person, paragraphs 1 and 2 of this article shall apply as if the consignee were the sender and that other person were the consignee.

Article 16

1   The carrier shall be entitled to recover the cost of his request for instructions and any expenses entailed in carrying out such instructions, unless such expenses were caused by the wrongful act or neglect of the carrier.

2   In the cases referred to in article 14, paragraph 1, and in article 15, the carrier may immediately unload the goods for account of the person entitled to dispose of them and thereupon the carriage shall be deemed to be at an end. The carrier shall then hold the goods on behalf of the person so entitled. He may however entrust them to a third party, and in that case he shall not be under any liability except for the exercise of reasonable care in the choice of such third party. The charges due under the consignment note and all other expenses shall remain chargeable against the goods.

3   The carrier may sell the goods, without awaiting instructions from the person entitled to dispose of them, if the goods are perishable or their condition warrants such a course, or when the storage expenses would be out of proportion to the value of the goods. He may also proceed to the sale of the goods in other cases if after the expiry of a reasonable period he has not received from the person entitled to dispose of the goods instructions to the contrary which he may reasonably be required to carry out.

4   If the goods have been sold pursuant to this article, the proceeds of sale, after deduction of the expenses chargeable against the goods, shall be placed at the disposal of the person entitled to dispose of the goods. If these charges exceed the proceeds of sale, the carrier shall be entitled to the difference.

5   The procedure in the case of sale shall be determined by the law or custom of the place where the goods are situated.

CHAPTER IV
Liability of the carrier

Article 17

1   The carrier shall be liable for the total or partial loss of the goods and for damage thereto occurring between the time when he takes over the goods and the time of delivery, as well as for any delay in delivery.

2   The carrier shall however be relieved of liability if the loss, damage or delay
was caused by the wrongful act or neglect of the claimant, by the instructions of
the claimant given otherwise than as the result of a wrongful act or neglect on the
part of the carrier, by inherent vice of the goods or through circumstances which
the carrier could not avoid and the consequences of which he was unable to
prevent.

3   The carrier shall not be relieved of liability by reason of the defective condition of the vehicle used by him in order to perform the carriage, or by reason of
the wrongful act or neglect of the person from whom he may have hired the
vehicle or of the agents or servants of the latter.

4   Subject to article 18, paragraphs 2 to 5 the carrier shall be relieved of liability
when the loss or damage arises from the special risks inherent in one or more of
the following circumstances:

(a)   use of open unsheeted vehicles, when their use has been expressly
agreed and specified in the consignment note;

(b)   the lack of, or defective condition of packing in the case of goods which,
by their nature, are liable to wastage or to be damaged when not packed or
when not properly packed;

(c)   handling, loading, stowage or unloading of the goods by the sender, the
consignee or person acting on behalf of the sender or consignee;

(d)   the nature of certain kinds of goods which particularly exposes them to
total or partial loss or to damage, especially through breakage, rust, decay,
desiccation, leakage, normal wastage, or the action of moth or vermin;

(e)   insufficiency or inadequacy of marks or numbers on the packages;

(f)   the carriage of livestock.

5   Where under this article the carrier is not under any liability in respect of
some of the factors causing the loss, damage or delay, he shall only be liable to the
extent that those factors for which he is liable under this article have contributed to
the loss, damage or delay.

Article 18

1   The burden of proving that loss, damage or delay was due to one of the
causes specified in article 17, paragraph 2, shall rest upon the carrier.

2   When the carrier establishes that in the circumstances of the case, the loss or
damage could be attributed to one or more of the special risks referred to in article
17, paragraph 4, it shall be presumed that it was so caused. The claimant shall
however be entitled to prove that the loss or damage was not, in fact, attributable
either wholly or partly to one of these risks.

3   This presumption shall not apply in the circumstances set out in article 17,
paragraph 4(a), if there has been an abnormal shortage, or a loss of any package.

4   If the carriage is performed in vehicles specially equipped to protect the
goods from the effects of heat, cold, variations in temperature or the humidity of
the air, the carrier shall not be entitled to claim the benefit of article 17, paragraph
4(d) unless he proves that all steps incumbent on him in the circumstances with
respect to the choice, maintenance and use of such equipment were taken and that
he complied with any special instructions issued to him.

5   The carrier shall not be entitled to claim the benefit of article 17, paragraph
4(f), unless he proves that all steps normally incumbent on him in the circumstances were taken and that he complied with any special instructions issued to
him.

Article 19

Delay in delivery shall be said to occur when the goods have not been delivered
within the agreed time-limit or when, failing an agreed time-limit, the actual duration of the carriage having regard to the circumstances of the case, and in particular, in the case of partial loads, the time required for making up a complete load

in the normal way, exceeds the time it would be reasonable to allow a diligent carrier.

Article 20

1   The fact that the goods have not been delivered within thirty days following the expiry of the agreed time-limit, or if there is no agreed time-limit, within sixty days from the time when the carrier took over the goods, shall be conclusive evidence of the loss of the goods, and the person entitled to make a claim may thereupon treat them as lost.

2   The person so entitled may, on receipt of compensation for the missing goods, request in writing that he shall be notified immediately should the goods be recovered in the course of the year following the payment of compensation. He shall be given a written acknowledgement of such request.

3   Within the thirty days following receipt of such notification, the person entitled as aforesaid may require the goods to be delivered to him against payment of the charges shown to be due on the consignment note and also against refund of the compensation he received less any charges included therein but without prejudice to any claims to compensation for delay in delivery under article 23 and, where applicable, article 26.

4   In the absence of the request mentioned in paragraph 2 or of any instructions given within the period of thirty days specified in paragraph 3, or if the goods are not recovered until more than one year after the payment of compensation, the carrier shall be entitled to deal with them in accordance with the law of the place where the goods are situated.

Article 21

Should the goods have been delivered to the consignee without collection of the 'cash on delivery' charge which should have been collected by the carrier under the terms of the contract of carriage, the carrier shall be liable to the sender for compensation not exceeding the amount of such charge without prejudice to his right of action against the consignee.

Article 22

1   When the sender hands goods of a dangerous nature to the carrier, he shall inform the carrier of the exact nature of the danger and indicate, if necessary, the precautions to be taken. If this information has not been entered in the consignment note, the burden of proving, by some other means, that the carrier knew the exact nature of the danger constituted by the carriage of the said goods shall rest upon the sender or the consignee.

2   Goods of a dangerous nature which, in the circumstances referred to in paragraph 1 of this article, the carrier did not know were dangerous, may, at any time or place, be unloaded, destroyed or rendered harmless by the carrier without compensation; further, the sender shall be liable for all expenses, loss or damage arising out of their handing over for carriage or of their carriage.

Article 23

1   When, under the provisions of this Convention, a carrier is liable for compensation in respect of total or partial loss of goods, such compensation shall be calculated by reference to the value of the goods at the place and time at which they were accepted for carriage.

2   The value of the goods shall be fixed according to the commodity exchange price or, if there is no such price, according to the current market price, or, if there is no commodity exchange price or current market price, by reference to the normal value of goods of the same kind and quality.

[3   Compensation shall not, however, exceed 8.33 units of account per kilogram of gross weight short.]

4   In addition, the carriage charges, Customs duties and other charges incurred in respect of the carriage of the goods shall be refunded in full in case of total loss

and in proportion to the loss sustained in case of partial loss, but no further damages shall be payable.

5   In the case of delay, if the claimant proves that damage has resulted therefrom the carrier shall pay compensation for such damage not exceeding the carriage charges.

6   Higher compensation may only be claimed where the value of the goods or a special interest in delivery has been declared in accordance with articles 24 and 26.

[7   The unit of account mentioned in this Convention is the Special Drawing Right as defined by the International Monetary Fund. The amount mentioned in paragraph 3 of this article shall be converted into the national currency of the State of the Court seised of the case on the basis of the value of that currency on the date of judgment or the date agreed upon by the Parties.]

Article 24
The sender may, against payment of a surcharge to be agreed upon, declare in the consignment note a value for the goods exceeding the limit laid down in article 23, paragraph 3, and in that case the amount of the declared value shall be substituted for that limit.

Article 25
1   In case of damage, the carrier shall be liable for the amount by which the goods have diminished in value, calculated by reference to the value of the goods fixed in accordance with article 23, paragraphs 1, 2 and 4.

2   The compensation may not, however, exceed:
   (a)   if the whole consignment has been damaged, the amount payable in the case of total loss;
   (b)   if part only of the consignment has been damaged, the amount payable in the case of loss of the part affected.

Article 26
1   The sender may, against payment of a surcharge to be agreed upon, fix the amount of a special interest in delivery in the case of loss or damage or of the agreed time-limit being exceeded, by entering such amount in the consignment note.

2   If a declaration of a special interest in delivery has been made, compensation for the additional loss or damage proved may be claimed, up to the total amount of the interest declared, independently of the compensation provided for in articles 23, 24 and 25.

Article 27
1   The claimant shall be entitled to claim interest on compensation payable. Such interest, calculated at five per centum per annum, shall accrue from the date on which the claim was sent in writing to the carrier or, if no such claim has been made, from the date on which legal proceedings were instituted.

2   When the amounts on which the calculation of the compensation is based are not expressed in the currency of the country in which payment is claimed, conversion shall be at the rate of exchange applicable on the day and at the place of payment of compensation.

Article 28
1   In cases where, under the law applicable, loss, damage or delay arising out of carriage under this Convention gives rise to an extra-contractual claim, the carrier may avail himself of the provisions of this Convention which exclude his liability or which fix or limit the compensation due.

2   In cases where the extra-contractual liability for loss, damage or delay of one of the persons for whom the carrier is responsible under the terms of article 3 is in issue, such person may also avail himself of the provisions of this Convention

which exclude the liability of the carrier or which fix or limit the compensation due.

Article 29

1   The carrier shall not be entitled to avail himself of the provisions of this chapter which exclude or limit his liability or which shift the burden of proof if the damage was caused by his wilful misconduct or by such default on his part as, in accordance with the law of the court or tribunal seised of the case, is considered as equivalent to misconduct.

2   The same provision shall apply if the wilful misconduct or default is committed by the agents or servants of the carrier or by any other persons of whose services he makes use for the performance of the carriage, when such agents, servants or other persons are acting within the scope of their employment. Furthermore, in such a case such agents, servants or other persons shall not be entitled to avail themselves, with regard to their personal liability, of the provisions of this chapter referred to in paragraph 1.

CHAPTER V

Claims and actions

Article 30

1   If the consignee takes delivery of the goods without duly checking their condition with the carrier or without sending him reservations giving a general indication of the loss or damage, not later than the time of delivery in the case of apparent loss or damage and within seven days of delivery, Sundays and public holidays excepted, in the case of loss or damage which is not apparent, the fact of his taking delivery shall be prima facie evidence that he has received the goods in the condition described in the consignment note. In the case of loss or damage which is not apparent the reservations referred to shall be made in writing.

2   When the condition of the goods has been duly checked by the consignee and the carrier, evidence contradicting the result of this checking shall only be admissible in the case of loss or damage which is not apparent and provided that the consignee has duly sent reservations in writing to the carrier within seven days, Sundays and public holidays excepted, from the date of checking.

3   No compensation shall be payable for delay in delivery unless a reservation has been sent in writing to the carrier, within twenty-one days from the time that the goods were placed at the disposal of the consignee.

4   In calculating the time-limits provided for in this article the date of delivery, or the date of checking, or the date when the goods were placed at the disposal of the consignee, as the case may be, shall not be included.

5   The carrier and the consignee shall give each other every reasonable facility for making the requisite investigations and checks.

Article 31

1   In legal proceedings arising out of carriage under this Convention, the plaintiff may bring an action in any court or tribunal of a contracting country designated by agreement between the parties and, in addition, in the courts or tribunals of a country within whose territory:

(a)   the defendant is ordinarily resident, or has his principal place of business, or the branch or agency through which the contract of carriage was made, or

(b)   the place where the goods were taken over by the carrier or the place designated for delivery is situated,

and in no other courts or tribunals.

2   Where in respect of a claim referred to in paragraph 1 of this article an action is pending before a court or tribunal competent under that paragraph, or where in respect of such a claim a judgment has been entered by such a court or tribunal no

new action shall be started between the same parties on the same grounds unless the judgment of the court or tribunal before which the first action was brought is not enforceable in the country in which the fresh proceedings are brought.

3   When a judgment entered by a court or tribunal of a contracting country in any such action as is referred to in paragraph 1 of this article has become enforceable in that country, it shall also become enforceable in each of the other contracting States, as soon as the formalities required in the country concerned have been complied with. These formalities shall not permit the merits of the case to be re-opened.

4   The provisions of paragraph 3 of this article shall apply to judgments after trial, judgments by default and settlements confirmed by an order of the court, but shall not apply to interim judgments or to awards of damages, in addition to costs against a plaintiff who wholly or partly fails in his action.

5   Security for costs shall not be required in proceedings arising out of carriage under this Convention from nationals of contracting countries resident or having their place of business in one of those countries.

Article 32

1   The period of limitation for an action arising out of carriage under this Convention shall be one year. Nevertheless, in the case of wilful misconduct, or such default as in accordance with the law of the court or tribunal seised of the case, is considered as equivalent to wilful misconduct, the period of limitation shall be three years. The period of limitation shall begin to run:

(a)   in the case of partial loss, damage or delay in delivery, from the date of delivery;

(b)   in the case of total loss, from the thirtieth day after the expiry of the agreed time-limit or where there is no agreed time-limit from the sixtieth day from the date on which the goods were taken over by the carrier;

(c)   in all other cases, on the expiry of a period of three months after the making of the contract of carriage.

The day on which the period of limitation begins to run shall not be included in the period.

2   A written claim shall suspend the period of limitation until such date as the carrier rejects the claim by notification in writing and returns the documents attached thereto. If a part of the claim is admitted the period of limitation shall start to run again only in respect of that part of the claim still in dispute. The burden of proof of the receipt of the claim, or of the reply and of the return of the documents, shall rest with the party relying upon these facts. The running of the period of limitation shall not be suspended by further claims having the same object.

3   Subject to the provisions of paragraph 2 above, the extension of the period of limitation shall be governed by the law of the court or tribunal seised of the case. That law shall also govern the fresh accrual rights of action.

4   A right of action which has become barred by lapse of time may not be exercised by way of counter-claim or set-off.

Article 33

The contract of carriage may contain a clause conferring competence on an arbitration tribunal if the clause conferring competence on the tribunal provides that the tribunal shall apply this Convention.

CHAPTER VI
Provisions relating to carriage performed by successive carriers

Article 34

If carriage governed by a single contract is performed by successive road carriers, each of them shall be responsible for the performance of the whole operation, the second carrier and each succeeding carrier becoming a party to the contract of carriage, under the terms of the consignment note, by reason of his acceptance of the goods and the consignment note.

Article 35

1   A carrier accepting the goods from a previous carrier shall give the latter a dated and signed receipt. He shall enter his name and address on the second copy of the consignment note. Where applicable, he shall enter on the second copy of the consignment note and on the receipt reservations of the kind provided for in article 8, paragraph 2.

2   The provisions of article 9 shall apply to the relations between successive carriers.

Article 36

Except in the case of a counter-claim or a set-off raised in an action concerning a claim based on the same contract of carriage, legal proceedings in respect of liability for loss, damage or delay may only be brought against the first carrier, the last carrier or the carrier who was performing that portion of the carriage during which the event causing the loss, damage or delay occurred; an action may be brought at the same time against several of these carriers.

Article 37

A carrier who has paid compensation in compliance with the provisions of this Convention, shall be entitled to recover such compensation, together with interest thereon and all costs and expenses incurred by reason of the claim, from the other carriers who have taken part in the carriage, subject to the following provisions:

(a)   the carrier responsible for the loss or damage shall be solely liable for the compensation whether paid by himself or by another carrier;

(b)   when the loss or damage has been caused by the action of two or more carriers, each of them shall pay an amount proportionate to his share of liability; should it be impossible to apportion the liability, each carrier shall be liable in proportion to the share of the payment for the carriage which is due to him;

(c)   if it cannot be ascertained to which carriers liability is attributable for the loss or damage, the amount of the compensation shall be apportioned between all the carriers as laid down in (b) above.

Article 38

If one of the carriers is insolvent, the share of the compensation due from him and unpaid by him shall be divided among the other carriers in proportion to the share of the payment for the carriage due to them.

Article 39

1   No carrier against whom a claim is made under articles 37 and 38 shall be entitled to dispute the validity of the payment made by the carrier making the claim if the amount of the compensation was determined by judicial authority after the first mentioned carrier had been given due notice of the proceedings and afforded an opportunity of entering an appearance.

2   A carrier wishing to take proceedings to enforce his right of recovery may make his claim before the competent court or tribunal of the country in which one of the carriers concerned is ordinarily resident, or has his principal place of business or the branch or agency through which the contract of carriage was made. All the carriers concerned may be made defendants in the same action.

3   The provisions of article 31, paragraphs 3 and 4 shall apply to judgments entered in the proceedings referred to in articles 37 and 38.

4   The provisions of article 32 shall apply to claims between carriers. The period of limitation shall, however, begin to run either on the date of the final judicial decision fixing the amount of compensation payable under the provisions of this

Convention, or, if there is no such judicial decision, from the actual date of payment.

Article 40
Carriers shall be free to agree among themselves on provisions other than those laid down in articles 37 and 38.

CHAPTER VII
Nullity of stipulations contrary to the Convention

Article 41
1   Subject to the provisions of article 40, any stipulation which would directly or indirectly derogate from the provisions of this Convention shall be null and void. The nullity of such a stipulation shall not involve the nullity of the other provisions of the contract.

2   In particular, a benefit of insurance in favour of the carrier or any other similar clause, or any clause shifting the burden of proof shall be null and void.

[Chapter VIII deals with the coming into force of the Convention, the settlement of disputes between the high contracting parties and related matters.]

TRADE DESCRIPTIONS ACT 1968
(1968, c 29)

Prohibition of false trade descriptions

1   Prohibition of false trade descriptions
(1)   Any person who, in the course of a trade or business,—
  (a)   applies a false trade description to any goods; or
  (b)   supplies or offers to supply any goods to which a false trade description is applied;
shall, subject to the provisions of this Act, be guilty of an offence.

(2)   Sections 2 to 6 of this Act shall have effect for the purposes of this section and for the interpretation of expressions used in this section, wherever they occur in this Act.

2   Trade description
(1)   A trade description is an indication, direct or indirect, and by whatever means given, of any of the following matters with respect to any goods or parts of goods, that is to say—
  (a)   quantity, size or gauge;
  (b)   method of manufacture, production, processing or re-conditioning;
  (c)   composition;
  (d)   fitness for purpose, strength, performance, behaviour or accuracy;
  (e)   any physical characteristics not included in the preceding paragraphs;
  (f)   testing by any person and results thereof;
  (g)   approval by any person or conformity with a type approved by any person;
  (h)   place or date of manufacture, production, processing or reconditioning;
  (i)   person by whom manufactured, produced, processed or reconditioned;
  (j)   other history, including previous ownership or use.
(2)   The matters specified in subsection (1) of this section shall be taken—
  (a)   in relation to any animal, to include sex, breed or cross, fertility and soundness;
  (b)   in relation to any semen, to include the identity and characteristics of the animal from which it was taken and measure of dilution.

(3)   In this section 'quantity' includes length, width, height, area, volume, capacity, weight and number.

(4)   Notwithstanding anything in the preceding provisions of this section, the following shall be deemed not to be trade descriptions, that is to say, any description or mark applied in pursuance of—

[. . .]

(b)   section 2 of the Agricultural Produce (Grading and Marking) Act 1928 (as amended by the Agricultural Produce (Grading and Marking) Amendment Act 1931) or any corresponding enactment of the Parliament of Northern Ireland;

(c)   the Plant Varieties and Seeds Act 1964;

(d)   the Agriculture and Horticulture Act 1964 [or any Community grading rules within the meaning of Part III of that Act];

(e)   the Seeds Act (Northern Ireland) 1965;

(f)   the Horticulture Act (Northern Ireland) 1966;

[(g)   the Consumer Protection Act 1987;

(h)   the Plant Varieties Act 1997;

any statement made in respect of, or mark applied to, any material in pursuance of Part IV of the Agriculture Act 1970, any name or expression to which a meaning has been assigned under section 70 of that Act when applied to any material in the circumstances specified in that section] [. . .] any mark prescribed by a system of classification compiled under section 5 of the Agriculture Act 1967 [and any designation, mark or description applied in pursuance of a scheme brought into force under section 6(1) or an order made under section 25(1) of the Agriculture Act 1970.]

(5)   Notwithstanding anything in the preceding provisions of this section,

(a)   where provision is made under [the Food Safety Act 1990] or the Food and Drugs Act (Northern Ireland) 1958 [or the Consumer Protection Act 1987] prohibiting the application of a description except to goods in the case of which the requirements specified in that provision are complied with, that description, when applied to such goods, shall be deemed not to be a trade description.

[(b)   where by virtue of any provision made under Part V of the Medicines Act 1968 (or made under any provisions of the said Part V as applied by an order made under section 104 or section 105 of that Act) anything which in accordance with this Act, constitutes the application of a trade description to goods is subject to any requirements or restrictions imposed by that provision, any particular description specified in that provision, when applied to goods in circumstances to which those requirements or restrictions are applicable, shall be deemed not to be a trade description.]

3   False trade description
(1)   A false trade description is a trade description which is false to a material degree.

(2)   A trade description which, though not false, is misleading, that is to say, likely to be taken for such an indication of any of the matters specified in section 2 of this Act as would be false to a material degree, shall be deemed to be a false trade description.

(3)   Anything which, though not a trade description, is likely to be taken for an indication of any of those matters and, as such an indication, would be false to a material degree, shall be deemed to be a false trade description.

(4)   A false indication, or anything likely to be taken as an indication which would be false, that any goods comply with a standard specified or recognised by any person or implied by the approval of any person shall be deemed to be a false trade description, if there is no such person or no standard so specified, recognised or implied.

4 Applying a trade description to goods

(1)   A person applies a trade description to goods if he—

(a)   affixes or annexes it to or in any manner marks it on or incorporates it with—

(i)   the goods themselves, or

(ii)   anything in, on or with which the goods are supplied; or

(b)   places the goods in, on or with anything which the trade description has been affixed or annexed to, marked on or incorporated with, or places any such thing with the goods; or

(c)   uses the trade description in any manner likely to be taken as referring to the goods.

(2)   An oral statement may amount to the use of a trade description.

(3)   Where goods are supplied in pursuance of a request in which a trade description is used and the circumstances are such as to make it reasonable to infer that the goods are supplied as goods corresponding to that trade description, the person supplying the goods shall be deemed to have applied the trade description to the goods.

5 Trade descriptions used in advertisements

(1)   The following provisions of this section shall have effect where in an advertisement a trade description is used in relation to any class of goods.

(2)   The trade description shall be taken as referring to all goods of the class, whether or not in existence at the time the advertisement is published—

(a)   for the purpose of determining whether an offence has been committed under paragraph (a) of section 1(1) of this Act; and

(b)   where goods of the class are supplied or offered to be supplied by a person publishing or displaying the advertisement, also for the purpose of determining whether an offence has been committed under paragraph (b) of the said section 1(1).

(3)   In determining for the purposes of this section whether any goods are of a class to which a trade description used in an advertisement relates regard shall be had not only to the form and content of the advertisement but also to the time, place, manner and frequency of its publication and all other matters making it likely or unlikely that a person to whom the goods are supplied would think of the goods as belonging to the class in relation to which the trade description is used in the advertisement.

6 Offer to supply

A person exposing goods for supply or having goods in his possession for supply shall be deemed to offer to supply them.

14 False or misleading statements as to services, etc

(1)   It shall be an offence for any person in the course of any trade or business—

(a)   to make a statement which he knows to be false; or

(b)   recklessly to make a statement which is false;

as to any of the following matters, that is to say,—

(i)   the provision in the course of any trade or business of any services, accommodation or facilities;

(ii)   the nature of any services, accommodation or facilities provided in the course of any trade or business;

(iii)   the time at which, manner in which or persons by whom any services, accommodation or facilities are so provided;

(iv)   the examination, approval or evaluation by any person of any services, accommodation or facilities so provided; or

(v)   the location or amenities of any accommodation so provided.

(2)   For the purpose of this section—

(a)   anything (whether or not a statement as to any of the matters specified in the preceding subsection) likely to be taken for such a statement as to any of those matters as would be false shall be deemed to be a false statement as to that matter; and

(b)   a statement made regardless of whether it is true or false shall be deemed to be made recklessly, whether or not the person making it had reasons for believing that it might be false.

(3)   In relation to any services consisting of or including the application of any treatment or process or the carrying out of any repair, the matters specified in subsection (1) of this section shall be taken to include the effect of the treatment, process or repair.

(4)   In this section 'false' means false to a material degree and 'services' does not include anything done under a contract of service.

18   Penalty for offences

A person guilty of an offence under this Act for which no other penalty is specified shall be liable—

(a)   on summary conviction, to a fine not exceeding [the prescribed sum]; and

(b)   on conviction on indictment, to a fine or imprisonment for a term not exceeding two years or both.

CARRIAGE OF GOODS BY SEA ACT 1971
(1971, c 19)

1   Application of Hague Rules as amended

(1)   In this Act, 'the Rules' means the International Convention for the unification of certain rules of law relating to bills of lading signed at Brussels on 25th August 1924, as amended by the Protocol signed at Brussels on 23rd February 1968 [and by the protocol signed at Brussels on 21st December 1979].

(2)   The provisions of the Rules, as set out in the Schedule to this Act, shall have the force of law.

(3)   Without prejudice to subsection (2) above, the said provisions shall have effect (and have the force of law) in relation to and in connection with the carriage of goods by sea in ships where the port of shipment is a port in the United Kingdom, whether or not the carriage is between ports in two different States within the meaning of Article X of the Rules.

(4)   Subject to subsection (6) below, nothing in this section shall be taken as applying anything in the Rules to any contract for the carriage of goods by sea, unless the contract expressly or by implication provides for the issue of a bill of lading or any similar document of title.

[. . .]

(6)   Without prejudice to Article X(c) of the Rules, the Rules shall have the force of law in relation to—

(a)   any bill of lading if the contract contained in or evidenced by it expressly provides that the Rules shall govern the contract, and

(b)   any receipt which is a non-negotiable document marked as such if the contract contained in or evidenced by it is a contract for the carriage of goods by sea which expressly provides that the Rules are to govern the contract as if the receipt were a bill of lading, but subject, where paragraph (b) applies, to any necessary modifications and in particular with the omission in Article III of the Rules of the second sentence of paragraph 4 and of paragraph 7.

(7)   If and so far as the contract contained in or evidenced by a bill of lading or receipt within paragraph (a) or (b) of subsection (6) above applies to deck cargo or live animals, the Rules as given the force of law by that subsection shall have effect as if Article I(c) did not exclude deck cargo and live animals.

In this subsection 'deck cargo' means cargo which by the contract of carriage is stated as being carried on deck and is so carried.

2 Contracting States, etc

(1)   If Her Majesty by Order in Council certifies to the following effect, that is to say, that for the purposes of the Rules—

(a)   a State specified in the Order is a contracting State, or is a contracting State in respect of any place or territory so specified; or

(b)   any place or territory specified in the Order forms part of a State so specified (whether a contracting State or not),

the Order shall, except so far as it has been superseded by a subsequent Order, be conclusive evidence of the matters so certified.

(2)   An Order in Council under this section may be varied or revoked by a subsequent Order in Council.

3 Absolute warranty of seaworthiness not to be implied in contracts to which Rules apply

There shall not be implied in any contract for the carriage of goods by sea to which the Rules apply by virtue of this Act any absolute undertaking by the carrier of the goods to provide a seaworthy ship.

4 Application of Act to British possessions, etc

(1)   Her Majesty may by Order in Council direct that this Act shall extend, subject to such exceptions, adaptations and modifications as may be specified in the Order, to all or any of the following territories, that is—

(a)   any colony (not being a colony for whose external relations a country other than the United Kingdom is responsible),

(b)   any country outside Her Majesty's dominions in which Her Majesty has jurisdiction in right of Her Majesty's Government of the United Kingdom.

(2)   An Order in Council under this section may contain such transitional and other consequential and incidental provisions as appear to Her Majesty to be expedient, including provisions amending or repealing any legislation about the carriage of goods by sea forming part of the law of any of the territories mentioned in paragraphs (a) and (b) above.

(3)   An Order in Council under this section may be varied or revoked by a subsequent Order in Council.

5 Extension of application of Rules to carriage from ports in British possessions, etc

(1)   Her Majesty may by Order in Council provide that section 1(3) of this Act shall have effect as if the reference therein to the United Kingdom included a reference to all or any of the following territories, that is—

(a)   the Isle of Man;

(b)   any of the Channel Islands specified in the Order;

(c)   any colony specified in the Order (not being a colony for whose external relations a country other than the United Kingdom is responsible);

[. . .]

(e)   any country specified in the Order, being a country outside Her Majesty's dominions in which Her Majesty has jurisdiction in right of Her Majesty's Government of the United Kingdom.

(2)   An Order in Council under this section may be varied or revoked by a subsequent Order in Council.

6 Supplemental

(1)   This Act may be cited as the Carriage of Goods by Sea Act 1971.

(2)   It is hereby declared that this Act extends to Northern Ireland.

(3)   The following enactments shall be repealed, that is—

(a)   the Carriage of Goods by Sea Act 1924,

(b)   section 12(4)(a) of the Nuclear Installations Act 1965,
and without prejudice to section 38(1) of the Interpretation Act 1889, the reference
to the said Act of 1924 in section 1(1)(i)(ii) of the Hovercraft Act 1968 shall include
a reference to this Act.

(4)   It is hereby declared that for the purposes of Article VIII of the Rules
[section 18 of the Merchant Shipping Act 1979 (which] entirely exempts ship-
owners and others in certain circumstances from liability for loss of, or damage to,
goods) is a provision relating to limitation of liability.

(5)   This Act shall come into force on such day as Her Majesty may by Order in
Council appoint, and, for the purposes of the transition from the law in force
immediately before the day appointed under this subsection to the provisions of
this Act, the Order appointing the day may provide that those provisions shall
have effect subject to such transitional provisions as may be contained in the
Order.

SCHEDULE

THE HAGUE RULES AS AMENDED BY
THE BRUSSELS PROTOCOL 1968

Article I
In these Rules the following words are employed, with the meanings set out
below:—

(a)   'Carrier' includes the owner or the charterer who enters into a contract of
carriage with a shipper.

(b)   'Contract of carriage' applies only to contracts of carriage covered by a
bill of lading or any similar document of title, in so far as such document relates
to the carriage of goods by sea, including any bill of lading or any similar
document as aforesaid issued under or pursuant to a charter party from the
moment at which such bill of lading or similar document of title regulates the
relations between a carrier and a holder of the same.

(c)   'Goods' includes goods, wares, merchandise, and articles of every kind
whatsoever except live animals and cargo which by the contract of carriage is
stated as being carried on deck and is so carried.

(d)   'Ship' means any vessel used for the carriage of goods by sea.

(e)   'Carriage of goods' covers the period from the time when the goods are
loaded on to the time they are discharged from the ship.

Article II
Subject to the provisions of Article VI, under every contract of carriage of goods by
sea the carrier, in relation to the loading, handling, stowage, carriage, custody, care
and discharge of such goods, shall be subject to the responsibilities and liabilities,
and entitled to the rights and immunities hereinafter set forth.

Article III
(1)   The carrier shall be bound before and at the beginning of the voyage to
exercise due diligence to—

(a)   Make the ship seaworthy.

(b)   Properly man, equip and supply the ship.

(c)   Make the holds, refrigerating and cool chambers, and all other parts of
the ship in which goods are carried, fit and safe for their reception, carriage and
preservation.

(2)   Subject to the provisions of Article IV, the carrier shall properly and carefully load, handle, stow, carry, keep, care for, and discharge the goods carried.

(3)   After receiving the goods into his charge the carrier or the master or agent
of the carrier shall, on demand of the shipper, issue to the shipper a bill of lading
showing among other things—

(a)   The leading marks necessary for identification of the goods as the same are furnished in writing by the shipper before the loading of such goods starts, provided such marks are stamped or otherwise shown clearly upon the goods if uncovered, or on the cases or coverings in which such goods are contained, in such a manner as should ordinarily remain legible until the end of the voyage.

(b)   Either the number of packages or pieces, or the quantity, or weight, as the case may be, as furnished in writing by the shipper.

(c)   The apparent order and condition of the goods.

Provided that no carrier, master or agent of the carrier shall be bound to state or show in the bill of lading any marks, number, quantity, or weight which he has reasonable ground for suspecting not accurately to represent the goods actually received, or which be has had no reasonable means of checking.

(4)   Such a bill of lading shall be prima facie evidence of the receipt by the carrier of the goods as therein described in accordance with paragraph 3(a), (b) and (c). However, proof to the contrary shall not be admissible when the bill of lading has been transferred to a third party acting in good faith.

(5)   The shipper shall be deemed to have guaranteed to the carrier the accuracy at the time of shipment of the marks, number, quantity and weight, as furnished by him, and the shipper shall indemnify the carrier against all loss, damages and expenses arising or resulting from inaccuracies in such particulars. The right of the carrier to such indemnity shall in no way limit his responsibility and liability under the contract of carriage to any person other than the shipper.

(6)   Unless notice of loss or damage and the general nature of such loss or damage be given in writing to the carrier or his agent at the port of discharge before or at the time of the removal of the goods into the custody of the person entitled to delivery thereof under the contract of carriage, or, if the loss or damage be not apparent, within three days, such removal shall be prima facie evidence of the delivery by the carrier of the goods as described in the bill of lading.

The notice in writing need not be given if the state of the goods has, at the time of their receipt, been the subject of joint survey or inspection.

Subject to paragraph 6bis the carrier and the ship shall in any event be discharged from all liability whatsoever in respect of the goods, unless suit is brought within one year of their delivery or of the date when they should have been delivered. This period may, however, be extended if the parties so agree after the cause of action has arisen.

In the case of any actual or apprehended loss or damage the carrier and the receiver shall give all reasonable facilities to each other for inspecting and tallying the goods.

(6bis)   An action for indemnity against a third person may be brought even after the expiration of the year provided for in the preceding paragraph if brought within the time allowed by the law of the court seised of the case. However, the time allowed shall be not less than three months, commencing from the day when the person bringing such action for indemnity has settled the claim or has been served with process in the action against himself.

(7)   After the goods are loaded the bill of lading to be issued by the carrier, master, or agent of the carrier, to the shipper shall, if the shipper so demands, be a 'shipped' bill of lading, provided that if the shipper shall have previously taken up any document of title to such goods, he shall surrender the same as against the issue of the 'shipped' bill of lading, but at the option of the carrier such document of title may be noted at the port of shipment by the carrier, master, or agent with the name or names of the ship or ships upon which the goods have been shipped and the date or dates of shipment, and when so noted if it shows the particulars mentioned in paragraph 3 of Article III, shall for the purpose of this article be deemed to constitute a 'shipped' bill of lading.

(8)   Any clause, covenant, or agreement in a contract of carriage relieving the carrier or the ship from liability for loss or damage to, or in connection with, goods

arising from negligence, fault, or failure in the duties and obligations provided in this article or lessening such liability otherwise than as provided in these Rules, shall be null and void and of no effect. A benefit of insurance in favour of the carrier or similar clause shall be deemed to be a clause relieving the carrier from liability.

Article IV

(1)   Neither the carrier nor the ship shall be liable for loss or damage arising or resulting from unseaworthiness unless caused by want of due diligence on the part of the carrier to make the ship seaworthy, and to secure that the ship is properly manned, equipped and supplied, and to make the holds, refrigerating and cool chambers and all other parts of the ship in which goods are carried fit and safe for their reception, carriage and preservation in accordance with the provisions of paragraph 1 of Article III. Whenever loss or damage has resulted from unseaworthiness the burden of proving the exercise of due diligence shall be on the carrier or other person claiming exemption under this article.

(2)   Neither the carrier nor the ship shall be responsible for loss or damage arising or resulting from—

(a)   Act, neglect, or default of the master, mariner, pilot, or the servants of the carrier in the navigation or in the management of the ship.

(b)   Fire, unless caused by the actual fault or privity of the carrier.

(c)   Perils, dangers and accidents of the sea or other navigable waters.

(d)   Act of God.

(e)   Act of war.

(f)   Act of public enemies.

(g)   Arrest or restraint of princes, rulers or people, or seizure under legal process.

(h)   Quarantine restrictions.

(i)   Act or omission of the shipper or owner of the goods, his agent or representative.

(j)   Strikes or lockouts or stoppage or restraint of labour from whatever cause, whether partial or general.

(k)   Riots and civil commotions.

(l)   Saving or attempting to save life or property at sea.

(m)   Wastage in bulk or weight or any other loss or damage arising from inherent defect, quality or vice of the goods.

(n)   Insufficiency of packing.

(o)   Insufficiency or inadequacy of marks.

(p)   Latent defects not discoverable by due diligence.

(q)   Any other cause arising without the actual fault or privity of the carrier, or without the fault or neglect of the agents or servants of the carrier, but the burden of proof shall be on the person claiming the benefit of this exception to show that neither the actual fault or privity of the carrier nor the fault or neglect of the agents or servants of the carrier contributed to the loss or damage.

(3)   The shipper shall not be responsible for the loss or damage sustained by the carrier or the ship arising or resulting from any cause without the act, fault or neglect of the shipper, his agents or his servants.

(4)   Any deviation in saving or attempting to save life or property at sea or any reasonable deviation shall not be deemed to be an infringement or breach of these Rules or of the contract of carriage, and the carrier shall not be liable for any loss or damage resulting therefrom.

(5)(a)   Unless the nature and value of such goods have been declared by the shipper before shipment and inserted in the bill of lading, neither the carrier nor the ship shall in any event be or become liable for any loss or damage to or in connection with the goods in an amount exceeding [666.67 units of account] per package or unit or [2 units of account per kilogramme] of gross weight of the goods lost or damaged, whichever is the higher.

(b)   The total amount recoverable shall be calculated by reference to the value of such goods at the place and time at which the goods are discharged from the ship in accordance with the contract or should have been so discharged.

The value of the goods shall be fixed according to the commodity exchange price, or, if there be no such price, according to the current market price, or, if there be no commodity exchange price or current market price, by reference to the normal value of goods of the same kind and quality.

(c)   Where a container, pallet or similar article of transport is used to consolidate goods, the number of packages or units enumerated in the bill of lading as packed in such article of transport shall be deemed the number of packages or units for the purpose of this paragraph as far as these packages or units are concerned. Except as aforesaid such article of transport shall be considered the package or unit.

[(d)   The unit of account mentioned in this Article is the special drawing right as defined by the International Monetary Fund. The amounts mentioned in sub-paragraph (a) of this paragraph shall be converted into national currency on the basis of the value of that currency on a date to be determined by the law of the court seised of the case.]

(e)   Neither the carrier nor the ship shall be entitled to the benefit of the limitation of liability provided for in this paragraph if it is proved that the damage resulted from an act or omission of the carrier done with intent to cause damage, or recklessly and with knowledge that damage would probably result.

(f)   The declaration mentioned in sub-paragraph (a) of this paragraph, if embodied in the bill of lading, shall be prima facie evidence, but shall not be binding or conclusive on the carrier.

(g)   By agreement between the carrier, master or agent of the carrier and the shipper other maximum amounts than those mentioned in sub-paragraph (a) of this paragraph may be fixed, provided that no maximum amount so fixed shall be less than the appropriate maximum mentioned in that sub-paragraph.

(h)   Neither the carrier nor the ship shall be responsible in any event for loss or damage to, or in connection with, goods if the nature or value thereof has been knowingly mis-stated by the shipper in the bill of lading.

(6)   Goods of an inflammable, explosive or dangerous nature to the shipment whereof the carrier, master or agent of the carrier has not consented with knowledge of their nature and character, may at any time before discharge be landed at any place, or destroyed or rendered innocuous by the carrier without compensation and the shipper of such goods shall be liable for all damages and expenses directly or indirectly arising out of or resulting from such shipment. If any such goods shipped with such knowledge and consent shall become a danger to the ship or cargo, they may in like manner be landed at any place, or destroyed or rendered innocuous by the carrier without liability on the part of the carrier except to general average, if any.

Article IV bis

(1)   The defences and limits of liability provided for in these Rules shall apply in any action against the carrier in respect of loss or damage to goods covered by a contract of carriage whether the action be founded in contract or in tort.

(2)   If such an action is brought against a servant or agent of the carrier (such servant or agent not being an independent contractor), such servant or agent shall be entitled to avail himself of the defences and limits of liability which the carrier is entitled to invoke under these Rules.

(3)   The aggregate of the amounts recoverable from the carrier, and such servants and agents, shall in no case exceed the limit provided for in these Rules.

(4)   Nevertheless, a servant or agent of the carrier shall not be entitled to avail

himself of the provisions of this article, if it is proved that the damage resulted from an act or omission of the servant or agent done with intent to cause damage or recklessly and with knowledge that damage would probably result.

Article V
A carrier shall be at liberty to surrender in whole or in part all or any of his rights and immunities or to increase any of his responsibilities and obligations under these Rules, provided such surrender or increase shall be embodied in the bill of lading issued to the shipper. The provisions of the Rules shall not be applicable to charter parties, but if bills of lading are issued in the case of a ship under a charter party they shall comply with the terms of these Rules. Nothing in these Rules shall be held to prevent the insertion in a bill of lading of any lawful provisions regarding general average.

Article VI
Notwithstanding the provisions of the preceding articles, a carrier, master or agent of the carrier and a shipper shall in regard to any particular goods be at liberty to enter into any agreement in any terms as to the responsibility and liability of the carrier for such goods, and as to the rights and immunities of the carrier in respect of such goods, or his obligation as to seaworthiness, so far as this stipulation is not contrary to public policy, or the care or diligence of his servants or agents in regard to the loading, handling, stowage, carriage, custody, care and discharge of the goods carried by sea, provided that in this case no bill of lading has been or shall be issued and that the terms agreed shall be embodied in a receipt which shall be a non-negotiable document and shall be marked as such.

Any agreement so entered into shall have full legal effect.

Provided that this article shall not apply to ordinary commercial shipment made in the ordinary course of trade, but only to other shipments where the character or condition of the property to be carried or the circumstances, terms and conditions under which the carriage is to be performed are such as reasonably to justify a special agreement.

Article VII
Nothing herein contained shall prevent a carrier or a shipper from entering into any agreement, stipulation, condition, reservation or exemption as to the responsibility and liability of the carrier or the ship for the loss or damage to, or in connection with, the custody and care and handling of goods prior to the loading on, and subsequent to the discharge from, the ship on which the goods are carried by sea.

Article VIII
The provisions of these Rules shall not affect the rights and obligations of the carrier under any statute for the time being in force relating to the limitation of the liability of owners of sea-going vessels.

Article IX
These rules shall not affect the provisions of any international Convention or national law governing liability for nuclear damage.

Article X
The provisions of these Rules shall apply to every bill of lading relating to the carriage of goods between ports in two different States if:
    (a)   the bill of lading is issued in a contracting State, or
    (b)   the carriage is from a port in a contracting State, or
    (c)   the contract contained in or evidenced by the bill of lading provides that these Rules or legislation of any State giving effect to them are to govern the contract, whatever may be the nationality of the ship, the carrier, the shipper, the consignee, or any other interested person.

[The last two paragraphs of this article require contracting States to apply the Rules to

bills of lading mentioned in the article and authorise them to apply the Rules to other bills of lading.]

[Articles XI to XVI deal with the coming into force of the Convention, procedure for ratification, accession and denunciation and the right to call for a fresh conference to consider amendments to the Rules contained in the Convention.]

UNSOLICITED GOODS AND SERVICES ACT 1971
(1971, c 30)

[. . .]

2 Demands and threats regarding payment

(1) A person who, not having reasonable cause to believe there is a right to payment, in the course of any trade or business makes a demand for payment, or asserts a present or prospective right to payment, for what he knows are unsolicited goods sent (after the commencement of this Act) to another person with a view to his acquiring them [for the purposes of his trade or business], shall be guilty of an offence and on summary conviction shall be liable to a fine not exceeding [level 4 on the standard scale].

(2) A person who, not having reasonable cause to believe there is a right to payment, in the course of any trade or business and with a view to obtaining any payment for what he knows are unsolicited goods sent as aforesaid—

(a) threatens to bring any legal proceedings; or

(b) places or causes to be placed the name of any person on a list of defaulters or debtors or threatens to do so; or

(c) invokes or causes to be invoked any other collection procedure or threatens to do so,

shall be guilty of an offence and shall be liable on summary conviction to a fine not exceeding [level 5 on the standard scale].

3 Directory entries

[(1) A person ('the purchaser') shall not be liable to make any payment, and shall be entitled to recover any payment made by him, by way of charge for including or arranging for the inclusion in a directory of an entry relating to that person or his trade or business, unless—

(a) there has been signed by the purchaser or on his behalf an order complying with this section,

(b) there has been signed by the purchaser or on his behalf a note complying with this section of his agreement to the charge and before the note was signed, a copy of it was supplied, for retention by him, to him or a person acting on his behalf,

(c) there has been transmitted by the purchaser or a person acting on his behalf an electronic communication which includes a statement that the purchaser agrees to the charge and the relevant condition is satisfied in relation to that communication, [or

(d) the charge arises under a contract in relation to which the conditions in section 3B(1) (renewed and extended contracts) are met.]

(2) A person shall be guilty of an offence punishable on summary conviction with a fine not exceeding [level 5 on the standard scale] if, in a case where a payment in respect of a charge would [. . .] be recoverable from him in accordance with the terms of subsection (1) above, he demands payment, or asserts a present or prospective right to payment, of the charge or any part of it, without knowing or having reasonable cause to believe [that—

(a) the entry to which the charge relates was ordered in accordance with this section,

(b) a proper note of the agreement has been duly signed, or

(c)   the requirements set out in subsection (1)(c) [or (d)] above have been met.]

(3)   For the purposes of [this section—

(a)] an order for an entry in a directory must be made by means of an order form or other stationery belonging to the [purchaser, which may be sent electronically but which must bear his name and address (or one or more of his addresses)]; and

[b]   the note [of a person's agreement to a charge must—

(i)   specify the particulars set out in Part 1 of the Schedule to the Regulatory Reform (Unsolicited Goods and Services Act 1971) (Directory Entries and Demands for Payment) Order 2005, and

(ii)   give reasonable particulars of the entry in respect of which the charge would be payable].

[(3A)   In relation to an electronic communication which includes a statement that the purchaser agrees to a charge for including or arranging the inclusion in a directory of any entry, the relevant condition is that—

(a)   before the electronic communication was transmitted the information referred to in subsection (3B) below was communicated to the purchaser, and

(b)   the electronic communication can readily be produced and retained in a visible and legible form.

(3B)   that information is—

(a)   the following particulars—

(i)   the amount of the charge;

(ii)   the name of the directory or proposed directory;

(iii)   the name of the person producing the directory;

(iv)   the geographic address at which that person is established;

(v)   if the directory is or is to be available in printed form, the proposed date of publication of the directory or of the issue in which the entry is to be included;

(vi)   if the directory or the issue in which the entry is to be included is to be put on sale, the price at which it is to be offered for sale and the minimum number of copies which are to be available for sale;

(vii)   if the directory or the issue in which the entry is to be included is to be distributed free of charge (whether or not it is also to be put on sale), the minimum number of copies which are to be so distributed;

(viii)   if the directory is or is to be available in a form other than in printed form, adequate details of how it may be accessed; and

(b)   reasonable particulars of the entry in respect of which the charge would be payable.

(3C)   In this section 'electronic communication' has the same meaning as in the Electronic Communications Act 2000.]

[. . .]

[3B   Renewed and extended contracts

(1)   The conditions referred to in section 3(1)(e) above are met in relation to a contract ('the new contract') if—

(a)   a person ('the purchaser') has entered into an earlier contract ('the earlier contract') for including or arranging for the inclusion in a particular issue or version of a directory ('the earlier directory') of an entry ('the earlier entry') relating to him or his trade or business;

(b)   the purchaser was liable to make a payment by way of a charge arising under the earlier contract for including or arranging for the inclusion of the earlier entry in the earlier directory;

(c)   the new contract is a contract for including or arranging for the inclusion in a later issue or version of a directory ('the later directory') of an entry ('the later entry') relating to the purchaser or his trade or business;

(d)   the form, content and distribution of the later directory is materially the same as the form, content and distribution of the earlier directory;

(e)   the form and content of the later entry is materially the same as the form and content of the earlier entry;

(f)   if the later directory is published other than in electronic form—

(i)   the earlier directory was the last, or the last but one, issue or version of the directory to be published before the later directory, and

(ii)   the date of publication of the later directory is not more than 13 months after the date of publication of the earlier directory;

(g)   if the later directory is published in electronic form, the first date on which the new contract requires the later entry to be published is not more than the relevant period after the last date on which the earlier contract required the earlier entry to be published;

(h)   if it was a term of the earlier contract that the purchaser renew or extend the contract—

(i)   before the start of the new contract the relevant publisher has given notice in writing to the purchaser containing the information set out in Part 3 of the Schedule to the Regulatory Reform (Unsolicited Goods and Services Act 1971) (Directory Entries and Demands for Payment) Order 2005; and

(ii)   the purchaser has not written to the relevant publisher withdrawing his agreement to the renewal or extension of the earlier contract within the period of 21 days starting when he receives the notice referred to in sub-paragraph (i); and

(i)   if the parties to the earlier contract and the new contract are different—

(i)   the parties to both contracts have entered into a novation agreement in respect of the earlier contract; or

(ii)   the relevant publisher has given the purchaser the information set out in Part 4 of the Schedule to the Regulatory Reform (Unsolicited Goods and Services Act 1971) (Directory Entries and Demands for Payment) Order 2005.

(2)   For the purposes of subsection (1)(d) and (e), the form, content or distribution of the later directory, or the form or content of the later entry, shall be taken to be materially the same as that of the earlier directory or the earlier entry (as the case may be), if a reasonable person in the position of the purchaser would—

(a)   view the two as being materially the same; or

(b)   view that of the later directory or the later entry as being an improvement on that of the earlier directory or the earlier entry.

(3)   For the purposes of subsection (1)(g) 'the relevant period' means the period of 13 months or (if shorter) the term of the earlier contract.

(4)   For the purposes of subsection (1)(h) and (i) 'the relevant publisher' is the person with whom the purchaser has entered into the new contract.

(5)   The information referred to in subsection (1)(i)(ii) must be given to the purchaser prior to the conclusion of the new contract.]

4   Unsolicited publications

(1)   A person shall be guilty of an offence if he sends or causes to be sent to another person any book, magazine or leaflet (or advertising material for any such publication) which he knows or ought reasonably to know is unsolicited and which describes or illustrates human sexual techniques.

(2)   A person found guilty of an offence under this section shall be liable on summary conviction to a fine not exceeding [level 5 on the standard scale].

(3)   A prosecution for an offence under this section shall not in England and Wales be instituted except by, or with the consent of, the Director of Public Prosecutions.

5   Offences by corporations

(1)   Where an offence under this Act which has been committed by a body corporate is proved to have been committed with the consent or connivance of, or to

be attributable to any neglect on the part of, any director, manager, secretary, or other similar officer of the body corporate, or of any person who was purporting to act in any such capacity, he as well as the body corporate shall be guilty of that offence and shall be liable to be proceeded against and punished accordingly.

(2)   Where the affairs of a body corporate are managed by its members, this section shall apply in relation to the acts or defaults of a member in connection with his functions of management as if he were a director of the body corporate.

6   Interpretation

(1)   In this Act, unless the context or subject matter otherwise requires,—

'acquire' includes hire;

'send' includes deliver, and 'sender' shall be construed accordingly;

'unsolicited' means, in relation to goods sent to any person, that they are sent without any prior request made by him or on his behalf.

[(2)   For the purposes of this Act any invoice or similar document stating the amount of any payment shall be regarded as asserting a right to the payment unless it complies with the conditions set out in Part 2 of the Schedule to the Regulatory Reform (Unsolicited Goods and Services Act 1971) (Directory Entries and Demands for Payment) Order 2005.

(3)   Nothing in sections 3 or 3B shall affect the rights of any consumer under the Consumer Protection (Distance Selling) Regulations 2000.]

7   Citation, commencement and extent

(1)   This Act may be cited as the Unsolicited Goods and Services Act 1971.

(2)   This Act shall come into force at the expiration of three months beginning with the day on which it is passed.

(3)   This Act does not extend to Northern Ireland.

SUPPLY OF GOODS (IMPLIED TERMS) ACT 1973
(1973, c 13)

8   Implied terms as to title

[(1)   In every hire-purchase agreement, other than one to which subsection (2) below applies, there is—

(a)   an implied term on the part of the creditor that he will have a right to sell the goods at the time when the property is to pass; and

(b)   an implied term that—

(i)   the goods are free, and will remain free until the time when the property is to pass, from any charge or encumbrance not disclosed or known to the person to whom the goods are bailed or (in Scotland) hired before the agreement is made, and

(ii)   that person will enjoy quiet possession of the goods except so far as it may be disturbed by any person entitled to the benefit of any charge or encumbrance so disclosed or known.

(2)   In a hire-purchase agreement, in the case of which there appears from the agreement or is to be inferred from the circumstances of the agreement an intention that the creditor should transfer only such title as he or a third person may have, there is—

(a)   an implied term that all charges or encumbrances known to the creditor and not known to the person to whom the goods are bailed or hired have been disclosed to that person before the agreement is made; and

(b)   an implied term that neither—

(i)   the creditor; nor

(ii)   in a case where the parties to the agreement intend that any title which may be transferred shall be only such title as a third person may have, that person; nor

(iii)   anyone claiming through or under the creditor or that third person

not otherwise than under a charge or encumbrance disclosed or known to the
person to whom the goods are bailed or hired, before the agreement is made;
will disturb the quiet possession of the person to whom the goods are bailed
or hired.

(3)   As regards England and Wales and Northern Ireland, the term implied by
subsection (1)(a) above is a condition and the terms implied by subsections (1)(b),
(2)(a) and (2)(b) above are warranties.]

9   Bailing or hiring by description

[(1)   Where under a hire-purchase agreement goods are bailed or (in Scotland)
hired by description, there is an implied term that the goods will correspond with
the description, and if under the agreement the goods are bailed or hired by reference to a sample as well as a description, it is not sufficient that the bulk of the
goods corresponds with the sample if the goods do not also correspond with the
description.

(1A)   As regards England and Wales and Northern Ireland, the term implied by
subsection (1) above is a condition.

(2)   Goods shall not be prevented from being bailed or hired by description by
reason only that, being exposed for sale, bailment or hire, they are selected by the
person to whom they are bailed or hired.]

10   Implied undertakings as to quality or fitness

[(1)   Except as provided by this section and section 11 below and subject to the
provisions of any other enactment, including any enactment of the Parliament of
Northern Ireland or the Northern Ireland Assembly, there is no implied term as to
the quality or fitness for any particular purpose of goods bailed or (in Scotland)
hired under a hire-purchase agreement.

(2)   Where the creditor bails or hires goods under a hire-purchase agreement in
the course of a business, there is an implied term that the goods supplied under
the agreement are of satisfactory quality.

(2A)   For the purposes of this Act, goods are of satisfactory quality if they meet
the standard that a reasonable person would regard as satisfactory, taking account
of any description of the goods, the price (if relevant) and all the other relevant
circumstances.

(2B)   For the purposes of this Act, the quality of goods includes their state and
condition and the following (among others) are in appropriate cases aspects of the
quality of goods—

(a)   fitness for all the purposes for which goods of the kind in question are
commonly supplied,

(b)   appearance and finish,

(c)   freedom from minor defects,

(d)   safety, and

(e)   durability.

(2C)   The term implied by subsection (2) above does not extend to any matter
making the quality of goods unsatisfactory—

(a)   which is specifically drawn to the attention of the person to whom the
goods are bailed or hired before the agreement is made,

(b)   where that person examines the goods before the agreement is made,
which that examination ought to reveal, or

(c)   where the goods are bailed or hired by reference to a sample, which
would have been apparent on a reasonable examination of the sample.

[(2D)   If the person to whom the goods are bailed or hired deals as consumer
or, in Scotland, if the goods are hired to a person under a consumer contract, the
relevant circumstances mentioned in subsection (2A) above include any public
statements on the specific characteristics of the goods made about them by the
creditor, the producer or his representative, particularly in advertising or on
labelling.

(2E)   A public statement is not by virtue of subsection (2D) above a relevant circumstance for the purposes of subsection (2A) above in the case of a contract of hire-purchase, if the creditor shows that—

(a)   at the time the contract was made, he was not, and could not reasonably have been, aware of the statement,

(b)   before the contract was made, the statement had been withdrawn in public or, to the extent that it contained anything which was incorrect or misleading, it had been corrected in public, or

(c)   the decision to acquire the goods could not have been influenced by the statement.

(2F)   Subsections (2D) and (2E) above do not prevent any public statement from being a relevant circumstance for the purposes of subsection (2A) above (whether or not the person to whom the goods are bailed or hired deals as consumer or, in Scotland, whether or not the goods are hired to a person under a consumer contract) if the statement would have been such a circumstance apart from those subsections.]

(3)   Where the creditor bails or hires goods under a hire-purchase agreement in the course of a business and the person to whom the goods are bailed or hired, expressly or by implication, makes known—

(a)   to the creditor in the course of negotiations conducted by the creditor in relation to the making of the hire-purchase agreement, or

(b)   to a credit-broker in the course of negotiations conducted by that broker in relation to goods sold by him to the creditor before forming the subject matter of the hire-purchase agreement,

any particular purpose for which the goods are being bailed or hired, there is an implied term that the goods supplied under the agreement are reasonably fit for that purpose, whether or not that is a purpose for which such goods are commonly supplied, except where the circumstances show that the person to whom the goods are bailed or hired does not rely, or that it is unreasonable for him to rely, on the skill or judgment of the creditor or credit-broker.

(4)   An implied term as to quality or fitness for a particular purpose may be annexed to a hire-purchase agreement by usage.

(5)   The preceding provisions of this section apply to a hire-purchase agreement made by a person who in the course of a business is acting as agent for the creditor as they apply to an agreement made by the creditor in the course of a business, except where the creditor is not bailing or hiring in the course of a business and either the person to whom the goods are bailed or hired knows that fact or reasonable steps are taken to bring it to the notice of that person before the agreement is made.

(6)   In subsection (3) above and this subsection—

(a)   'credit-broker' means a person acting in the course of a business of credit brokerage;

(b)   'credit brokerage' means the effecting of introductions of individuals desiring to obtain credit—

(i)   to persons carrying on any business so far as it relates to the provision of credit, or

(ii)   to other persons engaged in credit brokerage.

(7)   As regards England and Wales and Northern Ireland, the terms implied by subsections (2) and (3) above are conditions.

[(8)   In Scotland, 'consumer contract' in this section has the same meaning as in section 12A(3) below.]

11   Samples

[(1)   Where under a hire-purchase agreement goods are bailed or (in Scotland) hired by reference to a sample, there is an implied term—

(a)   that the bulk will correspond with the sample in quality; and

(b)   that the person to whom the goods are bailed or hired will have a reasonable opportunity of comparing the bulk with the sample; and

(c)   that the goods will be free from any defect, making their quality unsatisfactory, which would not be apparent on reasonable examination of the sample.

(2)   As regards England and Wales and Northern Ireland, the term implied by subsection (1) above is a condition.]

[12   Exclusion of implied terms

An express term does not negative a term implied by this Act unless inconsistent with it.]

[12A   Remedies for breach of hire-purchase agreement as respects Scotland

(1)   Where in a hire-purchase agreement the creditor is in breach of any term of the agreement (express or implied), the person to whom the goods are hired shall be entitled—

(a)   to claim damages, and

(b)   if the breach is material, to reject any goods delivered under the agreement and treat it as repudiated.

(2)   Where a hire-purchase agreement is a consumer contract, then, for the purposes of subsection (1) above, breach by the creditor of any term (express or implied)—

(a)   as to the quality of the goods or their fitness for a purpose,

(b)   if the goods are, or are to be, hired by description, that the goods will correspond with the description,

(c)   if the goods are, or are to be, hired by reference to a sample, that the bulk will correspond with the sample in quality,

shall be deemed to be a material breach.

(3)   In subsection (2) above 'consumer contract' has the same meaning as in section 25(1) of the Unfair Contract Terms Act 1977; and for the purposes of that subsection the onus of proving that a hire-purchase agreement is not to be regarded as a consumer contract shall lie on the creditor.

(4)   This section applies to Scotland only.]

[. . .]

14   Special provisions as to conditional sale agreements

[(1)   Section 11(4) of the Sale of Goods Act 1979 (whereby in certain circumstances a breach of a condition in a contract of sale is treated only as a breach of warranty) shall not apply to [a conditional sale agreement] where the buyer deals as consumer within Part I of the Unfair Contract Terms Act 1977 or, in Scotland, the agreement is a consumer contract within Part II of that Act.]

15   Supplementary

[(1)   In sections 8 to 14 above and this section—

'business' includes a profession and the activities of any government department (including a Northern Ireland department), [or local or public authority];

'buyer' and 'seller' includes a person to whom rights and duties under a conditional sale agreement have passed by assignment or operation of law;

'conditional sale agreement' means an agreement for the sale of goods under which the purchase price or part of it is payable by instalments, and the property in the goods is to remain in the seller (notwithstanding that the buyer is to be in possession of the goods) until such conditions as to the payment of instalments or otherwise as may be specified in the agreement are fulfilled;

['consumer sale' has the same meaning as in section 55 of the Sale of Goods Act 1979 (as set out in paragraph 11 of Schedule 1 to that Act)];

'creditor' means the person by whom the goods are bailed or (in Scotland) hired

under a hire-purchase agreement or the person to whom his rights and duties under the agreement have passed by assignment or operation of law; and

'hire-purchase agreement' means an agreement, other than conditional sale agreement, under which—

(a) goods are bailed or (in Scotland) hired in return for periodical payments by the person to whom they are bailed or hired, and

(b) the property in the goods will pass to that person if the terms of the agreement are complied with and one or more of the following occurs—

(i) the exercise of an option to purchase by that person,

(ii) the doing of any other specified act by any party to the agreement,

(iii) the happening of any other specified event.

['producer' means the manufacturer of goods, the importer of goods into the European Economic Area or any person purporting to be a producer by placing his name, trade mark or other distinctive sign on the goods;]

(3) In section 14(2) above 'corresponding hire-purchase agreement' means, in relation to a conditional sale agreement, a hire-purchase agreement relating to the same goods as the conditional sale agreement and made between the same parties and at the same time and in the same circumstances and, as nearly as may be, in the same terms as the conditional sale agreement.

(4) Nothing in sections 8 to 13 above shall prejudice the operation of any other enactment including any enactment of the Parliament of Northern Ireland or the Northern Ireland Assembly or any rule of law whereby any term, other than one relating to quality or fitness, is to be implied in any hire-purchase agreement.]

CONSUMER CREDIT ACT 1974
(1974, c 39)

PART I
[OFFICE OF FAIR TRADING]

1 General functions of [OFT]

(1) It is the duty of [the Office of Fair Trading ('the OFT')]—

(a) to administer the licensing system set up by this Act,

(b) to exercise the adjudicating functions conferred on [it] by this Act in relation to the issue, renewal, variation, suspension and revocation of licences, and other matters,

[(ba) to monitor, as it sees fit, businesses being carried on under licences;]

(c) generally to superintend the working and enforcement of this Act, and regulations made under it, and

(d) where necessary or expedient, [itself] to take steps to enforce this Act, and regulations so made.

(2) It is the duty of the [OFT], so far as appears to [it] to be practicable and having regard both to the national interest and the interests of persons carrying on businesses to which this Act applies and their customers, to keep under review and from time to time advise the Secretary of State about—

(a) social and commercial developments in the United Kingdom and elsewhere relating to the provision of credit or bailment or (in Scotland) hiring of goods to individuals, and related activities; and

(b) the working and enforcement of this Act and orders and regulations made under it.

2 Powers of Secretary of State

(1) The Secretary of State may by order—

(a) confer on the [OFT] additional functions concerning the provision of credit or bailment or (in Scotland) hiring of goods to individuals, and related activities, and

(b)   regulate the carrying out by the [OFT] of [its] functions under this Act.

(2)   The Secretary of State may give general directions indicating considerations to which the [OFT] should have particular regard in carrying out [its] functions under this Act, and may give specific directions on any matter connected with the carrying out by the [OFT] of those functions.

(3)   The Secretary of State, on giving any directions under subsection (2), shall arrange for them to be published in such manner as he thinks most suitable for drawing them to the attention of interested persons.

(4)   With the approval of the Secretary of State and the Treasury, the [OFT] may charge, for any service or facility provided by [it] under this Act, a fee of an amount specified by general notice (the 'specified fee').

(5)   Provision may be made under subsection (4) for reduced fees, or no fees at all, to be paid for certain services or facilities by persons of a specified description, and references in this Act to the specified fee shall, in such cases, be construed accordingly.

(6)   An order under subsection (1)(a) shall be made by statutory instrument and shall be of no effect unless a draft of the order has been laid before and approved by each House of Parliament.

(7)   References in subsection (2) to the functions of the [OFT] under this Act do not include the making of a determination to which section 41 [. . .] (appeals from [OFT] to [the Tribunal]) applies.

[. . .]

4   Dissemination of information and advice

The [OFT] shall arrange for the dissemination, in such form and manner as [it] considers appropriate, of such information and advice as it may appear to [it] expedient to give to the public in the United Kingdom about the operation of this Act, [the consumer credit jurisdiction under Part 16 of the Financial Services and Markets Act 2000,] the credit facilities available to them, and other matters within the scope of [its] functions under this Act.

6   Form etc of applications

(1)   An application to the [OFT] under this Act is of no effect unless the requirements of this section are satisfied.

(2)   The application must be in writing, and in such form, and accompanied by such [information and documents], as the [OFT] may specify [or describe in a] general notice [. . .].

[(2A)   The application must also be accompanied—

(a)   in the case of an application for a licence or for the renewal of a licence, by the charge payable by virtue of section 6A;

(b)   in any other case, by the specified fee.]

(3)   [Where the OFT receives an application, it may by notice to the applicant at any time before the determination of the application require him to provide such information or documents relevant to the application as may be specified or described in the notice.]

(4)   The [OFT] may by notice require the applicant to publish details of his application at a time or times and in a manner specified in the notice.

[(5)   Subsection (6) applies where a general notice under subsection (2) comes into effect—

(a)   after an application has been made; but

(b)   before its determination.

(6)   The applicant shall, within such period as may be specified in the general notice, provide the OFT with any information or document—

(a)   which he has not previously provided in relation to the application by virtue of this section;

(b)   which he would have been required to provide with his application had it been made after the general notice came into effect; and

(c)   which the general notice requires to be provided for the purposes of this subsection.

(7)   An applicant shall notify the OFT, giving details, if before his application is determined—

(a)   any information or document provided by him in relation to the application by virtue of this section is, to any extent, superseded or otherwise affected by a change in circumstances; or

(b)   he becomes aware of an error in or omission from any such information or document.

(8)   A notification for the purposes of subsection (7) shall be given within the period of 28 days beginning with the day on which (as the case may be)—

(a)   the information or document is superseded;

(b)   the change in circumstances occurs; or

(c)   the applicant becomes aware of the error or omission.

(9)   Subsection (7) does not require an applicant to notify the OFT about—

(a)   anything of which he is required to notify it under section 36; or

(b)   an error in or omission from any information or document which is a clerical error or omission not affecting the substance of the information or document.]

[6A   Charge on applicants for licences etc

(1)   An applicant for a licence, or for the renewal of a licence, shall pay the OFT a charge towards the costs of carrying out its functions under this Act.

(2)   The amount of the charge payable by an applicant shall be determined in accordance with provision made by the OFT by general notice.

(3)   The provision that may be made by the OFT under subsection (2) includes—

(a)   different provision in relation to persons of different descriptions;

(b)   provision for no charge at all to be payable by persons of specified descriptions.

(4)   The approval of the Secretary of State and the Treasury is required for a general notice under subsection (2).]

[7   Penalty for false information

A person commits an offence if, for the purposes of, or in connection with, any requirement imposed or other provision made by or under this Act, he knowingly or recklessly gives information to the OFT, or to an officer of the OFT, which, in a material particular, is false or misleading.]

PART II
CREDIT AGREEMENTS, HIRE AGREEMENTS AND LINKED TRANSACTIONS

8   Consumer credit agreements

(1)   A [consumer] credit agreement is an agreement between an individual ('the debtor') and any other person ('the creditor') by which the creditor provides the debtor with credit of any amount.

[. . .]

(3)   A consumer credit agreement is a regulated agreement within the meaning of this Act if it is not an agreement (an 'exempt agreement') specified in or under section 16 [, 16A or 16B].

9   Meaning of credit

(1)   In this Act 'credit' includes a cash loan, and any other form of financial accommodation.

(2)   Where credit is provided otherwise than in sterling it shall be treated for the purposes of this Act as provided in sterling of an equivalent amount.

(3)   Without prejudice to the generality of subsection (1), the person by whom goods are bailed or (in Scotland) hired to an individual under a hire-purchase agreement shall be taken to provide him with fixed-sum credit to finance the transaction of an amount equal to the total price of the goods less the aggregate of the deposit (if any) and the total charge for credit.

(4)   For the purposes of this Act, an item entering into the total charge for credit shall not be treated as credit even though time is allowed for its payment.

10   Running-account credit and fixed-sum credit

(1)   For the purposes of this Act—

(a)   running-account credit is a facility under a [consumer] credit agreement whereby the debtor is enabled to receive from time to time (whether in his own person, or by another person) from the creditor or a third party cash, goods and services (or any of them) to an amount or value such that, taking into account payments made by or to the credit of the debtor, the credit limit (if any) is not at any time exceeded; and

(b)   fixed-sum credit is any other facility under a [consumer] credit agreement whereby the debtor is enabled to receive credit (whether in one amount or by instalments).

(2)   In relation to running-account credit, 'credit limit' means, as respects any period, the maximum debit balance which, under the credit agreement, is allowed to stand on the account during that period, disregarding any term of the agreement allowing that maximum to be exceeded merely temporarily.

(3)   For the purposes of [paragraph (a) of section 16B(1)], running-account credit shall be taken not to exceed the amount specified in that [paragraph] ('the specified amount') if—

(a)   the credit limit does not exceed the specified amount; or

(b)   whether or not there is a credit limit, and if there is, notwithstanding that it exceeds the specified amount,—

(i)   the debtor is not enabled to draw at any one time an amount which, so far as (having regard to section 9(4)) it represents credit, exceeds the specified amount, or

(ii)   the agreement provides that, if the debit balance rises above a given amount (not exceeding the specified amount), the rate of the total charge for credit increases or any other condition favouring the creditor or his associate comes into operation, or

(iii)   at the time the agreement is made it is probable, having regard to the terms of the agreement and any other relevant considerations, that the debit balance will not at any time rise above the specified amount.

11   Restricted-use credit and unrestricted-use credit

(1)   A restricted-use credit agreement is a regulated consumer credit agreement—

(a)   to finance a transaction between the debtor and the creditor, whether forming part of that agreement or not, or

(b)   to finance a transaction between the debtor and a person (the 'supplier') other than the creditor, or

(c)   to refinance any existing indebtedness of the debtor's, whether to the creditor or another person, and 'restricted-use credit' shall be construed accordingly.

(2)   An unrestricted-use credit agreement is a regulated consumer credit agreement not falling within subsection (1), and 'unrestricted-use credit' shall be construed accordingly.

(3)   An agreement does not fall within subsection (1) if the credit is in fact provided in such a way as to leave the debtor free to use it as he chooses, even though certain uses would contravene that or any other agreement.

(4)   An agreement may fall within subsection (1)(b) although the identity of the supplier is unknown at the time the agreement is made.

12   Debtor-creditor-supplier agreements
A debtor-creditor-supplier agreement is a regulated consumer credit agreement being—
(a)   a restricted-use credit agreement which falls within section 11(1)(a), or
(b)   a restricted-use credit agreement which falls within section 11(1)(b) and is made by the creditor under pre-existing arrangements, or in contemplation of future arrangements, between himself and the supplier, or
(c)   an unrestricted-use credit agreement which is made by the creditor under pre-existing arrangements between himself and a person (the 'supplier') other than the debtor in the knowledge that the credit is to be used to finance a transaction between the debtor and the supplier.

13   Debtor-creditor agreements
A debtor-creditor agreement is a regulated consumer credit agreement being—
(a)   a restricted-use credit agreement which falls within section 11(1)(b) but is not made by the creditor under pre-existing arrangements, or in contemplation of future arrangements, between himself and the supplier, or
(b)   a restricted-use credit agreement which falls within section 11(1)(c), or
(c)   an unrestricted-use credit agreement which is not made by the creditor under pre-existing arrangements between himself and a person (the 'supplier') other than the debtor in the knowledge that the credit is to be used to finance a transaction between the debtor and the supplier.

14   Credit-token agreements
(1)   A credit-token is a card, check, voucher, coupon, stamp, form, booklet or other document or thing given to an individual by a person carrying on a consumer credit business, who undertakes—
(a)   that on the production of it (whether or not some other action is also required) he will supply cash, goods and services (or any of them) on credit, or
(b)   that where, on the production of it to a third party (whether or not any other action is also required), the third party supplies cash, goods and services (or any of them), he will pay the third party for them (whether or not deducting any discount or commission), in return for payment to him by the individual.
(2)   A credit-token agreement is a regulated agreement for the provision of credit in connection with the use of a credit-token.
(3)   Without prejudice to the generality of section 9(1), the person who gives to an individual an undertaking falling within subsection (1)(b) shall be taken to provide him with credit drawn on whenever a third party supplies him with cash, goods or services.
(4)   For the purposes of subsection (1), use of an object to operate a machine provided by the person giving the object or a third party shall be treated as the production of the object to him.

15   Consumer hire agreements
(1)   A consumer hire agreement is an agreement made by a person with an individual (the 'hirer') for the bailment or (in Scotland) the hiring of goods to the hirer, being an agreement which—
(a)   is not a hire-purchase agreement, and
(b)   is capable of subsisting for more than three months, [. . .].
(2)   A consumer hire agreement is a regulated agreement if it is not an exempt agreement.

16   Exempt agreements
(1)   This Act does not regulate a consumer credit agreement where the creditor

is a local authority [. . .], or a body specified, or of a description specified, in an order made by the Secretary of State, being—

    (a) [an insurer],
    (b) a friendly society,
    (c) an organisation of employers or organisation of workers,
    (d) a charity,
    (e) a land improvement company,
    (f) a body corporate named or specifically referred to in any public general Act,

    [(ff) a body corporate named or specifically referred to in an order made under—

      section 156(4) or 447(2)(a) of the Housing Act 1985,

      section 156(4) of that Act as it has effect by virtue of section 17 of the Housing Act 1996 (the right to acquire),

      section 223 or 229 of the Housing (Scotland) Act 1987, or

      Article 154(1)(a) or 156AA of the Housing (Northern Ireland) Order 1981

      Article 10(6A) of the Housing (Northern Ireland) Order 1983; or

    (g) a building society, or
    (h) a deposit-taker.]

  (2) Subsection (1) applies only where the agreement is—

    (a) a debtor-creditor-supplier agreement financing—

      (i) the purchase of land, or

      (ii) the provision of dwellings on any land, and secured by a land mortgage on that land; or

    (b) a debtor-creditor agreement secured by any land mortgage; or

    (c) a debtor-creditor-supplier agreement financing a transaction which is a linked transaction in relation to—

      (i) an agreement falling within paragraph (a), or

      (ii) an agreement falling within paragraph (b) financing—

        (aa) the purchase of any land, or

        (bb) the provision of dwellings on any land, and secured by a land mortgage on the land referred to in paragraph (a) or, as the case may be, the land referred to in sub-paragraph (ii).

  [(3) Before he makes, varies or revokes an order under subsection (1), the Secretary of State must undertake the necessary consultation.

  (3A) The necessary consultation means consultation with the bodies mentioned in the following table in relation to the provision under which the order is to be made, varied or revoked:

Provision of subsection (1)	Consultee
Paragraph (a) or (b)	The Financial Services Authority
Paragraph (d)	The Charity Commissioners
Paragraph (e), (f) or (ff)	Any Minister of the Crown with responsibilities in relation to the body in question
Paragraph (g) or (h)	The Treasury and the Financial Services Authority]

  (4) An order under subsection (1) relating to a body may be limited so as to apply only to agreements by that body of a description specified in the order.

  (5) The Secretary of State may by order provide that this Act shall not regulate other consumer credit agreements where—

(a)   the number of payments to be made by the debtor does not exceed the number specified for that purpose in the order, or

(b)   the rate of the total charge for credit does not exceed the rate so specified, or

(c)   an agreement has a connection with a country outside the United Kingdom.

(6)   The Secretary of State may by order provide that this Act shall not regulate consumer hire agreements of a description specified in the order where—

(a)   the owner is a body corporate authorised by or under any enactment to supply electricity, gas or water, and

(b)   the subject of the agreement is a meter or metering equipment [or where the owner is a provider of a public electronic communications service who is specified in the order].

[(6A)   This Act does not regulate a consumer credit agreement where the creditor is a housing authority and the agreement is secured by a land mortgage of a dwelling.

(6B)   In subsection (6A) 'housing authority' means—

(a)   as regards England and Wales, the Housing Corporation, . . . and an authority or body within section 80(1) of the Housing Act 1985 (the landlord condition for secure tenancies), other than a housing association or a housing trust which is a charity;

(b)   as regards Scotland, a development corporation established under an order made, or having effect as if made under the New Towns (Scotland) Act 1968, the Scottish Special Housing Association or the Housing Corporation;

(c)   as regards Northern Ireland, the Northern Ireland Housing Executive.

(6C)   This Act does not regulate a consumer credit agreement, if—

(a)   it is secured by a land mortgage; and

(b)   entering into that agreement as lender is a regulated activity for the purposes of the Financial Services and Markets Act 2000.

(6D)   But section 126, and any other provision so far as it related to section 126, applies to an agreement which would (but for subsection (6C)) be a regulated agreement.

(6E)   Subsection (6C) must be read with—

(a)   section 22 of the Financial Services and Markets Act 2000 (regulated activities; power to specify classes of activity and categories of investment);

(b)   any order for the time being in force under that section; and

(c)   Schedule 2 to that Act.]

[. . .]

[(7A)   Nothing in this section affects the application of sections 140A to 140C.]

(8)   [In the application of this section to Scotland subsection (3A) shall have effect as if the reference to the Charity Commissioners were a reference to the Lord Advocate.]

(9)   In the application of this section to Northern Ireland subsection [(3A)] shall have effect as if any reference to a Minister of the Crown were a reference to a Northern Ireland department, [. . .] and any reference to the Charity Commissioners were a reference to the Department of Finance for Northern Ireland.

[(10)   In this section—

(a)   'deposit-taker' means—

(i)   a person who has permission under Part 4 of the Financial Services and Markets Act 2000 to accept deposits,

(ii)   an EEA firm of the kind mentioned in paragraph 5(b) of Schedule 3 to that Act which has permission under paragraph 15 of that Schedule (as a result of qualifying for authorisation under paragraph 12 of that Schedule) to accept deposits,

(iii)   any wholly owned subsidiary (within the meaning of the Companies Act 1985) of a person mentioned in sub-paragraph (i), or

(iv) any undertaking which, in relation to a person mentioned in sub-paragraph (ii), is a subsidiary undertaking within the meaning of any rule of law in force in the EEA State in question for purposes connected with the implementation of the European Council Seventh Company Law Directive of 13 June 1983 on consolidated accounts (No 83/349/EEC), and which has no members other than that person;

(b) 'insurer' means—

(i) a person who has permission under Part 4 of the Financial Services and Markets Act 2000 to effect or carry out contracts of insurance, or

(ii) an EEA firm of the kind mentioned in paragraph 5(d) of Schedule 3 to that Act, which has permission under paragraph 15 of that Schedule (as a result of qualifying for authorisation under paragraph 12 of that Schedule) to effect or carry out contracts of insurance,

but does not include a friendly society or an organisation of workers or of employers.

(11) Subsection (10) must be read with—

(a) section 22 of the Financial Services and Markets Act 2000;

(b) any relevant order under that section; and

(c) Schedule 2 to that Act.]

[16A   Exemption relating to high net worth debtors and hirers

(1) The Secretary of State may by order provide that this Act shall not regulate a consumer credit agreement or a consumer hire agreement where—

(a) the debtor or hirer is a natural person;

(b) the agreement includes a declaration made by him to the effect that he agrees to forgo the protection and remedies that would be available to him under this Act if the agreement were a regulated agreement;

(c) a statement of high net worth has been made in relation to him; and

(d) that statement is current in relation to the agreement and a copy of it was provided to the creditor or owner before the agreement was made.

(2) For the purposes of this section a statement of high net worth is a statement to the effect that, in the opinion of the person making it, the natural person in relation to whom it is made—

(a) received during the previous financial year income of a specified description totalling an amount of not less than the specified amount; or

(b) had throughout that year net assets of a specified description with a total value of not less than the specified value.

(3) Such a statement—

(a) may not be made by the person in relation to whom it is made;

(b) must be made by a person of a specified description; and

(c) is current in relation to an agreement if it was made during the period of one year ending with the day on which the agreement is made.

(4) An order under this section may make provision about—

(a) how amounts of income and values of net assets are to be determined for the purposes of subsection (2)(a) and (b);

(b) the form, content and signing of—

(i) statements of high net worth;

(ii) declarations for the purposes of subsection (1)(b).

(5) Where an agreement has two or more debtors or hirers, for the purposes of paragraph (c) of subsection (1) a separate statement of high net worth must have been made in relation to each of them; and paragraph (d) of that subsection shall have effect accordingly.

(6) In this section—

'previous financial year' means, in relation to a statement of high net worth, the financial year immediately preceding the financial year during which the statement is made;

'specified' means specified in an order under this section.

(7) In subsection (6) 'financial year' means a period of one year ending with 31st March.

(8) Nothing in this section affects the application of sections 140A to 140C.

16B Exemption relating to businesses

(1) This Act does not regulate—

(a) a consumer credit agreement by which the creditor provides the debtor with credit exceeding £25,000, or

(b) a consumer hire agreement that requires the hirer to make payments exceeding £25,000,

if the agreement is entered into by the debtor or hirer wholly or predominantly for the purposes of a business carried on, or intended to be carried on, by him.

(2) If an agreement includes a declaration made by the debtor or hirer to the effect that the agreement is entered into by him wholly or predominantly for the purposes of a business carried on, or intended to be carried on, by him, the agreement shall be presumed to have been entered into by him wholly or predominantly for such purposes.

(3) But that presumption does not apply if, when the agreement is entered into—

(a) the creditor or owner, or

(b) any person who has acted on his behalf in connection with the entering into of the agreement,

knows, or has reasonable cause to suspect, that the agreement is not entered into by the debtor or hirer wholly or predominantly for the purposes of a business carried on, or intended to be carried on, by him.

(4) The Secretary of State may by order make provision about the form, content and signing of declarations for the purposes of subsection (2).

(5) Where an agreement has two or more creditors or owners, in subsection (3) references to the creditor or owner are references to any one or more of them.

(6) Nothing in this section affects the application of sections 140A to 140C.]

17 Small agreements

(1) A small agreement is—

(a) a regulated consumer credit agreement for credit not exceeding [£50], other than a hire-purchase or conditional sale agreement; or

(b) a regulated consumer hire agreement which does not require the hirer to make payments exceeding [£50],

being an agreement which is either unsecured or secured by a guarantee or indemnity only (whether or not the guarantee or indemnity is itself secured).

(2) Section 10(3)(a) applies for the purposes of subsection (1) as it applies for the purposes of section [16B(1)(a)].

(3) Where—

(a) two or more small agreements are made at or about the same time between the same parties, and

(b) it appears probable that they would instead have been made as a single agreement but for the desire to avoid the operation of provisions of this Act which would have applied to that single agreement but, apart from this subsection, are not applicable to the small agreements,

this Act applies to the small agreements as if they were regulated agreements other small agreements.

(4) If, apart from this subsection, subsection (3) does not apply to any agreements but would apply if, for any party or parties to any of the agreements, there were substituted an associate of that party, or associates of each of those parties, as the case may be, then subsection (3) shall apply to the agreements.

18   Multiple agreements

(1)   This section applies to an agreement (a 'multiple agreement') if its terms are such as—

(a)   to place a part of it within one category of agreement mentioned in this Act, and another part of it within a different category of agreement so mentioned, or within a category of agreement not so mentioned, or

(b)   to place it, or a part of it, within two or more categories of agreement so mentioned.

(2)   Where a part of an agreement falls within subsection (1), that part shall be treated for the purposes of this Act as a separate agreement.

(3)   Where an agreement falls within subsection (1)(b), it shall be treated as an agreement in each of the categories in question, and this Act shall apply to it accordingly.

(4)   Where under subsection (2) a part of a multiple agreement is to be treated as a separate agreement, the multiple agreement shall (with any necessary modifications) be construed accordingly; and any sum payable under the multiple agreement, if not apportioned by the parties, shall for the purposes of proceedings in any court relating to the multiple agreement be apportioned by the court as may be requisite.

(5)   In the case of an agreement for running-account credit, a term of the agreement allowing the credit limit to be exceeded merely temporarily shall not be treated as a separate agreement or as providing fixed-sum credit in respect of the excess.

(6)   This Act does not apply to a multiple agreement so far as the agreement relates to goods if under the agreement payments are to be made in respect of the goods in the form of rent (other than a rentcharge) issuing out of land.

19   Linked transactions

(1)   A transaction entered into by the debtor or hirer, or a relative of his, with any other person ('the other party'), except one for the provision of security, is a linked transaction in relation to an actual or prospective regulated agreement (the 'principal agreement') of which it does not form part if—

(a)   the transaction is entered into in compliance with a term of the principal agreement; or

(b)   the principal agreement is a debtor-creditor-supplier agreement and the transaction is financed, or to be financed, by the principal agreement; or

(c)   the other party is a person mentioned in subsection (2), and a person so mentioned initiated the transaction by suggesting it to the debtor or hirer, or his relative, who enters into it—

(i)   to induce the creditor or owner to enter into the principal agreement, or

(ii)   for another purpose related to the principal agreement, or

(iii)   where the principal agreement is a restricted-use credit agreement, for a purpose related to a transaction financed, or to be financed, by the principal agreement.

(2)   The persons referred to in subsection (1)(c) are—

(a)   the creditor or owner, or his associate;

(b)   a person who, in the negotiation of the transaction, is represented by a credit-broker who is also a negotiator in antecedent negotiations for the principal agreement;

(c)   a person who, at the time the transaction is initiated, knows that the principal agreement has been made or contemplates that it might be made.

(3)   A linked transaction entered into before the making of the principal agreement has no effect until such time (if any) as that agreement is made.

(4)   Regulations may exclude linked transactions of the prescribed description from the operation of subsection (3).

20 Total charge for credit

(1)   The Secretary of State shall make regulations containing such provisions as appear to him appropriate for determining the true cost to the debtor of the credit provided or to be provided under an actual or prospective consumer credit agreement (the 'total charge for credit'), and regulations so made shall prescribe—

(a)   what items are to be treated as entering into the total charge for credit, and how their amount is to be ascertained;

(b)   the method of calculating the rate of the total charge for credit.

(2)   Regulations under subsection (1) may provide for the whole or part of the amount payable by the debtor or his relative under any linked transaction to be included in the total charge for credit, whether or not the creditor is a party to the transaction or derives benefit from it.

PART III
LICENSING OF CREDIT AND HIRE BUSINESSES

Licensing principles

21 Businesses needing a licence

(1)   Subject to this section, a licence is required to carry on a consumer credit business [a consumer hire business or an ancillary credit business].

(2)   A local authority does not need a licence to carry on a business.

(3)   A body corporate empowered by a public general Act naming it to carry on a business does not need a licence to do so.

22 Standard and group licences

(1)   A licence may be—

(a)   a standard licence, that is a licence issued by the [OFT] to a person named in the licence on an application made by him, which, [whilst the licence is in effect], covers such activities as are described in the licence, or

(b)   a group licence, that is a licence issued by the [OFT] (whether on the application of any person or of [its] own motion), which, [whilst the licence is in effect], covers such persons and activities as are described in the licence.

[(1A)   The terms of a licence shall specify—

(a)   whether it has effect indefinitely or only for a limited period; and

(b)   if it has effect for a limited period, that period.

(1B)   For the purposes of subsection (1A)(b) the period specified shall be such period not exceeding the prescribed period as the OFT thinks fit (subject to subsection (1E)).

(1C)   A standard licence shall have effect indefinitely unless—

(a)   the application for its issue requests that it have effect for a limited period only; or

(b)   the OFT otherwise thinks there is good reason why it should have effect for such a period only.

(1D)   A group licence shall have effect for a limited period only unless the OFT thinks there is good reason why it should have effect indefinitely.

(1E)   Where a licence which has effect indefinitely is to be varied under section 30 or 31 for the purpose of limiting the licence's duration, the variation shall provide for the licence to expire—

(a)   in the case of a variation under section 30, at the end of such period from the time of the variation as is set out in the application for the variation; or

(b)   in the case of a variation under section 31, at the end of such period from the time of the variation as the OFT thinks fit;

but a period mentioned in paragraph (a) or (b) shall not exceed the prescribed period.]

(2)   A licence is not assignable or, subject to section 37, transmissible on death or in any other way.

(3)   Except in the case of a partnership or an unincorporated body of persons, a standard licence shall not be issued to more than one person.

(4)   A standard licence issued to a partnership or an unincorporated body of persons shall be issued in the name of the partnership or body.

(5)   The [OFT] may issue a group licence only if it appears to [it] that the public interest is better served by doing so than by obliging the persons concerned to apply separately for standard licences.

[(5A)   A group licence to carry on a business may limit the activities it covers in any way the OFT thinks fit.]

(6)   The persons covered by a group licence may be described by general words, whether or not coupled with the exclusion of named persons, or in any other way the [OFT] thinks fit.

(7)   The fact that a person is covered by a group licence in respect of certain activities does not prevent a standard licence being issued to him in respect of those activities or any of them.

(8)   A group licence issued on the application of any person shall be issued to that person, and general notice shall be given of the issue of any group licence (whether on application or not).

[. . .]

23   Authorisation of specific activities

(1)   Subject to [the terms of the licence], a licence to carry on a business covers all lawful activities done in the course of that business, whether by the licensee or other persons on his behalf.

[. . .]

(3)   A licence covers the canvassing off trade premises of debtor-creditor-supplier agreements or regulated consumer hire agreements only if, and to the extent that, the licence specifically so provides; and such provision shall not be included in a group licence.

(4)   [The OFT may by general notice specify] other activities which, if engaged in by or on behalf of the person carrying on a business, require to be covered by an express term in his licence.

24   Control of name of business

A standard licence authorises the licensee to carry on a business under the name or names specified in the licence, but not under any other name.

[24A   Applications for standard licences

(1)   An application for a standard licence shall, in relation to each type of business which is covered by the application, state whether the applicant is applying—

(a)   for the licence to cover the carrying on of that type of business with no limitation; or

(b)   for the licence to cover the carrying on of that type of business only so far as it falls within one or more descriptions of business.

(2)   An application within subsection (1)(b) in relation to a type of business shall set out the description or descriptions of business in question.

(3)   References in this Part to a type of business are references to a type of business within subsection (4).

(4)   The types of business within this subsection are—

(a)   a consumer credit business;

(b)   a consumer hire business;

(c)   a business so far as it comprises or relates to credit brokerage;

(d)   a business so far as it comprises or relates to debt-adjusting;

(e)   a business so far as it comprises or relates to debt-counselling;

(f)   a business so far as it comprises or relates to debt-collecting;

(g)   a business so far as it comprises or relates to debt administration;

(h)   a business so far as it comprises or relates to the provision of credit information services;

(i)   a business so far as it comprises or relates to the operation of a credit reference agency.

(5)   The OFT—

(a)   shall by general notice specify the descriptions of business which can be set out in an application for the purposes of subsection (2) in relation to a type of business;

(b)   may by general notice provide that applications within subsection (1)(b) cannot be made in relation to one or more of the types of business within subsection (4)(c) to (i).

(6)   The power of the OFT under subsection (5) includes power to make different provision for different cases or classes of case.]

25   Licensee to be a fit person

[(1)   If an applicant for a standard licence—

(a)   makes an application within section 24A(1)(a) in relation to a type of business, and

(b)   satisfies the OFT that he is a fit person to carry on that type of business with no limitation,

he shall be entitled to be issued with a standard licence covering the carrying on of that type of business with no limitation.

(1AA)   If such an applicant—

(a)   makes an application within subsection (1)(b) of section 24A in relation to a type of business, and

(b)   satisfies the OFT that he is a fit person to carry on that type of business so far as it falls within the description or descriptions of business set out in his application in accordance with subsection (2) of that section,

he shall be entitled to be issued with a standard licence covering the carrying on of that type of business so far as it falls within the description or descriptions in question.

(1AB)   If such an applicant makes an application within section 24A(1)(a) or (b) in relation to a type of business but fails to satisfy the OFT as mentioned in subsection (1) or (1AA) (as the case may be), he shall nevertheless be entitled to be issued with a standard licence covering the carrying on of that type of business so far as it falls within one or more descriptions of business if—

(a)   he satisfies the OFT that he is a fit person to carry on that type of business so far as it falls within the description or descriptions in question;

(b)   he could have applied for the licence to be limited in that way; and

(c)   the licence would not cover any activity which was not covered by his application.

(1AC)   In this section 'description of business' means, in relation to a type of business, a description of business specified in a general notice under section 24A(5)(a).

(1AD)   An applicant shall not, by virtue of this section, be issued with a licence unless he satisfies the OFT that the name or names under which he would be licensed is or are not misleading or otherwise undesirable.]

[. . .]

(1B)   If an application for the grant of a standard licence—

(a)   is made by a person with permission under Part 4 of the Financial Services and Markets Act 2000 to accept deposits, and

(b)   relates to a listed activity,

the Financial Services Authority may, if it considers that the [OFT] ought to refuse the application, notify [it] of that fact.

(1C)   In subsection (1B) 'listed activity' means an activity listed in Annex 1 to the banking consolidation directive (2000/12/EC) or in the Annex to the investment services directive (93/22/EEC) and references to deposits and to their acceptance must be read with—

    (a)   section 22 of the Financial Services and Markets Act 2000;

    (b)   any relevant order under that section; and

    (c)   Schedule 2 to that Act.]

[(2) In determining whether an applicant for a licence is a fit person for the purposes of this section the OFT shall have regard to any matters appearing to it to be relevant including (amongst other things)—

    (a)   the applicant's skills, knowledge and experience in relation to consumer credit businesses, consumer hire businesses or ancillary credit businesses;

    (b)   such skills, knowledge and experience of other persons who the applicant proposes will participate in any business that would be carried on by him under the licence;

    (c)   practices and procedures that the applicant proposes to implement in connection with any such business;

    (d)   evidence of the kind mentioned in subsection (2A).

(2A) That evidence is evidence tending to show that the applicant, or any of the applicant's employees, agents or associates (whether past or present) or, where the applicant is a body corporate, any person appearing to the OFT to be a controller of the body corporate or an associate of any such person, has—

    (a)   committed any offence involving fraud or other dishonesty or violence;

    (b)   contravened any provision made by or under—

        (i) this Act;

        (ii) Part 16 of the Financial Services and Markets Act 2000 so far as it relates to the consumer credit jurisdiction under that Part;

        (iii) any other enactment regulating the provision of credit to individuals or other transactions with individuals;

    (c)   contravened any provision in force in an EEA State which corresponds to a provision of the kind mentioned in paragraph (b);

    (d)   practised discrimination on grounds of sex, colour, race or ethnic or national origins in, or in connection with, the carrying on of any business; or

    (e)   engaged in business practices appearing to the OFT to be deceitful or oppressive or otherwise unfair or improper (whether unlawful or not).

(2B) For the purposes of subsection (2A)(e), the business practices which the OFT may consider to be deceitful or oppressive or otherwise unfair or improper include practices in the carrying on of a consumer credit business that appear to the OFT to involve irresponsible lending.]

(3) In subsection [(2A)], 'associate', in addition to the persons specified in section 184, includes a business associate.

[25A Guidance on fitness test

(1) The OFT shall prepare and publish guidance in relation to how it determines, or how it proposes to determine, whether persons are fit persons as mentioned in section 25.

(2) If the OFT revises the guidance at any time after it has been published, the OFT shall publish it as revised.

(3) The guidance shall be published in such manner as the OFT thinks fit for the purpose of bringing it to the attention of those likely to be affected by it.

(4) In preparing or revising the guidance the OFT shall consult such persons as it thinks fit.

(5) In carrying out its functions under this Part the OFT shall have regard to the guidance as most recently published.]

[26 Conduct of business

(1) Regulations may be made as to—

    (a)   the conduct by a licensee of his business; and

(b)   the conduct by a consumer credit EEA firm of its business in the United Kingdom.

(2)   The regulations may in particular specify—

(a)   the books or other records to be kept by any person to whom the regulations apply;

(b)   the information to be furnished by such a person to those persons with whom—

(i)   that person does business, or

(ii)   that person seeks to do business,

and the way in which that information is to be furnished.]

Issue of licences

27   Determination of applications

(1)   Unless the [OFT] determines to issue a licence in accordance with an application [it] shall, before determining the application by notice—

(a)   inform the applicant, giving [its] reasons, that, as the case may be, [it] is minded to refuse the application, or to grant it in terms different from those applied for, describing them, and

(b)   invite the applicant to submit to the [OFT] representations in support of his application in accordance with section 34.

(2)   If the [OFT] grants the application in terms different from those applied for then, whether or not the applicant appeals, the [OFT] shall issue the licence in the terms approved by [it] unless the applicant by notice informs [it] that he does not desire a licence in those terms.

[27A   Consumer credit EEA firms

(1)   Where—

(a)   a consumer credit EEA firm makes an application for a standard licence, and

(b)   the activities covered by the application are all permitted activities, the OFT shall refuse the application.

(2)   Subsection (3) applies where—

(a)   a consumer credit EEA firm makes an application for a standard licence; and

(b)   some (but not all) of the activities covered by the application are permitted activities.

(3)   In order to be entitled to be issued with a standard licence in accordance with section 25(1) to (1AB) in relation to a type of business, the firm need not satisfy the OFT that it is a fit person to carry on that type of business so far as it would involve any of the permitted activities covered by the application.

(4)   A standard licence held by a consumer credit EEA firm does not at any time authorise the carrying on of an activity which is a permitted activity at that time.

(5)   In this section 'permitted activity' means, in relation to a consumer credit EEA firm, an activity for which the firm has, or could obtain, permission under paragraph 15 of Schedule 3 to the Financial Services and Markets Act 2000.]

28   Exclusion from group licence

Where the [OFT] is minded to issue a group licence (whether on the application of any person or not), and in doing so to exclude any person from the group by name, [it] shall, before determining the matter,—

(a)   give notice of that fact to the person proposed to be excluded, giving [its] reasons, and

(b)   invite that person to submit to the [OFT] representations against his exclusion in accordance with section 34.

[Charges for indefinite licences

28A   Charges to be paid by licensees etc before end of payment periods
(1)   The licensee under a standard licence which has effect indefinitely shall, before the end of each payment period of his, pay the OFT a charge towards the costs of carrying out its functions under this Act.
(2)   The original applicant for a group licence which has effect indefinitely shall, before the end of each payment period of his, pay the OFT such a charge.
(3)   The amount of the charge payable by a person under subsection (1) or (2) before the end of a payment period shall be determined in accordance with provision which—
      (a)   is made by the OFT by general notice; and
      (b)   is current on such day as may be determined in accordance with provision made by regulations.
(4)   The provision that may be made by the OFT under subsection (3)(a) includes—
      (a)   different provision in relation to persons of different descriptions (including persons whose payment periods end at different times);
      (b)   provision for no charge at all to be payable by persons of specified descriptions.
(5)   The approval of the Secretary of State and the Treasury is required for a general notice under subsection (3)(a).
(6)   For the purposes of this section a person's payment periods are to be determined in accordance with provision made by regulations.

28B   Extension of period to pay charge under s 28A
(1)   A person who is required under section 28A to pay a charge before the end of a period may apply once to the OFT for that period to be extended.
(2)   The application shall be made before such day as may be determined in accordance with provision made by the OFT by general notice.
(3)   If the OFT is satisfied that there is a good reason—
      (a)   why the applicant has not paid that charge prior to his making of the application, and
      (b)   why he cannot pay that charge before the end of that period,
it may, if it thinks fit, by notice to him extend that period by such time as it thinks fit having regard to that reason.
(4)   The power of the OFT under this section to extend a period in relation to a charge—
      (a)   includes the power to extend the period in relation to a part of the charge only;
      (b)   may be exercised even though the period has ended.

28C   Failure to pay charge under s 28A
(1)   This section applies if a person (the 'defaulter') fails to pay a charge—
      (a)   before the end of a period (the 'payment period') as required under section 28A; or
      (b)   where the payment period is extended under section 28B, before the end of the payment period as extended (subject to subsection (2)).
(2)   Where the payment period is extended under section 28B in relation to a part of the charge only, this section applies if the defaulter fails—
      (a)   to pay so much of the charge as is not covered by the extension before the end of the payment period disregarding the extension; or
      (b)   to pay so much of the charge as is covered by the extension before the end of the payment period as extended.
(3)   Subject to subsection (4), if the charge is a charge under section 28A(1), the defaulter's licence terminates.

(4)   If the defaulter has applied to the OFT under section 28B for the payment period to be extended and that application has not been determined—

(a)   his licence shall not terminate before the application has been determined and the OFT has notified him of the determination; and

(b)   if the OFT extends the payment period on that application, this section shall have effect accordingly.

(5)   If the charge is a charge under section 28A(2), the charge shall be recoverable by the OFT.]

Renewal, variation, suspension and revocation of licences

29   Renewal

(1)   If the licensee under a standard licence [of limited duration], or the original applicant for, or any licensee under, a group licence of limited duration, wishes the [OFT] to renew the licence, whether on the same terms (except as to expiry) or on varied terms, he must, during the period specified by the [OFT] by general notice or such longer period as the [OFT] may allow, make an application to the [OFT] for its renewal.

(2)   The [OFT] may of [its] own motion renew any group licence.

(3)   The preceding provisions of this Part apply to the renewal of a licence as they apply to the issue of a licence, except that section 28 does not apply to a person who was already excluded in the licence up for renewal.

[(3A)   In its application to the renewal of standard licences by virtue of subsection (3) of this section, section 27(1) shall have effect as if for paragraph (b) there were substituted—

'(b)   invite the applicant to submit to the OFT in accordance with section 34 representations—

(i)   in support of his application; and

(ii)   about the provision (if any) that should be included under section 34A as part of the determination were the OFT to refuse the application or grant it in terms different from those applied for.']

(4)   Until the determination of an application under subsection (1) and, where an appeal lies from the determination, until the end of the appeal period, the licence shall continue [to have effect], notwithstanding that apart from this subsection it would expire earlier.

[. . .]

(6)   General notice shall be given of the renewal of a group licence.

30   Variation by request

(1)   [If it thinks fit, the OFT may by notice to the licensee under a standard licence—

(a)   in the case of a licence which covers the carrying on of a type of business only so far as it falls within one or more descriptions of business, vary the licence by—

(i)   removing that limitation;

(ii)   adding a description of business to that limitation; or

(iii)   removing a description of business from that limitation;

(b)   in the case of a licence which covers the carrying on of a type of business with no limitation, vary the licence so that it covers the carrying on of that type of business only so far as it falls within one or more descriptions of business;

(c)   vary the licence so that it no longer covers the carrying on of a type of business at all;

(d)   vary the licence so that a type of business the carrying on of which is not covered at all by the licence is covered either—

(i)   with no limitation; or

(ii)   only so far as it falls within one or more descriptions of business; or

(e)   vary the licence in any other way except for the purpose of varying the descriptions of activities covered by the licence.

(1A)   The OFT may vary a licence under subsection (1) only in accordance with an application made by the licensee.

(1B)   References in this section to a description of business in relation to a type of business—

(a)   are references to a description of business specified in a general notice under section 24A(5)(a); and

(b)   in subsection (1)(a) (apart from sub-paragraph (ii)) include references to a description of business that was, but is no longer, so specified.]

(2)   In the case of a group licence issued on the application of any person, the [OFT], on an application made by that person, may if [it] thinks fit by notice to that person vary the terms of the licence in accordance with the application; but the [OFT] shall not vary a group licence under this subsection by excluding a named person, other than the person making the request, unless that named person consents in writing to his exclusion.

(3)   In the case of a group licence from which (whether by name or description) a person is excluded, the [OFT], on an application made by that person, may if [it] thinks fit, by notice to that person, vary the terms of the licence so as to remove the exclusion.

(4)   Unless the [OFT] determines to vary a licence in accordance with an application [it] shall, before determining the application, by notice—

(a)   inform the applicant, giving [its] reasons, that [it] is minded to refuse the application, and

(b)   invite the applicant to submit to the [OFT] representations in support of his application in accordance with section 34.

[. . .]

31   Compulsory variation

(1)   Where at a time during the currency of a licence the [OFT] is of the opinion that, if the licence had expired at that time, [(assuming, in the case of a licence which has effect indefinitely, that it were a licence of limited duration) it] would on an application for its renewal or further renewal on the same terms (except as to expiry), have been minded to grant the application but on different terms, and that therefore [it should take steps mentioned in subsection (1A)], [it] shall proceed as follows.

[(1A)   Those steps are—

(a)   in the case of a standard licence, steps mentioned in section 30(1)(a)(ii) and (iii), (b), (c) and (e);

(b)   in the case of a group licence, the varying of terms of the licence.

(1B)   The OFT shall also proceed as follows if, having regard to section 22(1B) to (1E), it is of the opinion—

(a)   that a licence which has effect indefinitely should have its duration limited; or

(b)   in the case of a licence of limited duration, that the period during which it has effect should be shortened.]

(2)   In the case of a standard licence the [OFT] shall, by notice—

(a)   inform the licensee of the variations the [OFT] is minded to make in the terms of the licence, stating [its] reasons, and

[(b)   invite him to submit to the OFT in accordance with section 34 representations—

(i)   as to the proposed variations; and

(ii)   about the provision (if any) that should be included under section 34A as part of the determination were the OFT to vary the licence.]

(3)   In the case of a group licence the [OFT] shall—

(a)   give general notice of the variations [it] is minded to make in the terms of the licence, stating [its] reasons, and

(b)   in the notice invite any licensee to submit to [it] representations as to the proposed variations in accordance with section 34.

(4)   In the case of a group licence issued on application the [OFT] shall also—

(a)   inform the original applicant of the variations the [OFT] is minded to make in the terms of the licence, stating [its] reasons, and

(b)   invite him to submit to the [OFT] representations as to the proposed variations in accordance with section 34.

(5)   If the [OFT] is minded to vary a group licence by excluding any person (other than the original applicant) from the group by name the [OFT] shall, in addition, take the like steps under section 28 as are required in the case mentioned in that section.

(6)   General notice shall be given that a variation of any group licence has been made under this section.

(7)   A variation under this section shall not take effect before the end of the appeal period.

[(8)   Subsection (1) shall have effect in relation to a standard licence as if an application could be made for the renewal or further renewal of the licence on the same terms (except as to expiry) even if such an application could not be made because of provision made in a general notice under section 24A(5).

(9)   Accordingly, in applying subsection (1AA) of section 25 in relation to the licence for the purposes of this section, the OFT shall treat references in that subsection to the description or descriptions of business in relation to a type of business as references to the description or descriptions of business included in the licence in relation to that type of business, notwithstanding that provision under section 24A(5).]

32   Suspension and revocation

(1)   Where at a time during the currency of a licence the [OFT] is of the opinion that if the licence had expired at that time [(assuming, in the case of a licence which has effect indefinitely, that it were a licence of limited duration) it] would have been minded not to renew it, and that therefore it should be revoked or suspended, [it] shall proceed as follows.

(2)   In the case of a standard licence the [OFT] shall, by notice—

(a)   inform the licensee that, as the case may be, the [OFT] is minded to revoke the licence, or suspend it until a specified date or indefinitely, stating [its] reasons, and

[(b)   invite him to submit to the OFT in accordance with section 34 representations—

(i)   as to the proposed revocation or suspension; and

(ii)   about the provision (if any) that should be included under section 34A as part of the determination were the OFT to revoke or suspend the licence.]

(3)   In the case of a group licence the [OFT] shall—

(a)   give general notice that, as the case may be, [it] is minded to revoke the licence, or suspend it until a specified date or indefinitely, stating [its] reasons, and

(b)   in the notice invite any licensee to submit to [it] representations as to the proposed revocation or suspension in accordance with section 34.

(4)   In the case of a group licence issued on application the [OFT] shall also—

(a)   inform the original applicant that, as the case may be, the [OFT] is minded to revoke the licence, or suspend it until a specified date or indefinitely, stating [its] reasons, and

(b)   invite him to submit representations as to the proposed revocation or suspension in accordance with section 34.

[. . .]

(6)   General notice shall be given of the revocation or suspension of a group licence.

(7)   A revocation or suspension under this section shall not take effect before the end of the appeal period.

(8)   Except for the purposes of section 29, a licensee under a suspended licence shall be treated, in respect of the period of suspension, as if the licence had not been issued; and where the suspension is not expressed to end on a specified date it may, if the [OFT] thinks fit, be ended by notice given by [it] to the licensee or, in the case of a group licence, by general notice.

[(9)   The OFT has no power to revoke or to suspend a standard licence simply because, by virtue of provision made in a general notice under section 24A(5), a person cannot apply for the renewal of such a licence on terms which are the same as the terms of the licence in question.]

33   Application to end suspension

(1)   On an application made by a licensee the [OFT] may, if [it] thinks fit, by notice to the licensee end the suspension of a licence, whether the suspension was for a fixed or indefinite period.

(2)   Unless the [OFT] determines to end the suspension in accordance with the application [it] shall, before determining the application, by notice—

   (a)   inform the applicant, giving [its] reasons, that [it] is minded to refuse the application, and

   (b)   invite the applicant to submit to the [OFT] representations in support of his application in accordance with section 34.

(3)   General notice shall be given that a suspension of a group licence has been ended under this section.

(4)   In the case of a group licence issued on application—

   (a)   the references in subsection (1) to a licensee include the original applicant;

   (b)   the [OFT] shall inform the original applicant that a suspension of a group licence has been ended under this section.

[Further powers of OFT to regulate conduct of licensees etc

33A   Power of OFT to impose requirements on licensees

(1)   This section applies where the OFT is dissatisfied with any matter in connection with—

   (a)   a business being carried on, or which has been carried on, by a licensee or by an associate or a former associate of a licensee;

   (b)   a proposal to carry on a business which has been made by a licensee or by an associate or a former associate of a licensee; or

   (c)   any conduct not covered by paragraph (a) or (b) of a licensee or of an associate or a former associate of a licensee.

(2)   The OFT may by notice to the licensee require him to do or not to do (or to cease doing) anything specified in the notice for purposes connected with—

   (a)   addressing the matter with which the OFT is dissatisfied; or

   (b)   securing that matters of the same or a similar kind do not arise.

(3)   A requirement imposed under this section on a licensee shall only relate to a business which the licensee is carrying on, or is proposing to carry on, under the licence under which he is a licensee.

(4)   Such a requirement may be framed by reference to a named person other than the licensee.

(5)   For the purposes of subsection (1) it is immaterial whether the matter with which the OFT is dissatisfied arose before or after the licensee became a licensee.

(6)   If—

   (a)   a person makes an application for a standard licence, and

   (b)   while dealing with that application the OFT forms the opinion that, if

such a licence were to be issued to that person, it would be minded to impose
on him a requirement under this section,
the OFT may, before issuing such a licence to that person, do (in whole or in part)
anything that it must do under section 33D or 34(1) or (2) in relation to the imposing of the requirement.

(7)   In this section 'associate', in addition to the persons specified in section 184,
includes a business associate.

33B   Power of OFT to impose requirements on supervisory bodies

(1)   This section applies where the OFT is dissatisfied with the way in which a
responsible person in relation to a group licence—

(a)   is regulating or otherwise supervising, or has regulated or otherwise
supervised, persons who are licensees under that licence; or

(b)   is proposing to regulate or otherwise to supervise such persons.

(2)   The OFT may by notice to the responsible person require him to do or not
to do (or to cease doing) anything specified in the notice for purposes connected
with—

(a)   addressing the matters giving rise to the OFT's dissatisfaction; or

(b)   securing that matters of the same or a similar kind do not arise.

(3)   A requirement imposed under this section on a responsible person in relation to a group licence shall only relate to practices and procedures for regulating or otherwise supervising licensees under the licence in connection with their
carrying on of businesses under the licence.

(4)   For the purposes of subsection (1) it is immaterial whether the matters
giving rise to the OFT's dissatisfaction arose before or after the issue of the group
licence in question.

(5)   If—

(a)   a person makes an application for a group licence, and

(b)   while dealing with that application the OFT forms the opinion that, if
such a licence were to be issued to that person, it would be minded to impose
on him a requirement under this section,
the OFT may, before issuing such a licence to that person, do (in whole or in part)
anything that it must do under section 33D or 34(1) or (2) in relation to the imposing of the requirement.

(6)   For the purposes of this Part a person is a responsible person in relation to
a group licence if—

(a)   he is the original applicant for it; and

(b)   he has a responsibility (whether by virtue of an enactment, an agreement
or otherwise) for regulating or otherwise supervising persons who are licensees
under the licence.

33C   Supplementary provision relating to requirements

(1)   A notice imposing a requirement under section 33A or 33B may include
provision about the time at or by which, or the period during which, the requirement is to be complied with.

(2)   A requirement imposed under section 33A or 33B shall not have effect after
the licence by reference to which it is imposed has itself ceased to have effect.

(3)   A person shall not be required under section 33A or 33B to compensate, or
otherwise to make amends to, another person.

(4)   The OFT may by notice to the person on whom a requirement has been
imposed under section 33A or 33B vary or revoke the requirement (including any
provision made under subsection (1) of this section in relation to it) with effect
from such date as may be specified in the notice.

(5)   The OFT may exercise its power under subsection (4) in relation to a
requirement either on its own motion or on the application of a person falling
within subsection (6) or (7) in relation to the requirement.

(6)   A person falls within this subsection in relation to a requirement if he is the person on whom the requirement is imposed.

(7)   A person falls within this subsection in relation to a requirement if—

(a)   the requirement is imposed under section 33A;

(b)   he is not the person on whom the requirement is imposed;

(c)   the requirement is framed by reference to him by name; and

(d)   the effect of the requirement is—

(i)   to prevent him being an employee of the person on whom the requirement is imposed;

(ii)   to restrict the activities that he may engage in as an employee of that person; or

(iii)   otherwise to prevent him from doing something, or to restrict his doing something, in connection with a business being carried on by that person.

33D   Procedure in relation to requirements

(1)   Before making a determination—

(a)   to impose a requirement on a person under section 33A or 33B,

(b)   to refuse an application under section 33C(5) in relation to a requirement imposed under either of those sections, or

(c)   to vary or to revoke a requirement so imposed,

the OFT shall proceed as follows.

(2)   The OFT shall give a notice to every person to whom subsection (3) applies in relation to the determination—

(a)   informing him, with reasons, that it is minded to make the determination; and

(b)   inviting him to submit to it representations as to the determination under section 34.

(3)   This subsection applies to a person in relation to the determination if he falls within, or as a consequence of the determination would fall within, section 33C(6) or (7) in relation to the requirement in question.

(4)   This section does not require the OFT to give a notice to a person if the determination in question is in the same terms as a proposal made to the OFT by that person (whether as part of an application under this Part or otherwise).

33E   Guidance on requirements

(1)   The OFT shall prepare and publish guidance in relation to how it exercises, or how it proposes to exercise, its powers under sections 33A to 33C.

(2)   If the OFT revises the guidance at any time after it has been published, the OFT shall publish it as revised.

(3)   The guidance shall be published in such manner as the OFT thinks fit for the purpose of bringing it to the attention of those likely to be affected by it.

(4)   In preparing or revising the guidance the OFT shall consult such persons as it thinks fit.

(5)   In exercising its powers under sections 33A to 33C the OFT shall have regard to the guidance as most recently published.]

Miscellaneous

34   Representations to [OFT]

(1)   Where this section applies to an invitation by the [OFT] to any person to submit representations, the [OFT] shall invite that person, within 21 days after the notice containing the invitation is given to him or published, or such longer period as the [OFT] may allow—

(a)   to submit his representations in writing to the [OFT], and

(b)   to give notice to the [OFT], if he thinks fit, that he wishes to make representations orally, and where notice is given under paragraph (b) the [OFT] shall arrange for the oral representations to be heard.

(2)   In reaching [its] determination the [OFT] shall take into account any representations submitted or made under this section.

(3)   The [OFT] shall give notice of [its] determination to the persons who were required to be invited to submit representations about it or, where the invitation to submit representations was required to be given by general notice, shall give general notice of the determination.

[34A   Winding-up of standard licensee's business

(1)   If it thinks fit, the OFT may, for the purpose of enabling the licensee's business, or any part of his business, to be transferred or wound up, include as part of a determination to which subsection (2) applies provision authorising the licensee to carry on for a specified period—

(a)   specified activities, or

(b)   activities of specified descriptions,

which, because of that determination, the licensee will no longer be licensed to carry on.

(2)   This subsection applies to the following determinations—

(a)   a determination to refuse to renew a standard licence in accordance with the terms of the application for its renewal;

(b)   a determination to vary such a licence under section 31;

(c)   a determination to suspend or revoke such a licence.

(3)   Such provision—

(a)   may specify different periods for different activities or activities of different descriptions;

(b)   may provide for persons other than the licensee to carry on activities under the authorisation;

(c)   may specify requirements which must be complied with by a person carrying on activities under the authorisation in relation to those activities;

and, if a requirement specified under paragraph (c) is not complied with, the OFT may by notice to a person carrying on activities under the authorisation terminate the authorisation (in whole or in part) from a specified date.

(4)   Without prejudice to the generality of paragraph (c) of subsection (3), a requirement specified under that paragraph may have the effect of—

(a)   preventing a named person from being an employee of a person carrying on activities under the authorisation, or restricting the activities he may engage in as an employee of such a person;

(b)   preventing a named person from doing something, or restricting his doing something, in connection with activities being carried on by a person under the authorisation;

(c)   securing that access to premises is given to officers of the OFT for the purpose of enabling them to inspect documents or to observe the carrying on of activities.

(5)   Activities carried on under an authorisation shall be treated for the purposes of sections 39(1), 40, 148 and 149 as if carried on under a standard licence.]

35   The register

(1)   The [OFT] shall establish and maintain a register, in which [it] shall cause to be kept particulars of—

(a)   applications not yet determined for the issue, variation or renewal of licences, or for ending the suspension of a licence;

(b)   licences which are in [effect], or have at any time been suspended or revoked [or terminated by section 28C], with details of any variation of the terms of a licence;

[(ba)   requirements imposed under section 33A or 33B which are in effect or which have been in effect, with details of any variation of such a requirement;]

(c)   decisions given by [it] under this Act, and any appeal from those decisions; and

(d)   such other matters (if any) as [it] thinks fit.

[(1A)   The [OFT] shall also cause to be kept in the register any copy of any notice or other document relating to a consumer credit EEA firm which is given to the [OFT] by the Financial Services Authority for inclusion in the register.]

(2)   The [OFT] shall give general notice of the various matters required to be entered in the register, and of any change in them made under subsection (1)(d).

(3)   Any person shall be entitled on payment of the specified fee—

(a)   to inspect the register during ordinary office hours and take copies of any entry, or

(b)   to obtain from the [OFT] a copy, certified by the [OFT] to be correct, of any entry in the register.

(4)   The [OFT] may, if [it] thinks fit, determine that the right conferred by subsection (3)(a) shall be exercisable in relation to a copy of the register instead of, or in addition to, the original.

(5)   The [OFT] shall give general notice of the place or places where, and times when, the register or a copy of it may be inspected.

36   Duty to notify changes

(1)   Within 21 working days after change takes place in any particulars entered in the register in respect of a standard licence or the licensee under section 35(1)(d) (not being a change resulting from action taken by the [OFT]), the licensee shall give the [OFT] notice of the change; and the [OFT] shall cause any necessary amendment to be made in the register.

(2)   Within 21 working days after—

(a)   any change takes place in the officers of—

(i)   a body corporate, or an unincorporated body of persons, which is the licensee under a standard licence, or

(ii)   a body corporate which is a controller of a body corporate which is such a licensee, or

(b)   a body corporate which is such a licensee becomes aware that a person has become or ceased to be a controller of the body corporate, or

(c)   any change takes place in the members of a partnership which is such a licensee (including a change on the amalgamation of the partnership with another firm, or a change whereby the number of partners is reduced to one), the licensee shall give the [OFT] notice of the change.

(3)   Within 14 working days after any change takes place in the officers of a body corporate which is a controller of another body corporate which is a licensee under a standard licence, the controller shall give the licensee notice of the change.

(4)   Within 14 working days after a person becomes or ceases to be a controller of a body corporate which is a licensee under a standard licence, that person shall give the licensee notice of the fact.

(5)   Where a change in a partnership has the result that the business ceases to be carried on under the name, or any of the names, specified in a standard licence the licence shall cease to have effect.

[. . .]

36A   Further duties to notify changes etc

(1)   Subsections (2) to (4) apply where a general notice under section 6(2) comes into effect.

(2)   A person who is the licensee under a standard licence or who is the original applicant for a group licence shall, in relation to each relevant application which he has made and which was determined before the general notice came into effect, provide the OFT with any information or document—

(a)   which he would have been required to provide with the application had the application been made after the general notice came into effect; and

(b)   which the general notice requires to be provided for the purposes of this subsection.

(3)   Any such information or document shall be provided within such period as may be specified in the general notice.

(4)   Subsection (2) does not require a person to provide any information or document—

(a)   which he provided in relation to the application by virtue of section 6;

(b)   which he has previously provided in relation to the application by virtue of this section; or

(c)   which he would have been required to provide in relation to the application by virtue of subsection (5) but for subsection (6).

(5)   A person who is the licensee under a standard licence or who is the original applicant for a group licence shall, in relation to each relevant application which he has made, notify the OFT giving details if, after the application is determined, any information or document which he—

(a)   provided in relation to the application by virtue of section 6, or

(b)   has so provided by virtue of this section,

is, to any extent, superseded or otherwise affected by a change in circumstances.

(6)   Subsection (5) does not require a person to notify the OFT about a matter unless it falls within a description of matters specified by the OFT in a general notice.

(7)   A description may be specified for the purposes of subsection (6) only if the OFT is satisfied that the matters which would fall within that description are matters which would be relevant to the question of—

(a)   whether, having regard to section 25(2), a person is a fit person to carry on a business under a standard licence; or

(b)   whether the public interest is better served by a group licence remaining in effect than by obliging the licensees under it to apply separately for standard licences.

(8)   A person who is the licensee under a standard licence or who is the original applicant for a group licence shall, in relation to each relevant application which he has made, notify the OFT about every error or omission—

(a)   in or from any information or document which he provided by virtue of section 6, or which he has provided by virtue of this section, in relation to the application; and

(b)   of which he becomes aware after the determination of the application.

(9)   A notification for the purposes of subsection (5) or (8) shall be given within the period of 28 days beginning with the day on which (as the case may be)—

(a)   the information or document is superseded;

(b)   the change in circumstances occurs; or

(c)   the licensee or the original applicant becomes aware of the error or omission.

(10)   This section does not require a person to notify the OFT about—

(a)   anything of which he is required to notify it under section 36; or

(b)   an error in or omission from any information or document which is a clerical error or omission not affecting the substance of the information or document.

(11)   In this section 'relevant application' means, in relation to a person who is the licensee under a standard licence or who is the original applicant for a group licence—

(a)   the original application for the licence; or

(b)   an application for its renewal or for its variation.

36B   Power of OFT to require information generally

(1)   The OFT may by notice to a person require him—

(a)   to provide such information as may be specified or described in the notice; or

(b)   to produce such documents as may be so specified or described.

(2)   The notice shall set out the reasons why the OFT requires the information or documents to be provided or produced.

(3)   The information or documents shall be provided or produced—

(a)   before the end of such reasonable period as may be specified in the notice; and

(b)   at such place as may be so specified.

(4)   A requirement may be imposed under subsection (1) on a person who is—

(a)   the licensee under a standard licence, or

(b)   the original applicant for a group licence,

only if the provision or production of the information or documents in question is reasonably required for purposes connected with the OFT's functions under this Act.

(5)   A requirement may be imposed under subsection (1) on any other person only if—

(a)   an act or omission mentioned in subsection (6) has occurred or the OFT has reason to suspect that such an act or omission has occurred; and

(b)   the provision or production of the information or documents in question is reasonably required for purposes connected with—

(i)   the taking by the OFT of steps under this Part as a consequence; or

(ii)   its consideration of whether to take such steps as a consequence.

(6)   Those acts or omissions are acts or omissions which—

(a)   cast doubt on whether, having regard to section 25(2), a person is a fit person to carry on a business under a standard licence;

(b)   cast doubt on whether the public interest is better served by a group licence remaining in effect, or being issued, than by obliging the persons who are licensees under it, or who would be licensees under it, to apply separately for standard licences;

(c)   give rise, or are likely to give rise, to dissatisfaction for the purposes of section 33A(1) or 33B(1); or

(d)   constitute or give rise to a failure of the kind mentioned in section 39A(1).

36C   Power of OFT to require access to premises

(1)   The OFT may by notice to a licensee under a licence require him to secure that access to the premises specified or described in the notice is given to an officer of an enforcement authority in order for the officer—

(a)   to observe the carrying on of a business under the licence by the licensee; or

(b)   to inspect such documents of the licensee relating to such a business as are—

(i)   specified or described in the notice; and

(ii)   situated on the premises.

(2)   The notice shall set out the reasons why the access is required.

(3)   The premises which may be specified or described in the notice—

(a)   include premises which are not premises of the licensee if they are premises from which he carries on activities in connection with the business in question; but

(b)   do not include premises which are used only as a dwelling.

(4)   The licensee shall secure that the required access is given at such times as the OFT reasonably requires.

(5)   The OFT shall give reasonable notice of those times.

(6)   Where an officer is given access to any premises by virtue of this section, the licensee shall also secure that persons on the premises give the officer such

assistance or information as he may reasonably require in connection with his observation or inspection of documents (as the case may be).

(7)   The assistance that may be required under subsection (6) includes (amongst other things) the giving to the officer of an explanation of a document which he is inspecting.

(8)   A requirement may be imposed under subsection (1) on a person who is—

(a)   the licensee under a standard licence, or

(b)   the original applicant for a group licence,

only if the observation or inspection in question is reasonably required for purposes connected with the OFT's functions under this Act.

(9)   A requirement may be imposed under subsection (1) on any other person only if—

(a)   an act or omission mentioned in section 36B(6) has occurred or the OFT has reason to suspect that such an act or omission has occurred; and

(b)   the observation or inspection in question is reasonably required for purposes connected with—

(i)   the taking by the OFT of steps under this Part as a consequence; or

(ii)   its consideration of whether to take such steps as a consequence.

(10)   In this section—

(a)   references to a licensee under a licence include, in relation to a group licence issued on application, references to the original applicant; and

(b)   references to a business being carried on under a licence by a licensee include, in relation to the original applicant for a group licence, activities being carried on by him for the purpose of regulating or otherwise supervising (whether by virtue of an enactment, an agreement or otherwise) licensees under that licence in connection with their carrying on of businesses under that licence.

36D   Entry to premises under warrant

(1)   A justice of the peace may issue a warrant under this section if satisfied on information on oath given on behalf of the OFT that there are reasonable grounds for believing that the following conditions are satisfied.

(2)   Those conditions are—

(a)   that there is on the premises specified in the warrant information or documents in relation to which a requirement could be imposed under section 36B; and

(b)   that if such a requirement were to be imposed in relation to the information or documents—

(i)   it would not be complied with; or

(ii)   the information or documents would be tampered with.

(3)   A warrant under this section shall authorise an officer of an enforcement authority—

(a)   to enter the premises specified in the warrant;

(b)   to search the premises and to seize and detain any information or documents appearing to be information or documents specified in the warrant or information or documents of a description so specified;

(c)   to take any other steps which may appear to be reasonably necessary for preserving such information or documents or preventing interference with them; and

(d)   to use such force as may be reasonably necessary.

(4)   An officer entering premises by virtue of this section may take such persons and equipment with him as he thinks necessary.

(5)   In the application of this section to Scotland—

(a)   the reference to a justice of the peace includes a reference to a sheriff;

(b)   for 'information on oath' there is substituted 'evidence on oath'.

(6)   In the application of this section to Northern Ireland the reference to a justice of the peace shall be construed as a reference to a lay magistrate.

36E   Failure to comply with information requirement

(1)   If on an application made by the OFT it appears to the court that a person (the 'information defaulter') has failed to do something that he was required to do by virtue of section 36B or 36C, the court may make an order under this section.

(2)   An order under this section may require the information defaulter—

(a)   to do the thing that it appears he failed to do within such period as may be specified in the order;

(b)   otherwise to take such steps to remedy the consequences of the failure as may be so specified.

(3)   If the information defaulter is a body corporate, a partnership or an unincorporated body of persons which is not a partnership, the order may require any officer who is (wholly or partly) responsible for the failure to meet such costs of the application as are specified in the order.

(4)   In this section—

'court' means—

(a)   in England and Wales and Northern Ireland, the High Court or the county court;

(b)   in Scotland, the Court of Session or the sheriff;

'officer' means—

(a)   in relation to a body corporate, a person holding a position of director, manager or secretary of the body or any similar position;

(b)   in relation to a partnership or to an unincorporated body of persons, a member of the partnership or body.

(5)   In subsection (4) 'director' means, in relation to a body corporate whose affairs are managed by its members, a member of the body.

36F   Officers of enforcement authorities other than OFT

(1)   A relevant officer may only exercise powers by virtue of section 36C or 36D in pursuance of arrangements made with the OFT by or on behalf of the enforcement authority of which he is an officer.

(2)   Anything done or omitted to be done by, or in relation to, a relevant officer in the exercise or purported exercise of a power by virtue of section 36C or 36D shall be treated for all purposes as having been done or omitted to be done by, or in relation to, an officer of the OFT.

(3)   Subsection (2) does not apply for the purposes of any criminal proceedings brought against the officer, the enforcement authority of which he is an officer or the OFT in respect of anything done or omitted to be done by the officer.

(4)   A relevant officer shall not disclose to a person other than the OFT information obtained by his exercise of a power by virtue of section 36C or 36D unless—

(a)   he has the approval of the OFT to do so; or

(b)   he is under a duty to make the disclosure.

(5)   In this section 'relevant officer' means an officer of an enforcement authority other than the OFT.]

37   Death, bankruptcy etc of licensee

(1)   A licence held by one individual terminates if he—

(a)   dies,

[(b)   has his estate sequestrated, or

(c)   becomes incapable of managing his own affairs.]

[(1A)   A licence terminates if the licensee gives the OFT a notice under subsection (1B).

(1B)   A notice under this subsection shall—

(a)   be in such form as the OFT may by general notice specify;

(b)   contain such information as may be so specified;

(c)   be accompanied by the licence or give reasons as to why it is not accompanied by the licence; and

(d)   be signed by or on behalf of the licensee.]

(2)   In relation to a licence held by one individual, or a partnership or other unincorporated body of persons, or a body corporate, regulations may specify other events relating to the licensee on the occurrence of which the licence is to terminate.

(3)   Regulations may—

(a)   provide for the termination of a licence by subsection (1) [or (1A)], or under subsection (2), to be deferred for a period not exceeding 12 months, and

(b)   authorise the business of the licensee to be carried on under the licence by some other person during the period of deferment, subject to such conditions as may be prescribed.

(4)   This section does not apply to group licences.

38   Application of s 37 to Scotland and Northern Ireland

(1)   [Scottish provisions incorporated in s 37 above.]

39   Offences against Part III

(1)   A person who engages in any activities for which a licence is required when he is not a licensee under a licence covering those activities commits an offence.

(2)   A licensee under a standard licence who carries on business under a name not specified in the licence commits an offence.

(3)   A person who fails to give the [OFT] or a licensee notice under section 36 within the period required commits an offence.

[39A   Power of OFT to impose civil penalties

(1)   Where the OFT is satisfied that a person (the 'defaulter') has failed or is failing to comply with a requirement imposed on him by virtue of section 33A, 33B or 36A, it may by notice to him (a 'penalty notice') impose on him a penalty of such amount as it thinks fit.

(2)   The penalty notice shall—

(a)   specify the amount of the penalty that is being imposed;

(b)   set out the OFT's reasons for imposing a penalty and for specifying that amount;

(c)   specify how the payment of the penalty may be made to the OFT; and

(d)   specify the period within which the penalty is required to be paid.

(3)   The amount of the penalty shall not exceed £50,000.

(4)   The period specified in the penalty notice for the purposes of subsection (2)(d) shall not end earlier than the end of the period during which an appeal may be brought against the imposition of the penalty under section 41.

(5)   If the defaulter does not pay the penalty to the OFT within the period so specified—

(a)   the unpaid balance from time to time shall carry interest at the rate for the time being specified in section 17 of the Judgments Act 1838; and

(b)   the penalty and any interest payable on it shall be recoverable by the OFT.

39B   Further provision relating to civil penalties

(1)   Before determining to impose a penalty on a person under section 39A the OFT shall give a notice to that person—

(a)   informing him that it is minded to impose a penalty on him;

(b)   stating the proposed amount of the penalty;

(c)   setting out its reasons for being minded to impose a penalty on him and for proposing that amount;

(d)   setting out the proposed period for the payment of the penalty; and

(e)   inviting him to submit representations to it about the matters mentioned in the preceding paragraphs in accordance with section 34.

(2)   In determining whether and how to exercise its powers under section 39A

in relation to a person's failure, the OFT shall have regard to (amongst other things)—

    (a)   any penalty or fine that has been imposed on that person by another body in relation to the conduct giving rise to the failure;

    (b)   other steps that the OFT has taken or might take under this Part in relation to that conduct.

(3)   General notice shall be given of the imposition of a penalty under section 39A on a person who is a responsible person in relation to a group licence.

(4)   That notice shall include the matters set out in the notice imposing the penalty in accordance with section 39A(2)(a) and (b).

39C   Statement of policy in relation to civil penalties

(1)   The OFT shall prepare and publish a statement of policy in relation to how it exercises, or how it proposes to exercise, its powers under section 39A.

(2)   If the OFT revises the statement of policy at any time after it has been published, the OFT shall publish it as revised.

(3)   No statement of policy shall be published without the approval of the Secretary of State.

(4)   The statement of policy shall be published in such manner as the OFT thinks fit for the purpose of bringing it to the attention of those likely to be affected by it.

(5)   In preparing or revising the statement of policy the OFT shall consult such persons as it thinks fit.

(6)   In determining whether and how to exercise its powers under section 39A in relation to a person's failure, the OFT shall have regard to the statement of policy as most recently published at the time the failure occurred.

(7)   The OFT shall not impose a penalty on a person under section 39A in relation to a failure occurring before it has published a statement of policy.]

40   Enforcement of agreements made by unlicensed trader

[(1)   A regulated agreement is not enforceable against the debtor or hirer by a person acting in the course of a consumer credit business or a consumer hire business (as the case may be) if that person is not licensed to carry on a consumer credit business or a consumer hire business (as the case may be) of a description which covers the enforcement of the agreement.

(1A)   Unless the OFT has made an order under subsection (2) which applies to the agreement, a regulated agreement is not enforceable against the debtor or hirer if—

    (a)   it was made by the creditor or owner in the course of a consumer credit business or a consumer hire business (as the case may be); and

    (b)   at the time the agreement was made he was not licensed to carry on a consumer credit business or a consumer hire business (as the case may be) of a description which covered the making of the agreement.

(2)   Where—

    (a)   during any period a person (the 'trader' has made regulated agreements in the course of a consumer credit business or a consumer hire business (as the case may be), and

    (b)   during that period he was not licensed to carry on a consumer credit business or a consumer hire business (as the case may be) of a description which covered the making of those agreements,

he or his successor in title may apply to the OFT for an order that the agreements are to be treated for the purposes of subsection (1A) as if he had been licensed as required.]

(3)   Unless the [OFT] determines to make an order under subsection (2) in accordance with the application, [it] shall, before determining the application, by notice—

    (a)   inform the applicant, giving [its] reasons, that, as the case may be, [it] is minded to refuse the application, or to grant it in terms different from those applied for, describing them, and

(b)   invite the applicant to submit to the [OFT] representations in support of his application in accordance with section 34.

(4)   In determining whether or not to make an order under subsection (2) in respect of any period the [OFT] shall consider, in addition to any other relevant factors—

(a)   how far, if at all, debtors or hirers under [the regulated agreements in question] made by the trader during that period were prejudiced by the trader's conduct,

(b)   whether or not the [OFT] would have been likely to grant a licence covering [the making of those agreements during] that period on an application by the trader, and

(c)   the degree of culpability for the failure to [be licensed as required].

(5)   If the [OFT] thinks fit, [it] may in an order under subsection (2)—

(a)   limit the order to specified agreements, or agreements of a specified description or made at a specified time;

(b)   make the order conditional on the doing of specified acts by the applicant.

[(6)   This section [(apart from subsection (1))] does not apply to a regulated agreement [. . .] made by a consumer credit EEA firm unless at the time it was made that firm was precluded from entering into it as a result of—

(a)   a consumer credit prohibition imposed under section 203 of the Financial Services and Markets Act 2000; or

(b)   a restriction imposed on the firm under section 204 of that Act.]

[(7)   Subsection (1) does not apply to the enforcement of a regulated agreement by a consumer credit EEA firm unless that firm is precluded from enforcing it as a result of a prohibition or restriction mentioned in subsection (6)(a) or (b).

(8)   This section (apart from subsection (1)) does not apply to a regulated agreement made by a person if by virtue of section 21(2) or (3) he was not required to be licensed to make the agreement.

(9)   Subsection (1) does not apply to the enforcement of a regulated agreement by a person if by virtue of section 21(2) or (3) he is not required to be licensed to enforce the agreement.]

[*Appeals*

40A   The Consumer Credit Appeals Tribunal

(1)   There shall be a tribunal known as the Consumer Credit Appeals Tribunal ('the Tribunal').

(2)   The Tribunal shall have the functions conferred on it by or under this Part.

(3)   The Lord Chancellor may by rules make such provision as he thinks fit for regulating the conduct and disposal of appeals before the Tribunal.

(4)   Schedule A1 (which makes provision about the Tribunal and proceedings before it) shall have effect.

(5)   But that Schedule does not limit the Lord Chancellor's powers under subsection (3).]

41   Appeals to Secretary of State under Part III

(1)   If, in the case of a determination by the [OFT] such as is mentioned in column 1 of the table set out at the end of this section, a person mentioned in relation to that determination in column 2 of the table is aggrieved by the determination he may, within the [specified period, appeal to the Tribunal].

[(1A)   The means for making an appeal is by sending the Tribunal a notice of appeal.

(1B)   The notice of appeal shall—

(a)   be in the specified form;

(b)   set out the grounds of appeal in the specified manner; and
(c)   include the specified information and documents.
(1C)   An appeal to the Tribunal is to be by way of a rehearing of the determination appealed against.
(1D)   In this section 'specified' means specified by rules under section 40A(3).]
[. . .]

TABLE

Determination	Appellant
Refusal to issue, renew or vary licence in accordance with terms of application.	The applicant.
Exclusion of person from group licence.	The person excluded.
[. . .]	[. . .]
Compulsory variation, or suspension or revocation, of standard licence.	The licensee.
Compulsory variation, or suspension or revocation, of group licence.	The original applicant or any licensee.
Refusal to end suspension of licence in accordance with terms of application.	The applicant.
[Determination— (a) to impose a requirement under section 33A or 33B; (b) to refuse an application under section 33C(5) in relation to a requirement imposed under either of those sections; (c) to vary or revoke a requirement so imposed.	A person who falls within section 33C(6) or (7) in relation to the requirement unless the OFT was not required to give a notice to him in relation to the determination by virtue of section 33D(4).]
Refusal to make order under section 40(2) [, 148(2) or 149(2)] in accordance with terms of application.	The applicant.
[Imposition of, or refusal to withdraw, consumer credit prohibition under section 203 of the Financial Services and Markets Act 2000.	The consumer credit EEA firm concerned.
Imposition of, or refusal to withdraw, a restriction under section 204 of the Financial Services and Markets Act 2000.	The consumer credit EEA firm concerned.]

41A   Appeals from the Consumer Credit Appeals Tribunal
(1)   A party to an appeal to the Tribunal may with leave appeal—
(a)   in England and Wales and Northern Ireland, to the Court of Appeal, or
(b)   in Scotland, to the Court of Session,
on a point of law arising from a decision of the Tribunal.
(2)   For the purposes of subsection (1) leave to appeal may be given by—
(a)   the Tribunal; or
(b)   the Court of Appeal or the Court of Session.
(3)   An application for leave to appeal may be made to the Court of Appeal or
the Court of Session only if the Tribunal has refused such leave.
(4)   If on an appeal under this section the court considers that the decision of
the Tribunal was wrong in law, it may do one or more of the following—
(a)   quash or vary that decision;
(b)   substitute for that decision a decision of its own;
(c)   remit the matter to the Tribunal for rehearing and determination in
accordance with the directions (if any) given to it by the court.
(5)   An appeal may be brought from a decision of the Court of Appeal under

this section only if leave to do so is given by the Court of Appeal or the House of Lords.

(6)   Rules under section 40A(3) may make provision for regulating or prescribing any matters incidental to or consequential on an appeal under this section.

(7)   In this section 'party' means, in relation to an appeal to the Tribunal, the appellant or the OFT.]

[. . .]

PART IV

SEEKING BUSINESS

Advertising

43   Advertisements to which Part IV applies

(1)   This Part applies to any advertisement, published for the purposes of a business carried on by the advertiser, indicating that he is willing—

(a)   to provide credit, or

(b)   to enter into an agreement for the bailment or (in Scotland) the hiring of goods by him.

(2)   An advertisement does not fall within subsection (1) if the advertiser does not carry on—

(a)   a consumer credit business or consumer hire business, or

(b)   a business in the course of which he provides credit to individuals secured on land, or

(c)   a business which comprises or relates to unregulated agreements where—

(i)   the [law applicable to] the agreement is the law of a country outside the United Kingdom, and

(ii)   if the [law applicable to] the agreement were the law of a part of the United Kingdom it would be a regulated agreement.

(3)   An advertisement does not fall within subsection (1)(a) if it indicates—

[. . .]

(b)   that the credit is available only to a body corporate.

[(3A)   An advertisement does not fall within subsection (1)(a) in so far as it is a communication of an invitation or inducement to engage in investment activity within the meaning of section 21 of the Financial Services and Markets Act 2000, other than an exempt generic communication.

(3B)   An 'exempt generic communication' is a communication to which subsection (1) of section 21 of the Financial Services and Markets Act 2000 does not apply, as a result of an order under subsection (5) of that section, because it does not identify a person as providing an investment or as carrying on an activity to which the communication relates.]

(4)   An advertisement does not fall within subsection (1)(b) if it indicates that the advertiser is not willing to enter into a consumer hire agreement.

(5)   The Secretary of State may by order provide that this Part shall not apply to other advertisements of a description specified in the order.

44   Form and content of advertisements

(1)   The Secretary of State shall make regulations as to the form and content of advertisements to which this Part applies, and the regulations shall contain such provisions as appear to him appropriate with a view to ensuring that, having regard to its subject-matter and the amount of detail included in it, an advertisement conveys a fair and reasonably comprehensive indication of the nature of the credit or hire facilities offered by the advertiser and of their true cost to persons using them.

(2)   Regulations under subsection (1) may in particular—

(a)   require specified information to be included in the prescribed manner in advertisements, and other specified material to be excluded;

(b)   contain requirements to ensure that specified information is clearly brought to the attention of persons to whom advertisements are directed, and that one part of an advertisement is not given insufficient or excessive prominence compared with another.

45   Prohibition of advertisement where goods etc not sold for cash

If an advertisement to which this Part applies indicates that the advertiser is willing to provide credit under a restricted-use credit agreement relating to goods or services to be supplied by any person, but at the time when the advertisement is published that person is not holding himself out as prepared to sell the goods or provide the services (as the case may be) for cash, the advertiser commits an offence.

46   False or misleading advertisements

(1)   If an advertisement to which this Part applies conveys information which in a material respect is false or misleading the advertiser commits an offence.

(2)   Information stating or implying an intention on the advertiser's part which he has not got is false.

47   Advertising infringements

(1)   Where an advertiser commits an offence against regulations made under section 44 or against section 45 or 46 or would be taken to commit such an offence but for the defence provided by section 168, a like offence is committed by—

(a)   the publisher of the advertisement, and

(b)   any person who, in the course of a business carried on by him, devised the advertisement, or a part of it relevant to the first-mentioned offence, and

(c)   where the advertiser did not procure the publication of the advertisement, the person who did procure it.

(2)   In proceedings for an offence under subsection (1)(a) it is a defence for the person charged to prove that—

(a)   the advertisement was published in the course of a business carried on by him, and

(b)   he received the advertisement in the course of that business, and did not know and had no reason to suspect that its publication would be an offence under this Part.

Canvassing, etc

48   Definition of canvassing off trade premises (regulated agreements)

(1)   An individual (the 'canvasser') canvasses a regulated agreement off trade premises if he solicits the entry (as debtor or hirer) of another individual (the 'consumer') into the agreement by making oral representations to the consumer, or any other individual, during a visit by the canvasser to any place (not excluded by subsection (2)) where the consumer, or that other individual, as the case may be, is, being a visit—

(a)   carried out for the purpose of making such oral representations to individuals who are at that place, but

(b)   not carried out in response to a request made on a previous occasion.

(2)   A place is excluded from subsection (1) if it is a place where a business is carried on (whether on a permanent or temporary basis) by—

(a)   the creditor or owner, or

(b)   a supplier, or

(c)   the canvasser, or the person whose employee or agent the canvasser is, or

(d)   the consumer.

49   Prohibition of canvassing debtor-creditor agreements off trade premises

(1)   It is an offence to canvass debtor-creditor agreements off trade premises.

(2)   It is also an offence to solicit the entry of an individual (as debtor) into a debtor-creditor agreement during a visit carried out in response to a request made on a previous occasion, where—

(a)   the request was not in writing signed by or on behalf of the person making it, and

(b)   if no request for the visit had been made, the soliciting would have constituted the canvassing of a debtor-creditor agreement off trade premises.

(3)   Subsections (1) and (2) do not apply to any soliciting for an agreement enabling the debtor to overdraw on a current account of any description kept with the creditor, where—

(a)   the [OFT] has determined that current accounts of that description kept with the creditor are excluded from subsections (1) and (2), and

(b)   the debtor already keeps an account with the creditor (whether a current account or not).

(4)   A determination under subsection (3)(a)—

(a)   may be made subject to such conditions as the [OFT] thinks fit, and

(b)   shall be made only where the [OFT] is of opinion that it is not against the interests of debtors.

(5)   If soliciting is done in breach of a condition imposed under subsection (4)(a), the determination under subsection (3)(a) does not apply to it.

50   Circulars to minors

(1)   A person commits an offence who, with a view to financial gain, sends to a minor any document inviting him to—

(a)   borrow money, or

(b)   obtain goods on credit or hire, or

(c)   obtain services on credit, or

(d)   apply for information or advice on borrowing money or otherwise obtaining credit, or hiring goods.

(2)   In proceedings under subsection (1) in respect of the sending of a document to a minor, it is a defence for the person charged to prove that he did not know, and had no reasonable cause to suspect, that he was a minor.

(3)   Where a document is received by a minor at any school or other educational establishment for minors, a person sending it to him at that establishment knowing or suspecting it to be such an establishment shall be taken to have reasonable cause to suspect that he is a minor.

51   Prohibition of unsolicited credit-tokens

(1)   It is an offence to give a person a credit-token if he has not asked for it.

(2)   To comply with subsection (1) a request must be contained in a document signed by the person making the request, unless the credit-token agreement is a small debtor-creditor-supplier agreement.

(3)   Subsection (1) does not apply to the giving of a credit-token to a person—

(a)   for use under a credit-token agreement already made, or

(b)   in renewal or replacement of a credit-token previously accepted by him under a credit-token agreement which continues in force, whether or not varied.

Miscellaneous

52   Quotations

(1)   Regulations may be made—

(a)   as to the form and content of any document (a 'quotation') by which a person who carries on a consumer credit business or consumer hire business, or a business in the course of which he provides credit to individuals secured on land, gives prospective customers information about the terms on which he is prepared to do business;

(b) requiring a person carrying on such a business to provide quotations to such persons and in such circumstances as are prescribed.

(2) Regulations under subsection (1)(a) may in particular contain provisions relating to quotations such as are set out in relation to advertisements in section 44.

[(3) In this section, 'quotation' does not include—

(a) any document which is a communication of an invitation or inducement to engage in investment activity within the meaning of section 21 of the Financial Services and Markets Act 2000; or

(b) any document (other than one falling within paragraph (a)) provided by an authorised person (within the meaning of that Act) in connection with an agreement which would or might be an exempt agreement as a result of section 16(6C).]

53 Duty to display information
Regulations may require a person who carries on a consumer credit business or consumer hire business, or a business in the course of which he provides credit to individuals secured on land [(other than credit provided under an agreement which is an exempt agreement as a result of section 16(6C))], to display in the pre-scribed manner, at any premises where the business is carried on to which the public have access, prescribed information about the business.

54 Conduct of business regulations
Without prejudice to the generality of section 26, regulations under that section may include provisions further regulating the seeking of business by [a person to whom the regulations apply] who carries on a consumer credit business or a con-sumer hire business.

PART V
ENTRY INTO CREDIT OR HIRE AGREEMENTS

Preliminary matters

55 Disclosure of information
(1) Regulations may require specified information to be disclosed in the pre-scribed manner to the debtor or hirer before a regulated agreement is made.

(2) A regulated agreement is not properly executed unless regulations under subsection (1) were complied with before the making of the agreement.

56 Antecedent negotiations
(1) In this Act 'antecedent negotiations' means any negotiations with the debtor or hirer—

(a) conducted by the creditor or owner in relation to the making of any regulated agreement, or

(b) conducted by a credit-broker in relation to goods sold or proposed to be sold by the credit-broker to the creditor before forming the subject-matter of a debtor-creditor-supplier agreement within section 12(a), or

(c) conducted by the supplier in relation to a transaction financed or proposed to be financed by a debtor-creditor-supplier agreement within section 12(b) or (c), and 'negotiator' means the person by whom negotiations are so conducted with the debtor or hirer.

(2) Negotiations with the debtor in a case falling within subsection (1)(b) or (c) shall be deemed to be conducted by the negotiator in the capacity of agent of the creditor as well as in his actual capacity.

(3) An agreement is void if, and to the extent that, it purports in relation to an actual or prospective regulated agreement—

(a)   to provide that a person acting as, or on behalf of, a negotiator is to be treated as the agent of the debtor or hirer, or

(b)   to relieve a person from liability for acts or omissions of any person acting as, or on behalf of, a negotiator.

(4)   For the purposes of this Act, antecedent negotiations shall be taken to begin when the negotiator and the debtor or hirer first enter into communication (including communication by advertisement), and to include any representations made by the negotiator to the debtor or hirer and any other dealings between them.

57   Withdrawal from prospective agreement

(1)   The withdrawal of a party from a prospective regulated agreement shall operate to apply this Part to the agreement, any linked transaction and any other thing done in anticipation of the making of the agreement as it would apply if the agreement were made and then cancelled under section 69.

(2)   The giving to a party of a written or oral notice which, however expressed, indicates the intention of the other party to withdraw from a prospective regulated agreement operates as a withdrawal from it.

(3)   Each of the following shall be deemed to be the agent of the creditor or owner for the purpose of receiving a notice under subsection (2)—

(a)   a credit-broker or supplier who is the negotiator in antecedent negotiations, and

(b)   any person who, in the course of a business carried on by him, acts on behalf of the debtor or hirer in any negotiations for the agreement.

(4)   Where the agreement, if made, would not be a cancellable agreement, subsection (1) shall nevertheless apply as if the contrary were the case.

58   Opportunity for withdrawal from prospective land mortgage

(1)   Before sending to the debtor or hirer, for his signature, an unexecuted agreement in a case where the prospective regulated agreement is to be secured on land (the 'mortgaged land'), the creditor or owner shall give the debtor or hirer a copy of the unexecuted agreement which contains a notice in the prescribed form indicating the right of the debtor or hirer to withdraw from the prospective agreement, and how and when the right is exercisable, together with a copy of any other document referred to in the unexecuted agreement.

(2)   Subsection (1) does not apply to—

(a)   a restricted-use credit agreement to finance the purchase of the mortgaged land, or

(b)   an agreement for a bridging loan in connection with the purchase of the mortgaged land or other land.

59   Agreement to enter future agreement void

(1)   An agreement is void if, and to the extent that, it purports to bind a person to enter as debtor or hirer into a prospective regulated agreement.

(2)   Regulations may exclude from the operation of subsection (1) agreements such as are described in the regulations.

Making the agreement

60   Form and content of agreements

(1)   The Secretary of State shall make regulations as to the form and content of documents embodying regulated agreements, and the regulations shall contain such provisions as appear to him appropriate with a view to ensuring that the debtor or hirer is made aware of—

(a)   the rights and duties conferred or imposed on him by the agreement,

(b)   the amount and rate of the total charge for credit (in the case of a consumer credit agreement),

(c)   the protection and remedies available to him under this Act, and

(d)   any other matters which, in the opinion of the Secretary of State, it is desirable for him to know about in connection with the agreement.

(2)   Regulations under subsection (1) may in particular—

(a)   require specified information to be included in the prescribed manner in documents, and other specified material to be excluded;

(b)   contain requirements to ensure that specified information is clearly brought to the attention of the debtor or hirer, and that one part of a document is not given insufficient or excessive prominence compared with another.

(3)   If, on an application made to the [OFT] by a person carrying on a consumer credit business or a consumer hire business, it appears to the [OFT] impracticable for the applicant to comply with any requirement of regulations under subsection (1) in a particular case, [it] may, by notice to the applicant direct that the requirement be waived or varied in relation to such agreements, and subject to such conditions (if any), as [it] may specify, and this Act and the regulations shall have effect accordingly.

(4)   The [OFT] shall give a notice under subsection (3) only if [it] is satisfied that to do so would not prejudice the interests of debtors or hirers.

61   Signing of agreement

(1)   A regulated agreement is not properly executed unless—

(a)   a document in the prescribed form itself containing all the prescribed terms and conforming to regulations under section 60(1) is signed in the prescribed manner both by the debtor or hirer and by or on behalf of the creditor or owner, and

(b)   the document embodies all the terms of the agreement, other than implied terms, and

(c)   the document is, when presented or sent to the debtor or hirer for signature, in such a state that all its terms are readily legible.

(2)   In addition, where the agreement is one to which section 58(1) applies, it is not properly executed unless—

(a)   the requirements of section 58(1) were complied with, and

(b)   the unexecuted agreement was sent, for his signature, to the debtor or hirer [by an appropriate method] not less than seven days after a copy of it was given to him under section 58(1), and

(c)   during the consideration period, the creditor or owner refrained from approaching the debtor or hirer (whether in person, by telephone or letter, or in any other way) except in response to a specific request made by the debtor or hirer after the beginning of the consideration period, and

(d)   no notice of withdrawal by the debtor or hirer was received by the creditor or owner before the sending of the unexecuted agreement.

(3)   In subsection (2)(c), 'the consideration period' means the period beginning with the giving of the copy under section 58(1) and ending—

(a)   at the expiry of seven days after the day on which the unexecuted agreement is sent, for his signature, to the debtor or hirer, or

(b)   on its return by the debtor or hirer after signature by him, whichever first occurs.

(4)   Where the debtor or hirer is a partnership or an unincorporated body of persons, subsection (1)(a) shall apply with the substitution for 'by the debtor or hirer' of 'by or on behalf of the debtor or hirer'.

62   Duty to supply copy of unexecuted agreement

(1)   If the unexecuted agreement is presented personally to the debtor or hirer for his signature, but on the occasion when he signs it the document does not become an executed agreement, a copy of it, and of any other document referred to in it, must be there and then delivered to him.

(2)   If the unexecuted agreement is sent to the debtor or hirer for his signature,

a copy of it, and of any other document referred to in it, must be sent to him at the same time.

(3)   A regulated agreement is not properly executed if the requirements of this section are not observed.

63   Duty to supply copy of executed agreement

(1)   If the unexecuted agreement is presented personally to the debtor or hirer for his signature, and on the occasion when he signs it the document becomes an executed agreement, a copy of the executed agreement, and of any other document referred to in it, must be there and then delivered to him.

(2)   A copy of the executed agreement, and of any other document referred to in it, must be given to the debtor or hirer within the seven days following the making of the agreement unless—

(a)   subsection (1) applies, or

(b)   the unexecuted agreement was sent to the debtor or hirer for his signature and, on the occasion of his signing it, the document became an executed agreement.

(3)   In the case of a cancellable agreement, a copy under subsection (2) must be sent [by an appropriate method].

(4)   In the case of a credit-token agreement, a copy under subsection (2) need not be given within the seven days following the making of the agreement if it is given before or at the time when the credit-token is given to the debtor.

(5)   A regulated agreement is not properly executed if the requirements of this section are not observed.

64   Duty to give notice of cancellation rights

(1)   In the case of a cancellable agreement, a notice in the prescribed form indicating the right of the debtor or hirer to cancel the agreement, how and when that right is exercisable, and the name and address of a person to whom notice of cancellation may be given,—

(a)   must be included in every copy given to the debtor or hirer under section 62 or 63, and

(b)   except where section 63(2) applied, must also be sent [by an appropriate method] to the debtor or hirer within the seven days following the making of the agreement.

(2)   In the case of a credit-token agreement, a notice under subsection (1)(b) need not be sent [by an appropriate method] within the seven days following the making of the agreement if either—

(a)   it is sent by post to the debtor or hirer before the credit-token is given to him, or

(b)   it is sent by post to him together with the credit-token.

(3)   Regulations may provide that except where section 63(2) applied a notice sent under subsection (1)(b) shall be accompanied by a further copy of the executed agreement, and of any other document referred to in it.

(4)   Regulations may provide that subsection (1)(b) is not to apply in the case of agreements such as are described in the regulations, being agreements made by a particular person, if—

(a)   on an application by that person to the [OFT], the [OFT] has determined that, having regard to—

(i)   the manner in which antecedent negotiations for agreements with the applicant of that description are conducted, and

(ii)   the information provided to debtors or hirers before such agreements are made, the requirement imposed by subsection (1)(b) can be dispensed with without prejudicing the interests of debtors or hirers, and

(b)   any conditions imposed by the [OFT] in making the determination are complied with.

(5)   A cancellable agreement is not properly executed if the requirements of this section are not observed.

65   Consequences of improper execution

(1)   An improperly-executed regulated agreement is enforceable against the debtor or hirer on an order of the court only.

(2)   A retaking of goods or land to which a regulated agreement relates is an enforcement of the agreement.

66   Acceptance of credit-tokens

(1)   The debtor shall not be liable under a credit-token agreement for use made of the credit-token by any person unless the debtor had previously accepted the credit-token, or the use constituted an acceptance of it by him.

(2)   The debtor accepts a credit-token when—

    (a)   it is signed, or

    (b)   a receipt for it is signed, or

    (c)   it is first used,

either by the debtor himself or by a person who, pursuant to the agreement, is authorised by him to use it.

Cancellation of certain agreements within cooling-off period

67   Cancellable agreements

A regulated agreement may be cancelled by the debtor or hirer in accordance with this Part if the antecedent negotiations included oral representations made when in the presence of the debtor or hirer by an individual acting as, or on behalf of, the negotiator, unless—

    (a)   the agreement is secured on land, or is a restricted-use credit agreement to finance the purchase of land or is an agreement for a bridging loan in connection with the purchase of land, or

    (b)   the unexecuted agreement is signed by the debtor or hirer at premises at which any of the following is carrying on any business (whether on a permanent or temporary basis)—

        (i)   the creditor or owner;

        (ii)   any party to a linked transaction (other than the debtor or hirer or a relative of his);

        (iii)   the negotiator in any antecedent negotiations.

68   Cooling-off period

The debtor or hirer may serve notice of cancellation of a cancellable agreement between his signing of the unexecuted agreement and—

    (a)   the end of the fifth day following the day on which he received a copy under section 63(2) or a notice under section 64(1)(b), or

    (b)   if (by virtue of regulations made under section 64(4)) section 64(1)(b) does not apply, the end of the fourteenth day following the day on which he signed the unexecuted agreement.

69   Notice of cancellation

(1)   If within the period specified in section 68 the debtor or hirer under a cancellable agreement serves on—

    (a)   the creditor or owner, or

    (b)   the person specified in the notice under section 64(1), or

    (c)   a person who (whether by virtue of subsection (6) or otherwise) is the agent of the creditor or owner, a notice (a 'notice of cancellation') which, however expressed and whether or not conforming to the notice given under section 64(1), indicates the intention of the debtor or hirer to withdraw from the agreement, the notice shall operate—

        (i)   to cancel the agreement, and any linked transaction, and

(ii) to withdraw any offer by the debtor or hirer, or his relative, to enter into a linked transaction.

(2)   In the case of a debtor-creditor-supplier agreement for restricted-use credit financing—

(a)   the doing of work or supply of goods to meet an emergency, or

(b)   the supply of goods which, before service of the notice of cancellation, had by the act of the debtor or his relative become incorporated in any land or thing not comprised in the agreement or any linked transaction,

subsection (1) shall apply with the substitution of the following for paragraph (i)—

'(i)   to cancel only such provisions of the agreement and any linked transaction as—

(aa)   relate to the provision of credit, or

(bb)   require the debtor to pay an item in the total charge for credit, or

(cc)   subject the debtor to any obligation other than to pay for the doing of the said work, or the supply of the said goods.'

(3)   Except so far as is otherwise provided, references in this Act to the cancellation of an agreement or transaction do not include a case within subsection (2).

(4)   Except as otherwise provided by or under this Act, an agreement or transaction cancelled under subsection (1) shall be treated as if it had never been entered into.

(5)   Regulations may exclude linked transactions of the prescribed description from subsection (1)(i) or (ii).

(6)   Each of the following shall be deemed to be the agent of the creditor or owner for the purpose of receiving a notice of cancellation—

(a)   a credit-broker or supplier who is the negotiator in antecedent negotiations, and

(b)   any person who, in the course of a business carried on by him, acts on behalf of the debtor or hirer in any negotiations for the agreement.

[(7)   Whether or not it is actually received by him, a notice of cancellation sent to a person shall be deemed to be served on him—

(a)   in the case of a notice sent by post, at the time of posting, and

(b)   in the case of a notice transmitted in the form of an electronic communication in accordance with section 17A(1), at the time of the transmission.]

70   Cancellation: recovery of money paid by debtor or hirer

(1)   On the cancellation of a regulated agreement, and of any linked transaction,—

(a)   any sum paid by the debtor or hirer, or his relative, under or in contemplation of the agreement or transaction, including any item in the total charge for credit, shall become repayable, and

(b)   any sum, including any item in the total charge for credit, which but for the cancellation is, or would or might become, payable by the debtor or hirer, or his relative, under the agreement or transaction shall cease to be, or shall not become, so payable, and

(c)   in the case of a debtor-creditor-supplier agreement falling within section 12(b), any sum paid on the debtor's behalf by the creditor to the supplier shall become repayable to the creditor.

(2)   If, under the terms of a cancelled agreement or transaction, the debtor or hirer, or his relative, is in possession of any goods, he shall have a lien on them for any sum repayable to him under subsection (1) in respect of that agreement or transaction, or any other linked transaction.

(3)   A sum repayable under subsection (1) is repayable by the person to whom it was originally paid, but in the case of a debtor-creditor-supplier agreement falling within section 12(b) the creditor and the supplier shall be under a joint and several liability to repay sums paid by the debtor, or his relative, under the agree-

ment or under a linked transaction falling within section 19(1)(b) and accordingly, in such a case, the creditor shall be entitled, in accordance with rules of court, to have the supplier made a party to any proceedings brought against the creditor to recover any such sums.

(4) Subject to any agreement between them, the creditor shall be entitled to be indemnified by the supplier for loss suffered by the creditor in satisfying his liability under subsection (3), including costs reasonably incurred by him in defending proceedings instituted by the debtor.

(5) Subsection (1) does not apply to any sum which, if not paid by a debtor, would be payable by virtue of section 71, and applies to a sum paid or payable by a debtor for the issue of a credit-token only where the credit-token has been returned to the creditor or surrendered to a supplier.

(6) If the total charge for credit includes an item in respect of a fee or commission charged by a credit-broker, the amount repayable under subsection (1) in respect of that item shall be the excess over [£5] of the fee or commission.

(7) If the total charge for credit includes any sum payable or paid by the debtor to a credit-broker otherwise than in respect of a fee or commission charged by him, that sum shall for the purposes of subsection (6) be treated as if it were such a fee or commission.

(8) So far only as is necessary to give effect to section 69(2), this section applies to an agreement or transaction within that subsection as it applies to a cancelled agreement or transaction.

71 Cancellation: repayment of credit

(1) Notwithstanding the cancellation of a regulated consumer credit agreement, other than a debtor-creditor-supplier agreement for restricted-use credit, the agreement shall continue in force so far as it relates to repayment of credit and payment of interest.

(2) If, following the cancellation of a regulated consumer credit agreement, the debtor repays the whole or a portion of the credit—

(a) before the expiry of one month following service of the notice of cancellation, or

(b) in the case of a credit repayable by instalments, before the date on which the first instalment is due,

no interest shall be payable on the amount repaid.

(3) If the whole of a credit repayable by instalments is not repaid on or before the date specified in subsection (2)(b), the debtor shall not be liable to repay any of the credit except on receipt of a request in writing in the prescribed form, signed by or on behalf of the creditor, stating the amounts of the remaining instalments (recalculated by the creditor as nearly as may be in accordance with the agreement and without extending the repayment period), but excluding any sum other than principal and interest.

(4) Repayment of a credit, or payment of interest, under a cancelled agreement shall be treated as duly made if it is made to any person on whom, under section 69, a notice of cancellation could have been served, other than a person referred to in section 69(6)(b).

72 Cancellation: return of goods

(1) This section applies where any agreement or transaction relating to goods, being—

(a) a restricted-use debtor-creditor-supplier agreement, a consumer hire agreement, or a linked transaction to which the debtor or hirer under any regulated agreement is a party, or

(b) a linked transaction to which a relative of the debtor or hirer under any regulated agreement is a party,

is cancelled after the debtor or hirer (in a case within paragraph (a)) or the relative (in a case within paragraph (b)) has acquired possession of the goods by virtue of the agreement or transaction.

(2) In this section—

(a) 'the possessor' means the person who has acquired possession of the goods as mentioned in subsection (1),

(b) 'the other party' means the person from whom the possessor acquired possession, and

(c) 'the pre-cancellation period' means the period beginning when the possessor acquired possession and ending with the cancellation.

(3) The possessor shall be treated as having been under a duty throughout the pre-cancellation period—

(a) to retain possession of the goods, and

(b) to take reasonable care of them.

(4) On the cancellation, the possessor shall be under a duty, subject to any lien to restore the goods to the other party in accordance with this section, and meanwhile to retain possession of the goods and take reasonable care of them.

(5) The possessor shall not be under any duty to deliver the goods except at his own premises and in pursuance of a request in writing signed by or on behalf of the other party and served on the possessor either before, or at the time when, the goods are collected from those premises.

(6) If the possessor—

(a) delivers the goods (whether at his own premises or elsewhere) to any person on whom, under section 69, a notice of cancellation could have been served (other than a person referred to in section 69(6)(b)), or

(b) sends the goods at his own expense to such a person, he shall be discharged from any duty to retain the goods or deliver them to any person.

(7) Where the possessor delivers the goods as mentioned in subsection (6)(a), his obligation to take care of the goods shall cease; and if he sends the goods as mentioned in subsection (6)(b), he shall be under a duty to take reasonable care to see that they are received by the other party and not damaged in transit, but in other respects his duty to take care of the goods shall cease.

(8) Where, at any time during the period of 21 days following the cancellation, the possessor receives such a request as is mentioned in subsection (5), and unreasonably refuses or unreasonably fails to comply with it, his duty to take reasonable care of the goods shall continue until he delivers or sends the goods as mentioned in subsection (6), but if within that period he does not receive such a request his duty to take reasonable care of the goods shall cease at the end of that period.

(9) The preceding provisions of this section do not apply to—

(a) perishable goods, or

(b) goods which by their nature are consumed by use and which, before the cancellation, were so consumed, or

(c) goods supplied to meet an emergency, or

(d) goods which, before the cancellation, had become incorporated in any land or thing not comprised in the cancelled agreement or a linked transaction.

(10) Where the address of the possessor is specified in the executed agreement, references in this section to his own premises are to that address and no other.

(11) Breach of a duty imposed by this section is actionable as a breach of statutory duty.

73 Cancellation: goods given in part-exchange

(1) This section applies on the cancellation of a regulated agreement where, in antecedent negotiations, the negotiator agreed to take goods in part-exchange (the 'part-exchange goods') and those goods have been delivered to him.

(2) Unless, before the end of the period of ten days beginning with the date of cancellation, the part-exchange goods are returned to the debtor or hirer in a con-

dition substantially as good as when they were delivered to the negotiator, the debtor or hirer shall be entitled to recover from the negotiator a sum equal to the part-exchange allowance (as defined in subsection (7)(b)).

(3)   In the case of a debtor-creditor-supplier agreement within section 12(b), the negotiator and the creditor shall be under a joint and several liability to pay to the debtor a sum recoverable under subsection (2).

(4)   Subject to any agreement between them, the creditor shall be entitled to be indemnified by the negotiator for loss suffered by the creditor in satisfying his liability under subsection (3), including costs reasonably incurred by him in defending proceedings instituted by the debtor.

(5)   During the period of ten days beginning with the date of cancellation, the debtor or hirer, if he is in possession of goods to which the cancelled agreement relates, shall have a lien on them for—

(a)   delivery of the part-exchange goods, in a condition substantially as good as when they were delivered to the negotiator; or

(b)   a sum equal to the part-exchange allowance;

and if the lien continues to the end of that period it shall thereafter subsist only as a lien for a sum equal to the part-exchange allowance.

(6)   Where the debtor or hirer recovers from the negotiator or creditor, or both of them jointly, a sum equal to the part-exchange allowance, then, if the title of the debtor or hirer to the part-exchange goods has not vested in the negotiator, it shall so vest on the recovery of that sum.

(7)   For the purposes of this section—

(a)   the negotiator shall be treated as having agreed to take goods in part-exchange if, in pursuance of the antecedent negotiations, he either purchased or agreed to purchase those goods or accepted or agreed to accept them as part of the consideration for the cancelled agreement, and

(b)   the part-exchange allowance shall be the sum agreed as such in the antecedent negotiations or, if no such agreement was arrived at, such sum as it would have been reasonable to allow in respect of the part-exchange goods if no notice of cancellation had been served.

(8)   In an action brought against the creditor for a sum recoverable under subsection (2), he shall be entitled, in accordance with rules of court, to have the negotiator made a party to the proceedings.

Exclusion of certain agreements from Part V

74   Exclusion of certain agreements from Part V

(1)   This Part (except section 56) does not apply to—

(a)   a non-commercial agreement, or

(b)   a debtor-creditor agreement enabling the debtor to overdraw on a current account, or

(c)   a debtor-creditor agreement to finance the making of such payments arising on, or connected with, the death of a person as may be prescribed.

(2)   This Part (except sections 55 and 56) does not apply to a small debtor-creditor-supplier agreement for restricted-use credit.

[(2A)   In the case of an agreement to which the Consumer Protection (Cancellation of Contracts Concluded Away from Business Premises) Regulations 1987 apply the reference in subsection (2) to a small agreement shall be construed as if in section 17(1)(a) and (b) '£35' were substituted for '£50'.]

(3)   Subsection (1)(b) or (c) applies only where the [OFT] so determines, and such a determination—

(a)   may be made subject to such conditions as the [OFT] thinks fit, and

(b)   shall be made only if the [OFT] is of opinion that it is not against the interests of debtors.

[(3A)   Notwithstanding anything in subsection (3)(b) above, in relation to a debtor-creditor agreement under which the creditor is the Bank of England or a bank within the meaning of the Bankers' Books Evidence Act 1879, the [OFT] shall make a determination that subsection (1)(b) above applies unless [it] considers that it would be against the public interest to do so.]

(4)   If any term of an agreement falling within subsection [(1)(c)] or (2) is expressed in writing, regulations under section 60(1) shall apply to that term (subject to section 60(3)) as if the agreement were a regulated agreement not falling within subsection [(1)(c)] or (2).

PART VI
MATTERS ARISING DURING CURRENCY OF CREDIT OR HIRE AGREEMENTS

75   Liability of creditor for breaches by supplier

(1)   If the debtor under a debtor-creditor-supplier agreement falling within section 12(b) or (c) has, in relation to a transaction financed by the agreement, any claim against the supplier in respect of a misrepresentation or breach of contract, he shall have a like claim against the creditor, who, with the supplier, shall accordingly be jointly and severally liable to the debtor.

(2)   Subject to any agreement between them, the creditor shall be entitled to be indemnified by the supplier for loss suffered by the creditor in satisfying his liability under subsection (1), including costs reasonably incurred by him in defending proceedings instituted by the debtor.

(3)   Subsection (1) does not apply to a claim—

(a)   under a non-commercial agreement, or

(b)   so far as the claim relates to any single item to which the supplier has attached a cash price not exceeding [£100] or more than [£30,000].

(4)   This section applies notwithstanding that the debtor, in entering into the transaction, exceeded the credit limit or otherwise contravened any term of the agreement.

(5)   In an action brought against the creditor under subsection (1) he shall be entitled, in accordance with rules of court, to have the supplier made a party to the proceedings.

76   Duty to give notice before taking certain action

(1)   The creditor or owner is not entitled to enforce a term of a regulated agreement by—

(a)   demanding earlier payment of any sum, or

(b)   recovering possession of any goods or land, or

(c)   treating any right conferred on the debtor or hirer by the agreement as terminated, restricted or deferred,

except by or after giving the debtor or hirer not less than seven days' notice of his intention to do so.

(2)   Subsection (1) applies only where—

(a)   a period for the duration of the agreement is specified in the agreement, and

(b)   that period has not ended when the creditor or owner does an act mentioned in subsection (1),

but so applies notwithstanding that, under the agreement, any party is entitled to terminate it before the end of the period so specified.

(3)   A notice under subsection (1) is ineffective if not in the prescribed form.

(4)   Subsection (1) does not prevent a creditor from treating the right to draw on any credit as restricted or deferred and taking such steps as may be necessary to make the restriction or deferment effective.

(5)   Regulations may provide that subsection (1) is not to apply to agreements described by the regulations.

(6)   Subsection (1) does not apply to a right of enforcement arising by reason of any breach by the debtor or hirer of the regulated agreement.

77   Duty to give information to debtor under fixed-sum credit agreement

(1)   The creditor under a regulated agreement for fixed-sum credit, within the prescribed period after receiving a request in writing to that effect from the debtor and payment of a fee of [£1], shall give the debtor a copy of the executed agreement (if any) and of any other document referred to in it, together with a statement signed by or on behalf of the creditor showing, according to the information to which it is practicable for him to refer,—

(a)   the total sum paid under the agreement by the debtor;

(b)   the total sum which has become payable under the agreement by the debtor but remains unpaid, and the various amounts comprised in that total sum, with the date when each became due; and

(c)   the total sum which is to become payable under the agreement by the debtor, and the various amounts comprised in that total sum, with the date, or mode of determining the date, when each becomes due.

(2)   If the creditor possesses insufficient information to enable him to ascertain the amounts and dates mentioned in subsection (1)(c), he shall be taken to comply with that paragraph if his statement under subsection (1) gives the basis on which, under the regulated agreement, they would fall to be ascertained.

(3)   Subsection (1) does not apply to—

(a)   an agreement under which no sum is, or will or may become, payable by the debtor, or

(b)   a request made less than one month after a previous request under that subsection relating to the same agreement was complied with.

(4)   If the creditor under an agreement fails to comply with subsection (1)—

(a)   he is not entitled, while the default continues, to enforce the agreement; and

(b)   if the default continues for one month he commits an offence.

(5)   This section does not apply to a non-commercial agreement.

[77A   Statements to be provided in relation to fixed-sum credit agreements

(1)   The creditor under a regulated agreement for fixed-sum credit—

(a)   shall, within the period of one year beginning with the day after the day on which the agreement is made, give the debtor a statement under this section; and

(b)   after the giving of that statement, shall give the debtor further statements under this section at intervals of not more than one year.

(2)   Regulations may make provision about the form and content of statements under this section.

(3)   The debtor shall have no liability to pay any sum in connection with the preparation or the giving to him of a statement under this section.

(4)   The creditor is not required to give the debtor any statement under this section once the following conditions are satisfied—

(a)   that there is no sum payable under the agreement by the debtor; and

(b)   that there is no sum which will or may become so payable.

(5)   Subsection (6) applies if at a time before the conditions mentioned in subsection (4) are satisfied the creditor fails to give the debtor—

(a)   a statement under this section within the period mentioned in subsection (1)(a); or

(b)   such a statement within the period of one year beginning with the day after the day on which such a statement was last given to him.

(6)   Where this subsection applies in relation to a failure to give a statement under this section to the debtor—

(a)   the creditor shall not be entitled to enforce the agreement during the period of non-compliance;

(b)   the debtor shall have no liability to pay any sum of interest to the extent calculated by reference to the period of non-compliance or to any part of it; and

(c)   the debtor shall have no liability to pay any default sum which (apart from this paragraph)—

    (i)   would have become payable during the period of non-compliance; or

    (ii)   would have become payable after the end of that period in connection with a breach of the agreement which occurs during that period (whether or not the breach continues after the end of that period).

(7)   In this section 'the period of non-compliance' means, in relation to a failure to give a statement under this section to the debtor, the period which—

(a)   begins immediately after the end of the period mentioned in paragraph (a) or (as the case may be) paragraph (b) of subsection (5); and

(b)   ends at the end of the day on which the statement is given to the debtor or on which the conditions mentioned in subsection (4) are satisfied, whichever is earlier.

(8)   This section does not apply in relation to a non-commercial agreement or to a small agreement.]

78   Duty to give information to debtor under running-account credit agreement

(1)   The creditor under a regulated agreement for running-account credit, within the prescribed period after receiving a request in writing to that effect from the debtor and payment of a fee of [£1], shall give the debtor a copy of the executed agreement (if any) and of any other document referred to in it, together with a statement signed by or on behalf of the creditor showing, according to the information to which it is practicable for him to refer,—

(a)   the state of the account, and

(b)   the amount, if any, currently payable under the agreement by the debtor to the creditor, and

(c)   the amounts and due dates of any payments which, if the debtor does not draw further on the account, will later become payable under the agreement by the debtor to the creditor.

(2)   If the creditor possesses insufficient information to enable him to ascertain the amounts and dates mentioned in subsection (1)(c), he shall be taken to comply with that paragraph if his statement under subsection (1) gives the basis on which, under the regulated agreement, they would fall to be ascertained.

(3)   Subsection (1) does not apply to—

(a)   an agreement under which no sum is, or will or may become, payable by the debtor, or

(b)   a request made less than one month after a previous request under that subsection relating to the same agreement was complied with.

(4)   Where running-account credit is provided under a regulated agreement, the creditor shall give the debtor statements in the prescribed form, and with the prescribed contents—

(a)   showing according to the information to which it is practicable for him to refer, the state of the account at regular intervals of not more than twelve months, and

(b)   where the agreement provides, in relation to specified periods, for the making of payments by the debtor, or the charging against him of interest or any other sum, showing according to the information to which it is practicable for him to refer the state of the account at the end of each of those periods during which there is any movement in the account.

[(4A)   Regulations may require a statement under subsection (4) to contain also information in the prescribed terms about the consequences of the debtor—

(a)   failing to make payments as required by the agreement; or

(b)   only making payments of a prescribed description in prescribed circumstances.]

(5) A statement under subsection (4) shall be given within the prescribed period after the end of the period to which the statement relates.

(6) If the creditor under an agreement fails to comply with subsection (1)—

(a) he is not entitled, while the default continues, to enforce the agreement; and

(b) if the default continues for one month he commits an offence.

(7) This section does not apply to a non-commercial agreement, and subsections [(4) to (5)] do not apply to a small agreement.

79 Duty to give hirer information

(1) The owner under a regulated consumer hire agreement, within the prescribed period after receiving a request in writing to that effect from the hirer and payment of a fee of [£1], shall give to the hirer a copy of the executed agreement and of any other document referred to in it, together with a statement signed by or on behalf of the owner showing, according to the information to which it is practicable for him to refer, the total sum which has become payable under the agreement by the hirer but remains unpaid and the various amounts comprised in that total sum, with the date when each became due.

(2) Subsection (1) does not apply to—

(a) an agreement under which no sum is, or will or may become, payable by the hirer, or

(b) a request made less than one month after a previous request under that subsection relating to the same agreement was complied with.

(3) If the owner under an agreement fails to comply with subsection (1)—

(a) he is not entitled, while the default continues, to enforce the agreement; and

(b) if the default continues for one month he commits an offence.

(4) This section does not apply to a non-commercial agreement.

80 Debtor or hirer to give information about goods

(1) Where a regulated agreement, other than a non-commercial agreement, requires the debtor or hirer to keep goods to which the agreement relates in his possession or control, he shall, within seven working days after he has received a request in writing to that effect from the creditor or owner, tell the creditor or owner where the goods are.

(2) If the debtor or hirer fails to comply with subsection (1), and the default continues for 14 days, he commits an offence.

81 Appropriation of payments

(1) Where a debtor or hirer is liable to make to the same person payments in respect of two or more regulated agreements, he shall be entitled, on making any payment in respect of the agreements which is not sufficient to discharge the total amount then due under all the agreements, to appropriate the sum so paid by him—

(a) in or towards the satisfaction of the sum due under any one of the agreements, or

(b) in or towards the satisfaction of the sums due under any two or more of the agreements in such proportions as he thinks fit.

(2) If the debtor or hirer fails to make any such appropriation where one or more of the agreements is—

(a) a hire-purchase agreement or conditional sale agreement, or

(b) a consumer hire agreement, or

(c) an agreement in relation to which any security is provided,

the payment shall be appropriated towards the satisfaction of the sums due under the several agreements respectively in the proportions which those sums bear to one another.

82 Variation of agreements

(1) Where, under a power contained in a regulated agreement, the creditor or owner varies the agreement, the variation shall not take effect before notice of it is given to the debtor or hirer in the prescribed manner.

(2) Where an agreement (a 'modifying agreement') varies or supplements an earlier agreement, the modifying agreement shall for the purposes of this Act be treated as—

(a) revoking the earlier agreement, and

(b) containing provisions reproducing the combined effect of the two agreements, and obligations outstanding in relation to the earlier agreement shall accordingly be treated as outstanding instead in relation to the modifying agreement.

[(2A) Subsection (2) does not apply if the modifying agreement is an exempt agreement as a result of section 16(6C).]

(3) If the earlier agreement is a regulated agreement but (apart from this subsection) the modifying agreement is not then, [unless the modifying agreement is—

(a) for running account credit; or

(b) an exempt agreement as a result of section 16(6C), it shall be treated as a regulated agreement.]

(4) If the earlier agreement is a regulated agreement for running-account credit, and by the modifying agreement the creditor allows the credit limit to be exceeded but intends the excess to be merely temporary, Part V (except section 56) shall not apply to the modifying agreement.

(5) If—

(a) the earlier agreement is a cancellable agreement, and

(b) the modifying agreement is made within the period applicable under section 68 to the earlier agreement,

then, whether or not the modifying agreement would, apart from this subsection, be a cancellable agreement, it shall be treated as a cancellable agreement in respect of which a notice may be served under section 68 not later than the end of the period applicable under that section to the earlier agreement.

[(5A) Subsection (5) does not apply where the modifying agreement is an exempt agreement as a result of section 16(6C).]

(6) Except under subsection (5), a modifying agreement shall not be treated as a cancellable agreement.

(7) This section does not apply to a non-commercial agreement.

83 Liability for misuse of credit facilities

(1) The debtor under a regulated consumer credit agreement shall not be liable to the creditor for any loss arising from use of the credit facility by another person not acting, or to be treated as acting, as the debtor's agent.

(2) This section does not apply to a non-commercial agreement, or to any loss in so far as it arises from misuse of an instrument to which section 4 of the Cheques Act 1957 applies.

84 Misuse of credit-tokens

(1) Section 83 does not prevent the debtor under a credit-token agreement from being made liable to the extent of [£50] (or the credit limit if lower) for loss to the creditor arising from use of the credit-token by other persons during a period beginning when the credit-token ceases to be in the possession of any authorised person and ending when the credit-token is once more in the possession of an authorised person.

(2) Section 83 does not prevent the debtor under a credit-token agreement from being made liable to any extent for loss to the creditor from use of the credit-token by a person who acquired possession of it with the debtor's consent.

(3) Subsections (1) and (2) shall not apply to any use of the credit-token after

the creditor has been given oral or written notice that it is lost or stolen, or is for any other reason liable to misuse.

[(3A)   Subsections (1) and (2) shall not apply to any use, in connection with a distance contract (other than an excepted contract), of a card which is a credit-token.

(3B)   In subsection (3A), 'distance contract' and 'excepted contract' have the meanings given in the Consumer Protection (Distance Selling) Regulations 2000.

(3C)   Subsections (1) and (2) shall not apply to any use, in connection with a distance contract within the meaning of the Financial Services (Distance Marketing) Regulations 2004, of a card which is a credit-token.

(3D)   In subsection (3C), 'distance contract' and 'excepted contract' have the meanings given in the Financial Services (Distance Marketing) Regulations 2004.]

(4)   Subsections (1) and (2) shall not apply unless there are contained in the credit-token agreement in the prescribed manner particulars of the name, address and telephone number of a person stated to be the person to whom notice is to be given under subsection (3).

(5)   Notice under subsection (3) takes effect when received, but where it is given orally, and the agreement so requires, it shall be treated as not taking effect if not confirmed in writing within seven days.

(6)   Any sum paid by the debtor for the issue of the credit-token to the extent (if any) that it has not been previously offset by use made of the credit-token, shall be treated as paid towards satisfaction of any liability under subsection (1) or (2).

(7)   The debtor, the creditor, and any person authorised by the debtor to use the credit-token, shall be authorised persons for the purposes of subsection (1).

(8)   Where two or more credit-tokens are given under one credit-token agreement, the preceding provisions of this section apply to each credit-token separately.

85   Duty on issue of new credit-tokens

(1)   Whenever, in connection with a credit-token agreement, a credit-token (other than the first) is given by the creditor to the debtor, the creditor shall give the debtor a copy of the executed agreement (if any) and of any other document referred to in it.

(2)   If the creditor fails to comply with this section—

(a)   he is not entitled, while the default continues, to enforce the agreement, and

(b)   if the default continues for one month he commits an offence.

(3)   This section does not apply to a small agreement.

86   Death of debtor or hirer

(1)   The creditor or owner under a regulated agreement is not entitled, by reason of the death of the debtor or hirer, to do an act specified in paragraphs (a) to (e) of section 87(1) if at the death the agreement is fully secured.

(2)   If at the death of the debtor or hirer a regulated agreement is only partly secured or is unsecured, the creditor or owner is entitled, by reason of the death of the debtor or hirer, to do an act specified in paragraphs (a) to (e) of section 87(1) on an order of the court only.

(3)   This section applies in relation to the termination of an agreement only where—

(a)   a period for its duration is specified in the agreement, and

(b)   that period has not ended when the creditor or owner purports to terminate the agreement,

but so applies notwithstanding that, under the agreement, any party is entitled to terminate it before the end of the period so specified.

(4)   The section does not prevent the creditor from treating the right to draw on any credit as restricted or deferred, and taking such steps as may be necessary to make the restriction or deferment effective.

(5)   This section does not affect the operation of any agreement providing for payment of sums—

(a)   due under the regulated agreement, or

(b)   becoming due under it on the death of the debtor or hirer,

out of the proceeds of a policy of assurance on his life.

(6)   For the purposes of this section an act is done by reason of the death of the debtor or hirer if it is done under a power conferred by the agreement which is—

(a)   exercisable on his death, or

(b)   exercisable at will and exercised at any time after his death.

PART VII
DEFAULT AND TERMINATION

[Information sheets

86A   OFT to prepare information sheets on arrears and default

(1)   The OFT shall prepare, and give general notice of, an arrears information sheet and a default information sheet.

(2)   The arrears information sheet shall include information to help debtors and hirers who receive notices under section 86B or 86C.

(3)   The default information sheet shall include information to help debtors and hirers who receive default notices.

(4)   Regulations may make provision about the information to be included in an information sheet.

(5)   An information sheet takes effect for the purposes of this Part at the end of the period of three months beginning with the day on which general notice of it is given.

(6)   If the OFT revises an information sheet after general notice of it has been given, it shall give general notice of the information sheet as revised.

(7)   A revised information sheet takes effect for the purposes of this Part at the end of the period of three months beginning with the day on which general notice of it is given.

Sums in arrears and default sums

86B   Notice of sums in arrears under fixed-sum credit agreements etc

(1)   This section applies where at any time the following conditions are satisfied—

(a)   that the debtor or hirer under an applicable agreement is required to have made at least two payments under the agreement before that time;

(b)   that the total sum paid under the agreement by him is less than the total sum which he is required to have paid before that time;

(c)   that the amount of the shortfall is no less than the sum of the last two payments which he is required to have made before that time;

(d)   that the creditor or owner is not already under a duty to give him notices under this section in relation to the agreement; and

(e)   if a judgment has been given in relation to the agreement before that time, that there is no sum still to be paid under the judgment by the debtor or hirer.

(2)   The creditor or owner—

(a)   shall, within the period of 14 days beginning with the day on which the conditions mentioned in subsection (1) are satisfied, give the debtor or hirer a notice under this section; and

(b)   after the giving of that notice, shall give him further notices under this section at intervals of not more than six months.

(3)   The duty of the creditor or owner to give the debtor or hirer notices under this section shall cease when either of the conditions mentioned in subsection (4) is

satisfied; but if either of those conditions is satisfied before the notice required by subsection (2)(a) is given, the duty shall not cease until that notice is given.

(4)   The conditions referred to in subsection (3) are—

(a)   that the debtor or hirer ceases to be in arrears;

(b)   that a judgment is given in relation to the agreement under which a sum is required to be paid by the debtor or hirer.

(5)   For the purposes of subsection (4)(a) the debtor or hirer ceases to be in arrears when—

(a)   no sum, which he has ever failed to pay under the agreement when required, is still owing;

(b)   no default sum, which has ever become payable under the agreement in connection with his failure to pay any sum under the agreement when required, is still owing;

(c)   no sum of interest, which has ever become payable under the agreement in connection with such a default sum, is still owing; and

(d)   no other sum of interest, which has ever become payable under the agreement in connection with his failure to pay any sum under the agreement when required, is still owing.

(6)   A notice under this section shall include a copy of the current arrears information sheet under section 86A.

(7)   The debtor or hirer shall have no liability to pay any sum in connection with the preparation or the giving to him of a notice under this section.

(8)   Regulations may make provision about the form and content of notices under this section.

(9)   In the case of an applicable agreement under which the debtor or hirer must make all payments he is required to make at intervals of one week or less, this section shall have effect as if in subsection (1)(a) and (c) for 'two' there were substituted 'four'.

(10)   If an agreement mentioned in subsection (9) was made before the beginning of the relevant period, only amounts resulting from failures by the debtor or hirer to make payments he is required to have made during that period shall be taken into account in determining any shortfall for the purposes of subsection (1)(c).

(11)   In subsection (10) 'relevant period' means the period of 20 weeks ending with the day on which the debtor or hirer is required to have made the most recent payment under the agreement.

(12)   In this section 'applicable agreement' means an agreement which—

(a)   is a regulated agreement for fixed-sum credit or a regulated consumer hire agreement; and

(b)   is neither a non-commercial agreement nor a small agreement.

86C   Notice of sums in arrears under running-account credit agreements

(1)   This section applies where at any time the following conditions are satisfied—

(a)   that the debtor under an applicable agreement is required to have made at least two payments under the agreement before that time;

(b)   that the last two payments which he is required to have made before that time have not been made;

(c)   that the creditor has not already been required to give a notice under this section in relation to either of those payments; and

(d)   if a judgment has been given in relation to the agreement before that time, that there is no sum still to be paid under the judgment by the debtor.

(2)   The creditor shall, no later than the end of the period within which he is next required to give a statement under section 78(4) in relation to the agreement, give the debtor a notice under this section.

(3)   The notice shall include a copy of the current arrears information sheet under section 86A.

(4)   The notice may be incorporated in a statement or other notice which the creditor gives the debtor in relation to the agreement by virtue of another provision of this Act.

(5)   The debtor shall have no liability to pay any sum in connection with the preparation or the giving to him of the notice.

(6)   Regulations may make provision about the form and content of notices under this section.

(7)   In this section 'applicable agreement' means an agreement which—

(a)   is a regulated agreement for running-account credit; and

(b)   is neither a non-commercial agreement nor a small agreement.

86D   Failure to give notice of sums in arrears

(1)   This section applies where the creditor or owner under an agreement is under a duty to give the debtor or hirer notices under section 86B but fails to give him such a notice—

(a)   within the period mentioned in subsection (2)(a) of that section; or

(b)   within the period of six months beginning with the day after the day on which such a notice was last given to him.

(2)   This section also applies where the creditor under an agreement is under a duty to give the debtor a notice under section 86C but fails to do so before the end of the period mentioned in subsection (2) of that section.

(3)   The creditor or owner shall not be entitled to enforce the agreement during the period of non-compliance.

(4)   The debtor or hirer shall have no liability to pay—

(a)   ·any sum of interest to the extent calculated by reference to the period of non-compliance or to any part of it; or

(b)   any default sum which (apart from this paragraph)—

(i)   would have become payable during the period of non-compliance; or

(ii)   would have become payable after the end of that period in connection with a breach of the agreement which occurs during that period (whether or not the breach continues after the end of that period).

(5)   In this section 'the period of non-compliance' means, in relation to a failure to give a notice under section 86B or 86C to the debtor or hirer, the period which—

(a)   begins immediately after the end of the period mentioned in (as the case may be) subsection (1)(a) or (b) or (2); and

(b)   ends at the end of the day mentioned in subsection (6).

(6)   That day is—

(a)   in the case of a failure to give a notice under section 86B as mentioned in subsection (1)(a) of this section, the day on which the notice is given to the debtor or hirer;

(b)   in the case of a failure to give a notice under that section as mentioned in subsection (1)(b) of this section, the earlier of the following—

(i)   the day on which the notice is given to the debtor or hirer;

(ii)   the day on which the condition mentioned in subsection (4)(a) of that section is satisfied;

(c)   in the case of a failure to give a notice under section 86C, the day on which the notice is given to the debtor.

86E   Notice of default sums

(1)   This section applies where a default sum becomes payable under a regulated agreement by the debtor or hirer.

(2)   The creditor or owner shall, within the prescribed period after the default sum becomes payable, give the debtor or hirer a notice under this section.

(3)   The notice under this section may be incorporated in a statement or other

notice which the creditor or owner gives the debtor or hirer in relation to the agreement by virtue of another provision of this Act.

(4)   The debtor or hirer shall have no liability to pay interest in connection with the default sum to the extent that the interest is calculated by reference to a period occurring before the 29th day after the day on which the debtor or hirer is given the notice under this section.

(5)   If the creditor or owner fails to give the debtor or hirer the notice under this section within the period mentioned in subsection (2), he shall not be entitled to enforce the agreement until the notice is given to the debtor or hirer.

(6)   The debtor or hirer shall have no liability to pay any sum in connection with the preparation or the giving to him of the notice under this section.

(7)   Regulations may—
   (a)   provide that this section does not apply in relation to a default sum which is less than a prescribed amount;
   (b)   make provision about the form and content of notices under this section.

(8)   This section does not apply in relation to a non-commercial agreement or to a small agreement.

86F   Interest on default sums

(1)   This section applies where a default sum becomes payable under a regulated agreement by the debtor or hirer.

(2)   The debtor or hirer shall only be liable to pay interest in connection with the default sum if the interest is simple interest.]

Default notices

87   Need for default notice

(1)   Service of a notice on the debtor or hirer in accordance with section 88 (a 'default notice') is necessary before the creditor or owner can become entitled, by reason of any breach by the debtor or hirer of a regulated agreement,—
   (a)   to terminate the agreement, or
   (b)   to demand earlier payment of any sum, or
   (c)   to recover possession of any goods or land, or
   (d)   to treat any right conferred on the debtor or hirer by the agreement as terminated, restricted or deferred, or
   (e)   to enforce any security.

(2)   Subsection (1) does not prevent the creditor from treating the right to draw upon any credit as restricted or deferred, and taking such steps as may be necessary to make the restriction or deferment effective.

(3)   The doing of an act by which a floating charge becomes fixed is not enforcement of a security.

(4)   Regulations may provide that section (1) is not to apply to agreements described by the regulations.

88   Contents and effect of default notice

(1)   The default notice must be in the prescribed form and specify—
   (a)   the nature of the alleged breach;
   (b)   if the breach is capable of remedy, what action is required to remedy it and the date before which that action is to be taken;
   (c)   if the breach is not capable of remedy, the sum (if any) required to be paid as compensation for the breach, and the date before which it is to be paid.

(2)   A date specified under subsection (1) must not be less than [14] days after the date of service of the default notice, and the creditor or owner shall not take action such as is mentioned in section 87(1) before the date so specified or (if no requirement is made under subsection (1)) before those [14] days have elapsed.

(3)   The default notice must not treat as a breach failure to comply with a provision of the agreement which becomes operative only on breach of some other

provision, but if the breach of that other provision is not duly remedied or compensation demanded under subsection (1) is not duly paid, or (where no requirement is made under subsection (1)) if the [14] days mentioned in subsection (2) have elapsed, the creditor or owner may treat the failure as a breach and section 87(1) shall not apply to it.

(4)   The default notice must contain information in the prescribed terms about the consequences of failure to comply with it [and any other prescribed matters relating to the agreement].

[(4A)   The default notice must also include a copy of the current default information sheet under section 86A.]

(5)   A default notice making a requirement under subsection (1) may include a provision for the taking of action such as is mentioned in section 87(1) at any time after the restriction imposed by subsection (2) will cease, together with a statement that the provision will be ineffective if the breach is duly remedied or the compensation duly paid.

89   Compliance with default notice
If before the date specified for that purpose in the default notice the debtor or hirer takes the action specified under section 88(1)(b) or (c) the breach shall be treated as not having occurred.

Further restriction of remedies for default

90   Retaking of protected hire-purchase etc goods
(1)   At any time when—
   (a)   the debtor is in breach of a regulated hire-purchase or a regulated conditional sale agreement relating to goods, and
   (b)   the debtor has paid to the creditor one-third or more of the total price of the goods, and
   (c)   the property in the goods remains in the creditor,
the creditor is not entitled to recover possession of the goods from the debtor except on an order of the court.

(2)   Where under a hire-purchase or conditional sale agreement the creditor is required to carry out any installation and the agreement specifies, as part of the total price, the amount to be paid in respect of the installation (the 'installation charge') the reference in subsection (1)(b) to one-third of the total price shall be construed as a reference to the aggregate of the installation charge and one-third of the remainder of the total price.

(3)   In a case where—
   (a)   subsection (1)(a) is satisfied, but not subsection (1)(b), and
   (b)   subsection (1)(b) was satisfied on a previous occasion in relation to an earlier agreement, being a regulated hire-purchase or regulated conditional sale agreement, between the same parties, and relating to any of the goods comprised in the later agreement (whether or not other goods were also included),
subsection (1) shall apply to the later agreement with the omission of paragraph (b).

(4)   If the later agreement is a modifying agreement, subsection (3) shall apply with the substitution, for the second reference to the later agreement, of a reference to the modifying agreement.

(5)   Subsection (1) shall not apply, or shall cease to apply, to an agreement if the debtor has terminated, or terminates, the agreement.

(6)   Where subsection (1) applies to an agreement at the death of the debtor, it shall continue to apply (in relation to the possessor of the goods) until the grant of probate or administration, or (in Scotland) confirmation (on which the personal representative would fall to be treated as the debtor).

(7)   Goods falling within this section are in this Act referred to as 'protected goods'.

91   Consequences of breach of s 90
If goods are recovered by the creditor in contravention of section 90—

(a)   the regulated agreement, if not previously terminated, shall terminate, and

(b)   the debtor shall be released from all liability under the agreement, and shall be entitled to recover from the creditor all sums paid by the debtor under the agreement.

92   Recovery of possession of goods or land
(1)   Except under an order of the court, the creditor or owner shall not be entitled to enter any premises to take possession of goods subject to a regulated hire-purchase agreement, regulated conditional sale agreement or regulated consumer hire agreement.

(2)   At any time when the debtor is in breach of a regulated conditional sale agreement relating to land, the creditor is entitled to recover possession of the land from the debtor, or any person claiming under him, on an order of the court only.

(3)   An entry in contravention of subsection (1) or (2) is actionable as a breach of statutory duty.

93   Interest not to be increased on default
The debtor under a regulated consumer credit agreement shall not be obliged to pay interest on sums which, in breach of the agreement, are unpaid by him at a rate—

(a)   where the total charge for credit includes an item in respect of interest, exceeding the rate of that interest, or

(b)   in any other case, exceeding what would be the rate of the total charge for credit if any items included in the total charge for credit by virtue of section 20(2) were disregarded.

[93A   Summary diligence not competent in Scotland
Summary diligence shall not be competent in Scotland to enforce payment of a debt due under a regulated agreement or under any security related thereto.]

Early payment by debtor

94   Right to complete payments ahead of time
(1)   The debtor under a regulated consumer credit agreement is entitled at any time, by notice to the creditor and the payment to the creditor of all amounts payable by the debtor to him under the agreement (less any rebate allowable under section 95), to discharge the debtor's indebtedness under the agreement.

(2)   A notice under subsection (1) may embody the exercise by the debtor of any option to purchase goods conferred on him by the agreement, and deal with any other matter arising on, or in relation to, the termination of the agreement.

95   Rebate on early settlement
(1)   Regulations may provide for the allowance of a rebate of charges for credit to the debtor under a regulated consumer credit agreement where, under section 94, on refinancing, on breach of the agreement, or for any other reason, his indebtedness is discharged or becomes payable before the time fixed by the agreement, or any sum becomes payable by him before the time so fixed.

(2)   Regulations under subsection (1) may provide for calculation of the rebate by reference to any sums paid or payable by the debtor or his relative under or in connection with the agreement (whether to the creditor or some other person), including sums under linked transactions and other items in the total charge for credit.

96   Effect on linked transactions
(1)   Where for any reason the indebtedness of the debtor under a regulated consumer credit agreement is discharged before the time fixed by the agreement, he,

and any relative of his, shall at the same time be discharged from any liability under a linked transaction, other than a debt which has already become payable.

(2) Subsection (1) does not apply to a linked transaction which is itself an agreement providing the debtor or his relative with credit.

(3) Regulations may exclude linked transactions of the prescribed description from the operation of subsection (1).

97 Duty to give information

(1) The creditor under a regulated consumer credit agreement, within the prescribed period after he has received a request in writing to that effect from the debtor, shall give the debtor a statement in the prescribed form indicating, according to the information to which it is practicable for him to refer, the amount of the payment required to discharge the debtor's indebtedness under the agreement, together with the prescribed particulars showing how the amount is arrived at.

(2) Subsection (1) does not apply to a request made less than one month after a previous request under that subsection relating to the same agreement was complied with.

(3) If the creditor fails to comply with subsection (1)—

(a)   he is not entitled, while the default continues, to enforce the agreement; and

(b)   if the default continues for one month he commits an offence.

Termination of agreements

98 Duty to give notice of termination (non-default cases)

(1) The creditor or owner is not entitled to terminate a regulated agreement except by or after giving the debtor or hirer not less than seven days' notice of the termination.

(2) Subsection (1) applies only where—

(a)   a period for the duration of the agreement is specified in the agreement, and

(b)   that period has not ended when the creditor or owner does an act mentioned in subsection (1),

but so applies notwithstanding that, under the agreement, any party is entitled to terminate it before the end of the period so specified.

(3) A notice under subsection (1) is ineffective if not in the prescribed form.

(4) Subsection (1) does not prevent a creditor from treating the right to draw on any credit as restricted or deferred and taking such steps as may be necessary to make the restriction or deferment effective.

(5) Regulations may provide that subsection (1) is not to apply to agreements described by the regulations.

(6) Subsection (1) does not apply to the termination of a regulated agreement by reason of any breach by the debtor or hirer of the agreement.

99 Right to terminate hire-purchase etc agreements

(1) At any time before the final payment by the debtor under a regulated hire-purchase or regulated conditional sale agreement falls due, the debtor shall be entitled to terminate the agreement by giving notice to any person entitled or authorised to receive the sums payable under the agreement.

(2) Termination of an agreement under subsection (1) does not affect any liability under the agreement which has accrued before the termination.

(3) Subsection (1) does not apply to a conditional sale agreement relating to land after the title to the land has passed to the debtor.

(4) In the case of a conditional sale agreement relating to goods, where the property in the goods, having become vested in the debtor, is transferred to a person who does not become the debtor under the agreement, the debtor shall not thereafter be entitled to terminate the agreement under subsection (1).

(5)   Subject to subsection (4), where a debtor under a conditional sale agreement relating to goods terminates the agreement under this section after the property in the goods has become vested in him, the property in the goods shall thereupon vest in the person (the 'previous owner') in whom it was vested immediately before it became vested in the debtor:

Provided that if the previous owner has died, or any other event has occurred whereby that property, if vested in him immediately before that event, would thereupon have vested in some other person, the property shall be treated as having devolved as if it had been vested in the previous owner immediately before his death or immediately before that event, as the case may be.

100   Liability of debtor on termination of hire-purchase etc agreement

(1)   Where a regulated hire-purchase or regulated conditional sale agreement is terminated under section 99 the debtor shall be liable, unless the agreement provides for a smaller payment, or does not provide for any payment, to pay to the creditor the amount (if any) by which one-half of the total price exceeds the aggregate of the sums paid and the sums due in respect of the total price immediately before the termination.

(2)   Where under a hire-purchase or conditional sale agreement the creditor is required to carry out any installation and the agreement specifies, as part of the total price, the amount to be paid in respect of the installation (the 'installation charge') the reference in subsection (1) to one-half of the total price shall be construed as a reference to the aggregate of the installation charge and one-half of the remainder of the total price.

(3)   If in any action the court is satisfied that a sum less than the amount specified in subsection (1) would be equal to the loss sustained by the creditor in consequence of the termination of the agreement by the debtor, the court may make an order for the payment of that sum in lieu of the amount specified in subsection (1).

(4)   If the debtor has contravened an obligation to take reasonable care of the goods or land, the amount arrived at under subsection (1) shall be increased by the sum required to recompense the creditor for that contravention, and subsection (2) shall have effect accordingly.

(5)   Where the debtor, on the termination of the agreement, wrongfully retains possession of goods to which the agreement relates, then, in any action brought by the creditor to recover possession of the goods from the debtor, the court, unless it is satisfied that having regard to the circumstances it would not be just to do so, shall order the goods to be delivered to the creditor without giving the debtor an option to pay the value of the goods.

101   Right to terminate hire agreement

(1)   The hirer under a regulated consumer hire agreement is entitled to terminate the agreement by giving notice to any person entitled or authorised to receive the sums payable under the agreement.

(2)   Termination of an agreement under subsection (1) does not affect any liability under the agreement which has accrued before the termination.

(3)   A notice under subsection (1) shall not expire earlier than eighteen months after the making of the agreement, but apart from that the minimum period of notice to be given under subsection (1), unless the agreement provides for a shorter period, is as follows.

(4)   If the agreement provides for the making of payments by the hirer to the owner at equal intervals, the minimum period of notice is the length of one interval or three months, whichever is less.

(5)   If the agreement provides for the making of such payments at differing intervals, the minimum period of notice is the length of the shortest interval or three months, whichever is less.

(6)   In any other case, the minimum period of notice is three months.

(7)   This section does not apply to—

(a)   any agreement which provides for the making by the hirer of payments which in total (and without breach of the agreement) exceed [£1,500] in any year, or

(b)   any agreement where—

(i)   goods are bailed or (in Scotland) hired to the hirer for the purposes of a business carried on by him, or the hirer holds himself out as requiring the goods for those purposes, and

(ii)   the goods are selected by the hirer, and acquired by the owner for the purposes of the agreement at the request of the hirer from any person other than the owner's associate, or

(c)   any agreement where the hirer requires, or holds himself out as requiring, the goods for the purpose of bailing or hiring them to other persons in the course of a business carried on by him.

(8)   If, on an application made to the [OFT] by a person carrying on a consumer hire business, it appears to the [OFT] that it would be in the interest of hirers to do so, [it] may by notice to the applicant direct that [, subject to such conditions (if any) as it may specify, this section shall not apply to consumer hire agreements made by the applicant; and this Act shall have effect accordingly].

[(8A)   If it appears to the OFT that it would be in the interest of hirers to do so, it may by general notice direct that, subject to such conditions (if any) as it may specify, this section shall not apply to a consumer hire agreement if the agreement falls within a specified description; and this Act shall have effect accordingly.]

(9)   In the case of a modifying agreement, subsection (3) shall apply with the substitution for 'the making of the agreement' of 'the making of the original agreement'.

102   Agency for receiving notice of rescission

(1)   Where the debtor or hirer under a regulated agreement claims to have a right to rescind the agreement, each of the following shall be deemed to be the agent of the creditor owner for the purpose of receiving any notice rescinding the agreement which is served by the debtor or hirer—

(a)   a credit-broker or supplier who was the negotiator in antecedent negotiations, and

(b)   any person who, in the course of a business carried on by him, acted on behalf of the debtor or hirer in any negotiations for the agreement.

(2)   In subsection (1) 'rescind' does not include—

(a)   service of a notice of cancellation, or

(b)   termination of an agreement under section 99 or 101 or by the exercise of a right or power in that behalf expressly conferred by the agreement.

103   Termination statements

(1)   If an individual (the 'customer') serves on any person (the 'trader') a notice—

(a)   stating that—

(i)   the customer was the debtor or hirer under a regulated agreement described in the notice, and the trader was the creditor or owner under the agreement, and

(ii)   the customer has discharged his indebtedness to the trader under the agreement, and

(iii)   the agreement has ceased to have any operation; and

(b)   requiring the trader to give the customer a notice, signed by or on behalf of the trader, confirming that those statements are correct,

the trader shall, within the prescribed period after receiving the notice, either comply with it or serve on the customer a counter-notice stating that, as the case may be, he disputes the correctness of the notice or asserts that the customer is not indebted to him under the agreement.

(2)   Where the trader disputes the correctness of the notice he shall give particulars of the way in which he alleges it to be wrong.

(3)   Subsection (1) does not apply in relation to any agreement if the trader has previously complied with that subsection on the service of a notice under it with respect to that agreement.

(4)   Subsection (1) does not apply to a non-commercial agreement.

(5)   If the trader fails to comply with subsection (1), and the default continues for one month, he commits an offence.

104   Goods not to be treated as subject to landlord's hypothec in Scotland
Goods comprised in a hire-purchase agreement or goods comprised in a conditional sale agreement which have not become vested in the debtor shall not be treated in Scotland as subject to the landlord's hypothec—

(a)   during the period between the service of a default notice in respect of the goods and the date on which the notice expires or is earlier complied with; or

(b)   if the agreement is enforceable on an order of the court only, during the period between the commencement and termination of an action by the creditor to enforce the agreement.

PART VIII
SECURITY

General

105   Form and content of securities
(1)   Any security provided in relation to a regulated agreement shall be expressed in writing.

(2)   Regulations may prescribe the form and content of documents ('security instruments') to be made in compliance with subsection (1).

(3)   Regulations under subsection (2) may in particular—

(a)   require specified information to be included in the prescribed manner in documents, and other specified material to be excluded;

(b)   contain requirements to ensure that specified information is clearly brought to the attention of the surety, and that one part of a document is not given insufficient or excessive prominence compared with another.

(4)   A security instrument is not properly executed unless—

(a)   a document in the prescribed form, itself containing all the prescribed terms and conforming to regulations under subsection (2), is signed in the prescribed manner by or on behalf of the surety, and

(b)   the document embodies all the terms of the security, other than implied terms, and

(c)   the document, when presented or sent for the purpose of being signed by or on behalf of the surety, is in such state that its terms are readily legible, and

(d)   when the document is presented or sent for the purpose of being signed by or on behalf of the surety there is also presented or sent a copy of the document.

(5)   A security instrument is not properly executed unless—

(a)   where the security is provided after, or at the time when, the regulated agreement is made, a copy of the executed agreement, together with a copy of any other document referred to in it, is given to the surety at the time the security is provided, or

(b)   where the security is provided before the regulated agreement is made, a copy of the executed agreement, together with a copy of any other document referred to in it, is given to the surety within seven days after the regulated agreement is made.

(6)   Subsection (1) does not apply to a security provided by the debtor or hirer.

(7) If—
   (a)   in contravention of subsection (1) a security is not expressed in writing, or
   (b)   a security instrument is improperly executed,
the security, so far as provided in relation to a regulated agreement, is enforceable against the surety on an order of the court only.

(8) If an application for an order under subsection (7) is dismissed (except on technical grounds only) section 106 (ineffective securities) shall apply to the security.

(9) Regulations under section 60(1) shall include provision requiring documents embodying regulated agreements also to embody any security provided in relation to a regulated agreement by the debtor or hirer.

106 Ineffective securities

Where, under any provision of this Act, this section is applied to any security provided in relation to a regulated agreement, then, subject to section 177 (saving for registered charges)—
   (a)   the security, so far as it is so provided, shall be treated as never having effect;
   (b)   any property lodged with the creditor or owner solely for the purposes of the security as so provided shall be returned by him forthwith;
   (c)   the creditor or owner shall take any necessary action to remove or cancel an entry in any register, so far as the entry relates to the security as so provided; and
   (d)   any amount received by the creditor or owner on realisation of the security shall, so far as it is referable to the agreement, be repaid to the surety.

107 Duty to give information to surety under fixed-sum credit agreement

(1) The creditor under a regulated agreement for fixed-sum credit in relation to which security is provided, within the prescribed period after receiving a request in writing to that effect from the surety and payment of a fee of [£1], shall give to the surety (if a different person from the debtor)—
   (a)   a copy of the executed agreement (if any) and of any other document referred to in it;
   (b)   a copy of the security instrument (if any); and
   (c)   a statement signed by or on behalf of the creditor showing, according to the information to which it is practicable for him to refer,—
      (i)   the total sum paid under the agreement by the debtor,
      (ii)   the total sum which has become payable under the agreement by the debtor but remains unpaid, and the various amounts comprised in that total sum, with the date when each became due, and
      (iii)   the total sum which is to become payable under the agreement by the debtor, and the various amounts comprised in that total sum, with the date, or mode of determining the date, when each becomes due.

(2) If the creditor possesses insufficient information to enable him to ascertain the amounts and dates mentioned in subsection (1)(c)(iii), he shall be taken to comply with that sub-paragraph if his statement under subsection (1)(c) gives the basis on which, under the regulated agreement, they would fall to be ascertained.

(3) Subsection (1) does not apply to—
   (a)   an agreement under which no sum is, or will or may become, payable by the debtor, or
   (b)   a request made less than one month after a previous request under that subsection relating to the same agreement was complied with.

(4) If the creditor under an agreement fails to comply with subsection (1)—
   (a)   he is not entitled, while the default continues, to enforce the security, so far as provided in relation to the agreement; and
   (b)   if the default continues for one month he commits an offence.

(5)   This section does not apply to a non-commercial agreement.

108   Duty to give information to surety under running-account credit agreement

(1)   The creditor under a regulated agreement for running-account credit in relation to which security is provided, within the prescribed period after receiving a request in writing to that effect from the surety and payment of a fee of [£1], shall give to the surety (if a different person from the debtor)—

(a)   a copy of the executed agreement (if any) and of any other document referred to in it;

(b)   a copy of the security instrument (if any); and

(c)   a statement signed by or on behalf of the creditor showing, according to the information to which it is practicable for him to refer,—

(i)   the state of the account, and

(ii)   the amount if any, currently payable under the agreement by the debtor to the creditor, and

(iii)   the amounts and due dates of any payments which, if the debtor does not draw further on the account, will later become payable under the agreement by the debtor to the creditor.

(2)   If the creditor possesses insufficient information to enable him to ascertain the amounts and dates mentioned in subsection (1)(c)(iii), he shall be taken to comply with that sub-paragraph if his statement under subsection (1)(c) gives the basis on which, under the regulated agreement, they would fall to be ascertained.

(3)   Subsection (1) does not apply to—

(a)   an agreement under which no sum is, or will or may become, payable by the debtor, or

(b)   a request made less than one month after a previous request under that subsection relating to the same agreement was complied with.

(4)   If the creditor under an agreement fails to comply with subsection (1)—

(a)   he is not entitled, while the default continues, to enforce the security, so far as provided in relation to the agreement; and

(b)   if the default continues for one month he commits an offence.

(5)   This section does not apply to a non-commercial agreement.

109   Duty to give information to surety under consumer hire agreement

(1)   The owner under a regulated consumer hire agreement in relation to which security is provided, within the prescribed period after receiving a request in writing to that effect from the surety and payment of a fee of [£1], shall give to the surety (if a different person from the hirer)—

(a)   a copy of the executed agreement and of any other document referred to in it;

(b)   a copy of the security instrument (if any); and

(c)   a statement signed by or on behalf of the owner showing, according to the information to which it is practicable for him to refer, the total sum which has become payable under the agreement by the hirer but remains unpaid and the various amounts comprised in that total sum, with the date when each became due.

(2)   Subsection (1) does not apply to—

(a)   an agreement under which no sum is, or will or may become, payable by the hirer, or

(b)   a request made less than one month after a previous request under that subsection relating to the same agreement was complied with.

(3)   If the owner under an agreement fails to comply with subsection (1)—

(a)   he is not entitled, while the default continues, to enforce the security, so far as provided in relation to the agreement; and

(b)   if the default continues for one month he commits an offence.

(4)   This section does not apply to a non-commercial agreement.

110   Duty to give information to debtor or hirer

(1)   The creditor or owner under a regulated agreement, within the prescribed period after receiving a request in writing to that effect from the debtor or hirer and payment of a fee of [£1], shall give the debtor or hirer a copy of any security instrument executed in relation to the agreement after the making of the agreement.

(2)   Subsection (1) does not apply to—

(a)   a non-commercial agreement, or

(b)   an agreement under which no sum is, or will or may become, payable by the debtor or hirer, or

(c)   a request made less than one month after a previous request under subsection (1) relating to the same agreement was complied with.

(3)   If the creditor or owner under an agreement fails to comply with subsection (1)—

(a)   he is not entitled, while the default continues, to enforce the security (so far as provided in relation to the agreement); and

(b)   if the default continues for one month he commits an offence.

111   Duty to give surety copy of default etc notice

(1)   When a default notice or a notice under section 76(1) or 98(1) is served on a debtor or hirer, a copy of the notice shall be served by the creditor or owner on any surety (if a different person from the debtor or hirer).

(2)   If the creditor or owner fails to comply with subsection (1) in the case of any surety, the security is enforceable against the surety (in respect of the breach or other matter to which the notice relates) on an order of the court only.

112   Realisation of securities

Subject to section 121, regulations may provide for any matters relating to the sale or other realisation, by the creditor or owner, of property over which any right has been provided by way of security in relation to an actual or prospective regulated agreement, other than a non-commercial agreement.

113   Act not to be evaded by use of security

(1)   Where a security is provided in relation to an actual or prospective regulated agreement, the security shall not be enforced so as to benefit the creditor or owner, directly or indirectly, to an extent greater (whether as respects the amount of any payment or the time or manner of its being made) than would be the case if the security were not provided and any obligations of the debtor or hirer, or his relative, under or in relation to the agreement were carried out to the extent (if any) to which they would be enforced under this Act.

(2)   In accordance with subsection (1), where a regulated agreement is enforceable on an order of the court or the [OFT] only, any security provided in relation to the agreement is enforceable (so far as provided in relation to the agreement) where such an order has been made in relation to the agreement, but not otherwise.

(3)   Where—

(a)   a regulated agreement is cancelled under section 69(1) or becomes subject to section 69(2), or

(b)   a regulated agreement is terminated under section 91, or

(c)   in relation to any agreement an application for an order under section 40(2), 65(1), 124(1) or 149(2) is dismissed (except on technical grounds only), or

(d)   a declaration is made by the court under section 142(1) (refusal of enforcement order) as respects any regulated agreement,

section 106 shall apply to any security provided in relation to the agreement.

(4)   Where subsection (3)(d) applies and the declaration relates to a part only of the regulated agreement, section 106 shall apply to the security only so far as it concerns that part.

(5)   In the case of a cancelled agreement, the duty imposed on the debtor or hirer by section 71 or 72 shall not be enforceable before the creditor or owner has discharged any duty imposed on him by section 106 (as applied by subsection (3)(a)).

(6)   If the security is provided in relation to a prospective agreement or trans-action, the security shall be enforceable in relation to the agreement or transaction only after the time (if any) when the agreement is made; and until that time the person providing the security shall be entitled, by notice to the creditor or owner, to require that section 106 shall thereupon apply to the security.

(7)   Where an indemnity [or guarantee] is given in a case where the debtor or hirer is a minor, or [an indemnity is given in a case where he] is otherwise not of full capacity, the reference in subsection (1) to the extent to which his obligations would be enforced shall be read in relation to the indemnity [or guarantee] as a reference to the extent to which [those obligations] would be enforced if he were of full capacity.

(8)   Subsections (1) and (3) also apply where a security is provided in relation to an actual or prospective linked transaction, and in that case—

(a)   references to the agreement shall be read as references to the linked transaction, and

(b)   references to the creditor or owner shall be read as references to any person (other than the debtor or hirer, or his relative) who is a party, or prospective party, to the linked transaction.

Pledges

114   Pawn-receipts

(1)   At the time he receives the article, a person who takes any article in pawn under a regulated agreement shall give to the person from whom he receives it a receipt in the prescribed form (a 'pawn-receipt').

(2)   A person who takes any article in pawn from an individual whom he knows to be, or who appears to be and is, a minor commits an offence.

(3)   This section and sections 115 to 122 do not apply to—

(a)   a pledge of documents of title [or of bearer bonds], or

(b)   a non-commercial agreement.

115   Penalty for failure to supply copies of pledge agreement, etc

If the creditor under a regulated agreement to take any article in pawn fails to observe the requirements of section 62 to 64 or 114(1) in relation to the agreement he commits an offence.

116   Redemption period

(1)   A pawn is redeemable at any time within six months after it was taken.

(2)   Subject to subsection (1), the period within which a pawn is redeemable shall be the same as the period fixed by the parties for the duration of the credit secured by the pledge, or such longer period as they may agree.

(3)   If the pawn is not redeemed by the end of the period laid down by sub-sections (1) and (2) (the 'redemption period'), it nevertheless remains redeemable until it is realised by the pawnee under section 121 except where under section 120(1)(a) the property in it passes to the pawnee.

(4)   No special charge shall be made for redemption of a pawn after the end of the redemption period, and charges in respect of the safe keeping of the pawn shall not be at a higher rate after the end of the redemption period than before.

117   Redemption procedure

(1)   On surrender of the pawn-receipt, and payment of the amount owing, at any time when the pawn is redeemable, the pawnee shall deliver the pawn to the bearer of the pawn-receipt.

(2)   Subsection (1) does not apply if the pawnee knows or has reasonable cause

to suspect that the bearer of the pawn-receipt is neither the owner of the pawn nor authorised by the owner to redeem it.

(3)   The pawnee is not liable to any person in tort or delict for delivering the pawn where subsection (1) applies, or refusing to deliver it where the person demanding delivery does not comply with subsection (1) or, by reason of subsection (2), subsection (1) does not apply.

118   Loss etc of pawn-receipt

(1)   A person (the 'claimant') who is not in possession of the pawn-receipt but claims to be the owner of the pawn, or to be otherwise entitled or authorised to redeem it, may do so at any time when it is redeemable by tendering to the pawnee in place of the pawn-receipt—

(a)   a statutory declaration made by the claimant in the prescribed form, and with the prescribed contents, or

(b)   where the pawn is security for fixed-sum credit not exceeding [£75] or running-account credit on which the credit limit does not exceed [£75], and the pawnee agrees, a statement in writing in the prescribed form, and with the prescribed contents, signed by the claimant.

(2)   On compliance by the claimant with subsection (1), section 117 shall apply as if the declaration or statement were the pawn-receipt, and the pawn-receipt itself shall become inoperative for the purposes of section 117.

119   Unreasonable refusal to deliver pawn

(1)   If a person who has taken a pawn under a regulated agreement refuses without reasonable cause to allow the pawn to be redeemed, he commits an offence.

(2)   On the conviction in England and Wales of a pawnee under subsection (1) where the offence does not amount to theft, [section 148 of the Powers of Criminal Courts (Sentencing) Act 2000 (restitution orders)] shall apply as if the pawnee had been convicted of stealing the pawn.

(3)   On the conviction in Northern Ireland of a pawnee under subsection (1) where the offence does not amount to theft, section 27 (orders for restitution) of the Theft Act (Northern Ireland) 1969, and any provision of the Theft Act (Northern Ireland) 1969 relating to that section, shall apply as if the pawnee had been convicted of stealing the pawn.

120   Consequence of failure to redeem

(1)   If at the end of the redemption period the pawn has not been redeemed—

(a)   notwithstanding anything in section 113, the property in the pawn passes to the pawnee where the redemption period is six months and the pawn is security for fixed-sum credit not exceeding [£75] or running-account credit on which the credit limit does not exceed [£75]; or

(b)   in any other case the pawn becomes realisable by the pawnee.

(2)   Where the debtor or hirer is entitled to apply to the court for a time order under section 129, subsection (1) shall apply with the substitution, for 'at the end of the redemption period' of 'after the expiry of five days following the end of the redemption period'.

121   Realisation of pawn

(1)   When a pawn has become realisable by him, the pawnee may sell it, after giving to the pawnor (except in such cases as may be prescribed) not less than the prescribed period of notice of the intention to sell, indicating in the notice the asking price and such other particulars as may be prescribed.

(2)   Within the prescribed period after the sale takes place, the pawnee shall give the pawnor the prescribed information in writing as to the sale, its proceeds and expenses.

(3)   Where the net proceeds of sale are not less than the sum which, if the pawn had been redeemed on the date of the sale, would have been payable for its

redemption, the debt secured by the pawn is discharged and any surplus shall be paid by the pawnee to the pawnor.

(4)   Where subsection (3) does not apply, the debt shall be treated as from the date of sale as equal to the amount by which the net proceeds of sale fall short of the sum which would have been payable for the redemption of the pawn on that date.

(5)   In this section the 'net proceeds of sale' is the amount realised (the 'gross amount') less the expenses (if any) of the sale.

(6)   If the pawnor alleges that the gross amount is less than the true market value of the pawn on the date of sale, it is for the pawnee to prove that he and any agents employed by him in the sale used reasonable care to ensure that the true market value was obtained, and if he fails to do so subsections (3) and (4) shall have effect as if the reference in subsection (5) to the gross amount were a reference to the true market value.

(7)   If the pawnor alleges that the expenses of the sale were unreasonably high, it is for the pawnee to prove that they were reasonable, and if he fails to do so subsections (3) and (4) shall have effect as if the reference in subsection (5) to expenses were a reference to reasonable expenses.

122   Order in Scotland to deliver pawn

(1)   As respects Scotland where—
(a)   a pawn is either—
(i)   an article which has been stolen, or
(ii)   an article which has been obtained by fraud, and a person is convicted of any offence in relation to the theft or, as the case may be, the fraud; or
(b)   a person is convicted of an offence under section 119(1), the court by which that person is so convicted may order delivery of the pawn to the owner or the person otherwise entitled thereto.

(2)   A court making an order under subsection (1)(a) for delivery of a pawn may make the order subject to such conditions as to payment of the debt secured by the pawn as it thinks fit.

Negotiable instruments

123   Restrictions on taking and negotiating instruments

(1)   A creditor or owner shall not take a negotiable instrument, other than a bank note or cheque, in discharge of any sum payable—
(a)   by the debtor or hirer under a regulated agreement, or
(b)   by any person as surety in relation to the agreement.

(2)   The creditor or owner shall not negotiate a cheque taken by him in discharge of a sum payable as mentioned in subsection (1) except to a banker (within the meaning of the Bills of Exchange Act 1882).

(3)   The creditor or owner shall not take a negotiable instrument as security for the discharge of any sum payable as mentioned in subsection (1).

(4)   A person takes a negotiable instrument as security for the discharge of a sum if the sum is intended to be paid in some other way, and the negotiable instrument is to be presented for payment only if the sum is not paid in that way.

(5)   This section does not apply where the regulated agreement is a non-commercial agreement.

(6)   The Secretary of State may by order provide that this section shall not apply where the regulated agreement has a connection with a country outside the United Kingdom.

124   Consequences of breach of s 123

(1)   After any contravention of section 123 has occurred in relation to a sum payable as mentioned in section 123(1)(a), the agreement under which the sum is payable is enforceable against the debtor or hirer on an order of the court only.

(2)   After any contravention of section 123 has occurred in relation to a sum payable by any surety, the security is enforceable on an order of the court only.

(3)   Where an application for an order under subsection (2) is dismissed (except on technical grounds only) section 106 shall apply to the security.

125   Holders in due course

(1)   A person who takes a negotiable instrument in contravention of section 123(1) or (3) is not a holder in due course, and is not entitled to enforce the instrument.

(2)   Where a person negotiates a cheque in contravention of section 123(2), his doing so constitutes a defect in his title within the meaning of the Bills of Exchange Act 1882.

(3)   If a person mentioned in section 123(1)(a) and (b) ('the protected person') becomes liable to a holder in due course of an instrument taken from the protected person in contravention of section 123(1) or (3), or taken from the protected person and negotiated in contravention of section 123(2), the creditor or owner shall indemnify the protected person in respect of that liability.

(4)   Nothing in this Act affects the rights of the holder in due course of any negotiable instrument.

Land mortgages

126   Enforcement of land mortgages

A land mortgage securing a regulated agreement is enforceable (so far as provided in relation to the agreement) on an order of the court only.

PART IX
JUDICIAL CONTROL

Enforcement of certain regulated agreements and securities

127   Enforcement orders in cases of infringement

(1)   In the case of an application for an enforcement order under—
   (a)   section 65(1) (improperly executed agreements), or
   (b)   section 105(7)(a) or (b) (improperly executed security instruments), or
   (c)   section 111(2) (failure to serve copy of notice on surety), or
   (d)   section 124(1) or (2) (taking of negotiable instrument in contravention of section 123),
the court shall dismiss the application if, but [. . .] only if, it considers it just to do so having regard to—
      (i)   prejudice caused to any person by the contravention in question, and the degree of culpability for it; and
      (ii)   the powers conferred on the court by subsection (2) and sections 135 and 136.

(2)   If it appears to the court just to do so, it may in an enforcement order reduce or discharge any sum payable by the debtor or hirer, or any surety, so as to compensate him for prejudice suffered as a result of the contravention in question.
   [. . .]

128   Enforcement orders on death of debtor or hirer

The court shall make an order under section 86(2) if, but only if, the creditor or owner proves that he has been unable to satisfy himself that the present and future obligations of the debtor or hirer under the agreement are likely to be discharged.

Extension of time

129   Time orders

(1)   [Subject to subsection (3) below,] if it appears to the court just to do so—

(a) on an application for an enforcement order; or

(b) on an application made by a debtor or hirer under this paragraph after service on him of—

  (i) a default notice, or

  (ii) a notice under section 76(1) or 98(1); or

[(ba) on an application made by a debtor or hirer under this paragraph after he has been given a notice under section 86B or 86C; or]

(c) in an action brought by a creditor or owner to enforce a regulated agreement or any security, or recover possession of any goods or land to which a regulated agreement relates,

the court may make an order under this section (a 'time order').

(2) A time order shall provide for one or both of the following, as the court considers just—

(a) the payment by the debtor or hirer or any surety of any sum owed under a regulated agreement or a security by such instalments, payable at such times, as the court having regard to the means of the debtor or hirer and any surety, considers reasonable;

(b) the remedying by the debtor or hirer of any breach of a regulated agreement (other than non-payment of money) within such period as the court may specify.

[(3) Where in Scotland a time to pay direction or a time order has been made in relation to a debt, it shall not thereafter be competent to make a time order in relation to the same debt.]

[129A Debtor or hirer to give notice of intent etc to creditor or owner

(1) A debtor or hirer may make an application under section 129(1)(ba) in relation to a regulated agreement only if—

(a) following his being given the notice under section 86B or 86C, he gave a notice within subsection (2) to the creditor or owner; and

(b) a period of at least 14 days has elapsed after the day on which he gave that notice to the creditor or owner.

(2) A notice is within this subsection if it—

(a) indicates that the debtor or hirer intends to make the application;

(b) indicates that he wants to make a proposal to the creditor or owner in relation to his making of payments under the agreement; and

(c) gives details of that proposal.]

130 Supplemental provisions about time orders

(1) Where in accordance with rules of court an offer to pay any sum by instalments is made by the debtor or hirer and accepted by the creditor or owner, the court may in accordance with rules of court make a time order under section 129(2)(a) giving effect to the offer without hearing evidence of means.

(2) In the case of a hire-purchase or conditional sale agreement only, a time order under section 129(2)(a) may deal with sums which, although not payable by the debtor at the time the order is made, would if the agreement continued in force become payable under it subsequently.

(3) A time order under section 129(2)(a) shall not be made where the regulated agreement is secured by a pledge if, by virtue of regulations made under section 76(5), 87(4) or 98(5), service of a notice is not necessary for enforcement of the pledge.

(4) Where, following the making of a time order in relation to a regulated hire-purchase or conditional sale agreement or a regulated consumer hire agreement, the debtor or hirer is in possession of the goods, he shall be treated (except in the case of a debtor to whom the creditor's title has passed) as a bailee or (in Scotland) a custodier of the goods under the terms of the agreement, notwithstanding that the agreement has been terminated.

(5) Without prejudice to anything done by the creditor or owner before the

commencement of the period specified in a time order made under section 129(2)(b) ('the relevant period'),—

(a)   he shall not while the relevant period subsists take in relation to the agreement any action such as is mentioned in section 87(1);

(b)   where—

(i)   a provision of the agreement ('the secondary provision') becomes operative only on breach of another provision of the agreement ('the primary provision'), and

(ii)   the time order provides for the remedying of such a breach of the primary provision within the relevant period,

he shall not treat the secondary provision as operative before the end of that period;

(c)   if while the relevant period subsists the breach to which the order relates is remedied it shall be treated as not having occurred.

(6)   On the application of any person affected by a time order, the court may vary or revoke the order.

[Interest

130A   Interest payable on judgment debts etc

(1)   If the creditor or owner under a regulated agreement wants to be able to recover from the debtor or hirer post-judgment interest in connection with a sum that is required to be paid under a judgment given in relation to the agreement (the 'judgment sum'), he—

(a)   after the giving of that judgment, shall give the debtor or hirer a notice under this section (the 'first required notice'); and

(b)   after the giving of the first required notice, shall give the debtor or hirer further notices under this section at intervals of not more than six months.

(2)   The debtor or hirer shall have no liability to pay post-judgment interest in connection with the judgment sum to the extent that the interest is calculated by reference to a period occurring before the day on which he is given the first required notice.

(3)   If the creditor or owner fails to give the debtor or hirer a notice under this section within the period of six months beginning with the day after the day on which such a notice was last given to the debtor or hirer, the debtor or hirer shall have no liability to pay post-judgment interest in connection with the judgment sum to the extent that the interest is calculated by reference to the whole or to a part of the period which—

(a)   begins immediately after the end of that period of six months; and

(b)   ends at the end of the day on which the notice is given to the debtor or hirer.

(4)   The debtor or hirer shall have no liability to pay any sum in connection with the preparation or the giving to him of a notice under this section.

(5)   A notice under this section may be incorporated in a statement or other notice which the creditor or owner gives the debtor or hirer in relation to the agreement by virtue of another provision of this Act.

(6)   Regulations may make provision about the form and content of notices under this section.

(7)   This section does not apply in relation to post-judgment interest which is required to be paid by virtue of any of the following—

(a)   section 4 of the Administration of Justice (Scotland) Act 1972;

(b)   Article 127 of the Judgments Enforcement (Northern Ireland) Order 1981;

(c)   section 74 of the County Courts Act 1984.

(8)   This section does not apply in relation to a non-commercial agreement or to a small agreement.

(9)   In this section 'post-judgment interest' means interest to the extent calcu-

lated by reference to a period occurring after the giving of the judgment under which the judgment sum is required to be paid.]

Protection of property pending proceedings

131   Protection orders
The court, on application of the creditor or owner under a regulated agreement, may make such orders as it thinks just for protecting any property of the creditor or owner, or property subject to any security, from damage or depreciation pending the determination of any proceedings under this Act, including orders restricting or prohibiting use of the property or giving directions as to its custody.

Hire and hire-purchase etc agreements

132   Financial relief for hirer
(1)   Where the owner under a regulated consumer hire agreement recovers possession of goods to which the agreement relates otherwise than by action, the hirer may apply to the court for an order that—
    (a)   the whole or part of any sum paid by the hirer to the owner in respect of the goods shall be repaid, and
    (b)   the obligation to pay the whole or part of any sum owed by the hirer to the owner in respect of the goods shall cease,
and if it appears to the court just to do so, having regard to the extent of the enjoyment of the goods by the hirer, the court shall grant the application in full or in part.
(2)   Where in proceedings relating to a regulated consumer hire agreement the court makes an order for the delivery to the owner of goods to which the agreement relates the court may include in the order the like provision as may be made in an order under subsection (1).

133   Hire-purchase etc agreements: special powers of court
(1)   If, in relation to a regulated hire-purchase or conditional sale agreement, it appears to the court just to do so—
    (a)   on an application for an enforcement order or time order; or
    (b)   in an action brought by the creditor to recover possession of goods to which the agreement relates,
the court may—
        (i)   make an order (a 'return order') for the return to the creditor of goods to which the agreement relates;
        (ii)   make an order (a 'transfer order') for the transfer to the debtor of the creditor's title to certain goods to which the agreement relates ('the transferred goods'), and the return to the creditor of the remainder of the goods.
(2)   In determining for the purposes of this section how much of the total price has been paid ('the paid-up sum'), the court may—
    (a)   treat any sum paid by the debtor, or owed by the creditor, in relation to the goods as part of the paid-up sum;
    (b)   deduct any sum owed by the debtor in relation to the goods (otherwise than as part of the total price) from the paid-up sum,
and make corresponding reductions in amounts so owed.
(3)   Where a transfer order is made, the transferred goods shall be such of the goods to which the agreement relates as the court thinks just; but a transfer order shall be made only where the paid-up sum exceeds the part of the total price referable to the transferred goods by an amount equal to at least one-third of the unpaid balance of the total price.
(4)   Notwithstanding the making of a return order or transfer order, the debtor may at any time before the goods enter the possession of the creditor, on payment

of the balance of the total price and the fulfilment of any other necessary conditions, claim the goods ordered to be returned to the creditor.

(5) When, in pursuance of a time order or under this section, the total price of goods under a regulated hire-purchase agreement or regulated conditional sale agreement is paid and any other necessary conditions are fulfilled, the creditor's title to the goods vests in the debtor.

(6) If, in contravention of a return order or transfer order, any goods to which the order relates are not returned to the creditor, the court, on the application of the creditor, may—

(a)   revoke so much of the order as relates to those goods, and

(b)   order the debtor to pay the creditor the unpaid portion of so much of the total price as is referable to those goods.

(7) For the purposes of this section, the part of the total price referable to any goods is the part assigned to those goods by the agreement or (if no such assignment is made) the part determined by the court to be reasonable.

134   Evidence of adverse detention in hire-purchase etc cases

(1) Where goods are comprised in a regulated hire-purchase agreement, regulated conditional sale agreement or regulated consumer hire agreement, and the creditor or owner—

(a)   brings an action or makes an application to enforce a right to recover possession of the goods from the debtor or hirer, and

(b)   proves that a demand for the delivery of the goods was included in the default notice under section 88(5), or that, after the right to recover possession of the goods accrued but before the action was begun or the application was made, he made a request in writing to the debtor or hirer to surrender the goods,

then, for the purposes of the claim of the creditor or owner to recover possession of the goods, the possession of them by the debtor or hirer shall be deemed to be adverse to the creditor or owner.

(2) In subsection (1) 'the debtor or hirer' includes a person in possession of the goods at any time between the debtor's or hirer's death and the grant of probate or administration, or (in Scotland) confirmation.

(3) Nothing in this section affects a claim for damages for conversion or (in Scotland) for delict.

Supplemental provisions as to orders

135   Power to impose conditions, or suspend operation of order

(1) If it considers it just to do so, the court may in an order made by it in relation to a regulated agreement include provisions—

(a)   making the operation of any term of the order conditional on the doing of specified acts by any party to the proceedings;

(b)   suspending the operation of any term of the order either—

(i)   until such time as the court subsequently directs, or

(ii)   until the occurrence of a specified act or omission.

(2) The court shall not suspend the operation of a term requiring the delivery up of goods by any person unless satisfied that the goods are in his possession or control.

(3) In the case of a consumer hire agreement, the court shall not so use its powers under subsection (1)(b) as to extend the period for which, under the terms of the agreement, the hirer is entitled to possession of the goods to which the agreement relates.

(4) On the application of any person affected by a provision included under subsection (1), the court may vary the provision.

136   Power to vary agreements and securities

(1) The court may in an order made by it under this Act include such pro-

vision as it considers just for amending any agreement or security in consequence of a term of the order.

[. . .]

[*Unfair relationships*

140A   Unfair relationships between creditors and debtors
(1)   The court may make an order under section 140B in connection with a credit agreement if it determines that the relationship between the creditor and the debtor arising out of the agreement (or the agreement taken with any related agreement) is unfair to the debtor because of one or more of the following—
  (a)   any of the terms of the agreement or of any related agreement;
  (b)   the way in which the creditor has exercised or enforced any of his rights under the agreement or any related agreement;
  (c)   any other thing done (or not done) by, or on behalf of, the creditor (either before or after the making of the agreement or any related agreement).
(2)   In deciding whether to make a determination under this section the court shall have regard to all matters it thinks relevant (including matters relating to the creditor and matters relating to the debtor).
(3)   For the purposes of this section the court shall (except to the extent that it is not appropriate to do so) treat anything done (or not done) by, or on behalf of, or in relation to, an associate or a former associate of the creditor as if done (or not done) by, or on behalf of, or in relation to, the creditor.
(4)   A determination may be made under this section in relation to a relationship notwithstanding that the relationship may have ended.
(5)   An order under section 140B shall not be made in connection with a credit agreement which is an exempt agreement by virtue of section 16(6C).

140B   Powers of court in relation to unfair relationships
(1)   An order under this section in connection with a credit agreement may do one or more of the following—
  (a)   require the creditor, or any associate or former associate of his, to repay (in whole or in part) any sum paid by the debtor or by a surety by virtue of the agreement or any related agreement (whether paid to the creditor, the associate or the former associate or to any other person);
  (b)   require the creditor, or any associate or former associate of his, to do or not to do (or to cease doing) anything specified in the order in connection with the agreement or any related agreement;
  (c)   reduce or discharge any sum payable by the debtor or by a surety by virtue of the agreement or any related agreement;
  (d)   direct the return to a surety of any property provided by him for the purposes of a security;
  (e)   otherwise set aside (in whole or in part) any duty imposed on the debtor or on a surety by virtue of the agreement or any related agreement;
  (f)   alter the terms of the agreement or of any related agreement;
  (g)   direct accounts to be taken, or (in Scotland) an accounting to be made, between any persons.
(2)   An order under this section may be made in connection with a credit agreement only—
  (a)   on an application made by the debtor or by a surety;
  (b)   at the instance of the debtor or a surety in any proceedings in any court to which the debtor and the creditor are parties, being proceedings to enforce the agreement or any related agreement; or
  (c)   at the instance of the debtor or a surety in any other proceedings in any court where the amount paid or payable under the agreement or any related agreement is relevant.

(3)   An order under this section may be made notwithstanding that its effect is to place on the creditor, or any associate or former associate of his, a burden in respect of an advantage enjoyed by another person.

(4)   An application under subsection (2)(a) may only be made—
   (a)   in England and Wales, to the county court;
   (b)   in Scotland, to the sheriff court;
   (c)   in Northern Ireland, to the High Court (subject to subsection (6)).

(5)   In Scotland such an application may be made in the sheriff court for the district in which the debtor or surety resides or carries on business.

(6)   In Northern Ireland such an application may be made to the county court if the credit agreement is an agreement under which the creditor provides the debtor with—
   (a)   fixed-sum credit not exceeding £15,000; or
   (b)   running-account credit on which the credit limit does not exceed £15,000.

(7)   Without prejudice to any provision which may be made by rules of court made in relation to county courts in Northern Ireland, such rules may provide that an application made by virtue of subsection (6) may be made in the county court for the division in which the debtor or surety resides or carries on business.

(8)   A party to any proceedings mentioned in subsection (2) shall be entitled, in accordance with rules of court, to have any person who might be the subject of an order under this section made a party to the proceedings.

(9)   If, in any such proceedings, the debtor or a surety alleges that the relationship between the creditor and the debtor is unfair to the debtor, it is for the creditor to prove to the contrary.

140C   Interpretation of ss 140A and 140B

(1)   In this section and in sections 140A and 140B 'credit agreement' means any agreement between an individual (the 'debtor') and any other person (the 'creditor') by which the creditor provides the debtor with credit of any amount.

(2)   References in this section and in sections 140A and 140B to the creditor or to the debtor under a credit agreement include—
   (a)   references to the person to whom his rights and duties under the agreement have passed by assignment or operation of law;
   (b)   where two or more persons are the creditor or the debtor, references to any one or more of those persons.

(3)   The definition of 'court' in section 189(1) does not apply for the purposes of sections 140A and 140B.

(4)   References in sections 140A and 140B to an agreement related to a credit agreement (the 'main agreement') are references to—
   (a)   a credit agreement consolidated by the main agreement;
   (b)   a linked transaction in relation to the main agreement or to a credit agreement within paragraph (a);
   (c)   a security provided in relation to the main agreement, to a credit agreement within paragraph (a) or to a linked transaction within paragraph (b).

(5)   In the case of a credit agreement which is not a regulated consumer credit agreement, for the purposes of subsection (4) a transaction shall be treated as being a linked transaction in relation to that agreement if it would have been such a transaction had that agreement been a regulated consumer credit agreement.

(6)   For the purposes of this section and section 140B the definitions of 'security' and 'surety' in section 189(1) apply (with any appropriate changes) in relation to—
   (a)   a credit agreement which is not a consumer credit agreement as if it were a consumer credit agreement; and
   (b)   a transaction which is a linked transaction by virtue of subsection (5).

(7)   For the purposes of this section a credit agreement (the 'earlier agreement') is consolidated by another credit agreement (the 'later agreement') if—

(a)   the later agreement is entered into by the debtor (in whole or in part) for purposes connected with debts owed by virtue of the earlier agreement; and

(b)   at any time prior to the later agreement being entered into the parties to the earlier agreement included—

(i)   the debtor under the later agreement; and

(ii)   the creditor under the later agreement or an associate or a former associate of his.

(8)   Further, if the later agreement is itself consolidated by another credit agreement (whether by virtue of this subsection or subsection (7)), then the earlier agreement is consolidated by that other agreement as well.

140D   Advice and information

The advice and information published by the OFT under section 229 of the Enterprise Act 2002 shall indicate how the OFT expects sections 140A to 140C of this Act to interact with Part 8 of that Act.]

Miscellaneous

141   Jurisdiction and parties

(1)   In England and Wales the county court shall have jurisdiction to hear and determine—

(a)   any action by the creditor or owner to enforce a regulated agreement or any security relating to it;

(b)   any action to enforce any linked transaction against the debtor or hirer or his relative,

and such an action shall not be brought in any other court.

(2)   Where an action or application is brought in the High Court which, by virtue of this Act, ought to have been brought in the county court it shall not be treated as improperly brought, but shall be transferred to the county court.

[(3)   In Scotland the sheriff court shall have jurisdiction to hear and determine any action falling within subsection (1) and such an action shall not be brought in any other court.

(3A)   Subject to subsection (3B) an action which is brought in the sheriff court by virtue of subsection (3) shall be brought only in one of the following courts, namely—

(a)   the court for the place where the debtor or hirer is domiciled (within the meaning of section 41 or 42 of the Civil Jurisdiction and Judgments Act 1982);

(b)   the court for the place where the debtor or hirer carries on business; and

(c)   where the purpose of the action is to assert, declare or determine proprietary or possessory rights, or rights of security, in or over moveable property, or to obtain authority to dispose of moveable property, the court for the place where the property is situated.

(3B)   Subsection (3A) shall not apply—

(a)   where rule 3 of Schedule 8 to the said Act of 1982 applies; or

(b)   where the jurisdiction of another court has been prorogated by an agreement entered into after the dispute has arisen.]

(4)   In Northern Ireland the county court shall have jurisdiction to hear and determine any action or application falling within subsection (1).

(5)   Except as may be provided by rules of court, all the parties to a regulated agreement, and any surety, shall be made parties to any proceedings relating to the agreement.

142   Power to declare rights of parties

(1)   Where under any provision of this Act a thing can be done by a creditor or owner on an enforcement order only, and either—

(a)   the court dismisses (except on technical grounds only) an application for an enforcement order, or

(b)   where no such application has been made or such an application has been dismissed on technical grounds only an interested party applies to the court for a declaration under this subsection,

the court may if it thinks just make a declaration that the creditor or owner is not entitled to do that thing, and thereafter no application for an enforcement order in respect of it shall be entertained.

(2)   Where—

(a)   a regulated agreement or linked transaction is cancelled under section 69(1), or becomes subject to section 69(2), or

(b)   a regulated agreement is terminated under section 91, and an interested party applies to the court for a declaration under this subsection, the court may make a declaration to that effect.

143, 144   [*Apply to Northern Ireland*]

PART X
ANCILLARY CREDIT BUSINESSES

Definitions

145   Types of ancillary credit business

(1)   An ancillary credit business is any business so far as it comprises or relates to—

(a)   credit brokerage,

(b)   debt-adjusting,

(c)   debt-counselling,

(d)   debt-collecting,

[(da) debt administration;]

(db) the provision of credit information services, or

(e)   the operation of a credit reference agency.

(2)   Subject to section 146(5) [and (5A)], credit brokerage is the effecting of introductions—

(a)   of individuals desiring to obtain credit—

(i)   to persons carrying on businesses to which this sub-paragraph applies, or

(ii)   in the case of an individual desiring to obtain credit to finance the acquisition or provision of a dwelling occupied by himself or his relative, to any person carrying on a business in the course of which he provides credit secured on land, or

(b)   of individuals desiring to obtain goods on hire to persons carrying on businesses to which this paragraph applies, or

(c)   of individuals desiring to obtain credit, or to obtain goods on hire, to other credit-brokers.

(3)   Subsection (2)(a)(i) applies to—

(a)   a consumer credit business;

(b)   a business which comprises or relates to consumer credit agreements being, otherwise than by virtue of section 16(5)(a), exempt agreements;

(c)   a business which comprises or relates to unregulated agreements where—

(i)   the [law applicable to] the agreement is the law of a country outside the United Kingdom, and

(ii)   if the [law applicable to] the agreement were the law of a part of the United Kingdom it would be a regulated consumer credit agreement.

(4)   Subsection (2)(b) applies to—

(a)   a consumer hire business;

[(aa) a business which comprises or relates to consumer hire agreements being, otherwise than by virtue of section 16(6), exempt agreements,]

(b)   a business which comprises or relates to unregulated agreements where—

    (i)   the [law applicable to] the agreement is the law of a country outside the United Kingdom, and

    (ii)   if the [law applicable to] the agreement were the law of a part of the United Kingdom it would be a regulated consumer hire agreement.

(5)   Subject to [section 146(5B) and (6)], debt-adjusting is, in relation to debts due under consumer credit agreements or consumer hire agreements,—

(a)   negotiating with the creditor or owner, on behalf of the debtor or hirer, terms for the discharge of a debt, or

(b)   taking over, in return for payments by the debtor or hirer, his obligation to discharge a debt, or

(c)   any similar activity concerned with the liquidation of a debt.

(6)   Subject to section 146(6), debt-counselling is the giving of advice to debtors or hirers about the liquidation of debts due under consumer credit agreements or consumer hire agreements.

(7)   Subject to [section 146(5C) and (6)], debt-collecting is the taking of steps to procure payment of debts due under consumer credit agreements or consumer hire agreements.

[(7A)   Subject to section 146(7), debt administration is the taking of steps—

(a)   to perform duties under a consumer credit agreement or a consumer hire agreement on behalf of the creditor or owner, or

(b)   to exercise or to enforce rights under such an agreement on behalf of the creditor or owner,

so far as the taking of such steps is not debt-collecting.

(7B)   A person provides credit information services if—

(a)   he takes any steps mentioned in subsection (7C) on behalf of an individual; or

(b)   he gives advice to an individual in relation to the taking of any such steps.

(7C)   Those steps are taken with a view—

(a)   to ascertaining whether a credit information agency (other than that person himself if he is one) holds information relevant to the financial standing of an individual;

(b)   to ascertaining the contents of such information held by such an agency;

(c)   to securing the correction of, the omission of anything from, or the making of any other kind of modification of, such information so held; or

(d)   to securing that such agency which holds such information—

    (i)   stops holding it; or

    (ii)   does not provide it to another person.

(7D)   In subsection (7C) 'credit information agency' means—

(a)   a person carrying on a consumer credit business or a consumer hire business;

(b)   a person carrying on a business so far as it comprises or relates to credit brokerage, debt-adjusting, debt-counselling, debt-collecting, debt administration or the operation of a credit reference agency;

(c)   a person carrying on a business which would be a consumer credit business except that it comprises or relates to consumer credit agreements being, otherwise than by virtue of section 16(5)(a), exempt agreements; or

(d)   a person carrying on a business which would be a consumer hire business except that it comprises or relates to consumer hire agreements being, otherwise than by virtue of section 16(6), exempt agreements.]

(8)   A credit reference agency is a person carrying on a business comprising the furnishing of persons with information relevant to the financial standing of individuals, being information collected by the agency for that purpose.

146 Exceptions from section 145

(1) A barrister or advocate acting in that capacity is not to be treated as doing so in the course of any ancillary credit business.

(2) A solicitor engaging in contentious business (as defined in [section 87(1) of the Solicitors Act 1974]) is not to be treated as doing so in the course of any ancillary credit business.

(3) A solicitor within the meaning of the [Solicitors (Scotland) Act 1980] engaging in business done in or for the purposes of proceedings before a court or before an arbiter is not to be treated as doing so in the course of any ancillary credit business.

(4) A solicitor in Northern Ireland engaging in [contentious business (as defined in Article 3(2) of the Solicitors (Northern Ireland) Order 1976], is not to be treated as doing so in the course of any ancillary credit business.

(5) For the purposes of section 145(2), introductions effected by an individual by canvassing off trade premises either debtor-creditor-supplier agreements falling within section 12(a) or regulated consumer hire agreements shall be disregarded if—

   (a) the introductions are not effected by him in the capacity of an employee, and

   (b) he does not by any other method effect introductions falling within section 145(2).

[5(A) It is not credit brokerage for a person to effect the introduction of an individual desiring to obtain credit if the introduction is made—

   (a) to an authorised person, within the meaning of the 2000 Act, who has permission under that Act to enter as lender into relevant agreements; or

   (b) to a qualifying broker,

with a view to that individual obtaining credit under a relevant agreement.

(5B) It is not debt-adjusting for a person to carry on an activity mentioned in paragraph (a), (b) or (c) of section 145(5) if—

   (a) the debt in question is due under a relevant agreement; and

   (b) that activity is a regulated activity for the purposes of the 2000 Act.

(5C) It is not debt-counselling for a person to give advice to debtors about the liquidation of debts if—

   (a) the debt in question is due under a relevant agreement; and

   (b) giving that advice is a regulated activity for the purposes of the 2000 Act.

(5D) In this section—

'the 2000 Act' means the Financial Services and Markets Act 2000;

'relevant agreement' means [an] agreement which is secured by a land mortgage, where entering into that agreement as lender is a regulated activity for the purposes of the 2000 Act;

'qualifying broker' means a person who may effect introductions of the kind mentioned in subsection (5A) without contravening the general prohibition, within the meaning of section 19 of the 2000 Act,

and references to 'regulated activities' and the definition of 'qualifying broker' must be read with—

   (a) section 22 of the 2000 Act (regulated activities: power to specify classes of activity and categories of investment);

   (b) any order for the time being in force under that section; and

   (c) Schedule 2 to that Act.].

(6) It is not debt-adjusting, debt-counselling or debt-collecting for a person to do anything in relation to a debt arising under an agreement if [any of the following conditions is satisfied]—

   [(aa) that he is the creditor or owner under the agreement, or]

   (c) that he is the supplier in relation to the agreement, or

   (d) that he is a credit-broker who has acquired the business of the person who was the supplier in relation to the agreement, or

(e)   that he is a person prevented by subsection (5) from being treated as a credit-broker, and the agreement was made in consequence of an introduction (whether made by him or another person) which, under subsection (5), is to be disregarded.

[(7)   It is not debt administration for a person to take steps to perform duties, or to exercise or enforce rights, under an agreement on behalf of the creditor or owner if any of the conditions mentioned in subsection (6)(aa) to (e) is satisfied in relation to that person.]

Licensing

147   Application of Part III

[. . .]

(2)   Without prejudice to the generality of section 26, regulations under that section [. . .] may include provisions regulating the collection and dissemination of information by credit reference agencies.

148   Agreement for services of unlicensed trader

(1)   An agreement for the services of a person carrying on ancillary credit business (the 'trader'), if made when the trader was unlicensed, is enforceable against the other party (the 'customer') only where the [OFT] has made an order under subsection (2) which applies to the agreement.

(2)   The trader or his successor in title may apply to the [OFT] for an order that agreements within subsection (1) are to be treated as if made when the trader was licensed.

(3)   Unless the [OFT] determines to make an order under subsection (2) in accordance with the application, [it] shall, before determining the application, by notice—

(a)   inform the trader, giving [its] reasons, that, as the case may be, [it] is minded to refuse the application, or to grant it in terms different from those applied for, describing them, and

(b)   invite the trader to submit to the [OFT] representations in support of his application in accordance with section 34.

(4)   In determining whether or not to make an order under subsection (2) in respect of any period the [OFT] shall consider, in addition to any other relevant factors,—

(a)   how far, if at all, customers under agreements made by the trader during that period were prejudiced by the trader's conduct,

(b)   whether or not the [OFT] would have been likely to grant a licence covering that period on an application by the trader, and

(c)   the degree of culpability for the failure to obtain a licence.

(5)   If the [OFT] thinks fit, [it] may in an order under subsection (2)—

(a)   limit the order to specified agreements, or agreements of a specified description or made at a specified time;

(b)   make the order conditional on the doing of specified acts by the trader.

[(6)   This section does not apply to an agreement made by a consumer credit EEA firm unless at the time it was made that firm was precluded from entering into it as a result of—

(a)   a consumer credit prohibition imposed under section 203 of the Financial Services and Markets Act 2000; or

(b)   a restriction imposed on the firm under section 204 of that Act.]

149   Regulated agreements made on introductions by unlicensed credit-broker

(1)   A regulated agreement made by a debtor or hirer who, for the purpose of making that agreement, was introduced to the creditor or owner by an unlicensed credit-broker is enforceable against the debtor or hirer only where—

(a)   on the application of the credit-broker, the [OFT] has made an order under section 148(2) in respect of a period including the time when the introduction was made, and the order does not (whether in general terms or specifically) exclude the application of this paragraph to the regulated agreement, or

(b)   the [OFT] has made an order under subsection (2) which applies to the agreement.

(2)   Where during any period individuals were introduced to a person carrying on a consumer credit business or consumer hire business by an unlicensed credit-broker for the purpose of making regulated agreements with the person carrying on that business, that person or his successor in title may apply to the [OFT] for an order that regulated agreements so made are to be treated as if the credit-broker had been licensed at the time of the introduction.

(3)   Unless the [OFT] determines to make an order under subsection (2) in accordance with the application, [it] shall, before determining the application, by notice—

(a)   inform the applicant, giving [its] reasons, that, as the case may be, [it] is minded to refuse the application, or to grant it in terms different from those applied for, describing them, and

(b)   invite the applicant to submit to the [OFT] representations in support of his application in accordance with section 34.

(4)   In determining whether or not to make an order under subsection (2) the [OFT] shall consider, in addition to any other relevant factors—

(a)   how far, if at all, debtors or hirers under regulated agreements to which the application relates were prejudiced by the credit-broker's conduct, and

(b)   the degree of culpability of the applicant in facilitating the carrying on by the credit-broker of his business when unlicensed.

(5)   If the [OFT] thinks fit, [it] may in an order under subsection (2)—

(a)   limit the order to specified agreements, or agreements of a specified description or made at a specified time;

(b)   make the order conditional on the doing of specified acts by the applicant.

[(6)   For the purposes of this section 'unlicensed credit-broker' does not include a consumer credit EEA firm unless at the time the introduction was made that firm was precluded from making it as a result of—

(a)   a consumer credit prohibition imposed under section 203 of the Financial Services and Markets Act 2000; or

(b)   a restriction imposed on the firm under section 204 of that Act.]

[. . .]

Seeking business

151   Advertisements

(1)   Sections 44 to 47 apply to an advertisement published for the purposes of a business of credit brokerage carried on by any person, whether it advertises the services of that person or the services of persons to whom he effects introductions, as they apply to an advertisement to which Part IV applies.

(2)   Sections 44, 46 and 47 apply to an advertisement, published for the purposes of a business carried on by the advertiser, indicating that he is willing to advise on debts, [to] engage in transactions concerned with the liquidation of debts [or to provide credit information services], as they apply to an advertisement to which Part IV applies.

[(2A)   An advertisement does not fall within subsection (1) or (2) in so far as it is a communication of an invitation or inducement to engage in investment activity within the meaning of section 21 of the Financial Services and Markets Act 2000, other than an exempt generic communication (as defined in section 43(3B).]

(3)   The Secretary of State may by order provide that an advertisement pub-

lished for the purposes of a business of credit brokerage, debt-adjusting [debt-counselling or the provision of credit information services] shall not fall within subsection (1) or (2) if it is of a description specified in the order.

(4)   An advertisement [(other than one for credit information services)] does not fall within subsection (2) if it indicates that the advertiser is not willing to act in relation to consumer credit agreements and consumer hire agreements.

(5)   In subsections (1) and (3) 'credit brokerage' includes the effecting of introductions of individuals desiring to obtain credit to any person carrying on a business in the course of which he provides credit secured on land.

152   Application of sections 52 to 54 to credit brokerage etc

(1)   Sections 52 to 54 apply to a business of credit brokerage, debt-adjusting [, debt-counselling or the provision of credit information services] as they apply to a consumer credit business.

(2)   In their application to a business of credit brokerage, sections 52 and 53 shall apply to the giving of quotations and information about the business of any person to whom the credit-broker effects introductions as well as to the giving of quotations and information about his own business.

153   Definition of canvassing off trade premises (agreements for ancillary credit services)

(1)   An individual (the 'canvasser') canvasses off trade premises the services of a person carrying on an ancillary credit business if he solicits the entry of another individual (the 'consumer') into an agreement for the provision to the consumer of those services by making oral representations to the consumer, or any other individual, during a visit by the canvasser to any place (not excluded by subsection (2)) where the consumer, or that other individual as the case may be, is, being a visit—

    (a)   carried out for the purpose of making such oral representations to individuals who are at that place, but

    (b)   not carried out in response to a request made on a previous occasion.

(2)   A place is excluded from subsection (1) if it is a place where (whether on a permanent or temporary basis)—

    (a)   the ancillary credit business is carried on, or

    (b)   any business is carried on by the canvasser or the person whose employee or agent the canvasser is, or by the consumer.

154   Prohibition of canvassing certain ancillary credit services off trade premises

It is an offence to canvass off trade premises the services of a person carrying on a business of credit-brokerage, debt-adjusting [, debt-counselling or the provision of credit information services].

155   Right to recover brokerage fees

(1)   [Subject to subsection (2A)] the excess over [£5] of a fee or commission for his services charged by a credit-broker to an individual to whom this subsection applies shall cease to be payable or, as the case may be, shall be recoverable by the individual if the introduction does not result in his entering into a relevant agreement within the six months following the introduction (disregarding any agreement which is cancelled under section 69(1) or becomes subject to section 69(2)).

(2)   Subsection (1) applies to an individual who sought an introduction for a purpose which would have been fulfilled by his entry into—

    (a)   a regulated agreement, or

    (b)   in the case of an individual such as is referred to in section 145(2)(a)(ii), an agreement for credit secured on land, or

    (c)   an agreement such as is referred to in section 145(3)(b) or (c) or (4)(b).

[(2A)   But subsection (1) does not apply where—

(a)   the fee or commission relates to the effecting of an introduction of a kind mentioned in section 146(5A); and

(b)   the person charging that fee or commission is an authorised person or an appointed representative, within the meaning of the Financial Services and Markets Act 2000.]

(3)   An agreement is a relevant agreement for the purposes of subsection (1) in relation to an individual if it is an agreement such as is referred to in subsection (2) in relation to that individual.

(4)   In the case of an individual desiring to obtain credit under a consumer credit agreement, any sum payable or paid by him to a credit-broker otherwise than as a fee or commission for the credit-broker's services shall for the purposes of subsection (1) be treated as such a fee or commission if it enters, or would enter, into the total charge for credit.

Entry into agreements

156   Entry into agreements
Regulations may make provision, in relation to agreements entered into in the course of a business of credit brokerage, debt-adjusting [, debt-counselling or the provision of credit information services], corresponding, with such modifications as the Secretary of State thinks fit, to the provision which is or may be made by or under sections 55, 60, 61, 62, 63, 65, 127, 179 or 180 in relation to agreements to which those sections apply.

Credit reference agencies

157   Duty to disclose name etc of agency
(1)   A creditor, owner or negotiator, within the prescribed period after receiving a request in writing to that effect from the debtor or hirer, shall give him notice of the name and address of any credit reference agency from which the creditor, owner or negotiator has, during the antecedent negotiations, applied for information about his financial standing.

(2)   Subsection (1) does not apply to a request received more than 28 days after the termination of the antecedent negotiations, whether on the making of the regulated agreement or otherwise.

(3)   If the creditor, owner or negotiator fails to comply with subsection (1) he commits an offence.

158   Duty of agency to disclose filed information
(1)   A credit reference agency, within the prescribed period after receiving,—

(a)   [a request in writing to that effect from a consumer], and

(b)   such particulars as the agency may reasonably require to enable them to identify the file, and

(c)   a fee of [£2],

shall give the consumer a copy of the file relating to [it] kept by the agency.

(2)   When giving a copy of the file under subsection (1), the agency shall also give the consumer a statement in the prescribed form of [the consumer's] rights under section 159.

(3)   If the agency does not keep a file relating to [the consumer] it shall give the consumer notice of that fact, but need not return any money paid.

(4)   If the agency contravenes any provision of this section it commits an offence.

[(4A)   In this section 'consumer' means—

(a)   a partnership consisting of two or three persons not all of whom are bodies corporate; or

(b)   an unincorporated body of persons which does not consist entirely of bodies corporate and is not a partnership.]

(5)   In this Act 'file', in relation to an individual, means all the information about him kept by a credit reference agency, regardless of how the information is stored, and 'copy of the file', as respects information not in plain English, means a transcript reduced into plain English.

159   Correction of wrong information

[(1)   Any individual (the 'objector') given—

(a)   information under section 7 of the Data Protection Act 1998 by a credit reference agency, or

(b)   information under section 158,

who considers that an entry in his file is incorrect, and that if it is not corrected he is likely to be prejudiced, may give notice to the agency requiring it either to remove the entry from the file or amend it.]

(2)   Within 28 days after receiving a notice under subsection (1), the agency shall by notice inform the [objector] that it has—

(a)   removed the entry from the file, or

(b)   amended the entry, or

(c)   taken no action,

and if the notice states that the agency has amended the entry it shall include a copy of the file so far as it comprises the amended entry.

(3)   Within 28 days after receiving a notice under subsection (2), or where no such notice was given, within 28 days after the expiry of the period mentioned in subsection (2), the [objector] may, unless he has been informed by the agency that it has removed the entry from his file, serve a further notice on the agency requiring it to add to the file an accompanying notice of correction (not exceeding 200 words) drawn up by the [objector], and include a copy of it when furnishing information included in or based on that entry.

(4)   Within 28 days after receiving a notice under subsection (3), the agency, unless it intends to apply to the [the relevant authority] under subsection (5), shall by notice inform the [objector] that it has received the notice under subsection (3) and intends to comply with it.

(5)   If—

(a)   the [objector] has not received a notice under subsection (4) within the time required, or

(b)   it appears to the agency that it would be improper for it to publish a notice of correction because it is incorrect, or unjustly defames any person, or is frivolous or scandalous, or is for any other reason unsuitable, the [objector] or, as the case may be, the agency may, in the prescribed manner and on payment of the specified fee, apply to [the relevant authority], who may make such order on the application as it thinks fit.

(6)   If a person to whom an order under this section is directed fails to comply with it within the period specified in the order he commits an offence.

[(7)   The Information Commissioner may vary or revoke any order made by him under this section.

(8)   In this section 'the relevant authority' means—

(a)   where the objector is a partnership or other unincorporated body of persons, the [OFT], and

(b)   in any other case, the Information Commissioner.]

160   Alternative procedure for business consumers

(1)   The [OFT], on an application made by a credit reference agency, may direct that this section shall apply to the agency if [it] is satisfied—

(a)   that compliance with section 158 in the case of consumers who carry on a business would adversely affect the service provided to its customers by the agency, and

(b)   that, having regard to the methods employed by the agency and to any other relevant facts, it is probable that consumers carrying on a business would not be prejudiced by the making of the direction.

(2) Where an agency to which this section applies receives a request, particulars and a fee under section 158(1) from a consumer who carries on a business and section 158(3) does not apply, the agency, instead of complying with section 158, may elect to deal with the matter under the following subsections.

(3) Instead of giving the consumer a copy of the file, the agency shall within the prescribed period give notice to the consumer that it is proceeding under this section, and by notice give the consumer such information included in or based on entries in the file as the [OFT] may direct, together with a statement in the prescribed form of the consumer's rights under subsections (4) and (5).

(4) If within 28 days after receiving the information given [to the consumer] under subsection (3), or such longer period as the [OFT] may allow, the consumer—

(a)   gives notice to the [OFT] that [the consumer] is dissatisfied with the information, and

(b)   satisfies the [OFT] that [the consumer] has taken such steps in relation to the agency as may be reasonable with a view to removing the cause of [the consumer's] dissatisfaction, and

(c)   pays the [OFT] the specified fee,

the [OFT] may direct the agency to give the [OFT] a copy of the file, and the [OFT] may disclose to the consumer such of the information on the file as the [OFT] thinks fit.

(5) Section 159 applies with any necessary modifications to information given to the consumer under this section as it applies to information given under section 158.

(6) If an agency making an election under subsection (2) fails to comply with subsection (3) or (4) it commits an offence.

[(7)   In this section 'consumer' has the same meaning as in section 158.]

PART XI
ENFORCEMENT OF ACT

161   Enforcement authorities

(1) The following authorities ('enforcement authorities') have a duty to enforce this Act and regulations made under it—

(a)   the [OFT],

(b)   in Great Britain, the local weights and measures authority,

(c)   in Northern Ireland, the Department of Commerce for Northern Ireland.

[. . .]

(3) Every local weights and measures authority shall, whenever the [OFT] requires, report to [it] in such form and with such particulars as [it] requires on the exercise of their functions under this Act.

[. . .]

162   Powers of entry and inspection

(1) A duly authorised officer of an enforcement authority, at all reasonable hours and on production, if required, of his credentials, may—

(a)   in order to ascertain whether a breach of any provision of or under this Act has been committed, inspect any goods and enter any premises (other than premises used only as a dwelling);

(b)   if he has reasonable cause to suspect that a breach of any provision of or under this Act has been committed, in order to ascertain whether it has been committed, require any person—

(i)   carrying on, or employed in connection with, a business to produce any [. . .] documents relating to it; or

(ii) having control of any information relating to a business [to provide him with that information] [. . .];

(c)   if he has reasonable cause to believe that a breach of any provision of or under this Act has been committed, seize and detain any goods in order to ascertain (by testing or otherwise) whether such a breach has been committed;

(d)   seize and detain any goods, [. . .] or documents which he has reason to believe may be required as evidence in proceedings for an offence under this Act;

(e)   for the purpose of exercising his powers under this subsection to seize goods, [. . .] or documents, but only if and to the extent that it is reasonably necessary for securing that the provision of this Act and of any regulations made under it are duly observed, require any person having authority to do so to break open any container and, if that person does not comply, break it open himself.

(2)   An officer seizing goods, [. . .] or documents in exercise of his powers under this section shall not do so without informing the person he seizes them from.

(3)   If a justice of the peace, on sworn information in writing, or, in Scotland, a sheriff or a magistrate or justice of the peace, on evidence on oath,—

(a)   is satisfied that there is reasonable ground to believe either—

(i) that any goods, [. . .] or documents which a duly authorised officer has power to inspect under this section are on any premises and their inspection is likely to disclose evidence of a breach of any provision of or under this Act; or

(ii) that a breach of any provision of or under this Act has been, is being or is about to be committed on any premises; and

(b)   is also satisfied either—

(i) that admission to the premises has been or is likely to be refused and that notice of intention to apply for a warrant under this subsection has been given to the occupier; or

(ii) that an application for admission, or the giving of such a notice, would defeat the object of the entry or that the premises are unoccupied or that the occupier is temporarily absent and it might defeat the object of the entry to wait for his return, the justice or, as the case may be, the sheriff or magistrate may by warrant under his hand, which shall continue in force for a period of one month, authorise an officer of an enforcement authority to enter the premises (by force if need be).

(4)   An officer entering premises by virtue of this section may take such other persons and equipment with him as he thinks necessary; and on leaving premises entered by virtue of a warrant under subsection (3) shall, if they are unoccupied or the occupier is temporarily absent, leave them as effectively secured against trespassers as he found them.

(5)   Regulations may provide that, in cases described by the regulations, an officer of a local weights and measures authority is not to be taken to be duly authorised for the purposes of this section unless he is authorised by the [OFT].

(6)   A person who is not a duly authorised officer of an enforcement authority, but purports to act as such under this section, commits an offence.

[. . .]

[(8)   References in this section to a breach of any provision of or under this Act do not include references to—

(a)   a failure to comply with a requirement imposed under section 33A or 33B;

(b)   a failure to comply with section 36A; or

(c)   a failure in relation to which the OFT can apply for an order under section 36E.]

163   Compensation for loss

(1)   Where, in exercising his powers under section 162, an officer of an enforcement authority seizes and detains goods and their owner suffers loss by reason of—

(a)   that seizure, or

(b)   the loss, damage or deterioration of the goods during detention,

then, unless the owner is convicted of an offence under this Act committed in relation to the goods, the authority shall compensate him for the loss so suffered.

(2)   Any dispute as to the right to or amount of any compensation under subsection (1) shall be determined by arbitration.

164   Power to make test purchases etc

(1)   An enforcement authority may—

(a)   make, or authorise any of their officers to make on their behalf, such purchases of goods; and

(b)   authorise any of their officers to procure the provision of such services or facilities or to enter into such agreements or other transactions, as may appear to them expedient for determining whether any provisions made by or under this Act are being complied with.

(2)   Any act done by an officer authorised to do it under subsection (1) shall be treated for the purposes of this Act as done by him as an individual on his own behalf.

(3)   Any goods seized by an officer under this Act may be tested, and in the event of such a test he shall inform the person mentioned in section 162(2) of the test results.

(4)   Where any test leads to proceedings under this Act, the enforcement authority shall—

(a)   if the goods were purchased, inform the person they were purchased from of the test results, and

(b)   allow any person against whom the proceedings are taken to have the goods tested on his behalf if it is reasonably practicable to do so.

165   Obstruction of authorised officers

(1)   Any person who—

(a)   wilfully obstructs an officer of an enforcement authority acting in pursuance of this Act; or

(b)   wilfully fails to comply with any requirement properly made to him by such an officer under section 162; or

(c)   without reasonable cause fails to give such an officer (so acting) other assistance or information he may reasonably require in performing his functions under this Act, commits an offence.

[(1A)   A failure to give assistance or information shall not constitute an offence under subsection (1)(c) if it is also—

(a)   a failure to comply with a requirement imposed under section 33A or 33B;

(b)   a failure to comply with section 36A; or

(c)   a failure in relation to which the OFT can apply for an order under section 36E.]

(2)   If any person, in giving such information as is mentioned in subsection (1)(c), makes any statement which he knows to be false, he commits an offence.

(3)   Nothing in this section requires a person to answer any question or give any information if to do so might incriminate that person or (where that person is [married or a civil partner) the spouse or civil partner] of that person.

166   Notification of convictions and judgments to [OFT]

Where a person is convicted of an offence or has a judgment given against him by or before any court in the United Kingdom and it appears to the court—

(a)   having regard to the functions of the [OFT] under this Act, that the conviction or judgment should be brought to the [OFT's] attention, and

(b)   that it may not be brought to [its] attention unless arrangements for that purpose are made by the court,

the court may make such arrangements notwithstanding that the proceedings have been finally disposed of.

167   Penalties

(1)   An offence under a provision of this Act specified in column 1 of Schedule 1 is triable in the mode or modes indicated in column 3, and on conviction is punishable as indicated in column 4 (where a period of time indicates the maximum term of imprisonment, and a monetary amount indicates the maximum fine, for the offence in question).

(2)   A person who contravenes any regulations made under section 44, 52, 53, or 112, or made under section 26 by virtue of section 54, commits an offence.

168   Defences

(1)   In any proceedings for an offence under this Act it is a defence for the person charged to prove—

(a)   that his act or omission was due to a mistake, or to reliance on information supplied to him, or to an act or omission by another person, or to an accident or some other cause beyond his control, and

(b)   that he took all reasonable precautions and exercised all due diligence to avoid such an act or omission by himself or any person under his control.

(2)   If in any case the defence provided by subsection (1) involves the allegation that the act or omission was due to an act or omission by another person or to reliance on information supplied by another person, the person charged shall not, without leave of the court, be entitled to rely on that defence unless, within a period ending seven clear days before the hearing, he has served on the prosecutor a notice giving such information identifying or assisting in the identification of that other person as was then in his possession.

169   Offences by bodies corporate

Where at any time a body corporate commits an offence under this Act with the consent or connivance of, or because of neglect by, any individual, the individual commits the like offence if at that time—

(a)   he is a director, manager, secretary or similar officer of the body corporate, or

(b)   he is purporting to act as such an officer, or

(c)   the body corporate is managed by its members of whom he is one.

170   No further sanctions for breach of Act

(1)   A breach of any requirement made (otherwise than by any court) by or under this Act shall incur no civil or criminal sanction as being such a breach, except to the extent (if any) expressly provided by or under this Act.

(2)   In exercising [its] functions under this Act the [OFT] may take account of any matter appearing to [it] to constitute a breach of a requirement made by or under this Act, whether or not any sanction for that breach is provided by or under this Act and, if it is so provided, whether or not proceedings have been brought in respect of the breach.

(3)   Subsection (1) does not prevent the grant of an injunction, or the making of an order of certiorari, mandamus or prohibition or as respects Scotland the grant of an interdict or of an order under [section 45 of the Court of Session Act 1988] (order for specific performance of statutory duty).

171   Onus of proof in various proceedings

(1)   If an agreement contains a term signifying that in the opinion of the parties

section 10(3)(b)(iii) does not apply to the agreement, it shall be taken not to apply unless the contrary is proved.

(2)   It shall be assumed in any proceedings, unless the contrary is proved, that when a person initiated a transaction as mentioned in section 19(1)(c) he knew the principal agreement had been made, or contemplated that it might be made.

(3)   Regulations under section 44 or 52 may make provision as to the onus of proof in any proceedings to enforce the regulations.

(4)   In proceedings brought by the creditor under a credit-token agreement—

(a)   it is for the creditor to prove that the credit-token was lawfully supplied to the debtor, and was accepted by him, and

(b)   if the debtor alleges that any use made of the credit-token was not authorised by him, it is for the creditor to prove either—

(i)   that the use was so authorised, or

(ii)   that the use occurred before the creditor had been given notice under section 84(3).

(5)   In proceedings under section 50(1) in respect of a document received by a minor at any school or other educational establishment for minors, it is for the person sending it to him at that establishment to prove that he did not know or suspect it to be such an establishment.

(6)   In proceedings under section 119(1) it is for the pawnee to prove that he had reasonable cause to refuse to allow the pawn to be redeemed.

[. . .]

172   Statements by creditor or owner to be binding

(1)   A statement by a creditor or owner is binding on him if given under—
section 77(1),
section 78(1),
section 79(1),
section 97(1),
section 107(1)(c),
section 108(1)(c), or
section 109(1)(c).

(2)   Where a trader—

(a)   gives a customer a notice in compliance with section 103(1)(b), or

(b)   gives a customer a notice under section 103(1) asserting that the customer is not indebted to him under an agreement,
the notice is binding on the trader.

(3)   Where in proceedings before any court—

(a)   it is sought to reply on a statement or notice given as mentioned in subsection (1) or (2), and

(b)   the statement or notice is shown to be incorrect, the court may direct such relief (if any) to be given to the creditor or owner from the operation of subsection (1) or (2) as appears to the court to be just.

173   Contracting-out forbidden

(1)   A term contained in a regulated agreement or linked transaction, or in any other agreement relating to an actual or prospective regulated agreement or linked transaction, is void if, and to the extent that, it is inconsistent with a provision for the protection of the debtor or hirer or his relative or any surety contained in this Act or in any regulation made under this Act.

(2)   Where a provision specifies the duty or liability of the debtor or hirer or his relative or any surety in certain circumstances, a term is inconsistent with that provision if it purports to impose, directly or indirectly, an additional duty or liability on him in those circumstances.

(3)   Notwithstanding subsection (1), a provision of this Act under which a thing may be done in relation to any person on an order of the court or the [OFT] only shall not be taken to prevent its being done at any time with that person's consent

given at that time, but the refusal of such consent shall not give rise to any liability.

PART XII
SUPPLEMENTAL

[. . .]

174A Powers to require provision of information or documents etc

(1)   Every power conferred on a relevant authority by or under this Act (however expressed) to require the provision or production of information or documents includes the power—

(a)   to require information to be provided or produced in such form as the authority may specify, including, in relation to information recorded otherwise than in a legible form, in a legible form;

(b)   to take copies of, or extracts from, any documents provided or produced by virtue of the exercise of the power;

(c)   to require the person who is required to provide or produce any information or document by virtue of the exercise of the power—

(i)   to state, to the best of his knowledge and belief, where the information or document is;

(ii)   to give an explanation of the information or document;

(iii)   to secure that any information provided or produced, whether in a document or otherwise, is verified in such manner as may be specified by the authority;

(iv)   to secure that any document provided or produced is authenticated in such manner as may be so specified;

(d)   to specify a time at or by which a requirement imposed by virtue of paragraph (c) must be complied with.

(2)   Every power conferred on a relevant authority by or under this Act (however expressed) to inspect or to seize documents at any premises includes the power to take copies of, or extracts from, any documents inspected or seized by virtue of the exercise of the power.

(3)   But a relevant authority has no power under this Act—

(a)   to require another person to provide or to produce,

(b)   to seize from another person, or

(c)   to require another person to give access to premises for the purposes of the inspection of,

any information or document which the other person would be entitled to refuse to provide or produce in proceedings in the High Court on the grounds of legal professional privilege or (in Scotland) in proceedings in the Court of Session on the grounds of confidentiality of communications.

(4)   In subsection (3) 'communications' means—

(a)   communications between a professional legal adviser and his client;

(b)   communications made in connection with or in contemplation of legal proceedings and for the purposes of those proceedings.

(5)   In this section 'relevant authority' means—

(a)   the OFT or an enforcement authority (other than the OFT);

(b)   an officer of the OFT or of an enforcement authority (other than the OFT).]

175   Duty of persons deemed to be agents

Where under this Act a person is deemed to receive a notice or payment as agent of the creditor or owner under a regulated agreement, he shall be deemed to be under a contractual duty to the creditor or owner to transmit the notice, or remit the payment, to him forthwith.

176 Service of documents

(1) A document to be served under this Act by one person ('the server') on another person ('the subject') is to be treated as properly served on the subject if dealt with as mentioned in the following subsections.

(2) The document may be delivered or sent [by an appropriate method] to the subject, or addressed to him by name and left at his proper address.

(3) For the purposes of this Act, a document sent [by an appropriate method] to, or left at, the address last known to the server as the address of a person shall be treated as sent by post to, or left at, his proper address.

(4) Where the document is to be served on the subject as being the person having any interest in land, and it is not practicable after reasonable inquiry to ascertain the subject's name or address, the document may be served by—

(a) addressing it to the subject by the description of the person having that interest in the land (naming it), and

(b) delivering the document to some responsible person on the land or affixing it, or a copy of it, in a conspicuous position on the land.

(5) Where a document to be served on the subject as being a debtor, hirer or surety, or as having any other capacity relevant for the purposes of this Act, is served at any time on another person who—

(a) is the person last known to the server as having that capacity, but

(b) before that time had ceased to have it, the document shall be treated as having been served at that time on the subject.

(6) Anything done to a document in relation to a person who (whether to the knowledge of the server or not) has died shall be treated for the purposes of subsection (5) as service of the document on that person if it would have been so treated had he not died.

[(7) The following enactments shall not be construed as authorising service on the Public Trustee (in England and Wales) or the Probate Judge (in Northern Ireland) of any document which is to be served under this Act—

section 9 of the Administration of Estates Act 1925;

section 3 of the Administration of Estates Act (Northern Ireland) 1955.]

(8) References in the preceding subsections to the serving of a document on a person include the giving of the document to that person.

[176A Electronic transmission of documents

(1) A document is transmitted in accordance with this subsection if—

(a) the person to whom it is transmitted agrees that it may be delivered to him by being transmitted to a particular electronic address in a particular electronic form,

(b) it is transmitted to that address in that form, and

(c) the form in which the document is transmitted is such that any information in the document which is addressed to the person to whom the document is transmitted is capable of being stored for future reference for an appropriate period in a way which allows the information to be reproduced without change.

(2) A document transmitted in accordance with subsection (1) shall, unless the contrary is proved, be treated for the purposes of this Act, except section 69, as having been delivered on the working day immediately following the day on which it is transmitted.

(3) In this section, 'electronic address' includes any number of addresses used for the purposes of receiving electronic communications.]

177 Saving for registered charges

(1) Nothing in this Act affects the rights of a creditor in a heritable security who—

(a) became the creditor under a transfer for value without notice of any defect in the title arising (apart from this section) by virtue of this Act; or

(b)   derives title from such a creditor.

(2)   Nothing in this Act affects the operation of section 41 of the Conveyancing (Scotland) Act 1924 (protection of purchasers), or of that section as applied to standard securities by section 32 of the Conveyancing and Feudal Reform (Scotland) Act 1970.

(3)   Subsection (1) does not apply to a creditor carrying on [a consumer credit business, a consumer hire business or a business of debt-collecting or debt administration].

(4)   Where, by virtue of subsection (1), a land mortgage is enforced which apart from this section would be treated as never having effect, the original creditor or owner shall be liable to indemnify the debtor or hirer against any loss thereby suffered by him.

(5)   [Substitutes subsections (1) to (3) for Scotland.]

(6)   [Applies to Northern Ireland.]

178   Local Acts

The Secretary of State or the Department of Commerce for Northern Ireland may by order make such amendments or repeals of any provision of any local Act as appears to the Secretary of State or, as the case may be, the Department, necessary or expedient in consequence of the replacement by this Act of the enactments relating to pawnbrokers and moneylenders.

Regulations, orders, etc

179   Power to prescribe form etc of secondary documents

(1)   Regulations may be made as to the form and content of credit-cards, trading-checks, receipts, vouchers and other documents or things issued by creditors, owners or suppliers under or in connection with regulated agreements or by other persons in connection with linked transactions, and may in particular—

(a)   require specified information to be included in the prescribed manner in documents, and other specified material to be excluded;

(b)   contain requirements to ensure that specified information is clearly brought to the attention of the debtor or hirer, or his relative, and that one part of a document is not given insufficient or excessive prominence compared with another.

(2)   If a person issues any document or thing in contravention of regulations under subsection (1) then, as from the time of the contravention but without prejudice to anything done before it, this Act shall apply as if the regulated agreement had been improperly executed by reason of a contravention of regulations under section 60(1).

180   Power to prescribe form etc of copies

(1)   Regulations may be made as to the form and content of documents to be issued as copies of any executed agreement, security instrument or other document referred to in this Act, and may in particular—

(a)   require specified information to be included in the prescribed manner in any copy, and contain requirements to ensure that such information is clearly brought to the attention of a reader of the copy;

(b)   authorise the omission from a copy of certain material contained in the original, or the inclusion of such material in condensed form.

(2)   A duty imposed by any provision of this Act (except section 35) to supply a copy of any document—

(a)   is not satisfied unless the copy supplied is in the prescribed form and conforms to the prescribed requirements;

(b)   is not infringed by the omission of any material, or its inclusion in condensed form, if that is authorised by regulations;

and references in this Act to copies shall be construed accordingly.

(3)   Regulations may provide that a duty imposed by this Act to supply a copy of a document referred to in an unexecuted agreement or an executed agreement shall not apply to documents of a kind specified in the regulations.

181   Power to alter monetary limits etc

(1)   The Secretary of State may by order made by statutory instrument amend, or further amend, any of the following provisions of this Act so as to reduce or increase a sum mentioned in that provision, namely, sections [16B(1)], 70(6), 75(3)(b), 77(1), 78(1), 79(1), 84(1), 101(7)(a), 107(1), 108(1), 109(1), 110(1), 118(1)(b), 120(1)(a), 140B(6), [. . .], 155(1) and 158(1).

(2)   An order under subsection (1) amending section [16B(1)], 75(3)(b) or 140B(6), [. . .] shall be of no effect unless a draft of the order has been laid before and approved by each House of Parliament.

182   Regulations and orders

(1)   Any power of the Secretary of State to make regulations or orders under this Act, except the power conferred by sections 2(1)(a), 181 and 192 shall be exercisable by statutory instrument subject to annulment in pursuance of a resolution of either House of Parliament.

[(1A)   The power of the Lord Chancellor to make rules under section 40A(3) shall be exercisable by statutory instrument subject to annulment in pursuance of a resolution of either House of Parliament.]

(2)   Where a power to make regulations or orders [or rules] is exercisable by the Secretary of State [or by the Lord Chancellor] by virtue of this Act, regulations or orders [or rules] made in the exercise of that power may—

(a)   make different provision in relation to different cases or classes of case, and

(b)   exclude certain cases or classes of case, and

(c)   contain such transitional provision as the [person making them] thinks fit.

(3)   Regulations may provide that specified expressions, when used as described by the regulations, are to be given the prescribed meaning, notwithstanding that another meaning is intended by the person using them.

(4)   Any power conferred on the Secretary of State by this Act to make orders includes power to vary or revoke an order so made.

183   Determinations etc by [OFT]

[(1)   The OFT may vary or revoke any determination made, or direction given, by it under this Act.

(2)   Subsection (1) does not apply to—

(a)   a determination to issue, renew or vary a licence;

(b)   a determination to extend a period under section 28B or to refuse to extend a period under that section;

(c)   a determination to end a suspension under section 33;

(d)   a determination to make an order under section 40(2), 148(2) or 149(2);

(e)   a determination mentioned in column 1 of the Table in section 41.]

Interpretation

184   Associates

[(1)   A person is an associate of an individual if that person is—

(a)   the individual's husband or wife or civil partner,

(b)   a relative of—

(i)   the individual, or

(ii)   the individual's husband or wife or civil partner, or

(c)   the husband or wife or civil partner of a relative of—

(i)   the individual, or

(ii)   the individual's husband or wife or civil partner.]

(2)   A person is an associate of any person with whom he is in partnership, and of the husband or wife [or civil partner] or a relative of any individual with whom he is in partnership.

(3)   A body corporate is an associate of another body corporate—

(a)   if the same person is a controller of both, or a person is a controller of one and persons who are his associates, or he and persons who are his associates, are controllers of the other; or

(b)   if a group of two or more persons is controller of each company, and the groups either consist of the same persons or could be regarded as consisting of the same persons by treating (in one or more cases) a member of either group as replaced by a person of whom he is an associate.

(4)   A body corporate is an associate of another person if that person is a controller of it or if that person and persons who are his associates together are controllers of it.

(5)   In this section 'relative' means brother, sister, uncle, aunt, nephew, niece, lineal ancestor or lineal descendant, references to a husband [or wife, and references to a civil partner include a former civil partner,] include a former husband or wife and a reputed husband or wife; and for the purposes of this subsection a relationship shall be established as if any illegitimate child, step-child or adopted child of a person [were the legitimate child of the relationship in question].

185   Agreement with more than one debtor or hirer

(1)   Where an actual or prospective regulated agreement has two or more debtors or hirers (not being a partnership or an unincorporated body of persons)—

(a)   anything required by or under this Act to be done to or in relation to the debtor or hirer shall be done to or in relation to each of them; and

(b)   anything done under this Act by or on behalf of one of them shall have effect as if done by or on behalf of all of them.

[(2)   Notwithstanding subsection (1)(a), where credit is provided under an agreement to two or more debtors jointly, in performing his duties—

(a)   in the case of fixed-sum credit, under section 77A, or

(b)   in the case of running-account credit, under section 78(4),

the creditor need not give statements to any debtor who has signed and given to him a notice (a 'dispensing notice') authorising him not to comply in the debtor's case with section 77A or (as the case may be) 78(4).

(2A)   A dispensing notice given by a debtor is operative from when it is given to the creditor until it is revoked by a further notice given to the creditor by the debtor.

(2B)   But subsection (2) does not apply if (apart from this subsection) dispensing notices would be operative in relation to all of the debtors to whom the credit is provided.

(2C)   Any dispensing notices operative in relation to an agreement shall cease to have effect if any of the debtors dies.

(2D)   A dispensing notice which is operative in relation to an agreement shall be operative also in relation to any subsequent agreement which, in relation to the earlier agreement, is a modifying agreement.]

(3)   Subsection (1)(b) does not apply for the purposes of section 61(1)(a) [. . .].

(4)   Where a regulated agreement has two or more debtors or hirers (not being a partnership or an unincorporated body of persons), section 86 applies to the death of any of them.

(5)   An agreement for the provision of credit, or the bailment or (in Scotland) the hiring of goods, to two or more persons jointly where—

(a)   one or more of those persons is an individual, and

(b)   one or more of them is [not an individual],

is a consumer credit agreement or consumer hire agreement if it would have been one had they all been individuals; and [each person within paragraph (b)] shall accordingly be included among the debtors or hirers under the agreement.

(6)   Where subsection (5) applies, references in this Act to the signing of any document by the debtor or hirer shall be construed in relation to a body corporate [within paragraph (b) of that subsection] as referring to a signing on behalf of the body corporate.

186   Agreement with more than one creditor or owner
Where an actual or prospective regulated agreement has two or more creditors or owners, anything required by or under this Act to be done to, or in relation to, or by, the creditor or owner shall be effective if done to, or in relation to, or by, any one of them.

187   Arrangements between creditor and supplier
(1)   A consumer credit agreement shall be treated as entered into under pre-existing arrangements between a creditor and a supplier if it is entered into in accordance with, or in furtherance of, arrangements previously made between persons mentioned in subsection (4)(a), (b) or (c).

(2)   A consumer credit agreement shall be treated as entered into in contemplation of future arrangements between a creditor and a supplier if it is entered into in the expectation that arrangements will subsequently be made between persons mentioned in subsection (4)(a), (b) or (c) for the supply of cash, goods and services (or any of them) to be financed by the consumer credit agreement.

(3)   Arrangements shall be disregarded for the purposes of subsection (1) or (2) if—
   (a)   they are arrangements for the making, in specified circumstances, of payments to the supplier by the creditor, and
   (b)   the creditor holds himself out as willing to make, in such circumstances, payments of the kind to suppliers generally.

[(3A)   Arrangements shall also be disregarded for the purposes of subsections (1) and (2) if they are arrangements for the electronic transfer of funds from a current account at a bank within the meaning of the Bankers' Books Evidence Act 1879.]

(4)   The persons referred to in subsections (1) and (2) are—
   (a)   the creditor and the supplier;
   (b)   one of them and an associate of the other's;
   (c)   an associate of one and an associate of the other's.

(5)   Where the creditor is an associate of the supplier's, the consumer credit agreement shall be treated, unless the contrary is proved, as entered into under pre-existing arrangements between the creditor and the supplier.

[187A   Definition of 'default sum'
(1)   In this Act 'default sum' means, in relation to the debtor or hirer under a regulated agreement, a sum (other than a sum of interest) which is payable by him under the agreement in connection with a breach of the agreement by him.

(2)   But a sum is not a default sum in relation to the debtor or hirer simply because, as a consequence of his breach of the agreement, he is required to pay it earlier than he would otherwise have had to.]

188   Examples of use of new terminology
(1)   Schedule 2 shall have effect for illustrating the use of terminology employed in this Act.

(2)   The examples given in Schedule 2 are not exhaustive.

(3)   In the case of conflict between Schedule 2 and any other provision of this Act, that other provision shall prevail.

(4)   The Secretary of State may by order amend Schedule 2 by adding further examples or in any other way.

189   Definitions

(1)   In this Act, unless the context otherwise requires—

'advertisement' includes every form of advertising, whether in a publication, by television or radio, by display of notices, signs, labels, showcards or goods, by distribution of samples, circulars, catalogues, price lists or other material, by exhibition of pictures, models or films, or in any other way, and references to the publishing of advertisements shall be construed accordingly;

'advertiser' in relation to an advertisement, means any person indicated by the advertisement as willing to enter into transactions to which the advertisement relates;

'ancillary credit business' has the meaning given by section 145(1);

'antecedent negotiations' has the meaning given by section 56;

'appeal period' means the period beginning on the first day on which an appeal to the [Tribunal] may be brought and ending on the last day on which it may be brought or, if it is brought, ending on its final determination, or abandonment;

['appropriate method' means—

    (a)   post, or

    (b)   transmission in the form of an electronic communication within the meaning of the Electronic Communications Act 2000 (c 7).]

'assignment', in relation to Scotland, means assignation;

'associate' shall be construed in accordance with section 184;

[. . .]

'bill of sale' has the meaning given by section 4 of the Bills of Sale Act 1878 or, for Northern Ireland, by section 4 of the Bills of Sale (Ireland) Act 1879;

['building society' means a building society within the meaning of the Building Societies Act 1986;]

'business' includes profession or trade, and references to a business apply subject to subsection (2);

'cancellable agreement' means a regulated agreement which, by virtue of section 67, may be cancelled by the debtor or hirer;

'canvass' shall be construed in accordance with sections 48 and 153;

'cash' includes money in any form;

'charity' means as respects England and Wales a charity registered under [the Charities Act 1993] or an exempt charity (within the meaning of that Act), and as respects Scotland and Northern Ireland an institution or other organisation established for charitable purposes only ('organisation' including any persons administering a trust and 'charitable' being construed in the same way as if it were contained in the Income Tax Acts);

'conditional sale agreement' means an agreement for the sale of goods or land under which the purchase price or part of it is payable by instalments, and the property in the goods or land is to remain in the seller (notwithstanding that the buyer is to be in possession of the goods or land) until such conditions as to the payment of instalments or otherwise as may be specified in the agreement are fulfilled;

'consumer credit agreement' has the meaning given by section 8, and includes a consumer credit agreement which is cancelled under section 69(1), or becomes subject to section 69(2), so far as the agreement remains in force;

['consumer credit business' means any business being carried on by a person so far as it comprises or relates to—

    (a)   the provision of credit by him, or

    (b)   otherwise his being a creditor,

under regulated consumer credit agreements];

'consumer hire agreement' has the meaning given by section 15;

['consumer hire business' means any business being carried on by a person so far as it comprises or relates to—

    (a)   the bailment or (in Scotland) the hiring of goods by him, or

    (b)   otherwise his being an owner,

under regulated consumer hire agreements];
    'controller', in relation to a body corporate, means a person—
    (a) in accordance with whose directions or instructions the directors of the body corporate or of another body corporate which is its controller (or any of them) are accustomed to act, or
    (b) who, either alone or with any associate or associates, is entitled to exercise, or control the exercise of, one third or more of the voting power at any general meeting of the body corporate or of another body corporate which is its controller;
    'copy' shall be construed in accordance with section 180;
    [. . .]
    'court' means in relation to England and Wales the county court, in relation to Scotland the sheriff court and in relation to Northern Ireland the High Court or the county court;
    'credit' shall be construed in accordance with section 9;
    'credit-broker' means a person carrying on a business of credit-brokerage;
    'credit-brokerage' has the meaning given by section 145(2);
    ['credit information service' has the meaning given by section 145(7B);]
    'credit limit' has the meaning given by section 10(2);
    'creditor' means the person providing credit under a consumer credit agreement or the person to whom his rights and duties under the agreement have passed by assignment or operation of law, and in relation to a prospective consumer agreement, includes the prospective creditor;
    'credit reference agency' has the meaning given by section 145(8);
    'credit-sale agreement' means an agreement for the sale of goods, under which the purchase price or part of it is payable by instalments, but which is not a conditional sale agreement;
    'credit-token' has the meaning given by section 14(1);
    'credit-token agreement' means a regulated agreement for the provision of credit in connection with the use of a credit-token;
    'debt-adjusting' has the meaning given by section 145(5);
    ['debt administration' has the meaning given by section 145(7A);]
    'debt-collecting' has the meaning given by section 145(7);
    'debt-counselling' has the meaning given by section 145(6);
    'debtor' means the individual receiving credit under a consumer credit agreement or the person to whom his rights and duties under the agreement have passed by assignment or operation of law, and in relation to a prospective consumer credit agreement includes the prospective debtor;
    'debtor-creditor agreement' has the meaning given by section 13;
    'debtor-creditor-supplier agreement' has the meaning given by section 12;
    'default notice' has the meaning given by section 87(1);
    ['default sum' has the meaning given by section 187A;]
    'deposit' means [(except in sections 16(10) and 25(1B))] any sum payable by a debtor or hirer by way of deposit or downpayment, or credited or to be credited to him on account of any deposit or downpayment, whether the sum is to be or has been paid to the creditor or owner or any other person, or is to be or has been discharged by a payment of money or a transfer or delivery of goods or by any other means;
    ['documents' includes information recorded in any form;]
    [. . .]
    'electric line' has the meaning given by [the Electricity Act 1989] or, for Northern Ireland the Electricity Supply (Northern Ireland) Order 1972;
    ['electronic communication' means an electronic communication within the meaning of the Electronic Communications Act 2000 (c 7).]
    'embodies' and related words shall be construed in accordance with subsection (4);

'enforcement authority' has the meaning given by section 161(1);

'enforcement order' means an order under section 65(1), 105(7)(a) or (b), 111(2) or 124(1) or (2);

'executed agreement' means a document, signed by or on behalf of the parties, embodying the terms of a regulated agreement, or such of them as have been reduced to writing;

'exempt agreement' means an agreement specified in or under section 16 [, 16A or 16B];

'finance' means to finance wholly or partly, and 'financed' and 'refinanced' shall be construed accordingly;

'file' and 'copy of the file' have the meanings given by section 158(5);

'fixed-sum credit' has the meaning given by section 10(1)(b);

'friendly society' means a society registered [or treated as registered under the Friendly Societies Act 1974 or the Friendly Societies Act 1992];

'future arrangements' shall be construed in accordance with section 187;

'general notice' means a notice published by the [OFT] at a time and in a manner appearing to [it] suitable for securing that the notice is seen within a reasonable time by persons likely to be affected by it;

'give' means deliver or send [by an appropriate method] to;

'goods' has the meaning given by [section 61(1) of the Sale of Goods Act 1979];

'group licence' has the meaning given by section 22(1)(b);

'High Court' means Her Majesty's High Court of Justice, or the Court of Session in Scotland or the High Court of Justice in Northern Ireland;

'hire-purchase agreement' means an agreement, other than a conditional sale agreement, under which—

(a)   goods are bailed or (in Scotland) hired in return for periodical payments by the person to whom they are bailed or hired, and

(b)   the property in the goods will pass to that person if the terms of the agreement are complied with and one or more of the following occurs—

(i)   the exercise of an option to purchase by that person,

(ii)   the doing of any other specified act by any party to the agreement,

(iii)   the happening of any other specified event;

'hirer' means the individual to whom goods are bailed or (in Scotland) hired under a consumer hire agreement, or the person to whom his rights and duties under the agreement have passed by assignment or operation of law, and in relation to a prospective consumer hire agreement includes the prospective hirer;

['individual' includes—

(a)   a partnership consisting of two or three persons not all of whom are bodies corporate; and

(b)   an unincorporated body of persons which does not consist entirely of bodies corporate and is not a partnership.]

'installation' means—

(a)   the installing of any electric line or any gas or water pipe,

(b)   the fixing of goods to the premises where they are to be used, and the alteration of premises to enable goods to be used on them,

(c)   where it is reasonably necessary that goods should be constructed or erected on the premises where they are to be used, any work carried out for the purpose of constructing or erecting them on those premises;

[. . .]

'judgment' includes an order or decree made by any court;

'land' includes an interest in land, and in relation to Scotland includes heritable subjects of whatever description;

'land improvement company' means an improvement company as defined by section 7 of the improvement of Land Act 1899;

'land mortgage' includes any security charged on land;

'licence' means a licence under Part III [. . .];

'licensed', in relation to any act, means authorised by a licence to do the act or cause or permit another person to do it;

'licensee', in the case of a group licence, includes any person covered by the licence;

'linked transaction' has the meaning given by section 19(1);

'local authority', in relation to England and Wales, means the Greater London Council, a county council, a London borough council, a district council, the Common Council of the City of London, or the Council of the Isles of Scilly, and in relation to Scotland, means a [council constituted under section 2 of the Local Government etc (Scotland) Act 1994], and, in relation to Northern Ireland, means a district council;

'modifying agreement' has the meaning given by section 82(2);

'mortgage', in relation to Scotland, includes any heritable security;

'multiple agreement' has the meaning given by section 18(1);

'negotiator' has the meaning given by section 56(1);

'non-commercial agreement' means a consumer credit agreement or a consumer hire agreement not made by the creditor or owner in the course of a business carried on by him;

'notice' means notice in writing;

'notice of cancellation' has the meaning given by section 69(1);

['OFT' means the Office of Fair Trading;]

'owner' means a person who bails or (in Scotland) hires out goods under a consumer hire agreement or the person to whom his rights and duties under the agreement have passed by assignment or operation of law, and in relation to a prospective consumer hire agreement, includes the prospective bailor or person from whom the goods are to be hired;

'pawn' means any article subject to a pledge;

'pawn-receipt' has the meaning given by section 114;

'pawnee' and 'pawnor' include any person to whom the rights and duties of the original pawnee or the original pawnor, as the case may be, have passed by assignment or operation of law;

'payment' includes tender;

[. . .]

'pledge' means the pawnee's rights over an article taken in pawn;

'prescribed' means prescribed by regulations made by the Secretary of State;

'pre-existing arrangements' shall be construed in accordance with section 187;

'principal agreement' has the meaning given by section 19(1);

'protected goods' has the meaning given by section 90(7);

'quotation' has the meaning given by section 52(1)(a);

'redemption period' has the meaning given by section 116(3);

'register' means the register kept by the [OFT] under section 35;

'regulated agreement' means a consumer credit agreement, or consumer hire agreement, other than an exempt agreement, and 'regulated' and 'unregulated' shall be construed accordingly;

'regulations' means regulations made by the Secretary of State;

'relative', except in section 184, means a person who is an associate by virtue of section 184(1);

'representation' includes any condition or warranty, and any other statement or undertaking, whether oral or in writing;

'restricted-use credit agreement' and 'restricted-use credit' have the meanings given by section 11(1);

'rules of court', in relation to Northern Ireland means, in relation to the High Court, rules made under section 7 of the Northern Ireland Act 1962, and, in relation to any other court, rules made by the authority having for the time being power to make rules regulating the practice and procedure in that court;

'running-account credit' shall be construed in accordance with section 10;

'security', in relation to an actual or prospective consumer credit agreement or consumer hire agreement, or any linked transaction, means a mortgage, charge, pledge, bond, debenture, indemnity, guarantee, bill, note or other right provided by the debtor or hirer, or at his request (express or implied), to secure the carrying out of the obligations of the debtor or hirer under the agreement;

'security instrument' has the meaning given by section 105(2);

'serve on' means deliver or send [by an appropriate method] to;

'signed' shall be construed in accordance with subsection (3);

'small agreement' has the meaning given by section 17(1), and 'small' in relation to an agreement within any category shall be construed accordingly;

'specified fee' shall be construed in accordance with section 2(4) and (5);

'standard licence' has the meaning given by section 22(1)(a);

'supplier' has the meaning given by section 11(1)(b) or 12(c) or 13(c) or, in relation to an agreement falling within section 11(1)(a), means the creditor, and includes a person to whom the rights and duties of a supplier (as so defined) have passed by assignment or operation of law, or (in relation to a prospective agreement) the prospective supplier;

'surety' means the person by whom any security is provided, or the person to whom his rights and duties in relation to the security have passed by assignment or operation of law;

'technical grounds' shall be construed in accordance with subsection (5);

'time order' has the meaning given by section 129(1);

'total charge for credit' means a sum calculated in accordance with regulations under section 20(1);

'total price' means the total sum payable by the debtor under a hire-purchase agreement or a conditional sale agreement, including any sum payable on the exercise of an option to purchase, but excluding any sum payable as a penalty or as compensation or damages for a breach of the agreement;

['the Tribunal' means the Consumer Credit Appeal Tribunal;]

'unexecuted agreement' means a document embodying the terms of a prospective regulated agreement, or such of them as it is intended to reduce to writing;

'unlicensed' means without a licence, but applies only in relation to acts for which a licence is required;

'unrestricted-use credit agreement' and 'unrestricted-use credit' have the meanings given by section 11(2);

'working day' means any day other than—
(a) Saturday or Sunday,
(b) Christmas Day or Good Friday,
(c) a bank holiday within the meaning given by section 1 of the Banking and Financial Dealings Act 1971.

[(1A) In sections 36E(3), 70(4), 73(4) and 75(2) and paragraphs 14 and 15 of Schedule A1 'costs', in relation to proceedings in Scotland, means expenses.]

(2) A person is not to be treated as carrying on a particular type of business merely because occasionally he enters into transactions belonging to a business of that type.

(3) Any provision of this Act requiring a document to be signed is complied with by a body corporate if the document is sealed by that body.

This subsection does not apply to Scotland.

(4) A document embodies a provision if the provision is set out either in the document itself or in another document referred to in it.

(5) An application dismissed by the court or the [OFT] shall, if the court or the [OFT] (as the case may be) so certifies, be taken to be dismissed on technical grounds only.

(6) Except in so far as the context otherwise requires, any reference in this Act to an enactment shall be construed as a reference to that enactment as amended by or under any other enactment, including this Act.

(7)   In this Act, except where otherwise indicated—

(a)   a reference to a numbered Part, section or Schedule is a reference to the Part or section of, or the Schedule to, this Act so numbered, and

(b)   a reference in a section to a numbered subsection is a reference to the subsection of that section so numbered, and

(c)   a reference in a section, subsection or Schedule to a numbered paragraph is a reference to the paragraph of that section, subsection or Schedule so numbered.

[189A   Meaning of 'consumer credit EEA firm'

In this Act 'consumer credit EEA firm' means an EEA firm falling within sub-paragraph (a), (b) or (c) of paragraph 5 of Schedule 3 to the Financial Services and Markets Act 2000 carrying on, or seeking to carry on, consumer credit business, consumer hire business or ancillary credit business for which a licence would be required under this Act but for paragraph 15(3) of Schedule 3 to the Financial Services and Markets Act 2000.]

190   Financial provisions

(1)   There shall be defrayed out of money provided by Parliament—

(a)   all expenses incurred by the Secretary of State in consequence of the provisions of this Act;

(b)   any expenses incurred in consequence of those provisions by any other Minister of the Crown or Government department;

(c)   any increase attributable to this Act in the sums payable out of money so provided under the Superannuation Act 1972 or the Fair Trading Act 1973.

(2)   Any fees [, charges, penalties or other sums] received by the Director under this Act shall be paid into the Consolidated Fund.

191   [Applies to Northern Ireland]

193   Short title and extent

(1)   This Act may be cited as the Consumer Credit Act 1974.

(2)   This Act extends to Northern Ireland.

SCHEDULES

SCHEDULE A1
THE CONSUMER CREDIT APPEALS TRIBUNAL

PART 1
INTERPRETATION

1   In this Schedule—

'the Deputy President' means the Deputy President of the Consumer Credit Appeals Tribunal;

'lay panel' means the panel established under paragraph 3(3);

'panel of chairmen' means the panel established under paragraph 3(1);

'party' means, in relation to an appeal, the appellant or the OFT;

'the President' means the President of the Consumer Credit Appeals Tribunal;

'rules' means rules under section 40A(3) of this Act;

'specified' means specified by rules.

PART 2
THE TRIBUNAL

The President and the Deputy President

2—(1)   The Lord Chancellor shall appoint one of the members of the panel of chairmen to preside over the discharge of the Tribunal's functions.

(2)   The person so appointed shall be known as the President of the Consumer Credit Appeals Tribunal.

(3)   The Lord Chancellor may appoint one of the members of the panel of chairmen to be the Deputy President of the Consumer Credit Appeals Tribunal.

(4)   The Deputy President shall have such functions in relation to the Tribunal as the President may assign to him.

(5)   If the President or the Deputy President ceases to be a member of the panel of chairmen, he shall also cease to be the President or (as the case may be) the Deputy President.

(6)   The functions of the President may, if he is absent or is otherwise unable to act, be discharged—

    (a)   by the Deputy President; or

    (b)   if there is no Deputy President or he too is absent or otherwise unable to act, by a person appointed for that purpose from the panel of chairmen by the Lord Chancellor.

Panels

3—(1)   The Lord Chancellor shall appoint a panel of persons for the purpose of serving as chairmen of the Tribunal.

(2)   A person shall not be appointed to the panel of chairmen unless he—

    (a)   has a seven year general qualification within the meaning of section 71 of the Courts and Legal Services Act 1990;

    (b)   is an advocate or solicitor in Scotland of at least seven years' standing; or

    (c)   is a member of the Bar of Northern Ireland, or a solicitor of the Supreme Court of Northern Ireland, of at least seven years' standing.

(3)   The Lord Chancellor shall also appoint a panel of persons who appear to him to be qualified by experience or otherwise to deal with appeals of the kind that may be made to the Tribunal.

Terms of office etc

4—(1)   Each member of the panel of chairmen or the lay panel shall hold and vacate office in accordance with the terms of his appointment.

(2)   The Lord Chancellor may remove a member of either panel from office on the ground of incapacity or misbehaviour.

(3)   A member of either panel—

    (a)   may at any time resign office by notice in writing to the Lord Chancellor;

    (b)   is eligible for re-appointment if he ceases to hold office.

Remuneration and allowances

5   The Lord Chancellor may pay to a person in respect of his service—

    (a)   as the President or the Deputy President,

    (b)   as a member of the Tribunal, or

    (c)   as a person appointed under paragraph 7(4),

such remuneration and allowances as the Lord Chancellor may determine.

Staff and costs

6—(1)   The Lord Chancellor may appoint such staff for the Tribunal as he may determine.

(2)   The Lord Chancellor shall defray—

    (a)   the remuneration of the Tribunal's staff; and

    (b)   such other costs of the Tribunal as he may determine.

PART 3
CONSTITUTION OF THE TRIBUNAL

7—(1) On an appeal to the Tribunal, the persons to act as members of the Tribunal for the purposes of the appeal shall be selected from the panel of chairmen or the lay panel.

(2) The selection shall be in accordance with arrangements made by the President for the purposes of this paragraph.

(3) Those arrangements shall provide for at least one member to be a person selected from the panel of chairmen.

(4) If it appears to the Tribunal that a matter before it involves a question of fact of special difficulty, it may appoint one or more experts to provide assistance.

PART 4
TRIBUNAL POWERS AND PROCEDURE

Sittings

8   The Tribunal shall sit at such times and in such places as the Lord Chancellor may direct.

Evidence

9—(1) Subject to sub-paragraph (2), the Tribunal may, on an appeal, consider any evidence that it thinks relevant, whether or not it was available to the OFT at the time it made the determination appealed against.

(2) Rules may make provision restricting the evidence that the Tribunal may consider on an appeal in specified circumstances.

Rules on procedure

10   Rules may include, amongst other things, provision—

(a)   about the withdrawal of appeals;

(b)   about persons who may appear on behalf of a party to an appeal;

(c)   about how an appeal is to be dealt with if a person acting as member of the Tribunal in respect of the appeal becomes unable to act;

(d)   setting time limits in relation to anything that is to be done for the purposes of an appeal or for such limits to be set by the Tribunal or a member of the panel of chairmen;

(e)   for time limits (including the period specified for the purposes of section 41(1) of this Act) to be extended by the Tribunal or a member of the panel of chairmen;

(f)   conferring powers on the Tribunal or a member of the panel of chairmen to give such directions to the parties to an appeal as it or he thinks fit for purposes connected with the conduct and disposal of the appeal;

(g)   about the holding of hearings by the Tribunal or a member of the panel of chairmen (including for such hearings to be held in private);

(h)   placing restrictions on the disclosure of information and documents or for such restrictions to be imposed by the Tribunal or a member of the panel of chairmen;

(i)   about the consequences of a failure to comply with a requirement imposed by or under any rule (including for the immediate dismissal or allowing of an appeal if the Tribunal or a member of the panel of chairmen thinks fit);

(j)   for proceedings on different appeals (including appeals with different appellants) to take place concurrently;

(k)   for the suspension of determinations of the OFT;

(l)   for the suspension of decisions of the Tribunal;

(m)   for the Tribunal to reconsider its decision disposing of an appeal where it has reason to believe that the decision was wrongly made because of an administrative error made by a member of its staff.

Council on Tribunals

11   A member of the Council on Tribunals or of its Scottish Committee shall be entitled—

  (a)   to attend any hearing held by the Tribunal or a member of the panel of chairmen whether or not it is held in public; and

  (b)   to attend any deliberations of the Tribunal in relation to an appeal.

Disposal of appeals

12—(1)   The Tribunal shall decide an appeal by reference to the grounds of appeal set out in the notice of appeal.

  (2)   In disposing of an appeal the Tribunal may do one or more of the following—

  (a)   confirm the determination appealed against;

  (b)   quash that determination;

  (c)   vary that determination;

  (d)   remit the matter to the OFT for reconsideration and determination in accordance with the directions (if any) given to it by the Tribunal;

  (e)   give the OFT directions for the purpose of giving effect to its decision.

  (3)   In the case of an appeal against a determination to impose a penalty, the Tribunal—

  (a)   has no power by virtue of sub-paragraph (2)(c) to increase the penalty;

  (b)   may extend the period within which the penalty is to be paid (including in cases where that period has already ended).

  (4)   Sub-paragraph (3) does not affect—

  (a)   the Tribunal's power to give directions to the OFT under sub-paragraph (2)(d); or

  (b)   what the OFT can do where a matter is remitted to it under sub-paragraph (2)(d).

  (5)   Where the Tribunal remits a matter to the OFT, it may direct that the requirements of section 34 of this Act are not to apply, or are only to apply to a specified extent, in relation to the OFT's reconsideration of the matter.

  (6)   Subject to sub-paragraphs (7) and (8), where the Tribunal remits an application to the OFT, section 6(1) and (3) to (9) of this Act shall apply as if the application had not been previously determined by the OFT.

  (7)   In the case of a general notice which came into effect after the determination appealed against was made but before the application was remitted, the applicant shall provide any information or document which he is required to provide under section 6(6) within—

  (a)   the period of 28 days beginning with the day on which the application was remitted; or

  (b)   such longer period as the OFT may allow.

  (8)   In the case of—

  (a)   any information or document which was superseded,

  (b)   any change in circumstances which occurred, or

  (c)   any error or omission of which the applicant became aware,

after the determination appealed against was made but before the application was remitted, any notification that is required to be given by the applicant under section 6(7) shall be given within the period of 28 days beginning with the day on which the application was remitted.

Decisions of the Tribunal

13—(1)   A decision of the Tribunal may be taken by majority.

  (2)   A decision of the Tribunal disposing of an appeal shall—

  (a)   state whether it was unanimous or taken by majority; and

(b)   be recorded in a document which—

(i)   contains a statement of the reasons for the decision and any other specified information; and

(ii)   is signed and dated by a member of the panel of chairmen.

(3)   Where the Tribunal disposes of an appeal it shall—

(a)   send to each party to the appeal a copy of the document mentioned in sub-paragraph (2)(b); and

(b)   publish that document in such manner as it thinks fit.

(4)   The Tribunal may exclude from what it publishes under sub-paragraph (3)(b) information of a specified description.

Costs

14—(1)   Where the Tribunal disposes of an appeal and—

(a)   it decides that the OFT was wrong to make the determination appealed against, or

(b)   during the course of the appeal the OFT accepted that it was wrong to make that determination,

it may order the OFT to pay to the appellant the whole or a part of the costs incurred by the appellant in relation to the appeal.

(2)   In determining whether to make such an order, and the terms of such an order, the Tribunal shall have regard to whether it was unreasonable for the OFT to make the determination appealed against.

15   Where—

(a)   the Tribunal disposes of an appeal or an appeal is withdrawn before the Tribunal disposes of it, and

(b)   the Tribunal thinks that a party to the appeal acted vexatiously, frivolously or unreasonably in bringing the appeal or otherwise in relation to the appeal,

it may order that party to pay to the other party the whole or a part of the costs incurred by the other party in relation to the appeal.

16   An order of the Tribunal under paragraph 14 or 15 may be enforced—

(a)   as if it were an order of the county court; or

(b)   in Scotland, as if it were an interlocutor of the Court of Session.

SCHEDULE 1. PROSECUTION AND PUNISHMENT OF OFFENCES

Section 167

1 Section	2 Offence	3 Mode of prosecution	4 Imprisonment or fine
7	.... Knowingly or recklessly giving false information to [the OFT].	(a) Summarily. (b) On indictment.	[The prescribed sum.] 2 years or a fine or both.
39(1)	.... Engaging in activities requiring a licence when not a licensee.	(a) Summarily. (b) On indictment.	[The prescribed sum.] 2 years or a fine or both.
39(2)	.... Carrying on a business under a name not specified in licence.	(a) Summarily. (b) On indictment.	[The prescribed sum.] 2 years or a fine or both.
39(3)	.... Failure to notify changes in registered particulars.	(a) Summarily. (b) On indictment.	[The prescribed sum.] 2 years or a fine or both.
45	.... Advertising credit where goods etc not available for cash.	(a) Summarily. (b) On indictment.	[The prescribed sum.] 2 years or a fine or both.
46(1)	.... False or misleading advertisements.	(a) Summarily. (b) On indictment.	[The prescribed sum.) 2 years or a fine or both.
47(1)	.... Advertising infringements.	(a) Summarily. (b) On indictment.	[The prescribed sum.] 2 years or a fine or both.
49(1)	.... Canvassing debtor-creditor agreements off trade premises.	(a) Summarily. (b) On indictment.	[The prescribed sum.] 1 year or a fine or both.
49(2)	.... Soliciting debtor-creditor agreements during visits made in response to previous oral requests.	(a) Summarily. (b) On indictment.	[The prescribed sum.] 1 year or a fine or both.
50(1)	.... Sending circulars to minors.	(a) Summarily. (b) On indictment.	[The prescribed sum.] 1 year or a fine or both.
51(1)	.... Supplying unsolicited credit-tokens.	(a) Summarily. (b) On indictment.	[The prescribed sum.] 2 years or a fine or both.
77(4)	.... Failure of creditor under fixed-sum credit agreement to supply copies of documents etc.	Summarily.	[Level 4 on the standard scale.]
78(6)	.... Failure of creditor under running-account credit agreement to supply copies of documents etc.	Summarily.	[Level 4 on the standard scale.]
79(3)	.... Failure of owner under consumer hire agreement to supply copies of documents etc.	Summarily.	[Level 4 on the standard scale.]
80(2)	.... Failure to tell creditor or owner whereabouts of goods.	Summarily.	[Level 3 on the standard scale.]

1 Section	2 Offence	3 Mode of prosecution	4 Imprisonment or fine
85(2)	Failure of creditor to supply copy of credit-token agreement.	Summarily.	[Level 4 on the standard scale.]
97(3)	Failure to supply debtor with statement of amount required to discharge agreement.	Summarily.	[Level 3 on the standard scale.]
103(5)	Failure to deliver notice relating to discharge of agreements.	Summarily.	[Level 3 on the standard scale.]
107(4)	Failure of creditor to give information to surety under fixed-sum credit agreement.	Summarily.	[Level 4 on the standard scale.]
108(4)	Failure of creditor to give information to surety under running-account credit agreement.	Summarily.	[Level 4 on the standard scale.]
109(3)	Failure of owner to give information to surety under consumer hire agreement.	Summarily.	[Level 4 on the standard scale.]
110(3)	Failure of creditor or owner to supply a copy of any security instrument to debtor or hirer.	Summarily.	[Level 4 on the standard scale.]
114(2)	Taking pledges from minors.	(a) Summarily. (b) On indictment.	[The prescribed sum.] 1 year or a fine or both.
115	Failure to supply copies of a pledge agreement or pawn-receipt.	Summarily.	[Level 4 on the standard scale.]
119(1)	Unreasonable refusal to allow pawn to be redeemed.	Summarily.	[Level 4 on the standard scale.]
154	Canvassing ancillary credit services of trade premises.	(a) Summarily. (b) On indictment.	[The prescribed sum.] 1 year or a fine or both.
157(3)	Refusal to give name etc of credit reference agency.	Summarily.	[Level 4 on the standard scale.]
158(4)	Failure of credit reference agency to disclose filed information.	Summarily.	[Level 4 on the standard scale.]
159(6)	Failure of credit reference agency to correct information.	Summarily.	[Level 4 on the standard scale.]
160(6)	Failure of credit reference agency to comply with section 160(3) or (4).	Summarily.	[Level 4 on the standard scale.]
162(6)	Impersonation of enforcement authority officers.	(a) Summarily. (b) On indictment.	[The prescribed sum.] 1 year or a fine or both.
165(1)	Obstruction of enforcement authority officers.	Summarily.	[Level 4 on the standard scale.]
165(2)	Giving false information to enforcement authority officers.	(a) Summarily. (b) On indictment.	[The prescribed sum.] 2 years or a fine or both.
167(2)	Contravention of regulations under section 44, 52, 53, 54, or 112.	(a) Summarily. (b) On indictment.	[The prescribed sum.] 2 years or a fine or both.
174(5)	Wrongful disclosure of information.	(a) Summarily. (b) On indictment.	[The prescribed sum.] 2 years or a fine or both.

SCHEDULE 2
EXAMPLES OF USE OF NEW TERMINOLOGY

Section 188(1)

PART I
LIST OF TERMS

Term	Defined in section	Illustrated by examples(s)
Advertisement	189(1)	2
Advertiser	189(1)	2
Antecedent negotiations	56	1, 2, 3, 4
Cancellable agreement	67	4
Consumer credit agreement	8	5, 6, 7, 15, 19, 21
Consumer hire agreement	15	20, 24
Credit	9	16, 19, 21
Credit-broker	189(1)	2
Credit limit	10(2)	6, 7, 19, 22, 23
Creditor	189(1)	1, 2, 3, 4
Credit-sale agreement	189(1)	5
Credit-token	14	3, 14, 16
Credit-token agreement	14	3, 14, 16, 22
Debtor-creditor agreement	13	8, 16, 17, 18
Debtor-creditor-supplier agreement	12	8, 16
Fixed-sum credit	10	9, 10, 17, 23
Hire-purchase agreement	189(1)	10
Individual	189(1)	19, 24
Linked transaction	19	11
Modifying agreement	82(2)	24
Multiple agreement	18	16, 18
Negotiator	56(1)	1, 2, 3, 4
[. . .]		
Pre-existing arrangements	187	8, 21
Restricted-use credit	11	10, 12, 13, 14, 16
Running-account credit	10	15, 16, 18, 23
Small agreement	17	16, 17, 22
Supplier	189(1)	3, 14
Total charge for credit	20	5, 10
Total price	189(1)	10
Unrestricted-use credit	11	8, 12, 16, 17, 18

PART II
EXAMPLES

Example 1

Facts Correspondence passes between an employee of a money-lending company (writing on behalf of the company) and an individual about the terms on which the company would grant him a loan under a regulated agreement.

Analysis The correspondence constitutes antecedent negotiations falling within section 56(1)(a), the money-lending company being both creditor and negotiator.

Example 2

Facts Representations are made about goods in a poster displayed by a shopkeeper near the goods, the goods being selected by a customer who has read the poster and then sold by the shopkeeper to a finance company introduced by him (with whom he has a business relationship). The goods are disposed of by the finance company to the customer under a regulated hire-purchase agreement.

Analysis The representations in the poster constitute antecedent negotiations falling within section 56(1)(b), the shopkeeper being the credit-broker and negotiator and the finance company being the creditor. The poster is an advertisement and the shopkeeper is the advertiser.

Example 3

Facts Discussions take place between a shopkeeper and a customer about goods the customer wishes to buy using a credit-card issued by the D Bank under a regulated agreement.

Analysis The discussions constitute antecedent negotiations falling within section 36(1)(c), the shopkeeper being the supplier and negotiator and the D Bank the creditor. The credit-card is a credit-token as defined in section 14(1), and the regulated agreement under which it was issued is a credit-token agreement as defined in section 14(2).

Example 4

Facts Discussions take place and correspondence passes between a second-hand car dealer and a customer about a car, which is then sold by the dealer to the customer under a regulated conditional sale agreement. Subsequently, on a revocation of that agreement by consent, the car is resold by the dealer to a finance company introduced by him (with whom he has a business relationship), who in turn dispose of it to the same customer under a regulated hire-purchase agreement.

Analysis The discussions and correspondence constitute antecedent negotiations in relation both to the conditional sale agreement and the hire-purchase agreement. They fall under section 56(1)(a) in relation to the conditional sale agreement, the dealer being the creditor and the negotiator. In relation to the hire-purchase agreement they fall within section 56(1)(b), the dealer continuing to be treated as the negotiator but the finance company now being the creditor. Both agreements are cancellable if the discussions took place when the individual conducting the negotiations (whether the 'negotiator' or his employee or agent) was in the presence of the debtor, unless the unexecuted agreement was signed by the debtor at trade premises (as defined in section 67(b)). If the discussions all took place by telephone however, or the unexecuted agreement was signed by the debtor on trade premises (as so defined) the agreements are not cancellable.

Example 5

Facts E agrees to sell to F (an individual) an item of furniture in return for 24 monthly instalments of £10 payable in arrear. The property in the goods passes to F immediately.

Analysis This is a credit-sale agreement (see definition of 'credit-sale agreement' in section 189(1)). The credit provided amounts to £240 less the amount which, according to regulations made under section 20(1), constitutes the total charge for credit. (This amount is required to be deducted by section 9(4).) Accordingly the agreement falls within section 8(2) and is a consumer credit agreement.

Example 6

Facts The G Bank grants H (an individual) an unlimited over-draft, with an increased rate of interest on so much of any debit balance as exceeds £2,000.

Analysis Although the overdraft purports to be unlimited, the stipulation for increased interest above £2,000 brings the agreement within section 10(3)(b)(ii) and it is a consumer credit agreement.

Example 7

Facts J is an individual who owns a small shop which usually carries a stock worth about £1,000. K makes a stocking agreement under which he undertakes to provide on short-term credit the stock needed from time to time by J without any specified limit.

Analysis Although the agreement appears to provide unlimited credit, it is probable, having regard to the stock usually carried by J, that his indebtedness to K will not at any time rise above £5,000. Accordingly the agreement falls within section 10(3)(b)(iii) and is a consumer credit agreement.

Example 8

Facts U, a moneylender, lends £500 to V (an individual) knowing he intends to use it to buy office equipment from W. W introduced V to U, it being his practice to introduce customers needing finance to him. Sometimes U gives W a commission for this and sometimes not. U pays the £500 direct to V.

Analysis Although this appears to fall under section 11(1)(b), it is excluded by section 11(3) and is therefore (by section 11(2)) an unrestricted-use credit agreement. Whether it is a debtor-creditor agreement (by section 13(c)) or a debtor-creditor-supplier agreement (by section 12(c)) depends on whether the previous dealings between U and W amount to 'pre-existing arrangements', that is whether the agreement can be taken to have been entered into 'in accordance with, or in furtherance of' arrangements previously made between U and W, as laid down in section 187(1).

Example 9

Facts A agrees to lend B (an individual) £4,500 in nine monthly instalments of £500.

Analysis This is a cash loan and is a form of credit (see section 9 and definition of 'cash' in section 189(1)). Accordingly it falls within section 10(1)(b) and is fixed-sum credit amounting to £4,500.

Example 10

Facts C (in England) agrees to bail goods to D (an individual) in return for periodical payments. The agreement provides for the property in the goods to pass to D on payment of a total of £7,500 and the exercise by D of an option to purchase. The sum of £7,500 includes a down-payment of £1,000. It also includes an amount which, according to regulations made under section 20(1), constitutes a total charge for credit of £1,500.

Analysis This is a hire-purchase agreement with a deposit of £1,000 and a total price of £7,500 (see definitions of 'hire-purchase agreement', 'deposit' and 'total price' in section 189(1)). By section 9(3), it is taken to provide credit amounting to £7,500 − (£1,500 + £1,000), which equals £5,000. Under section 8(2), the agreement is therefore a consumer credit agreement, and under sections 9(3) and 11(1) it is a restricted-use credit agreement for fixed-sum credit. A similar result would follow if the agreement by C had been a hiring agreement in Scotland.

Example 11

Facts X (an individual) borrows £500 from Y (Finance). As a condition of the granting of the loan X is required—

    (a)   to execute a second mortgage on his house in favour of Y (Finance), and

    (b)   to take out a policy of insurance on his life with Y (Insurances).

In accordance with the loan agreement, the policy is charged to Y (Finance) as collateral security for the loan. The two companies are associates within the meaning of section 184(3).

Analysis The second mortgage is a transaction for the provision of security and accordingly does not fall within section 19(1), but the taking out of the insurance policy is a linked transaction falling within section 19(1)(a). The charging of the policy is a separate transaction (made between different parties) for the provision of security and again is excluded from section 19(1). The only linked transaction is therefore the taking out of the insurance policy. If X had not been required by the loan agreement to take out the policy, but it had been done at the suggestion of Y (Finance) to induce them to enter into the loan agreement, it would have been a linked transaction under section 19(1)(c)(i) by virtue of section 19(2)(a).

Example 12

Facts   The N Bank agrees to lend O (an individual) £2,000 to buy a car from P. To make sure the loan is used as intended, the N Bank stipulates that the money must be paid by it direct to P.

Analysis   The agreement is a consumer credit agreement by virtue of section 8(2). Since it falls within section 11(1)(b), it is a restricted-use credit agreement, P being the supplier. If the N Bank had not stipulated for direct payment to the supplier, section 11(3) would have operated and made the agreement into one for unrestricted-use credit.

Example 13

Facts   Q, a debt-adjuster, agrees to pay off debts owed by R (an individual) to various moneylenders. For this purpose the agreement provides for the making of a loan by Q to R in return for R's agreeing to repay the loan by instalments with interest. The loan money is not paid over to R but retained by Q and used to pay off the money lenders.

Analysis   This is an agreement to refinance existing indebtedness of the debtor's, and if the loan by Q does not exceed £5,000 is a restricted-use credit agreement falling within section 11(1)(c).

Example 14

Facts   On payment of £1, S issues to T (an individual) a trading check under which T can spend up to £20 at any shop which has agreed, or in future agrees, to accept S's trading checks.

Analysis   The trading check is a credit-token falling within section 14(1)(b). The credit-token agreement is a restricted-use credit agreement within section 11(1)(b), any shop in which the credit-token is used being the 'supplier'. The fact that further shops may be added after the issue of the credit-token is irrelevant in view of section 11(4).

Example 15

Facts   A retailer L agrees with M (an individual) to open an account in M's name and, in return for M's promise to pay a specified minimum sum into the account each month and to pay a monthly charge for credit, agrees to allow to be debited to the account, in respect of purchases made by M from L, such sums as will not increase the debit balance at any time beyond the credit limit, defined in the agreement as a given multiple of the specified minimum sum.

Analysis   This agreement provides credit falling within the definition of running-account credit in section 10(1)(a). Provided the credit limit is not over £5,000, the agreement falls within section 8(2) and is a consumer credit agreement for running-account credit.

Example 16

Facts   Under an unsecured agreement, A (Credit), an associate of the A Bank, issues to B (an individual) a credit-card for use in obtaining cash on credit from A (Credit), to be paid by branches of the A Bank (acting as agent of A (Credit)), or goods or cash from suppliers or banks who have agreed to honour credit-cards issued by A (Credit). The credit limit is £30.

Analysis This is a credit-token agreement falling within section 14(1)(a) and (b). It is a regulated consumer credit agreement for running-account credit. Since the credit limit does not exceed £30, the agreement is a small agreement. So far as the agreement relates to goods it is a debtor-creditor-supplier agreement within section 12(b), since it provides restricted-use credit under section 11(1)(b). So far as it relates to cash it is a debtor-creditor agreement within section 13(c) and the credit it provides is unrestricted-use credit. This is therefore a multiple agreement. In that the whole agreement falls within several of the categories of agreement mentioned in this Act, it is, by section 18(3), to be treated as an agreement in each of those categories. So far as it is a debtor-creditor-supplier agreement providing restricted-use credit it is, by section 18(2), to be treated as a separate agreement; and similarly so far as it is a debtor-creditor agreement providing unrestricted-use credit. (See also Example 22.)

Example 17

Facts The manager of the C Bank agrees orally with D (an individual) to open a current account in D's name. Nothing is said about overdraft facilities. After maintaining the account in credit for some weeks, D draws a cheque in favour of E for an amount exceeding D's credit balance by £20. E presents the cheque and the Bank pay it.

Analysis In drawing the cheque D, by implication, requests the Bank to grant him an overdraft of £20 on its usual terms as to interest and other charges. In deciding to honour the cheque, the Bank by implication accept the offer. This constitutes a regulated small consumer credit agreement for unrestricted-use, fixed sum credit. It is a debtor-creditor agreement, and falls within section 74(1)(b) if covered by a determination under section 74(3). (Compare Example 18.)

Example 18

Facts F (an individual) has had a current account with the G Bank for many years. Although usually in credit, the account has been allowed by the Bank to become overdrawn from time to time. The maximum such overdraft has been is about £1,000. No explicit agreement has ever been made about overdraft facilities. Now, with a credit balance of £500, F draws a cheque for £1,300.

Analysis It might well be held that the agreement with F (express or implied) under which the Bank operate his account includes an implied term giving him the right to overdraft facilities up to say £1,000. If so, the agreement is a regulated consumer credit agreement for unrestricted-use, running-account credit. It is a debtor-creditor agreement, and falls within section 74(1)(b) if covered by a direction under section 74(3). It is also a multiple agreement, part of which (i.e. the part not dealing with the overdraft), as referred to in section 18(1)(a), falls within a category of agreement not mentioned in this Act. (Compare Example 17.)

Example 19

Facts H (a finance house) agrees with J (a partnership of individuals) to open an unsecured loan account in J's name on which the debit balance is not to exceed £7,500 (having regard to payments into the account made from time to time by J). Interest is to be payable in advance on this sum, with provision for yearly adjustments. H is entitled to debit the account with interest, a 'setting-up' charge, and other charges. Before J has an opportunity to draw on the account it is initially debited with £2,250 for advance interest and other charges.

Analysis This is a personal running-account credit agreement (see sections 8(1) and 10(1)(a), and definition of 'individual' in section 189(1)). By section 10(2) the credit limit is £7,000. By section 9(4) however the initial debit of £2,250, and any other charges later debited to the account by H, are not to be treated as credit even though time is allowed for their payment. Effect is given to this by section 10(3). Although the credit limit of £7,000 exceeds the amount (£5,000) specified in section 8(2) as the maximum for a consumer credit agreement, so that the agreement is not within section 10(3)(a), it is caught by section 10(3)(b)(i). At the beginning J can effectively draw (as credit) no more than £4,750, so the agreement is a consumer credit agreement.

Example 20

Facts K (in England) agrees with L (an individual) to bail goods to L for a period of three years certain at £2,200 a year, payable quarterly. The agreement contains no provision for the passing of the property in the goods to L.

Analysis This is not a hire-purchase agreement (see paragraph (b) of the definition of that term in section 189(1)), and is capable of subsisting for more than three months. Paragraphs (a) and (b) of section 15(1) are therefore satisfied, but paragraph (c) is not. The payments by L must exceed £5,000 if he conforms to the agreement. It is true that under section 101 L has a right to terminate the agreement on giving K three months' notice expiring not earlier than eighteen months after the making of the agreement, but that section applies only where the agreement is a regulated consumer hire agreement apart from the section (see subsection (1)). So the agreement is not a consumer hire agreement, though it would be if the hire charge were say £1,500 a year, or there were a 'break' clause in it operable by either party before the hire charges exceeded £5,000. A similar result would follow if the agreement by K had been a hiring agreement in Scotland.

Example 21

Facts The P Bank decides to issue cheque cards to its customers under a scheme whereby the bank undertakes to honour cheques of up to £30 in every case where the payee has taken the cheque in reliance on the cheque card, whether the customer has funds in his account or not. The P Bank writes to the major retailers advising them of this scheme and also publicises it by advertising. The Bank issues a cheque card to Q (an individual), who uses it to pay by cheque for goods costing £20 bought by Q from R, a major retailer. At the time, Q has £500 in his account at the P Bank.

Analysis The agreement under which the cheque card is issued to Q is a consumer credit agreement even though at all relevant times Q has more than £30 in his account. This is because Q is free to draw out his whole balance and then use the cheque card, in which case the Bank has bound itself to honour the cheque. In other words the cheque card agreement provides Q with credit, whether he avails himself of it or not. Since the amount of the credit is not subject to any express limit, the cheque card can be used any number of times. It may be presumed however that section 10(3)(b)(iii) will apply. The agreement is an unrestricted-use debtor-creditor agreement (by section 13(c)). Although the P Bank wrote to R informing R of the P Bank's willingness to honour any cheque taken by R in reliance on a cheque card, this does not constitute pre-existing arrangements as mentioned in section 13(c) because section 187(3) operates to prevent it. The agreement is not a credit-token agreement within section 14(1)(b) because payment by the P Bank to R, would be a payment of the cheque and not a payment for the goods.

Example 22

Facts The facts are as in Example 16. On one occasion B uses the credit-card in a way which increases his debit balance with A (Credit) to £40. A (Credit) writes to B agreeing to allow the excess on that occasion only, but stating that it must be paid off within one month.

Analysis In exceeding his credit limit B, by implication, requests A (Credit) to allow him a temporary excess (compare Example 17). A (Credit) is thus faced by B's action with the choice of treating it as a breach of contract or granting his

implied request. He does the latter. If he had done the former, B would be treated
as taking credit to which he was not entitled (see section 14(3)) and, subject to the
terms of his contract with A (Credit), would be liable to damages for breach of
contract. As it is, the agreement to allow the excess varies the original credit-token
agreement by adding a new term. Under section 10(2), the new term is to be disregarded in arriving at the credit limit, so that the credit-token agreement at no
time ceases to be a small agreement. By section 82(2) the later agreement is
deemed to revoke the original agreement and contain provisions reproducing the
combined effect of the two agreements. By section 82(4), this later agreement is
exempted from Part V (except section 56).

Example 23

Facts   Under an oral agreement made on 10th January, X (an individual) has an
overdraft on his current account at the Y bank with a credit limit of £100. On 15th
February, when his overdraft stands at £90, X draws a cheque for £25. It is the first
time that X has exceeded his credit limit, and on 16th February the bank honours
the cheque.

Analysis   The agreement of 10th January is a consumer credit agreement for
running-account credit. The agreement of 15th–16th February varies the earlier
agreement by adding a term allowing the credit limit to be exceeded merely temporarily. By section 82(2) the later agreement is deemed to revoke the earlier agreement and reproduce the combined effect of the two agreements. By section 82(4),
Part V of this Act (except section 56) does not apply to the later agreement. By
section 18(5), a term allowing a merely temporary excess over the credit limit is
not to be treated as a separate agreement, or as providing fixed-sum credit. The
whole of the £115 owed to the bank by X on 16th February is therefore running-
account credit.

Example 24

Facts   On 1st March 1975 Z (in England) enters into an agreement with A (an
unincorporated body of persons) to bail to A equipment consisting of two components (component P and component Q). The agreement is not a hire-purchase
agreement and is for a fixed term of 3 years, so paragraphs (a) and (b) of section
15(1) are both satisfied. The rental is payable monthly at a rate of £2,400 a year, but
the agreement provides that this is to be reduced to £1,200 a year for the remainder of the agreement if at any time during its currency A returns component Q to
the owner Z. On 5th May 1976 A is incorporated as A Ltd, taking over A's assets
and liabilities. On 1st March 1977, A Ltd returns component Q. On 1st January
1978, Z and A Ltd agree to extend the earlier agreement by one year, increasing
the rental for the final year by £250 to £1,450.

Analysis   When entered into on 1st March 1975, the agreement is a consumer
hire agreement. A falls within the definition of 'individual' in section 189(1) and if
A returns component Q before 1st May 1976 the total rental will not exceed £5,000
(see section 15(1)(c)). When this date is passed without component Q having been
returned it is obvious that the total rental must now exceed £5,000. Does this mean
that the agreement then ceases to be a consumer hire agreement? The answer is
no, because there has been no change in the terms of the agreement, and without
such a change the agreement cannot move from one category to the other. Similarly, the fact that A's rights and duties under the agreement pass to a body corporate on 5th May 1976 does not cause the agreement to cease to be a consumer hire
agreement (see definition of 'hirer' in section 189(1)).

The effect of the modifying agreement of 1st January 1978 is governed by section
82(2), which requires it to be treated as containing provisions reproducing the
combined effect of the two actual agreements, that is to say as providing that—

>   (a)   obligations outstanding on 1st January 1978 are to be treated as out-
> standing under the modifying agreement;

(b)   the modifying agreement applies at the old rate of hire for the months of January and February 1978, and

(c)   for the year beginning 1st March 1978 A Ltd will be the bailee of component P at a rental of £1,450.

The total rental under the modifying agreement is £1,850. Accordingly the modifying agreement is a regulated agreement. Even if the total rental under the modifying agreement exceeded £5,000 it would still be regulated because of the provisions of section 82(3).

UNFAIR CONTRACT TERMS ACT 1977
(1977, c 50)

PART II
AMENDMENT OF LAW FOR SCOTLAND

15 Scope of Part II

(1)   This Part of this Act [. . .] is subject to Part III of this Act and does not affect the validity of any discharge or indemnity given by a person in consideration of the receipt by him of compensation in settlement of any claim which he has.

(2)   Subject to subsection (3) below, sections 16 to 18 of this Act apply to any contract only to the extent that the contract—

(a)   relates to the transfer of the ownership or possession of goods from one person to another (with or without work having been done on them);

(b)   constitutes a contract of service or apprenticeship;

(c)   relates to services of whatever kind, including (without prejudice to the foregoing generality) carriage, deposit and pledge, care and custody, mandate, agency, loan and services relating to the use of land;

(d)   relates to the liability of an occupier of land to persons entering upon or using that land;

(e)   relates to a grant of any right or permission to enter upon or use land not amounting to an estate or interest in the land.

(3)   Notwithstanding anything in subsection (2) above, sections 16 to 18—

(a)   do not apply to any contract to the extent that the contract—

(i)   is a contract of insurance (including a contract to pay an annuity on human life);

(ii)   relates to the formation, constitution or dissolution of any body corporate or unincorporated association or partnership;

(b)   apply to—

a contract of marine salvage or towage;

a charter party of a ship or hovercraft;

a contract for the carriage of goods by ship or hovercraft; or

a contract to which subsection (4) below relates,

only to the extent that—

(i)   both parties deal or hold themselves out as dealing in the course of a business (and then only in so far as the contract purports to exclude or restrict liability for breach of duty in respect of death or personal injury); or

(ii)   the contract is a consumer contract (and then only in favour of the consumer).

(4)   This subsection relates to a contract in pursuance of which goods are carried by ship or hovercraft and which either—

(a)   specifies ship or hovercraft as the means of carriage over part of the journey to be covered; or

(b)   makes no provision as to the means of carriage and does not exclude ship or hovercraft as that means,

in so far as the contract operates for and in relation to the carriage of the goods by that means.

16   Liability for breach of duty

(1)   [Subject to subsection (1A) below,] where a term of a contract [, or a provision of a notice given to persons generally or to particular persons,] purports to exclude or restrict liability for breach of duty arising in the course of any business or from the occupation of any premises used for business purposes of the occupier, that term [or provision]—

(a)   shall be void in any case where such exclusion or restriction is in respect of death or personal injury;

(b)   shall, in any other case, have no effect if it was not fair and reasonable to incorporate the term in the contract [or, as the case may be, if it is not fair and reasonable to allow reliance on the provision].

[(1A)   Nothing in paragraph (b) of subsection (1) above shall be taken as implying that a provision of a notice has effect in circumstances where, apart from that paragraph, it would not have effect.]

(2)   Subsection (1)(a) above does not affect the validity of any discharge and indemnity given by a person, on or in connection with an award to him of compensation for pneumoconiosis attributable to employment in the coal industry, in respect of any further claim arising from his contracting that disease.

(3)   Where under subsection (1) above a term of a contract [or a provision of a notice] is void or has no effect, the fact that a person agreed to, or was aware of, the term [or provision] shall not of itself be sufficient evidence that he knowingly and voluntarily assumed any risk.

17   Control of unreasonable exemptions in consumer or standard form contracts

(1)   Any term of a contract which is a consumer contract or a standard form contract shall have no effect for the purpose of enabling a party to the contract—

(a)   who is in breach of a contractual obligation, to exclude or restrict any liability of his to the consumer or customer in respect of the breach;

(b)   in respect of a contractual obligation, to render no performance, or to render a performance substantially different from that which the consumer or customer reasonably expected from the contract;

if it was not fair and reasonable to incorporate the term in the contract.

(2)   In this section 'customer' means a party to a standard form contract who deals on the basis of written standard terms of business of the other party to the contract who himself deals in the course of a business.

18   Unreasonable indemnity clauses in consumer contracts

(1)   Any term of a contract which is a consumer contract shall have no effect for the purpose of making the consumer indemnify another person (whether a party to the contract or not) in respect of liability which that other person may incur as a result of breach of duty or breach of contract, if it was not fair and reasonable to incorporate the term in the contract.

(2)   In this section 'liability' means liability arising in the course of any business or from the occupation of any premises used for business purposes of the occupier.

19   'Guarantee' of consumer goods

(1)   This section applies to a guarantee—

(a)   in relation to goods which are of a type ordinarily supplied for private use or consumption; and

(b)   which is not a guarantee given by one party to the other party to a contract under or in pursuance of which the ownership or possession of the goods to which the guarantee relates is transferred.

(2)   A term of a guarantee to which this section applies shall be void in so far as it purports to exclude or restrict liability for loss or damage (including death or personal injury)—

(a)   arising from the goods proving defective while—

(i)   in use otherwise than exclusively for the purposes of a business; or

(ii)   in the possession of a person for such use; and

(b)   resulting from the breach of duty of a person concerned in the manufacture or distribution of the goods.

(3)   For the purposes of this section, any document is a guarantee if it contains or purports to contain some promise or assurance (however worded or presented) that defects will be made good by complete or partial replacement, or by repair, monetary compensation or otherwise.

20 Obligations implied by law in sale and hire-purchase contracts

(1)   Any term of a contract which purports to exclude or restrict liability for breach of the obligations arising from—

(a)   section 12 of the Sale of Goods Act [1979] (seller's implied undertakings as to title etc);

(b)   section 8 of the Supply of Goods (Implied Terms) Act 1973 (implied terms as to title in hire-purchase agreements),

shall be void.

(2)   Any term of a contract which purports to exclude or restrict liability for breach of the obligations arising from—

(a)   section 13, 14 or 15 of the said Act of [1979] (seller's implied undertakings as to conformity of goods with description or sample, or as to their quality or fitness for a particular purpose);

(b)   section 9, 10 or 11 of the said Act of 1973 (the corresponding provisions in relation to hire-purchase),

shall—

(i)   in the case of a consumer contract, be void against the consumer;

(ii)   in any other case, have no effect if it was not fair and reasonable to incorporate the term in the contract.

21 Obligations implied by law in other contracts for the supply of goods

(1)   Any term of a contract to which this section applies purporting to exclude or restrict liability for breach of an obligation—

(a)   such as is referred to in subsection (3)(a) below—

(i)   in the case of a consumer contract, shall be void against the consumer, and

(ii)   in any other case, shall have no effect if it was not fair and reasonable to incorporate the term in the contract;

(b)   such as is referred to in subsection (3)(b) below, shall have no effect if it was not fair and reasonable to incorporate the term in the contract.

(2)   This section applies to any contract to the extent that it relates to any such matter as is referred to in section 15(2)(a) of this Act, but does not apply to—

(a)   a contract of sale of goods or a hire-purchase agreement; or

(b)   a charterparty of a ship or hovercraft unless it is a consumer contract (and then only in favour of the consumer).

(3)   An obligation referred to in this subsection is an obligation incurred under a contract in the course of a business and arising by implication of law from the nature of the contract which relates—

(a)   to the correspondence of goods with description or sample, or to the quality or fitness of goods for any particular purpose; or

(b)   to any right to transfer ownership or possession of goods, or to the enjoyment of quiet possession of goods.

[(3A)   Notwithstanding anything in the foregoing provisions of this section, any term of a contract which purports to exclude or restrict liability for breach of the obligations arising under section 11B of the Supply of Goods and Services Act 1982 (implied terms about title, freedom from encumbrances and quiet possession in certain contracts for the transfer of property in goods) shall be void.]

[. . .]

22   Consequence of breach

For the avoidance of doubt, where any provision of this Part of this Act requires that the incorporation of a term in a contract must be fair and reasonable for that term to have effect—

(a)   if that requirement is satisfied, the term may be given effect to notwithstanding that the contract has been terminated in consequence of breach of that contract;

(b)   for the term to be given effect to, that requirement must be satisfied even where a party who is entitled to rescind the contract elects not to rescind it.

23   Evasion by means of secondary contract

Any term of any contract shall be void which purports to exclude or restrict, or has the effect of excluding or restricting—

(a)   the exercise, by a party to any other contract, of any right or remedy which arises in respect of that other contract in consequence of breach of duty, or of obligation, liability for which could not by virtue of the provisions of this Part of this Act be excluded or restricted by a term of that other contract;

(b)   the application of the provisions of this Part of this Act in respect of that or any other contract.

24   The 'reasonableness' test

(1)   In determining for the purposes of this Part of this Act whether it was fair and reasonable to incorporate a term in a contract, regard shall be had only to the circumstances which were, or ought reasonably to have been, known to or in the contemplation of the parties to the contract at the time the contract was made.

(2)   In determining for the purposes of section 20 or 21 of this Act whether it was fair and reasonable to incorporate a term in a contract, regard shall be had in particular to the matters specified in Schedule 2 to this Act; but this sub-section shall not prevent a court or arbiter from holding in accordance with any rule of law, that a term which purports to exclude or restrict any relevant liability is not a term of the contract.

[(2A)   In determining for the purposes of this Part of this Act whether it is fair and reasonable to allow reliance on a provision of a notice (not being a notice having contractual effect), regard shall be had to all the circumstances obtaining when the liability arose or (but for the provision) would have arisen.]

(3)   Where a term in a contract [or a provision of a notice] purports to restrict liability to a specified sum of money, and the question arises for the purposes of this Part of this Act whether it was fair and reasonable to incorporate the term in the contract [or whether it is fair and reasonable to allow reliance on the provision], then, without prejudice to subsection (2) above [in the case of a term in a contract], regard shall be had in particular to—

(a)   the resources which the party seeking to rely on that term [or provision] could expect to be available to him for the purpose of meeting the liability should it arise;

(b)   how far it was open to that party to cover himself by insurance.

(4)   The onus of proving that it was fair and reasonable to incorporate a term in a contract [or that it is fair and reasonable to allow reliance on a provision of a notice] shall lie on the party so contending.

25   Interpretation of Part II

(1)   In this Part of this Act—

'breach of duty' means the breach—

(a)   of any obligation, arising from the express or implied terms of a contract, to take reasonable care or exercise reasonable skill in the performance of the contract;

(b)   of any common law duty to take reasonable care or exercise reasonable skill;

(c)   of the duty of reasonable care imposed by section 2(1) of the Occupiers' Liability (Scotland) Act 1960;

'business' includes a profession and the activities of any government department or local or public authority;

'consumer' has the meaning assigned to that expression in the definition in this section of 'consumer contract';

'consumer contract' means [subject to subsections (1A) and (1B) below] a contract [. . .] in which—

(a)   one party to the contract deals, and the other party to the contract ('the consumer') does not deal or hold himself out as dealing, in the course of a business, and

(b)   in the case of a contract such as is mentioned in section 15(2)(a) of this Act, the goods are of a type ordinarily supplied for private use or consumption; and for the purposes of this Part of this Act the onus of proving that a contract is not to be regarded as a consumer contract shall lie on the party so contending;

'goods' has the same meaning as in the Sale of Goods Act [1979];

'hire-purchase agreement' has the same meaning as in section 189(1) of the Consumer Credit Act 1974;

['notice' includes an announcement, whether or not in writing, and any other communication or pretended communication;]

'personal injury' includes any disease and any impairment of physical or mental condition.

[(1A)   Where the consumer is an individual, paragraph (b) in the definition of 'consumer contract' in subsection (1) must be disregarded.

(1B)   The expression of 'consumer contract' does not include a contract in which—

(a)   the buyer is an individual and the goods are second hand goods sold by public auction at which individuals have the opportunity of attending in person; or

(b)   the buyer is not an individual and the goods are sold by auction or competitive tender.]

(2)   In relation to any breach of duty or obligation, it is immaterial for any purpose of this Part of this Act whether the act or omission giving rise to that breach was inadvertent or intentional or whether liability for it arises directly or vicariously.

(3)   In this Part of this Act, any reference to excluding or restricting any liability includes—

(a)   making the liability or its enforcement subject to any restrictive or onerous conditions;

(b)   excluding or restricting any right or remedy in respect of the liability, or subjecting a person to any prejudice in consequence of his pursuing any such right or remedy;

(c)   excluding or restricting any rule of evidence or procedure;

[. . .]

(5)   In section 15 and 16 and 19 to 21 of this Act, any reference to excluding or restricting liability for breach of any obligation or duty shall include a reference to excluding or restricting the obligation or duty itself.

PART III
PROVISIONS APPLYING TO WHOLE OF UNITED KINGDOM

26   International supply contracts

(1)   The limits imposed by this Act on the extent to which a person may exclude or restrict liability by reference to a contract term do not apply to liability arising under such a contract as is described in subsection (3) below.

(2)   The terms of such a contract are not subject to any requirement of reasonableness under section 3 or 4: and nothing in Part II of this Act should

require the incorporation of the terms of such a contract to be fair and reasonable for them to have effect.

(3)   Subject to subsection (4), that description of contract is one whose characteristics are the following—

(a)   either it is a contract of sale of goods or it is one under or in pursuance of which the possession of ownership of goods passes, and

(b)   it is made by parties whose places of business (or, if they have none, habitual residences) are in the territories of different States (the Channel Islands and the Isle of Man being treated for this purpose as different States from the United Kingdom).

(4)   A contract falls within subsection (3) above only if either—

(a)   the goods in question are, at the time of the conclusion of the contract, in the course of carriage, or will be carried, from the territory of one State to the territory of another; or

(b)   the acts constituting the offer and acceptance have been done in the territories of different States; or

(c)   the contract provides for the goods to be delivered to the territory of a state other than that within whose territory those acts were done.

27   Choice of law clauses

(1)   Where the [law applicable to] a contract is the law of any part of the United Kingdom only by choice of the parties (and apart from that choice would be the law of some country outside the United Kingdom) sections 2 to 7 and 16 to 21 of this Act do not operate as part [of the law applicable to the contract].

(2)   This Act has effect notwithstanding any contract term which applies or purports to apply the law of some country outside the United Kingdom, where (either or both)—

(a)   the term appears to the court, or arbitrator or arbiter to have been imposed wholly or mainly for the purpose of enabling the party imposing it to evade the operation of this Act; or

(b)   in the making of the contract one of the parties dealt as consumer, and he was then habitually resident in the United Kingdom, and the essential steps necessary for the making of the contract were taken there, whether by him or by others on his behalf.

29   Saving for other relevant legislation

(1)   Nothing in this Act removes or restricts the effect of, or prevents reliance upon, any contractual provision which—

(a)   is authorised or required by the express terms or necessary implication of an enactment; or

(b)   being made with a view to compliance with an international agreement to which the United Kingdom is a party, does not operate more restrictively than is contemplated by the agreement.

(2)   A contract term is to be taken—

(a)   for the purposes of Part I of this Act, as satisfying the requirement of reasonableness [. . .]

if it is incorporated or approved by, or incorporated pursuant to a decision or ruling of, a competent authority acting in the exercise of any statutory jurisdiction or function and is not a term in a contract to which the competent authority is itself a party.

(3)   In this section—

'competent authority' means any court, arbitrator or arbiter, government department or public authority;

'enactment' means any legislation (including subordinate legislation) of the United Kingdom or Northern Ireland and any instrument having effect by virtue of such legislation; and

'statutory' means conferred by an enactment.

SCHEDULE 2
'GUIDELINES' FOR APPLICATION OF REASONABLENESS TEST
Sections 11(2) and 24(2)

The matters to which regard is to be had in particular for the purposes of sections 6(3), 7(3) and (4), 20 and 21 are any of the following which appear to be relevant—

(a) the strength of the bargaining positions of the parties relative to each other, taking into account (among other things) alternative means by which the customer's requirements could have been met;

(b) whether the customer received an inducement to agree to the terms, or in accepting it had an opportunity of entering into a similar contract with other persons, but without having to accept similar terms;

(c) whether the customer knew or ought reasonably to have known of the existence and extent of the term (having regard, among other things, to any customs of the trade and any previous course of dealing between the parties);

(d) where the term excludes or restricts any relevant liability if some condition is not complied with, whether it was reasonable at the time of the contract to expect that compliance with that condition would be practicable;

(e) whether the goods were manufactured, processed or adapted to the special order of the customer.

SALE OF GOODS ACT 1979
(1979, c 54)

PART I
CONTRACTS TO WHICH ACT APPLIES

1 Contracts to which Act applies
(1) This Act applies to contracts of sale of goods made on or after (but not to those made before) 1 January 1894.

(2) In relation to contracts made on certain dates, this Act applies subject to the modification of certain of its sections as mentioned in Schedule 1 below.

(3) Any such modification is indicated in the section concerned by a reference to Schedule 1 below.

(4) Accordingly, where a section does not contain such a reference, this Act applies in relation to the contract concerned without such modification of the section.

PART II
FORMATION OF THE CONTRACT

Contract of sale

2 Contract of sale
(1) A contract of sale of goods is a contract by which the seller transfers or agrees to transfer the property in goods to the buyer for a money consideration, called the price.

(2) There may be a contract of sale between one part owner and another.

(3) A contract of sale may be absolute or conditional.

(4) Where under a contract of sale the property in the goods is transferred from the seller to the buyer the contract is called a sale.

(5) Where under a contract of sale the transfer of the property in the goods is to take place at a future time or subject to some condition later to be fulfilled the contract is called an agreement to sell.

(6) An agreement to sell becomes a sale when the time elapses or the conditions are fulfilled subject to which the property in the goods is to be transferred.

3 Capacity to buy and sell

(1) Capacity to buy and sell is regulated by the general law concerning capacity to contract and to transfer and acquire property.

(2) Where necessaries are sold and delivered [. . .] to a person who by reason of mental incapacity or drunkenness is incompetent to contract, he must pay a reasonable price for them.

(3) In subsection (2) above 'necessaries' means goods suitable to the condition in life of the [. . .] person concerned and to his actual requirements at the time of the sale and delivery.

Formalities of contract

4 How contract of sale is made

(1) Subject to this and any other Act, a contract of sale may be made in writing (either with or without seal), or by word of mouth, or partly in writing and partly by word of mouth, or may be implied from the conduct of the parties.

(2) Nothing in this section affects the law relating to corporations.

Subject matter of contract

5 Existing or future goods

(1) The goods which form the subject of a contract of sale may be either existing goods, owned or possessed by the seller, or goods to be manufactured or acquired by him after the making of the contract of sale, in this Act called future goods.

(2) There may be a contract for the sale of goods the acquisition of which by the seller depends on a contingency which may or may not happen.

(3) Where by a contract of sale the seller purports to effect a present sale of future goods, the contract operates as an agreement to sell the goods.

6 Goods which have perished

Where there is a contract for the sale of specific goods, and the goods without the knowledge of the seller have perished at the time when a contract is made, the contract is void.

7 Goods perishing before sale but after agreement to sell

Where there is an agreement to sell specific goods and subsequently the goods, without any fault on the part of the seller or buyer, perish before the risk passes to the buyer, the agreement is avoided.

The price

8 Ascertainment of price

(1) The price in a contract of sale may be fixed by the contract, or may be left to be fixed in a manner agreed by the contract, or may be determined by the course of dealing between the parties.

(2) Where the price is not determined as mentioned in subsection (1) above the buyer must pay a reasonable price.

(3) What is a reasonable price is a question of fact dependent on the circumstances of each particular case.

9 Agreement to sell at valuation

(1) Where there is an agreement to sell goods on the terms that the price is to be fixed by the valuation of a third party, and he cannot or does not make the valuation, the agreement is avoided; but if the goods or any part of them have been delivered to and appropriated by the buyer he must pay a reasonable price for them.

(2) Where the third party is prevented from making the valuation by the fault

of the seller or buyer, the party not at fault may maintain an action for damages against the party at fault.

[Implied terms etc]

10 Stipulations about time

(1)   Unless a different intention appears from the terms of the contract, stipulations as to time of payment are not of the essence of a contract of sale.

(2)   Whether any other stipulation as to time is or is not of the essence of the contract depends on the terms of the contract.

(3)   In a contract of sale 'month' prima facie means calendar month.

11 [*Does not apply to Scotland.*]

12 Implied terms about title, etc

(1)   In a contract of sale, other than one to which subsection (3) below applies, there is an implied [term] on the part of the seller that in the case of a sale he has a right to sell the goods, and in the case of an agreement to sell he will have such a right at the time when the property is to pass.

(2)   In a contract of sale, other than one to which subsection (3) below applies, there is also an implied [term] that—

(a)   the goods are free, and will remain free until the time when the property is to pass, from any charge or encumbrance not disclosed or known to the buyer before the contract is made, and

(b)   the buyer will enjoy quiet possession of the goods except so far as it may be disturbed by the owner or other person entitled to the benefit of any charge or encumbrance so disclosed or known.

(3)   This subsection applies to a contract of sale in the case of which there appears from the contract or is to be inferred from its circumstances an intention that the seller should transfer only such title as he or a third person may have.

(4)   In a contract to which subsection (3) above applies there is an implied [term] that all charges or encumbrances known to the seller and not known to the buyer have been disclosed to the buyer before the contract is made.

(5)   In a contract to which subsection (3) above applies there is also an implied [term] that none of the following will disturb the buyer's quiet possession of the goods, namely—

(a)   the seller;

(b)   in a case where the parties to the contract intend that the seller should transfer only such title as a third person may have, that person;

(c)   anyone claiming through or under the seller or that third person otherwise than under a charge or encumbrance disclosed or known to the buyer before the contract is made.

[(5A)   As regards England and Wales and Northern Ireland, the term implied by subsection (1) above is a condition and the terms implied by subsections (2), (4) and (5) above are warranties.]

(6)   Paragraph 3 of Schedule 1 below applies in relation to a contract made before 18 May 1973.

13 Sale by description

(1)   Where there is a contract for the sale of goods by description, there is an implied [term] that the goods will correspond with the description.

[(1A)   As regards England and Wales and Northern Ireland, the term implied by subsection (1) above is a condition.]

(2)   If the sale is by sample as well as by description it is not sufficient that the bulk of the goods corresponds with the sample if the goods do not also correspond with the description.

(3)   A sale of goods is not prevented from being a sale by description by reason only that, being exposed for sale or hire, they are selected by the buyer.

(4) Paragraph 4 of Schedule 1 below applies in relation to a contract made before 18 May 1973.

14 Implied terms about quality or fitness

(1) Except as provided by this section and section 15 below and subject to any other enactment, there is no implied [term] about the quality or fitness for any particular purpose of goods supplied under a contract of sale.

[(2) Where the seller sells goods in the course of a business, there is an implied term that the goods supplied under the contract are of satisfactory quality.

(2A) For the purposes of this Act, goods are of satisfactory quality if they meet the standard that a reasonable person would regard as satisfactory, taking account of any description of the goods, the price (if relevant) and all the other relevant circumstances.

(2B) For the purposes of this Act, the quality of goods includes their state and condition and the following (among others) are in appropriate cases aspects of the quality of goods—

(a) fitness for all the purposes for which goods of the kind in question are commonly supplied,

(b) appearance and finish,

(c) freedom from minor defects,

(d) safety, and

(c) durability.

(2C) The term implied by subsection (2) above does not extend to any matter making the quality of goods unsatisfactory—

(a) which is specifically drawn to the buyer's attention before the contract is made,

(b) where the buyer examines the goods before the contract is made, which that examination ought to reveal, or

(c) in the case of a contract for sale by sample, which would have been apparent on a reasonable examination of the sample.]

[(2D) If the buyer deals as consumer or, in Scotland, if a contract of sale is a consumer contract, the relevant circumstances mentioned in subsection (2A) above include any public statements on the specific characteristics of the goods made about them by the seller, the producer or his representative, particularly in advertising or on labelling.

(2E) A public statement is not by virtue of subsection (2D) above a relevant circumstance for the purposes of subsection (2A) above in the case of a contract of sale, if the seller shows that—

(a) at the time the contract was made, he was not, and could not reasonably have been, aware of the statement,

(b) before the contract was made, the statement had been withdrawn in public or, to the extent that it contained anything which was incorrect or misleading, it had been corrected in public, or

(c) the decision to buy the goods could not have been influenced by the statement.

(2F) Subsections (2D) and (2E) above do not prevent any public statement from being a relevant circumstance for the purposes of subsection (2A) above (whether or not the buyer deals as consumer or, in Scotland, whether or not the contract of sale is a consumer contract) if the statement would have been such a circumstance apart from those subsections.]

(3) Where the seller sells goods in the course of a business and the buyer, expressly or by implication, makes known—

(a) to the seller, or

(b) where the purchase price or part of it is payable by instalments and the goods were previously sold by a credit-broker to the seller, to that credit-broker, any particular purpose for which the goods are being bought, there is an implied [term] that the goods supplied under the contract are reason-ably fit for that purpose, whether or not that is a purpose for which such goods are commonly supplied, except where the circumstances show that the buyer does not rely, or that it is unreasonable for him to rely, on the skill or judgment of the seller or credit-broker.

(4)   An implied [term] about quality or fitness for a particular purpose may be annexed to a contract of sale by usage.

(5)   The preceding provisions of this section apply to a sale by a person who in the course of a business is acting as agent for another as they apply to a sale by a principal in the course of a business, except where that other is not selling in the course of a business and either the buyer knows that fact or reasonable steps are taken to bring it to the notice of the buyer before the contract is made.

[(6)   As regards England and Wales and Northern Ireland, the terms implied by subsections (2) and (3) above are conditions.]

(7)   Paragraph 5 of Schedule 1 below applies in relation to a contract made on or after 18 May 1973 and before the appointed day, and paragraph 6 in relation to one made before 18 May 1973.

(8)   In subsection (7) above and paragraph 5 of Schedule 1 below references to the appointed day are to the day appointed for the purposes of those provisions by an order of the Secretary of State made by statutory instrument.

Sale by sample

15   Sale by sample

(1)   A contract of sale is a contract for sale by sample where there is an express or implied term to that effect in the contract.

(2)   In the case of a contract for sale by sample there is an implied [term]—
   (a)   that the bulk will correspond with the sample in quality;
   [. . .]
   (c)   that the goods will be free from any defect, making their quality unsatisfactory, which would not be apparent on reasonable examination of the sample.

[(3)   As regards England and Wales and Northern Ireland, the term implied by subsection (2) above is a condition.]

(4)   Paragraph 7 of Schedule 1 below applies in relation to a contract made before 18 May 1973.

Miscellaneous

15A   [*Does not apply to Scotland.*]

[15B   Remedies for breach of contract as respects Scotland

(1)   Where in a contract of sale the seller is in breach of any term of the contract (express or implied), the buyer shall be entitled—
   (a)   to claim damages, and
   (b)   if the breach is material, to reject any goods delivered under the contract and treat it as repudiated.

(2)   Where a contract of sale is a consumer contract, then, for the purposes of subsection (1)(b) above, breach by the seller of any term (express or implied)—
   (a)   as to the quality of the goods or their fitness for a purpose,
   (b)   if the goods are, or are to be, sold by description, that the goods will correspond with the description,
   (c)   if the goods are, or are to be, sold by reference to a sample, that the bulk will correspond with the sample in quality,
shall be deemed to be a material breach.

(3)   This section applies to Scotland only.]

PART III
EFFECTS OF THE CONTRACT

Transfer of property as between seller and buyer

16 Goods must he ascertained
[Subject to section 20A below] where there is a contract for the sale of unascertained goods no property in the goods is transferred to the buyer unless and until the goods are ascertained.

17 Property passes when intended to pass
(1) Where there is a contract for the sale of specific or ascertained goods the property in them is transferred to the buyer at such time as the parties to the contract intend it to be transferred.

(2) For the purpose of ascertaining the intention of the parties regard shall be had to the terms of the contract, the conduct of the parties and the circumstances of the case.

18 Rules for ascertaining intention
Unless a different intention appears, the following are rules for ascertaining the intention of the parties as to the time at which the property in the goods is to pass to the buyer.

Rule 1.—Where there is an unconditional contract for the sale of specific goods in a deliverable state the property in the goods passes to the buyer when the contract is made, and it is immaterial whether the time of payment or the time of delivery, or both, be postponed.

Rule 2.—Where there is a contract for the sale of specific goods and the seller is bound to do something to the goods for the purpose of putting them into a deliverable state, the property does not pass until the thing is done and the buyer has notice that it has been done.

Rule 3.—Where there is a contract for the sale of specific goods in a deliverable state but the seller is bound to weigh, measure, test, or do some other act or thing with reference to the goods for the purpose of ascertaining the price, the property does not pass until the act or thing is done and the buyer has notice that it has been done.

Rule 4.—When goods are delivered to the buyer on approval or on sale or return or other similar terms the property in the goods passes to the buyer:—

(a) when he signifies his approval or acceptance to the seller or does any other act adopting the transaction;

(b) if he does not signify his approval or acceptance to the seller but retains the goods without giving notice of rejection, then, if a time has been fixed for the return of the goods, on the expiration of that time, and, if no time has been fixed, on the expiration of a reasonable time.

Rule 5.—(1) Where there is a contract for the sale of unascertained or future goods by description, and goods of that description and in a deliverable state are unconditionally appropriated to the contract, either by the seller with the assent of the buyer or by the buyer with the assent of the seller, the property in the goods then passes to the buyer; and the assent may be express or implied, and may be given either before or after the appropriation is made.

(2) Where, in pursuance of the contract, the seller delivers the goods to the buyer or to a carrier or other bailee or custodier (whether named by the buyer or not) for the purpose of transmission to the buyer, and does not reserve the right of disposal, he is to be taken to have unconditionally appropriated the goods to the contract.

[(3) Where there is a contract for the sale of a specified quantity of unascertained goods in a deliverable state forming part of a bulk which is identified either in the contract or by subsequent agreement between the parties and the bulk is reduced to (or to less than) that quantity, then, if the buyer under that contract is the only buyer to whom goods are then due out of the bulk—

(a)   the remaining goods are to be taken as appropriated to that contract at the time when the bulk is so reduced; and

(b)   the property in those goods then passes to that buyer.

(4)   Paragraph (3) above applies also (with the necessary modifications) where a bulk is reduced to (or to less than) the aggregate of the quantities due to a single buyer under separate contracts relating to that bulk and he is the only buyer to whom goods are then due out of that bulk.]

19   Reservation of right of disposal

(1)   Where there is a contract for the sale of specific goods or where goods are subsequently appropriated to the contract, the seller may, by the terms of the contract or appropriation, reserve the right of disposal of the goods until certain conditions are fulfilled; and in such a case, notwithstanding the delivery of the goods to the buyer, or to a carrier or other bailee or custodier for the purpose of transmission to the buyer, the property in the goods does not pass to the buyer until the conditions imposed by the seller are fulfilled.

(2)   Where goods are shipped, and by the bill of lading the goods are deliverable to the order of the seller or his agent, the seller is prima facie to be taken to reserve the right of disposal.

(3)   Where the seller of goods draws on the buyer for the price, and transmits the bill of exchange and bill of lading to the buyer together to secure acceptance or payment of the bill of exchange, the buyer is bound to return the bill of lading if he does not honour the bill of exchange, and if he wrongfully retains the bill of lading the property in the goods does not pass to him.

20   [Passing of risk]

(1)   Unless otherwise agreed, the goods remain at the seller's risk until the property in them is transferred to the buyer, but when the property in them is transferred to the buyer the goods are at the buyer's risk whether delivery has been made or not.

(2)   But where delivery has been delayed through the fault of either buyer or seller the goods are at the risk of the party at fault as regards any loss which might not have occurred but for such fault.

(3)   Nothing in this section affects the duties or liabilities of either seller or buyer as a bailee or custodier of the goods of the other party.

[(4)   In a case where the buyer deals as consumer or, in Scotland, where there is a consumer contract in which the buyer is a consumer, subsections (1) to (3) above must be ignored and the goods remain at the seller's risk until they are delivered to the consumer.]

[20A   Undivided shares in goods forming part of a bulk

(1)   This section applies to a contract for the sale of a specified quantity of unascertained goods if the following conditions are met—

(a)   the goods or some of them form part of a bulk which is identified either in the contract or by subsequent agreement between the parties; and

(b)   the buyer has paid the price for some or all of the goods which are the subject of the contract and which form part of the bulk.

(2)   Where this section applies, then (unless the parties agree otherwise), as soon as the conditions specified in paragraphs (a) and (b) of subsection (1) above are met or at such later time as the parties may agree—

(a)   property in an undivided share in the bulk is transferred to the buyer; and

(b)   the buyer becomes an owner in common of the bulk.

(3)   Subject to subsection (4) below, for the purposes of this section, the undivided share of a buyer in a bulk at any time shall be such share as the quantity

of goods paid for and due to the buyer out of the bulk bears to the quantity of goods in the bulk at that time.

(4)   Where the aggregate of the undivided shares of buyers in a bulk deter-mined under subsection (3) above would at any time exceed the whole of the bulk at that time, the undivided share in the bulk of each buyer shall be reduced pro-portionately so that the aggregate of the undivided shares is equal to the whole bulk.

(5)   Where a buyer has paid the price for only some of the goods due to him out of a bulk, any delivery to the buyer out of the bulk shall, for the purposes of this section, be ascribed in the first place to the goods in respect of which payment has been made.

(6)   For the purpose of this section payment of part of the price for any goods shall be treated as payment for a corresponding part of the goods.]

[20B   Deemed consent by co-owner to dealings in bulk goods

(1)   A person who has become an owner in common of a bulk by virtue of section 20A above shall be deemed to have consented to—

(a)   any delivery of goods out of the bulk to any other owner in common of the bulk, being goods which are due to him under his contract;

(b)   any removal, dealing with, delivery or disposal of goods in the bulk by any other person who is an owner in common of the bulk in so far as the goods fall within that co-owner's undivided share in the bulk at the time of the removal, dealing, delivery or disposal.

(2)   No cause of action shall accrue to anyone against a person by reason of that person having acted in accordance with paragraph (a) or (b) of subsection (1) above in reliance on any consent deemed to have been given under that subsection.

(3)   Nothing in this section or section 20A above shall—

(a)   impose an obligation on a buyer of goods out of a bulk to compensate any other buyer of goods out of that bulk for any shortfall in the goods received by that other buyer;

(b)   affects any contractual arrangement between buyers of goods out of a bulk for adjustments between themselves; or

(c)   affect the rights of any buyer under his contract.]

Transfer of title

21   Sale by person not the owner

(1)   Subject to this Act, where goods are sold by a person who is not their owner, and who does not sell them under the authority or with the consent of the owner, the buyer acquires no better title to the goods than the seller had, unless the owner of the goods is by his conduct precluded from denying the seller's authority to sell.

(2)   Nothing in this Act affects—

(a)   the provisions of the Factors Acts or any enactment enabling the apparent owner of goods to dispose of them as if he were their true owner;

(b)   the validity of any contract of sale under any special common law or statutory power of sale or under the order of a court of competent jurisdiction.

22   [*Does not apply to Scotland.*]

23   Sale under voidable title

When the seller of goods has a voidable title to them, but his title has not been avoided at the time of the sale, the buyer acquires a good title to the goods, pro-vided he buys them in good faith and without notice of the seller's defect of title.

24   Seller in possession after sale

Where a person having sold goods continues or is in possession of the goods, or of the documents of title to the goods, the delivery or transfer by that person, or by a mercantile agent acting for him, of the goods or documents of title under any sale, pledge, or other disposition thereof, to any person receiving the same in good faith and without notice of the previous sale, has the same effect as if the person making the delivery or transfer were expressly authorised by the owner of the goods to make the same.

25 Buyer in possession after sale

(1) Where a person having bought or agreed to buy goods obtains, with the consent of the seller, possession of the goods or the documents of title to the goods, the delivery or transfer by that person, or by a mercantile agent acting for him, of the goods or documents of title, under any sale, pledge, or other disposition thereof, to any person receiving the same in good faith and without notice of any lien or other right of the original seller in respect of the goods, has the same effect as if the person making the delivery or transfer were a mercantile agent in possession of the goods or documents of title with the consent of the owner.

(2) For the purposes of subsection (1) above—

(a) the buyer under a conditional sale agreement is to be taken not to be a person who has bought or agreed to buy goods, and

(b) 'conditional sale agreement' means an agreement for the sale of goods which is a consumer credit agreement within the meaning of the Consumer Credit Act 1974 under which the purchase price or part of it is payable by instalments, and the property in the goods is to remain in the seller (notwithstanding that the buyer is to be in possession of the goods) until such conditions as to the payment of instalments or otherwise as may be specified in the agreement are fulfilled.

(3) Paragraph 9 of Schedule 1 below applies in relation to a contract under which a person buys or agrees to buy goods and which is made before the appointed day.

(4) In subsection (3) above and paragraph 9 of Schedule 1 below references to the appointed day are to the day appointed for the purposes of those provisions by an order of the Secretary of State made by statutory instrument.

26 Supplementary to sections 24 and 25

In sections 24 and 25 above 'mercantile agent' means a mercantile agent having in the customary course of his business as such agent authority either—

(a) to sell goods, or

(b) to consign goods for the purpose of sale, or

(c) to buy goods, or

(d) to raise money on the security of goods.

PART IV
PERFORMANCE OF THE CONTRACT

27 Duties of seller and buyer

It is the duty of the seller to deliver the goods, and of the buyer to accept and pay for them, in accordance with the terms of the contract of sale.

28 Payment and delivery are concurrent conditions

Unless otherwise agreed, delivery of the goods and payment of the price are concurrent conditions, that is to say, the seller must be ready and willing to give possession of the goods to the buyer in exchange for the price and the buyer must be ready and willing to pay the price in exchange for possession of the goods.

29 Rules about delivery

(1) Whether it is for the buyer to take possession of the goods or for the seller to send them to the buyer is a question depending in each case on the contract, express or implied, between the parties.

(2)   Apart from any such contract, express or implied, the place of delivery is the seller's place of business if he has one, and if not, his residence; except that, if the contract is for the sale of specific goods, which to the knowledge of the parties when the contract is made are in some other place, then that place is the place of delivery.

(3)   Where under the contract of sale the seller is bound to send the goods to the buyer, but no time for sending them is fixed, the seller is bound to send them within a reasonable time.

(4)   Where the goods at the time of sale are in the possession of a third person, there is no delivery by seller to buyer unless and until the third person acknowledges to the buyer that he holds the goods on his behalf; but nothing in this section affects the operation of the issue or transfer of any document of title to goods.

(5)   Demand or tender of delivery may be treated as ineffectual unless made at a reasonable hour, and what is a reasonable hour is a question of fact.

(6)   Unless otherwise agreed, the expenses of and incidental to putting the goods into a deliverable state must be borne by the seller.

30   Delivery of wrong quantity

(1)   Where the seller delivers to the buyer a quantity of goods less than he contracted to sell, the buyer may reject them, but if the buyer accepts the goods so delivered he must pay for them at the contract rate.

(2)   Where the seller delivers to the buyer a quantity of goods larger than he contracted to sell, the buyer may accept the goods included in the contract and reject the rest, or he may reject the whole.

. . .

[(2C)   Subsections (2A) and (2B) above do not apply to Scotland.

(2D)   Where the seller delivers a quantity of goods—

(a)   less than he contracted to sell, the buyer shall not be entitled to reject the goods under subsection (1) above,

(b)   larger than he contracted to sell, the buyer shall not be entitled to reject the whole under subsection (2) above,

unless the shortfall or excess is material.

(2E)   Subsection (2D) above applies to Scotland only.]

(3)   Where the seller delivers to the buyer a quantity of goods larger than he contracted to sell and the buyer accepts the whole of the goods so delivered he must pay for them at the contract rate.

[. . .]

(5)   This section is subject to any usage of trade, special agreement, or course of dealing between the parties.

31   Instalment deliveries

(1)   Unless otherwise agreed, the buyer of goods is not bound to accept delivery of them by instalments.

(2)   Where there is a contract for the sale of goods to be delivered by stated instalments, which are to be separately paid for, and the seller makes defective deliveries in respect of one or more instalments, or the buyer neglects or refuses to take delivery of or pay for one or more instalments, it is a question in each case depending on the terms of the contract and the circumstances of the case whether the breach of contract is a repudiation of the whole contract or whether it is a severable breach giving rise to a claim for compensation but not to a right to treat the whole contract as repudiated.

32   Delivery to carrier

(1)   Where, in pursuance of a contract of sale, the seller is authorised or required to send the goods to the buyer, delivery of the goods to a carrier (whether

named by the buyer or not) for the purpose of transmission to the buyer is prima facie deemed to be delivery of the goods to the buyer.

(2)   Unless otherwise authorised by the buyer, the seller must make such contact with the carrier on behalf of the buyer as may be reasonable having regard to the nature of the goods and the other circumstances of the case; and if the seller omits to do so, and the goods are lost or damaged in course of transit, the buyer may decline to treat the delivery to the carrier as a delivery to himself or may hold the seller responsible in damages.

(3)   Unless otherwise agreed, where goods are sent by the seller to the buyer by a route involving sea transit, under circumstances in which it is usual to insure, the seller must give such notice to the buyer as may enable him to insure them during their sea transit, and if the seller fails to do so, the goods are at his risk during such sea transit.

[(4)   In a case where the buyer deals as consumer or, in Scotland, where there is a consumer contract in which the buyer is a consumer, subsections (1) to (3) above must be ignored, but if in pursuance of a contract of sale the seller is authorised or required to send the goods to the buyer, delivery of the goods to the carrier is not delivery of the goods to the buyer.]

33   Risk where goods are delivered at distant place
Where the seller of goods agrees to deliver them at his own risk at a place other than that where they are when sold, the buyer must nevertheless (unless otherwise agreed) take any risk of deterioration in the goods necessarily incident to the course of transit.

34   Buyer's right of examining the goods
[Unless otherwise agreed, when the seller tenders delivery of goods to the buyer, he is bound on request to afford the buyer a reasonable opportunity of examining the goods for the purpose of ascertaining whether they are in conformity with the contract and, in the case of a contract for sale by sample, of comparing the bulk with the sample.]

35   Acceptance
(1)   The buyer is deemed to have accepted the goods [subject to subsection (2) below—
   (a)   when he intimates to the seller that he has accepted them, or
   (b)   when the goods have been delivered to him and he does any act in relation to them which is inconsistent with the ownership of the seller.

(2)   Where goods are delivered to the buyer, and he has not previously examined them, he is not deemed to have accepted them under subsection (1) above until he has had a reasonable opportunity of examining them for the purpose—
   (a)   of ascertaining whether they are in conformity with the contract, and
   (b)   in the case of a contract for sale by sample, of comparing the bulk with the sample.

(3)   Where the buyer deals as consumer or (in Scotland) the contract of sale is a consumer contract, the buyer cannot lose his right to rely on subsection (2) above by agreement, waiver or otherwise.

(4)   The buyer is also deemed to have accepted the goods when after the lapse of a reasonable time he retains the goods without intimating to the seller that he has rejected them.

(5)   The questions that are material in determining for the purposes of subsection (4) above whether a reasonable time has elapsed include whether the buyer has had a reasonable opportunity of examining the goods for the purpose mentioned in subsection (2) above.

(6)   The buyer is not by virtue of this section deemed to have accepted the goods merely because—

(a)   he asks for, or agrees to, their repair by or under an arrangement with the seller, or

(b)   the goods are delivered to another under a sub-sale or other disposition.

(7)   Where the contract is for the sale of goods making one or more commercial units, a buyer accepting any goods included in a unit is deemed to have accepted all the goods making the unit; and in this subsection 'commercial unit' means a unit division of which would materially impair the value of the goods or the character of the unit.

(8)]   Paragraph 10 of Schedule 1 below applies in relation to a contract made before 22 April 1967 or (in the application of this Act to Northern Ireland) 28 July 1967.

[35A   Right of partial rejection

(1)   If the buyer—

(a)   has the right to reject the goods by reason of a breach on the part of the seller that affects some or all of them, but

(b)   accepts some of the goods, including, where there are any goods unaffected by the breach, all such goods,

he does not by accepting them lose his right to reject the rest.

(2)   In the case of a buyer having the right to reject an instalment of goods, subsection (1) above applies as if references to the goods were references to the goods comprised in the instalment.

(3)   For the purposes of subsection (1) above, goods are affected by a breach if by reason of the breach they are not in conformity with the contract.

(4)   This section applies unless a contrary intention appears in, or is to be implied from, the contract.]

36   Buyer not bound to return rejected goods

Unless otherwise agreed, where goods are delivered to the buyer, and he refuses to accept them, having the right to do so, he is not bound to return them to the seller, but it is sufficient if he intimates to the seller that he refuses to accept them.

37   Buyer's liability for not taking delivery of goods

(1)   When the seller is ready and willing to deliver the goods, and requests the buyer to take delivery, and the buyer does not within a reasonable time after such request take delivery of the goods, he is liable to the seller for any loss occasioned by his neglect or refusal to take delivery, and also for a reasonable charge for the care and custody of the goods.

(2)   Nothing in this section affects the rights of the seller where the neglect or refusal of the buyer to take delivery amounts to a repudiation of the contract.

PART V
RIGHTS OF UNPAID SELLER AGAINST THE GOODS

Preliminary

38   Unpaid seller defined

(1)   The seller of goods is an unpaid seller within the meaning of this Act—

(a)   when the whole of the price has not been paid or tendered;

(b)   when a bill of exchange or other negotiable instrument has been received as conditional payment, and the condition on which it was received has not been fulfilled by reason of the dishonour of the instrument or otherwise.

(2)   In this Part of this Act 'seller' includes any person who is in the position of a seller, as, for instance, an agent of the seller to whom the bill of lading has been indorsed, or a consignor or agent who has himself paid (or is directly responsible for) the price.

39   Unpaid seller's rights

(1)   Subject to this and any other Act, notwithstanding that the property in the goods may have passed to the buyer, the unpaid seller of goods, as such, has by implication of law—

(a)   a lien on the goods or right to retain them for the price while he is in possession of them;

(b)   in the case of the insolvency of the buyer, a right of stopping the goods in transit after he has parted with the possession of them;

(c)   a right of re-sale as limited by this Act.

(2)   Where the property in goods has not passed to the buyer, the unpaid seller has (in addition to his other remedies) a right of withholding delivery similar to and coextensive with his rights of lien or retention and stoppage in transit where the property has passed to the buyer.

[. . .]

Unpaid seller's lien

41   Seller's lien

(1)   Subject to this Act, the unpaid seller of goods who is in possession of them is entitled to retain possession of them until payment or tender of the price in the following cases:—

(a)   where the goods have been sold without any stipulation as to credit;

(b)   where the goods have been sold on credit but the term of credit has expired;

(c)   where the buyer becomes insolvent.

(2)   The seller may exercise his lien or right of retention notwithstanding that he is in possession of the goods as agent or bailee or custodier for the buyer.

42   Part delivery

Where an unpaid seller has made part delivery of the goods, he may exercise his lien or right of retention on the remainder, unless such part delivery has been made under such circumstances as to show an agreement to waive the lien or right of retention.

43   Termination of lien

(1)   The unpaid seller of goods loses his lien or right of retention in respect of them—

(a)   when he delivers the goods to a carrier or other bailee or custodier for the purpose of transmission to the buyer without reserving the right of disposal of the goods;

(b)   when the buyer or his agent lawfully obtains possession of the goods;

(c)   by waiver of the lien or right of retention.

(2)   An unpaid seller of goods who has a lien or right of retention in respect of them does not lose his lien or right of retention by reason only that he has obtained judgment or decree for the price of the goods.

Stoppage in transit

44   Right of stoppage in transit

Subject to this Act, when the buyer of goods becomes insolvent the unpaid seller who has parted with the possession of the goods has the right of stopping them in transit, that is to say, he may resume possession of the goods as long as they are in course of transit, and may retain them until payment or tender of the price.

45   Duration of transit

(1)   Goods are deemed to be in course of transit from the time when they are delivered to a carrier or other bailee or custodier for the purpose of transmission to the buyer, until the buyer or his agent in that behalf takes delivery of them from the carrier or other bailee or custodier.

(2)   If the buyer or his agent in that behalf obtains delivery of the goods before their arrival at the appointed destination, the transit is at an end.

(3)   If, after the arrival of the goods at the appointed destination, the carrier or other bailee or custodier acknowledges to the buyer or his agent that he holds the goods on his behalf and continues in possession of them as bailee or custodier for the buyer or his agent, the transit is at an end, and it is immaterial that a further destination for the goods may have been indicated by the buyer.

(4)   If the goods are rejected by the buyer, and the carrier or other bailee or custodier continues in possession of them, the transit is not deemed to be at an end, even if the seller has refused to receive them back.

(5)   When goods are delivered to a ship chartered by the buyer it is a question depending on the circumstances of the particular case whether they are in the possession of the master as a carrier or as agent to the buyer.

(6)   Where the carrier or other bailee or custodier wrongfully refuses to deliver the goods to the buyer or his agent in that behalf, the transit is deemed to be at an end.

(7)   Where part delivery of the goods has been made to the buyer or his agent in that behalf, the remainder of the goods may be stopped in transit, unless such part delivery has been made under such circumstances as to show an agreement to give up possession of the whole of the goods.

46   How stoppage in transit is effected

(1)   The unpaid seller may exercise his right of stoppage in transit either by taking actual possession of the goods or by giving notice of his claim to the carrier or other bailee or custodier in whose possession the goods are.

(2)   The notice may be given either to the person in actual possession of the goods or to his principal.

(3)   If given to the principal, the notice is ineffective unless given at such time and under such circumstances that the principal, by the exercise of reasonable diligence, may communicate it to his servant or agent in time to prevent a delivery to the buyer.

(4)   When notice of stoppage in transit is given by the seller to the carrier or other bailee or custodier in possession of the goods, he must re-deliver the goods to, or according to the directions of, the seller; and the expenses of the re-delivery must be borne by the seller.

Re-sale etc by buyer

47   Effect of sub-sale etc by buyer

(1)   Subject to this Act, the unpaid seller's right of lien or retention or stoppage in transit is not affected by any sale or other disposition of the goods which the buyer may have made, unless the seller has assented to it.

(2)   Where a document of title to goods has been lawfully transferred to any person as buyer or owner of the goods, and that person transfers the document to a person who takes it in good faith and for valuable consideration, then—

(a)   if the last-mentioned transfer was by way of sale the unpaid seller's right of lien or retention or stoppage in transit is defeated; and

(b)   if the last-mentioned transfer was made by way of pledge or other disposition for value, the unpaid seller's right of lien or retention of stoppage in transit can only be exercised subject to the rights of the transferee.

Rescission: and re-sale by seller

48   Rescission: and re-sale by seller

(1)   Subject to this section, a contract of sale is not rescinded by the mere exercise by an unpaid seller of his right of lien or retention or stoppage in transit.

(2)   Where an unpaid seller who has exercised his right of lien or retention or

stoppage in transit re-sells the goods, the buyer acquires a good title to them as against the original buyer.

(3)   Where the goods are of a perishable nature, or where the unpaid seller gives notice to the buyer of his intention to re-sell, and the buyer does not within a reasonable time pay or tender the price, the unpaid seller may re-sell the goods and recover from the original buyer damages for any loss occasioned by his breach of contract.

(4)   Where the seller expressly reserves the right of re-sale in case the buyer should make default, and on the buyer making default re-sells the goods, the original contract of sale is rescinded but without prejudice to any claim the seller may have for damages.

[PART VA
ADDITIONAL RIGHTS OF BUYER IN CONSUMER CASES

48A   Introductory
(1)   This section applies if—

(a)   the buyer deals as consumer or, in Scotland, there is a consumer contract in which the buyer is a consumer, and

(b)   the goods do not conform to the contract of sale at the time of delivery.

(2)   If this section applies, the buyer has the right—

(a)   under and in accordance with section 48B below, to require the seller to repair or replace the goods, or

(b)   under and in accordance with section 48C below—

(i)   to require the seller to reduce the purchase price of the goods to the buyer by an appropriate amount, or

(ii)   to rescind the contract with regard to the goods in question.

(3)   For the purposes of subsection (1)(b) above goods which do not conform to the contract of sale at any time within the period of six months starting with the date on which the goods were delivered to the buyer must be taken not to have so conformed at that date.

(4)   Subsection (3) above does not apply if—

(a)   it is established that the goods did so conform at that date;

(b)   its application is incompatible with the nature of the goods or the nature of the lack of conformity.

48B   Repair or replacement of the goods
(1)   If section 48A above applies, the buyer may require the seller—

(a)   to repair the goods, or

(b)   to replace the goods.

(2)   If the buyer requires the seller to repair or replace the goods, the seller must—

(a)   repair or, as the case may be, replace the goods within a reasonable time but without causing significant inconvenience to the buyer;

(b)   bear any necessary costs incurred in doing so (including in particular the cost of any labour, materials or postage).

(3)   The buyer must not require the seller to repair or, as the case may be, replace the goods if that remedy is—

(a)   impossible, or

(b)   disproportionate in comparison to the other of those remedies, or

(c)   disproportionate in comparison to an appropriate reduction in the purchase price under paragraph (a), or rescission under paragraph (b), of section 48C(1) below.

(4)   One remedy is disproportionate in comparison to the other if the one imposes costs on the seller which, in comparison to those imposed on him by the other, are unreasonable, taking into account—

(a)   the value which the goods would have if they conformed to the contract of sale,

(b)   the significance of the lack of conformity, and

(c)   whether the other remedy could be effected without significant inconvenience to the buyer.

(5)   Any question as to what is a reasonable time or significant inconvenience is to be determined by reference to—

(a)   the nature of the goods, and

(b)   the purpose for which the goods were acquired.

48C   Reduction of purchase price or rescission of contract

(1)   If section 48A above applies, the buyer may—

(a)   require the seller to reduce the purchase price of the goods in question to the buyer by an appropriate amount, or

(b)   rescind the contract with regard to those goods,

if the condition in subsection (2) below is satisfied.

(2)   The condition is that—

(a)   by virtue of section 48B(3) above the buyer may require neither repair nor replacement of the goods; or

(b)   the buyer has required the seller to repair or replace the goods, but the seller is in breach of the requirement of section 48B(2)(a) above to do so within a reasonable time and without significant inconvenience to the buyer.

(3)   For the purposes of this Part, if the buyer rescinds the contract, any reimbursement to the buyer may be reduced to take account of the use he has had of the goods since they were delivered to him.

48D   Relation to other remedies etc

(1)   If the buyer requires the seller to repair or replace the goods the buyer must not act under subsection (2) until he has given the seller a reasonable time in which to repair or replace (as the case may be) the goods.

(2)   The buyer acts under this subsection if—

(a)   in England and Wales or Northern Ireland he rejects the goods and terminates the contract for breach of condition;

(b)   in Scotland he rejects any goods delivered under the contract and treats it as repudiated;

(c)   he requires the goods to be replaced or repaired (as the case may be).

48E   Powers of the court

(1)   In any proceedings in which a remedy is sought by virtue of this Part the court, in addition to any other power it has, may act under this section.

(2)   On the application of the buyer the court may make an order requiring specific performance or, in Scotland, specific implement by the seller of any obligation imposed on him by virtue of section 48B above.

(3)   Subsection (4) applies if—

(a)   the buyer requires the seller to give effect to a remedy under section 48B or 48C above or has claims to rescind under section 48C, but

(b)   the court decides that another remedy under section 48B or 48C is appropriate.

(4)   The court may proceed—

(a)   as if the buyer had required the seller to give effect to the other remedy, or if the other remedy is rescission under section 48C; or

(b)   as if the buyer had claimed to rescind the contract under that section.

(5)   If the buyer has claimed to rescind the contract the court may order that any reimbursement to the buyer is reduced to take account of the use he has had of the goods since they were delivered to him.

(6)   The court may make an order under this section unconditionally or on such

terms and conditions as to damages, payment of the price and otherwise as it thinks just.

48F   Conformity with the contract
For the purposes of this Part, goods do not conform to a contract of sale if there is, in relation to the goods, a breach of an express term of the contract or a term implied by section 13, 14 or 15 above.]

PART VI
ACTIONS FOR BREACH OF THE CONTRACT

Seller's remedies

49   Action for price
(1)   Where, under a contract of sale, the property in the goods has passed to the buyer and he wrongfully neglects or refuses to pay for the goods according to the terms of the contract, the seller may maintain an action against him for the price of the goods.

(2)   Where, under a contract of sale, the price is payable on a day certain irrespective of delivery and the buyer wrongfully neglects or refuses to pay such price, the seller may maintain an action for the price, although the property in goods has not passed and the goods have not been appropriated to the contract.

(3)   Nothing in this section prejudices the right of the seller in Scotland to recover interest on the price from the date of tender of the goods, or from the date on which the price was payable, as the case may be.

50   Damages for non-acceptance
(1)   Where the buyer wrongfully neglects or refuses to accept and pay for the goods, the seller may maintain an action against him for damages for non-acceptance.

(2)   The measure of damages is the estimated loss directly and naturally resulting in the ordinary course of events, from the buyer's breach of contract.

(3)   Where there is an available market for the goods in question the measure of damages is prima facie to be ascertained by the difference between the contract price and the market or current price at the time or times when the goods ought to have been accepted or (if no time was fixed for acceptance) at the time of the refusal to accept.

Buyer's remedies

51   Damages for non-delivery
(1)   Where the seller wrongfully neglects or refuses to deliver the goods to the buyer, the buyer may maintain an action against the seller for damages for non-delivery.

(2)   The measure of damages is the estimated loss directly and naturally resulting, in the ordinary course of events, from the seller's breach of contract.

(3)   Where there is an available market for the goods in question the measure of damages is prima facie to be ascertained by the difference between the contract price and the market or current price of the goods at the time or times when they ought to have been delivered or (if no time was fixed) at the time of the refusal to deliver.

52   Specific performance
(1)   If any action for breach of contract to deliver specific or ascertained goods the court may, if it thinks fit, on the plaintiff's application, by its judgment or decree direct that the contract shall be performed specifically, without giving the defendant the option of retaining the goods on payment of damages.

(2)   The plaintiff's application may be made at any time before judgment or decree.

(3)   The judgment or decree may be unconditional, or on such terms and conditions as to damages, payment of the price and otherwise as seem just to the court.

(4)   The provisions of this section shall be deemed to be supplementary to, and not in derogation of, the right of specific implement in Scotland.

53   [*Does not apply to Scotland.*]

[53A   Measure of damages as respects Scotland

(1)   The measure of damages for the seller's breach of contract is the estimated loss directly and naturally resulting, in the ordinary course of events, from the breach.

(2)   Where the seller's breach consists of the delivery of goods which are not of the quality required by the contract and the buyer retains the goods, such loss as aforesaid is prima facie the difference between the value of the goods at the time of delivery to the buyer and the value they would have had if they had fulfilled the contract.

(3)   This section applies to Scotland only.]

Interest, etc

54   Interest, etc

Nothing in this Act affects the right of the buyer or the seller to recover interest or special damages in any case where by law interest or special damages may be recoverable, or to recover money paid where the consideration for the payment of it has failed.

PART VII
SUPPLEMENTARY

55   Exclusion of implied terms

(1)   Where a right, duty or liability would arise under a contract of sale of goods by implication of law, it may (subject to the Unfair Contract Terms Act 1977) be negatived or varied by express agreement, or by the course of dealing between the parties, or by such usage as binds both parties to the contract.

(2)   An express [term] does not negative a [term] implied by this Act unless inconsistent with it.

(3)   Paragraph 11 of Schedule 1 below applies in relation to a contract made on or after 18 May 1973 and before 1 February 1978, and paragraph 12 in relation to one made before 18 May 1973.

56   Conflict of laws

Paragraph 13 of Schedule 1 below applies in relation to a contract made on or after 18 May 1973 and before 1 February 1978, so as to make provision about conflict of laws in relation to such a contract.

57   Auction sales

(1)   Where goods are put up for sale by auction in lots, each lot is prima facie deemed to be the subject of a separate contract of sale.

(2)   A sale by auction is complete when the auctioneer announces its completion by the fall of the hammer, or in other customary manner; and until the announcement is made any bidder may retract his bid.

(3)   A sale by auction may be notified to be subject to a reserve or upset price, and a right to bid may also be reserved expressly by or on behalf of the seller.

(4)   Where a sale by auction is not notified to be subject to a right to bid by or on behalf of the seller, it is not lawful for the seller to bid himself or to employ any

person to bid at the sale, or for the auctioneer knowingly to take any bid from the seller or any such person.

(5)   A sale contravening subsection (4) above may be treated as fraudulent by the buyer.

(6)   Where, in respect of a sale by auction, a right to bid is expressly reserved (but not otherwise) the seller or any one person on his behalf may bid at the auction.

58   Payment into court in Scotland
In Scotland where a buyer has elected to accept goods which he might have rejected, and to treat a breach of contract as only giving rise to a claim for damages, he may, in an action by the seller for the price, be required, in the discretion of the court before which the action depends, to consign or pay into court the price of the goods, or part of the price, or to give other reasonable security for its due payment.

59   Reasonable time a question of fact
Where a reference is made in this Act to a reasonable time the question what is a reasonable time is a question of fact.

60   Rights etc enforceable by action
Where a right, duty or liability is declared by this Act, it may (unless otherwise provided by this Act) be enforced by action.

61   Interpretation
(1)   In this Act, unless the context or subject matter otherwise requires,—

'action' includes counterclaim and set-off, and in Scotland condescendence and claim and compensation;

['bulk' means a mass or collection of goods of the same kind which—
    (a)   is contained in a defined space or area; and
    (b)   is such that any goods in the bulk are interchangeable with any other goods therein of the same number or quantity;]

'business' includes a profession and the activities of any government department (including a Northern Ireland department) or local or public authority;

'buyer' means a person who buys or agrees to buy goods;

['consumer contract' has the same meaning as in section 25(1) of the Unfair Contract Terms Act 1977; and for the purposes of this Act the onus of proving that a contract is not to be regarded as a consumer contract shall lie on the seller;]

'contract of sale' includes an agreement to sell as well as a sale;

'credit-broker' means a person acting in the course of a business of credit brokerage carried on by him, that is a business of effecting introductions of individuals desiring to obtain credit—
    (a)   to persons carrying on any business so far as it relates to the provision of credit, or
    (b)   to other persons engaged in credit brokerage;

'defendant' includes in Scotland defender, respondent, and claimant in a multiplepoinding;

'delivery' means voluntary transfer of possession from one person to another; [except that in relation to sections 20A and 20B above it includes such appropriation of goods to the contract as results in property in the goods being transferred to the buyer;]

'document of title to goods' has the same meaning as it has in the Factors Acts;

'Factors Acts' means the Factors Act 1889, the Factors (Scotland) Act 1890, and any enactment amending or substituted for the same;

'fault' means wrongful act or default;

'future goods' means goods to be manufactured or acquired by the seller after the making of the contract of sale;

'goods' includes all personal chattels other than things in action and money, and in Scotland all corporeal moveables except money; and in particular 'goods' includes emblements, industrial growing crops, and things attached to or forming part of the land which are agreed to be severed before sale or under the contract of sale; [and includes an undivided share in goods;]

'plaintiff' includes pursuer, complainer, claimant in a multiplepoinding and defendant or defender counter-claiming;

['producer' means the manufacturer of goods, the importer of goods into the European Economic Area or any person purporting to be a producer by placing his name, trade mark or other distinctive sign on the goods;]

'property' means the general property in goods, and not merely a special property;

['repair' means, in cases where there is a lack of conformity in goods for the purposes of section 48F of this Act, to bring the goods into conformity with the contract;]

'sale' includes a bargain and sale as well as a sale and delivery;

'seller' means a person who sells or agrees to sell goods;

'specific goods' means goods identified and agreed on at the time a contract of sale is made; [and includes an undivided share, specified as a fraction or percentage, of goods identified and agreed on as aforesaid;]

'warranty' (as regards England and Wales and Northern Ireland) means an agreement with reference to goods which are the subject of a contract of sale, but collateral to the main purpose of such contract, the breach of which gives rise to a claim for damages, but not to a right to reject the goods and treat the contract as repudiated.

[. . .]

(3) A thing is deemed to be done in good faith within the meaning of this Act when it is in fact done honestly, whether it is done negligently or not.

(4) A person is deemed to be insolvent within the meaning of this Act if he has either ceased to pay his debts in the ordinary course of business or he cannot pay his debts as they become due, [. . .]

(5) Goods are in a deliverable state within the meaning of this Act when they are in such a state that the buyer would under the contract be bound to take delivery of them.

[(5A) References in this Act to dealing as consumer are to be construed in accordance with Part I of the Unfair Contract Terms Act 1977; and, for the purposes of this Act, it is for a seller claiming that the buyer does not deal as consumer to show that he does not.]

(6) As regards the definition of 'business' in subsection (1) above, paragraph 14 of Schedule 1 below applies in relation to a contract made on or after 18 May 1973 and before 1 February 1978, and paragraph 15 in relation to one made before 18 May 1973,

62 Savings: rules of law etc

(1) The rules in bankruptcy relating to contracts of sale apply to those contracts, notwithstanding anything in this Act.

(2) The rules of the common law, including the law merchant, except in so far as they are inconsistent with the provisions of this Act, and in particular the rules relating to the law of principal and agent and the effect of fraud, misrepresentation, duress or coercion, mistake, or other invalidating cause, apply to contracts for the sale of goods.

(3) Nothing in this Act or the Sale of Goods Act 1893 affects the enactments relating to bills of sale, or any enactment relating to the sale of goods which is not expressly repealed or amended by this Act or that.

(4) The provisions of this Act about contracts of sale do not apply to a transaction in the form of a contract of sale which is intended to operate by way of mortgage, pledge, charge, or other security.

(5) Nothing in this Act prejudices or affects the landlord's right of hypothec or sequestration for rent in Scotland.

64 Short title and commencement
(1) This Act may be cited as the Sale of Goods Act 1979.
(2) This Act comes into force on 1 January 1980.

SUPPLY OF GOODS AND SERVICES ACT 1982
(1982, c 29)

[PART IA
SUPPLY OF GOODS AS RESPECTS SCOTLAND

Contracts for the transfer of property in goods

11A The contracts concerned
(1) In this Act in its application to Scotland a 'contract for the transfer of goods' means a contract under which one person transfers or agrees to transfer to another the property in goods, other than an excepted contract.
(2) For the purposes of this section an excepted contract means any of the following—
(a) a contract of sale of goods;
(b) a hire-purchase agreement;
[. . .]
(d) a transfer or agreement to transfer for which there is no consideration;
(e) a contract intended to operate by way of mortgage, pledge, charge or other security.
(3) For the purposes of this Act in its application to Scotland a contract is a contract for the transfer of goods whether or not services are also provided or to be provided under the contract, and (subject to subsection (2) above) whatever is the nature of the consideration for the transfer or agreement to transfer.

11B Implied terms about title, etc
(1) In a contract for the transfer of goods, other than one to which subsection (3) below applies, there is an implied term on the part of the transferor that in the case of a transfer of the property in the goods he has a right to transfer the property and in the case of an agreement to transfer the property in the goods he will have such a right at the time when the property is to be transferred.
(2) In a contract for the transfer of goods, other than one to which subsection (3) below applies, there is also an implied term that—
(a) the goods are free, and will remain free until the time when the property is to be transferred, from any charge or encumbrance not disclosed or known to the transferee before the contract is made, and
(b) the transferee will enjoy quiet possession of the goods except so far as it may be disturbed by the owner or other person entitled to the benefit of any charge or encumbrance so disclosed or known.
(3) This subsection applies to a contract for the transfer of goods in the case of which there appears from the contract or is to be inferred from its circumstances an intention that the transferor should transfer only such title as he or a third person may have.
(4) In a contract to which subsection (3) above applies there is an implied term that all charges or encumbrances known to the transferor and not known to the transferee have been disclosed to the transferee before the contract is made.
(5) In a contract to which subsection (3) above applies there is also an implied term that none of the following will disturb the transferee's quiet possession of the goods, namely—
(a) the transferor;

(b) in a case where the parties to the contract intend that the transferor should transfer only such title as a third person may have, that person;

(c) anyone claiming through or under the transferor or that third person otherwise than under a charge or encumbrance disclosed or known to the transferee before the contract is made.

(6) [*amends Unfair Contract Terms Act 1977*]

11C Implied terms where transfer is by description

(1) This section applies where, under a contract for the transfer of goods, the transferor transfers or agrees to transfer the property in the goods by description.

(2) In such a case there is an implied term that the goods will correspond with the description.

(3) If the transferor transfers or agrees to transfer the property in the goods by reference to a sample as well as by description it is not sufficient that the bulk of the goods corresponds with the sample if the goods do not also correspond with the description.

(4) A contract is not prevented from falling within subsection (1) above by reason only that, being exposed for supply, the goods are selected by the transferee.

11D Implied terms about quality or fitness

(1) Except as provided by this section and section 11E below and subject to the provisions of any other enactment, there is no implied term about the quality or fitness for any particular purpose of goods supplied under a contract for the transfer of goods.

(2) Where, under such a contract, the transferor transfers the property in goods in the course of a business, there is an implied term that the goods supplied under the contract are of satisfactory quality.

(3) For the purposes of this section and section 11E below, goods are of satisfactory quality if they meet the standard that a reasonable person would regard as satisfactory, taking account of any description of the goods, the price (if relevant) and all the other relevant circumstances.

[(3A) If the contract for the transfer of goods is a consumer contract, the relevant circumstances mentioned in subsection (3) above include any public statements on the specific characteristics of the goods made about them by the transferor, the producer or his representative, particularly in advertising or on labelling.

(3B) A public statement is not by virtue of subsection (3A) above a relevant circumstance for the purposes of subsection (3) above in the case of a contract for the transfer of goods, if the transferor shows that—

(a) at the time the contract was made, he was not, and could not reasonably have been, aware of the statement,

(b) before the contract was made, the statement had been withdrawn in public or, to the extent that it contained anything which was incorrect or misleading, it had been corrected in public, or

(c) the decision to acquire the goods could not have been influenced by the statement.

(3C) Subsections (3A) and (3B) above do not prevent any public statement from being a relevant circumstance for the purposes of subsection (3) above (whether or not the contract for the transfer of goods is a consumer contract) if the statement would have been such a circumstance apart from those subsections.]

(4) The term implied by subsection (2) above does not extend to any matter making the quality of goods unsatisfactory—

(a) which is specifically drawn to the transferee's attention before the contract is made,

(b) where the transferee examines the goods before the contract is made, which that examination ought to reveal, or

(c)   where the property in the goods is, or is to be, transferred by reference to a sample, which would have been apparent on a reasonable examination of the sample.

(5)   Subsection (6) below applies where, under a contract for the transfer of goods, the transferor transfers the property in goods in the course of a business and the transferee, expressly or by implication, makes known—

(a)   to the transferor, or

(b)   where the consideration or part of the consideration for the transfer is a sum payable by instalments and the goods were previously sold by a credit-broker to the transferor, to that credit-broker,

any particular purpose for which the goods are being acquired.

(6)   In that case there is (subject to subsection (7) below) an implied term that the goods supplied under the contract are reasonably fit for the purpose, whether or not that is a purpose for which such goods are commonly supplied.

(7)   Subsection (6) above does not apply where the circumstances show that the transferee does not rely, or that it is unreasonable for him to rely, on the skill or judgment of the transferor or credit-broker.

(8)   An implied term about quality or fitness for a particular purpose may be annexed by usage to a contract for the transfer of goods.

(9)   The preceding provisions of this section apply to a transfer by a person who in the course of a business is acting as agent for another as they apply to a transfer by a principal in the course of a business, except where that other is not transferring in the course of a business and either the transferee knows that fact or reasonable steps are taken to bring it to the transferee's notice before the contract concerned is made.

[(10)   For the purposes of this section, 'consumer contract' has the same meaning as in section 11F(3) below.]

11E   Implied terms where transfer is by sample

(1)   This section applies where, under a contract for the transfer of goods, the transferor transfers or agrees to transfer the property in the goods by reference to a sample.

(2)   In such a case there is an implied term—

(a)   that the bulk will correspond with the sample in quality;

(b)   that the transferee will have a reasonable opportunity of comparing the bulk with the sample; and

(c)   that the goods will be free from any defect, making their quality unsatisfactory, which would not be apparent on reasonable examination of the sample.

(3)   For the purposes of this section a transferor transfers or agrees to transfer the property in goods by reference to a sample where there is an express or implied term to that effect in the contract concerned.

11F   Remedies for breach of contract

(1)   Where in a contract for the transfer of goods a transferor is in breach of any term of the contract (express or implied), the other party to the contract (in this section referred to as 'the transferee') shall be entitled—

(a)   to claim damages; and

(b)   if the breach is material, to reject any goods delivered under the contract and treat it as repudiated.

(2)   Where a contract for the transfer of goods is a consumer contract and the transferee is the consumer, then, for the purposes of subsection (1)(b) above, breach by the transferor of any term (express or implied)—

(a)   as to the quality of the goods or their fitness for a purpose;

(b)   if the goods are, or are to be, transferred by description, that the goods will correspond with the description;

(c)   if the goods are, or are to be, transferred by reference to a sample, that the bulk will correspond with the sample in quality,
shall be deemed to be a material breach.

(3)   In subsection (2) above, 'consumer contract' has the same meaning as in section 25(1) of the 1977 Act; and for the purposes of that subsection the onus of proving that a contract is not to be regarded as a consumer contract shall lie on the transferor.

Contracts for the hire of goods

11G   The contracts concerned

(1)   In this Act in its application to Scotland a 'contract for the hire of goods' means a contract under which one person ('the supplier') hires or agrees to hire goods to another, other than [a hire-purchase agreement].

[. . .]

(3)   For the purposes of this Act in its application to Scotland a contract is a contract for the hire of goods whether or not services are also provided or to be provided under the contract, and [. . .] whatever is the nature of the consideration for the hire or agreement to hire.

11H   Implied terms about right to transfer possession etc

(1)   In a contract for the hire of goods there is an implied term on the part of the supplier that—

(a)   in the case of a hire, he has a right to transfer possession of the goods by way of hire for the period of the hire; and

(b)   in the case of an agreement to hire, he will have such a right at the time of commencement of the period of the hire.

(2)   In a contract for the hire of goods there is also an implied term that the person to whom the goods are hired will enjoy quiet possession of the goods for the period of the hire except so far as the possession may be disturbed by the owner or other person entitled to the benefit of any charge or encumbrance disclosed or known to the person to whom the goods are hired before the contract is made.

(3)   The preceding provisions of this section do not affect the right of the supplier to repossess the goods under an express or implied term of the contract.

11I   Implied terms where hire is by description

(1)   This section applies where, under a contract for the hire of goods, the supplier hires or agrees to hire the goods by description.

(2)   In such a case there is an implied term that the goods will correspond with the description.

(3)   If under the contract the supplier hires or agrees to hire the goods by reference to a sample as well as by description it is not sufficient that the bulk of the goods corresponds with the sample if the goods do not also correspond with the description.

(4)   A contract is not prevented from falling within subsection (1) above by reason only that, being exposed for supply, the goods are selected by the person to whom the goods are hired.

11J   Implied terms about quality or fitness

(1)   Except as provided by this section and section 11K below and subject to the provisions of any other enactment, there is no implied term about the quality or fitness for any particular purpose of goods hired under a contract for the hire of goods.

(2)   Where, under such a contract, the supplier hires goods in the course of a business, there is an implied term that the goods supplied under the contract are of satisfactory quality.

(3)   For the purposes of this section and section 11K below, goods are of satis-

factory quality if they meet the standard that a reasonable person would regard as satisfactory, taking account of any description of the goods, the consideration for the hire (if relevant) and all the other relevant circumstances.

[(3A)   If the contract for the transfer of goods is a consumer contract, the relevant circumstances mentioned in subsection (3) above include any public statements on the specific characteristics of the goods made about them by the transferor, the producer or his representative, particularly in advertising or on labelling.

(3B)   A public statement is not by virtue of subsection (3A) above a relevant circumstance for the purposes of subsection (3) above in the case of a contract for the transfer of goods, if the transferor shows that—

(a)   at the time the contract was made, he was not, and could not reasonably have been, aware of the statement,

(b)   before the contract was made, the statement had been withdrawn in public or, to the extent that it contained anything which was incorrect or misleading, it had been corrected in public, or

(c)   the decision to acquire the goods could not have been influenced by the statement.

(3C)   Subsections (3A) and (3B) above do not prevent any public statement from being a relevant circumstance for the purposes of subsection (3) above (whether or not the contract for the transfer of goods is a consumer contract) if the statement would have been such a circumstance apart from those subsections.]

(4)   The term implied by subsection (2) above does not extend to any matter making the quality of goods unsatisfactory—

(a)   which is specifically drawn to the attention of the person to whom the goods are hired before the contract is made, or

(b)   where that person examines the goods before the contract is made, which that examination ought to reveal; or

(c)   where the goods are hired by reference to a sample, which would have been apparent on reasonable examination of the sample.

(5)   Subsection (6) below applies where, under a contract for the hire of goods, the supplier hires goods in the course of a business and the person to whom the goods are hired, expressly or by implication, makes known—

(a)   to the supplier in the course of negotiations conducted by him in relation to the making of the contract; or

(b)   to a credit-broker in the course of negotiations conducted by that broker in relation to goods sold by him to the supplier before forming the subject matter of the contract,

any particular purpose for which the goods are being hired.

(6)   In that case there is (subject to subsection (7) below) an implied term that the goods supplied under the contract are reasonably fit for that purpose, whether or not that is a purpose for which such goods are commonly supplied.

(7)   Subsection (6) above does not apply where the circumstances show that the person to whom the goods are hired does not rely, or that it is unreasonable for him to rely, on the skill or judgment of the hirer or credit-broker.

(8)   An implied term about quality or fitness for a particular purpose may be annexed by usage to a contract for the hire of goods.

(9)   The preceding provisions of this section apply to a hire by a person who in the course of a business is acting as agent for another as they apply to a hire by a principal in the course of a business, except where that other is not hiring in the course of a business and either the person to whom the goods are hired knows that fact or reasonable steps are taken to bring it to that person's notice before the contract concerned is made.

[(10)   For the purposes of this section, 'consumer contract' has the same meaning as in section 11F(3) above.]

11K Implied terms where hire is by sample

(1) This section applies where, under a contract for the hire of goods, the supplier hires or agrees to hire the goods by reference to a sample.

(2) In such a case there is an implied term—

(a) that the bulk will correspond with the sample in quality; and

(b) that the person to whom the goods are hired will have a reasonable opportunity of comparing the bulk with the sample; and

(c) that the goods will be free from any defect, making their quality unsatisfactory, which would not be apparent on reasonable examination of the sample.

(3) For the purposes of this section a supplier hires or agrees to hire goods by reference to a sample where there is an express or implied term to that effect in the contract concerned.

Exclusion of implied terms, etc

11L Exclusion of implied terms etc

(1) Where a right, duty or liability would arise under a contract for the transfer of goods or a contract for the hire of goods by implication of law, it may (subject to subsection (2) below and the 1977 Act) be negatived or varied by express agreement, or by the course of dealing between the parties, or by such usage as binds both parties to the contract.

(2) An express term does not negative a term implied by the preceding provisions of this Part of this Act unless inconsistent with it.

(3) Nothing in the preceding provisions of this Part of this Act prejudices the operation of any other enactment or any rule of law whereby any term (other than one relating to quality or fitness) is to be implied in a contract for the transfer of goods or a contract for the hire of goods.]

[PART IB
ADDITIONAL RIGHTS OF TRANSFEREE IN CONSUMER CASES

11M Introductory

(1) This section applies if—

(a) the transferee deals as consumer or, in Scotland, there is a consumer contract in which the transferee is a consumer, and

(b) the goods do not conform to the contract for the transfer of goods at the time of delivery.

(2) If this section applies, the transferee has the right—

(a) under and in accordance with section 11N below, to require the transferor to repair or replace the goods, or

(b) under and in accordance with section 11P below—

(i) to require the transferor to reduce the amount to be paid for the transfer by the transferee by an appropriate amount, or

(ii) to rescind the contract with regard to the goods in question.

(3) For the purposes of subsection (1)(b) above, goods which do not conform to the contract for the transfer of goods at any time within the period of six months starting with the date on which the goods were delivered to the transferee must be taken not to have so conformed at that date.

(4) Subsection (3) above does not apply if—

(a) it is established that the goods did so conform at that date;

(b) its application is incompatible with the nature of the goods or the nature of the lack of conformity.

(5) For the purposes of this section, 'consumer contract' has the same meaning as in section 11F(3) above.

11N Repair or replacement of the goods

(1) If section 11M above applies, the transferee may require the transferor—

    (a) to repair the goods, or

    (b) to replace the goods.

(2) If the transferee requires the transferor to repair or replace the goods, the transferor must—

    (a) repair or, as the case may be, replace the goods within a reasonable time but without causing significant inconvenience to the transferee;

    (b) bear any necessary costs incurred in doing so (including in particular the cost of any labour, materials or postage).

(3) The transferee must not require the transferor to repair or, as the case may be, replace the goods if that remedy is—

    (a) impossible,

    (b) disproportionate in comparison to the other of those remedies, or

    (c) disproportionate in comparison to an appropriate reduction in the purchase price under paragraph (a), or rescission under paragraph (b), of section 11P(1) below.

(4) One remedy is disproportionate in comparison to the other if the one imposes costs on the transferor which, in comparison to those imposed on him by the other, are unreasonable, taking into account—

    (a) the value which the goods would have if they conformed to the contract for the transfer of goods,

    (b) the significance of the lack of conformity to the contract for the transfer of goods, and

    (c) whether the other remedy could be effected without significant inconvenience to the transferee.

(5) Any question as to what is a reasonable time or significant inconvenience is to be determined by reference to—

    (a) the nature of the goods, and

    (b) the purpose for which the goods were acquired.

11P Reduction of purchase price or rescission of contract

(1) If section 11M above applies, the transferee may—

    (a) require the transferor to reduce the purchase price of the goods in question to the transferee by an appropriate amount, or

    (b) rescind the contract with regard to those goods,

if the condition in subsection (2) below is satisfied.

(2) The condition is that—

    (a) by virtue of section 11N(3) above the transferee may require neither repair nor replacement of the goods, or

    (b) the transferee has required the transferor to repair or replace the goods, but the transferor is in breach of the requirement of section 11N(2)(a) above to do so within a reasonable time and without significant inconvenience to the transferee.

(3) If the transferee rescinds the contract, any reimbursement to the transferee may be reduced to take account of the use he has had of the goods since they were delivered to him.

11Q Relation to other remedies etc

(1) If the transferee requires the transferor to repair or replace the goods the transferee must not act under subsection (2) until he has given the transferor a reasonable time in which to repair or replace (as the case may be) the goods.

(2) The transferee acts under this subsection if—

    (a) in England and Wales or Northern Ireland he rejects the goods and terminates the contract for breach of condition;

    (b) in Scotland he rejects any goods delivered under the contract and treats it as repudiated; or (c)	he requires the goods to be replaced or repaired (as the case may be).

## 11R	Powers of the court

(1)	In any proceedings in which a remedy is sought by virtue of this Part the court, in addition to any other power it has, may act under this section.

(2)	On the application of the transferee the court may make an order requiring specific performance or, in Scotland, specific implement by the transferor of any obligation imposed on him by virtue of section 11N above.

(3)	Subsection (4) applies if—

(a)	the transferee requires the transferor to give effect to a remedy under section 11N or 11P above or has claims to rescind under section 11P, but

(b)	the court decides that another remedy under section 11N or 11P is appropriate.

(4)	The court may proceed—

(a)	as if the transferee had required the transferor to give effect to the other remedy, or if the other remedy is rescission under section 11P,

(b)	as if the transferee had claimed to rescind the contract under that section.

(5)	If the transferee has claimed to rescind the contract the court may order that any reimbursement to the transferee is reduced to take account of the use he has had of the goods since they were delivered to him.

(6)	The court may make an order under this section unconditionally or on such terms and conditions as to damages, payment of the price and otherwise as it thinks just.

## 11S	Conformity with the contract

(1)	Goods do not conform to a contract for the supply or transfer of goods if—

(a)	there is, in relation to the goods, a breach of an express term of the contract or a term implied by section 3, 4 or 5 above or, in Scotland, by section 11C, 11D or 11E above, or

(b)	installation of the goods forms part of the contract for the transfer of goods, and the goods were installed by the transferor, or under his responsibility, in breach of the term implied by section 13 below or (in Scotland) in breach of any term implied by any rule of law as to the manner in which the installation is carried out.]

BANKRUPTCY (SCOTLAND) ACT 1985
(1985, c 66)

## 1	Accountant in Bankruptcy

[(1)	The Accountant in Bankruptcy shall be appointed by the Scottish Ministers.

(2)	The Scottish Ministers may appoint a member of the staff of the Accountant in Bankruptcy to be Depute Accountant in Bankruptcy to exercise all of the functions of the Accountant in Bankruptcy at any time when the Accountant in Bankruptcy is unable to do so.]

## [1A	Supervisory functions of the Accountant in Bankruptcy

(1)	The Accountant in Bankruptcy shall have the following general functions in the administration of sequestration and personal insolvency—

(a)	the supervision of the performance by—

(i)	interim trustees (not being the Accountant in Bankruptcy);

(ii)	permanent trustees; and

(iii)	commissioners,

of the functions conferred on them by this Act or any other enactment (including an enactment contained in subordinate legislation) or any rule of law and the investigation of any complaints made against them;

(b)	the maintenance of a register (in this Act referred to as the 'register of

insolvencies'), in such form as may be prescribed by the Court of Session by act
of sederunt, which shall contain particulars of—
    (i) estates which have been sequestrated; and
    (ii) trust deeds which have been sent to him for registration under
paragraph 5(1)(e) of Schedule 5 to this Act; [and
    (iii) the winding up and receivership of business associations which the
Court of Session has jurisdiction to wind up];
    (c) the preparation of an annual report which shall be presented to the
Secretary of State and the Court of Session and shall contain—
    (i) statistical information relating to the state of all sequestrations [and the
winding up and receiverships of business associations] of which particulars
have been registered in the register of insolvencies during the year to which
the report relates;
    (ii) particulars of trust deeds registered as protected trust deeds in that
year; and
    (iii) particulars of the performance of the Accountant in Bankruptcy's
functions under this Act;
    (d) such other functions as may from time to time be conferred on him by
the Secretary of State [; and
    (e) in this subsection 'business association' has the meaning given in Section
C2 of Part II of Schedule 5 to the Scotland Act 1998].
(2) If it appears to the Accountant in Bankruptcy that a person mentioned in
paragraph (a) of subsection (1) above has failed without reasonable excuse to perform a duty imposed on him by any provision of this Act or by any other enactment (including an enactment contained in subordinate legislation) or by any rule
of law, he shall report the matter to the court which, after hearing that person on
the matter, may remove him from office or censure him or make such other order
as the circumstances of the case may require.
(3) Where the Accountant in Bankruptcy has reasonable grounds to suspect
that an offence has been committed—
    (a) by a person mentioned in paragraph (a) of subsection (1) above in the
performance of his functions under this Act or any other enactment (including
an enactment contained in subordinate legislation) or any rule of law; or
    (b) in relation to a sequestration, by the debtor in respect of his assets, his
dealings with them or his conduct in relation to his business or financial affairs;
or
    (c) in relation to a sequestration, by a person other than the debtor in that
person's dealings with the debtor, the interim trustee or the permanent trustee
in respect of the debtor's assets, business or financial affairs,
he shall report the matter to the Lord Advocate.
(4) The Accountant in Bankruptcy shall—
    (a) make the register of insolvencies, at all reasonable times, available for
inspection; and
    (b) provide any person, on request, with a certified copy of any entry in the
register.

1B Performance of certain functions of the Accountant in Bankruptcy
(1) The functions of the Accountant in Bankruptcy, other than functions conferred by section 1A of this Act, may be carried out on his behalf by any member
of his staff authorised by him to do so.
(2) Without prejudice to subsection (1) above, the Accountant in Bankruptcy
may appoint on such terms and conditions as he considers appropriate such
persons as he considers fit to perform on his behalf any of his functions in respect
of the sequestration of the estate of any debtor.
(3) A person appointed under subsection (2) above shall comply with such
general or specific directions as the Accountant in Bankruptcy may from time to

time give to such person as to the performance of his functions in relation to any sequestration.

(4)　The Accountant in Bankruptcy may pay to a person appointed under subsection (2) above such fee as he may consider appropriate.

1C　Directions

(1)　The Secretary of State may, after consultation with the Lord President of the Court of Session, give to the Accountant in Bankruptcy general directions as to the performance of his functions under this Act.

(2)　Directions under this section may be given in respect of all cases or any class or description of cases, but may not be given in respect of any particular case.

(3)　The Accountant in Bankruptcy shall comply with any directions given to him under this section.]

2　Appointment and functions of interim trustee

[(1)　Where the court awards sequestration of the debtor's estate and the petition for the sequestration—

(a)　nominates a person to be interim trustee;

(b)　states that the person satisfies the conditions mentioned in subsection (3) below; and

(c)　has annexed to it a copy of the undertaking mentioned in subsection (3)(c) below,

the court may, if it appears to the court that the person satisfies those conditions and if no interim trustee has been appointed in pursuance of subsection (5) below, appoint that person to be interim trustee in the sequestration.

(2)　Where the court awards sequestration of the debtor's estate and—

(a)　it does not appoint a person to be interim trustee in pursuance of subsection (1) above; and

(b)　no interim trustee has been appointed in pursuance of subsection (5) below,

the court shall appoint the Accountant in Bankruptcy to be interim trustee in the sequestration.

(3)　The conditions referred to in subsection (1) above are that the person—

(a)　resides within the jurisdiction of the Court of Session;

(b)　is qualified to act as an insolvency practitioner; and

(c)　has given an undertaking, in writing, that he will act—

(i)　as interim trustee; and

(ii)　where no permanent trustee is elected, as permanent trustee, in the sequestration.

(4)　The interim trustee's general functions shall be—

(a)　to safeguard the debtor's estate pending the appointment of a permanent trustee under this Act;

(b)　to ascertain the reasons for the debtor's insolvency and the circumstances surrounding it;

(c)　to ascertain the state of the debtor's liabilities and assets;

(d)　to administer the sequestration process pending the appointment of a permanent trustee; and

(e)　whether or not he is still acting in the sequestration, to supply the Accountant in Bankruptcy with such information as the Accountant in Bankruptcy considers necessary to enable him to discharge his functions under this Act.

(5)　Where a petition for sequestration is presented by a creditor or a trustee acting under a trust deed, the court may appoint an interim trustee before sequestration is awarded—

(a)　if the debtor consents; or

(b)　if the trustee acting under the trust deed or any creditor shows cause.

(6)   For the purposes of the appointment of an interim trustee under subsection (5) above—
(a)   where a person is nominated as mentioned in subsection (1)(a) above and the provisions of that subsection apply, the court may appoint that person; and
(b)   where such a person is not appointed, the court shall appoint the Accountant in Bankruptcy.
(7)   Where the petition for sequestration was presented by a creditor or the trustee acting under a trust deed, the interim trustee shall, as soon as practicable, notify the debtor of his appointment.]

3   Permanent trustee

(1)   In every sequestration there shall be a permanent trustee whose general functions shall be—
(a)   to recover, manage and realise the debtor's estate, whether situated in Scotland or elsewhere;
(b)   to distribute the estate among the debtor's creditors according to their respective entitlements;
(c)   to ascertain the reasons for the debtor's insolvency and the circumstances surrounding it;
(d)   to ascertain the state of the debtor's liabilities and assets;
(e)   to maintain a sederunt book during his term of office for the purpose of providing an accurate record of the sequestration process;
(f)   to keep regular accounts of his intromissions with the debtor's estate, such accounts being available for inspection at all reasonable times by the commissioners (if any), the creditors and the debtor; and
(g)   whether or not he is still acting in the sequestration, to supply the Accountant in Bankruptcy with such information as the Accountant in Bankruptcy considers necessary to enable him to discharge his functions under this Act.
(2)   A permanent trustee in performing his functions under this Act shall have regard to advice offered to him by the commissioners (if any).
(3)   If the permanent trustee has reasonable grounds to suspect that an offence has been committed in relation to a sequestration—
(a)   by the debtor in respect of his assets, his dealings with them or his conduct in relation to his business or financial affairs; or
(b)   by a person other than the debtor in that person's dealings with the debtor, the interim trustee or the permanent trustee in respect of the debtor's assets, business or financial affairs,
he shall report the matter to the Accountant in Bankruptcy.
(4)   A report under subsection (3) above shall be absolutely privileged.
[(5)   Paragraph (g) of subsection (1) above and subsection (3) above shall not apply in any case where the permanent trustee is the Accountant in Bankruptcy.
(6)   A permanent trustee may apply to the sheriff for directions in relation to any particular matter arising in the sequestration.
(7)   Where the debtor, a creditor or any other person having an interest is dissatisfied with any act, omission or decision of the permanent trustee, he may apply to the sheriff and, on such an application being made, the sheriff may confirm, annul or modify any act or decision of the permanent trustee or may give him directions or make such order as he thinks fit.]

4   Commissioners

In any sequestration (other than one to which Schedule 2 to this Act applies) commissioners, whose general functions shall be to supervise the intromissions of the permanent trustee with the sequestrated estate and to advise him, may be elected in accordance with section 30 of this Act.

Petitions for sequestration

5 Sequestration of the estate of living or deceased debtor
(1) The estate of a debtor may be sequestrated in accordance with the provisions of this Act.
[(2) The sequestration of the estate of a living debtor shall be on the petition of—
(a) the debtor, if either subsection (2A) or (2B) below applies to him;
(b) a qualified creditor or qualified creditors, if the debtor is apparently insolvent;
[(ba) a temporary administrator;
(bb) a member State liquidator appointed in main proceedings;] or
(c) the trustee acting under a trust deed if, and only if, one or more of the conditions in subsection (2C) below is satisfied.
(2A) This subsection applies to the debtor if a qualified creditor or qualified creditors concur in the petition.
(2B) This subsection applies to the debtor where—
(a) the total amount of his debts (including interest) at the date of presentation of the petition is not less than £1,500;
(b) an award of sequestration has not been made against him in the period of 5 years ending on the day before the date of presentation of the petition; and
(c) the debtor either—
(i) is apparently insolvent; or
(ii) has granted a trust deed and the trustee has complied with the requirements of sub-sub-paragraphs (a) to (c) of paragraph 5(1) of Schedule 5 to this Act but has received notification as mentioned in sub-sub-paragraph (d) of that paragraph, and for the purposes of this paragraph a debtor shall not be apparently insolvent by reason only that he has granted a trust deed or that he has given notice to his creditors as mentioned in paragraph (b) of section 7(1) of this Act.
(2C) The conditions mentioned in subsection (2)(c) above are—
(a) that the debtor has failed to comply—
(i) with any obligation imposed on him under the trust deed with which he could reasonably have complied; or
(ii) with any instruction or requirement reasonably given to or made of him by the trustee for the purposes of the trust deed; or
(b) that the trustee avers in his petition that it would be in the best interests of the creditors that an award of sequestration be made.]
(3) The sequestration of the estate of a deceased debtor shall be on the petition of—
(a) an executor or a person entitled to be appointed as executor on the estate;
(b) a qualified creditor or qualified creditors of the deceased debtor;
[(ba) a temporary administrator;
(bb) a member State liquidator appointed in main proceedings;] or
(c) the trustee acting under a trust deed.
(4) In this Act 'qualified creditor' means a creditor who, at the date of the presentation of the petition, is a creditor of the debtor in respect of liquid or illiquid debts (other than contingent or future debts [or amounts payable under a confiscation order]), whether secured or unsecured, which amount (or of one such debt which amounts) to not less than [£1,500] or such sum as may be prescribed; and 'qualified creditors' means creditors who at the said date are creditors of the debtor in respect of such debts as aforesaid amounting in aggregate to not less than [£1,500] or such sum as may be prescribed [; and in the foregoing provisions of this subsection 'confiscation order' [means a confiscation order under Part 2, 3, or 4 of the Proceeds of Crime Act 2002].

[(4A) In this Act, 'trust deed' means a voluntary trust deed granted by or on behalf of the debtor whereby his estate (other than such of his estate as would not, under section 33(1) of this Act, vest in the permanent trustee if his estate were sequestrated) is conveyed to the trustee for the benefit of his creditors generally.]

(5) Paragraphs 1(1) and (3), 2(1)(a) and (2) and 6 of Schedule 1 to this Act shall apply in order to ascertain the amount of the debt or debts for the purposes of subsection (4) above as they apply in order to ascertain the amount which a creditor is entitled to claim, but as if for any reference to the date of sequestration there were substituted a reference to the date of presentation of the petition.

(6) The petitioner shall [on the day the petition for sequestration is presented under this section, send a copy of the petition] to the Accountant in Bankruptcy.

[(6A) Where the petitioner is the debtor—
(a) he shall lodge with the petition a statement of assets and liabilities; and
(b) he shall, on the day the petition is presented, send to the Accountant in Bankruptcy such statement of assets and liabilities as was lodged in court in pursuance of paragraph (a) above.]

(7) Where, after a petition for sequestration has been presented but before the sequestration has been awarded, the debtor dies then—
(a) if the petitioner was the debtor, the petition shall fall;
(b) if the petitioner is a creditor, the proceedings shall continue in accordance with this Act so far as circumstances will permit.

(8) Where, after a petition for sequestration has been presented under this section but before the sequestration has been awarded, a creditor who—
(a) is the petitioner or concurs in a petition by the debtor; or
(b) has lodged answers to the petition,
withdraws or dies, there may be sisted in the place of—
(i) the creditor mentioned in paragraph (a) above, any creditor who was a qualified creditor at the date when the petition was presented and who remains so qualified at the date of the sist;
(ii) the creditor mentioned in paragraph (b) above, any other creditor.

[(9) If the debtor—
(a) fails to send to the Accountant in Bankruptcy in accordance with subsection (6A)(b) above such statement of assets and liabilities; or
(b) fails to disclose any material fact in such statement of assets and liabilities; or
(c) makes a material misstatement in such statement of assets and liabilities,
he shall be guilty of an offence and liable on summary conviction to a fine not exceeding level 5 on the standard scale or to imprisonment for a term not exceeding 3 months or to both such fine and imprisonment.

(10) In any proceedings for an offence under subsection (9) above, it shall be a defence for the accused to show that he had a reasonable excuse for—
(a) failing to send to the Accountant in Bankruptcy in accordance with subsection (6A)(b) above such statement of assets and liabilities; or
(b) failing to disclose a material fact; or
(c) making a material misstatement.]

6 Sequestration of other estates

(1) Subject to subsection (2) below, the estate belonging to or held for or jointly by the members of any of the following entities may be sequestrated—
(a) a trust in respect of debts incurred by it;
(b) a partnership, including a dissolved partnership;
(c) a body corporate or an unincorporated body;
(d) a limited partnership (including a dissolved partnership) within the meaning of the Limited Partnerships Act 1907.

(2) It shall not be competent to sequestrate the estate of any of the following entities—

(a)   a company registered under the Companies Act 1985 or under the former Companies Acts (within the meaning of that Act); or

(b)   an entity in respect of which an enactment provides, expressly or by implication, that sequestration is incompetent.

(3)   The sequestration of a trust estate in respect of debts incurred by the trust shall be on the petition of—

(a)   a majority of the trustees, with the concurrence of a qualified creditor or qualified creditors;

[(aa) a temporary administrator;

(ab) a member State liquidator appointed in main proceedings;] or

(b)   a qualified creditor or qualified creditors, if the trustees as such are apparently insolvent.

(4)   The sequestration of the estate of a partnership shall be on the petition of—

(a)   the partnership, with the concurrence of a qualified creditor or qualified creditors;

[(aa) a temporary administrator;

(ab) a member State liquidator appointed in main proceedings;] or

(b)   a qualified creditor or qualified creditors, if the partnership is apparently insolvent.

(5)   A petition under [subsection (4)(aa) to (b)] above may be combined with a petition for the sequestration of the estate of any of the partners as an individual where that individual is apparently insolvent.

(6)   The sequestration of the estate of a body corporate or of an unincorporated body shall be on the petition of—

(a)   a person authorised to act on behalf of the body, with the concurrence of a qualified creditor or qualified creditors;

[(aa) a temporary administrator;

(ab) a member State liquidator appointed in main proceedings;] or

(b)   a qualified creditor or qualified creditors, if the body is apparently insolvent.

(7)   The application of this Act to the sequestration of the estate of a limited partnership shall be subject to such modifications as may be prescribed.

(8)   Subsections (6) and (8) of section 5 of this Act shall apply for the purposes of this section as they apply for the purposes of that section.

[6A   Petition for sequestration of estate: provision of information

(1)   A petitioner for sequestration of a debtor's estate shall, insofar as it is within the petitioner's knowledge, state in the petition—

(a)   whether or not the debtor's centre of main interests is situated—

(i)   in the United Kingdom; or

(ii)   in another member State; and

(b)   whether or not the debtor possesses an establishment—

(i)   in the United Kingdom; or

(ii)   in any other member State.

(2)   If, to the petitioner's knowledge, there is a member State liquidator appointed in main proceedings in relation to the debtor, the petitioner shall, as soon as reasonably practicable, send a copy of the petition to that member State liquidator.]

7   Meaning of apparent insolvency

(1)   A debtor's apparent insolvency shall be constituted (or, where he is already apparently insolvent, constituted anew) whenever—

(a)   his estate is sequestrated, or he is adjudged bankrupt in England or Wales or Northern Ireland; or

(b)   [not being a person whose property is for the time being affected by a restraint order or subject to a confiscation, or charging, order,] he gives written notice to his creditors that he has ceased to pay his debts in the ordinary course of business; or

[(ba)   he becomes subject to main proceedings in a member State other than the United Kingdom.]

(c)   any of the following circumstances occurs—

(i)   he grants a trust deed;

(ii)   following the service on him of a duly executed charge for payment of a debt, the days of charge expire without payment;

(iii)   following [an attachment (or an attempt to attach)] or seizure of any of his moveable property in pursuance of a summary warrant for the recovery of rates or taxes, 14 days elapse without payment;

(iv)   a decree of adjudication of any part of his estate is granted, either for payment or in security;

(v)   his effects are sold under a sequestration for rent due by him;

(vi)   a receiving order is made against him in England or Wales [; or

(vii)   a debt payment programme under the Debt Arrangement and Attachment (Scotland) Act 2002 is revoked, where any debt being paid under the programme is constituted by a decree or document of debt as defined in section 10 (attachment) of that Act;]

unless it is shown that at the time when any such circumstance occurred, the debtor was able and willing to pay his debts as they became due [or that but for his property being affected by a restraint order or subject to a confiscation, or charging, order he would be able to do so]; or

(d)   a creditor of the debtor, in respect of a liquid debt which amounts (or liquid debts which in aggregate amount) to not less than £750 or such sum as may be prescribed, has served on the debtor, by personal service by an officer of court, a demand in the prescribed form requiring him either to pay the debt (or debts) or to find security for its (or their) payment, and within 3 weeks after the date of service of the demand the debtor has not—

(i)   complied with the demand; or

(ii)   intimated to the creditor, by recorded delivery, that he denies that there is a debt or that the sum claimed by the creditor as the debt is immediately payable.

[In paragraph (d) above, 'liquid debt' does not include a sum payable under a confiscation order; and in the foregoing provisions of this subsection—

'charging order' has the meaning assigned by section 78(2) of the Criminal Justice Act 1988 or by section 27(2) of the Drug Trafficking Act 1994;

'confiscation order' and 'restraint order' mean a confiscation order or a restraint order under Part 2, 3, or 4 of the Proceeds of Crime Act 2002.]

(2)   A debtor's apparent insolvency shall continue, if constituted under—

(a)   subsection (1)(a) above, until his discharge; [. . .]

(b)   subsection (1)(b), (c) or (d) above, until he becomes able to pay his debts and pays them as they become due [; or

(c)   subsection (i)(ba), when main proceedings have ended.]

(3)   The apparent insolvency of—

(a)   a partnership shall be constituted either in accordance with the foregoing provisions of this section or if any of the partners is apparently insolvent for a debt of the partnership;

(b)   an unincorporated body shall be constituted if a person representing the body is apparently insolvent, or a person holding property of the body in a fiduciary capacity is apparently insolvent, for a debt of the body.

(4)   Notwithstanding subsection (2) of section 6 of this Act, the apparent insolvency of an entity such as is mentioned in paragraph (a) or (b) of that subsection may be constituted (or as the case may be constituted anew) under subsection (1) above; and any reference in the foregoing provisions of this section to a debtor

shall, except where the context otherwise requires, be construed as including a reference to such an entity.

8 Further provisions relating to presentation of petitions

(1) Subject to subsection (2) below, a petition for the sequestration of a debtor's estate (other than a deceased debtor's estate) may be presented—

[(a) at any time by—
(i) the debtor;
(ii) a trustee under a trust deed;
(iii) a temporary administrator; or
(iv) a member State liquidator appointed in main proceedings;]
(b) by a qualified creditor or qualified creditors, only if the apparent insolvency founded on in the petition was constituted within 4 months before the petition is presented.

(2) A petition for the sequestration of the estate of a limited partnership may be presented within such time as may be prescribed.

(3) A petition for the sequestration of the estate of a deceased debtor may be presented—

[(a) at any time by—
(i) an executor;
(ii) a person entitled to be appointed as executor of the estate;
(iii) a trustee acting under a trust deed;
(iv) a temporary administrator; or
(v) a member State liquidator appointed in main proceedings;]
(b) by a qualified creditor or qualified creditors of the deceased debtor—
(i) in a case where the apparent insolvency of the debtor was constituted within 4 months before his death, at any time;
(ii) in any other case (whether or not apparent insolvency has been constituted), not earlier than 6 months after the debtor's death.

(4) If an executor does not petition for sequestration of the deceased debtor's estate or for the appointment of a judicial factor to administer the estate within a reasonable period after he knew or ought to have known that the estate was absolutely insolvent and likely to remain so, any intromission by him with the estate after the expiry of that period shall be deemed to be an intromission without a title.

(5) The presentation of, or the concurring in, a petition for sequestration shall bar the effect of any enactment or rule of law relating to the limitation of actions in any part of the United Kingdom.

(6) Where before sequestration is awarded it becomes apparent that a petitioning or concurring creditor was ineligible so to petition or concur he shall withdraw, or as the case may be withdraw from, the petition but another creditor may be sisted in his place.

9 Jurisdiction

(1) The Court of Session shall have jurisdiction in respect of the sequestration of the estate of a living debtor or of a deceased debtor if the debtor had an established place of business in Scotland, or was habitually resident there, at the relevant time.

(2) The Court of Session shall have jurisdiction in respect of the sequestration of the estate of any entity which may be sequestrated by virtue of section 6 of this Act, if the entity—

(a) had an established place of business in Scotland at the relevant time; or
(b) was constituted or formed under Scots law, and at any time carried on business in Scotland.

(3) Notwithstanding that the partner of a firm, whether alive or deceased, does not fall within subsection (1) above, the Court of Session shall have jurisdiction in respect of the sequestration of his estate if a petition has been presented for the

sequestration of the estate of the firm of which he is, or was at the relevant time before his decease, a partner and the process of that sequestration is still current.

(4)   The provisions of this section shall apply to the sheriff as they apply to the Court of Session but as if for the word 'Scotland' wherever it occurs there were substituted the words 'the sheriffdom' and in subsection (3) after the word 'presented' there were inserted the words 'in the sheriffdom'.

(5)   In this section 'the relevant time' means at any time in the year immediately preceding the date of presentation of the petition or the date of death, as the case may be.

[(6)   This section is subject to Article 3 of the EC Regulation.]

10   Concurrent proceedings for sequestration or analogous remedy

(1)   If, in the course of sequestration proceedings, the petitioner for sequestration, the debtor or a creditor concurring in the petition (the petition in such proceedings being hereafter in this section referred to as the 'instant petition') is, or becomes, aware that—

(a)   another petition for sequestration of the debtor's estate is before a court or such sequestration has been awarded; or

(b)   a petition for the appointment of a judicial factor on the debtor's estate is before a court or such a judicial factor has been appointed; or

(c)   [a petition is before a court for the winding up of the debtor under Part IV or V of the Insolvency Act 1986 or section 372 of the Financial Services and Markets Act 2000]; or

(d)   an application for an analogous remedy in respect of the debtor's estate is proceeding or such an analogous remedy is in force,

he shall as soon as possible bring that fact to the notice of the court to which the instant petition was presented.

(2)   If a petitioner (not being the debtor) or a creditor concurring in the petition fails to comply with subsection (1) above, he may be made liable for the expenses of presenting the petition for sequestration; and, if the debtor fails to comply with subsection (1) above, he shall be guilty of an offence and liable, on summary conviction, to a fine not exceeding level 5 on the standard scale.

(3)   Where in the course of sequestration proceedings any of the circumstances mentioned in paragraph (a), (b) or (c) of subsection (1) above exists then—

(a)   the court to which the instant petition was presented may, on its own motion or at the instance of the debtor or any creditor or other person having an interest, allow that petition to proceed or may sist or dismiss it; or

(b)   without prejudice to paragraph (a) above, the Court of Session may, on its own motion or on application by the debtor or any creditor or other person having an interest, direct the sheriff before whom the instant petition is pending, or the court before which the other petition is pending, to sist or dismiss the instant petition or, as the case may be, the other petition, or may order the petitions to be heard together.

(4)   Where in respect of the same estate—

(a)   a petition for sequestration is pending before a court; and

(b)   an application for an analogous remedy is proceeding or an analogous remedy is in force,

the court, on its own motion or at the instance of the debtor or any creditor or other person having an interest, may allow the petition for sequestration to proceed or may sist or dismiss it.

(5)   In this section 'analogous remedy' means a bankruptcy order under the Bankruptcy Act 1914 or under the Insolvency Act 1985 or an administration order under section 112 of the County Courts Act 1984 in England and Wales or under any enactment having the like effect in Northern Ireland or a remedy analogous to either of the aforesaid remedies, or to sequestration, in any other country.

11   Creditor's oath

(1)   Every creditor, being a petitioner for sequestration, a creditor who concurs in a petition by a debtor or a qualified creditor who becomes sisted under sub-section (8)(i) of section 5 of this Act or under that subsection as applied by section 6(8) of this Act, shall produce an oath in the prescribed form made by him or on his behalf.

(2)   The oath may be made—

(a)   in the United Kingdom, before any person entitled to administer an oath there;

(b)   outwith the United Kingdom, before a British diplomatic or consular officer or any person authorised to administer an oath or affirmation under the law of the place where the oath is made.

(3)   The identity of the person making the oath and the identity of the person before whom the oath is made and their authority to make and to administer the oath respectively shall be presumed to be correctly stated, and any seal or sig-nature on the oath shall be presumed to be authentic, unless the contrary is established.

(4)   If the oath contains any error or has omitted any fact, the court to which the petition for sequestration was presented may, at any time before sequestration is awarded, allow another oath to be produced rectifying the original oath; and this section shall apply to the making of that other oath as it applies to the making of the original oath.

(5)   Every creditor must produce along with the oath an account or voucher (according to the nature of the debt) which constitutes *prima facie* evidence of the debt; and a petitioning creditor shall in addition produce such evidence as is avail-able to him to show the apparent insolvency of the debtor.

Award of sequestration and appointment and resignation of interim trustee

12   When sequestration is awarded

[(1)   Where a petition for the sequestration of his estate is presented by the debtor, unless cause is shown why sequestration cannot competently be awarded, the court shall award sequestration forthwith if it is satisfied—

(a)   that the petition has been presented in accordance with the provisions of this Act;

(b)   that either subsection (2A) or (2B) of section 5 of this Act applies to the debtor; and

(c)   that the provisions of subsections (6) and (6A) of that section have been complied with.

(1A)   Where a petition is presented as mentioned in subsection (1) above, the Accountant in Bankruptcy may, not later than 7 days after the date on which sequestration is awarded, apply to the court for the grant of a certificate for the summary administration of the sequestration of the debtor's estate.]

(2)   Where a petition for sequestration of a debtor's estate is presented by a creditor or a trustee acting under a trust deed, the court to which the petition is presented shall grant warrant to cite the debtor to appear before it on such date as shall be specified in the warrant, being a date not less than 6 nor more than 14 days after the date of citation, to show cause why sequestration should not be awarded.

[(3)   Where, on a petition for sequestration presented by a creditor or a trustee acting under a trust deed, the court is satisfied—

(a)   that, if the debtor has not appeared, proper citation has been made of the debtor;

(b)   that the petition has been presented in accordance with the provisions of this Act;

(c)   that the provisions of subsection (6) of section 5 of this Act have been complied with;

(d)   that, in the case of a petition by a creditor, the requirements of this Act relating to apparent insolvency have been fulfilled; and

(e)   that, in the case of a petition by a trustee, the averments in his petition as to any of the conditions in subsection (2C) of the said section 5 are true,

it shall, subject to subsection (3A) below, award sequestration forthwith.

(3A)   Sequestration shall not be awarded in pursuance of subsection (3) above if—

(a)   cause is shown why sequestration cannot competently be awarded; or

(b)   the debtor forthwith pays or satisfies, or produces written evidence of the payment or satisfaction of, or gives or shows that there is sufficient security for the payment of—

(i)   the debt in respect of which he became apparently insolvent; and

(ii)   any other debt due by him to the petitioner and any creditor concurring in the petition.]

[(4)   In this Act 'the date of sequestration' means—

(a)   where the petition for sequestration is presented by the debtor, the date on which sequestration is awarded;

(b)   where the petition for sequestration is presented by a creditor or a trustee acting under a trust deed—

(i)   the date on which the court grants warrant under subsection (2) above to cite the debtor; or

(ii)   where more than one such warrant is granted, the date on which the first such warrant is granted.]

[13   Resignation, removal etc of interim trustee

(1)   Where, under section 1A(2) of this Act, the court removes from office an interim trustee, the court shall, on the application of the Accountant in Bankruptcy, appoint a new interim trustee.

(2)   Without prejudice to section 1A(2) of this Act or to subsection (1) above, where the court is satisfied that an interim trustee—

(a)   is unable to act (whether by, under or by virtue of a provision of this Act or from any other cause whatsoever); or

(b)   has so conducted himself that he should no longer continue to act in the sequestration, the court, on the application of the debtor, a creditor or the Accountant in Bankruptcy, shall remove from office the interim trustee and appoint a new interim trustee.

(3)   An interim trustee (not being the Accountant in Bankruptcy) may apply to the court for authority to resign office; and if the court is satisfied that the grounds mentioned in paragraph (a) or (b) of subsection (2) above apply in relation to the interim trustee, it shall grant the application.

(4)   Where, following an application under subsection (3) above, the interim trustee resigns office, the court shall appoint a new interim trustee.

(5)   Where the interim trustee has died, the court, on the application of the debtor, a creditor or the Accountant in Bankruptcy, shall appoint a new interim trustee.

(6)   No one (other than the Accountant in Bankruptcy) shall act as interim trustee in a sequestration if he would, by virtue of section 24(2) of this Act, be disqualified from acting as permanent trustee in that sequestration; but where an interim trustee is, by virtue of this subsection, prohibited from so acting, he shall forthwith make an application under subsection (3) above.

(7)   Subsections (1) and (2) of section 2 of this Act shall apply as regards the appointment of an interim trustee under this section as if for any reference to—

(a)   the court awarding sequestration of the debtor's estate, there was substituted a reference to the court appointing a new interim trustee; and

(b)   the petition for sequestration there was substituted a reference to the application under this section for the appointment of a new interim trustee.]

14   Registration of court order

(1)   The clerk of the court shall forthwith after the date of sequestration send—

(a)   a certified copy of the relevant court order to the keeper of the register of inhibitions and adjudications for recording in that register; and

(b)   a copy of the order to the Accountant in Bankruptcy.

[(c)   a copy of that order to the DAS administrator (as defined in regulation 2(1) of the Debt Arrangement Scheme (Scotland) Regulations 2004), where the debtor is taking part in a debt payment programme under Part 1 of the Debt Arrangement and Attachment (Scotland) Act 2002.]

(2)   Recording under subsection (1)(a) above shall have the effect as from the date of sequestration of an inhibition and of a citation in an adjudication of the debtor's heritable estate at the instance of the creditors who subsequently have claims in the sequestration accepted under section 49 of this Act.

(3)   The effect mentioned in subsection (2) above shall expire—

(a)   on the recording under section 15(5)(a) or 17(8)(a) of, or by virtue of paragraph 11 of Schedule 4 to, this Act of a certified copy of an order; or

(b)   subject to subsection (4) below, if the effect has not expired by virtue of paragraph (a) above, at the end of the period of 3 years beginning with the date of sequestration.

(4)   The permanent trustee, if not discharged, [may] before the end of the period of 3 years mentioned in subsection (3)(b) above send a memorandum in a form prescribed by the Court of Session by act of sederunt to the keeper of the register of inhibitions and adjudications for recording in that register, and such recording shall renew the effect mentioned in subsection (2) above; and thereafter the said effect shall continue to be preserved only if such a memorandum is so recorded before the expiry of every subsequent period of 3 years.

(5)   In this section 'relevant court order' means, if the petition for sequestration is presented by—

(a)   the debtor, the order of the court awarding sequestration; or

(b)   a creditor or the trustee acting under a trust deed, the order of the court granting warrant under section 12(2) of this Act.

15   Further provisions relating to award of sequestration

(1)   Where sequestration has been awarded by the Court of Session, it shall remit the sequestration to such sheriff as in all the circumstances of the case it considers appropriate.

(2)   The Court of Session may at any time after sequestration has been awarded, on application being made to it, transfer the sequestration from the sheriff before whom it is depending or to whom it has been remitted to any other sheriff.

(3)   Where the court makes an order refusing to award sequestration, the petitioner or a creditor concurring in the petition for sequestration may appeal against the order within 14 days of the date of making of the order.

(4)   Without prejudice to any right to bring an action of reduction of an award of sequestration, such an award shall not be subject to review otherwise than by recall under sections 16 and 17 of this Act.

(5)   Where a petition for sequestration is presented by a creditor or a trustee acting under a trust deed, the clerk of the court shall—

(a)   on the final determination or abandonment of any appeal under subsection (3) above in relation to the petition, or if there is no such appeal on the expiry of the 14 days mentioned in that subsection, send a certified copy of an order refusing to award sequestration to the keeper of the register of inhibitions and adjudications for recording in that register;

[(b)   forthwith send a copy of the order refusing or awarding sequestration to—

       (i)   the Accountant in Bankruptcy,

      (ii)   the DAS administrator (as defined in regulation 2(1) of the Debt Arrangement Scheme (Scotland) Regulations 2004), where the debtor is taking part in a debt payment programme under Part 1 of the Debt Arrangement and Attachment (Scotland) Act 2002.]

    [(6)   The interim trustee shall, as soon as an award of sequestration has been granted, publish in the Edinburgh Gazette a notice—

      (a)   stating that sequestration of the debtor's estate has been awarded;

      (b)   inviting the submission of claims to him; and

      (c)   giving such other information as may be prescribed.]

    (7)   Where sequestration has been awarded, the process of sequestration shall not fall asleep.

    (8)   Where a debtor learns, whether before or after the date of sequestration, that he may derive benefit from another estate, he shall as soon as practicable after that date inform—

      (a)   the permanent trustee or, if the permanent trustee has not yet been elected or appointed, the interim trustee of that fact; and

      (b)   the person who is administering that other estate of the sequestration.

    (9)   If the debtor fails to comply with subsection (8) above, he shall be guilty of an offence and liable, on summary conviction, to a fine not exceeding level 5 on the standard scale.

16 Petitions for recall of sequestration

    (1)   A petition for recall of an award of sequestration may be presented to the Court of Session by—

      (a)   the debtor, any creditor or any other person having an interest (notwithstanding that he was a petitioner, or concurred in the petition, for the sequestration);

      (b)   the interim trustee, the permanent trustee, or the Accountant in Bankruptcy.

    (2)   The petitioner shall serve upon the debtor, any person who was a petitioner, or concurred in the petition, for the sequestration, the interim trustee or permanent trustee and the Accountant in Bankruptcy, a copy of the petition along with a notice stating that the recipient of the notice may lodge answers to the petition within 14 days of the service of the notice.

    (3)   At the same time as service is made under subsection (2) above, the petitioner shall publish a notice in the Edinburgh Gazette stating that a petition has been presented under this section and that any person having an interest may lodge answers to the petition within 14 days of the publication of the notice.

    (4)   Subject to [sections 41(1)(b) and 41A(1)(b)] of this Act, a petition under this section may be presented—

      (a)   within 10 weeks after the date of [the award of] sequestration; but

      (b)   at any time if the petition is presented on any of the grounds mentioned in paragraphs (a) to (c) of section 17(1) of this Act.

    (5)   Notwithstanding that a petition has been presented under this section, the proceedings in the sequestration shall continue (subject to section 17(6) of this Act) as if that petition had not been presented until the recall is granted.

    (6)   Where—

      (a)   a petitioner under this section; or

      (b)   a person who has lodged answers to the petition,

withdraws or dies, any person entitled to present or, as the case may be, lodge answers to a petition under this section may be sisted in his place.

17 Recall of sequestration

    (1)   The Court of Session may recall an award of sequestration if it is satisfied that in all the circumstances of the case (including those arising after the date of

the award of sequestration) it is appropriate to do so and, without prejudice to the foregoing generality, may recall the award if it is satisfied that—

(a) the debtor has paid his debts in full or has given sufficient security for their payment;

(b) a majority in value of the creditors reside in a country other than Scotland and that it is more appropriate for the debtor's estate to be administered in that other country; or

(c) one or more other awards of sequestration of the estate or analogous remedies (as defined in section 10(5) of this Act) have been granted.

(2) Where one or more awards of sequestration of the debtor's estate have been granted, the Court may, after such intimation as it considers necessary, recall an award whether or not the one in respect of which the petition for recall was presented.

(3) On recalling an award of sequestration, the Court—

(a) shall make provision for the payment of the outlays and remuneration of the interim trustee and permanent trustee by directing that such payment shall be made out of the debtor's estate or by requiring any person who was a party to the petition for sequestration to pay the whole or any part of the said outlays and remuneration;

(b) without prejudice to subsection (7) below, may direct that payment of the expenses of a creditor who was a petitioner, or concurred in the petition, for sequestration shall be made out of the debtor's estate;

(c) may make any further order that it considers necessary or reasonable in all the circumstances of the case.

(4) Subject to subsection (5) below, the effect of the recall of an award of sequestration shall be, so far as practicable, to restore the debtor and any other person affected by the sequestration to the position he would have been in if the sequestration had not been awarded.

(5) A recall of an award of sequestration shall not—

(a) affect the interruption of prescription caused by the presentation of the petition for sequestration or the submission of a claim under section 22 or 48 of this Act;

(b) invalidate any transaction entered into before such recall by the interim trustee or permanent trustee with a person acting in good faith.

(6) Where the Court considers that it is inappropriate to recall or to refuse to recall an award of sequestration forthwith, it may order that the proceedings in the sequestration shall continue but shall be subject to such conditions as it may think fit.

(7) The Court may make such order in relation to the expenses in a petition for recall as it thinks fit.

(8) The clerk of court shall send—

(a) a certified copy of any order recalling an award of sequestration to the keeper of the register of inhibitions and adjudications for recording in that register; and

(b) a copy of any order recalling or refusing to recall an award of sequestration, or of any order under section 41(1)(b)(ii) [or 41A(1)(b)(ii)] of this Act, to—

(i) the Accountant in Bankruptcy; and

(ii) the permanent trustee (if any) who shall insert it in the sederunt book.

Period between award of sequestration and statutory meeting of creditors

18 Interim preservation of estate

(1) The interim trustee may give general or particular directions to the debtor relating to the management of the debtor's estate.

(2)   In exercising the functions conferred on him by section [2(4)(a)] of this Act, an interim trustee may—

(a)   require the debtor to deliver up to him any money or valuables, or any document relating to the debtor's business or financial affairs, belonging to or in the possession of the debtor or under his control;

(b)   place in safe custody anything mentioned in paragraph (a) above;

(c)   require the debtor to deliver up to him any perishable goods belonging to the debtor or under his control and may arrange for the sale or disposal of such goods;

(d)   make or cause to be made an inventory or valuation of any property belonging to the debtor;

(e)   require the debtor to implement any transaction entered into by the debtor;

(f)   effect or maintain insurance policies in respect of the business or property of the debtor;

(g)   close down the debtor's business;

[(h)   carry on any business of the debtor or borrow money in so far as it is necessary for the interim trustee to do so to safeguard the debtor's estate].

(3)   The court, on the application of the interim trustee, may—

[. . .]

(b)   on cause shown, grant a warrant authorising the interim trustee to enter the house where the debtor resides or his business premises and to search for and take possession of anything mentioned in paragraphs (a) and (c) of subsection (2) above, if need be by opening shut and lock-fast places; or

(c)   make such other order to safeguard the debtor's estate as it thinks appropriate.

(4)   The court, on an application by the debtor on the grounds that a direction under subsection (1) above is unreasonable, may—

(a)   if it considers the direction to be unreasonable, set aside the direction; and

(b)   in any event, give such directions to the debtor regarding the management of his estate as it considers appropriate;

but, subject to any interim order of the court, the debtor shall comply with the direction appealed against pending the final determination of the appeal.

(5)   The debtor shall be guilty of an offence if—

(a)   he fails without reasonable excuse to comply with—

(i)   a direction under subsection (1) or (4)(b) above; or

(ii)   a requirement under subsection 2(a), (c) or (e) above; or

(b)   he obstructs the interim trustee where the interim trustee is acting in pursuance of subsection (3)(b) above.

(6)   A person convicted of an offence under subsection (5) above shall be liable—

(a)   on summary conviction to a fine not exceeding the statutory maximum or—

(i)   to imprisonment for a term not exceeding 3 months; or

(ii)   if he has previously been convicted of an offence inferring dishonest appropriation of property or an attempt at such appropriation, to imprisonment for a term not exceeding 6 months,

or (in the case of either sub-paragraph) to both such fine and such imprisonment; or

(b)   on conviction on indictment to a fine or to imprisonment for a term not exceeding 2 years or to both.

19   [Statement of assets and liabilities etc

(1)   Where the petitioner for sequestration is the debtor he shall, not later than 7 days after the appointment of the interim trustee (where he is not the Accountant

in Bankruptcy), send to the interim trustee such statement of assets and liabilities as was lodged in court in pursuance of section 5(6A)(a) of this Act.

(2) Where the petitioner for sequestration is a creditor or a trustee acting under a trust deed, the debtor shall, not later than 7 days after having been notified by the interim trustee as mentioned in section 2(7) of this Act, send to the interim trustee a statement of assets and liabilities.

(3) If the debtor—

(a) fails to send to the interim trustee in accordance with subsection (1) or (2) above such statement of assets and liabilities; or

(b) fails to disclose any material fact in such statement of assets and liabilities; or

(c) makes a material misstatement in such statement of assets and liabilities,

he shall be guilty of an offence and liable on summary conviction to a fine not exceeding level 5 on the standard scale or to imprisonment for a term not exceeding 3 months or to both such fine and imprisonment.

(4) In any proceedings for an offence under subsection (3) above, it shall be a defence for the accused to show that he had a reasonable excuse for—

(a) failing to send to the interim trustee in accordance with subsection (1) or (2) above such statement of assets and liabilities; or

(b) failing to disclose a material fact; or

(c) making a material misstatement.]

20   Trustee's duties on receipt of list of assets and liabilities

[(1) When the interim trustee has received the statement of assets and liabilities, he shall, as soon as practicable, prepare a statement of the debtor's affairs so far as within the knowledge of the interim trustee and shall indicate in the statement of the debtor's affairs whether, in his opinion, the debtor's assets are unlikely to be sufficient to pay any dividend whatsoever in respect of the debts mentioned in paragraphs (e) to (h) of section 51(1) of this Act.]

(2) The interim trustee shall, not later than 4 days before the date fixed for the statutory meeting, send to the Accountant in Bankruptcy—

(a) [a statement] of assets and liabilities; and

(b) a copy of the [. . .] statement of the debtor's affairs; and

(c) written comments by the interim trustee indicating what in his opinion are the causes of the insolvency and to what extent the conduct of the debtor may have contributed to the insolvency.

(3) The written comments made under subsection (2)(c) above shall be absolutely privileged.

(4) The interim trustee may request—

(a) the debtor to appear before him and to give information relating to his assets, his dealings with them or his conduct in relation to his business or financial affairs; or

(b) the debtor's spouse [or civil partner] or any other person who the interim trustee believes can give such information to give that information,

and if the interim trustee considers it necessary he may apply to the sheriff for an order requiring the debtor, spouse [, civil partner] or other person to appear before the sheriff for private examination.

(5) Subsections (2) to (4) of section 44 and sections 46 and 47 of this Act shall apply, subject to any necessary modifications, in respect of private examination under subsection (4) above as they apply in respect of private examination under the said subsection (2).

[(5A) Subsections (2) and (3) above do not apply in any case where the Accountant in Bankruptcy is the interim trustee.]

[20A   Statutory meeting

A meeting of creditors called by the interim trustee under section 21 or 21A of this Act shall, in this Act, be referred to as 'the statutory meeting'.]

Statutory meeting of creditors and confirmation of permanent trustee

21 Calling of statutory meeting

(1) [Where the interim trustee is not the Accountant in Bankruptcy he shall call the statutory meeting] to be held within 60 days, or such longer period as the sheriff on cause shown may allow, after the date of the award of sequestration.

[(1A) The statutory meeting shall be held at such time and place as the interim trustee determines.]

(2) Not less than 7 days before the date fixed for the statutory meeting, the interim trustee shall notify—

(a) every creditor known to him; and

(b) the Accountancy in Bankruptcy,

of the date, time and place of the meeting, and shall in the notification to creditors invite the submission of such claims as have not already been submitted and inform them of his duties under section 23(3) and (5) of this Act.

(3) The creditors may continue the statutory meeting to a date not later than 7 days after the end of the period—

(a) of [60] days mentioned in subsection (1) above; or (as the case may be),

(b) allowed by the sheriff under that subsection.

[(4) This section does not apply in any case where the Accountant in Bankruptcy is the interim trustee.]

[21A Calling of statutory meeting where interim trustee is Accountant in Bankruptcy

(1) Subject to subsections (5) and (6) below, where the interim trustee is the Accountant in Bankruptcy, the statutory meeting may be held at such time and place as the interim trustee may determine.

(2) Not later than 60 days after the date of the sequestration, or such longer period as the sheriff may on cause shown allow, the interim trustee shall give notice to every creditor known to him of whether he intends to call the statutory meeting.

(3) A notice given under subsection (2) above shall—

(a) be accompanied by a copy of the interim trustee's statement of the debtor's affairs; and

(b) where the interim trustee is notifying his intention not to hold the statutory meeting, inform creditors—

(i) of the effect of subsections (4) and (5) below; and

(ii) whether he intends to apply for the grant of a certificate for the summary administration of the sequestration of the debtor's estate.

(4) Within 7 days of the giving of notice under subsection (2) above, any creditor may request the interim trustee to call the statutory meeting.

(5) Where a request or requests under subsection (4) above are made by not less than one quarter in value of the debtor's creditors, the interim trustee shall call the statutory meeting not later than 28 days, or such other period as the sheriff may on cause shown allow, after the giving of notice under subsection (2) above.

(6) Where the interim trustee gives notice under subsection (2) above that he intends to call the statutory meeting, such meeting shall be called not later than 28 days after the giving of such notice.

(7) Not less than 7 days before the date fixed for the statutory meeting, the interim trustee shall notify every creditor known to him of the date, time and place of the meeting, and shall in such notice invite the submission of such claims as have not already been submitted and inform them of his duties under section 23(3) of this Act.

(8) The creditors may continue the statutory meeting to a date not later than 7 days after the end of the period mentioned in subsection (6) above or such longer period as the sheriff may on cause shown allow.

(9) This section applies in any case where the Accountant in Bankruptcy is the interim trustee.

21B Procedure where no statutory meeting called
(1) Where the interim trustee does not call the statutory meeting and the period mentioned in section 21A(4) of this Act has expired, he shall—
    (a) forthwith make a report to the sheriff on the circumstances of the sequestration; and
    (b) provide to the sheriff a copy of the interim trustee's statement of the debtor's affairs.
(2) In the case of a sequestration which falls within subsection (1) above—
    (a) section 25A of this Act shall apply; and
    (b) the interim trustee may apply to the sheriff for the grant of a certificate for the summary administration of the sequestration of the debtor's estate.]

22 Submission of claims for voting purposes at statutory meeting
(1) For the purposes of voting at the statutory meeting, a creditor shall submit a claim in accordance with this section to the interim trustee at or before the meeting.
(2) A creditor shall submit a claim under this section by producing to the interim trustee—
    (a) a statement of claim in the prescribed form; and
    (b) an account or voucher (according to the nature of the debt) which constitutes *prima facie* evidence of the debt:
Provided that the interim trustee may dispense with any requirement under this subsection in respect of any debt or any class of debt.
(3) Where a creditor neither resides nor has a place of business in the United Kingdom, the interim trustee—
    (a) shall, if he knows where the creditor resides or has a place of business and if no notification has been given to that creditor under section 21(2) of this Act, write to him informing him that he may submit a claim under this section;
    (b) may allow the creditor to submit an informal claim in writing.
(4) A creditor who has produced a statement of claim in accordance with subsection (2) above may at any time before the statutory meeting produce in place of that statement of claim another such statement of claim specifying a different amount for his claim.
(5) If a creditor produces under this section a statement of claim, account, voucher or other evidence which is false—
    (a) the creditor shall be guilty of an offence unless he shows that he neither knew nor had reason to believe that the statement of claim, account, voucher or other evidence was false;
    (b) the debtor shall be guilty of an offence if he—
      (i) knew or became aware that the statement of claim, account, voucher or other evidence was false; and
      (ii) failed as soon as practicable after acquiring such knowledge to report it to the interim trustee or permanent trustee.
(6) A creditor may, in such circumstances as may be prescribed, state the amount of his claim in foreign currency.
(7) The interim trustee shall, on production of any document to him under this section, initial the document and keep a record of it stating the date when it was produced to him, and, if requested by the sender, shall return it (if it is not a statement of claim) to him.
(8) The submission of a claim under this section shall bar the effect of any enactment or rule of law relating to the limitation of actions in any part of the United Kingdom.
(9) Schedule 1 to this Act shall have effect for determining the amount in respect of which a creditor shall be entitled to claim.

(10) A person convicted of an offence under subsection (5) above shall be liable—

(a) on summary conviction to a fine not exceeding the statutory maximum or—

    (i) to imprisonment for a term not exceeding 3 months; or

    (ii) if he has previously been convicted of an offence inferring dishonest appropriation of property or an attempt at such appropriation, to imprisonment for a term not exceeding 6 months,

or (in the case of either sub-paragraph) to both such fine and such imprisonment; or

(b) on conviction on indictment to a fine or to imprisonment for a term not exceeding 2 years or to both.

23 Proceedings at statutory meeting before election of permanent trustee

(1) At the commencement of the statutory meeting, the chairman shall be the interim trustee who as chairman shall—

(a) for the purposes of subsection (2) below, accept or reject in whole or in part the claim of each creditor, and, if the amount of a claim is stated in foreign currency, he shall convert that amount into sterling, in such manner as may be prescribed, at the rate of exchange prevailing at the close of business on the date of sequestration;

(b) invite the creditors thereupon to elect one of their number as chairman in his place and shall preside over the election:

    Provided that if a chairman is not elected in pursuance of this paragraph, the interim trustee shall remain the chairman throughout the meeting; and

(c) arrange for a record to be made of the proceedings at the meeting.

(2) The acceptance of a claim in whole or in part under subsection (1) above shall, subject to section 24(3) of this Act, determine the entitlement of a creditor to vote at the statutory meeting.

(3) On the conclusion of the proceedings under subsection (1) above, the interim trustee—

[(a) shall make available for inspection—

    (i) the statement of assets and liabilities; and

    (ii) his statement of the debtor's affairs prepared under section 20(1) of this Act;]; and

(b) shall answer to the best of his ability any questions, and shall consider any representations, put to him by the creditors relating to the debtor's assets, business or financial affairs or his conduct in relation thereto;

(c) shall, after considering any such representations as are mentioned in paragraph (b) above, indicate whether, in his opinion, the debtor's assets are unlikely to be sufficient as mentioned in section 20(1) of this Act; and

[(d) shall determine whether it is necessary to revise his statement of the debtor's affairs and, if he determines that it is necessary to revise the statement, he shall do so either at, or as soon as possible after, the statutory meeting.]

[. . .]

[(5) Where the interim trustee has revised his statement of the debtor's affairs, he shall, as soon as possible after the statutory meeting, send a copy of the revised statement to every creditor known to him.]

[23A Summary administration

(1) Where an application is made to the court under this Act for the grant of a certificate for the summary administration of the sequestration of the debtor's estate, the court shall, subject to subsection (9) below, grant such a certificate where it appears to the court that—

(a) the aggregate amount of the debtor's liabilities does not exceed £20,000; and

(b) the aggregate amount of the debtor's assets does not exceed £2,000.

(2) In calculating—

(a) the aggregate amount of the debtor's liabilities under paragraph (a) of subsection (1) above, no account shall be taken of any debt to the extent that a creditor holds a security for that debt; and

(b) the aggregate amount of the debtor's assets under paragraph (b) of that subsection, no account shall be taken of—

(i) any heritable property of his; or

(ii) any property of his which, under section 33(1) of this Act, does not vest in the permanent trustee.

(3) For the purposes of an application under subsection (1) above made by—

(a) the Accountant in Bankruptcy; or

(b) an interim trustee who is not the Accountant in Bankruptcy,

a certificate by the Accountant in Bankruptcy or, as the case may be, the interim trustee as to the aggregate amounts of the debtor's liabilities and assets shall be sufficient evidence of such aggregate amounts.

(4) Where a certificate for the summary administration of the sequestration of the debtor's estate is granted—

(a) in any case where the application for the certificate was made by the Accountant in Bankruptcy, section 25A of this Act; and

(b) in every case, Schedule 2A to this Act (which modifies the duties of the permanent trustee), shall apply to the sequestration.

(5) The debtor, a creditor, the permanent trustee or the Accountant in Bankruptcy may, at any time, apply to the sheriff to withdraw the certificate for the summary administration of the sequestration of the debtor's estate.

(6) Where an application is made under subsection (5) above by a person who is not the permanent trustee, the applicant shall send a copy of the application to the permanent trustee who shall prepare and present to the sheriff a report on all of the circumstances of the sequestration.

(7) If it appears to the sheriff, on considering an application under subsection (5) above and any report under subsection (6) above, that it is no longer appropriate for the sequestration to be subject to summary administration, he shall withdraw the certificate and the sequestration of the estate shall proceed as if the certificate had not been granted.

(8) The sheriff clerk shall send to the permanent trustee and, where he is not the permanent trustee, the Accountant in Bankruptcy a copy of the sheriff's decision on any application under subsection (5) above.

(9) The court shall not grant an application as mentioned in subsection (1) above—

(a) in any case where the application is made by the Accountant in Bankruptcy and the court has appointed as interim trustee a person who is not the Accountant in Bankruptcy; or

(b) in any other case—

(i) where a person has been elected as permanent trustee, before the sheriff has confirmed the election of that person as permanent trustee; or

(ii) where no such person has been elected, unless the court at the same time appoints the interim trustee as permanent trustee.]

24 Election of permanent trustee

[(1) At the statutory meeting, the creditors shall, at the conclusion of the proceedings under section 23(3) of this Act, proceed to the election of the permanent trustee.]

(2) None of the following persons shall be eligible for election as permanent trustee, nor shall anyone who becomes such a person after having been elected as permanent trustee be qualified to continue to act as permanent trustee—

(a) the debtor;

(b) a person who is not qualified to act as an insolvency practitioner or who, though qualified to act as an insolvency practitioner, is not qualified to act as such in relation to the debtor;

(c)   a person who holds an interest opposed to the general interests of the creditors;

(d)   a person who resides outwith the jurisdiction of the Court of Session.

[(e)   a person who has not given an undertaking, in writing, to act as permanent trustee;

(f)   the Accountant in Bankruptcy.]

(3)   The following persons shall not be entitled to vote in the election of the permanent trustee—

(a)   anyone acquiring a debt due by the debtor, otherwise than by succession, after the date of sequestration;

(b)   any creditor to the extent that his debt is a postponed debt.

[(3A)   In any case where the Accountant in Bankruptcy is the interim trustee, if—

(a)   no creditor entitled to vote in the election of the permanent trustee attends the statutory meeting; or

(b)   no permanent trustee is elected, the Accountant in Bankruptcy shall forthwith report the proceedings at the statutory meeting to the sheriff and section 25A of this Act shall apply.

(3B)   Where a report is made in pursuance of subsection (3A) above, the Accountant in Bankruptcy may apply to the sheriff for the grant of a certificate for the summary administration of the sequestration of the debtor's estate.]

(4)   [In any case where the Accountant in Bankruptcy is not the interim trustee] if no creditor entitled to vote in the election of the permanent trustee attends the statutory meeting or if no permanent trustee is elected, the interim trustee shall forthwith—

(a)   so notify the Accountant in Bankruptcy; and

(b)   report the proceedings at the statutory meeting to the sheriff, who shall thereupon appoint the interim trustee as the permanent trustee.

[(4A)   Where a report is made in pursuance of subsection (4) above, the interim trustee may apply to the sheriff for the grant of a certificate for the summary administration of the sequestration of the debtor's estate.]

(5)   Where subsection (4) above applies, the provisions of this Act shall have effect as regards the sequestration subject to such modifications, and with such further provisions, as are set out in Schedule 2 to this Act.

25 Confirmation of permanent trustee

(1)   On the election of the permanent trustee—

(a)   the interim trustee shall forthwith make a report of the proceedings at the statutory meeting to the sheriff; and

(b)   the debtor, a creditor, the interim trustee, the permanent trustee or the Accountant in Bankruptcy may, within 4 days after the statutory meeting, object to any matter connected with the election; and such objection shall be by summary application to the sheriff, specifying the grounds on which the objection is taken.

(2)   If there is no timeous objection under subsection (1)(b) above, the sheriff shall forthwith declare the elected person to be the permanent trustee; and the sheriff shall confirm his election and the sheriff clerk shall issue to him an act and warrant in a form prescribed by the Court of Session by act of sederunt and send a copy of the act and warrant to the Accountant in Bankruptcy.

[(2A)   Where a report is made in pursuance of subsection (1) above, the interim trustee may apply to the sheriff for the grant of a certificate for the summary administration of the sequestration of the debtor's estate.]

(3)   If there is a timeous objection under subsection (1)(b) above, the sheriff

shall forthwith give parties an opportunity to be heard thereon and shall give his decision.

(4) If in his decision under subsection (3) above the sheriff—

(a) rejects the objection, subsection (2) above shall apply as if there had been no timeous objection;

(b) sustains the objection, he shall order the interim trustee to arrange a new meeting for the election of a permanent trustee; and sections 23 and 24 of this Act and this section shall apply in relation to such a meeting.

(5) Any declaration, confirmation or decision of the sheriff under this section shall be final, and no expense in objecting under this section shall fall on the debtor's estate.

(6) The permanent trustee shall—

(a) insert a copy of the said act and warrant in the sederunt book; and

(b) where he is not the same person as the interim trustee, publish a notice in the Edinburgh Gazette [. . .] stating that he has been confirmed in office as permanent trustee [and giving such other information as may be prescribed].

[25A Appointment of permanent trustee in certain cases

(1) Where this section applies as mentioned in section 21B(2), 23A(4) or 24(3A) of this Act, the court shall appoint as permanent trustee—

(a) the Accountant in Bankruptcy; or

(b) such person as may be nominated by the Accountant in Bankruptcy (being a person who is not ineligible for election as permanent trustee under section 24(2) of this Act) if that person consents to the nomination.

(2) Where this section applies as mentioned in section 28(5) of this Act, if either of the persons mentioned in paragraphs (a) and (b) of subsection (1) above applies to the sheriff for appointment as permanent trustee, the sheriff shall so appoint such person.

(3) Where a person is appointed to be permanent trustee under this section, the provisions of this Act shall apply to the sequestration subject to such modifications, and with such further provisions, as are set out in Schedule 2 to this Act.]

26 Provisions relating to termination of interim trustee's functions

(1) Where the interim trustee does not himself become the permanent trustee, he shall, on confirmation of the permanent trustee in office, hand over to him everything in his possession which relates to the sequestration (including [the statement of assets and liabilities, and a copy] of the statement prepared under section 23(3)(d), and of the written comments sent under section 20(2)(c) of this Act) and shall thereupon cease to act in the sequestration.

(2) Within 3 months of the confirmation in office of the permanent trustee, the interim trustee shall—

(a) submit to the Accountant in Bankruptcy—

(i) his accounts of his intromissions (if any) with the debtor's estate; and

(ii) a claim for outlays reasonably incurred, and for remuneration for work reasonably undertaken, by him; and

(b) send to the permanent trustee (unless the interim trustee has himself become the permanent trustee), a copy of what is submitted to the Accountant in Bankruptcy under paragraph (a) above.

(3) On a submission being made to him under subsection (2) above, the Accountant in Bankruptcy—

(a) shall—

(i) audit the accounts; and

(ii) issue a determination fixing the amount of the outlays and remuneration payable to the interim trustee; and

(b) shall send a copy of—

(i) the said determination to the interim trustee (except where the interim trustee has himself become the permanent trustee); and

(ii)   the interim trustee's audited accounts and of the said determination to the permanent trustee, who shall insert the copies in the sederunt book.

(4)   The interim trustee, the permanent trustee, the debtor or any creditor may appeal to the sheriff against a determination under subsection (3)(a)(ii) above within 14 days of its issue [and the decision of the sheriff on such an appeal shall be final].

(5)   The permanent trustee, on being confirmed in office, shall make such insertions in the sederunt book as are appropriate to provide a record of the sequestration process before his confirmation, but he shall make no insertion therein relating to the written comments made by the interim trustee under section 20(2)(c) of this Act.

[(5A)   This section does not apply in any case where the Accountant in Bankruptcy is the interim trustee.]

[26A   Accountant in Bankruptcy to account for intromissions

(1)   This section applies in any case where the Accountant in Bankruptcy was the interim trustee and some other person becomes the permanent trustee.

(2)   The Accountant in Bankruptcy shall, on confirmation of the permanent trustee in office, hand over to the permanent trustee everything in his possession which relates to the sequestration and which he obtained in his capacity as interim trustee (including the statement of assets and liabilities); and thereupon he shall cease to act as interim trustee.

(3)   The Accountant in Bankruptcy shall, not later than 3 months after the confirmation in office of the permanent trustee, supply to the permanent trustee—

(a)   his accounts of his intromissions (if any) as interim trustee with the debtor's estate;

(b)   a determination of his fees and outlays calculated in accordance with regulations made under section 69A of this Act; and

(c)   a copy of the notice mentioned in subsection (4)(b) below.

(4)   The Accountant in Bankruptcy shall send to the debtor and to all creditors known to him—

(a)   a copy of the determination mentioned in subsection (3)(b) above; and

(b)   a notice in writing stating—

(i)   that the Accountant in Bankruptcy has commenced the procedure under this Act leading to discharge in respect of his actings as interim trustee;

(ii)   that the accounts of his intromissions (if any) with the debtor's estate are available for inspection at such address as the Accountant in Bankruptcy may determine;

(iii)   that an appeal may be made to the sheriff under subsection (5) below; and

(iv)   the effect of subsection (7) below.

(5)   The permanent trustee, the debtor and any creditor may appeal to the sheriff against—

(a)   the determination of the Accountant in Bankruptcy mentioned in subsection (3)(b) above;

(b)   the discharge of the Accountant in Bankruptcy in respect of his actings as interim trustee; or

(c)   both such determination and discharge.

(6)   An appeal under subsection (5) above shall be made not more than 14 days after the issue of the notice mentioned in subsection (4)(b) above; and the decision of the sheriff on such an appeal shall be final.

(7)   Where—

(a)   the requirements of this section have been complied with; and

(b)   no appeal is made to the sheriff under subsection (5) above or such an appeal is made but is refused as regards the discharge of the Accountant in Bankruptcy, the Accountant in Bankruptcy shall be discharged from all liability (other than any liability arising from fraud) to the creditors or to the debtor in respect of any act or omission of the Accountant in Bankruptcy in exercising the functions of interim trustee in the sequestration.

(8)   The permanent trustee, on being confirmed in office, shall make such insertions in the sederunt book as are appropriate to provide a record of the sequestration process before his confirmation.]

27   Discharge of interim trustee

(1)   On receiving a copy of the Accountant in Bankruptcy's determination sent under subsection (3)(b)(i) of section 26 of this Act the interim trustee may apply to him for a certificate of discharge.

(2)   The interim trustee shall send notice of an application under subsection (1) above to the debtor and to the permanent trustee and shall inform the debtor—

(a)   that he, the permanent trustee or any creditor may make written representations relating to the application to the Accountant in Bankruptcy within a period of 14 days after such notification;

(b)   that the audited accounts of his intromissions (if any) with the debtor's estate are available for inspection at the office of the interim trustee and that a copy of those accounts has been sent to the permanent trustee for insertion in the sederunt book; and

(c)   of the effect mentioned in subsection (5) below.

(3)   On the expiry of the period mentioned in subsection (2)(a) above the Accountant in Bankruptcy, after considering any representations duly made to him, shall—

(a)   grant or refuse to grant the certificate of discharge; and

(b)   notify (in addition to the interim trustee) the debtor, the permanent trustee, and all creditors who have made such representations, accordingly.

(4)   The interim trustee, the permanent trustee, the debtor or any creditor who has made representations under subsection (2)(a) above may, within 14 days after the issuing of the determination under subsection (3) above, appeal therefrom to the sheriff and if the sheriff determines that a certificate of discharge which has been refused should be granted he shall order the Accountant in Bankruptcy to grant it; and the sheriff clerk shall send a copy of the decree of the sheriff to the Accountant in Bankruptcy.

[(4A)   The decision of the sheriff in an appeal under subsection (4) above shall be final.]

(5)   The grant of a certificate of discharge under this section by the Accountant in Bankruptcy shall have the effect of discharging the interim trustee from all liability (other than any liability arising from fraud) to the creditors or to the debtor in respect of any act or omission of the interim trustee in exercising the functions conferred on him by this Act.

(6)   Where a certificate of discharge is granted under this section, the permanent trustee shall make an appropriate entry in the sederunt book.

(7)   Where the interim trustee has died, resigned office or been removed from office, then once the accounts of his intromissions (if any) with the debtor's estate are or have been submitted to and audited by the Accountant in Bankruptcy, the Accountant in Bankruptcy shall issue a determination fixing the amount of the outlays and remuneration payable to the interim trustee and the provisions of subsection (4) of section 26 of this Act and the foregoing provisions of this section shall, subject to any necessary modifications, apply in relation to that interim trustee or, if he has died, to his executor as they apply in relation to an interim trustee receiving a copy of such a determination under subsection (3)(b)(i) of that section.

[(7A) This section does not apply in any case where the Accountant in Bankruptcy is the interim trustee.]

Replacement of permanent trustee

28 Resignation and death of permanent trustee

[(1) The permanent trustee may apply to the sheriff for authority to resign office and, where the sheriff is satisfied that either of the grounds mentioned in paragraphs (a) and (b) of section 13(2) of this Act applies to the permanent trustee, he shall grant the application.

(1A) The sheriff may make the granting of an application under subsection (1) above subject to the election of a new permanent trustee and to such conditions as he thinks appropriate in all the circumstances of the case.]

(2) Where the sheriff grants an application under [. . .] subsection (1) above—

(a)   except where paragraph (b) below applies, the commissioners, or if there are no commissioners, the Accountant in Bankruptcy, shall call a meeting of the creditors, to be held not more than 28 days after the permanent trustee has resigned, for the election by them of a new permanent trustee;

(b)   if the application has been granted subject to the election of a new permanent trustee, the resigning permanent trustee shall himself call a meeting of the creditors, to be held not more than 28 days after the granting of the application, for the purpose referred to in paragraph (a) above.

(3)   Where the commissioners become, or if there are no commissioners, the Accountant in Bankruptcy becomes, aware that the permanent trustee has died, they or as the case may be the Accountant in Bankruptcy shall as soon as practicable after becoming so aware call a meeting of creditors for the election by the creditors of a new permanent trustee.

(4)   The foregoing provisions of this Act relating to the election and confirmation in office of the permanent trustee shall, subject to any necessary modifications, apply in relation to the election and confirmation in office of a new permanent trustee in pursuance of subsection (1), [(1A)], (2) or (3) above.

[(5)   Where no new permanent trustee is elected in pursuance of subsection (2) or (3) above, the provisions of section 25A of this Act shall apply.]

(6)   The new permanent trustee may require—

(a)   delivery to him of all documents relating to the sequestration in the possession of the former trustee or his representatives, except the former trustee's accounts of which he shall be entitled to delivery of only a copy;

(b)   the former trustee or his representatives to submit the trustee's accounts for audit to the commissioners or, if there are no commissioners, to the Accountant in Bankruptcy, and the commissioners or the Accountant in Bankruptcy shall issue a determination fixing the amount of the outlays and remuneration payable to the trustee or representatives in accordance with section 53 of this Act.

(7)   The former trustee or his representatives, the new permanent trustee, the debtor or any creditor may appeal against a determination issued under subsection (6)(b) above within 14 days after it is issued—

(a)   where it is a determination of the commissioners, to the Accountant in Bankruptcy; and

(b)   where it is a determination of the Accountant in Bankruptcy, to the sheriff;

and the determination of the Accountant in Bankruptcy under paragraph (a) above shall be appealable to the sheriff.

[(8)   The decision of the sheriff on an appeal under subsection (7) above shall be final.]

29 Removal of permanent trustee and trustee not acting

(1)   The permanent trustee may be removed from office—

(a)   by the creditors (other than any such person as is mentioned in section 24(3) of this Act) at a meeting called for the purpose if they also elect forthwith a new permanent trustee; or

(b) without prejudice to section [1A(2)] of this Act, by order of the sheriff, on the application of—

(i) the Accountant in Bankruptcy;

(ii) the commissioners; or

(iii) a person representing not less than one quarter in value of the creditors,

if the sheriff is satisfied that cause has been shown on the basis of circumstances other than those to which subsection (9) below applies.

(2) The sheriff shall order any application under subsection (1)(b) above to be served on the permanent trustee and intimated in the Edinburgh Gazette, and before disposing of the application shall give the permanent trustee an opportunity of being heard.

(3) On an application under subsection (1)(b) above, the sheriff may, in ordering the removal of the permanent trustee from office, make such further order as he thinks fit or may, instead of removing the permanent trustee from office, make such other order as he thinks fit.

(4) The permanent trustee, the Accountant in Bankruptcy, the commissioners or any creditor may appeal against the decision of the sheriff on an application under subsection (1)(b) above within 14 days after the date of that decision.

(5) If the permanent trustee has been removed from office under subsection (1)(b) above or under section [1A(2)] of this Act or following an appeal under subsection (4) above, the commissioners or, if there are no commissioners, the Accountant in Bankruptcy shall call a meeting of creditors, to be held not more than 28 days after such removal, for the election by them of a new permanent trustee.

(6) Without prejudice to section [1A(2)] of this Act, where the sheriff is satisfied of any of the circumstances to which subsection (9) below applies he may, on the application of a commissioner, the debtor, a creditor or the Accountant in Bankruptcy, and after such intimation as the sheriff considers necessary—

(a) declare the office of permanent trustee to have become or to be vacant; and

(b) make any necessary order to enable the sequestration to proceed or to safeguard the estate pending the election of a new permanent trustee;

and thereafter the commissioners or, if there are no commissioners, the Accountant in Bankruptcy shall call a meeting of creditors, to be held not more than 28 days after such declaration, for the election by them of a new permanent trustee.

(7) The foregoing provisions of this Act relating to the election and confirmation in office of the permanent trustee shall, subject to any necessary modifications, apply in relation to the election and confirmation in office of a new permanent trustee in pursuance of subsection (5) or (6) above.

(8) Subsections (5) to (7) of section 28 of this Act shall apply for the purposes of this section as they apply for the purposes of that section.

(9) The circumstances to which this subsection applies are that the permanent trustee—

(a) is unable to act (whether by, under or by virtue of a provision of this Act or from any other cause whatsoever other than death); or

(b) has so conducted himself that he should no longer continue to act in the sequestration.

Election, resignation and removal of commissioners

30 Election, resignation and removal of commissioners

(1) At the statutory meeting or any subsequent meeting of creditors, the creditors (other than any such person as is mentioned in section 24(3) of this Act) may, from among the creditors or their mandatories, elect one or more commissioners (or new or additional commissioners); but not more than 5 commissioners shall hold office in any sequestration at any one time.

(2) None of the following persons shall be eligible for election as a commissioner, nor shall anyone who becomes such a person after having been elected as a commissioner be entitled to continue to act as a commissioner—

(a) any person mentioned in paragraph (a) or (c) of section 24(2) of this Act as not being eligible for election;

(b) a person who is an associate of the debtor or of the permanent trustee.

(3) A commissioner may resign office at any time.

(4) Without prejudice to section [1A(2)] of this Act, a commissioner may be removed from office—

(a) if he is a mandatory of a creditor, by the creditor recalling the mandate and intimating in writing its recall to the permanent trustee;

(b) by the creditors (other than any such person as is mentioned in section 24(3) of this Act) at a meeting called for the purpose.

Vesting of estate in permanent trustee

31 Vesting of estate at date of sequestration

(1) Subject to section 33 of this Act [and section 91(3) of the Pensions Act 1995], the whole estate of the debtor shall vest as at the date of sequestration in the permanent trustee for the benefit of the creditors; and—

(a) the estate shall so vest by virtue of the act and warrant issued on confirmation of the permanent trustee's appointment; and

(b) the act and warrant shall, in respect of the heritable estate in Scotland of the debtor, have the same effect as if a decree of adjudication in implement of sale, as well as a decree of adjudication for payment and in security of debt, subject to no legal reversion, had been pronounced in favour of the permanent trustee.

(2) The exercise by the permanent trustee of any power conferred on him by this Act in respect of any heritable estate vested in him by virtue of the act and warrant shall not be challengeable on the ground of any prior inhibition (reserving any effect of such inhibition on ranking).

(3) Where the debtor has an uncompleted title to any heritable estate in Scotland, the permanent trustee may complete title thereto either in his own name or in the name of the debtor, but completion of title in the name of the debtor shall not validate by accretion any unperfected right in favour of any person other than the permanent trustee.

(4) Any moveable property, in respect of which but for this subsection—

(a) delivery or possession; or

(b) intimation of its assignation,

would be required in order to complete title to it, shall vest in the permanent trustee by virtue of the act and warrant as if at the date of sequestration the permanent trustee had taken delivery or possession of the property or had made intimation of its assignation to him, as the case may be.

(5) Any non-vested contingent interest which the debtor has shall vest in the permanent trustee as if an assignation of that interest had been executed by the debtor and intimation thereof made at the date of sequestration.

(6) Any person claiming a right to any estate claimed by the permanent trustee may apply to the court for the estate to be excluded from such vesting, a copy of the application being served on the permanent trustee; and the court shall grant the application if it is satisfied that the estate should not be so vested.

(7) Where any successor of a deceased debtor whose estate has been sequestrated has made up title to, or is in possession of, any part of that estate, the court may, on the application of the permanent trustee, order the successor to convey such estate to him.

(8) In subsection (1) above [, subject to section 31A of this Act,] the 'whole

estate of the debtor' means [subject to subsection (9) below] his whole estate at the date of sequestration, wherever situated, including—

(a)   any income or estate vesting in the debtor on that date; and

(b)   the capacity to exercise and to take proceedings for exercising, all such powers in, over, or in respect of any property as might have been exercised by the debtor for his own benefit as at, or on, the date of sequestration or might be exercised on a relevant date (within the meaning of section 32(10) of this Act).

[(9)   Subject to subsection (10) below, the 'whole estate of the debtor' does not include any interest of the debtor as tenant under any of the following tenancies—

(a)   a tenancy which is an assured tenancy within the meaning of Part II of the Housing (Scotland) Act 1988, or

(b)   a protected tenancy within the meaning of the Rent (Scotland) Act 1984 in respect of which, by virtue of any provision of Part VIII of that Act, no premium can lawfully be required as a condition of the assignation, or

(c)   a Scottish secure tenancy within the meaning of the Housing (Scotland) Act 2001 (asp 10).

(10)   On the date on which the permanent trustee serves notice to that effect on the debtor, the interest of this debtor as tenant under any of the tenancies referred to in subsection (9) above shall form part of his estate and vest in the permanent trustee as if it had vested in him under section 32(6) of this Act.]

[31A   Proceedings under EC Regulation: modified definition of 'estate'

In the application of this Act to insolvency proceedings under the EC Regulation, a reference to 'estate' is a reference to estate which may be dealt with in those proceedings.]

[31A   Property subject to restraint order

(1)   This section applies where—

(a)   property is excluded from the debtor's estate by virtue of section 420(2)(a) of the Proceeds of Crime Act 2002 (property subject to a restraint order),

(b)   an order under section 50, 52, 128, 198 or 200 of that Act has not been made in respect of the property, and

(c)   the restraint order is discharged.

(2)   On the discharge of the restraint order the property vests in the permanent trustee as part of the debtor's estate.

(3)   But subsection (2) does not apply to the proceeds of property realised by a management receiver under section 49(2)(d) or 197(2)(d) of that Act (realisation of property to meet receiver's remuneration and expenses).

31B   Property in respect of which receivership or administration order is made

(1)   This section applies where—

(a)   property is excluded from the debtor's estate by virtue of section 420(2)(b), (c) or (d) of the Proceeds of Crime Act 2002 (property in respect of which an order for the appointment of a receiver or administrator under certain provisions of that Act is in force), and

(b)   a confiscation order is made under section 6, 92 or 156 of that Act,

(c)   the amount payable under the confiscation order is fully paid, and

(d)   any of the property remains in the hands of the receiver or administrator (as the case may be).

(2)   The property vests in the permanent trustee as part of the debtor's estate.

31C   Property subject to certain orders where confiscation order discharged or quashed

(1)   This section applies where—

(a)   property is excluded from the debtor's estate by virtue of section 420(2)(a), (b), (c) or (d) of the Proceeds of Crime Act 2002 (property in respect of which a restraint order or an order for the appointment of a receiver or administrator under that Act is in force),

(b)   a confiscation order is made under section 6, 92 or 156 of that Act, and

(c)   the confiscation order is discharged under section 30, 114 or 180 of that Act (as the case may be) or quashed under that Act or in pursuance of any enactment relating to appeals against conviction or sentence.

(2)   Any property in the hands of a receiver appointed under Part 2 or 4 of that Act or an administrator appointed under Part 3 of that Act vests in the permanent trustee as part of the debtor's estate.

(3)   But subsection (2) does not apply to the proceeds of property realised by a management receiver under section 49(2)(d) or 197(2)(d) of that Act (realisation of property to meet receiver's remuneration and expenses).]

32 Vesting of estate, and dealings of debtor, after sequestration

(1)   Subject to subsection (2) below, any income of whatever nature received by the debtor on a relevant date, other than income arising from the estate which is vested in the permanent trustee, shall vest in the debtor.

(2)   [Notwithstanding anything in section 11 or 12 of the Welfare Reform and Pensions Act 1999] the sheriff, on the application of the permanent trustee, may, after having regard to all the circumstances, determine a suitable amount to allow for—

(a)   aliment for the debtor; and

(b)   the debtor's relevant obligations;

and if the debtor's income is in excess of the total amount so allowed the sheriff shall fix the amount of the excess and order it to be paid to the permanent trustee.

[(2A)   The amount allowed for the purposes specified in paragraphs (a) and (b) of subsection (2) above shall not be less than the total amount of any income received by the debtor—

(a)   by way of guaranteed minimum pension; and

(b)   in respect of his protected rights as a member of a pension scheme, 'guaranteed minimum pension' and 'protected rights' having the same meanings as in the Pension Schemes Act 1993.]

(3)   The debtor's relevant obligations referred to in paragraph (b) of subsection (2) above are—

(a)   any obligation of aliment owed by him ('obligation of aliment' having the same meaning as in the Family Law (Scotland) Act 1985);

(b)   any obligation of his to make a periodical allowance to a former spouse [or civil partner];

[(c)   any obligation of his to pay child support maintenance under the Child Support Act 1991;]

but any amount allowed under that subsection for the relevant obligations [referred to in paragraphs (a) and (b) above] need not be sufficient for compliance with a subsisting order or agreement as regards such aliment or periodical allowance.

(4)   In the event of any change in the debtor's circumstances, the sheriff, on the application of the permanent trustee, the debtor or any other interested person, may vary or recall any order under subsection (2) above.

(5)   Diligence [(which, for the purposes of this section, includes the making of a deduction from earnings order under the Child Support Act 1991)] in respect of a debt or obligation of which the debtor would be discharged under section 55 of this Act were he discharged under section 54 thereof shall not be competent against income vesting in him under subsection (1) above.

(6)   Without prejudice to subsection (1) above, any estate, wherever situated, which—

(a)   is acquired by the debtor on a relevant date; and

(b)   would have vested in the permanent trustee if it had been part of the debtor's estate on the date of sequestration,

shall vest in the permanent trustee for the benefit of the creditors as at the date of acquisition; and any person who holds any such estate shall, on production to him of a copy of the act and warrant certified by the sheriff clerk confirming the permanent trustee's appointment, convey or deliver the estate to the permanent trustee:

Provided that—

(i)   if such a person has in good faith and without knowledge of the sequestration conveyed the estate to the debtor or to anyone on the instructions of the debtor, he shall incur no liability to the permanent trustee except to account for any proceeds of the conveyance which are in his hands; and

(ii)   this subsection shall be without prejudice to any right or interest acquired in the estate in good faith and for value.

(7)   The debtor shall immediately notify the permanent trustee of any assets acquired by him on a relevant date or of any other substantial change in his financial circumstances; and, if the debtor fails to comply with this subsection, he shall be guilty of an offence and liable on summary conviction to a fine not exceeding level 5 on the standard scale or to imprisonment for a term not exceeding 3 months or to both.

(8)   Subject to subsection (9) below, any dealing of or with the debtor relating to his estate vested in the permanent trustee under section 31 of this Act shall be of no effect in a question with the permanent trustee.

(9)   Subsection (8) above shall not apply where the person seeking to uphold the dealing establishes—

(a)   that the permanent trustee—

(i)   has abandoned to the debtor the property to which the dealing relates;

(ii)   has expressly or impliedly authorised the dealing; or

(iii)   is otherwise personally barred from challenging the dealing, or

(b)   that the dealing is—

(i)   the performance of an obligation undertaken before the date of sequestration by a person obliged to the debtor in the obligation;

(ii)   the purchase from the debtor of goods for which the purchaser has given value to the debtor or is willing to give value to the permanent trustee; or

(iii)   a banking transaction in the ordinary course of business between the banker and the debtor,

and that the person dealing with the debtor was, at the time when the dealing occurred, unaware of the sequestration and had at that time no reason to believe that the debtor's estate had been sequestrated or was the subject of sequestration proceedings.

(10)   In this section 'a relevant date' means a date after the date of sequestration and before the date on which the debtor's discharge becomes effective.

33   Limitations on vesting

(1)   The following property of the debtor shall not vest in the permanent trustee—

(a)   [any property kept outwith a dwellinghouse in respect of which attachment is, by virtue of section 11(1) of the Debt Arrangement and Attachment (Scotland) Act 2002 (asp 17), incompetent;

(aa)   any property kept in a dwellinghouse which is not a non-essential asset for the purposes of Part 3 of that Act;]

(b)   property held on trust by the debtor for any other person.

(2)   The vesting of a debtor's estate in a permanent trustee shall not affect the right of hypothec of a landlord.

(3) Sections 31 and 32 of this Act are without prejudice to the right of any secured creditor which is preferable to the rights of the permanent trustee.

Safeguarding of interests of creditors of insolvent persons

34 Gratuitous alienations

(1) Where this subsection applies, an alienation by a debtor shall be challengeable by—

(a) any creditor who is a creditor by virtue of a debt incurred on or before the date of sequestration, or before the granting of the trust deed or the debtor's death, as the case may be; or

(b) the permanent trustee, the trustee acting under the trust deed or the judicial factor, as the case may be.

(2) Subsection (1) above applies where—

(a) by the alienation, whether before or after the coming into force of this section, any of the debtor's property has been transferred or any claim or right of the debtor has been discharged or renounced; and

(b) any of the following has occurred—

(i) his estate has been sequestrated (other than, in the case of a natural person, after his death); or

(ii) he has granted a trust deed which has become a protected trust deed; or

(iii) he has died and within 12 months after his death, his estate has been sequestrated; or

(iv) he has died and within the said 12 months, a judicial factor has been appointed under section 11A of the Judicial Factors (Scotland) Act 1889 to administer his estate and the estate was absolutely insolvent at the date of death; and

(c) the alienation took place on a relevant day.

(3) For the purposes of paragraph (c) of subsection (2) above, the day on which an alienation took place shall be the day on which the alienation became completely effectual; and in that paragraph 'relevant day' means, if the alienation has the effect of favouring—

(a) a person who is an associate of the debtor, a day not earlier than 5 years before the date of sequestration, the granting of the trust deed or the debtor's death, as the case may be; or

(b) any other person, a day not earlier than 2 years before the said date.

(4) On a challenge being brought under subsection (1) above, the court shall grant decree of reduction or for such restoration of property to the debtor's estate or other redress as may be appropriate, but the court shall not grant such a decree if the person seeking to uphold the alienation establishes—

(a) that immediately, or at any other time, after the alienation the debtor's assets were greater than his liabilities, or

(b) that the alienation was made for adequate consideration; or

(c) that the alienation—

(i) was a birthday, Christmas or other conventional gift; or

(ii) was a gift made, for a charitable purpose, to a person who is not an associate of the debtor,

which having regard to all the circumstances, it was reasonable for the debtor to make:

Provided that this subsection shall be without prejudice to any right or interest acquired in good faith and for value from or through the transferee in the alienation.

(5) In subsection (4) above, 'charitable purpose' means any charitable, benevolent or philanthropic purpose whether or not it is charitable within the meaning of any rule of law.

(6)   For the purposes of the foregoing provisions of this section, an alienation in implementation of a prior obligation shall be deemed to be one for which there was no consideration or no adequate consideration to the extent that the prior obligation was undertaken for no consideration or no adequate consideration.

(7)   This section is without prejudice to the operation of section 2 of the Married Women's Policies of Assurance (Scotland) Act 1880 (policy of assurance may be effected in trust for spouse, future spouse and children) [including the operation of that section as applied by section 132 of the Civil Partnership Act 2004].

(8)   A permanent trustee, the trustee acting under a protected trust deed and a judicial factor appointed under section 11A of the Judicial Factors (Scotland) Act 1889 shall have the same right as a creditor has under any rule of law to challenge an alienation of a debtor made for no consideration or for no adequate consideration.

(9)   The permanent trustee shall insert in the sederunt book a copy of any decree under this section affecting the sequestrated estate.

35   Recalling of order for payment of capital sum on divorce

(1)   This section applies where—

(a)   a court has made an order, whether before or after the coming into force of this section, under section 5 of the Divorce (Scotland) Act 1976 or section 8(2) of the Family Law (Scotland) Act 1985, for the payment by a debtor of a capital sum or [a court has, under the said section 8(2), made an order for the transfer of property by him or made a pension sharing order];

(b)   on the date of the making of the order the debtor was absolutely insolvent or was rendered so by implementation of the order; and

(c)   within 5 years after the making of the order—

(i)   the debtor's estate has been sequestrated other than after his death; or

(ii)   he has granted a trust deed which has (whether or not within the 5 years) become a protected trust deed; or

(iii)   he has died and, within 12 months after his death, his estate has been sequestrated; or

(iv)   he has died and, within the said 12 months, a judicial factor has been appointed under section 11A of the Judicial Factors (Scotland) Act 1889 to administer his estate.

(2)   Where this section applies, the court, on an application brought by the permanent trustee, the trustee acting under the trust deed or the judicial factor, may make an order for recall of the order made under the said section 5 or 8(2) and for the repayment to the applicant of the whole or part of any sum already paid, or as the case may be for the return to the applicant of all or part of any property already transferred, under that order, or, where such property has been sold, for payment to the applicant of all or part of the proceeds of sale:

Provided that before making an order under this subsection the court shall have regard to all the circumstances including, without prejudice to the generality of this proviso, the financial, and other, circumstances (in so far as made known to the court) of the person against whom the order would be made.

(3)   Where an application is brought under this section in a case where the debtor's estate has been sequestrated, the permanent trustee shall insert a copy of the decree of recall in the sederunt book.

36   Unfair preferences

(1)   Subject to subsection (2) below, subsection (4) below applies to a transaction entered into by a debtor, whether before or after the coming into force of this section, which has the effect of creating a preference in favour of a creditor to the prejudice of the general body of creditors, being a preference created not earlier than 6 months before—

(a)   the date of sequestration of the debtor's estate (if, in the case of a natural person, a date within his lifetime); or

(b)   the granting by him of a trust deed which has become a protected trust deed; or

(c)   his death where, within 12 months after his death—

(i)   his estate has been sequestrated, or

(ii)   a judicial factor has been appointed under section 11A of the Judicial Factors (Scotland) Act 1889 to administer his estate and his estate was absolutely insolvent at the date of death.

(2)   Subsection (4) below shall not apply to any of the following transactions—

(a)   a transaction in the ordinary course of trade or business;

(b)   a payment in cash for a debt which when it was paid had become payable unless the transaction was collusive with the purpose of prejudicing the general body of creditors;

(c)   a transaction whereby the parties thereto undertake reciprocal obligations (whether the performance by the parties of their respective obligations occurs at the same time or at different times) unless the transaction was collusive as aforesaid;

(d)   the granting of a mandate by a debtor authorising an arrestee to pay over the arrested funds or part thereof to the arrester where—

(i)   there has been a decree for payment or a warrant for summary diligence; and

(ii)   the decree or warrant has been preceded by an arrestment on the dependence of the action or followed by an arrestment in execution.

(3)   For the purposes of subsection (1) above, the day on which a preference was created shall be the day on which the preference became completely effectual.

(4)   A transaction to which this subsection applies shall be challengeable by—

(a)   any creditor who is a creditor by virtue of a debt incurred on or before the date of sequestration, the granting of the protected trust deed or the debtor's death, as the case may be; or

(b)   the permanent trustee, the trustee acting under the protected trust deed, or the judicial factor, as the case may be.

(5)   On a challenge being brought under subsection (4) above, the court, if satisfied that the transaction challenged is a transaction to which this section applies, shall grant decree of reduction or for such restoration of property to the debtor's estate or other redress as may be appropriate:

Provided that this subsection shall be without prejudice to any right or interest acquired in good faith and for value from or through the creditor in whose favour the preference was created.

(6)   A permanent trustee, the trustee acting under a protected trust deed and a judicial factor appointed under section 11A of the Judicial Factors (Scotland) Act 1889 shall have the same right as a creditor has under any rule of law to challenge a preference created by a debtor.

(7)   The permanent trustee shall insert in the sederunt book a copy of any decree under this section affecting the sequestrated estate.

[36A   Recovery of excessive pension contributions

(1)   Where a debtor's estate has been sequestrated and he—

(a)   has rights under an approved pension arrangement, or

(b)   has excluded rights under an unapproved pension arrangement, the permanent trustee may apply to the court for an order under this section.

(2)   If the court is satisfied—

(a)   that the rights under the arrangement are to any extent, and whether directly or indirectly, the fruits of relevant contributions, and

(b)   that the making of any of the relevant contributions ('the excessive contributions') has unfairly prejudiced the debtor's creditors,

the court may make such order as it thinks fit for restoring the position to what it would have been had the excessive contributions not been made.

(3) Subsection (4) applies where the court is satisfied that the value of the rights under the arrangement is, as a result of rights of the debtor under the arrangement or any other pension arrangement having at any time become subject to a debit under section 29(1)(a) of the Welfare Reform and Pensions Act 1999 (debits giving effect to pension-sharing), less than it would otherwise have been.

(4) Where this subsection applies—

(a) any relevant contributions which were represented by the rights which became subject to the debit shall, for the purposes of subsection (2), be taken to be contributions of which the rights under the arrangement are the fruits, and

(b) where the relevant contributions represented by the rights under the arrangement (including those so represented by virtue of paragraph (a)) are not all excessive contributions, relevant contributions which are represented by the rights under the arrangement otherwise than by virtue of paragraph (a) shall be treated as excessive contributions before any which are so represented by virtue of that paragraph.

(5) In subsections (2) to (4) 'relevant contributions' means contributions to the arrangement or any other pension arrangement—

(a) which the debtor has at any time made on his own behalf, or

(b) which have at any time been made on his behalf.

(6) The court shall, in determining whether it is satisfied under subsection (2)(b), consider in particular—

(a) whether any of the contributions were made for the purpose of putting assets beyond the reach of the debtor's creditors or any of them, and

(b) whether the total amount of any contributions—

(i) made by or on behalf of the debtor to pension arrangements, and

(ii) represented (whether directly or indirectly) by rights under approved pension arrangements or excluded rights under unapproved pension arrangements,

is an amount which is excessive in view of the debtor's circumstances when those contributions were made.

(7) For the purposes of this section and sections 36B and 36C ('the recovery provisions'), rights of a debtor under an unapproved pension arrangement are excluded rights if they are rights which are excluded from his estate by virtue of regulations under section 12 of the Welfare Reform and Pensions Act 1999.

(8) In the recovery provisions—

'approved pension arrangement' has the same meaning as in section 11 of the Welfare Reform and Pensions Act 1999;

'unapproved pension arrangement' has the same meaning as in section 12 of that Act.

36B Orders under section 36A

(1) Without prejudice to the generality of section 36A(2) an order under section 36A may include provision—

(a) requiring the person responsible for the arrangement to pay an amount to the permanent trustee,

(b) adjusting the liabilities of the arrangement in respect of the debtor,

(c) adjusting any liabilities of the arrangement in respect of any other person that derive, directly or indirectly, from rights of the debtor under the arrangement,

(d) for the recovery by the person responsible for the arrangement (whether by deduction from any amount which that person is ordered to pay or otherwise) of costs incurred by that person in complying in the debtor's case with any requirement under section 36C(1) or in giving effect to the order.

(2) In subsection (1), references to adjusting the liabilities of the arrangement in respect of a person include (in particular) reducing the amount of any benefit or future benefit to which that person is entitled under the arrangement.

(3)   In subsection (1)(c), the reference to liabilities of the arrangement does not include liabilities in respect of a person which result from giving effect to an order or provision falling within section 28(1) of the Welfare Reform and Pensions Act 1999 (pension sharing orders and agreements).

(4)   The maximum amount which the person responsible for an arrangement may be required to pay by an order under section 36A is the lesser of—
(a)   the amount of the excessive contributions, and
(b)   the value of the debtor's rights under the arrangement (if the arrangement is an approved pension arrangement) or of his excluded rights under the arrangement (if the arrangement is an unapproved pension arrangement).

(5)   An order under section 36A which requires the person responsible for an arrangement to pay an amount ('the restoration amount') to the permanent trustee must provide for the liabilities of the arrangement to be correspondingly reduced.

(6)   For the purposes of subsection (5), liabilities are correspondingly reduced if the difference between—
(a)   the amount of the liabilities immediately before the reduction, and
(b)   the amount of the liabilities immediately after the reduction, is equal to the restoration amount.

(7)   An order under section 36A in respect of an arrangement—
(a)   shall be binding on the person responsible for the arrangement; and
(b)   overrides provisions of the arrangement to the extent that they conflict with the provisions of the order.

36C   Orders under section 36A: supplementary
(1)   The person responsible for—
(a)   an approved pension arrangement under which a debtor has rights,
(b)   an unapproved pension arrangement under which a debtor has excluded rights, or
(c)   a pension arrangement under which a debtor has at any time had rights,
shall, on the permanent trustee making a written request, provide the permanent trustee with such information about the arrangement and rights as the permanent trustee may reasonably require for, or in connection with, the making of applications under section 36A.

(2)   Nothing in—
(a)   any provision of section 159 of the Pensions Schemes Act 1993 or section 91 of the Pensions Act 1995 (which prevent assignation and the making of orders that restrain a person from receiving anything which he is prevented from assigning),
(b)   any provision of any enactment (whether passed or made before or after the passing of the Welfare Reform and Pensions Act 1999) corresponding to any of the provisions mentioned in paragraph (a), or
(c)   any provision of the arrangement in question corresponding to any of those provisions, applies to a court exercising its powers under section 36A.

(3)   Where any sum is required by an order under section 36A to be paid to the permanent trustee, that sum shall be comprised in the debtor's estate.

(4)   Regulations may, for the purposes of the recovery provisions, make provision about the calculation and verification of—
(a)   any such value as is mentioned in section 36B(4)(b);
(b)   any such amounts as are mentioned in section 36B(6)(a) and (b).

(5)   The power conferred by subsection (4) includes power to provide for calculation or verification—
(a)   in such manner as may, in the particular case, be approved by a prescribed person; or
(b)   in accordance with guidance—
(i)   from time to time prepared by a prescribed person, and
(ii)   approved by the Secretary of State.

(6)   References in the recovery provisions to the person responsible for a pension arrangement are to—

(a)   the trustees, managers or provider of the arrangement, or

(b)   the person having functions in relation to the arrangement corresponding to those of a trustee, manager or provider.

(7)   In this section and sections 36A and 36B—

'the recovery provisions' means this section and sections 36A and 36B;

'regulations' means regulations made by the Secretary of State.

(8)   Regulations under the recovery provisions may contain such incidental, supplemental and transitional provisions as appear to the Secretary of State necessary or expedient.

36D   Recovery of excessive contributions in pension-sharing cases

(1)   For the purposes of section 34 of this Act, a pension-sharing transaction shall be taken—

(a)   to be a transaction, entered into by the transferor with the transferee, by which the appropriate amount is transferred by the transferor to the transferee; and

(b)   to be capable of being an alienation challengeable under that section only so far as it is a transfer of so much of the appropriate amount as is recoverable.

(2)   For the purposes of section 35 of this Act, a pension-sharing transaction shall be taken—

(a)   to be a pension sharing order made by the court under section 8(2) of the Family Law (Scotland) Act 1985; and

(b)   to be an order capable of being recalled under that section only so far as it is a payment or transfer of so much of the appropriate amount as is recoverable.

(3)   For the purposes of section 36 of this Act, a pension-sharing transaction shall be taken—

(a)   to be something (namely a transfer of the appropriate amount to the transferee) done by the transferor; and

(b)   to be capable of being an unfair preference given to the transferee only so far as it is a transfer of so much of the appropriate amount as is recoverable.

(4)   Where—

(a)   an alienation is challenged under section 34;

(b)   an application is made under section 35 for the recall of an order made in divorce proceedings; or

(c)   a transaction is challenged under section 36,

if any question arises as to whether, or the extent to which, the appropriate amount in the case of a pension-sharing transaction is recoverable, the question shall be determined in accordance with subsections (5) to (9).

(5)   The court shall first determine the extent (if any) to which the transferor's rights under the shared arrangement at the time of the transaction appear to have been (whether directly or indirectly) the fruits of contributions ('personal contributions')—

(a)   which the transferor has at any time made on his own behalf, or

(b)   which have at any time been made on the transferor's behalf,

to the shared arrangement or any other pension arrangement.

(6)   Where it appears that those rights were to any extent the fruits of personal contributions, the court shall then determine the extent (if any) to which those rights appear to have been the fruits of personal contributions whose making has unfairly prejudiced the transferor's creditors ('the unfair contributions').

(7)   If it appears to the court that the extent to which those rights were the fruits of the unfair contributions is such that the transfer of the appropriate amount could have been made out of rights under the shared arrangement which were not

the fruits of the unfair contributions, then the appropriate amount is not recoverable.

(8) If it appears to the court that the transfer could not have been wholly so made, then the appropriate amount is recoverable to the extent to which it appears to the court that the transfer could not have been so made.

(9) In making the determination mentioned in subsection (6) the court shall consider in particular—

(a) whether any of the personal contributions were made for the purpose of putting assets beyond the reach of the transferor's creditors or any of them; and

(b) whether the total amount of any personal contributions represented, at the time the pension sharing arrangement was made, by rights under pension arrangements is an amount which is excessive in view of the transferor's circumstances when those contributions were made.

(10) In this section and sections 36E and 36F—

'appropriate amount', in relation to a pension-sharing transaction, means the appropriate amount in relation to that transaction for the purposes of section 29(1) of the Welfare Reform and Pensions Act 1999 (creation of pension credits and debits);

'pension-sharing transaction' means an order or provision falling within section 28(1) of the Welfare Reform and Pensions Act 1999 (orders and agreements which activate pension-sharing);

'shared arrangement', in relation to a pension-sharing transaction, means the pension arrangement to which the transaction relates;

'transferee', in relation to a pension-sharing transaction, means the person for whose benefit the transaction is made;

'transferor', in relation to a pension-sharing transaction, means the person to whose rights the transaction relates.

36E Recovery orders

(1) In this section and section 36F of this Act, 'recovery order' means—

(a) a decree granted under section 34(4) of this Act;

(b) an order made under section 35(2) of this Act;

(c) a decree granted under section 36(5) of this Act,

in any proceedings to which section 36D of this Act applies.

(2) Without prejudice to the generality of section 34(4), 35(2) or 36(5) a recovery order may include provision—

(a) requiring the person responsible for a pension arrangement in which the transferee has acquired rights derived directly or indirectly from the pension-sharing transaction to pay an amount to the permanent trustee,

(b) adjusting the liabilities of the pension arrangement in respect of the transferee,

(c) adjusting any liabilities of the pension arrangement in respect of any other person that derive, directly or indirectly, from rights of the transferee under the arrangement,

(d) for the recovery by the person responsible for the pension arrangement (whether by deduction from any amount which that person is ordered to pay or otherwise) of costs incurred by that person in complying in the debtor's case with any requirement under section 36F(1) or in giving effect to the order.

(3) In subsection (2), references to adjusting the liabilities of a pension arrangement in respect of a person include (in particular) reducing the amount of any benefit or future benefit to which that person is entitled under the arrangement.

(4) The maximum amount which the person responsible for an arrangement may be required to pay by a recovery order is the smallest of—

(a) so much of the appropriate amount as, in accordance with section 36D of this Act, is recoverable,

(b) so much (if any) of the amount of the unfair contributions (within the meaning given by section 36D(6)) as is not recoverable by way of an order under section 36A of this Act containing provision such as is mentioned in section 36B(1)(a), and

(c)   the value of the debtor's rights under the arrangement acquired by the transferee as a consequence of the transfer of the appropriate amount.

(5)   A recovery order which requires the person responsible for an arrangement to pay an amount ('the restoration amount') to the permanent trustee must provide for the liabilities of the arrangement to be correspondingly reduced.

(6)   For the purposes of subsection (5), liabilities are correspondingly reduced if the difference between—

(a)   the amount of the liabilities immediately before the reduction, and

(b)   the amount of the liabilities immediately after the reduction is equal to the restoration amount.

(7)   A recovery order in respect of an arrangement—

(a)   shall be binding on the person responsible for the arrangement, and

(b)   overrides provisions of the arrangement to the extent that they conflict with the provisions of the order.

36F   Recovery orders: supplementary

(1)   The person responsible for a pension arrangement under which the transferee has, at any time, acquired rights by virtue of the transfer of the appropriate amount shall, on the permanent trustee making a written request, provide the trustee with such information about the arrangement and the rights under it of the transferor and transferee as the permanent trustee may reasonably require for, or in connection with, the making of an application for a recovery order.

(2)   Nothing in—

(a)   any provision of section 159 of the Pension Schemes Act 1993 or section 91 of the Pensions Act 1995 (which prevent assignation and the making of orders which restrain a person from receiving anything which he is prevented from assigning),

(b)   any provision of any enactment (whether passed or made before or after the passing of the Welfare Reform and Pensions Act 1999) corresponding to any of the provisions mentioned in paragraph (a), or

(c)   any provision of the arrangement in question corresponding to any of those provisions, applies to a court exercising its power to make a recovery order.

(3)   Regulations may, for the purposes of the recovery provisions, make provision about the calculation and verification of—

(a)   any such value as is mentioned in section 36E(4)(c);

(b)   any such amounts as are mentioned in section 36E(6)(a) and (b).

(4)   The power conferred by subsection (3) includes power to provide for calculation or verification—

(a)   in such manner as may, in the particular case, be approved by a prescribed person; or

(b)   in accordance with guidance—

(i)   from time to time prepared by a prescribed person, and

(ii)   approved by the Secretary of State.

(5)   References in the recovery provisions to the person responsible for a pension arrangement are to—

(a)   the trustees, managers or provider of the arrangement, or

(b)   the person having functions in relation to the arrangement corresponding to those of a trustee, manager or provider.

(6)   In this section—

'prescribed' means prescribed by regulations;

'the recovery provisions' means this section and sections 34, 35, 36 and 36E of this Act;

'regulations' means regulations made by the Secretary of State.

(7)   Regulations under the recovery provisions may—

(a)   make different provision for different cases;

(b)   contain such incidental, supplemental and transitional provisions as appear to the Secretary of State necessary or expedient.

(8)   Regulations under the recovery provisions shall be made by statutory instrument subject to annulment in pursuance of a resolution of either House of Parliament.]

Effect of sequestration on diligence

37   Effect of sequestration on diligence

(1)   The order of the court awarding sequestration shall as from the date of sequestration have the effect, in relation to diligence done (whether before or after the date of sequestration) in respect of any part of the debtor's estate, of—

(a)   a decree of adjudication of the heritable estate of the debtor for payment of his debts which has been duly recorded in the register of inhibitions and adjudications on that date; and

(b)   an arrestment in execution and decree of furthcoming, an arrestment in execution and warrant of sale, and a completed poinding,

in favour of the creditors according to their respective entitlements.

(2)   No inhibition on the estate of the debtor which takes effect within the period of 60 days before the date of sequestration shall be effectual to create a preference for the inhibitor and any relevant right of challenge shall, at the date of sequestration, vest in the permanent trustee as shall any right of the inhibitor to receive payment for the discharge of the inhibition:

Provided that this subsection shall neither entitle the trustee to receive any payment made to the inhibitor before the date of sequestration nor affect the validity of any thing done before that date in consideration of such payment.

(3)   In subsection (2) above, 'any relevant right of challenge' means any right to challenge a deed voluntarily granted by the debtor if it is a right which vested in the inhibitor by virtue of the inhibition.

(4)   No arrestment or [attachment] of the estate of the debtor (including any estate vesting in the permanent trustee under section 32(6) of this Act) executed—

(a)   within the period of 60 days before the date of sequestration and whether or not subsisting at that date; or

(b)   on or after the date of sequestration,

shall be effectual to create a preference for the arrester or [attacher]; and the estate so arrested or [attached], or the proceeds of sale thereof, shall be handed over to the permanent trustee.

(5)   An arrester or [attacher] whose arrestment or [attachment] is executed within the said period of 60 days shall be entitled to payment, out of the arrested or [attached] estate or out of the proceeds of the sale thereof, of the expenses incurred—

(a)   in obtaining the extract of the decree or other document on which the arrestment or [attachment] proceeded;

(b)   in executing the arrestment or [attachment]; and

(c)   in taking any further action in respect of the diligence.

[(5A)   Nothing in subsection (4) or (5) above shall apply to an earnings arrestment, a current maintenance arrestment, a conjoined arrestment order or a deduction from earnings order under the Child Support Act 1991.]

(6)   No poinding of the ground in respect of the estate of the debtor (including any estate vesting in the permanent trustee under section 32(6) of this Act) executed within the period of 60 days before the date of sequestration or on or after that date shall be effectual in a question with the permanent trustee, except for the interest on the debt of a secured creditor, being interest for the current half-yearly

term and arrears of interest for one year immediately before the commencement of that term.

(7) The foregoing provisions of this section shall apply to the estate of a deceased debtor which—

(a)   has been sequestrated; or

(b)   was absolutely insolvent at the date of death and in respect of which a judicial factor has been appointed under section 11A of the Judicial Factors (Scotland) Act 1889,

within 12 months after his death, but as if for any reference to the date of sequestration and the debtor there were substituted respectively a reference to the date of the deceased's death and to the deceased debtor.

(8) It shall be incompetent on or after the date of sequestration for any creditor to raise or insist in an adjudication against the estate of a debtor (including any estate vesting in the permanent trustee under section 32(6) of this Act) or to be confirmed as executor-creditor on the estate.

(9) Where—

(a)   a deceased debtor's estate is sequestrated; or

(b)   a judicial factor is appointed under section 11A of the Judicial Factors (Scotland) Act 1889 to administer his estate (in a case where the estate is absolutely insolvent),

within 12 months after the debtor's death, no confirmation as executor-creditor on that estate at any time after the debtor's death shall be effectual in a question with the permanent trustee or the judicial factor; but the executor-creditor shall be entitled out of that estate, or out of the proceeds of sale thereof, to the expenses incurred by him in obtaining the confirmation.

Administration of estate by permanent trustee

38 Taking possession of estate by permanent trustee

(1) The permanent trustee shall—

(a)   as soon as may be after his confirmation in office, for the purpose of recovering the debtor's estate under section 3(1)(a) of this Act, and subject to section 40 of this Act, take possession of the debtor's whole estate so far as vesting in the permanent trustee under sections 31 and 32 of this Act and any document in the debtor's possession or control relating to his assets or his business or financial affairs;

(b)   make up and maintain an inventory and valuation of the estate which he shall record in the sederunt book; and

(c)   forthwith thereafter send a copy of any such inventory and valuation to the Accountant in Bankruptcy.

(2) The permanent trustee shall be entitled to have access to all documents relating to the assets or the business or financial affairs of the debtor sent by or on behalf of the debtor to a third party and in that third party's hands and to make copies of any such documents.

(3) If any person obstructs a permanent trustee who is exercising, or attempting to exercise, a power conferred by subsection (2) above, the sheriff, on the application of the permanent trustee, may order that person to cease so to obstruct the permanent trustee.

(4) The permanent trustee may require delivery to him of any title deed or other document of the debtor, notwithstanding that a right of lien is claimed over the title deed or document; but this subsection is without prejudice to any preference of the holder of the lien.

39 Management and realisation of estate

(1) As soon as may be after his confirmation in office, the permanent trustee shall consult with the commissioners or, if there are no commissioners, with the

Accountant in Bankruptcy concerning the exercise of his functions under section 3(1)(a) of this Act; and, subject to subsection (6) below, the permanent trustee shall comply with any general or specific directions given to him, as the case may be—

(a) by the creditors;

(b) on the application under this subsection of the commissioners, by the court; or

(c) if there are no commissioners, by the Accountant in Bankruptcy,

as to the exercise by him of such functions.

(2) The permanent trustee may, but if there are commissioners only with the consent of the commissioners, the creditors or the court, do any of the following things if he considers that its doing would be beneficial for the administration of the estate—

(a) carry on any business of the debtor;

(b) bring, defend or continue any legal proceedings relating to the estate of the debtor;

(c) create a security over any part of the estate;

(d) where any right, option or other power forms part of the debtor's estate, make payments or incur liabilities with a view to obtaining, for the benefit of the creditors, any property which is the subject of the right, option or power.

(3) Any sale of the debtor's estate by the permanent trustee may be by either public sale or private bargain.

(4) The following rules shall apply to the sale of any part of the debtor's heritable estate over which a heritable security is held by a creditor or creditors if the rights of the secured creditor or creditors are preferable to those of the permanent trustee—

(a) the permanent trustee may sell that part only with the concurrence of every such creditor unless he obtains a sufficiently high price to discharge every such security;

(b) subject to paragraph (c) below, the following acts shall be precluded—

(i) the taking of steps by a creditor to enforce his security over that part after the permanent trustee has intimated to the creditor that he intends to sell it;

(ii) the commencement by the permanent trustee of the procedure for the sale of that part after a creditor has intimated to the permanent trustee that he intends to commence the procedure for its sale;

(c) where the permanent trustee or a creditor has given intimation under paragraph (b) above, but has unduly delayed in proceeding with the sale, then, if authorised by the court in the case of intimation under—

(i) sub-paragraph (i) of that paragraph, any creditor to whom intimation has been given may enforce his security; or

(ii) sub-paragraph (ii) of that paragraph, the permanent trustee may sell that part.

(5) The function of the permanent trustee under section 3(1)(a) of this Act to realise the debtor's estate shall include the function of selling, with or without recourse against the estate, debts owing to the estate.

(6) The permanent trustee may sell any perishable goods without complying with any directions given to him under subsection (1)(a) or (c) above if the permanent trustee considers that compliance with such directions would adversely affect the sale.

(7) The validity of the title of any purchaser shall not be challengeable on the ground that there has been a failure to comply with a requirement of this section.

(8) It shall be incompetent for the permanent trustee or an associate of his or for any commissioner, to purchase any of the debtor's estate in pursuance of this section.

40 Power of permanent trustee in relation to the debtor's family home

(1)   Before the permanent trustee sells or disposes of any right or interest in the debtor's family home he shall—

(a)   obtain the relevant consent; or

(b)   where he is unable to do so, obtain the authority of the court in accordance with subsection (2) below.

(2)   Where the permanent trustee requires to obtain the authority of the court in terms of subsection (1)(b) above, the court, after having regard to all the circumstances of the case, including—

(a)   the needs and financial resources of the debtor's spouse or former spouse;

[(aa)   the needs and financial resources of the debtor's civil partnership or former civil partner;]

(b)   the needs and financial resources of any child of the family;

(c)   the interests of the creditors;

(d)   the length of the period during which (whether before or after the relevant date) the family home was used as a residence by any of the persons referred to in [paragraphs (a) to (b)] above,

may refuse to grant the application or may postpone the granting of the application for such period (not exceeding twelve months) as it may consider reasonable in the circumstances or may grant the application subject to such conditions as it may prescribe.

(3)   Subsection (2) above shall apply—

(a)   to an action for division and sale of the debtor's family home; or

(b)   to an action for the purpose of obtaining vacant possession of the debtor's family home,

brought by the permanent trustee as it applies to an application under subsection (1)(b) above and, for the purposes of this subsection, any reference in the said subsection (2) to that granting of the application shall be construed as a reference to the granting of decree in the action.

(4)   In this section—

(a)   'family home' means any property in which, at the relevant date, the debtor had (whether alone or in common with any other person) a right or interest, being property which was occupied at that date as a residence by the debtor and his spouse [or civil partner] or by the debtor's spouse [or civil partner] or former spouse [or civil partner] (in any case with or without a child of the family) or by the debtor with a child of the family;

(b)   'child of the family' includes any child or grandchild of either the debtor or his spouse [or civil partner] or former spouse [or civil partner], and any person who has been brought up or accepted by either the debtor or his spouse [or civil partner] or former spouse [or civil partner] as if he or she were a child of the debtor, spouse [or civil partner] or former spouse [or civil partner] whatever the age of such a child, grandchild or person may be;

(c)   'relevant consent' means in relation to the sale or disposal of any right or interest in a family home—

(i)   in a case where the family home is occupied by the debtor's spouse [or civil partner] or former spouse [or civil partner], the consent of the spouse [or civil partner], or, as the case may be, the former spouse [or civil partner], whether or not the family home is also occupied by the debtor;

(ii)   where sub-paragraph (i) above does not apply, in a case where the family home is occupied by the debtor with a child of the family, the consent of the debtor; and

(d)   'relevant date' means the day immediately preceding the date of sequestration.

41 Protection of rights of spouse against arrangements intended to defeat them

(1) If a debtor's sequestrated estate includes a matrimonial home of which the debtor, immediately before the date of issue of the act and warrant of the permanent trustee (or, if more than one such act and warrant is issued in the sequestration, of the first such issue) was an entitled spouse and the other spouse is a non-entitled spouse—

(a) the permanent trustee shall, where he—

(i) is aware that the entitled spouse is married to the non-entitled spouse; and

(ii) knows where the non-entitled spouse is residing,

inform the non-entitled spouse, within the period of 14 days beginning with that date, of the fact that sequestration of the entitled spouse's estate has been awarded, of the right of petition which exists under section 16 of this Act and of the effect of paragraph (b) below; and

(b) the Court of Session, on the petition under section 16 of this Act of the non-entitled spouse presented either within the period of 40 days beginning with that date or within the period of 10 weeks beginning with the date of sequestration may—

(i) under section 17 of this Act recall the sequestration; or

(ii) make such order as it thinks appropriate to protect the occupancy rights of the non-entitled spouse;

if it is satisfied that the purpose of the petition for sequestration was wholly or mainly to defeat the occupancy rights of the non-entitled spouse.

(2) In subsection (1) above—

'entitled spouse' and 'non-entitled spouse' have the same meanings as in section 6 of the Matrimonial Homes (Family Protection) (Scotland) Act 1981;

'matrimonial home' has the meaning assigned by section 22 of that Act as amended by the Law Reform (Miscellaneous Provisions) (Scotland) Act 1985; and

'occupancy rights' has the meaning assigned by section 1(4) of the said Act of 1981.

[41A Protection of rights of civil partner against arrangements intended to defeat them

(1) If a debtor's sequestrated estate includes a family home of which the debtor, immediately before the date of issue of the act and warrant of the permanent trustee (or, if more than one such act and warrant is issued in the sequestration, of the first such issue) was an entitled partner and the other partner in the civil partnership is a non-entitled partner—

(a) the permanent trustee shall, where he—

(i) is aware that the entitled partner is in civil partnership with the non-entitled partner; and

(ii) knows where the non-entitled partner is residing,

inform the non-entitled partner, within the period of 14 days beginning with that date, of the fact that sequestration of the entitled partner's estate has been awarded, of the right of petition which exists under section 16 of this Act and of the effect of paragraph (b) below; and

(b) the Court of Session, on the petition under section 16 of this Act of the non-entitled partner presented either within the period of 40 days beginning with that date or within the period of 10 weeks beginning with the date of sequestration may—

(i) under section 17 of this Act recall the sequestration; or

(ii) make such order as it thinks appropriate to protect the occupancy rights of the non-entitled partner, if it is satisfied that the purpose of the petition for sequestration was wholly or mainly to defeat the occupancy rights of the non-entitled partner.

(2)   In subsection (1) above—

'entitled partner' and 'non-entitled partner' have the same meanings as in section 101 of the Civil Partnership Act 2004;

'family home' has the meaning assigned by section 135 of the 2004 Act; and 'occupancy rights' means the rights conferred by subsection (1) of that section 101.]

42   Contractual powers of permanent trustee

(1)   Subject to subsections (2) and (3) below, the permanent trustee may adopt any contract entered into by the debtor before the date of sequestration where he considers that its adoption would be beneficial to the administration of the debtor's estate, except where the adoption is precluded by the express or implied terms of the contract, or may refuse to adopt any such contract.

(2)   The permanent trustee shall, within 28 days from the receipt by him of a request in writing from any party to a contract entered into by the debtor or within such longer period of that receipt as the court on application by the permanent trustee may allow, adopt or refuse to adopt the contract.

(3)   If the permanent trustee does not reply in writing to the request under subsection (2) above within the said period of 28 days or longer period, as the case may be, he shall be deemed to have refused to adopt the contract.

(4)   The permanent trustee may enter into any contract where he considers that this would be beneficial for the administration of the debtor's estate.

43   Money received by permanent trustee

(1)   Subject to subsection (2) below, all money received by the permanent trustee in the exercise of his functions shall be deposited by him in the name of the debtor's estate in an appropriate bank or institution.

(2)   The permanent trustee may at any time retain in his hands a sum not exceeding £200 or such other sum as may be prescribed.

Examination of debtor

44   Private examination

(1)   The permanent trustee may request—

(a)   the debtor to appear before him and to give information relating to his assets, his dealings with them or his conduct in relation to his business or financial affairs; or

(b)   the debtor's spouse [or civil partner] or any other person who the permanent trustee believes can give such information (in this Act such spouse [, civil partner] or other person being referred to as a 'relevant person'), to give that information.

and, if he considers it necessary, the permanent trustee may apply to the sheriff for an order to be made under subsection (2) below.

(2)   Subject to section 46(2) of this Act, on application to him under subsection (1) above the sheriff may make an order requiring the debtor or a relevant person to attend for private examination before him on a date (being not earlier than 8 days nor later than 16 days after the date of the order) and at a time specified in the order.

(3)   A person who fails without reasonable excuse to comply with an order made under subsection (2) above shall be guilty of an offence and liable on summary conviction to a fine not exceeding level 5 on the standard scale or to imprisonment for a term not exceeding 3 months or to both.

(4)   Where the debtor is an entity whose estate may be sequestrated by virtue of section 6(1) of this Act, the references in this section and in sections 45 to 47 of this Act to the debtor shall be construed, unless the context otherwise requires, as references to a person representing the entity.

45 Public examination

(1) Not less than 8 weeks before the end of the first accounting period, the permanent trustee—

(a) may; or

(b) if requested to do so by the Accountant in Bankruptcy or the commissioners (if any) or one quarter in value of the creditors, shall,

apply to the sheriff for an order for the public examination before the sheriff of the debtor or of a relevant person relating to the debtor's assets, his dealings with them or his conduct in relation to his business or financial affairs:

Provided that, on cause shown, such application may be made by the permanent trustee at any time.

(2) Subject to section 46(2) of this Act, the sheriff, on an application under subsection (1) above, shall make an order requiring the debtor or relevant person to attend for examination before him in open court on a date (being not earlier than 8 days nor later than 16 days after the date of the order) and at a time specified in the order.

(3) On the sheriff making an order under subsection (2) above, the permanent trustee shall—

(a) publish in the Edinburgh Gazette a notice in such form and containing such particulars as may be prescribed; and

(b) send a copy of the said notice—

(i) to every creditor known to the permanent trustee; and

(ii) where the order is in respect of a relevant person, to the debtor, and

inform the creditor and, where applicable, the debtor that he may participate in the examination.

(4) A person who fails without reasonable excuse to comply with an order made under subsection (2) above shall be guilty of an offence and liable on summary conviction to a fine not exceeding level 5 on the standard scale or to imprisonment for a term not exceeding 3 months or to both.

46 Provisions ancillary to sections 44 and 45

(1) If the debtor or relevant person is residing—

(a) in Scotland, the sheriff may, on the application of the permanent trustee, grant a warrant which may be executed by a messenger-at-arms or sheriff officer anywhere in Scotland [to apprehend]; or

(b) in any other part of the United Kingdom, the Court of Session or the sheriff may, on the application of the permanent trustee, [grant a warrant for the arrest of],

[. . .] the debtor or relevant person to have him taken to the place of the examination:

Provided that a warrant under [this subsection shall not be granted] unless the court is satisfied that it is necessary to do so to secure the attendance of the debtor or relevant person at the examination.

(2) If the debtor or a relevant person is for any good reason prevented from attending for examination, the sheriff may, without prejudice to subsection (3) below, grant a commission to take his examination (the commissioner being in this section and section 47 below referred to as an 'examining commissioner').

(3) The sheriff or the examining commissioner may at any time adjourn the examination to such day as the sheriff or the examining commissioner may fix.

(4) The sheriff or the examining commissioner may order the debtor or a relevant person to produce for inspection any document in his custody or control relating to the debtor's assets, his dealings with them or his conduct in relation to his business or financial affairs, and to deliver the document or a copy thereof to the permanent trustee for further examination by him.

47 Conduct of examination

(1) The examination, whether before the sheriff or an examining commissioner, shall be taken on oath.

(2) At the examination—

(a) the permanent trustee or a solicitor or counsel acting on his behalf and, in the case of public examination, any creditor may question the debtor or a relevant person; and

(b) the debtor may question a relevant person,

as to any matter relating to the debtor's assets, his dealings with them or his conduct in relation to his business or financial affairs.

(3) The debtor or a relevant person shall be required to answer any question relating to the debtor's assets, his dealings with them or his conduct in relation to his business or financial affairs and shall not be excused from answering any such question on the ground that the answer may incriminate or tend to incriminate him or on the ground of confidentiality:

Provided that—

(a) a statement made by the debtor or a relevant person in answer to such a question shall not be admissible in evidence in any subsequent criminal proceedings against the person making the statement, except where the proceedings are in respect of a charge of perjury relating to the statement;

(b) a person subject to examination shall not be required to disclose any information which he has received from a person who is not called for examination if the information is confidential between them.

(4) [The rules relating to the recording of evidence in ordinary causes specified in the First Schedule to the Sheriff Courts (Scotland) Act 1907] shall apply in relation to the recording of evidence at the examination before the sheriff or the examining commissioner.

(5) The debtor's deposition at the examination shall be subscribed by himself and by the sheriff (or, as the case may be, the examining commissioner) and shall be inserted in the sederunt book.

(6) The permanent trustee shall insert a copy of the record of the examination in the sederunt book and send a copy of the record to the Accountant in Bankruptcy.

(7) A relevant person shall be entitled to fees or allowances in respect of his attendance at the examination as if he were a witness in an ordinary civil cause in the sheriff court:

Provided that, if the sheriff thinks that it is appropriate in all the circumstances, he may disallow or restrict the entitlement to such fees or allowances.

Submission and adjudication of claims

48 Submission of claims to permanent trustee

(1) Subject to subsection (2) below and subsections (8) and (9) of section 52 of this Act, a creditor in order to obtain an adjudication as to his entitlement—

(a) to vote at a meeting of creditors other than the statutory meeting; or

(b) (so far as funds are available), to a dividend out of the debtor's estate in respect of any accounting period,

shall submit a claim in accordance with this section to the permanent trustee respectively—

(i) at or before the meeting; or

(ii) not later than 8 weeks before the end of the accounting period.

(2) A claim submitted by a creditor—

(a) under section 22 of this Act and accepted in whole or in part by the interim trustee for the purpose of voting at the statutory meeting; or

(b) under this section and accepted in whole or in part by the permanent

trustee for the purpose of voting at a meeting or of drawing a dividend in respect of any accounting period,
shall be deemed to have been re-submitted for the purpose of obtaining an adjudication as to his entitlement both to vote at any subsequent meeting and (so far as funds are available) to a dividend in respect of an accounting period, or, as the case may be, any subsequent accounting period.

(3) Subsections (2) and (3) of section 22 of this Act shall apply for the purposes of this section but as if in the proviso to subsection (2) for the words 'interim trustee' there were substituted the words 'permanent trustee with the consent of the commissioners, if any', and for any other reference to the interim trustee there were substituted a reference to the permanent trustee.

(4) A creditor who has submitted a claim under this section (or under section 22 of this Act, a statement of claim which has been deemed re-submitted as mentioned in subsection (2) above) may at any time submit a further claim under this section specifying a different amount for his claim:

Provided that a secured creditor shall not be entitled to produce a further claim specifying a different value for the security at any time after the permanent trustee requires the creditor to discharge, or convey or assign, the security under paragraph 5(2) of Schedule 1 to this Act.

(5) The permanent trustee, for the purpose of satisfying himself as to the validity or amount of a claim submitted by a creditor under this section, may require—

(a) the creditor to produce further evidence; or

(b) any other person who he believes can produce relevant evidence, to produce such evidence,

and, if the creditor or other person refuses or delays to do so, the permanent trustee may apply to the sheriff for an order requiring the creditor or other person to attend for his private examination before the sheriff.

(6) Sections 44(2) and (3) and 47(1) of this Act shall apply, subject to any necessary modifications, to the examination of the creditor or other person as they apply to the examination of a relevant person; and references in this subsection and subsection (5) above to a creditor in a case where the creditor is an entity mentioned in section 6(1) of this Act shall be construed, unless the context otherwise requires, as references to a person representing the entity.

(7) Subsections (5) to (10) of section 22 of this Act shall apply for the purposes of this section but as if—

(a) in subsection (5) the words 'interim trustee or' were omitted;

(b) in subsection (7) for the words 'interim' and 'keep a record of it' there were substituted respectively the words 'permanent' and 'make an insertion relating thereto in the sederunt book'.

(8) At any private examination under subsection (5) above, a solicitor or counsel may act on behalf of the permanent trustee or he may appear himself.

49 Adjudication of claims

(1) At the commencement of every meeting of creditors (other than the statutory meeting), the permanent trustee shall, for the purposes of section 50 of this Act so far as it relates to voting at that meeting, accept or reject the claim of each creditor.

(2) Where funds are available for payment of a dividend out of the debtor's estate in respect of an accounting period, the permanent trustee for the purpose of determining who is entitled to such a dividend shall, not later than 4 weeks before the end of the period, accept or reject every claim submitted or deemed to have been re-submitted to him under this Act; and shall at the same time make a decision on any matter requiring to be specified under paragraph (a) or (b) of subsection (5) below.

(3) If the amount of a claim is stated in foreign currency the permanent trustee in adjudicating on the claim under subsection (1) or (2) above shall convert the

amount into sterling, in such manner as may be prescribed, at the rate of exchange prevailing at the close of business on the date of sequestration.

(4) Where the permanent trustee rejects a claim, he shall forthwith notify the creditor giving reasons for the rejection.

(5) Where the permanent trustee accepts or rejects a claim, he shall record in the sederunt book his decision on the claim specifying—

(a) the amount of the claim accepted by him,

(b) the category of debt, and the value of any security, as decided by him, and

(c) if he is rejecting the claim, his reasons therefor.

(6) The debtor of any creditor may, if dissatisfied with the acceptance or rejection of any claim (or, in relation to such acceptance or rejection, with a decision in respect of any matter requiring to be specified under subsection (5)(a) or (b) above), appeal therefrom to the sheriff—

(a) if the acceptance or rejection is under subsection (1) above, within 2 weeks of that acceptance or rejection;

(b) if the acceptance or rejection is under subsection (2) above, not later than 2 weeks before the end of the accounting period,

and the permanent trustee shall record the sheriff's decision in the sederunt book.

(7) Any reference in this section to the acceptance or rejection of a claim shall be construed as a reference to the acceptance or rejection of the claim in whole or in part.

Entitlement to vote and draw dividend

50 Entitlement to vote and draw dividend

[(1)] A creditor who has had his claim accepted in whole or in part by the permanent trustee or on appeal under subsection (6) of section 49 of this Act shall be entitled—

(a) subject to sections 29(1)(a) and 30(1) and (4)(b) of this Act, in a case where the acceptance is under (or on appeal arising from) subsection (1) of the said section 49, to vote on any matter at the meeting of creditors for the purpose of voting at which the claim is accepted; and

(b) in a case where the acceptance is under (or on appeal arising from) subsection (2) of the said section 49, to payment out of the debtor's estate of a dividend in respect of the accounting period for the purposes of which the claim is accepted; but such entitlement to payment shall arise only in so far as that estate has funds available to make that payment, having regard to section 51 of this Act.

[(2) No vote shall be cast by virtue of a debt more than once on any resolution put to a meeting of creditors.

(3) Where a creditor—

(a) is entitled to vote under this section;

(b) has lodged his claim in one or more sets of other proceedings; and

(c) votes (either in person or by proxy) on a resolution put to the meeting, only the creditor's vote shall be counted.

(4) Where—

(a) a creditor has lodged his claim in more than one set of other proceedings; and

(b) more than one member State liquidator seeks to vote by virtue of that claim,

the entitlement to vote by virtue of that claim is exercisable by the member State liquidator in main proceedings, whether or not the creditor has lodged his claim in the main proceedings.

(5) For the purposes of subsections (3) and (4) above, 'other proceedings'

means main proceedings, secondary proceedings or territorial proceedings in a member State other than the United Kingdom.]

Distribution of debtor's estate

51 Order of priority in distribution

(1) The funds of the debtor's estate shall be distributed by the permanent trustee to meet the following debts in the order in which they are mentioned—

(a) the outlays and remuneration of the interim trustee in the administration of the debtor's estate;

(b) the outlays and remuneration of the permanent trustee in the administration of the debtor's estate;

(c) where the debtor is a deceased debtor, deathbed and funeral expenses reasonably incurred and expenses reasonably incurred in administering the deceased's estate;

(d) the expenses reasonably incurred by a creditor who is a petitioner, or concurs in the petition, for sequestration;

(e) preferred debts (excluding any interest which has accrued thereon to the date of sequestration);

(f) ordinary debts, that is to say a debt which is neither a secured debt nor a debt mentioned in any other paragraph of this subsection;

(g) interest at the rate specified in subsection (7) below on—

(i) the preferred debts;

(ii) the ordinary debts,

between the date of sequestration and the date of payment of the debt;

(h) any postponed debt.

(2) In this Act 'preferred debt' means a debt listed in Part I of Schedule 3 to this Act; and Part II of that Schedule shall have effect for the interpretation of the said Part I.

(3) In this Act 'postponed debt' means—

(a) a loan made to the debtor, in consideration of a share of the profits in his business, which is postponed under section 3 of the Partnership Act 1890 to the claims of other creditors;

(b) a loan made to the debtor by the debtor's spouse [or civil partner];

(c) a creditor's right to anything vesting in the permanent trustee by virtue of a successful challenge under section 34 of this Act or to the proceeds of sale of such a thing.

(4) Any debt falling within any of paragraphs (c) to (h) of subsection (1) above shall have the same priority as any other debt falling within the same paragraph and, where the funds of the estate are inadequate to enable the debts mentioned in the paragraph to be paid in full, they shall abate in equal proportions.

(5) Any surplus remaining, after all the debts mentioned in this section have been paid in full, shall be made over to the debtor or to his successors or assignees; and in this subsection 'surplus' includes any kind of estate but does not include any unclaimed dividend.

[(5A) Subsection (5) above is subject to Article 35 of the EC Regulation (surplus in secondary proceedings to be transferred to main proceedings).]

(6) Nothing in this section shall affect—

(a) the right of a secured creditor which is preferable to the rights of the permanent trustee; or

(b) any preference of the holder of a lien over a title deed or other document which has been delivered to the permanent trustee in accordance with a requirement under section 38(4) of this Act.

(7) The rate of interest referred to in paragraph (g) of subsection (1) above shall be whichever is the greater of—

(a) the prescribed rate at the date of sequestration; and

(b)   the rate applicable to that debt apart from the sequestration.

52   Estate to be distributed in respect of accounting periods
[(1)   The permanent trustee shall make up accounts of his intromissions with the debtor's estate in respect of each accounting period.

(2)   In this Act 'accounting period' shall be construed as follows—

(a)   the first accounting period shall be the period of 6 months beginning with the date of sequestration; and

(b)   any subsequent accounting period shall be the period of 6 months beginning with the end of the last accounting period; except that—

(i)   in a case where the Accountant in Bankruptcy is not the permanent trustee, the permanent trustee and the commissioners or, if there are no commissioners, the Accountant in Bankruptcy agree; or

(ii)   in a case where the Accountant in Bankruptcy is the permanent trustee, he determines,

that the accounting period shall be such other period beginning with the end of the last accounting period as may be agreed or, as the case may be determined, it shall be that other period.

(2A)   An agreement or determination under subsection (2)(b)(i) or (ii) above—

(a)   may be made in respect of one or more than one accounting period;

(b)   may be made before the beginning of the accounting period in relation to which it has effect and, in any event, shall not have effect unless made before the day on which such accounting period would, but for the agreement or determination, have ended;

(c)   may provide for different accounting periods to be of different durations, and shall be recorded in the sederunt book by the permanent trustee.]

(3)   Subject to the following provisions of this section, the permanent trustee shall, if the funds of the debtor's estate are sufficient and after making allowance for future contingencies, pay under section 53(7) of this Act a dividend out of the estate to the creditors in respect of each accounting period.

(4)   The permanent trustee may pay—

(a)   the debts mentioned in subsection (1)(a) to (d) of section 51 of this Act, other than his own remuneration, at any time;

(b)   the preferred debts at any time but only with the consent of the commissioners or, if there are no commissioners, of the Accountant in Bankruptcy.

(5)   If the permanent trustee—

(a)   is not ready to pay a dividend in respect of an accounting period; or

(b)   considers it would be inappropriate to pay such a dividend because the expense of doing so would be disproportionate to the amount of the dividend,

he may, with the consent of the commissioners, or if there are no commissioners of the Accountant in Bankruptcy, postpone such payment to a date not later than the time for payment of a dividend in respect of the next accounting period.

[. . .]

(7)   Where an appeal is taken under section 49(6)(b) of this Act against the acceptance or rejection of a creditor's claim, the permanent trustee shall, at the time of payment of dividends and until the appeal is determined, set aside an amount which would be sufficient, if the determination in the appeal were to provide for the claim being accepted in full, to pay a dividend in respect of that claim.

(8)   Where a creditor—

(a)   has failed to produce evidence in support of his claim earlier than 8 weeks before the end of an accounting period on being required by the permanent trustee to do so under section 48(5) of this Act; and

(b)   has given a reason for such failure which is acceptable to the permanent trustee,

the permanent trustee shall set aside, for such time as is reasonable to enable him to produce that evidence or any other evidence that will enable the permanent trustee to be satisfied under the said section 48(5), an amount which would be sufficient, if the claim were accepted in full, to pay a dividend in respect of that claim.

(9) Where a creditor submits a claim to the permanent trustee later than 8 weeks before the end of an accounting period but more than 8 weeks before the end of a subsequent accounting period in respect of which, after making allowance for contingencies, funds are available for the payment of a dividend, the permanent trustee shall, if he accepts the claim in whole or in part, pay to the creditor—

(a) the same dividend or dividends as has or have already been paid to creditors of the same class in respect of any accounting period or periods; and

(b) whatever dividend may be payable to him in respect of the said subsequent accounting period:

Provided that paragraph (a) above shall be without prejudice to any dividend which has already been paid.

[(10) In the declaration of and payment of a dividend, no payments shall be made more than once by virtue of the same debt.

(11) Any dividend paid in respect of a claim should be paid to the creditor.]

53 Procedure after end of accounting period

(1) Within 2 weeks after the end of an accounting period, the permanent trustee shall in respect of that period submit to the commissioners or, if there are no commissioners, to the Accountant in Bankruptcy—

(a) his accounts of his intromissions with the debtor's estate for audit and, where funds are available after making allowance for contingencies, a scheme of division of the divisible funds; and

(b) a claim for the outlays reasonably incurred by him and for his remuneration;

and, where the said documents are submitted to the commissioners, he shall send a copy of them to the Accountant in Bankruptcy.

[(2) Subject to subsection (2A) below, all accounts in respect of legal services incurred by the permanent trustee shall, before payment thereof by him, be submitted for taxation to the auditor of the court before which the sequestration is pending.

(2A) Where—

(a) any such account has been agreed between the permanent trustee and the person entitled to payment in respect of that account (in this subsection referred to as 'the payee');

(b) the permanent trustee is not an associate of the payee; and

(c) the commissioners have not determined that the account should be submitted for taxation,

the permanent trustee may pay such account without submitting it for taxation.]

(3) Within 6 weeks after the end of an accounting period—

(a) the commissioners or, as the case may be, the Accountant in Bankruptcy—

(i) [may] audit the accounts; and

(ii) [shall] issue a determination fixing the amount of the outlays and the remuneration payable to the permanent trustee; and

(b) the permanent trustee shall make the audited accounts, scheme of division and the said determination available for inspection by the debtor and the creditors.

(4) The basis for fixing the amount of the remuneration payable to the permanent trustee may be a commission calculated by reference to the value of the debtor's estate which has been realised by the permanent trustee, but there shall in any event be taken into account—

(a) the work which, having regard to that value, was reasonably undertaken by him; and

(b) the extent of his responsibilities in administering the debtor's estate.

(5) In fixing the amount of such remuneration in respect of [any] accounting period, the commissioners or, as the case may be, the Accountant in Bankruptcy may take into account any adjustment which the commissioners or the Accountant in Bankruptcy may wish to make in the amount of the remuneration fixed in respect of any earlier accounting period.

(6) Not later than 8 weeks after the end of an accounting period, the permanent trustee, the debtor or any creditor may appeal against a determination issued under subsection (3)(a)(ii) above—

(a) where it is a determination of the commissioners, to the Accountant in Bankruptcy; and

(b) where it is a determination of the Accountant in Bankruptcy, to the sheriff;

and the determination of the Accountant in Bankruptcy under paragraph (a) above shall be appealable to the sheriff [and the decision of the sheriff on such an appeal shall be final].

(7) On the expiry of the period within which an appeal may be taken under subsection (6) above or, if an appeal is so taken, on the final determination of the last such appeal, the permanent trustee shall pay to the creditors their dividends in accordance with the scheme of division.

(8) Any dividend—

(a) allocated to a creditor which is not cashed or uplifted; or

(b) dependent on a claim in respect of which an amount has been set aside under subsection (7) or (8) of section 52 of this Act,

shall be deposited by the permanent trustee in an appropriate bank or institution.

(9) If a creditor's claim is revalued, the permanent trustee may—

(a) in paying any dividend to that creditor, make such adjustment to it as he considers necessary to take account of that revaluation; or

(b) require the creditor to repay to him the whole or part of a dividend already paid to him.

(10) The permanent trustee shall insert in the sederunt book the audited accounts, the scheme of division and the final determination in relation to the permanent trustee's outlays and remuneration.

Discharge of debtor

54 Automatic discharge after 3 years

(1) Subject to the following provisions of this section, the debtor shall be discharged on the expiry of 3 years from the date of sequestration.

(2) Every debtor who has been discharged under or by virtue of this section or section 75(4) of this Act may apply to the Accountant in Bankruptcy for a certificate that he has been so discharged; and the Accountant in Bankruptcy, if satisfied of such discharge, shall grant a certificate of discharge in the prescribed form.

(3) The permanent trustee or any creditor may, not later than 2 years and 9 months after the date of sequestration, apply to the sheriff for a deferment of the debtor's discharge by virtue of subsection (1) above.

(4) On an application being made to him under subsection (3) above, the sheriff shall order—

(a) the applicant to serve the application on the debtor and (if he is not himself the applicant and is not discharged) the permanent trustee; and

(b) the debtor to lodge in court a declaration—

(i) that he has made a full and fair surrender of his estate and a full disclosure of all claims which he is entitled to make against other persons; and

(ii) that he has delivered to the interim or permanent trustee every document under his control relating to his estate or his business or financial affairs;

and, if the debtor fails to lodge such a declaration in court within 14 days of being required to do so, the sheriff shall defer his discharge without a hearing for a period not exceeding 2 years.

(5) If the debtor lodges the declaration in court within the said period of 14 days, the sheriff shall—

(a)   fix a date for a hearing not earlier than 28 days after the date of the lodging of the declaration; and

(b)   order the applicant to notify the debtor and the permanent trustee or (if he has been discharged) the Accountant in Bankruptcy of the date of the hearing;

and the permanent trustee or (if he has been discharged) the Accountant in Bankruptcy shall, not later than 7 days before the date fixed under paragraph (a) above, lodge in court a report upon the debtor's assets and liabilities, his financial and business affairs and his conduct in relation thereto and upon the sequestration and his conduct in the course of it.

(6)   After considering at the hearing any representations made by the applicant, the debtor or any creditor, the sheriff shall make an order either deferring the discharge for such period not exceeding 2 years as he thinks appropriate or dismissing the application:

Provided that the applicant or the debtor may appeal against an order under this subsection within 14 days after it is made.

(7)   Where the discharge is deferred under subsection (4) or (6) above, the clerk of the court shall send—

(a)   a certified copy of the order of the sheriff deferring discharge to the keeper of the register of inhibitions and adjudications for recording in that register; and

(b)   a copy of such order to—

(i)   the Accountant in Bankruptcy; and

(ii)   the permanent trustee (if not discharged) for insertion in the sederunt book.

(8)   A debtor whose discharge has been deferred under subsection (4) or (6) above may, at any time thereafter and provided that he lodges in court a declaration as to the matters mentioned in sub-paragraphs (i) and (ii) of paragraph (b) of the said subsection (4), petition the sheriff for his discharge; and subsections (5) to (7) above shall, with any necessary modifications, apply in relation to the proceedings which shall follow the lodging of a declaration under this subsection as they apply in relation to the proceedings which follow the timeous lodging of a declaration under the said paragraph (b).

(9)   The permanent trustee or any creditor may, not later than 3 months before the end of a period of deferment, apply to the sheriff for a further deferment of the discharge; and subsections (4) to (8) above and this subsection shall apply in relation to that further deferment.

55   Effect of discharge under section 54

(1)   Subject to [subsections (2) and (3)] below, on the debtor's discharge under section 54 of this Act, the debtor shall be discharged within the United Kingdom of all debts and obligations contracted by him, or for which he was liable, at the date of sequestration.

(2)   The debtor shall not be discharged by virtue of subsection (1) above from—

(a)   any liability to pay a fine or other penalty due to the Crown;

[(aa)   any liability to pay a fine imposed on a district court;

(ab)   any liability under a compensation order within the meaning of section 249 of the Criminal Procedure (Scotland) Act 1995;]

(b) any liability to forfeiture of a sum of money deposited in court under section 1(3) of the Bail etc (Scotland) Act 1980;

(c) any liability incurred by reason of fraud or breach of trust;

(d) any obligation to pay aliment or any sum of an alimentary nature under any enactment or rule of law or any periodical allowance payable on divorce by virtue of a court order or under an obligation, not

(i) being aliment or a periodical allowance which could be included in the amount of a creditor's claim under paragraph 2 of Schedule 1 to this Act; [or

(ii) child support maintenance within the meaning of the Child Support Act 1991 which was unpaid in respect of any period before the date of sequestration of—(aa) any person by whom it was due to be paid; or (bb) any employer by whom it was, or was due to be, deducted under section 31(5) of that Act].

(e) the obligation imposed on him by section 64 of this Act.

[(3) In subsection (2)(a) above the reference to a fine or other penalty due to the Crown includes a reference to a confiscation order made under Part 2, 3 or 4 of the Proceeds of Crime Act 2002.]

[(3) The discharge of the debtor under the said section 54 shall not affect any right of a secured creditor—

(a) for a debt in respect of which the debtor has been discharged to enforce his security for payment of the debt and any interest due and payable on the debt until the debt is paid in full; or

(b) for an obligation in respect of which the debtor has been discharged to enforce his security in respect of the obligation.]

56 Discharge on composition
Schedule 4 to this Act shall have effect in relation to an offer of composition by or on behalf of the debtor to the permanent trustee in respect of his debts and his discharge and the discharge of the permanent trustee where the offer is approved.

Discharge of permanent trustee

57 Discharge of permanent trustee
(1) After the permanent trustee has made a final division of the debtor's estate and has inserted his final audited accounts in the sederunt book, he—

(a) shall deposit any unclaimed dividends and any unapplied balances in an appropriate bank or institution;

(b) shall thereafter send to the Accountant in Bankruptcy the sederunt book, a copy of the audited accounts and a receipt for the deposit of the unclaimed dividends and unapplied balances; and

(c) may at the same time as sending the said documents apply to the Accountant in Bankruptcy for a certificate of discharge.

(2) The permanent trustee shall send notice of an application under subsection (1)(c) above to the debtor and to all the creditors known to the permanent trustee and shall inform the debtor and such creditors—

(a) that they may make written representations relating to the application to the Accountant in Bankruptcy within a period of 14 days after such notification;

(b) that the sederunt book is available for inspection at the office of the Accountant in Bankruptcy and contains the audited accounts of, and scheme of division in, the sequestration; and

(c) of the effect mentioned in subsection (5) below.

(3) On the expiry of the period mentioned in subsection (2)(a) above, the Accountant in Bankruptcy, after examining the documents sent to him and considering any representations duly made to him, shall—

(a) grant or refuse to grant the certificate of discharge; and

(b)   notify (in addition to the permanent trustee) the debtor and all creditors who have made such representations accordingly.

(4)   The permanent trustee, the debtor or any creditor who has made representations under subsection (2)(a) above, may within 14 days after the issuing of the determination under subsection (3) above, appeal therefrom to the sheriff and if the sheriff determines that a certificate of discharge which has been refused should be granted he shall order the Accountant in Bankruptcy to grant it; and the sheriff clerk shall send a copy of the decree of the sheriff to the Accountant in Bankruptcy.

[(4A)   The decision of the sheriff on an appeal under subsection (4) above shall be final.]

(5)   The grant of a certificate of discharge under this section by the Accountant in Bankruptcy shall have the effect of discharging the permanent trustee from all liability (other than any liability arising from fraud) to the creditors or to the debtor in respect of any act or omission of the permanent trustee in exercising the functions conferred on him by this Act including, where he was also the interim trustee, the functions conferred on him as interim trustee.

(6)   Where a certificate of discharge is granted under this section, the Accountant in Bankruptcy shall make an appropriate entry in the register of insolvencies and in the sederunt book.

(7)   Where the permanent trustee has died, resigned office or been removed from office, the provisions of this section shall, subject to any necessary modifications, apply in relation to that permanent trustee or, if he has died, to his executor as they apply to a permanent trustee who has made a final division of the debtor's estate in accordance with the foregoing provisions of this Act.

[(8)   This section does not apply in any case where the Accountant in Bankruptcy is the permanent trustee.]

58   Unclaimed dividends

(1)   Any person, producing evidence of his right, may apply to the Accountant in Bankruptcy to receive a dividend deposited under section 57(1)(a) [or 58A(3)] of this Act, if the application is made not later than 7 years after the date of such deposit.

(2)   If the Accountant in Bankruptcy is satisfied of the applicant's right to the dividend, he shall authorise the appropriate bank or institution to pay to the applicant the amount of that dividend and of any interest which has accrued thereon.

(3)   The Accountant in Bankruptcy shall, at the expiry of 7 years from the date of deposit of any unclaimed dividend or unapplied balance under section 57(1)(a) [or 58A(3)] of this Act, hand over the deposit receipt or other voucher relating to such dividend or balance to the Secretary of State, who shall thereupon be entitled to payment of the amount due, principal and interest, from the bank or institution in which the deposit was made.

[58A   Discharge of Accountant in Bankruptcy

(1)   This section applies where the Accountant in Bankruptcy has acted as the permanent trustee in any sequestration.

(2)   After the Accountant in Bankruptcy has made a final division of the debtor's estate, he shall insert in the sederunt book—

(a)   his final accounts of his intromissions (if any) with the debtor's estate;
(b)   the scheme of division (if any); and
(c)   a determination of his fees and outlays calculated in accordance with regulations made under section 69A of this Act.

(3)   The Accountant in Bankruptcy shall deposit any unclaimed dividends and any unapplied balances in an appropriate bank or institution.

(4)   The Accountant in Bankruptcy shall send to the debtor and to all creditors known to him—

(a)   a copy of the determination mentioned in subsection (2)(c) above; and

(b)   a notice in writing stating—

  (i) that the Accountant in Bankruptcy has commenced the procedure under this Act leading to discharge in respect of his actings as permanent trustee;

  (ii) that the sederunt book relating to the sequestration is available for inspection at such address as the Accountant in Bankruptcy may determine;

  (iii) that an appeal may be made to the sheriff under subsection (5) below; and

  (iv) the effect of subsection (7) below.

(5)   The debtor and any creditor may appeal to the sheriff against—

(a)   the determination of the Accountant in Bankruptcy mentioned in sub-section (2)(c) above;

(b)   the discharge of the Accountant in Bankruptcy in respect of his actings as permanent trustee; or

(c)   both such determination and discharge.

(6)   An appeal under subsection (5) above shall be made not more than 14 days after the issue of the notice mentioned in subsection (4)(b) above; and the decision of the sheriff on such an appeal shall be final.

(7)   Where—

(a)   the requirements of this section have been complied with; and

(b)   no appeal to the sheriff is made under subsection (5) above or such an appeal is made but is refused as regards the discharge of the Accountant in Bankruptcy,

the Accountant in Bankruptcy shall be discharged from all liability (other than any liability arising from fraud) to the creditors or to the debtor in respect of any act or omission of the Accountant in Bankruptcy in exercising the functions of permanent trustee in the sequestration.

(8)   Where the Accountant in Bankruptcy is discharged from all liability as mentioned in subsection (7) above, he shall make an entry in the sederunt book recording such discharge.

(9)   Where the Accountant in Bankruptcy—

(a)   has acted as both interim trustee and permanent trustee in a sequestration;

(b)   has not been discharged under section 26A(7) of this Act, references in this section to his acting as or exercising the functions of permanent trustee shall be construed as including references to his acting as or exercising the functions of interim trustee; and subsection (7) above shall have effect accordingly.]

Voluntary trust deeds for creditors

59   Voluntary trust deeds for creditors
Schedule 5 to this Act shall have effect in relation to trust deeds executed after the commencement of this section.

59A   Petition for conversion into sequestration
(1)   Where a member State liquidator proposes to petition the court for the conversion under Article 37 of the EC Regulation (conversion of earlier proceedings) of a protected trust deed into sequestration, an affidavit complying with section 59B of this Act must be prepared and sworn, and lodged in court in support of the petition.

(2)   The petition and the affidavit required under subsection (1) above shall be served upon—

(a)   the debtor;

(b)   the trustee;

(c)   such other person as may be prescribed.

59B   Contents of affidavit
(1)   The affidavit shall—
(a)   state that main proceedings have been opened in relation to the debtor in a member State other than the United Kingdom;
(b)   state that the member State liquidator believes that the conversion of the trust deed into a sequestration would prove to be in the interests of the creditors in the main proceedings;
(c)   contain such other information the member State liquidator considers will be of assistance to the court—
(i)   in deciding whether to make an order under section 59C; and
(ii)   if the court were to do so, in considering the need for any consequential provision that would be necessary or desirable; and
(d)   contain any other matters as may be prescribed.
(2)   An affidavit under this section shall be sworn by, or on behalf of, the member State liquidator.

59C   Power of court
(1)   On hearing the petition for conversion of a trust deed into a sequestration the court may make such order as it thinks fit.
(2)   If the court makes an order for conversion into sequestration the order may contain all such consequential provisions as the court deems necessary or desirable.
(3)   Where the court makes an order for conversion into sequestration under subsection (1) above, any expenses properly incurred as expenses of the administration of the trust deed in question shall be a first charge on the debtor's estate.]

Miscellaneous and supplementary

60   Liabilities and rights of co-obligants
(1)   Where a creditor has an obligant (in this section referred to as the 'co-obligant') bound to him along with the debtor for the whole or part of the debt, the co-obligant shall not be freed or discharged from his liability for the debt by reason of the discharge of the debtor or by virtue of the creditor's voting or drawing a dividend or assenting to, or not opposing—
(a)   the discharge of the debtor; or
(b)   any composition.
(2)   Where—
(a)   a creditor has had a claim accepted in whole or in part; and
(b)   a co-obligant holds a security over any part of the debtor's estate,
the co-obligant shall account to the permanent trustee so as to put the estate in the same position as if the co-obligant had paid the debt to the creditor and thereafter had had his claim accepted in whole or in part in the sequestration after deduction of the value of the security.
(3)   Without prejudice to any right under any rule of law of a co-obligant who has paid the debt, the co-obligant may require and obtain at his own expense from the creditor an assignation of the debt on payment of the amount thereof, and thereafter may in respect of that debt submit a claim, and vote and draw a dividend, if otherwise legally entitled to do so.
(4)   In this section a 'co-obligant' includes a cautioner.

[60A   Member State liquidator deemed creditor
For the purposes of this Act, and without prejudice to the generality of the right to participate referred to in paragraph 3 of Article 32 of the EC Regulation (exercise of creditors' rights) a member State liquidator appointed in relation to the debtor is deemed to be a creditor in the sum due to creditors in proceedings in relation to which he holds office.

60B   Trustee's duties concerning notices and copies of documents

(1)   This section applies where a member State liquidator has been appointed in relation to the debtor.

(2)   Where an interim or a permanent trustee is obliged to give notice to, or provide a copy of a document (including an order of court) to, the court or the Accountant in Bankruptcy, the trustee shall give notice or provide copies, as appropriate, to the member State liquidator.

(3)   Subsection (2) above is without prejudice to the generality of the obligations imposed by Article 31 of the EC Regulation (duty to co-operate and communicate information).]

61   Extortionate credit transactions

(1)   This section applies where the debtor is or has been a party to a transaction for, or involving, the provision to him of credit and his estate is sequestrated.

(2)   The court may, on the application of the permanent trustee, make an order with respect to the transaction if the transaction is or was extortionate and was not entered into more than three years before the date of sequestration.

(3)   For the purposes of this section a transaction is extortionate if, having regard to the risk accepted by the person providing the credit—

(a)   the terms of it are or were such as to require grossly exorbitant payments to be made (whether unconditionally or in certain contingencies) in respect of the provision of the credit; or

(b)   it otherwise grossly contravened ordinary principles of fair dealing; and it shall be presumed, unless the contrary is proved, that a transaction with respect to which an application is made under this section is, or as the case may be was, extortionate.

(4)   An order under this section with respect to any transaction may contain such one or more of the following as the court thinks fit—

(a)   provision setting aside the whole or part of any obligation created by the transaction;

(b)   provision otherwise varying the terms of the transaction or varying the terms on which any security for the purposes of the transaction is held;

(c)   provision requiring any person who is a party to the transaction to pay to the permanent trustee any sums paid to that person, by virtue of the transaction, by the debtor;

(d)   provision requiring any person to surrender to the permanent trustee any property held by him as security for the purposes of the transaction;

(e)   provision directing accounts to be taken between any persons.

(5)   Any sums or property required to be paid or surrendered to the permanent trustee in accordance with an order under this section shall vest in the permanent trustee.

(6)   [. . .] The powers conferred by this section shall be exercisable in relation to any transaction concurrently with any powers exercisable under this Act in relation to that transaction as a gratuitous alienation or unfair preference.

(7)   In this section 'credit' has the same meaning as in the said Act of 1974.

62   Sederunt book and other documents

(1)   Subject to subsection (2) below, whoever by virtue of this Act for the time being holds the sederunt book shall make it available for inspection at all reasonable hours by any interested person.

(2)   As regards any case in which the person on whom a duty is imposed by subsection (1) above is the Accountant in Bankruptcy, the Court of Session may by act of sederunt—

(a)   limit the period for which the duty is so imposed; and

(b)   prescribe conditions in accordance with which the duty shall be carried out.

(3)   Any entry in the sederunt book shall be sufficient evidence of the facts

stated therein, except where it is founded on by the permanent trustee in his own interest.

(4) Notwithstanding any provision of this Act, the permanent trustee shall not be bound to insert in the sederunt book any document of a confidential nature.

(5) The permanent trustee shall not be bound to exhibit to any person other than a commissioner or the Accountant in Bankruptcy any document in his possession of a confidential nature.

(6) An extract from the register of insolvencies bearing to be signed by the Accountant in Bankruptcy shall be sufficient evidence of the facts stated therein.

63　Power to cure defects in procedure

(1) The sheriff may, on the application of any person having an interest—

(a)　if there has been a failure to comply with any requirement of this Act or any regulations made under it, make an order waiving any such failure and, so far as practicable, restoring any person prejudiced by the failure to the position he would have been in but for the failure;

(b)　if for any reason anything required or authorised to be done in, or in connection with, the sequestration process cannot be done, make such order as may be necessary to enable that thing to be done.

(2) The sheriff, in an order under subsection (1) above, may impose such conditions, including conditions as to expenses, as he thinks fit and may—

(a)　authorise or dispense with the performance of any act in the sequestration process;

(b)　appoint as permanent trustee on the debtor's estate a person who would be eligible to be elected under section 24 of this Act, whether or not in place of an existing trustee;

(c)　extend or waive any time limit specified in or under this Act.

(3) An application under subsection (1) above—

(a)　may at any time be remitted by the sheriff to the Court of Session, of his own accord or on an application by any person having an interest;

(b)　shall be so remitted, if the Court of Session so directs on an application by any such person,

if the sheriff or the Court of Session, as the case may be, considers that the remit is desirable because of the importance or complexity of the matters raised by the application.

(4) The permanent trustee shall record in the sederunt book the decision of the sheriff or the Court of Session under this section.

64　Debtor to co-operate with permanent trustee

(1) The debtor shall take every practicable step, and in particular shall execute any document, which may be necessary to enable the permanent trustee to perform the functions conferred on him by this Act.

(2) If the sheriff, on the application of the permanent trustee, is satisfied that the debtor has failed—

(a)　to execute any document in compliance with subsection (1) above, he may authorise the sheriff clerk to do so; and the execution of a document by the sheriff clerk under this paragraph shall have the like force and effect in all respects as if the document had been executed by the debtor;

(b)　to comply in any other respect with subsection (1) above, he may order the debtor to do so.

(3) If the debtor fails to comply with an order of the sheriff under subsection (2) above, he shall be guilty of an offence.

(4) In this section 'debtor' includes a debtor discharged under this Act.

(5) A person convicted of an offence under subsection (3) above shall be liable—

(a)　on summary conviction, to a fine not exceeding the statutory maximum or—

(i)   to imprisonment for a term not exceeding 3 months; or

(ii) if he has previously been convicted of an offence inferring dishonest appropriation of property or an attempt at such appropriation, to imprisonment for a term not exceeding 6 months,

or (in the case of either sub-paragraph) to both such fine and such imprisonment; or

(b)   on conviction on indictment to a fine or to imprisonment for a term not exceeding 2 years or to both.

65 Arbitration and compromise

(1)   The permanent trustee may (but if there are commissioners only with the consent of the commissioners, the creditors or the court)—

(a)   refer to arbitration any claim or question of whatever nature which may arise in the course of the sequestration; or

(b)   make a compromise with regard to any claim of whatever nature made against or on behalf of the sequestrated estate;

and the decree arbitral or compromise shall be binding on the creditors and the debtor.

(2)   Where any claim or question is referred to arbitration under this section, the Accountant in Bankruptcy may vary any time limit in respect of which any procedure under this Act has to be carried out.

(3)   The permanent trustee shall insert a copy of the decree arbitral, or record the compromise, in the sederunt book.

66 Meetings of creditors and commissioners

Part I of Schedule 6 to this Act shall have effect in relation to meetings of creditors other than the statutory meeting; Part II of that Schedule shall have effect in relation to all meetings of creditors under this Act; and Part III of that Schedule shall have effect in relation to meetings of commissioners.

67 General offences by debtor etc

(1)   A debtor who during the relevant period makes a false statement in relation to his assets or his business or financial affairs to any creditor or to any person concerned in the administration of his estate shall be guilty of an offence, unless he shows that he neither knew nor had reason to believe that his statement was false.

(2)   A debtor, or other person acting in his interest whether with or without his authority, who during the relevant period destroys, damages, conceals or removes from Scotland any part of the debtor's estate or any document relating to his assets or his business or financial affairs shall be guilty of an offence, unless the debtor or other person shows that he did not do so with intent to prejudice the creditors.

(3)   A debtor who is absent from Scotland and who after the date of sequestration of his estate fails, when required by the court, to come to Scotland for any purpose connected with the administration of his estate, shall be guilty of an offence.

(4)   A debtor, or other person acting in his interest whether with or without his authority, who during the relevant period falsifies any document relating to the debtor's assets or his business or financial affairs, shall be guilty of an offence, unless the debtor or other person shows that he had no intention to mislead the permanent trustee, a commissioner or any creditor.

(5)   If a debtor whose estate is sequestrated—

(a)   knows that a person has falsified any document relating to the debtor's assets or his business or financial affairs; and

(b)   fails, within one month of the date of acquiring such knowledge, to report his knowledge to the interim or permanent trustee,

he shall be guilty of an offence.

(6)   A person who is absolutely insolvent and who during the relevant period

transfers anything to another person for an inadequate consideration or grants any unfair preference to any of his creditors shall be guilty of an offence, unless the transferor or grantor shows that he did not do so with intent to prejudice the creditors.

(7)   A debtor who is engaged in trade or business shall be guilty of an offence if at any time in the period of one year ending with the date of sequestration of his estate, he pledges or disposes of, otherwise than in the ordinary course of his trade or business, any property which he has obtained on credit and has not paid for unless he shows that he did not intend to prejudice his creditors.

(8)   A debtor who is engaged in trade or business shall be guilty of an offence if at any time in the period of 2 years ending with the date of sequestration, he has failed to keep or preserve such records as are necessary to give a fair view of the state of his assets or his business and financial affairs and to explain his trans-actions, unless he shows that such failure was neither reckless nor dishonest:

Provided that a debtor shall not be guilty of an offence under this subsection if, at the date of sequestration, his unsecured liabilities did not exceed the prescribed amount; but, for the purposes of this proviso, if at any time the amount of a debt (or part of a debt) over which a security is held exceeds the value of the security, that debt (or part) shall be deemed at that time to be unsecured to the extent of the excess.

(9)   If a debtor, either alone or jointly with another person, obtains credit to the extent of £100 (or such other sum as may be prescribed) or more without giving the person from whom he obtained it the relevant information about his status he shall be guilty of an offence.

(10)   For the purposes of subsection (9) above—
  (a)   'debtor' means—
    (i)   a debtor whose estate has been sequestrated, or
    (ii)   a person who has been adjudged bankrupt in England and Wales or Northern Ireland,
and who, in either case, has not been discharged;
  (b)   the reference to the debtor obtaining credit includes a reference to a case where goods are hired to him under a hire-purchase agreement or agreed to be sold to him under a conditional sale agreement; and
  (c)   the relevant information about the status of the debtor is the information that his estate has been sequestrated and that he has not received his discharge or, as the case may be, that he is an undischarged bankrupt in England and Wales or Northern Ireland.

(11)   In this section—
  (a)   'the relevant period' means the period commencing one year immediately before the date of sequestration of the debtor's estate and ending with his discharge;
  (b)   references to intent to prejudice creditors shall include references to intent to prejudice an individual creditor.

(12)   A person convicted of any offence under this section shall be liable—
  (a)   on summary conviction, to a fine not exceeding the statutory maximum or—
    (i)   to imprisonment for a term not exceeding 3 months; or
    (ii)   if he has previously been convicted of an offence inferring dishonest appropriation of property or an attempt at such appropriation, to imprison-ment for a term not exceeding 6 months,
or (in the case of either sub-paragraph) to both such fine and such imprison-ment; or
  (b)   on conviction on indictment to a fine or—
    (i)   in the case of an offence under subsection (1), (2), (4) or (7) above to imprisonment for a term not exceeding 5 years,
    (ii)   in any other case to imprisonment for a term not exceeding 2 years,

or (in the case of either sub-paragraph) to both such fine and such imprisonment.

68 Summary proceedings

(1) [Subject to subsection (1A) below] summary proceedings for an offence under this Act may be commenced at any time within the period of [12] months after the date on which evidence sufficient in the opinion of the Lord Advocate to justify the proceedings comes to his knowledge.

[(1A) No such proceedings shall be commenced by virtue of this section more than three years after the commission of the offence.]

(2) Subsection (3) of [section 136 of the Criminal Procedure (Scotland) Act 1995] (date of commencement of summary proceedings) shall have effect for the purposes of [this section] as it has effect for the purposes of that section.

(3) For the purposes of subsection (1) above, a certificate of the Lord Advocate as to the date on which the evidence in question came to his knowledge is conclusive evidence of the date on which it did so.

69 Outlays of interim and permanent trustee

The Secretary of State may, by regulations, provide for the premium (or a proportionate part thereof) of any bond of caution or other security required, for the time being, to be given by an insolvency practitioner to be taken into account as part of the outlays of the insolvency practitioner in his actings as an interim trustee or permanent trustee.

[69A Fees for the Accountant in Bankruptcy

The Secretary of State may prescribe—

(a) the fees and outlays to be payable to the Accountant in Bankruptcy in respect of the exercise of any of his functions under this Act [or the Insolvency Act 1986];

(b) the time and manner in which such fees and outlays are to be paid; and

(c) the circumstances, if any, in which the Accountant in Bankruptcy may allow exemption from payment or the remission or modification of payment of any fees or outlays payable or paid to him.]

70 Supplies by utilities

(1) This section applies where on any day ('the relevant day')—

(a) sequestration is awarded in a case where the petition was presented by the debtor,

(b) a warrant is granted under section 12(2) of this Act in a case where the petition was presented by a creditor or a trustee acting under a trust deed; or

(c) the debtor grants a trust deed,

and in this section 'the office holder' means the interim trustee, the permanent trustee or the trustee acting under a trust deed, as the case may be.

(2) If a request falling within subsection (3) below is made for the giving after the relevant day of any of the supplies mentioned in subsection (4) below, the supplier—

(a) may make it a condition of the giving of the supply that the office holder personally guarantees the payment of any charges in respect of the supply; and

(b) shall not make it a condition of the giving of the supply, or do anything which has the effect of making it a condition of the giving of the supply, that any outstanding charges in respect of a supply given to the debtor before the relevant day are paid.

(3) A request falls within this subsection if it is made—

(a) by or with the concurrence of the office holder; and

(b) for the purposes of any business which is or has been carried on by or on behalf of the debtor.

(4) The supplies referred to in subsection (2) above are—

[(a) a gas supplier within the meaning of the Gas Act 1986;

(b)   an electricity supplier within the meaning of Part I of the Electricity Act 1989;]

(c)   a supply of water by [Scottish Water];

[(d)   a supply of telecommunication services by a provider of a public telecommunications service.

(5)   In subsection (4), 'communication services' do not include electronic communications services to the extent that they are used to broadcast or otherwise transmit programme services (within the meaning of the Communications Act 2003).]

71   Edinburgh Gazette
The keeper of the Edinburgh Gazette shall, on each day of its publication, send a free copy of it to—

(a)   the Accountant in Bankruptcy; and

(b)   the petition department of the Court of Session.

[71A   Further duty of Accountant in Bankruptcy
The Accountant in Bankruptcy shall, on receiving any notice under section 109(1) of the Insolvency Act 1986 in relation to a community interest company, forward a copy of that notice to the Regulator of Community Interest Companies.]

72   Regulations
Any power to make regulations under this Act shall be exercisable by statutory instrument subject to annulment in pursuance of a resolution of either House of Parliament; and the regulations may make different provision for different cases or classes of case.

[72ZA   Modification of regulation making powers
Any power in any provision of this Act to make regulations may, insofar as that provision relates to a matter to which the EC Regulation applies, be exercised for the purpose of making provision in consequence of the EC Regulation.]

[72A   Variation of references to time, money etc
For any reference in this Act to—

(a)   a period of time;

(b)   an amount of money; or

(c)   a fraction,

there shall be substituted a reference to such other period or, as the case may be, amount or fraction as may be prescribed.]

73   Interpretation
(1)   In this Act, unless the context otherwise requires—

'Accountant in Bankruptcy' shall be construed in accordance with section 1 of this Act;

'accounting period' shall be construed in accordance with section [52(2)] of this Act;

'apparent insolvency' and 'apparently insolvent' shall be construed in accordance with section 7 of this Act;

['appropriate bank or institution' means—

(a)   the Bank of England,

(b)   a person who has permission under Part 4 of the Financial Services and Markets Act 2000 to accept deposits,

(c)   an EEA firm of the kind mentioned in paragraph 5(b) of Schedule 3 to that Act which has permission under paragraph 15 of that Schedule (as a result of qualifying for authorisation under paragraph 12 of that Schedule) to accept deposits, or

(d)   a person who is exempt from the general prohibition in respect of accepting deposits as a result of an exemption order made under section 38(1) of that Act,

and the expressions in this definition must be read with section 22 of the
Financial Services and Markets Act 2000, any relevant order under that
section and Schedule 2 to that Act;]

'act and warrant' means an act and warrant issued under section 25(2) of, or
paragraph 2(2) of Schedule 2 to, this Act;

'associate' shall be construed in accordance with section 74 of this Act;

'business' means the carrying on of any activity, whether for profit or not;

['centre of main interests' has the same meaning as in the EC Regulation;]

'commissioner', except in the expression 'examining commissioner', shall be
construed in accordance with section 30(1) of this Act;

'court' means Court of Session or sheriff;

['creditor' includes a member State liquidator deemed to be a creditor under
section 60A of this Act;]

'date of sequestration' has the meaning assigned by section 12(4) of this Act;

'debtor' includes, without prejudice to the expression's generality, an entity
whose estate may be sequestrated by virtue of section 6 of this Act, a deceased
debtor or his executor or a person entitled to be appointed as executor to a
deceased debtor;

['the EC Regulation' means Council Regulation (EC) No 1346/2000 of 29th
May 2000 on insolvency proceedings;

'establishment' has the meaning given by Article 2(h) of the EC Regulation;]

'examination' means a public examination under section 45 of this Act or a
private examination under section 44 of this Act;

'examining commissioner' shall be construed in accordance with section 46(2)
of this Act;

'interim trustee' shall be construed in accordance with section 2 of this Act;

[. . .]

['main proceedings' means proceedings opened in accordance with Article
3(1) of the EC Regulation and falling within the definition of insolvency
proceedings in Article 2(a) of the EC Regulation and—

    (a)   in relation to England and Wales and Scotland, set out in Annex A
    to the EC Regulation under the heading 'United Kingdom'; and

    (b)   in relation to another member State, set out in Annex A to the EC
    Regulation under the heading relating to that member State;

'member State liquidator' means a person falling within the definition of
liquidator in Article 2(b) of the EC Regulation appointed in proceedings to
which it applies in a member State other than the United Kingdom;]

'ordinary debt' shall be construed in accordance with section 51(1)(f) of this
Act;

'permanent trustee' shall be construed in accordance with section 3 of this Act;

'postponed debt' has the meaning assigned by section 51(3) of this Act;

'preferred debt' has the meaning assigned by section 51(2) of this Act;

'prescribed' means prescribed by regulations made by the Secretary of State;

'protected trust deed' shall be construed in accordance with paragraph 8 of
Schedule 5 to this Act;

'qualified creditor' and 'qualified creditors' shall be construed in accordance
with section 5(4) of this Act;

'qualified to act as an insolvency practitioner' means being, in accordance with
section 2 of the Insolvency Act 1985 (qualifications of insolvency practitioners),
so qualified:

    Provided that, until the coming into force of that section the expression
    shall instead mean satisfying such requirements (which, without prejudice
    to the generality of this definition, may include requirements as to the
    finding of caution) as may be prescribed for the purposes of this Act;

'register of insolvencies' has the meaning assigned by section [1A(1)(b)] of this
Act;

'relevant person' has the meaning assigned by section 44(1)(b) of this Act;

['secondary proceedings' means proceedings opened in accordance with Articles 3(2) and 3(3) of the EC Regulation and falling within the definition of winding-up proceedings in Article 2(c) of the EC Regulation, and—

(a) in relation to England and Wales and Scotland, set out in Annex B to the EC Regulation under the heading 'United Kingdom'; and

(b) in relation to another member State, set out in Annex B to the EC Regulation under the heading relating to that member State;]

'secured creditor' means a creditor who holds a security for his debt over any part of the debtor's estate;

'security' means any security, heritable or moveable, or any right of lien, retention or preference;

'sederunt book' means the sederunt book maintained under section 3(1)(e) of this Act;

'standard scale' means the standard scale as defined in section 75(b) of the Criminal Justice Act 1982;

['statement of assets and liabilities' means a document (including a copy of a document) in such form as may be prescribed containing—

(i) a list of the debtor's assets and liabilities;

(ii) a list of his income and expenditure; and

(iii) such other information as may be prescribed;]

'statutory meeting' has the meaning assigned by [section 20A] of this Act;

'statutory maximum' has the meaning assigned by section 74(2) of the Criminal Justice Act 1982;

['temporary administrator' means a temporary administrator referred to by Article 38 of the EC Regulation; and

'territorial proceedings' means proceedings opened in accordance with Articles 3(2) and 3(4) of the EC Regulation and falling within the definition of insolvency proceedings in Article 2(a) of the EC Regulation, and—

(a) in relation to England and Wales and Scotland, set out in Annex A to the EC Regulation under the heading 'United Kingdom'; and

(b) in relation to another member State, set out in Annex A to the EC Regulation under the heading relating to that member State.]

['trust deed' has the meaning assigned by section 5(4A) of this Act]; and

'unfair preference' means a preference created as is mentioned in subsection (1) of section 36 of this Act by a transaction to which subsection (4) of that section applies.

(2) Any reference in this Act to a debtor being absolutely insolvent shall be construed as a reference to his liabilities being greater than his assets, and any reference to a debtor's estate being absolutely insolvent shall be construed accordingly.

(3) Any reference in this Act to value of the creditors is, in relation to any matter, a reference to the value of their claims as accepted for the purposes of that matter.

(4) Any reference in this Act to 'the creditors' in the context of their giving consent or doing any other thing shall, unless the context otherwise requires, be construed as a reference to the majority in value of such creditors as vote in that context at a meeting of creditors.

(5) Any reference in this Act to any of the following acts by a creditor barring the effect of any enactment or rule of law relating to the limitation of actions in any part of the United Kingdom, namely—

(a) the presentation of a petition for sequestration;

(b) the concurrence in such a petition; and

(c) the submission of a claim,

shall be construed as a reference to that act having the same effect, for the purposes of any such enactment or rule of law, as an effective acknowledgement of the creditor's claim; and any reference in this Act to any such enactment shall not include a reference to an enactment which implements or gives effect to any international agreement or obligation.

[(6)   Any reference in this Act, howsoever expressed, to the time when a petition for sequestration is presented shall be construed as a reference to the time when the petition is received by the clerk of the court.]

74   Meaning of 'associate'

(1)   Subject to subsection (7) below, for the purposes of this Act any question whether a person is an associate of another person shall be determined in accordance with the following provisions of this section (any reference, whether in those provisions or in regulations under the said subsection (7), to a person being an associate of another person being taken to be a reference to their being associates of each other).

(2)   A person is an associate of an individual if that person is the individual's [husband, wife or civil partner], or is a relative, or the husband or wife of a relative, of the individual or of the individual's husband or wife.

(3)   A person is an associate of any person with whom he is in partnership, and of the husband or wife or a relative of any individual with whom he is in partnership; and a firm is an associate of any person who is a member of the firm.

(4)   For the purposes of this section a person is a relative of an individual if he is that individual's brother, sister, uncle, aunt, nephew, niece, lineal ancestor or lineal descendant treating—

(a)   any relationship of the half blood as a relationship of the whole blood and the stepchild or adopted child of any person as his child; and

(b)   an illegitimate child as the legitimate child of his mother and reputed father,

and references in this section to a [husband, wife or civil partner] include a former [husband, wife or civil partner] and a reputed [husband, wife or civil partner].

(5)   A person is an associate of any person whom he employs or by whom he is employed; and for the purposes of this subsection any director or other officer of a company shall be treated as employed by that company.

(6)   In subsection (5) above, 'company' includes any body corporate (whether incorporated in Great Britain or elsewhere).

(7)   The Secretary of State may by regulations—

(a)   amend the foregoing provisions of this section so as to provide further categories of persons who, for the purposes of this Act, are to be associates of other persons; and

(b)   provide that any or all of subsections (2) to (6) above (or any subsection added by virtue of paragraph (a) above) shall cease to apply, whether in whole or in part, or shall apply subject to such modifications as he may specify in the regulations;

and he may in the regulations make such incidental or transitional provision as he considers appropriate.

75   [*Amendments, repeals and transitional provisions*]

76   Receipts and expenses

(1)   Any—

(a)   payments received by the Secretary of State under section 58(3) of this Act; or

(b)   amounts handed over to him in accordance with section 53 of this Act by virtue of the insertion provided for in paragraph 9 of Schedule 2 to this Act,

shall be paid by him into the Consolidated Fund.

(2)   There shall be paid out of moneys provided by Parliament—

(a)   any amount of outlays and remuneration payable in accordance with section 53 of this Act by virtue of the insertion mentioned in subsection (1)(b) above;

(b)   any administrative expenses incurred by the Secretary of State under this Act; and

(c)   any increase attributable to this Act in the sums so payable under any other Act.

77   Crown application
The application of this Act to the Crown is to the Crown as creditor only.

78   Short title, commencement and extent
(1)   This Act may be cited as the Bankruptcy (Scotland) Act 1985.

(2)   This Act, except this section, shall come into force on such day as the Secretary of State may by order made by statutory instrument appoint; and different days may be so appointed for different purposes and for different provisions.

(3)   An order under subsection (2) above may contain such transitional provisions and savings as appear to the Secretary of State necessary or expedient in connection with the provisions brought into force (whether wholly or partly) by the order.

(4)   Without prejudice to section 75(3) to (5) of this Act, this Act applies to sequestrations as regards which the petition—

(a)   is presented on or after the date of coming into force of section 5 of this Act; or

(b)   was presented before, but in respect of which no award of sequestration has been made by, that date.

(5)   This Act, except the provisions mentioned in subsection (6) below, extends to Scotland only.

(6)   The provisions referred to in subsection (5) above are sections 8(5), 22(8) (including that subsection as applied by section 48(7)), 46, 55 and 73(5), paragraph 16(b) of Schedule 4 and paragraph 3 of Schedule 5.

SCHEDULES

SCHEDULE 1
DETERMINATION OF AMOUNT OF CREDITOR'S CLAIM
Sections 5(5) and 22(9)

Amount which may be claimed generally

1—(1)   Subject to the provisions of this Schedule, the amount in respect of which a creditor shall be entitled to claim shall be the accumulated sum of principal and any interest which is due on the debt as at the date of sequestration.

(2)   If a debt does not depend on a contingency but would not be payable but for the sequestration until after the date of sequestration, the amount of the claim shall be calculated as if the debt were payable on the date of sequestration but subject to the deduction of interest at the rate specified in section 51(7) of this Act from the said date until the date for payment of the debt.

(3)   In calculating the amount of his claim, a creditor shall deduct any discount (other than any discount for payment in cash) which is allowable by contract or course of dealing between the creditor and the debtor or by the usage of trade.

Claims for aliment and periodical allowance on divorce

2—(1)   A person entitled to aliment, however arising, from a living debtor as at the date of sequestration, or from a deceased debtor immediately before his death, shall not be entitled to include in the amount of his claim—

(a)   any unpaid aliment for any period before the date of sequestration unless the amount of the aliment has been quantified by court decree or by any legally binding obligation which is supported by evidence in writing, and,

[(i)] in the case of spouses (or, where the aliment is payable to a divorced person in respect of a child, former spouses) they were living apart during that period;

[(ii) in the case of civil partners (or, where the aliment is payable to a former civil partner in respect of a child after dissolution of a civil partnership, former civil partners),]

(b)   any aliment for any period after the date of sequestration.

(2)   Sub-paragraph (1) above shall apply to a periodical allowance payable on divorce [or on dissolution of a civil partnership]—

(a)   by virtue of a court order; or

(b)   under any legally binding obligation which is supported by evidence in writing,

as it applies to aliment and as if for the words from 'in the case' to 'they' there were substituted the words 'the payer and payee'.

Debts depending on contingency

3—(1)   Subject to sub-paragraph (2) below, the amount which a creditor shall be entitled to claim shall not include a debt in so far as its existence or amount depends upon a contingency.

(2)   On an application by the creditor—

(a)   to the permanent trustee; or

(b)   if there is no permanent trustee, to the sheriff,

the permanent trustee or sheriff shall put a value on the debt in so far as it is contingent, and the amount in respect of which the creditor shall then be entitled to claim shall be that value but no more; and, where the contingent debt is an annuity, a cautioner may not then be sued for more than that value.

(3)   Any interested person may appeal to the sheriff against a valuation under sub-paragraph (2) above by the permanent trustee, and the sheriff may affirm or vary that valuation.

Debts due under composition contracts

4   Where in the course of a sequestration the debtor is discharged following approval by the sheriff of a composition offered by the debtor but the sequestration is subsequently revived, the amount in respect of which a creditor shall be entitled to claim shall be the same amount as if the composition had not been so approved less any payment already made to him under the composition contract.

Secured debts

5—(1)   In calculating the amount of his claim, a secured creditor shall deduct the value of any security as estimated by him:

Provided that if he surrenders, or undertakes in writing to surrender, a security for the benefit of the debtor's estate, he shall not be required to make a deduction of the value of that security.

(2)   The permanent trustee may, at any time after the expiry of 12 weeks from the date of sequestration, require a secured creditor at the expense of the debtor's estate to discharge the security or convey or assign it to the permanent trustee on payment to the creditor of the value specified by the creditor; and the amount in

respect of which the creditor shall then be entitled to claim shall be any balance of his debt remaining after receipt of such payment.

(3) In calculating the amount of his claim, a creditor whose security has been realised shall deduct the amount (less the expenses of realisation) which he has received, or is entitled to receive, from the realisation.

Valuation of claims against partners for debts of the partnership

6 Where a creditor claims in respect of a debt of a partnership, against the estate of one of its partners, the creditor shall estimate the value of—

(a) the debt to the creditor from the firm's estate where that estate has not been sequestrated; or

(b) the creditor's claim against that estate where it has been sequestrated,

and deduct that value from his claim against the partner's estate; and the amount in respect of which he shall be entitled to claim on the partner's estate shall be the balance remaining after that deduction has been made.

SCHEDULE 2
ADAPTATION OF PROCEDURE ETC UNDER THIS ACT WHERE PERMANENT TRUSTEE NOT ELECTED
Sections 23(4), 24(5) and 28(5)

1 [Except where the permanent trustee is the Accountant in Bankruptcy] section 24(2) shall, in so far as it relates to qualifications for continuing to act as permanent trustee, apply to a permanent trustee appointed, as it applies to one elected, under this Act.

[2—(1) In place of section 25, sub-paragraph (2) below shall have effect.

(2) The sheriff clerk shall issue to the permanent trustee an act and warrant in such form as shall be prescribed by the Court of Session by act of sederunt.

2A Sections 26 and 26A shall apply as if for any reference to the confirmation of the permanent trustee in office there was substituted a reference to the permanent trustee receiving the act and warrant issued in pursuance of paragraph 2(2) above.

3—(1) In place of subsections (1A) to (5) of section 28, sub-paragraph (2) below shall have effect.

(2) Where the permanent trustee resigns under subsection (1) of section 28 of this Act or dies—

(a) the Accountant in Bankruptcy; or

(b) such person as may be nominated by the Accountant in Bankruptcy (being a person who is not ineligible for election as permanent trustee under section 24(2) of this Act) if that person consents to the nomination,

may apply to the sheriff for appointment as permanent trustee; and, on such an application being made, the sheriff shall appoint the Accountant in Bankruptcy or, as the case may be, the person nominated by him to be the permanent trustee.

4—(1) Section 29 shall have effect as follows.

(2) Where the permanent trustee is the Accountant in Bankruptcy, subsections (1) to (6) shall not have effect.

(3) In any other case—

(a) subsection (5) shall not have effect but sub-paragraph (2) of paragraph 3 above shall apply where the permanent trustee has been removed from office under subsection (1)(b) of section 29 of this Act or following an appeal under subsection (4) of that section as that sub-paragraph applies where he resigns or dies; and

(b) subsection (6) shall have effect as if for the words from '(b)' to the end there were substituted the words—

    '(b) appoint as permanent trustee—

        (i) the Accountant in Bankruptcy; or

        (ii) such person as may be nominated by the Accountant in Bankruptcy (being a person who is not ineligible for election as permanent trustee under section 24(2) of this Act) if that person consents to the nomination.'

(4) In every case—

    (a) subsection (7) shall not have effect; and

    (b) subsection (8) shall have effect as if for the word '(5)' there were substituted the word '(6)'.]

5 Where an appointment is made under paragraph 3(3), or by virtue of paragraph [4(3)(a) or (b)], above the provisions of this Act shall continue to have effect as regards the sequestration subject to such modifications and with such further provisions as are set out in this Schedule.

6 Section 30 shall not have effect, and, in any sequestration to which this Schedule applies by virtue of section 28(5) of this Act, any commissioners already holding office shall cease to do so.

7 In section 39 [subsection (1) shall not have effect where the permanent trustee is the Accountant in Bankruptcy and]—

    (a) in subsection (1), the reference to the permanent trustee's confirmation in office shall be construed as a reference to his receiving the act and warrant issued under paragraph 2(2) of this Schedule;

    [(b) in subsection (2) the words 'but if there are commissioners only with the consent of the commissioners, the creditors or the court' shall not have effect, and—

        (i) if the permanent trustee is the Accountant in Bankruptcy, no consent shall be required for the actings mentioned in that subsection; and

        (ii) in any other case, the consent of the Accountant in Bankruptcy shall be required for such actings.]

[7A In section 43 (money received by permanent trustee) for subsection (1) there shall be substituted the following subsection—

    '(1) Subject to subsection (2) below, all money received by—

    (a) the Accountant in Bankruptcy in respect of his actings as permanent trustee shall be deposited by him in the name of the debtor's estate or in the name of the Secretary of State in an appropriate bank or institution;

    (b) the permanent trustee (where he is not the Accountant in Bankruptcy) in the exercise of his functions shall be deposited by him in the name of the debtor's estate in an appropriate bank or institution.']

8 [Except where the permanent trustee is the Accountant in Bankruptcy] any power under section 44 or 45 to apply to the sheriff for an order requiring attendance shall be exerciseable only with the consent of the Accountant in Bankruptcy (unless in the case of section 45(1), the Accountant in Bankruptcy has requested the application).

[9—(1) Where the permanent trustee is the Accountant in Bankruptcy, section 53 shall have effect as follows.

(2) For subsections (1) to (7) there shall be substituted the following subsections—

    '(1) At the end of each accounting period, the Accountant in Bankruptcy shall prepare accounts of his intromissions with the debtor's estate, and he shall make a determination of his fees and outlays calculated in accordance with regulations made under section 69A of this Act.

(2) Such accounts and determination shall be available for inspection by the debtor and the creditors not later than 6 weeks after the end of the accounting period to which they relate.

(3) In making a determination as mentioned in subsection (1) above, the Accountant in Bankruptcy may take into account any adjustment which he may wish to make in the amount of his remuneration fixed in respect of any earlier accounting period.

(4) Not later than 8 weeks after the end of an accounting period, the debtor or any creditor may appeal to the sheriff against the determination of the Accountant in Bankruptcy; and the decision of the sheriff on such an appeal shall be final.

(5) On the expiry of the period within which an appeal may be made under subsection (4) above, the Accountant in Bankruptcy shall pay to the creditors their dividends in accordance with the scheme of division.'

(3) In subsection (10) for the words 'the audited' there shall be substituted the word 'his'.]

[SCHEDULE 2A
MODIFICATION OF DUTIES OF PERMANENT TRUSTEE IN SUMMARY ADMINISTRATION

1 The permanent trustee shall comply with the requirements of sections 3 and 39 of this Act only in so far as, in his view, it would be of financial benefit to the estate of the debtor and in the interests of creditors to do so.

2 The permanent trustee shall, until the debtor is discharged under this Act, at the end of—
    (a) the period of 6 months beginning with the date of sequestration; and
    (b) each subsequent period of 6 months,
require the debtor to give an account in writing of his current state of affairs.

3—(1) Where the Accountant in Bankruptcy is not the permanent trustee, the permanent trustee shall comply with any general or specific directions given to him by the Accountant in Bankruptcy.

(2) Directions given under this paragraph may be given in respect of any particular case, all cases or any class or description of case.]

4—(1) The permanent trustee shall, as soon as a certificate for the summary administration of the sequestration of the debtor's estate has been granted, publish in the Edinburgh Gazette a notice stating that such a certificate has been granted and that he has been appointed permanent trustee and, where no notice under section 15(6) of this Act has been published in respect of the sequestration—
    (a) stating that sequestration of the debtor's estate has been awarded; and
    (b) inviting the submission of claims to him.

(2) A notice under sub-paragraph (1) above shall also contain such additional information as may be prescribed.

5 Except in the case of an application for the grant of a certificate for the summary administration of the sequestration of the debtor's estate under section 25(2A) of this Act, Schedule 2 to this Act shall have effect in respect of a sequestration to which this Schedule applies.

SCHEDULE 3
PREFERRED DEBTS

Section 51

PART I
LIST OF PREFERRED DEBTS

[. . .]

Contributions to occupational pension schemes, etc

4   Any sum which is owed by the debtor and is a sum to which [Schedule 4 to the Pensions Schemes Act 1993] (contributions to occupational pension scheme and state scheme premiums) applies.

Remuneration of employees, etc

5—(1)   So much of any amount which—
(a)   is owed by the debtor to a person who is or has been an employee of the debtor, and
(b)   is payable by way of remuneration in respect of the whole or any part of the period of four months next before the relevant date,
as does not exceed the prescribed amount.
(2)   An amount owed by way of accrued holiday remuneration, in respect of any period of employment before the relevant date, to a person whose employment by the debtor has been terminated, whether before, on or after that date.
(3)   So much of any sum owed in respect of money advanced for the purpose as has been applied for the payment of a debt which, if it had not been paid, would have been a debt falling within sub-paragraph (1) or (2) above.

6   So much of any amount which—
(a)   is ordered, whether before or after the relevant date, to be paid by the debtor under the Reserve Forces (Safeguard of Employment) Act 1985; and
(b)   is so ordered in respect of a default made by the debtor before that date in the discharge of his obligations under that Act,
as does not exceed such amount as may be prescribed.

Levies on coal and steel production

[6A   Any sums due at the relevant date from the debtor in respect of—
(a)   the levies on the production of coal and steel referred to in Articles 49 and 50 of the ECSC Treaty, or
(b)   any surcharge for delay provided for in Article 50(3) of that Treaty and Article 6 of Decision 3/52 of the High Authority of the Coal and Steel Community.]

PART II
INTERPRETATION OF PART I

Meaning of 'the relevant date'

7   In Part I of this Schedule 'the relevant date' means—
(a)   in relation to a debtor (other than a deceased debtor), the date of sequestration; and
(b)   in relation to a deceased debtor, the date of his death.

[. . .]

Amounts payable by way of remuneration

9—(1)   For the purposes of paragraph 5 of Part I of this Schedule a sum is payable by the debtor to a person by way of remuneration in respect of any period if—

(a)   it is paid as wages or salary (whether payable for time or for piece work or earned wholly or partly by way of commission) in respect of services rendered to the debtor in that period; or

(b)   it is an amount falling within sub-paragraph (2) below and is payable by the debtor in respect of that period.

(2)   An amount falls within this sub-paragraph if it is—

(a)   a guarantee payment under section 12(1) of the Employment Protection (Consolidation) Act 1978 (employee without work to do for a day or part of a day),

(b)   remuneration on suspension on medical grounds under section 19 of that Act,

(c)   any payment for the time off under section 27(3) (trade-union duties), 31(3) (looking for work, etc) or 31A(4) (ante-natal care) of that Act,

(d)   [. . .]

(e)   remuneration under a protective award made by an industrial tribunal under section 101 of the Employment Protection Act 1975 (redundancy dismissal with compensation).

(3)   For the purposes of paragraph 5(2) of Part I of this Schedule, holiday remuneration shall be deemed, in the case of a person whose employment has been terminated by or in consequence of the award of sequestration of his employer's estate, to have accrued to that person in respect of any period of employment if, by virtue of that person's contract of employment or of any enactment (including an order made or direction given under any enactment), that remuneration would have accrued in respect of that period if that person's employment had continued until he became entitled to be allowed the holiday.

(4)   Without prejudice to the preceding provisions of this paragraph—

(a)   any remuneration payable by the debtor to a person in respect of a period of holiday or of absence from work through sickness or other good cause is deemed to be wages or, as the case may be, salary in respect of services rendered to the debtor in that period; and

(b)   references in this paragraph to remuneration in respect of a period of holiday include references to any sums which, if they had been paid, would have been treated for the purposes of the enactments relating to social services as earnings in respect of that period.

Transitional provisions

10   Regulations under paragraph 5 or 6 of Part I of this Schedule may contain such transitional provisions as may appear to the Secretary of State necessary or expedient.

SCHEDULE 4
DISCHARGE ON COMPOSITION

Section 56

1—(1)   At any time after the sheriff clerk issues the act and warrant to the permanent trustee, an offer of composition may be made by or on behalf of the debtor, in respect of his debts, to the permanent trustee.

(2)   Any offer of composition shall specify caution or other security to be provided for its implementation.

2   The permanent trustee [where he is not the Accountant in Bankruptcy] shall submit the offer of composition along with a report thereon to the commissioners or, if there are no commissioners, to the Accountant in Bankruptcy.

3   The commissioners or, if there are no commissioners, the Accountant in Bankruptcy—
    (a)   if they consider (or he considers) that the offer of composition will be timeously implemented and that, if the rules set out in section 51 of, and Schedule 1 to, this Act were applicable, its implementation would secure payment of a dividend of at least 25p in the £ in respect of the ordinary debts, and
    (b)   if satisfied with the caution or other security specified in the offer,
shall recommend that the offer should be placed before the creditors.

4   Where a recommendation is made that the offer of composition should be placed before the creditors, the permanent trustee shall—
    (a)   intimate the recommendation to the debtor and record it in the sederunt book;
    (b)   publish in the Edinburgh Gazette a notice stating that an offer of composition has been made and where its terms may be inspected;
    (c)   invite every creditor known to him to accept or reject the offer by completing a prescribed form sent by the permanent trustee with the invitation and returning the completed form to him; and
    (d)   send along with the prescribed form a report—
        (i)   summarising the offer and the present state of the debtor's affairs and the progress in realising his estate; and
        (ii)   estimating, if the offer is accepted, the expenses to be met in concluding the sequestration proceedings and the dividend which would be payable in respect of the ordinary debts if the rules set out in section 51 of, and Schedule 1 to, this Act were applied.

5—(1)   The permanent trustee shall determine from the completed prescribed forms duly received by him that the offer of composition has been accepted by the creditors, if a majority in number and not less than two-thirds in value of the creditors known to him have accepted it, and otherwise shall determine that they have rejected it.
    (2)   For the purposes of this paragraph, a prescribed form shall be deemed to be duly received by the permanent trustee if it is received by him not later than 14 days after the date on which it was sent to the creditor.
    (3)   The permanent trustee shall intimate in writing his determination under this paragraph to the debtor and any other person by whom the offer of composition was made and shall insert his determination in the sederunt book.

6   Where the permanent trustee determines that the creditors have accepted the offer of composition, he shall submit to the sheriff—
    (a)   a statement that he has so determined;
    (b)   a copy of the report mentioned in paragraph 4(d) of this Schedule; and
    (c)   a declaration by the debtor as to the matters mentioned in sub-paragraphs (i) and (ii) of section 54(4)(b) of this Act.

7—(1)   The sheriff shall, on receipt by him of the documents mentioned in paragraph 6 of this Schedule, fix a date and time for a hearing to consider whether or not to approve the offer of composition.
    (2)   The permanent trustee shall then send to every creditor known to him a notice in writing stating—
    (a)   that he has determined that the creditors have accepted the offer of composition;

(b) that a hearing has been fixed by the sheriff to consider whether or not to approve the offer;

(c) the place, date and time of the hearing; and

(d) that the recipient of the notice may make representations at the hearing as to whether or not the offer of composition should be approved.

8—(1) At the hearing the sheriff shall examine the documents and hear any representations and thereafter shall make an order—

(a) if he is satisfied that a majority in number and not less than two-thirds in value of the creditors known to the permanent trustee have accepted the offer of composition and that the terms of the offer are reasonable, approving the offer; and

(b) if he is not so satisfied, refusing to approve the offer of composition.

(2) The sheriff may make an order approving the offer of composition, notwithstanding that there has been a failure to comply with any provision of this Schedule.

(3) The debtor or any creditor may within 14 days of the order being made appeal against an order approving or refusing to approve the offer of composition.

9—(1) Where the offer of composition is approved, the permanent trustee [where he is not the Accountant in Bankruptcy] shall—

(a) submit to the commissioners or, if there are no commissioners, to the Accountant in Bankruptcy, his accounts of his intromissions with the debtor's estate for audit and a claim for the outlays reasonably incurred by him and for his remuneration; and where the said documents are submitted to the commissioners, he shall send a copy of them to the Accountant in Bankruptcy;

(b) take all reasonable steps to ensure that the interim trustee (where he is a different person) has submitted, or submits, to the Accountant in Bankruptcy his accounts and his claim for his outlays and remuneration.

[(1A) Where the offer of composition is approved and the permanent trustee is the Accountant in Bankruptcy, the permanent trustee shall prepare accounts of his intromissions with the debtor's estate and he shall make a determination of his fees and outlays calculated in accordance with regulations made under section 69A of this Act];

(2) Subsections (3), (4), (6) and (10) of section 53 of this Act shall apply, subject to any necessary modifications, in respect of the accounts and claim submitted under sub-paragraph (1)(a) above as they apply in respect of the accounts and claim submitted under section 53(1) of this Act.

[(3) Subsections (2), (3), (4), (5) and (10) of section 53 of this Act as adapted by paragraph 9(2) and (3) of Schedule 2 to this Act shall apply, subject to any necessary modifications, in respect of the accounts and determination prepared under sub-paragraph (1A) above as they apply in respect of the accounts and determination prepared under the said section 53 as so adapted.]

10 As soon as the procedure under paragraph 9 of this Schedule has been completed, there shall be lodged with the sheriff clerk—

(a) by the permanent trustee, a declaration that all necessary charges in connection with the sequestration have been paid or that satisfactory provision has been made in respect of the payment of such charges;

(b) by or on behalf of the debtor, the bond of caution or other security for payment of the composition.

11 Once the documents have been lodged under paragraph 10 of this Schedule, the sheriff shall make an order discharging the debtor and the permanent trustee; and subsection (7) of section 54 of this Act shall apply in relation to an order

under this paragraph as it applies in relation to an order under subsection (6) of that section.

12   An order under paragraph 11 of this Schedule discharging the permanent trustee shall have the effect of discharging him from all liability (other than any liability arising from fraud) to the creditors or to the debtor in respect of any act or omission of the permanent trustee in exercising the functions conferred on him, by this Act.

13   Notwithstanding that an offer of composition has been made, the sequestration shall proceed as if no such offer of composition has been made until the discharge of the debtor becomes effective; and the sequestration shall thereupon cease.

14   A creditor who has not submitted a claim under section 48 of this Act before the sheriff makes an order approving an offer of composition shall not be entitled to make any demand against a person offering the composition on behalf of the debtor or against a cautioner in the offer; but this paragraph is without prejudice to any right of such a creditor to a dividend out of the debtor's estate equal to the dividend which creditors of the same class are entitled to receive under the composition.

15   A debtor may make two, but no more than two, offers of composition in the course of a sequestration.

16—(1)   On an order under paragraph 11 of this Schedule discharging the debtor becoming effective—
    (a)   the debtor shall be re-invested in his estate as existing at the date of the order;
    (b)   the debtor shall, subject to paragraph 14 of this Schedule, be discharged of all debts for which he was liable at the date of sequestration (other than any debts mentioned in section 55(2) of this Act); and
    (c)   the claims of creditors in the sequestration shall be converted into claims for their respective shares in the composition.
    [(2)   The discharge of the debtor by virtue of an order under paragraph 11 above shall not affect any right of a secured creditor—
    (a)   for a debt in respect of which the debtor has been discharged to enforce his security for payment of the debt and any interest due and payable on the debt until the debt is paid in full; or
    (b)   for an obligation in respect of which the debtor has been discharged to enforce his security in respect of the obligation.]

17—(1)   Without prejudice to any rule of law relating to the reduction of court decrees, the Court of Session, on the application of any creditor, may recall the order of the sheriff approving the offer of composition and discharging the debtor and the permanent trustee where it is satisfied—
    (a)   that there has been, or is likely to be, default in payment of the composition or of any instalment thereof; or
    (b)   that for any reason the composition cannot be proceeded with or cannot be proceeded with without undue delay or without injustice to the creditors.
    (2)   The effect of a decree of recall under this paragraph where the debtor has already been discharged shall be to revive the sequestration:
    Provided that the revival of the sequestration shall not affect the validity of any transaction which has been entered into by the debtor since his discharge with a person who has given value and has acted in good faith.
    (3)   Where the permanent trustee has been discharged, the Court may, on pro-

nouncing a decree of recall under this paragraph, appoint a judicial factor to administer the debtor's estate, and give the judicial factor such order as it thinks fit as to that administration.

(4) The clerk of court shall send a copy of a decree of recall under this paragraph to the permanent trustee or judicial factor for insertion in the sederunt book.

18—(1) Without prejudice to any rule of law relating to the reduction of court decrees, the Court of Session, on the application of any creditor, may reduce an order under paragraph 11 of this Schedule discharging a debtor where it is satisfied that a payment was made or a preference granted or that a payment or preference was promised for the purpose of facilitating the obtaining of the debtor's discharge.

(2) The Court may, whether or not it pronounces a decree of reduction under this paragraph, order a creditor who has received a payment or preference in connection with the debtor's discharge to surrender the payment or the value of the preference to the debtor's estate.

(3) Where the permanent trustee has been discharged, the Court may, on pronouncing a decree of reduction under this paragraph, appoint a judicial factor to administer the debtor's estate, and give the judicial factor such order as it thinks fit as to that administration.

(4) The clerk of court shall send a copy of a decree of reduction under this paragraph to the permanent trustee or judicial factor for insertion in the sederunt book.

SCHEDULE 5
VOLUNTARY TRUST DEEDS FOR CREDITORS
Section 59

Remuneration of trustee

1 Whether or not provision is made in the trust deed for auditing the trustee's accounts and for determining the method of fixing the trustee's remuneration or whether or not the trustee and the creditors have agreed on such auditing and the method of fixing the remuneration, the debtor, the trustee or any creditor may, at any time before the final distribution of the debtor's estate among the creditors, have the trustee's accounts audited by and his remuneration fixed by the Accountant in Bankruptcy.

Registration of notice of inhibition

2—(1) The trustee, from time to time after the trust deed has been delivered to him, may cause a notice in such form as shall be prescribed by the Court of Session by act of sederunt to be recorded in the register of inhibitions and adjudications; and such recording shall have the same effect as the recording in that register of letters of inhibition against the debtor.

(2) The trustee, after the debtor's estate has been finally distributed among his creditors or the trust deed has otherwise ceased to be operative, shall cause to be so recorded a notice in such form as shall be prescribed as aforesaid recalling the notice recorded under sub-paragraph (1) above.

Lodging of claim to bar effect of limitation of actions

3 The submission of a claim by a creditor to the trustee acting under a trust deed shall bar the effect of any enactment or rule of law relating to limitation of actions in any part of the United Kingdom.

Valuation of claims

4   Unless the trust deed otherwise provides, Schedule 1 to this Act shall apply
in relation to a trust deed as it applies in relation to a sequestration but subject to
the following modifications—
    (a)   in paragraphs 1, 2 and 5 for the word 'sequestration' wherever it occurs
there shall be substituted the words 'granting of the trust deed';
    (b)   in paragraph 3—
        (i)   in sub-paragraph (2), for the words from the beginning of paragraph
    (a) to 'or sheriff' there shall be substituted the words 'the trustee'; and
        (ii)   in sub-paragraph (3), for the reference to the permanent trustee there
    shall be substituted a reference to the trustee;
    (c)   paragraph 4 shall be omitted; and
    (d)   in paragraph 5(2) for the references to the permanent trustee there shall
be substituted references to the trustee.

Protected trust deeds

[5—(1)   Paragraphs 6 and 7 of this Schedule shall apply in respect of a trust
deed if—
    (a)   the trustee is a person who would not be disqualified under section 24(2)
of this Act from acting as the permanent trustee if the debtor's estate were being
sequestrated;
    (b)   after the trust deed has been delivered to him, the trustee publishes in
the Edinburgh Gazette the notice specified in sub-paragraph (3) below;
    (c)   not later than one week after the date of publication of such notice, the
trustee sends to every creditor known to him—
        (i)   a copy of the trust deed;
        (ii)   a copy of the notice; and
        (iii)   such other information as may be prescribed;
    (d)   within the period of 5 weeks beginning with the date of publication of
such notice, the trustee has not received notification in writing from a majority
in number or not less than one third in value of the creditors that they object to
the trust deed and do not wish to accede to it; and
    (e)   immediately after the expiry of the said period of 5 weeks, the trustee
sends to the Accountant in Bankruptcy for registration in the register of
insolvencies a copy of the trust deed with a certificate endorsed thereon that it is
a true copy and that he has not received notification as mentioned in sub-sub-
paragraph (d) above.
(2)   Any creditor who has been sent a copy of the notice referred to in sub-
paragraph (1)(b) above and who has not notified the trustee as mentioned in
sub-paragraph (1)(d) above that he objects to the trust deed shall be treated for
all purposes as if he had acceded to the trust deed; and any reference in this
Act to a creditor who has acceded to a trust deed shall include a reference to a
creditor who is treated for all purposes as if he had so acceded.
(3)   The notice mentioned in sub-paragraph (1)(b) above shall be in the prescribed form and shall contain such information as may be prescribed.
(4)   The Secretary of State may by regulations amend sub-paragraphs (1) to (3)
above by replacing them, varying them or adding to or deleting anything from
them.
(5)   Regulations made under sub-paragraph (4) above may contain such amendments of this Act as appear to the Secretary of State to be necessary in consequence
of any amendment made by the regulations to the said sub-paragraphs (1) to (3).]

6   Where the provisions of paragraph 5 of this Schedule have been fulfilled,
then—

[(a)   subject to paragraph 7 of this Schedule, a creditor who has—

(i)   not been sent a copy of the notice as mentioned in paragraph 5(1)(c) above; or

(ii)   notified the trustee of his objection to the trust deed as mentioned in paragraph 5(1)(d) above, shall have no higher right to recover his debt than a creditor who has acceded to the trust deed;]

(b)   the debtor may not petition for the sequestration of his estate while the trust deed subsists.

7—(1)   A qualified creditor [who has not been sent a copy of the notice as mentioned in paragraph 5(1)(c) above or who has notified the trustee of his objection to the trust deed as mentioned in paragraph 5(1)(d) above] may present a petition for sequestration of the debtor's estate—

(a)   not later than 6 weeks after the date of publication of the notice under [paragraph 5(1)(b)] of this Schedule; but

(b)   subject to section 8(1)(b) of this Act, at any time if he avers that the provision for distribution of the estate is or is likely to be unduly prejudicial to a creditor or class of creditors.

(2)   The court may award sequestration in pursuance of sub-paragraph (1)(a) above if it considers that to do so would be in the best interests of the creditors.

(3)   The court shall award sequestration in pursuance of sub-paragraph (1)(b) above if, but only if, it is satisfied that the creditor's said averment is correct.

8   In this Act a trust deed in respect of which paragraphs 6 and 7 of this Schedule apply is referred to as a 'protected trust deed'.

9   Where the trustee under a protected trust deed has made the final distribution of the estate among the creditors, he shall, not more than 28 days after the final distribution, send to the Accountant in Bankruptcy for registration in the register of insolvencies—

(a)   a statement in the prescribed form indicating how the estate was realised and distributed; and

(b)   a certificate to the effect that the distribution was in accordance with the trust deed.

10   Where the trustee under a protected trust deed has obtained a discharge from the creditors who have acceded to the trust deed he shall forthwith give notice of the discharge—

(a)   by sending the notice by recorded delivery to every creditor known to him [who has not been sent a copy of the notice as mentioned in paragraph 5(1)(c) above or who has notified the trustee of his objection to the trust deed as mentioned in paragraph 5(1)(d) above]; and

(b)   by sending the notice to the Accountant in Bankruptcy who shall register the fact of the discharge in the register of insolvencies,

and, except where the court makes an order under paragraph 12 below, the sending of such notice to a creditor [who has not been sent a copy of the notice as mentioned in paragraph 5(1)(c) above or who has notified the trustee of his objection to the trust deed as mentioned in paragraph 5(1)(d) above] shall be effective to make the discharge binding upon that creditor.

Creditors not acceding to protected trust deed

11   A creditor who [has not been sent a copy of the notice as mentioned in paragraph 5(1)(c) above or who has notified the trustee of his objection to the trust deed as mentioned in paragraph 5(1)(d) above] may, not more than 28 days after

notice has been sent under paragraph 10 above, apply to the court for an order under paragraph 12 below.

12   Where, on an application by a creditor under paragraph 11 above, the court is satisfied (on grounds other than those on which a petition under paragraph 7(1)(b) above was or could have been presented by that creditor) that the intromissions of the trustee under the protected trust deed with the estate of the debtor have been so unduly prejudicial to that creditor's claim that he should not be bound by the discharge it may order that he shall not be so bound.

13   Where the court makes an order under paragraph 12 above, the clerk of court shall send a copy of the order to—
    (a)   the trustee; and
    (b)   the Accountant in Bankruptcy who shall register the copy of the order in the register of insolvencies.

SCHEDULE 7

PART II
RE-ENACTMENT OF CERTAIN PROVISIONS OF BANKRUPTCY (SCOTLAND) ACT 1913 (c 20)

Arrestments and poindings

24—(1)   Subject to sub-paragraph (2) below, all arrestments and [attachments] which have been executed within 60 days prior to the constitution of the apparent insolvency of the debtor, or within four months thereafter, shall be ranked *pari passu* as if they had all been executed on the same date.
    (2)   Any such arrestment which is executed on the dependence of an action shall be followed up without undue delay.
    (3)   Any creditor judicially producing in a process relative to the subject of such arrestment or [attachment] liquid grounds of debt or decree of payment within the 60 days or four months referred to in sub-paragraph (1) above shall be entitled to rank as if he had executed an arrestment or [an attachment]; and if the first or any subsequent arrester obtains in the meantime a decree of furthcoming, and recovers payment, or [an attaching] creditor carries through [an auction], he shall be accountable for the sum recovered to those who, by virtue of this Act, may be eventually found to have a right to a ranking *pari passu* thereon, and shall be liable in an action at their instance for payment to them proportionately, after allowing out of the fund the expense of such recovery.
    (4)   Arrestments executed for attaching the same effects of the debtor after the period of four months subsequent to the constitution of his apparent insolvency shall not compete with those within the said periods prior or subsequent thereto, but may rank with each other on any reversion of the fund attached in accordance with any enactment or rule of law relating thereto.
    (5)   Any reference in the foregoing provisions of this paragraph to a debtor shall be construed as including a reference to any entity whose apparent insolvency may, by virtue of subsection (5) of section 7 of this Act, be constituted under subsection (1) of that section.
    (6)   This paragraph shall apply in respect of arrestments and poindings which have been executed either before or after the coming into force of this paragraph.
    (7)   The repeal of the Bankruptcy (Scotland) Act 1913 shall not affect the equalisation of arrestments and poindings (whether executed before or after the coming into force of this paragraph) in consequence of the constitution of notour bankruptcy under that Act.

[(8) Nothing in this paragraph shall apply to an earnings arrestment, a current maintenance arrestment or a conjoined arrestment order.]

Exemptions from stamp duty or other duties for conveyances, deeds etc relating to sequestrated estates

25 Any—
(a) conveyance, assignation, instrument, discharge, writing, or deed relating solely to the estate of a debtor which has been or may be sequestrated, either under this or any former Act, being estate which after the execution of such conveyance, assignation, instrument, discharge, writing, or deed, shall be and remain the property of such debtor, for the benefit of his creditors, or the interim or permanent trustee appointed or chosen under or by virtue of such sequestration,
(b) discharge to such debtor,
(c) deed, assignation, instrument, or writing for reinventing the debtor in the estate,
(d) article of roup or sale, or submission,
(e) other instrument or writing whatsoever relating solely to the estate of any such debtor; and
(f) other deed or writing forming part of the proceedings ordered under such sequestration,
shall be exempt from all stamp duties or other Government duty.

CONSUMER PROTECTION ACT 1987
(1987, c 43)

PART I
PRODUCT LIABILITY

1 Purpose and construction of Part I
(1) This Part shall have effect for the purpose of making such provision as is necessary in order to comply with the product liability Directive and shall be construed accordingly.
(2) In this Part, except in so far as the context otherwise requires—
[. . .]
'dependant' and 'relative' have the same meaning as they have in, respectively, the Fatal Accidents Act 1976 and the Damages (Scotland) Act 1976;
'producer', in relation to a product, means—
(a) the person who manufactured it;
(b) in the case of a substance which has not been manufactured but has been won or abstracted, the person who won or abstracted it;
(c) in the case of a product which has not been manufactured, won or abstracted but essential characteristics of which are attributable to an industrial or other process having been carried out (for example, in relation to agricultural produce), the person who carried out that process;
'product' means any goods or electricity and (subject to subsection (3) below) includes a product which is comprised in another product, whether by virtue of being a component part or raw material or otherwise; and
'the product liability Directive' means the Directive of the Council of the European Communities, dated 25th July 1985, (No 85/374/EEC) on the approximation of the laws, regulations and administrative provisions of the member States concerning liability for defective products.
(3) For the purposes of this Part a person who supplies any product in which products are comprised, whether by virtue of being component parts or raw

materials or otherwise, shall not be treated by reason only of his supply of that product as supplying any of the products so comprised.

2 Liability for defective products

(1) Subject to the following provisions of this Part, where any damage is caused wholly or partly by a defect in a product, every person to whom subsection (2) below applies shall be liable for the damage.

(2) This subsection applies to—

(a) the producer of the product;

(b) any person who, by putting his name on the product or using a trade mark or other distinguishing mark in relation to the product, has held himself out to be the producer of the product;

(c) any person who has imported the product into a member State from a place outside the member States in order, in the course of any business of his, to supply it to another.

(3) Subject as aforesaid, where any damage is caused wholly or partly by a defect in a product, any person who supplied the product (whether to the person who suffered the damage, to the producer of any product in which the product in question is comprised or to any other person) shall be liable for the damage if—

(a) the person who suffered the damage requests the supplier to identify one or more of the persons (whether still in existence or not) to whom subsection (2) above applies in relation to the product;

(b) that request is made within a reasonable period after the damage occurs and at a time when it is not reasonably practicable for the person making the request to identify all those persons; and

(c) the supplier fails, within a reasonable period after receiving the request, either to comply with the request or to identify the person who supplied the product to him.

[. . .]

(5) Where two or more persons are liable by virtue of this Part for the same damage, their liability shall be joint and several.

(6) This section shall be without prejudice to any liability arising otherwise than by virtue of this Part.

3 Meaning of 'defect'

(1) Subject to the following provisions of the section, there is a defect in a product for the purposes of this Part if the safety of the product is not such as persons generally are entitled to expect; and for those purposes 'safety', in relation to a product, shall include safety with respect to products comprised in that product and safety in the context of risks of damage to property, as well as in the context of risks of death or personal injury.

(2) In determining for the purposes of subsection (1) above what persons generally are entitled to expect in relation to a product all the circumstances shall be taken into account, including—

(a) the manner in which, and purposes for which, the product has been marketed, its get-up, the use of any mark in relation to the product and any instructions for, or warnings with respect to, doing or refraining from doing anything with or in relation to the product;

(b) what might reasonably be expected to be done with or in relation to the product; and

(c) the time when the product was supplied by its producer to another;

and nothing in this section shall require a defect to be inferred from the fact alone that the safety of a product which is supplied after that time is greater than the safety of the product in question.

4 Defences

(1) In any civil proceedings by virtue of this Part against any person ('the

person proceeded against') in respect of a defect in a product it shall be a defence for him to show—

(a)   that the defect is attributable to compliance with any requirement imposed by or under any enactment or with any Community obligation; or

(b)   that the person proceeded against did not at any time supply the product to another; or

(c)   that the following conditions are satisfied, that is to say—

(i)   that the only supply of the product to another by the person proceeded against was otherwise than in the course of a business of that person's; and

(ii)   that section 2(2) above does not apply to that person or applies to him by virtue only of things done otherwise than with a view to profit; or

(d)   that the defect did not exist in the product at the relevant time; or

(e)   that the state of scientific and technical knowledge at the relevant time was not such that a producer of products of the same description as the product in question might be expected to have discovered the defect if it had existed in his products while they were under his control; or

(f)   that the defect—

(i)   constituted a defect in a product ('the subsequent product') in which the product in question had been comprised; and

(ii)   was wholly attributable to the design of the subsequent product or to compliance by the producer of the product in question with instructions given by the producer of the subsequent product.

(2)   In this section 'the relevant time', in relation to electricity, means the time at which it was generated, being a time before it was transmitted or distributed, and in relation to any other product, means—

(a)   if the person proceeded against is a person to whom subsection (2) of section 2 above applies in relation to the product, the time when he supplied the product to another;

(b)   if that subsection does not apply to that person in relation to the product, the time when the product was last supplied by a person to whom that subsection does apply in relation to the product.

5   Damage giving rise to liability

(1)   Subject to the following provisions of this section, in this Part 'damages' means death or personal injury or any loss of or damage to any property (including land).

(2)   A person shall not be liable under section 2 above in respect of any defect in a product for the loss of or any damage to the product itself or for the loss of or any damage to the whole or any part of any product which has been supplied with the product in question comprised in it.

(3)   A person shall not be liable under section 2 above for any loss of or damage to any property which, at the time it is lost or damaged, is not—

(a)   of a description of property ordinarily intended for private use, occupation or consumption; and

(b)   intended by the person suffering the loss or damage mainly for his own private use, occupation or consumption.

(4)   No damages shall be awarded to any person by virtue of this Part in respect of any loss of or damage to any property if the amount which would fall to be so awarded to that person, apart from this subsection and any liability for interest, does not exceed £275.

. . .

(8)   Subsections (5) to (7) above shall not extend to Scotland.

6   Application of certain enactments etc

(1)   Any damage for which a person is liable under section 2 above shall be deemed to have been caused—

(a)   for the purposes of the Fatal Accidents Act 1976, by that person's wrongful act, neglect or default;

(b)   for the purposes of section 3 of the Law Reform (Miscellaneous Provisions) (Scotland) Act 1940 (contribution among joint wrongdoers), by that person's wrongful act or negligent act or omission;

(c)   for the purposes of section 1 of the Damages (Scotland) Act 1976 (rights of relatives of a deceased), by that person's act or omission, and

(d)   for the purposes of Part II of the Administration of Justice Act 1982 (damages for personal injuries, etc—Scotland), by an act or omission giving rise to liability in that person to pay damages.

(2)   Where—

(a)   a person's death is caused wholly or partly by a defect in a product, or a person dies after suffering damage which has been so caused;

(b)   a request such as mentioned in paragraph (a) of subsection (3) of section 2 above is made to a supplier of the product by that person's personal representatives or, in the case of a person whose death is caused wholly or partly by the defect, by any dependant or relative of that person; and

(c)   the conditions specified in paragraphs (b) and (c) of that subsection are satisfied in relation to that request,

this Part shall have effect for the purposes of the Law Reform (Miscellaneous Provisions) Act 1934, the Fatal Accidents Acts 1976 and the Damages (Scotland) Act 1976 as if liability of the supplier to that person under that subsection did not depend on that person having requested the supplier to identify certain persons or on the said conditions having been satisfied in relation to a request made by that person.

(3)   Section 1 of the Congenital Disabilities (Civil Liability) Act 1976 shall have effect for the purposes of this Part as if—

(a)   a person were answerable to a child in respect of an occurrence caused wholly or partly by a defect in a product if he is or has been liable under section 2 above in respect of any effect of the occurrence on a parent of the child, or would be so liable if the occurrence caused a parent of the child to suffer damage;

(b)   the provisions of this Part relating to liability under section 2 above applied in relation to liability by virtue of paragraph (a) above under the said section 1; and

(c)   subsection (6) of the said section 1 (exclusion of liability) were omitted.

(4)   Where any damage is caused partly by a defect in a product and partly by the fault of the person suffering the damage, the Law Reform (Contributory Negligence) Act 1945 and section 5 of the Fatal Accidents Act 1976 (contributory negligence) shall have effect as if the defect were the fault of every person liable by virtue of this Part for the damage caused by the defect.

(5)   In subsection (4) above 'fault' has the same meaning as in the said Act of 1945.

(6)   Schedule 1 to this Act shall have effect for the purpose of amending the Limitation Act 1980 and the Prescription and Limitation (Scotland) Act 1973 in their application in relation to the bringing of actions by virtue of this Part.

(7)   It is hereby declared that liability by virtue of this Part is to be treated as liability in tort for the purposes of any enactment conferring jurisdiction on any court with respect to any matter.

(8)   Nothing in this Part shall prejudice the operation of section 12 of the Nuclear Installations Act 1965 (rights to compensation for certain breaches of duties confined to rights under that Act).

7   Prohibition on exclusions from liability

The liability of a person by virtue of this Part to person who has suffered damage caused wholly or partly by a defect in a product, or to a dependant or relative of such a person, shall not be limited or excluded by any contract term, by any notice or by any other provision.

8 Power to modify Part I

(1) Her Majesty may by Order in Council make such modifications of this Part and of any other enactment (including an enactment contained in the following Parts of this Act, or in an Act passed after this Act) as appear to Her Majesty in Council to be necessary or expedient in consequence of any modification of the product liability Directive which is made at any time after the passing of this Act.

(2) An Order in Council under subsection (1) above shall not be submitted to Her Majesty in Council unless a draft of the Order has been laid before, and approved by a resolution of, each House of Parliament.

9 Application of Part I to Crown

(1) Subject to subsection (2) below, this Part shall bind the Crown.

(2) The Crown shall not, as regards the Crown's liability by virtue of this Part, be bound by this Part further than the Crown is made liable in tort or in reparation under the Crown Proceedings Act 1947, as that Act has effect from time to time.

PART II
CONSUMER SAFETY

[. . .]

11 Safety regulations

(1) The Secretary of State may by regulations under this section ('safety regulations') make such provision as he considers appropriate [. . .] for the purpose of securing—

(a) that goods to which this section applies are safe;

(b) that goods to which this section applies which are unsafe, or would be unsafe in the hands of persons of a particular description, are not made available to persons generally or, as the case may be, to persons of that description, and

(c) that appropriate information is, and inappropriate information is not, provided in relation to goods to which this section applies.

(2) Without prejudice to the generality of subsection (1) above, safety regulations may contain provision—

(a) with respect to the composition or contents, design, construction, finish or packing of goods to which this section applies, with respect to standards for such goods and with respect to other matters relating to such goods;

(b) with respect to the giving, refusal, alteration or cancellation of approvals of such goods, of descriptions of such goods or of standards for such goods;

(c) with respect to the conditions that may be attached to any approval given under the regulations;

(d) for requiring such fees as may be determined by or under the regulations to be paid on the giving or alteration of any approval under the regulations and on the making of an application for such an approval or alteration;

(e) with respect to appeals against refusals, alterations and cancellations of approvals given under the regulations and against the conditions contained in such approvals;

(f) for requiring goods to which this section applies to be approved under the regulations or to conform to the requirements of the regulations or to descriptions or standards specified in or approved by or under the regulations;

(g) with respect to the testing or inspection of goods to which this section applies (including provision for determining the standards to be applied in carrying out any test or inspection);

(h) with respect to the way of dealing with goods of which some or all do not satisfy a test required by or under the regulations or a standard connected with a procedure so required;

(i)   for requiring a mark, warning or instruction or any other information relating to goods to be put on or to accompany the goods or to be used or provided in some other manner in relation to the goods, and for securing that inappropriate information is not given in relation to goods either by means of misleading marks or otherwise;

(j)   for prohibiting persons from supplying, or from offering to supply, agreeing to supply, exposing for supply or possessing for supply, goods to which this section applies and component parts and raw materials for such goods;

(k)   for requiring information to be given to any such person as may be determined by or under the regulations for the purpose of enabling that person to exercise any function conferred on him by the regulations.

(3)   Without prejudice as aforesaid, safety regulations may contain provision—

(a)   for requiring persons on whom functions are conferred by or under section 27 below to have regard, in exercising their functions so far as relating to any provision of safety regulations, to matters specified in a direction issued by the Secretary of State with respect to that provision;

(b)   for securing that a person shall not be guilty of an offence under section 12 below unless it is shown that the goods in question do not conform to a particular standard;

(c)   for securing that proceedings for such an offence are not brought in England and Wales except by or with the consent of the Secretary of State or the Director of Public Prosecutions;

(d)   for securing that proceedings for such an offence are not brought in Northern Ireland except by or with consent of the Secretary of State or the Director of Public Prosecutions for Northern Ireland;

(e)   for enabling a magistrate's court in England and Wales or Northern Ireland to try an information or, in Northern Ireland, a complaint in respect of such an offence if the information was laid or the complaint made within twelve months from the time when the offence was committed;

(f)   for enabling summary proceedings for such an offence to be brought in Scotland at any time within twelve months from the time when the offence was committed; and

(g)   for determining the persons by whom, and the manner in which, anything required to be done by or under the regulations is to be done.

(4)   Safety regulations shall not provide for any contravention of the regulations to be an offence.

(5)   Where the Secretary of State proposes to make safety regulations it shall be his duty before he makes them—

(a)   to consult such organisations as appear to him to be representative of interests substantially affected by the proposal;

(b)   to consult such other persons as he considers appropriate; and

(c)   in the case of proposed regulations relating to goods suitable for use at work to consult the Health and Safety Commission in relation to the application of the proposed regulations to Great Britain;

but the preceding provisions of this subsection shall not apply in the case of regulations which provide for the regulations to cease to have effect at the end of a period of not more than twelve months beginning with the day on which they come into force and which contain a statement that it appears to the Secretary of State that the need to protect the public requires that the regulations should be made without delay.

(6)   The power to make safety regulations shall be exercisable by statutory instrument subject to annulment in pursuance of a resolution of either House of Parliament and shall include power—

(a)   to make different provision for different cases; and

(b)   to make such supplemental, consequential and transitional provision as the Secretary of State considers appropriate.

(7) This section applies to any goods other than—

(a) growing crops and things comprised in land by virtue of being attached to it;

(b) water, food, feeding stuff and fertiliser;

(c) gas which is, is to be or has been supplied by a person authorised to supply it by or under [section 7A of the Gas Act 1986 (licensing of gas suppliers and gas shippers)];

(d) controlled drugs and licensed medicinal products.

12 Offences against the safety regulations

(1) Where safety regulations prohibit a person from supplying or offering or agreeing to supply any goods or from exposing or possessing any goods for supply that person shall be guilty of an offence if he contravenes the prohibition.

(2) Where safety regulations require a person who makes or processes any goods in the course of carrying on a business—

(a) to carry out a particular test or use a particular procedure in connection with the making or processing of the goods with a view to ascertaining whether the goods satisfy any requirements of such regulations; or

(b) to deal or not to deal in a particular way with a quantity of the goods of which the whole or part does not satisfy such a test or does not satisfy standards connected with such a procedure,

that person shall be guilty of an offence if he does not comply with the requirement.

(3) If a person contravenes a provision of safety regulations which prohibits or requires the provision, by means of a mark or otherwise, of information of a particular kind in relation to goods, he shall be guilty of an offence.

(4) Where safety regulations require any person to give information to another for the purpose of enabling that other to exercise any function, that person shall be guilty of an offence if—

(a) he fails without reasonable cause to comply with the requirement; or

(b) in giving the information which is required of him—

(i) he makes any statement which he knows is false in a material particular; or

(ii) he recklessly makes any statement which is false in a material particular.

(5) A person guilty of an offence under this section shall be liable on summary conviction to imprisonment for a term not exceeding six months or to a fine not exceeding level 5 on the standard scale or to both.

13 Prohibition notices and notices to warn

(1) The Secretary of State may—

(a) serve on any person a notice ('a prohibition notice') prohibiting that person, except with the consent of the Secretary of State, from supplying, or from offering to supply, agreeing to supply or possessing for supply, any relevant goods which the Secretary of State considers are unsafe and which are described in the notice;

(b) serve on any person a notice ('a notice to warn') requiring that person at his own expense to publish, in a form and manner and on occasions specified in the notice, a warning about any relevant goods which the Secretary of State considers are unsafe, which that person supplies or has supplied and which are described in the notice.

(2) Schedule 2 to this Act shall have effect with respect to prohibition notices and notices to warn, and the Secretary of State may by regulations make provision specifying the manner in which information is to be given to any person under that Schedule.

(3) A consent given by the Secretary of State for the purposes of a prohibition

notice may impose such conditions on the doing of anything for which the consent is required as the Secretary of State considers appropriate.

(4)   A person who contravenes a prohibition notice or a notice to warn shall be guilty of an offence and liable on summary conviction to imprisonment for a term not exceeding six months or to a fine not exceeding level 5 on the standard scale or to both.

(5)   The power to make regulations under subsection (2) above shall be exercisable by statutory instrument subject to annulment in pursuance of a resolution of either House of Parliament and shall include power—

(a)   to make different provision for different cases; and

(b)   to make such supplemental, consequential and transitional provision as the Secretary of State considers appropriate.

(6)   In this section 'relevant goods' means—

(a)   in relation to a prohibition notice, any goods to which section 11 above applies; and

(b)   in relation to a notice to warn, any goods to which that section applies or any growing crops or things comprised in land by virtue of being attached to it.

[(7)   A notice may not be given under this section in respect of any aspect of the safety of goods, or any risk or category of risk associated with goods, concerning which provision is contained in the General Product Safety Regulations 2005.]

14   Suspension notices

(1)   Where an enforcement authority has reasonable grounds for suspecting that any safety provision has been contravened in relation to any goods, the authority may serve a notice ('suspension notice') prohibiting the person on whom it is served, for such period ending not more than six months after the date of the notice as is specified therein, from doing any of the following things without the consent of the authority, that is to say, supplying the goods, offering to supply them, agreeing to supply them or exposing them for supply.

(2)   A suspension notice served by an enforcement authority in respect of any goods shall—

(a)   describe the goods in a manner sufficient to identify them;

(b)   set out the grounds on which the authority suspects that a safety provision has been contravened in relation to the goods, and

(c)   state that, and the manner in which, the person on whom the notice is served may appeal against the notice under section 15 below.

(3)   A suspension notice served by an enforcement authority for the purpose of prohibiting a person for any period from doing the things mentioned in subsection (1) above in relation to any goods may also require that person to keep the authority informed of the whereabouts throughout that period of any of those goods in which he has an interest.

(4)   Where a suspension notice has been served on any person in respect of any goods, no further such notice shall be served on that person in respect of the same goods unless—

(a)   proceedings against that person for an offence in respect of a contravention in relation to the goods of a safety provision (not being an offence under this section); or

(b)   proceedings for the forfeiture of the goods under section 16 or 17 below, are pending at the end of the period specified in the first-mentioned notice.

(5)   A consent given by an enforcement authority for the purposes of subsection (1) above may impose such conditions on the doing of anything for which the consent is required as the authority considers appropriate.

(6)   Any person who contravenes a suspension notice shall be guilty of an offence and liable on summary conviction to imprisonment for a term not exceeding six months or to a fine not exceeding level 5 on the standard scale or to both.

(7)   Where an enforcement authority serves a suspension notice in respect of

any goods, the authority shall be liable to pay compensation to any person having an interest in the goods in respect of any loss or damage caused by reason of the service of the notice if—

(a)   there has been no contravention in relation to the goods of any safety provision; and

(b)   the exercise of the power is not attributable to any neglect or default by that person.

(8)   Any disputed question as to the right to or the amount of any compensation payable under this section shall be determined by arbitration or, in Scotland, by a single arbiter appointed, failing agreement between the parties, by the sheriff.

15   Appeals against suspension notices

(1)   Any person having an interest in any goods in respect of which a suspension notice is for the time being in force may apply for an order setting aside the notice.

(2)   An application under this section may be made—

(a)   to any magistrates' court in which proceedings have been brought in England and Wales or Northern Ireland—

(i)   for an offence in respect of a contravention in relation to the goods of any safety provision; or

(ii)   for the forfeiture of the goods under section 16 below;

(b)   where no such proceedings have been so brought, by way of complaint to a magistrates' court; or

(c)   in Scotland, by summary application to the sheriff.

(3)   On an application under this section to a magistrates' court in England and Wales or Northern Ireland the court shall make an order setting aside the suspension notice only if the court is satisfied that there has been no contravention in relation to the goods of any safety provision.

(4)   On an application under this section to the sheriff he shall make an order setting aside the suspension notice only if he is satisfied that at the date of making the order—

(a)   proceedings for an offence in respect of a contravention in relation to the goods of any safety provision; or

(b)   proceedings for the forfeiture of the goods under section 17 below, have not been brought or, having been brought, have been concluded.

(5)   Any person aggrieved by an order made under this section by a magistrates' court in England and Wales or Northern Ireland, or by a decision of such a court not to make such an order, may appeal against that order or decision—

(a)   in England and Wales, to the Crown Court;

(b)   in Northern Ireland, to the county court;

and an order so made may contain such provision as appears to the court to be appropriate for delaying the coming into force of the order pending the making and determination of any appeal (including any application under section III of the Magistrates' Courts Act 1980 or Article 146 of the Magistrates' Courts (Northern Ireland) Order 1981 (statement of case)).

16   [*Does not apply to Scotland.*]

17   Forfeiture: Scotland

(1)   In Scotland a sheriff may make an order for forfeiture of any goods in relation to which there has been a contravention of a safety provision—

(a)   on an application by the procurator-fiscal made in the manner specified in [section 134 of the Criminal Procedure (Scotland) Act 1995]; or

(b)   where a person is convicted of any offence in respect of any such contravention, in addition to any other penalty which the sheriff may impose.

(2)   The procurator-fiscal making an application under subsection (1)(a) above

shall serve on any person appearing to him to be the owner of, or otherwise to have an interest in, the goods to which the application relates a copy of the application, together with a notice giving him the opportunity to appear at the hearing of the application to show cause why the goods should not be forfeited.

(3)   Service under subsection (2) above shall be carried out, and such service may be proved, in the manner specified for citation of accused in summary proceedings under the [Criminal Procedure (Scotland) Act 1995].

(4)   Any person upon whom notice is served under subsection (2) above and any other person claiming to be the owner of, or otherwise to have an interest in, goods to which an application under this section relates shall be entitled to appear at the hearing of the application to show cause why the goods should not be forfeited.

(5)   The sheriff shall not make an order following an application under subsection (1)(a) above—

(a)   if any person on whom notice is served under subsection (2) above does not appear, unless service of the notice on that person is proved; or

(b)   if no notice under subsection (2) above has been served, unless the court is satisfied that in the circumstances it was reasonable not to serve notice on any person.

(6)   The sheriff shall make an order under this section only if he is satisfied that there has been a contravention in relation to those goods of a safety provision.

(7)   For the avoidance of doubt it is declared that the sheriff may infer for the purposes of this section that there has been a contravention in relation to any goods of a safety provision if he is satisfied that any such provision has been contravened in relation to any goods which are representative of those goods (whether by reason of being of the same design or part of the same consignment or batch or otherwise).

(8)   Where an order for the forfeiture of any goods is made following an application by the procurator-fiscal under subsection (1)(a) above, any person who appeared, or was entitled to appear, to show cause why goods should not be forfeited may, within twenty-one days of the making of the order, appeal to the High Court by Bill of Suspension on the ground of an alleged miscarriage of justice; [and section 182(5)(a) to (e) of the Criminal Procedure (Scotland) Act 1995 shall apply to an appeal under this subsection as it applies to a stated case under Part X of that Act].

(9)   An order following an application under subsection (1)(a) above shall not take effect—

(a)   until the end of the period of twenty-one days beginning with the day after the day on which the order is made; or

(b)   if an appeal is made under subsection (8) above within that period, until the appeal is determined or abandoned.

(10)   An order under subsection (1)(b) above shall not take effect—

(a)   until the end of the period within which an appeal against the order could be brought under the Criminal Procedure (Scotland) Act 1995; or

(b)   if an appeal is made within that period, until the appeal is determined or abandoned.

(11)   Subject to subsection (12) below, goods forfeited under this section shall be destroyed in accordance with such directions as the sheriff may give.

(12)   If he thinks fit the sheriff may direct that the goods be released, to such person as he may specify, on condition that that person does not supply those goods to any other person otherwise than as mentioned in section 46(7)(a) or (b) below.

18   Power to obtain information

(1)   If the Secretary of State considers that, for the purpose of deciding whether—

    (a)   to make, vary or revoke any safety regulations; or

    (b)   to serve, vary or revoke a prohibition notice; or

    (c)   to serve or revoke a notice to warn,

he requires information which another person is likely to be able to furnish, the Secretary of State may serve on the other person a notice under this section.

(2)   A notice served on any person under this section may require that person—

    (a)   to furnish to the Secretary of State, within a period specified in the notice, such information as is so specified;

    (b)   to produce such records as are specified in the notice at a time and place so specified and to permit a person appointed by the Secretary of State for the purpose to take copies of the records at that time and place.

(3)   A person shall be guilty of an offence if he—

    (a)   fails, without reasonable cause, to comply with a notice served on him under this section; or

    (b)   in purporting to comply with a requirement which by virtue of paragraph (a) of subsection (2) above is contained in such a notice—

        (i)   furnishes information which he knows is false in a material particular; or

        (ii)   recklessly furnishes information which is false in a material particular.

(4)   A person guilty of an offence under subsection (3) above shall—

    (a)   in the case of an offence under paragraph (a) of that subsection, be liable on summary conviction to a fine not exceeding level 5 on the standard scale; and

    (b)   in the case of an offence under paragraph (b) of that subsection be liable—

        (i)   on conviction on indictment, to a fine,

        (ii)   on summary conviction, to a fine not exceeding the statutory maximum.

19 Interpretation of Part II

(1)   in this Part—

'controlled drug' means a controlled drug within the meaning of the Misuse of Drugs Act 1971;

'feeding stuff' and 'fertiliser' have the same meaning as in Part IV of the Agriculture Act 1970;

'food' does not include anything containing tobacco but, subject to that, has the same meaning as in the [Food Safety Act 1990] or, in relation to Northern Ireland, the same meaning as in the Food and Drugs Act (Northern Ireland) 1958;

'licensed medicinal product' means—

    (a)   any medicinal product within the meaning of the Medicines Act 1968 in respect of which a product licence within the meaning of that Act is for the time being in force; or

    (b)   any other article or substance in respect of which any such licence is for the time being in force in pursuance of an order under section 104 or 105 of that Act (application of Act to other articles and substances);

'safe', in relation to any goods, means such that there is no risk, or no risk apart from one reduced to a minimum, that any of the following will (whether immediately or after a definite or indefinite period) cause the death of, or any personal injury to, any person whatsoever, that is to say—

    (a)   the goods;

    (b)   the keeping, use or consumption of the goods;

    (c)   the assembly of any of the goods which are, or are to be supplied unassembled;

    (d)   any emission or leakage from the goods or, as a result of the keeping, use or consumption of the goods, from anything else; or

    (e)   reliance on the accuracy of any measurement, calculation or other reading made by or by means of the goods, and [. . .] 'unsafe' shall be construed accordingly;

'tobacco' includes any tobacco product within the meaning of the Tobacco Products Duty Act 1979 and any article or substance containing tobacco and intended for oral or nasal use.

(2)   In the definition of 'safe' in subsection (1) above, references to the keeping, use or consumption of any goods are references to—

(a)   the keeping, use or consumption of the goods by the persons by whom, and in all or any of the ways or circumstances in which, they might reasonably be expected to be kept, used or consumed; and

(b)   the keeping, use or consumption of the goods either alone or in conjunction with other goods in conjunction with which they might reasonably be expected to be kept, used or consumed.

PART III
MISLEADING PRICE INDICATIONS

20   Offence of giving misleading indication

(1)   Subject to the following provisions of this Part, a person shall be guilty of an offence if, in the course of any business of his, he gives (by any means whatever) to any consumers an indication which is misleading as to the price at which any goods, services, accommodation or facilities are available (whether generally or from particular persons).

(2)   Subject as aforesaid, a person shall be guilty of an offence if—

(a)   in the course of any business of his, he has given an indication to any consumers which, after it was given, has become misleading as mentioned in subsection (1) above; and

(b)   some or all of those consumers might reasonably be expected to rely on the indication at a time after it has become misleading; and

(c)   he fails to take all such steps as are reasonable to prevent those consumers from relying on the indication.

(3)   For the purposes of this section it shall be immaterial—

(a)   whether the person who gives or gave the indication is or was acting on his own behalf or on behalf of another;

(b)   whether or not that person is the person, or included among the persons, from whom the goods, services, accommodation or facilities are available; and

(c)   whether the indication is or has become misleading in relation to all the consumers to whom it is or was given or only in relation to some of them.

(4)   A person guilty of an offence under subsection (1) or (2) above shall be liable—

(a)   on conviction on indictment, to a fine;

(b)   on summary conviction, to a fine not exceeding the statutory maximum.

(5)   No prosecution for an offence under subsection (1) or (2) above shall be brought after whichever is the earlier of the following, that is to say—

(a)   the end of the period of three years beginning with the day on which the offence was committed; and

(b)   the end of the period of one year beginning with the day on which the person bringing the prosecution discovered that the offence had been committed.

[(5A)   A person is not guilty of an offence under subsection (1) or (2) above if, in giving the misleading indication which would otherwise constitute an offence under either of those subsections, he is guilty of an offence under section 397 of the Financial Services and Markets Act 2000 (misleading statements and practices).]

(6)   In this Part—

'consumer'—

(a)   in relation to any goods, means any person who might wish to be supplied with the goods for his own private use or consumption;

(b)   in relation to any services or facilities, means any person who might wish to be provided with the services or facilities otherwise than for the purposes of any business of his; and

(c)   in relation to any accommodation, means any person who might wish to occupy the accommodation otherwise than for the purposes of any business of his;

'price', in relation to any goods, services, accommodation or facilities, means—

(a)   the aggregate of the sums required to be paid by a consumer for or otherwise in respect of the supply of the goods or the provision of the services, accommodation or facilities; or

(b)   except in section 21 below, any method which will be or has been applied for the purpose of determining that aggregate.

21   Meaning of 'misleading'

(1)   For the purposes of section 20 above an indication given to any consumers is misleading as to a price if what is conveyed by the indication, or what those consumers might reasonably be expected to infer from the indication or any omission from it, includes any of the following, that is to say—

(a)   that the price is less than in fact it is;

(b)   that the applicability of the price does not depend on facts or circumstances on which its applicability does in fact depend;

(c)   that the price covers matters in respect of which an additional charge is in fact made;

(d)   that a person who in fact has no such expectation—

(i)   expects the price to be increased or reduced (whether or not at a particular time or by a particular amount); or

(ii)   expects the price, or the price as increased or reduced, to be maintained (whether or not for a particular period); or

(e)   that the facts or circumstances by reference to which the consumers might reasonably be expected to judge the validity of any relevant comparison made or implied by the indication are not what in fact they are.

(2)   For the purpose of section 20 above, an indication given to any consumers is misleading as to a method of determining a price if what is conveyed by the indication, or what those consumers might reasonably be expected to infer from the indication or any omission from it, includes any of the following, that is to say—

(a)   that the method is not what in fact it is;

(b)   that the applicability of the method does not depend on facts or circumstances on which its applicability does in fact depend;

(c)   that the method takes into account matters in respect of which an additional charge will in fact be made;

(d)   that a person who in fact has no such expectation—

(i)   expects the method to be altered (whether or not at a particular time or in a particular respect); or

(ii)   expects the method, or that method as altered, to remain unaltered (whether or not for a particular period); or

(e)   that the facts or circumstances by reference to which the consumers might reasonably be expected to judge the validity of any relevant comparison made or implied by the indication are not what in fact they are.

(3)   For the purposes of subsection (1)(e) and (2)(e) above a comparison is a relevant comparison in relation to a price or method of determining a price if it is made between that price or that method, or any price which has been or may be determined by that method, and

(a)   any price or value which is stated or implied to be, to have been or to be likely to be attributed to the goods, services, accommodation or facilities in question or to any other goods, services, accommodation or facilities; or

(b)   any method, or other method, which is stated or implied to be, to have been or to be likely to be applied or applicable for the determination of the price or value of the goods, services, accommodation or facilities in question or of the price or value of any other goods, services, accommodation or facilities.

22   Application to provision of services and facilities

(1)   Subject to the following provisions of this section, references in this Part to services or facilities are references to any services or facilities whatever including, in particular—

(a)   the provision of credit or of banking or insurance services and the provision of facilities incidental to the provision of such services;

(b)   the purchase or sale of foreign currency;

(c)   the supply of electricity;

(d)   the provision of a place, other than on a highway, for the parking of a motor vehicle;

(e)   the making of arrangements for a person to put or keep a caravan on any land other than arrangements by virtue of which that person may occupy the caravan as his only or main residence.

(2)   References in this Part to services shall not include references to services provided to an employer under a contract of employment.

[. . .]

(4)   In relation to a service consisting in the purchase or sale of foreign currency, references in this Part to the method by which the price of the service is determined shall include references to the rate of exchange.

(5)   In this section—

[. . .]

'caravan' has the same meaning as in the Caravan Sites and Control of Development Act 1960;

'contract of employment' and 'employer' have the same meanings as in [the Employment Rights Act 1996];

'credit' has the same meaning as in the Consumer Credit Act 1974.

23   Application to provision of accommodation etc

(1)   Subject to subsection (2) below, references in this Part to accommodation or facilities being available shall not include references to accommodation or facilities being available to be provided by means of the creation or disposal of an interest in land except where—

(a)   the person who is to create or dispose of the interest will do so in the course of any business of his; and

(b)   the interest to be created or disposed of is a relevant interest in a new dwelling and is to be created or disposed of for the purpose of enabling that dwelling to be occupied as a residence, or one of the residences, of the person acquiring the interest.

(2)   Subsection (1) above shall not prevent the application of any provision of this Part in relation to—

(a)   the supply of any goods as part of the same transaction as any creation or disposal of an interest in land; or

(b)   the provision of any services or facilities for the purpose of, or in connection with, any transaction for the creation or disposal of such an interest.

(3)   In this section—

'new dwelling' means any building or part of a building in Great Britain which—

(a)   has been constructed or adapted to be occupied as a residence; and

(b)   has not previously been so occupied or has been so occupied only with other premises or as more than one residence, and includes any yard, garden, out-houses or appurtenances which belong to that building or part or are to be enjoyed with it;

'relevant interest'—

(a)   in relation to a new dwelling in England and Wales, means the freehold estate in the dwelling or a leasehold interest in the dwelling for a term of years absolute of more than twenty-one years, not being a term of which twenty-one years or less remains unexpired;

(b)   in relation to a new dwelling in Scotland, means the [ownership] of the land comprising the dwelling, or a leasehold interest in the dwelling where twenty-one years or more remains unexpired.

24   Defences

(1)   In any proceedings against a person for an offence under subsection (1) or (2) of section 20 above in respect of any indication it shall be a defence for that person to show that his acts or omissions were authorised for the purposes of this subsection by regulations made under section 26 below.

(2)   In proceedings against a person for an offence under subsection (1) or (2) of section 20 above in respect of an indication published in a book, newspaper, magazine [or film or in a programme included in a programme service (within the meaning of the Broadcasting Act 1990),] it shall be a defence for that person to show that the indication was not contained in an advertisement.

(3)   In proceedings against a person for an offence under subsection (1) or (2) of section 20 above in respect of an indication published in an advertisement it shall be a defence for that person to show that—

(a)   he is a person who carries on a business of publishing or arranging for the publication of advertisements;

(b)   he received the advertisement for publication in the ordinary course of that business; and

(c)   at the time of publication he did not know and had no grounds for suspecting that the publication would involve the commission of the offence.

(4)   In any proceedings against a person for an offence under subsection (1) of section 20 above in respect of any indication, it shall be a defence for that person to show that—

(a)   the indication did not relate to the availability from him of any goods, services, accommodation or facilities;

(b)   a price had been recommended to every person from whom the goods, services, accommodation or facilities were indicated as being available;

(c)   the indication related to that price and was misleading as to that price only by reason of a failure by any person to follow the recommendation; and

(d)   it was reasonable for the person who gave the indication to assume that the recommendation was for the most part being followed.

(5)   The provisions of this section are without prejudice to the provisions of section 39 below.

(6)   In this section—

'advertisement' includes a catalogue, a circular and a price list.

25   Code of practice

(1)   The Secretary of State may, after consulting the [Office of Fair Trading] and such other persons as the Secretary of State considers it appropriate to consult, by order approve any code of practice issued (whether by the Secretary of State or another person) for the purpose of—

(a)   giving practical guidance with respect to any of the requirements of section 20 above; and

(b)   promoting what appear to the Secretary of State to be desirable practices as to the circumstances and manner in which any person gives an indication as to the price at which any goods, services, accommodation or facilities are available or indicates any other matter in respect of which any such indication may be misleading.

(2)   A contravention of a code of practice approved under this section shall not of itself give rise to any criminal or civil liability, but in any proceedings against any person for an offence under section 20(1) or (2) above—

(a)   any contravention by that person of such a code may be relied on in relation to any matter for the purpose of establishing that that person committed the offence or of negativing any defence; and

(b)   compliance by that person with such a code may be relied on in relation to any matter for the purpose of showing that the commission of the offence by that person has not been established or that that person has a defence.

(3)   Where the Secretary of State approves a code of practice under this section he may, after such consultation as is mentioned in subsection (1) above, at any time by order—

(a)   approve any modification of the code; or

(b)   withdraw his approval;

and references in subsection (2) above to a code of practice approved under this section shall be construed accordingly.

(4)   The power to make an order under this section shall be exercisable by statutory instrument subject to annulment in pursuance of a resolution of either House of Parliament.

26   Power to make regulations

(1)   The Secretary of State may, after consulting the [Office of Fair Trading] and such other persons as the Secretary of State considers it appropriate to consult, by regulations make provision—

(a)   for the purpose of regulating the circumstances and manner in which any person—

(i)   gives any indication as to the price at which any goods, services, accommodation or facilities will be or are available or have been supplied or provided; or

(ii)   indicates any other matter in respect of which any such indication may be misleading;

(b)   for the purpose of facilitating the enforcement of the provisions of section 20 above or of any regulations made under this section.

(2)   The Secretary of State shall not make regulations by virtue of subsection (1)(a) above except in relation to—

(a)   indications given by persons in the course of business; and

(b)   such indications given otherwise than in the course of business as—

(i)   are given by or on behalf of persons by whom accommodation is provided to others by means of leases or licences; and

(ii)   relate to goods, services or facilities supplied or provided to those others in connection with the provision of the accommodation.

(3)   Without prejudice to the generality of subsection (1) above, regulations under this section may—

(a)   prohibit an indication as to a price from referring to such matters as may be prescribed by the regulations;

(b)   require an indication as to a price or other matter to be accompanied or supplemented by such explanation or such additional information as may be prescribed by the regulations;

(c)   require information or explanations with respect to a price or other matter to be given to an officer of an enforcement authority and to authorise such an officer to require such information or explanations to be given;

(d)   require any information or explanation provided for the purposes of any regulations made by virtue of paragraph (b) or (c) above to be accurate;

(e) prohibit the inclusion in indications as to a price or other matter of statements that the indications are not to be relied upon;

(f) provide that expressions used in any indication as to a price or other matter shall be construed in a particular way for the purposes of this Part;

(g) provide that a contravention of any provision of the regulations shall constitute a criminal offence punishable—

(i) on conviction on indictment, by a fine;

(ii) on summary conviction, by a fine not exceeding the statutory maximum;

(h) apply any provision of this Act which relates to a criminal offence created by virtue of paragraph (g) above.

(4) The power to make regulations under this section shall be exercisable by statutory instrument subject to annulment in pursuance of a resolution of either House of Parliament and shall include power—

(a) to make different provision for different cases, and

(b) to make such supplemental, consequential and transitional provision as the Secretary of State considers appropriate.

(5) In this section 'lease' includes a sub-lease and an agreement for a lease and a statutory tenancy (within the meaning of the Landlord and Tenant Act 1985 or the Rent (Scotland) Act 1984).

PART IV
ENFORCEMENT OF PARTS II AND III

27 Enforcement

(1) Subject to the following provisions of this section—

(a) it shall be the duty of every weights and measures authority in Great Britain to enforce within their area the safety provisions and the provisions made by or under Part III of this Act; and

(b) it shall be the duty of every district council in Northern Ireland to enforce within their area the safety provisions.

(2) The Secretary of State may by regulations—

(a) wholly or partly transfer any duty imposed by subsection (1) above on a weights and measures authority or a district council in Northern Ireland to such other person who has agreed to the transfer as is specified in the regulations;

(b) relieve such an authority or council of any such duty so far as it is exercisable in relation to such goods as may be described in the regulations.

(3) The power to make regulations under subsection (2) above shall be exercisable by statutory instrument subject to annulment in pursuance of a resolution of either House of Parliament and shall include power—

(a) to make different provision for different cases; and

(b) to make such supplemental, consequential and transitional provision as the Secretary of State considers appropriate.

(4) Nothing in this section shall authorise any weights and measures authority, or any person on whom functions are conferred by regulations under subsection (2) above, to bring proceedings in Scotland for an offence.

28 Test purchases

(1) An enforcement authority shall have power, for the purpose of ascertaining whether any safety provision or any provision made by or under Part III of this Act has been contravened in relation to any goods, services, accommodation or facilities—

(a) to make, or to authorise an officer of the authority to make, any purchase of any goods; or

(b) to secure, or to authorise an officer of the authority to secure, the provision of any services, accommodation or facilities.

(2) Where—

(a)   any goods purchased under this section by or on behalf of an enforcement authority are submitted to a test; and

(b)   the test leads to—

(i)   the bringing of proceedings for an offence in respect of a contravention in relation to the goods of any safety provision or of any provision made by or under Part III of this Act or for the forfeiture of the goods under section 16 or 17 above; or

(ii)   the serving of a suspension notice in respect of any goods; and

(c)   the authority is requested to do so and it is practicable for the authority to comply with the request,

the authority shall allow the person from whom the goods were purchased or any person who is a party to the proceedings or has an interest in any goods to which the notice relates to have the goods tested.

(3)   The Secretary of State may by regulations provide that any test of goods under this section by or on behalf of an enforcement authority shall—

(a)   be carried out at the expense of the authority in a manner and by a person prescribed by or determined under the regulations; or

(b)   be carried out either as mentioned in paragraph (a) above or by the authority in a manner prescribed by the regulations.

(4)   The power to make regulations under subsection (3) above shall be exercisable by statutory instrument subject to annulment in pursuance of a resolution of either House of Parliament and shall include power—

(a)   to make different provision for different cases; and

(b)   to make such supplemental, consequential and transitional provision as the Secretary of State considers appropriate.

(5)   Nothing in this section shall authorise the acquisition by or on behalf of an enforcement authority of any interest in land.

29   Powers of search etc

(1)   Subject to the following provisions of this Part, a duly authorised officer of an enforcement authority may at any reasonable hour and on production, if required, of his credentials exercise any of the powers conferred by the following provisions of this section.

(2)   The officer may, for the purpose of ascertaining whether there has been any contravention of any safety provision or of any provision made by or under Part III of this Act, inspect any goods and enter any premises other than premises occupied only as a person's residence.

(3)   The officer may, for the purpose of ascertaining whether there has been any contravention of any safety provision, examine any procedure (including any arrangements for carrying out a test) connected with the production of any goods.

(4)   If the officer has reasonable grounds for suspecting that any goods are manufactured or imported goods which have not been supplied in the United Kingdom since they were manufactured or imported he may—

(a)   for the purpose of ascertaining whether there has been any contravention of any safety provision in relation to the goods, require any person carrying on a business, or employed in connection with a business, to produce any records relating to the business;

(b)   for the purpose of ascertaining (by testing or otherwise) whether there has been any such contravention, seize and detain the goods;

(c)   take copies of, or of any entry in, any records produced by virtue of paragraph (a) above.

(5)   If the officer has reasonable grounds for suspecting that there has been a contravention in relation to any goods of any safety provision or of any provision made by or under Part III of this Act, he may—

(a)   for the purpose of ascertaining whether there has been any such contravention, require any person carrying on a business, or employed in connection with a business, to produce any records relating to the business;

(b) for the purpose of ascertaining (by testing or otherwise) whether there has been any such contravention, seize and detain the goods;

(c) take copies of, or of any entry in, any records produced by virtue of paragraph (a) above.

(6) The officer may seize and detain—

(a) any goods or records which he has reasonable grounds for believing may be required as evidence in proceedings for an offence in respect of a contravention of any safety provision or of any provision made by or under Part III of this Act;

(b) any goods which he has reasonable grounds for suspecting may be liable to be forfeited under section 16 or 17 above.

(7) If and to the extent that it is reasonably necessary to do so to prevent a contravention of any safety provision or of any provision made by or under Part III of this Act, the officer may, for the purpose of exercising his power under sub-section (4), (5) or (6) above to seize any goods or records—

(a) require any person having authority to do so to open any container or to open any vending machine; and

(b) himself open or break open any such container or machine where a requirement made under paragraph (a) above in relation to the container or machine has not been complied with.

30 Provisions supplemental to s 29

(1) An officer seizing any goods or records under section 29 above shall inform the following persons that the goods or records have been so seized, that is to say—

(a) the person from whom they are seized; and

(b) in the case of imported goods seized on any premises under the control of the Commissioners of Customs and Excise, the importer of those goods (within the meaning of the Customs and Excise Management Act 1979).

(2) If a justice of the peace—

(a) is satisfied by any written information on oath that there are reasonable grounds for believing either—

(i) that any goods or records which any officer has power to inspect under section 29 above are on any premises and that their inspection is likely to disclose evidence that there has been a contravention of any safety provision or of any provision made by or under Part III of this Act; or

(ii) that such a contravention has taken place, is taking place or is about to take place on any premises; and

(b) is also satisfied by any such information either—

(i) that admission to the premises has been or is likely to be refused and that notice of intention to apply for a warrant under this section has been given to the occupier; or

(ii) that an application for admission, or the giving of such a notice, would defeat the object of entry or that the premises are unoccupied or that the occupier is temporarily absent and it might defeat the object of the entry to await his return, the justice may by warrant under his hand, which shall continue in force for a period of one month, authorise any officer of an enforcement authority to enter the premises, if need be by force.

(3) An officer entering any premises by virtue of section 29 above or a warrant under subsection (2) above may take with him such other persons and such equipment as may appear to him necessary.

(4) On leaving any premises which a person is authorised to enter by a warrant under subsection (2) above, that person shall, if the premises are unoccupied or the

occupier is temporarily absent, leave the premises as effectively secured against trespassers as he found them.

(5) If any person who is not an officer of an enforcement authority purports to act as such under section 29 above of this section he shall be guilty of an offence and liable on summary conviction to a fine not exceeding level 5 on the standard scale.

(6) Where any goods seized by an officer under section 29 above are submitted to a test, the officer shall inform the persons mentioned in subsection (1) above of the result of the test and, if—

(a) proceedings are brought for an offence in respect of a contravention in relation to the goods of any safety provision or of any provision made by or under Part III of this Act or for the forfeiture of the goods under section 16 or 17 above, or a suspension notice is served in respect of any goods; and

(b) the officer is requested to do so and it is practicable to comply with the request, the officer shall allow any person who is a party to the proceedings or, as the case may be, has an interest in the goods to which the notice relates to have the goods tested.

(7) The Secretary of State may by regulations provide that any test of goods seized under section 29 above by an officer of an enforcement authority shall—

(a) be carried out at the expense of the authority in a manner and by a person prescribed by or determined under the regulations; or

(b) be carried out either as mentioned in paragraph (a) above or by the authority in a manner prescribed by the regulations.

(8) The power to make regulations under subsection (7) above shall be exercisable by statutory instrument subject to annulment in pursuance of a resolution of either House of Parliament and shall include power—

(a) to make different provision for different cases; and

(b) to make such supplemental, consequential and transitional provisions as the Secretary of State considers appropriate.

(9) In the application of this section to Scotland, the reference in subsection (2) above to a justice of the peace shall include a reference to a sheriff and the references to written information on oath shall be construed as references to evidence on oath.

(10) In the application of this section to Northern Ireland, the references in subsection (2) above to any information on oath shall be construed as references to any complaint on oath.

31 Power of customs officer to detain goods

(1) A customs officer may, for the purpose of facilitating the exercise by an enforcement authority or officer of such an authority of any functions conferred on the authority or officer by or under Part II of this Act, or by or under this Part in its application for the purposes of the safety provisions, seize any imported goods and detain them for not more than two working days.

(2) Anything seized and detained under this section shall be dealt with during the period of its detention in such manner as the Commissioners of Customs and Excise may direct.

(3) In subsection (1) above the reference to two working days is a reference to a period of forty-eight hours calculated from the time when the goods in question are seized but disregarding so much of any period as falls on a Saturday or Sunday or on Christmas Day, Good Friday or a day which is a bank holiday under the Banking and Financial Dealings Act 1971 in the part of the United Kingdom where the goods are seized.

(4) In this section and section 32 below 'customs officer' means any officer within the meaning of the Customs and Excise Management Act 1979.

32 Obstruction of authorised officer

(1) Any person who—

(a)   intentionally obstructs any officer of an enforcement authority who is acting in pursuance of any provision of this Part or any customs officer who is so acting; or

(b)   intentionally fails to comply with any requirements made of him by any officer of an enforcement authority under any provision of this Part, or

(c)   without reasonable cause fails to give any officer of an enforcement authority who is so acting any other assistance or information which the officer may reasonably require of him for the purposes of the exercise of the officer's functions under any provision of this Part,

shall be guilty of an offence and liable on summary conviction to a fine not exceeding level 5 on the standard scale.

(2)   A person shall be guilty of an offence if, in giving any information which is required of him by virtue of subsection (1)(c) above—

(a)   he makes any statement which he knows is false in a material particular, or

(b)   he recklessly makes a statement which is false in a material particular.

(3)   A person guilty of an offence under subsection (2) above shall be liable—

(a)   on conviction on indictment to a fine;

(b)   on summary conviction, to a fine not exceeding the statutory maximum.

33   Appeals against detention of goods

(1)   Any person having an interest in any goods which are for the time being detained under any provision of this Part by an enforcement authority or by an officer of such an authority may apply for an order requiring the goods to be released to him or to another person.

(2)   An application under this section may be made—

(a)   to any magistrates' court in which proceedings have been brought in England and Wales or Northern Ireland—

(i)   for an offence in respect of a contravention in relation to the goods of any safety provision or of any provision made by or under Part III of this Act; or

(ii)   for the forfeiture of the goods under section 16 above;

(b)   where no such proceedings have been so brought, by way of complaint to a magistrates' court; or

(c)   makes an order under section 16 or 17 above for the forfeiture of any goods.

(2)   The court may (in addition to any other order it may make as to costs or expenses) order the person convicted or, as the case may be, any person having an interest in the goods to reimburse an enforcement authority for any expenditure which has been or may be incurred by that authority—

(a)   in connection with any seizure or detention of the goods by or on behalf of the authority; or

(b)   in connection with any compliance by the authority with directions by the court for the purposes of any order for the forfeiture of the goods.

PART V
MISCELLANEOUS AND SUPPLEMENTAL

36   [*Amends Health and Safety at Work etc Act 1974*]

37   [Power of Commissioners for Revenue and Customs to disclose information]

(1)   If they think it appropriate to do so for the purpose of facilitating the exercise by any person to whom subsection (2) below applies of any function conferred on that person by or under Part II of this Act, or by or under Part IV of this Act in its application for the purposes of the safety provisions, [the Commissioners for Her Majesty's Revenue and Customs] may authorise the disclosure to that person

of any information obtained [or held] for the purposes of the exercise by [Her Majesty's Revenue and Customs] of their functions in relation to imported goods.

(2)   This subsection applies to an enforcement authority and to any officer of an enforcement authority.

(3)   A disclosure of information made to any person under subsection (1) above shall be made in such manner as may be directed by [Her Majesty's Revenue and Customs] and may be through such persons acting on behalf of that person as may be so directed.

(4)   Information may be disclosed to a person under subsection (1) above whether or not the disclosure of the information has been requested by or on behalf of that person.

[. . .]

39   Defence of due diligence

(1)   Subject to the following provisions of this section, in proceedings against any person for an offence to which this section applies it shall be a defence for that person to show that he took all reasonable steps and exercised all due diligence to avoid committing the offence.

(2)   Where in any proceedings against any person for such an offence the defence provided by subsection (1) above involves an allegation that the commission of the offence was due—

(a)   to the act or default of another; or

(b)   to reliance on information given by another,

that person shall not, without the leave of the court, be entitled to rely on the defence unless, not less than seven clear days before the hearing of the proceedings, he has served a notice under subsection (3) below on the person bringing the proceedings.

(3)   A notice under this subsection shall give such information identifying or assisting in the identification of the person who committed the act or default or gave the information as is in the possession of the person serving the notice at the time he serves it.

(4)   It is hereby declared that a person shall not be entitled to rely on the defence provided by subsection (1) above by reason of his reliance on information supplied by another, unless he shows that it was reasonable in all the circumstances for him to have relied on the information, having regard in particular—

(a)   to the steps which he took, and those which might reasonably have been taken, for the purpose of verifying the information, and

(b)   to whether he had any reason to disbelieve the information.

(5)   This section shall apply to an offence under section [. . .] 12(1), (2) or (3), 13(4), 14(6) or 20(1) above.

40   Liability of persons other than principal offender

(1)   Where the commission by any person of an offence to which section 39 above applies is due to an act or default committed by some other person in the course of any business of his, the other person shall be guilty of the offence and may be proceeded against and punished by virtue of this subsection whether or not proceedings are taken against the first-mentioned person.

(2)   Where a body corporate is guilty of an offence under this Act (including where it is so guilty by virtue of subsection (1) above) in respect of any act or default which is shown to have been committed with the consent or connivance of, or to be attributable to any neglect on the part of, any director, manager, secretary or other similar officer of the body corporate or any person who was purporting to act in any such capacity he, as well as the body corporate, shall be guilty of that offence and shall be liable to be proceeded against and punished accordingly.

(3)   Where the affairs of a body corporate are managed by its members, subsection (2) above shall apply in relation to the acts and defaults of a member in

connection with his functions of management as if he were a director of the body corporate.

41 Civil proceedings

(1) An obligation imposed by safety regulations shall be a duty owed to any person who may be affected by a contravention of the obligation and, subject to any provisions to the contrary in the regulations and to the defences and other incidents applying to actions for breach of statutory duty, a contravention of any such obligation shall be actionable accordingly.

(2) This Act shall not be construed as conferring any other right of action in civil proceedings, apart from the right conferred by virtue of Part I of this Act, in respect of any loss or damage suffered in consequence of a contravention of a safety provision or of a provision made by or under Part III of this Act.

(3) Subject to any provision to the contrary in the agreement itself, an agreement shall not be void or unenforceable by reason only of a contravention of a safety provision or of a provision made by or under Part III of this Act.

(4) Liability by virtue of subsection (1) above shall not be limited or excluded by any contract term, by any notice or (subject to the power contained in subsection (1) above to limit or exclude it in safety regulations) by any other provision.

(5) Nothing in subsection (1) above shall prejudice the operation of section 12 of the Nuclear Installations Act 1965 (rights to compensation for certain breaches of duties confined to rights under that Act).

(6) In this section 'damage' includes personal injury and death.

42 Reports etc

(1) It shall be the duty of the Secretary of State at least once in every five years to lay before each House of Parliament a report on the exercise during the period to which the report relates of the functions which under Part II of this Act, or under Part IV of this Act in its application for the purposes of the safety provisions, are exercisable by the Secretary of State, weights and measures authorities, district councils in Northern Ireland and persons on whom functions are conferred by regulations made under section 27(2) above.

(2) The Secretary of State may from time to time prepare and lay before each House of Parliament such other reports on the exercise of those functions as he considers appropriate.

(3) Every weights and measures authority, every district council in Northern Ireland and every person on whom functions are conferred by regulations under subsection (2) of section 27 above shall, whenever the Secretary of State so directs, make a report to the Secretary of State on the exercise of the functions exercisable by that authority or council under that section or by that person by virtue of any such regulations.

(4) A report under subsection (3) above shall be in such form and shall contain such particulars as are specified in the direction of the Secretary of State.

(5) The first report under subsection (1) above shall be laid before each House of Parliament not more than five years after the laying of the last report under section 8(2) of the Consumer Safety Act 1978.

43 Financial provisions

(1) There shall be paid out of money provided by Parliament—

(a) any expenses incurred or compensation payable by a Minister of the Crown or Government department in consequence of any provision of this Act; and

(b) any increase attributable to this Act in the sums payable out of money so provided under any other Act.

(2) Any sums received by a Minister of the Crown or Government department by virtue of this Act shall be paid into the Consolidated Fund.

44 Service of documents etc

(1) Any documents required or authorised by virtue of this Act to be served on a person may be so served—

(a) by delivering it to him or by leaving it at his proper address or by sending it by post to him at that address; or

(b) if the person is a body corporate, by serving it in accordance with paragraph (a) above on the secretary or clerk of that body; or

(c) if the person is a partnership, by serving it in accordance with that paragraph on a partner or on a person having control or management of the partnership business.

(2) For the purposes of subsection (1) above, and for the purposes of section 7 of the Interpretation Act 1978 (which relates to the service of documents by post) in its application to that subsection, the proper address of any person on whom a document is to be served by virtue of this Act shall be his last known address except that—

(a) in the case of service on a body corporate or its secretary or clerk, it shall be the address of the registered or principal office of the body corporate;

(b) in the case of service on a partnership or a partner or a person having the control or management of a partnership business, it shall be the principal office of the partnership; and for the purposes of this subsection the principal office of a company registered outside the United Kingdom or of a partnership carrying on business outside the United Kingdom is its principal office within the United Kingdom.

(3) The Secretary of State may by regulations make provision for the manner in which any information is to be given to any person under any provision of Part IV of this Act.

(4) Without prejudice to the generality of subsection (3) above regulations made by the Secretary of State may prescribe the person, or manner of determining the person, who is to be treated for the purposes of section 28(2) or 30 above as the person from whom goods were purchased or seized where the goods were purchased or seized from a vending machine.

(5) The power to make regulations under subsection (3) or (4) above shall be exercisable by statutory instrument subject to annulment in pursuance of a resolution of either House of Parliament and shall include power—

(a) to make different provision for different cases; and

(b) to make such supplemental, consequential and transitional provision as the Secretary of State considers appropriate.

45 Interpretation

(1) In this Act, except in so far as the context otherwise requires—

'aircraft' includes gliders, balloons and hovercraft;

'business' includes a trade or profession and the activities of a professional or trade association or of a local authority or other public authority;

'conditional sale agreement', 'credit-sale agreement' and 'hire-purchase agreement' have the same meanings as in the Consumer Credit Act 1974 but as if in the definitions in that Act 'goods' had the same meaning as in this Act;

'contravention' includes a failure to comply and cognate expressions shall be construed accordingly;

'enforcement authority' means the Secretary of State, any other Minister of the Crown in charge of a Government department, any such department and any authority, council or other person on whom functions under this Act are conferred by or under section 27 above;

'gas' has the same meaning as in Part I of the Gas Act 1986;

'goods' includes substances, growing crops and things comprised in land by virtue of being attached to it and any ship, aircraft or vehicle;

'information' includes accounts, estimates and returns;

'magistrates' court', in relation to Northern Ireland, means a court of summary jurisdiction;

'modifications' includes additions, alterations and omissions, and cognate expressions shall be construed accordingly;

'motor vehicle' has the same meaning as in the Road Traffic Act 1972;

'notice' means a notice in writing;

'notice to warn' means a notice under section 13(1)(b) above;

'officer', in relation to an enforcement authority, means a person authorised in writing to assist the authority in carrying out its functions under or for the purposes of the enforcement of any of the safety provisions or of any of the provisions made by or under Part III of this Act;

'personal injury' includes any disease and any other impairment of a person's physical or mental condition;

'premises' includes any place and any ship, aircraft or vehicle;

'prohibition notice' means a notice under section 13(1)(a) above;

'records' includes any books or documents and any records in non-documentary form;

'safety provision' means [. . .] any provision of safety regulations, a prohibition notice or a suspension notice;

'safety regulations' means regulations under section 11 above;

'ship' includes any boat and any other description of vessel used in navigation;

'subordinate legislation' has the same meaning as in the Interpretation Act 1978;

'substance' means any natural or artificial substance, whether in solid, liquid or gaseous form or in the form of a vapour, and includes substances that are comprised in or mixed with other goods;

'supply' and cognate expressions shall be construed in accordance with section 46 below;

'suspension notice' means a notice under section 14 above.

(2)   Except in so far as the context otherwise requires, references in this Act to a contravention of a safety provision shall, in relation to any goods, include references to anything which would constitute such a contravention if the goods were supplied to any person.

(3)   References in this Act to any goods in relation to which any safety provision has been or may have been contravened shall include references to any goods which it is not reasonably practicable to separate from any such goods.

(4)   Section 68(2) of the Trade Marks Act 1938 (construction of references to use of a mark) shall apply for the purposes of this Act as it applies for the purposes of that Act.

(5)   In Scotland, any reference in this Act to things comprised in land by virtue of being attached to it is a reference to moveables which have become heritable by accession to heritable property.

46   Meaning of 'supply'

(1)   Subject to the following provisions of this section, references in this Act to supplying goods shall be construed as references to doing any of the following, whether as principal or agent, that is to say—

(a)   selling, hiring out or lending the goods;

(b)   entering into a hire-purchase agreement to furnish the goods;

(c)   the performance of any contract for work and materials to furnish the goods;

(d)   providing the goods in exchange for any consideration [. . .] other than money;

(e)   providing the goods in or in connection with the performance of any statutory function; or

(f)   giving the goods as a prize or otherwise making a gift of the goods;

and, in relation to gas or water, those references shall be construed as including references to providing the service by which the gas or water is made available for use.

(2)   For the purposes of any reference in this Act to supplying goods, where a person ('the ostensible supplier') supplies goods to another person ('the customer') under a hire-purchase agreement, conditional sale agreement or credit-sale agreement or under an agreement for the hiring of goods (other than a hire-purchase agreement) and the ostensible supplier—

(a)   carries on the business of financing the provision of goods for others by means of such agreements; and

(b)   in the course of that business acquired his interest in the goods supplied to the customer as a means of financing the provision of them for the customer by a further person ('the effective supplier'),

the effective supplier and not the ostensible supplier shall be treated as supplying the goods to the customer.

(3)   Subject to subsection (4) below, the performance of any contract by the erection of any building or structure on any land or by the carrying out of any other building works shall be treated for the purposes of this Act as a supply of goods in so far as, but only in so far as, it involves the provision of any goods to any person by means of their incorporation into the building, structure or works.

(4)   Except for the purposes of, and in relation to, notices to warn or any provision made by or under Part III of this Act, references in this Act to supplying goods shall not include references to supplying goods comprised in land where the supply is effected by the creation or disposal of an interest in the land.

(5)   Except in Part I of this Act references in this Act to a person's supplying goods shall be confined to references to that person's supplying goods in the course of a business of his, but for the purposes of this subsection it shall be immaterial whether the business is a business of dealing in the goods.

(6)   For the purposes of subsection (5) above goods shall not be treated as supplied in the course of a business if they are supplied, in pursuance of an obligation arising under or in connection with the insurance of the goods, to the person with whom they were insured.

(7)   Except for the purposes of, and in relation to, prohibition notices or suspension notices, references in Parts II to IV of this Act to supplying goods shall not include—

(a)   references to supplying goods where the person supplied carries on a business of buying goods of the same description as those goods and repairing or reconditioning them,

(b)   references to supplying goods by a sale of articles as scrap (that is to say, for the value of materials included in the articles rather than for the value of the articles themselves).

(8)   Where any goods have at any time been supplied by being hired out or lent to any person, neither a continuation or renewal of the hire or loan (whether on the same or different terms) nor any transaction for the transfer after that time of any interest in the goods to the person to whom they were hired or lent shall be treated for the purposes of this Act as a further supply of the goods to that person.

(9)   A ship, aircraft or motor vehicle shall not be treated for the purposes of this Act as supplied to any person by reason only that services consisting in the carriage of goods or passengers in that ship, aircraft or vehicle, or in its use for any other purpose, are provided to that person in pursuance of an agreement relating to the use of the ship, aircraft or vehicle for a particular period or for particular voyages, flights or journeys.

47   Savings for certain privileges

(1)   Nothing in this Act shall be taken as requiring any person to produce any records if he would be entitled to refuse to produce those records in any proceedings in any court on the ground that they are the subject of legal professional

privilege or, in Scotland, that they contain a confidential communication made by or to an advocate or solicitor in that capacity, or as authorising any person to take possession of any records which are in the possession of a person who would be so entitled.

(2)   Nothing in this Act shall be construed as requiring a person to answer any question or give any information if to do so would incriminate that person or that person's spouse [or civil partner].

48   [*Minor and consequential amendments and repeals*]

49   [*Northern Ireland*]

50   Short title, commencement and transitional provision
(1)   This Act may be cited as the Consumer Protection Act 1987.
(2)   This Act shall come into force on such day as the Secretary of State may by order made by statutory instrument appoint, and different days may be so appointed for different provisions or for different purposes.
. . .

SCHEDULES

SCHEDULE 2
PROHIBITION NOTICES AND NOTICES TO WARN
Section 13

PART I
PROHIBITION NOTICES

1   A prohibition notice in respect of any goods shall—
(a)   state that the Secretary of State considers that the goods are unsafe;
(b)   set out the reasons why the Secretary of State considers that the goods are unsafe;
(c)   specify the day on which the notice is to come into force; and
(d)   state that the trader may at any time make representations in writing to the Secretary of State for the purpose of establishing that the goods are safe.
2—(1)   If representations in writing about a prohibition notice are made by the trader to the Secretary of State, it shall be the duty of the Secretary of State to consider whether to revoke the notice and—
(a)   if he decides to revoke it, to do so;
(b)   in any other case, to appoint a person to consider those representations, any further representations made (whether in writing or orally) by the trader about the notice and the statements of any witnesses examined under this Part of this Schedule.
(2)   Where the Secretary of State has appointed a person to consider representations about a prohibition notice, he shall serve a notification on the trader which—
(a)   states that the trader may make oral representations to the appointed person for the purpose of establishing that the goods to which the notice relates are safe; and
(b)   specifies the place and time at which the oral representations may be made.
(3)   The time specified in a notification served under sub-paragraph (2) above shall not be before the end of the period of twenty-one days beginning with the day on which the notification is served, unless the trader otherwise agrees.
(4)   A person on whom a notification has been served under sub-paragraph (2) above or his representative may, at the place and time specified in the notification—

(a)   make oral representations to the appointed person for the purpose of establishing that the goods in question are safe; and

(b)   call and examine witnesses in connection with representations.

3—(1)   Where representations in writing about a prohibition notice are made by the trader to the Secretary of State at any time after a person has been appointed to consider representations about that notice, then, whether or not the appointed person has made a report to the Secretary of State, the following provisions of this paragraph shall apply instead of paragraph 2 above.

(2)   The Secretary of State shall, before the end of the period of one month beginning with the day on which he receives the representations, serve a notification on the trader which states—

(a)   that the Secretary of State has decided to revoke the notice, has decided to vary it or, as the case may be, has decided neither to revoke nor to vary it; or

(b)   that, a person having been appointed to consider representations about the notice, the trader may, at a place and time specified in the notification, make oral representations to the appointed person for the purpose of establishing that the goods to which the notice relates are safe.

(3)   The time specified in a notification served for the purposes of sub-paragraph (2)(b) above shall not be before the end of the period of twenty-one days beginning with the day on which the notification is served, unless the trader otherwise agrees or the time is the time already specified for the purposes of paragraph 2(2)(b) above.

(4)   A person on whom a notification has been served for the purposes of sub-paragraph (2)(b) above or his representative may, at the place and time specified in the notification—

(a)   make oral representations to the appointed person for the purpose of establishing that the goods in question are safe; and

(b)   call and examine witnesses in connection with the representations.

4—(1)   Where a person is appointed to consider representations about a prohibition notice, it shall be his duty to consider—

(a)   any written representations made by the trader about the notice, other than those in respect of which a notification is served under paragraph 3(2)(a) above;

(b)   any oral representations made under paragraph 2(4) or 3(4) above; and

(c)   any statements made by witnesses in connection with the oral representations, and after considering any matters under this paragraph, to make a report (including recommendations) to the Secretary of State about the matters considered by him and the notice.

(2)   It shall be the duty of the Secretary of State to consider any report made to him under sub-paragraph (1) above and, after considering the report, to inform the trader of his decision with respect to the prohibition notice to which the report relates.

5—(1)   The Secretary of State may revoke or vary a prohibition notice by serving on the trader a notification stating that the notice is revoked or, as the case may be, is varied as specified in the notification.

(2)   The Secretary of State shall not vary a prohibition notice so as to make the effect of the notice more restrictive for the trader.

(3)   Without prejudice to the power conferred by section 13(2) of this Act, the service of a notification under sub-paragraph (1) above shall be sufficient to satisfy the requirement of paragraph 4(2) above that the trader shall be informed of the Secretary of State's decision.

PART II
NOTICES TO WARN

6—(1)   If the Secretary of State proposes to serve a notice to warn on any person in respect of any goods, the Secretary of State, before he serves the notice shall serve on that person a notification which—

(a)   contains a draft of the proposed notice;

(b)   states that the Secretary of State proposes to serve a notice in the form of the draft on that person;

(c)   states that the Secretary of State considers that the goods described in the draft are unsafe;

(d)   sets out the reasons why the Secretary of State considers that those goods are unsafe; and

(e)   states that that person may make representations to the Secretary of State for the purpose of establishing that the goods are safe if, before the end of the period of fourteen days beginning with the day on which the notification is served, he informs the Secretary of State—

(i)   of his intention to make representations; and

(ii)   whether the representations will be made only in writing or both in writing and orally.

(2)   Where the Secretary of State has served a notification containing a draft of a proposed notice to warn on any person, he shall not serve a notice to warn on that person in respect of the goods to which the proposed notice relates unless—

(a)   the period of fourteen days beginning with the day on which the notification was served expires without the Secretary of State being informed as mentioned in sub-paragraph (1)(e) above;

(b)   the period of twenty-eight days beginning with that day expires without any written representations being made by that person to the Secretary of State about the proposed notice; or

(c)   the Secretary of State has considered a report about the proposed notice by a person appointed under paragraph 7(1) below.

7—(1)   Where a person on whom a notification containing a draft of a proposed notice to warn has been served—

(a)   informs the Secretary of State as mentioned in paragraph 6(1)(e) above before the end of the period of fourteen days beginning with the day on which the notification was served; and

(b)   makes written representations to the Secretary of State about the proposed notice before the end of the period of twenty-eight days beginning with that day, the Secretary of State shall appoint a person to consider those representations, any further representations made by that person about the draft notice and the statements of any witnesses examined under this Part of this Schedule.

(2)   Where—

(a)   the Secretary of State has appointed a person to consider representations about a proposed notice to warn; and

(b)   the person whose representations are to be considered has informed the Secretary of State for the purposes of paragraph 6(1)(e) above that the representations he intends to make will include oral representations, the Secretary of State shall inform the person intending to make the representations of the place and time at which oral representations may be made to the appointed person.

(3)   Where a person on whom a notification containing a draft of a proposed notice to warn has been served is informed of a time for the purposes of sub-paragraph (2) above, that time shall not be—

(a)   before the end of the period of twenty-eight days beginning with the day on which the notification was served; or

(b)   before the end of the period of seven days beginning with the day on which that person is informed of the time.

(4)   A person who has been informed of a place and time for the purposes of sub-paragraph (2) above or his representative may, at that place and time—

(a)   make oral representations to the appointed person for the purpose of establishing that the goods to which the proposed notice relates are safe; and

(b)   call and examine witnesses in connection with the representations.

8—(1)   Where a person is appointed to consider representations about a proposed notice to warn, it shall be his duty to consider—

(a)   any written representations made by the person on whom it is proposed to serve the notice; and

(b)   in a case where a place and time has been appointed under paragraph 7(2) above for oral representations to be made by that person or his representative, any representations so made and any statements made by witnesses in connection with those representations,

and, after considering those matters to make a report (including recommendations) to the Secretary of State about the matters considered by him and the proposal to serve the notice.

(2)   It shall be the duty of the Secretary of State to consider any report made to him under sub-paragraph (1) above, and after considering the report, to inform the person on whom it was proposed that a notice to warn should be served of his decision with respect to the proposal.

(3)   If at any time after serving a notification on a person under paragraph 6 above the Secretary of State decides not to serve on that person either the proposed notice to warn or that notice with modifications, the Secretary of State shall inform that person of the decision, and nothing done for the purposes of any of the preceding provisions of this Part of this Schedule before that person was so informed shall—

(a)   entitle the Secretary of State subsequently to serve the proposed notice or the notice with modifications; or

(b)   require the Secretary of State, or any person appointed to consider representations about the proposed notice, subsequently to do anything in respect of, or in consequence of, any such representations.

(4)   Where a notification containing a draft of a proposed notice to warn is served on a person in respect of any goods, a notice to warn served on him in consequence of a decision made under sub-paragraph (2) above shall either be in the form of the draft or shall be less onerous than the draft.

9   The Secretary of State may revoke a notice to warn by serving on the person on whom the notice was served a notification stating that the notice is revoked.

PART III
GENERAL

10—(1)   Where in a notification served on any person under this Schedule the Secretary of State has appointed a time for the making of oral representations or the examination of witnesses, he may, by giving that person such notification as the Secretary of State considers appropriate, change that time to a later time or appoint further times at which further representations may be made or the examination of witnesses may be continued; and paragraphs 2(4), 3(4) and 7(4) above shall have effect accordingly.

(2)   For the purposes of this Schedule the Secretary of State may appoint a person (instead of the appointed person) to consider any representations or statements, if the person originally appointed, or last appointed under this sub-paragraph, to consider those representations or statements has died or appears to the Secretary of State to be otherwise unable to act.

11   In this Schedule—

'the appointed person' in relation to a prohibition notice or a proposal to serve a notice to warn, means the person for the time being appointed under this Schedule to consider representations about the notice or, as the case may be, about the proposed notice;

'notification' means a notification in writing;

'trader', in relation to a prohibition notice, means the person on whom the notice is or was served.

CONTRACTS (APPLICABLE LAW) ACT 1990
(1990, c 36)

1 Meaning of 'the Conventions'

In this Act—

(a) 'the Rome Convention' means the Convention on the law applicable to contractual obligations opened for signature in Rome on 19th June 1980 and signed by the United Kingdom on 7th December 1981;

(b) 'the Luxembourg Convention' means the Convention on the accession of the Hellenic Republic to the Rome Convention signed by the United Kingdom in Luxembourg on 10th April 1984; and

(c) 'the Brussels Protocol' means the first Protocol on the interpretation of the Rome Convention by the European Court signed by the United Kingdom in Brussels on 19th December 1988;

[(d) 'the Funchal Convention' means the Convention on the accession of the Kingdom of Spain and the Portuguese Republic to the Rome Convention and the Brussels Protocol, with adjustments made to the Rome Convention by the Luxembourg Convention, signed by the United Kingdom in Funchal on 18th May 1992;

(e) 'the 1996 Accession Convention' means the Convention on the accession of the Republic of Austria, the Republic of Finland and the Kingdom of Sweden to the Rome Convention and the Brussels Protocol, with the adjustments made to the Rome Convention by the Luxembourg Convention and the Funchal Convention, signed by the United Kingdom in Brussels on 29th November 1996;

and these Conventions and this Protocol are together referred to as 'the Conventions'.]

2 Conventions to have force of law

(1) Subject to subsections (2) and (3) below, the Conventions shall have the force of law in the United Kingdom.

[(1A) The internal law for the purposes of Article 1(3) of the Rome Convention is the provisions of the regulations for the time being in force under section 424(3) of the Financial Services and Markets Act 2000.]

(2) Articles 7(1) and 10(1)(e) of the Rome Convention shall not have the force of law in the United Kingdom.

(3) Notwithstanding Article 19(2) of the Rome Convention the Conventions shall apply in the case of conflicts between the laws of different parts of the United Kingdom.

(4) For ease of reference there are set out in Schedules [1, 2, 3, 3A and 3B to this Act respectively the English texts of—

(a) the Rome Convention;

(b) the Luxembourg Convention; [. . .]

(c) the Brussels Protocol;

[(d) the Funchal Convention; and

(e) the 1996 Accession Convention.]

3 Interpretation of Conventions

(1) Any question as to the meaning or effect of any provision of the Conventions shall, if not referred to the European Court in accordance with the Brussels Protocol, be determined in accordance with the principles laid down by and any relevant decision of, the European Court.

(2) Judicial notice shall be taken of any decision of, or expression of opinion by, the European Court on any such question.

(3)   Without prejudice to any practice of the courts as to the matters which may be considered apart from this subsection—

(a)   the report on the Rome Convention by Professor Mario Giuliano and Professor Paul Lagarde which is reproduced in the Official Journal of the Communities of 31st October 1980 may be considered in ascertaining the meaning or effect of any provision of that Convention; and

(b)   any report on the Brussels Protocol which is reproduced in the Official Journal of the Communities may be considered in ascertaining the meaning or effect of any provision of that Protocol.

4   Revision of Conventions etc

(1)   If at any time it appears to Her Majesty in Council that Her Majesty's Government in the United Kingdom—

(a)   have agreed to a revision of any of the Conventions (including, in particular, any revision connected with the accession to the Rome Convention of any state), or

(b)   have given notification in accordance with Article 22(3) of the Rome Convention that either or both of the provisions mentioned in section 2(2) above shall have the force of law in the United Kingdom,

Her Majesty may by Order in Council make such consequential modifications of this Act or any other statutory provision, whenever passed or made, as Her Majesty considers appropriate.

(2)   An Order in Council under subsection (1) above shall not be made unless a draft of the Order has been laid before Parliament and approved by a resolution of each House.

(3)   In subsection (1) above—

'modifications' includes additions, omissions and alterations;

'revision' means an omission from, addition to or alteration of any of the Conventions and includes replacement of any of the Conventions to any extent by another convention, protocol or other description of international agreement; and

'statutory provision' means any provision contained in an Act, or in any Northern Ireland legislation, or in—

(a)   subordinate legislation (as defined in section 21(1) of the Interpretation Act 1978); or

(b)   any instrument of a legislative character made under any Northern Ireland legislation.

5   Consequential amendments

The enactments specified in Schedule 4 to this Act shall have effect subject to the amendments specified in that Schedule.

6   Application to Crown

This Act binds the Crown.

7   Commencement

This Act shall come into force on such day as the Lord Chancellor and the Lord Advocate may by order made by statutory instrument appoint; and different days may be appointed for different provisions or different purposes.

8   Extent

(1)   This Act extends to Northern Ireland.

(2)   Her Majesty may by Order in Council direct that all or any of the provisions of this Act shall extend to any of the following territories, namely—

(a)   the Isle of Man;

(b)   any of the Channel Islands;

(c)   Gibraltar;

(d)   the Sovereign Base Areas of Akrotiri and Dhekelia (that is to say, the areas mentioned in section 2(1) of the Cyprus Act 1960).

(3)   An Order in Council under subsection (2) above may modify this Act in its application to any of the territories mentioned in that subsection and may contain such supplementary provisions as Her Majesty considers appropriate; and in this subsection 'modify' shall be construed in accordance with section 4 above.

9   Short title
This Act may be cited as the Contracts (Applicable Law) Act 1990.

SCHEDULES

SCHEDULE 1
THE ROME CONVENTION

The High Contracting Parties to the Treaty establishing the European Economic Community,

Anxious to continue in the field of private international law the work of unification of law which has already been done within the Community, in particular in the field of jurisdiction and enforcement of judgments,

Wishing to establish uniform rules concerning the law applicable to contractual obligations,

Have agreed as follows:

TITLE I
SCOPE OF THE CONVENTION

Article 1. Scope of the Convention

1   The rules of this Convention shall apply to contractual obligations in any situation involving a choice between the laws of different countries.

2   They shall not apply to:

(a)   questions involving the status or legal capacity of natural persons, without prejudice to Article 11;

(b)   contractual obligations relating to:

—wills and succession,

—rights in property arising out of a matrimonial relationship,

—rights and duties arising out of a family relationship, parentage, marriage or affinity, including maintenance obligations in respect of children who are not legitimate;

(c)   obligations arising under bills of exchange, cheques and promissory notes and other negotiable instruments to the extent that the obligations under such other negotiable instruments arise out of their negotiable character;

(d)   arbitration agreements and agreements on the choice of court;

(e)   questions governed by the law of companies and other bodies corporate or unincorporate such as the creation, by registration or otherwise, legal capacity, internal organisation or winding up of companies and other bodies corporate or unincorporate and the personal liability of officers and members as such for the obligations of the company or body;

(f)   the question whether an agent is able to bind a principal or an organ to bind a company or body corporate or unincorporate, to a third party;

(g)   the constitution of trusts and the relationship between settlers, trustees and beneficiaries;

(h)   evidence and procedure, without prejudice to Article 14.

3   The rules of this Convention do not apply to contracts of insurance which cover risks situated in the territories of the Member States of the European Economic Community. In order to determine whether a risk is situated in these territories the court shall apply its internal law.

4   The preceding paragraph does not apply to contracts of re-insurance.

Article 2. Application of law of non-contracting States
Any law specified by this Convention shall be applied whether or not it is the law of a Contracting State.

TITLE II
UNIFORM RULES

Article 3. Freedom of choice
1 A contract shall be governed by the law chosen by the parties. The choice must be express or demonstrated with reasonable certainty by the terms of the contract or the circumstances of the case. By their choice the parties can select the law applicable to the whole or a part only of the contract.

2 The parties may at any time agree to subject the contract to a law other than that which previously governed it, whether as a result of an earlier choice under this Article or of other provisions of this Convention. Any variation by the parties of the law to be applied made after the conclusion of the contract shall not prejudice its formal validity under Article 9 or adversely affect the rights of third parties.

3 The fact that the parties have chosen a foreign law, whether or not accompanied by the choice of a foreign tribunal, shall not, where all the other elements relevant to the situation at the time of the choice are connected with one country only, prejudice the application of rules of the law of that country which cannot be derogated from by contract, hereinafter called 'mandatory rules'.

4 The existence and validity of the consent of the parties as to the choice of the applicable law shall be determined in accordance with the provisions of Articles 8, 9 and 11.

Article 4. Applicable law in the absence of choice
1 To the extent that the law applicable to the contract has not been chosen in accordance with Article 3, the contract shall be governed by the law of the country with which it is most closely connected. Nevertheless, a severable part of the contract which has a closer connection with another country may by way of exception be governed by the law of that other country.

2 Subject to the provisions of paragraph 5 of this Article, it shall be presumed that the contract is most closely connected with the country where the party who is to effect the performance which is characteristic of the contract has, at the time of conclusion of the contract, his habitual residence, or, in the case of a body corporate or unincorporate, its central administration. However, if the contract is entered into in the course of that party's trade or profession, that country shall be the country in which the principal place of business is situated or, where under the terms of the contract the performance is to be effected through a place of business other than the principal place of business, the country in which that other place of business is situated.

3 Notwithstanding the provisions of paragraph 2 of this Article, to the extent that the subject matter of the contract is a right in immovable property or a right to use immovable property it shall be presumed that the contract is most closely connected with the country where the immovable property is situated.

4 A contract for the carriage of goods shall not be subject to the presumption in paragraph 2. In such a contract if the country in which, at the time the contract is concluded, the carrier has his principal place of business is also the country in which the place of loading or the place of discharge or the principal place of business of the consignor is situated, it shall be presumed that the contract is most closely connected with that country. In applying this paragraph single voyage charter-parties and other contracts the main purpose of which is the carriage of goods shall be treated as contracts for the carriage of goods.

5 Paragraph 2 shall not apply if the characteristic performance cannot be determined, and the presumptions in paragraphs 2, 3 and 4 shall be disregarded if it

appears from the circumstances as a whole that the contract is more closely connected with another country.

Article 5. Certain consumer contracts

1   This Article applies to a contract the object of which is the supply of goods or services to a person ('the consumer') for a purpose which can be regarded as being outside his trade or profession, or a contract for the provision of credit for that object.

2   Notwithstanding the provisions of Article 3, a choice of law made by the parties shall not have the result of depriving the consumer of the protection afforded to him by the mandatory rules of the law of the country in which he has his habitual residence:

—if in that country the conclusion of the contract was preceded by a specific invitation addressed to him or by advertising, and he had taken in that country all the steps necessary on his part for the conclusion of the contract, or

—if the other party or his agent received the consumer's order in that country, or

—if the contract is for the sale of goods and the consumer travelled from that country to another country and there gave his order, provided that the consumer's journey was arranged by the seller for the purpose of inducing the consumer to buy.

3   Notwithstanding the provisions of Article 4, a contract to which this Article applies shall, in the absence of choice in accordance with Article 3, be governed by the law of the country in which the consumer has his habitual residence if it is entered into in the circumstances described in paragraph 2 of this Article.

4   This Article shall not apply to:

(a)   a contract of carriage;

(b)   a contract for the supply of services where the services are to be supplied to the consumer exclusively in a country other than that in which he has his habitual residence.

5   Notwithstanding the provisions of paragraph 4, this Article shall apply to a contract which, for an inclusive price, provides for a combination of travel and accommodation.

Article 6. Individual employment contracts

1   Notwithstanding the provisions of Article 3, in a contract of employment a choice of law made by the parties shall not have the result of depriving the employee of the protection afforded to him by the mandatory rules of the law which would be applicable under paragraph 2 in the absence of choice.

2   Notwithstanding the provisions of Article 4, a contract of employment shall, in the absence of choice in accordance with Article 3, be governed:

(a)   by the law of the country in which the employee habitually carries out his work in performance of the contract, even if he is temporarily employed in another country; or

(b)   if the employee does not habitually carry out his work in any one country, by the law of the country in which the place of business through which he was engaged is situated;

unless it appears from the circumstances as a whole that the contract is more closely connected with another country, in which case the contract shall be governed by the law of that country.

Article 7. Mandatory rules

1   When applying under this Convention the law of a country, effect may be given to the mandatory rules of the law of another country with which the situation has a close connection, if and in so far as, under the law of the latter country, those rules must be applied whatever the law applicable to the contract. In considering whether to give effect to these mandatory rules, regard shall be had to

their nature and purpose and to the consequences of their application or non-application.

2   Nothing in this Convention shall restrict the application of the rules of the law of the forum in a situation where they are mandatory irrespective of the law otherwise applicable to the contract.

Article 8. Material validity

1   The existence and validity of a contract, or of any term of a contract, shall be determined by the law which would govern it under this Convention if the contract or term were valid.

2   Nevertheless a party may rely upon the law of the country in which he has his habitual residence to establish that he did not consent if it appears from the circumstances that it would not be reasonable to determine the effect of his conduct in accordance with the law specified in the preceding paragraph.

Article 9. Formal validity

1   A contract concluded between persons who are in the same country is formally valid if it satisfies the formal requirements of the law which governs it under this Convention or of the law of the country where it is concluded.

2   A contract concluded between persons who are in different countries is formally valid if it satisfies the formal requirements of the law which governs it under this Convention or of the law of one of those countries.

3   Where a contract is concluded by an agent, the country in which the agent acts is the relevant country for the purposes of paragraphs 1 and 2.

4   An act intended to have legal effect relating to an existing or contemplated contract is formally valid if it satisfies the formal requirements of the law which under this Convention governs or would govern the contract or of the law of the country where the act was done.

5   The provisions of the preceding paragraphs shall not apply to a contract to which Article 5 applies, concluded in the circumstances described in paragraph 2 of Article 5. The formal validity of such a contract is governed by the law of the country in which the consumer has his habitual residence.

6   Notwithstanding paragraphs 1 to 4 of this Article, a contract the subject matter of which is a right in immovable property or a right to use immovable property shall be subject to the mandatory requirements of form of the law of the country where the property is situated if by that law those requirements are imposed irrespective of the country where the contract is concluded and irrespective of the law governing the contract.

Article 10. Scope of the applicable law

1   The law applicable to a contract by virtue of Articles 3 to 6 and 12 of this Convention shall govern in particular:

   (a)   interpretation;
   (b)   performance;
   (c)   within the limits of the powers conferred on the court by its procedural law, the consequences of breach, including the assessment of damages in so far as it is governed by rules of law;
   (d)   the various ways of extinguishing obligations, and prescription and limitation of actions;
   (e)   the consequences of nullity of the contract.

2   In relation to the manner of performance and the steps to be taken in the event of defective performance regard shall be had to the law of the country in which performance takes place.

Article 11. Incapacity

In a contract concluded between persons who are in the same country, a natural person who would have capacity under the law of that country may invoke his incapacity resulting from another law only if the other party to the contract was aware of this incapacity at the time of the conclusion of the contract or was not aware thereof as a result of negligence.

Article 12. Voluntary assignment

1   The mutual obligations of assignor and assignee under a voluntary assignment of a right against another person ('the debtor') shall be governed by the law which under this Convention applies to the contract between the assignor and assignee.

2   The law governing the right to which the assignment relates shall determine its assignability, the relationship between the assignee and the debtor, the conditions under which the assignment can be invoked against the debtor and any question whether the debtor's obligations have been discharged.

Article 13. Subrogation

1   Where a person ('the creditor') has a contractual claim upon another ('the debtor'), and a third person has a duty to satisfy the creditor, or has in fact satisfied the creditor in discharge of that duty, the law which governs the third person's duty to satisfy the creditor shall determine whether the third person is entitled to exercise against the debtor the rights which the creditor had against the debtor under the law governing their relationship and, if so, whether he may do so in full or only to a limited extent.

2   The same rule applies where several persons are subject to the same contractual claim and one of them has satisfied the creditor.

Article 14. Burden of proof, etc

1   The law governing the contract under this Convention applies to the extent that it contains, in the law of contract, rules which raise presumptions of law or determine the burden of proof.

2   A contract or an act intended to have legal effect may be proved by any mode of proof recognised by the law of the forum or by any of the laws referred to in Article 9 under which that contract or act is formally valid, provided that such mode of proof can be administered by the forum.

Article 15. Exclusion of renvoi

The application of the law of any country specified by this Convention means the application of the rules of law in force in that country other than its rules of private international law.

Article 16. 'Ordre public'

The application of a rule of the law of any country specified by this Convention may be refused only if such application is manifestly incompatible with the public policy ('ordre public') of the forum.

Article 17. No retrospective effect

This Convention shall apply in a Contracting State to contracts made after the date on which this Convention has entered into force with respect to that State.

Article 18. Uniform interpretation

In the interpretation and application of the preceding uniform rules regard shall be had to their international character and to the desirability of achieving uniformity in their interpretation and application.

Article 19. States with more than one legal system

1   Where a State comprises several territorial units each of which has its own rules of law in respect of contractual obligations, each territorial unit shall be considered as a country for the purposes of identifying the law applicable under this Convention.

2   A State within which different territorial units have their own rules of law in respect of contractual obligations shall not be bound to apply this Convention to conflicts solely between the laws of such units.

Article 20. Precedence of Community law
This Convention shall not affect the application of provisions which, in relation to particular matters, lay down choice of law rules relating to contractual obligations and which are or will be contained in acts of the institutions of the European Communities or in national laws harmonised in implementation of such acts.

Article 21. Relationship with other conventions
This Convention shall not prejudice the application of international conventions to which a Contracting State is, or becomes, a party.

Article 22. Reservations
1   Any Contracting State may, at the time of signature, ratification, acceptance or approval, reserve the right not to apply:
    (a)   the provisions of Article 7(1);
    (b)   the provisions of Article 10(1)(e).
. . .
3   Any Contracting State may at any time withdraw a reservation which it has made; the reservation shall cease to have effect on the first day of the third calendar month after notification of the withdrawal.

TITLE III
FINAL PROVISIONS

Article 23
1   If, after the date on which this Convention has entered into force for a Contracting State, that State wishes to adopt any new choice of law rule in regard to any particular category of contract within the scope of this Convention, it shall communicate its intention to the other signatory States through the Secretary-General of the Council of the European Communities.
2   Any signatory State may, within six months from the date of the communication made to the Secretary-General, request him to arrange consultations between signatory States in order to reach agreement.
3   If no signatory State has requested consultations within this period or if within two years following the communication made to the Secretary-General no agreement is reached in the course of consultations, the Contracting State concerned may amend its law in the manner indicated. The measures taken by that State shall be brought to the knowledge of the other signatory States through the Secretary-General of the Council of the European Communities.

Article 24
1   If, after the date on which this Convention has entered into force with respect to a Contracting State, that State wishes to become a party to a multilateral convention whose principal aim or one of whose principal aims is to lay down rules of private international law concerning any of the matters governed by this Convention, the procedure set out in Article 23 shall apply. However, the period of two years, referred to in paragraph 3 of that Article, shall be reduced to one year.
2   The procedure referred to in the preceding paragraph need not be followed if a Contracting State or one of the European Communities is already a party to the multilateral convention, or if its object is to revise a convention to which the State concerned is already a party, or if it is a convention concluded within the framework of the Treaties establishing the European Communities.

Article 25
If a Contracting State considers that the unification achieved by this Convention is prejudiced by the conclusion of agreements not covered by Article 24(1), that State may request the Secretary-General of the Council of the European Communities to arrange consultations between the signatory States of this Convention.

Article 26
Any Contracting State may request the revision of this Convention. In this event a revision conference shall be convened by the President of the Council of the European Communities.

. . .

Article 28
  1   This Convention shall be open from 19 June 1980 for signature by the States party to the Treaty establishing the European Economic Community.
  2   This Convention shall be subject to ratification, acceptance or approval by the signatory States. The instruments of ratification, acceptance or approval shall be deposited with the Secretary-General of the Council of the European Communities.

Article 29
  1   This Convention shall enter into force on the first day of the third month following the deposit of the seventh instrument of ratification, acceptance or approval.
  2   This Convention shall enter into force for each signatory State ratifying, accepting or approving at a later date on the first day of the third month following the deposit of its instrument of ratification, acceptance or approval.

Article 30
  1   This Convention shall remain in force for 10 years from the date of its entry into force in accordance with Article 29(1), even for States for which it enters into force at a later date.
  2   If there has been no denunciation it shall be renewed tacitly every five years.
  3   A Contracting State which wishes to denounce shall, not less than six months before the expiration of the period of 10 or five years, as the case may be, give notice to the Secretary-General of the Council of the European Communities. . . .
  4   The denunciation shall have effect only in relation to the State which has notified it. The Convention will remain in force as between all other Contracting States.

Article 31
The Secretary-General of the Council of the European Communities shall notify the States party to the Treaty establishing the European Economic Community of:
  (a)   the signatures;
  (b)   the deposit of each instrument of ratification, acceptance or approval;
  (c)   the date of entry into force of this Convention;
  (d)   communications made in pursuance of Articles 23, 24, 25, 26 and 30;
  (e)   the reservations and withdrawals of reservations referred to in Article 22.

Article 32
The Protocol annexed to this Convention shall form an integral part thereof.

Article 33
This Convention, drawn up in a single original in the Danish, Dutch, English, French, German, Irish and Italian languages, these texts being equally authentic, shall be deposited in the archives of the Secretariat of the Council of the European Communities. The Secretary-General shall transmit a certified copy thereof to the Government of each signatory State.

[PROTOCOL

The High Contracting Parties have agreed upon the following provision which shall be annexed to the Convention:
  Notwithstanding the provisions of the Convention, Denmark, Sweden and Finland may retain national provisions concerning the law applicable to questions

relating to the carriage of goods by sea and may amend such provisions without following the procedure provided for in Article 23 of the Convention of Rome. The national provisions applicable in this respect are the following:
- in Denmark, paragraphs 252 and 321(3) and (4) of the 'Sølov' (maritime law);
- in Sweden, Chapter 13, Article 2(1) and (2), and Chapter 14, Article 1(3), of 'sjölagen' (maritime law);
- in Finland, Chapter 13, Article 2(1) and (2), and Chapter 14, Article 1(3) of 'merilaki'/'sjölagen' (maritime law).]

SCHEDULE 2
THE LUXEMBOURG CONVENTION

The High Contracting Parties to the Treaty establishing the European Economic Community,

Considering that the Hellenic Republic, in becoming a Member of the Community, undertook to accede to the Convention on the law applicable to contractual obligations, opened for signature in Rome on 19 June 1980,

Have decided to conclude this Convention, and to this end have designated as their plenipotentiaries:

(Designation of plenipotentiaries)

Who, meeting within the Council, having exchanged their full powers, found in good and due form,

Have agreed as follows:

Article 1
The Hellenic Republic hereby accedes to the Convention on the law applicable to contractual obligations, opened for signature in Rome on 19 June 1980.

Article 2
The Secretary-General of the Council of the European Communities shall transmit a certified copy of the Convention on the law applicable to contractual obligations in the Danish, Dutch, English, French, German, Irish and Italian languages to the Government of the Hellenic Republic.

The text of the Convention on the law applicable to contractual obligations in the Greek language is annexed hereto. The text in the Greek language shall be authentic under the same conditions as the other texts of the Convention on the law applicable to contractual obligations.

Article 3
This Convention shall be ratified by the Signatory States. The instruments of ratification shall be deposited with the Secretary-General of the Council of the European Communities.

Article 4
This Convention shall enter into force, as between the States which have ratified it, on the first day of the third month following the deposit of the last instrument of ratification by the Hellenic Republic and seven States which have ratified the Convention on the law applicable to contractual obligations.

This Convention shall enter into force for each Contracting State which subsequently ratifies it on the first day of the third month following the deposit of its instrument of ratification.

Article 5
The Secretary-General of the Council of the European Communities shall notify the Signatory States of:
(a) the deposit of each instrument of ratification;
(b) the dates of entry into force of this Convention for the Contracting States.

Article 6
This Convention, drawn up in a single original in the Danish, Dutch, English, French, German, Greek, Irish and Italian languages, all eight texts being equally authentic, shall be deposited in the archives of the General Secretariat of the Council of the European Communities. The Secretary-General shall transmit a certified copy to the Government of each Signatory State.

SCHEDULE 3
THE BRUSSELS PROTOCOL

The High Contracting Parties to the Treaty establishing the European Economic Community,
 Having regard to the Joint Declaration annexed to the Convention on the law applicable to contractual obligations, opened for signature in Rome on 19 June 1980,
 Have decided to conclude a Protocol conferring jurisdiction on the Court of Justice of the European Communities to interpret that Convention and to this end have designated as their Plenipotentiaries:
 (Designation of plenipotentiaries)
 Who, meeting within the Council of the European Communities, having exchanged their full powers, found in good and due form,
 Have agreed as follows:

Article 1
The Court of Justice of the European Communities shall have jurisdiction to give rulings on the interpretation of—
 (a) the Convention on the law applicable to contractual obligations, opened for signature in Rome on 19 June 1980, hereinafter referred to as 'the Rome Convention';
 (b) the Convention on accession to the Rome Convention by the States which have become Members of the European Communities since the date on which it was opened for signature;
 (c) this Protocol.

Article 2
Any of the courts referred to below may request the Court of Justice to give a preliminary ruling on a question raised in a case pending before it and concerning interpretation of the provisions contained in the instruments referred to in Article 1 if that court considers that a decision on the question is necessary to enable it to give judgment:
 (a) —in Belgium:
   la Cour de cassation (het Hof van Cassatie) and le Conseil d'Etat (de Raad van State),
  —in Denmark:
   Højesteret,
  —in the Federal Republic of Germany:
   die obersten Gerichtschöfe des Bundes,
  —in Greece:
   τα ανώτατα Αικαστήρια,
  —in Spain:
   el Tribunal Supremo,
  —in France:
   la Cour de cassation and le Conseil d'Etat,
  —in Ireland:
   the Supreme Court,
  —in Italy:
   la Corte suprema di cassazione and il Consiglio di Stato,

—in Luxembourg:
la Cour Supérieure de Justice, when sitting as Cour de cassation,
[—in Austria:
the Oberste Gerichtshof, the Verwaltungsgerichtshof and the Verfass-
ungsgerichtshof,]
—in the Netherlands:
de Hoge Raad,
—in Portugal:
o Supremo Tribunal de Justiça and o Supremo Tribunal Admini-
strativo,
[—in Finland:
korkein oikeus/högsta domstolen, korkein hallinto-oikeus/högsta
förvaltningsdomstolen, markkinatuomioistuin/marknadsdomstolen and
työtuomioistuin/arbetsdomstolen,
—in Sweden:
Högsta domstolen, Regeringsrätten, Arbetsdomstolen and Marknads-
domstolen]
—in the United Kingdom:
the House of Lords and other courts from which no further appeal is
possible;
(b)   the courts of the Contracting States when acting as appeal courts.

Article 3

1   The competent authority of a Contracting State may request the Court of
Justice to give a ruling on a question of interpretation of the provisions contained
in the instruments referred to in Article 1 if judgments given by courts of that State
conflict with the interpretation given either by the Court of Justice or in a judgment of one of the courts of another Contracting State referred to in Article 2. The
provisions of this paragraph shall apply only to judgments which have become *res
judicata*.

2   The interpretation given by the Court of Justice in response to such a request
shall not affect the judgments which gave rise to the request for interpretation.

3   The Procurators-General of the Supreme Courts of Appeal of the Contracting
States, or any other authority designated by a Contracting State, shall be entitled to
request the Court of Justice for a ruling on interpretation in accordance with
paragraph 1.

4   The Registrar of the Court of Justice shall give notice of the request to the
Contracting States, to the Commission and to the Council of the European Communities; they shall then be entitled within two months of the notification to
submit statements of case or written observations to the Court.

5   No fees shall be levied or any costs or expenses awarded in respect of the
proceedings provided for in this Article.

Article 4

1   Except where this Protocol otherwise provides, the provisions of the Treaty
establishing the European Economic Community and those of the Protocol on the
Statute of the Court of Justice annexed thereto, which are applicable when the
Court is requested to give a preliminary ruling, shall also apply to any proceedings for the interpretation of the instruments referred to in Article 1.

2   The Rules of Procedure of the Court of Justice shall, if necessary, be adjusted
and supplemented in accordance with Article 188 of the Treaty establishing the
European Economic Community.

Article 5

This Protocol shall be subject to ratification by the Signatory States. The instruments of ratification shall be deposited with the Secretary-General of the Council
of the European Communities.

Article 6

1   To enter into force, this Protocol must be ratified by seven States in respect of which the Rome Convention is in force. This Protocol shall enter into force on the first day of the third month following the deposit of the instrument of ratification by the last such State to take this step. If, however, the Second Protocol conferring on the Court of Justice of the European Communities certain powers to interpret the Convention on the law applicable to contractual obligations, opened for signature in Rome on 19 June 1980, concluded in Brussels on 19 December 1988, enters into force on a later date, this Protocol shall enter into force on the date of entry into force of the Second Protocol.

2   Any ratification subsequent to the entry into force of this Protocol shall take effect on the first day of the third month following the deposit of the instrument of ratification provided that the ratification, acceptance or approval of the Rome Convention by the State in question has become effective.

Article 7

The Secretary-General of the Council of the European Communities shall notify the Signatory States of:
  (a)   the deposit of each instrument of ratification;
  (b)   the date of entry into force of this Protocol;
  (c)   any designation communicated pursuant to Article 3(3);
  (d)   any communication made pursuant to Article 8.

Article 8

The Contracting States shall communicate to the Secretary-General of the Council of the European Communities the texts of any provisions of their laws which necessitate an amendment to the list of courts in Article 2(a).

Article 9

This Protocol shall have effect for as long as the Rome Convention remains in force under the conditions laid down in Article 30 of that Convention.

Article 10

Any Contracting State may request the revision of this Protocol. In this event, a revision conference shall be convened by the President of the Council of the European Communities.

Article 11

This Protocol, drawn up in a single original in the Danish, Dutch, English, French, German, Greek, Irish, Italian, Portuguese and Spanish languages, all 10 texts being equally authentic, shall be deposited in the archives of the General Secretariat of the Council of the European Communities. The Secretary-General shall transmit a certified copy to the Government of each Signatory State.

[SCHEDULE 3A
THE FUNCHAL CONVENTION

The High Contracting Parties to the Treaty establishing the European Economic Community.

Considering that the Kingdom of Spain and the Portuguese Republic, in becoming Members of the Community, undertook to accede to the Convention on the law applicable to contractual obligations, opened for signature in Rome on 19th June 1980.

Have decided to conclude this Convention, and to this end have designated as their plenipotentiaries:
(Designation of plenipotentiaries)

Who, meeting within the Council, having exchanged their full powers, found in good and due form.

Have agreed as follows:

Article 1

The Kingdom of Spain and the Portuguese Republic hereby accede to the Convention on the law applicable to contractual obligations, opened for signature in Rome on 19th June 1980.

Article 2

The Convention on the law applicable to contractual obligations is hereby amended as follows:

(1)   Article 22(2), Article 27 and the second sentence of Article 30(3) shall be deleted.

(2)   The reference to Article 27 in Article 31(d) shall be deleted.

Article 3

The Secretary-General of the Council of the European Communities shall transmit a certified copy of the Convention on the law applicable to contractual obligations in the Danish, Dutch, English, French, German, Greek, Irish and Italian languages to the Governments of the Kingdom of Spain and the Portuguese Republic.

Article 4

This Convention shall be ratified by the Signatory States. The instruments of ratification shall be deposited with the Secretary-General of the Council of the European Communities.

Article 5

This Convention shall enter into force, as between the States which have ratified it, on the first day of the third month following deposit of the last instrument of ratification by the Kingdom of Spain or the Portuguese Republic and by one State which has ratified the Convention on the law applicable to contractual obligations.

This Convention shall enter into force for each Contracting State which subsequently ratifies it on the first day of the third month following that of deposit of its instrument of ratification.

Article 6

The Secretary-General of the Council of the European Communities shall notify the Signatory States of:

(a)   the deposit of each instrument of ratification;

(b)   the dates of entry into force of this Convention for the Contracting States.

Article 7

This Convention, drawn up in a single original in the Danish, Dutch, English, French, German, Greek, Irish, Italian, Portuguese and Spanish languages, all ten texts being equally authentic, shall be deposited in the archives of the General Secretariat of the Council of the European Communities. The Secretary-General shall transmit a certified copy to the Government of each Signatory State.]

[SCHEDULE 3B
THE 1996 ACCESSION CONVENTION

Section 2

The High Contracting Parties to the Treaty establishing the European Community.

Considering that the Republic of Austria, the Republic of Finland and the Kingdom of Sweden, in becoming Members of the European Union, undertook to accede to the Convention on the Law applicable to Contractual Obligations, opened for signature in Rome on 19th June 1980, and to the First and Second Protocols on its interpretation by the Court of Justice,

Have agreed as follows:

TITLE I
GENERAL PROVISIONS

Article 1

The Republic of Austria, the Republic of Finland and the Kingdom of Sweden hereby accede to:

(a)   the Convention on the Law applicable to Contractual Obligations, opened for signature in Rome on 19th June 1980, hereinafter referred to as 'the Convention of 1980', as it stands following incorporation of all the adjustments and amendments made thereto by:

—the Convention signed in Luxembourg on 10th April 1984, hereinafter referred to as 'the Convention of 1984', on the accession of the Hellenic Republic to the Convention on the Law applicable to Contractual Obligations;

—the Convention signed in Funchal on 18th May 1992, hereinafter referred to as 'the Convention of 1992', on the accession of the Kingdom of Spain and the Portuguese Republic to the Convention on the Law applicable to Contractual Obligations;

(b)   the First Protocol, signed on 19th December 1988, hereinafter referred to as 'the First Protocol of 1988', on the interpretation by the Court of Justice of the European Communities of the Convention on the Law applicable to Contractual Obligations;

(c)   the Second Protocol, signed on 19th December 1988, hereinafter referred to as 'the Second Protocol of 1988', conferring on the Court of Justice of the European Communities certain powers to interpret the Convention on the Law applicable to Contractual Obligations.

[*Titles II and III make adjustments to, respectively, the Protocol annexed to the 1980 Convention and the First Protocol of 1988.*]

TITLE IV
FINAL PROVISIONS

Article 4

1   The Secretary-General of the Council of the European Union shall transmit a certified copy of the Convention of 1980, the Convention of 1984, the First Protocol of 1988, the Second Protocol of 1988 and the Convention of 1992 in the Danish, Dutch, English, French, German, Greek, Irish, Italian, Spanish and Portuguese languages to the Governments of the Republic of Austria, the Republic of Finland and the Kingdom of Sweden.

2   The text of the Convention of 1980, the Convention of 1984, the First Protocol of 1988, the Second Protocol of 1988 and the Convention of 1992 in the Finnish and Swedish languages shall be authentic under the same conditions as the other texts of the Convention of 1980, the Convention of 1984, the First Protocol of 1988, the Second Protocol of 1988 and the Convention of 1992.

Article 5

This Convention shall be ratified by the Signatory States. The instruments of ratification shall be deposited with the Secretary-General of the Council of the European Union.

Article 6

1   This Convention shall enter into force, as between the States which have ratified it, on the first day of the third month following the deposit of the last instrument of ratification by the Republic of Austria, the Republic of Finland or the

Kingdom of Sweden and by one Contracting State which has ratified the Convention on the Law applicable to Contractual Obligations.

2   This Convention shall enter into force for each Contracting State which subsequently ratifies it on the first day of the third month following the deposit of its instrument of ratification.

Article 7
The Secretary-General of the Council of the European Union shall notify the Signatory States of:
  (a)   the deposit of each instrument of ratification;
  (b)   the dates of entry into force of this Convention for the Contracting States.

Article 8
This Convention, drawn up in a single original in the Danish, Dutch, English, Finnish, French, German, Greek, Irish, Italian, Portuguese, Spanish and Swedish languages, all twelve texts being equally authentic, shall be deposited in the archives of the General Secretariat of the Council of the European Union. The Secretary-General shall transmit a certified copy to the Government of each Signatory State.'

CARRIAGE OF GOODS BY SEA ACT 1992
(1992, c 50)

1 Shipping documents etc to which Act applies
  (1) This Act applies to the following documents, that is to say—
    (a)   any bill of lading;
    (b)   any sea waybill; and
    (c)   any ship's delivery order.
  (2) References in this Act to a bill of lading—
    (a)   do not include references to a document which is incapable of transfer either by indorsement or, as a bearer bill, by delivery without indorsement; but
    (b)   subject to that, do include references to a received for shipment bill of lading.
  (3) References in this Act to a sea waybill are references to any document which is not a bill of lading but—
    (a)   is such a receipt for goods as contains or evidences a contract for the carriage of goods by sea; and
    (b)   identifies the person to whom delivery of the goods is to be made by the carrier in accordance with that contract.
  (4) References in this Act to a ship's delivery order are references to any document which is neither a bill of lading nor a sea waybill but contains an undertaking which—
    (a)   is given under or for the purposes of a contract for the carriage by sea of the goods to which the document relates, or of goods which include those goods; and
    (b)   is an undertaking by the carrier to a person identified in the document to deliver the goods to which the document relates to that person.
  (5) The Secretary of State may by regulations make provision for the application of this Act to cases where [an electronic communications network] or any other information technology is used for effecting transactions corresponding to—
    (a)   the issue of a document to which this Act applies;
    (b)   the indorsement, delivery or other transfer of such a document; or
    (c)   the doing of anything else in relation to such a document.
  (6) Regulations under subsection (5) above may—
    (a)   make such modifications of the following provisions of this Act as the

Secretary of State considers appropriate in connection with the application of this Act to any case mentioned in that subsection; and

(b)   contain supplemental, incidental, consequential and transitional provision;

and the power to make regulations under that subsection shall be exercisable by statutory instrument subject to annulment in pursuance of a resolution of either House of Parliament.

2   Rights under shipping documents

(1)   Subject to the following provisions of this section, a person who becomes—

(a)   the lawful holder of a bill of lading;

(b)   the person who (without being an original party to the contract of carriage) is the person to whom delivery of the goods to which a sea waybill relates is to be made by the carrier in accordance with that contract; or

(c)   the person to whom delivery of the goods to which a ship's delivery order relates is to be made in accordance with the undertaking contained in the order,

shall (by virtue of becoming the holder of the bill or, as the case may be, the person to whom delivery is to be made) have transferred to and vested in him all rights of suit under the contract of carriage as if he had been a party to that contract.

(2)   Where, when a person becomes the lawful holder of a bill of lading, possession of the bill no longer gives a right (as against the carrier) to possession of the goods to which the bill relates, that person shall not have any rights transferred to him by virtue of subsection (1) above unless he becomes the holder of the bill—

(a)   by virtue of a transaction effected in pursuance of any contractual or other arrangements made before the time when such a right to possession ceased to attach to possession of the bill; or

(b)   as a result of the rejection to that person by another person of goods or documents delivered to the other person in pursuance of any such arrangements.

(3)   The rights vested in any person by virtue of the operation of subsection (1) above in relation to a ship's delivery order—

(a)   shall be so vested subject to the terms of the order; and

(b)   where the goods to which the order relates form a part only of the goods to which the contract of carriage relates, shall be confined to rights in respect of the goods to which the order relates.

(4)   Where, in the case of any document to which this Act applies—

(a)   a person with any interest or right in or in relation to goods to which the document relates sustains loss or damage in consequence of a breach of the contract of carriage; but

(b)   subsection (1) above operates in relation to that document so that rights of suit in respect of that breach are vested in another person,

the other person shall be entitled to exercise those rights for the benefit of the person who sustained the loss or damage to the same extent as they could have been exercised if they had been vested in the person for whose benefit they are exercised.

(5)   Where rights are transferred by virtue of the operation of subsection (1) above in relation to any document, the transfer for which that subsection provides shall extinguish any entitlement to those rights which derives—

(a)   where that document is a bill of lading, from a person's having been an original party to the contract of carriage; or

(b)   in the case of any document to which this Act applies, from the previous operation of that subsection in relation to that document;

but the operation of that subsection shall be without prejudice to any rights which derive from a person's having been an original party to the contract contained in, or evidenced by, a sea waybill and, in relation to a ship's delivery order, shall be without prejudice to any rights deriving otherwise than from the previous operation of that subsection in relation to that order.

3 Liabilities under shipping documents

(1)   Where subsection (1) of section 2 of this Act operates in relation to any document to which this Act applies and the person in whom rights are vested by virtue of that subsection—

(a)   takes or demands delivery from the carrier of any of the goods to which the document relates;

(b)   makes a claim under the contract of carriage against the carrier in respect of any of those goods; or

(c)   is a person who, at a time before those rights were vested in him, took or demanded delivery from the carrier of any of those goods,

that person shall (by virtue of taking or demanding delivery or making the claim or, in a case falling within paragraph (c) above, of having the rights vested in him) become subject to the same liabilities under that contract as if he had been a party to that contract.

(2)   Where the goods to which a ship's delivery order relates form a part only of the goods to which the contract of carriage relates, the liabilities to which any person is subject by virtue of the operation of this section in relation to that order shall exclude liabilities in respect of any goods to which the order does not relate.

(3)   This section, so far as it imposes liabilities under any contract on any person, shall be without prejudice to the liabilities under the contract of any person as an original party to the contract.

4 Representations in bills of lading

A bill of lading which—

(a)   represents goods to have been shipped on board a vessel or to have been received for shipment on board a vessel; and

(b)   has been signed by the master of the vessel or by a person who was not the master but had the express, implied or apparent authority of the carrier to sign bills of lading,

shall, in favour of a person who has become the lawful holder of the bill, be conclusive evidence against the carrier of the shipment of the goods or, as the case may be, of their receipt for shipment.

5 Interpretation etc

(1)   In this Act—

'bill of lading', 'sea waybill' and 'ship's delivery order' shall be construed in accordance with section 1 above;

'the contract of carriage'—

(a)   in relation to a bill of lading or sea waybill, means the contract contained in or evidenced by that bill or waybill; and

(b)   in relation to a ship's delivery order, means the contract under or for the purposes of which the undertaking contained in the order is given;

'holder', in relation to a bill of lading, shall be construed in accordance with subsection (2) below;

'information technology' includes any computer or other technology by means of which information or other matter may be recorded or communicated without being reduced to documentary form.

[. . .]

(2)   References in this Act to the holder of a bill of lading are references to any of the following persons, that is to say—

(a)   a person with possession of the bill who, by virtue of being the person identified in the bill, is the consignee of the goods to which the bill relates;

(b)   a person with possession of the bill as a result of the completion, by delivery of the bill, of any indorsement of the bill or, in the case of a bearer bill, of any other transfer of the bill;

(c) a person with possession of the bill as a result of any transaction by virtue of which he would have become a holder falling within paragraph (a) or (b) above had not the transaction been effected at a time when possession of the bill no longer gave a right (as against the carrier) to possession of the goods to which the bill relates;

and a person shall be regarded for the purposes of this Act as having become the lawful holder of a bill of lading wherever he has become the holder of the bill in good faith.

(3) References in this Act to a person's being identified in a document include references to his being identified by a description which allows for the identity of the person in question to be varied, in accordance with the terms of the document, after its issue; and the reference in section 1(3)(b) of this Act to a document's identifying a person shall be construed accordingly.

(4) Without prejudice to sections 2(2) and 4 above, nothing in this Act shall preclude its operation in relation to a case where the goods to which a document relates—

(a) cease to exist after the issue of the document; or

(b) cannot be identified (whether because they are mixed with other goods or for any other reason);

and references in this Act to the goods to which a document relates shall be construed accordingly.

(5) The preceding provisions of this Act shall have effect without prejudice to the application, in relation to any case, of the rules (the Hague-Visby Rules) which for the time being have the force of law by virtue of section 1 of the Carriage of Goods by Sea Act 1971.

6 Short title, repeal, commencement and extent

(1) This Act may be cited as the Carriage of Goods by Sea Act 1992.

(2) The Bills of Lading Act 1855 is hereby repealed.

(3) This Act shall come into force at the end of the period of two months beginning with the day on which it is passed; but nothing in this Act shall have effect in relation to any document issued before the coming into force of this Act.

(4) This Act extends to Northern Ireland.

REQUIREMENTS OF WRITING (SCOTLAND) ACT 1995
(1995, c 7)

1 Writing required for certain contracts, obligations, trusts, conveyances and wills

(1) Subject to subsection (2) below and any other enactment, writing shall not be required for the constitution of a contract, unilateral obligation or trust.

(2) Subject to subsection (3) below, a written document complying with section 2 of this Act shall be required for—

(a) the constitution of—

(i) a contract or unilateral obligation for the creation, transfer, variation or extinction of [a real right] in land;

(ii) a gratuitous unilateral obligation except an obligation undertaken in the course of business; and

(iii) a trust whereby a person declares himself to be sole trustee of his own property or any property which he may acquire;

(b) the creation, transfer, variation or extinction of [a real right] in land otherwise than by the operation of a court decree, enactment or rule of law; and

(c) the making of any will, testamentary trust disposition and settlement or codicil.

(3) Where a contract, obligation or trust mentioned in subsection (2)(a) above is not constituted in a written document complying with section 2 of this Act, but one of the parties to the contract, a creditor in the obligation or a beneficiary under the trust ('the first person') has acted or refrained from acting in reliance on the contract, obligation or trust with the knowledge and acquiescence of the other party to the contract, the debtor in the obligation or the truster ('the second person')—

(a) the second person shall not be entitled to withdraw from the contract, obligation or trust; and

(b) the contract, obligation or trust shall not be regarded as invalid, on the ground that it is not so constituted, if the condition set out in subsection (4) below is satisfied.

(4) The condition referred to in subsection (3) above is that the position of the first person—

(a) as a result of acting or refraining from acting as mentioned in that subsection has been affected to a material extent; and

(b) as a result of such a withdrawal as is mentioned in that subsection would be adversely affected to a material extent.

(5) In relation to the constitution of any contract, obligation or trust mentioned in subsection (2)(a) above, subsections (3) and (4) above replace the rules of law known as *rei interventus* and homologation.

(6) This section shall apply to the variation of a contract, obligation or trust as it applies to the constitution thereof but as if in subsections (3) and (4) for the references to acting or refraining from acting in reliance on the contract, obligation or trust and withdrawing therefrom there were substituted respectively references to acting or refraining from acting in reliance on the variation of the contract, obligation or trust and withdrawing from the variation.

(7) In this section ['real right in land' means any real] right in or over land, including any right to occupy or to use land or to restrict the occupation or use of land, but does not include—

(a) a tenancy;

(b) a right to occupy or use land; or

(c) a right to restrict the occupation or use of land,

if the tenancy or right is not granted for more than one year, unless the tenancy or right is for a recurring period or recurring periods and there is a gap of more than one year between the beginning of the first, and the end of the last, such period.

(8) For the purposes of subsection (7) above 'land' does not include—

(a) growing crops; or

(b) a moveable building or other moveable structure.

2 Type of writing required for formal validity of certain documents

(1) No document required by section 1(2) of this Act shall be valid in respect of the formalities of execution unless it is subscribed by the granter of it or, if there is more than one granter, by each granter, but nothing apart from such subscription shall be required for the document to be valid as aforesaid.

(2) A contract mentioned in section 1(2)(a)(i) of this Act may be regarded as constituted or varied (as the case may be) if the offer is contained in one or more documents and the acceptance is contained in another document or other documents, and each document is subscribed by the granter or granters thereof.

(3) Nothing in this section shall prevent a document which has not been subscribed by the granter or granters of it from being used as evidence in relation to any right or obligation to which the document relates.

(4) This section is without prejudice to any other enactment which makes different provision in respect of the formalities of execution of a document to which this section applies.

DATA PROTECTION ACT 1998
(1998, c 29)

7 Right of access to personal data*

(1) Subject to the following provisions of this section and to [sections 8, 9 and 9A], an individual is entitled—

(a) to be informed by any data controller whether personal data of which that individual is the data subject are being processed by or on behalf of that data controller,

(b) if that is the case, to be given by the data controller a description of—

(i) the personal data of which that individual is the data subject,

(ii) the purposes for which they are being or are to be processed, and

(iii) the recipients or classes of recipients to whom they are or may be disclosed,

(c) to have communicated to him in an intelligible form—

(i) the information constituting any personal data of which that individual is the data subject, and

(ii) any information available to the data controller as to the source of those data, and

(d) where the processing by automatic means of personal data of which that individual is the data subject for the purpose of evaluating matters relating to him such as, for example, his performance at work, his creditworthiness, his reliability or his conduct, has constituted or is likely to constitute the sole basis for any decision significantly affecting him, to be informed by the data controller of the logic involved in that decision-taking.

(2) A data controller is not obliged to supply any information under subsection (1) unless he has received—

(a) a request in writing, and

(b) except in prescribed cases, such fee (not exceeding the prescribed maximum) as he may require.

[(3) Where a data controller—

(a) reasonably requires further information in order to satisfy himself as to the identity of the person making a request under this section and to locate the information which that person seeks, and

(b) has informed him of that requirement,

the data controller is not obliged to comply with the request unless he is supplied with that further information.]

(4) Where a data controller cannot comply with the request without disclosing information relating to another individual who can be identified from that information, he is not obliged to comply with the request unless—

(a) the other individual has consented to the disclosure of the information to the person making the request, or

(b) it is reasonable in all the circumstances to comply with the request without the consent of the other individual.

(5) In subsection (4) the reference to information relating to another individual includes a reference to information identifying that individual as the source of the information sought by the request; and that subsection is not to be construed as excusing a data controller from communicating so much of the information sought by the request as can be communicated without disclosing the identity of the other individual concerned, whether by the omission of names or other identifying particulars or otherwise.

---

*Section 7 is modified in relation to particular professions, namely health (SI 2000/413); education (SI 2000/414); and social work (SI 2000/415; SI 2005/467).

(6)   In determining for the purposes of subsection (4)(b) whether it is reasonable in all the circumstances to comply with the request without the consent of the other individual concerned, regard shall be had, in particular, to—

(a)   any duty of confidentiality owed to the other individual,

(b)   any steps taken by the data controller with a view to seeking the consent of the other individual,

(c)   whether the other individual is capable of giving consent, and

(d)   any express refusal of consent by the other individual.

(7)   An individual making a request under this section may, in such cases as may be prescribed, specify that his request is limited to personal data of any prescribed description.

(8)   Subject to subsection (4), a data controller shall comply with a request under this section promptly and in any event before the end of the prescribed period beginning with the relevant day.

(9)   If a court is satisfied on the application of any person who has made a request under the foregoing provisions of this section that the data controller in question has failed to comply with the request in contravention of those provisions, the court may order him to comply with the request.

(10)   In this section—

'prescribed' means prescribed by the [Secretary of State] by regulations;

'the prescribed maximum' means such amount as may be prescribed;

'the prescribed period' means forty days or such other period as may be prescribed;

'the relevant day', in relation to a request under this section, means the day on which the data controller receives the request or, if later, the first day on which the data controller has both the required fee and the information referred to in subsection (3).

(11)   Different amounts or periods may be prescribed under this section in relation to different cases.

ELECTRONIC COMMUNICATIONS ACT 2000
(2000, c 7)

PART II
FACILITATION OF ELECTRONIC COMMERCE, DATA STORAGE, ETC

7   Electronic signatures and related certificates

(1)   In any legal proceedings—

(a)   an electronic signature incorporated into or logically associated with a particular electronic communication or particular electronic data, and

(b)   the certification by any person of such a signature,

shall each be admissible in evidence in relation to any question as to the authenticity of the communication or data or as to the integrity of the communication or data.

(2)   For the purposes of this section an electronic signature is so much of anything in electronic form as—

(a)   is incorporated into or otherwise logically associated with any electronic communication or electronic data; and

(b)   purports to be so incorporated or associated for the purpose of being used in establishing the authenticity of the communication or data, the integrity of the communication or data, or both.

(3)   For the purposes of this section an electronic signature incorporated into or associated with a particular electronic communication or particular electronic data is certified by any person if that person (whether before or after the making of the communication) has made a statement confirming that—

(a)   the signature,

(b)   a means of producing, communicating or verifying the signature, or

(c)   a procedure applied to the signature,

is (either alone or in combination with other factors) a valid means of establishing the authenticity of the communication or data, the integrity of the communication or data, or both.

LIMITED LIABILITY PARTNERSHIPS ACT 2000
(2000, c 12)

Introductory

1 Limited liability partnerships

(1)   There shall be a new form of legal entity to be known as a limited liability partnership.

(2)   A limited liability partnership is a body corporate (with legal personality separate from that of its members) which is formed by being incorporated under this Act; and—

(a)   in the following provisions of this Act (except in the phrase 'oversea limited liability partnership'), and

(b)   in any other enactment (except where provision is made to the contrary or the context otherwise requires),

references to a limited liability partnership are to such a body corporate.

(3)   A limited liability partnership has unlimited capacity.

(4)   The members of a limited liability partnership have such liability to contribute to its assets in the event of its being wound up as is provided for by virtue of this Act.

(5)   Accordingly, except as far as otherwise provided by this Act or any other enactment, the law relating to partnerships does not apply to a limited liability partnership.

(6)   The Schedule (which makes provision about the names and registered offices of limited liability partnerships) has effect.

Incorporation

2 Incorporation document etc

(1)   For a limited liability partnership to be incorporated—

(a)   two or more persons associated for carrying on a lawful business with a view to profit must have subscribed their names to an incorporation document,

(b)   there must have been delivered to the registrar either the incorporation document or a copy authenticated in a manner approved by him, and

(c)   there must have been so delivered a statement in a form approved by the registrar, made by either a solicitor engaged in the formation of the limited liability partnership or anyone who subscribed his name to the incorporation document, that the requirement imposed by paragraph (a) has been complied with.

(2)   The incorporation document must—

(a)   be in a form approved by the registrar (or as near to such a form as circumstances allow),

(b)   state the name of the limited liability partnership,

(c)   state whether the registered office of the limited liability partnership is to be situated in England and Wales, in Wales or in Scotland,

(d)   state the address of that registered office,

(e)   state the name and address of each of the persons who are to be members of the limited liability partnership on incorporation, and

(f)   either specify which of those persons are to be designated members or state that every person who from time to time is a member of the limited liability partnership is a designated member.

[(2A) Where a confidentiality order, made under section 723B of the Companies Act 1985 as applied to limited liability partnerships is in force in respect of any individual named as a member of a limited liability partnership under subsection (2) that subsection shall have effect as if the reference to the address of the individual were a reference to the address for the time being notified by him under the Limited Liability Partnerships (Particulars of Usual Residential Address) (Confidentiality Orders) Regulations 2002 to any limited liability partnership of which he is a member or if he is not such a member either the address specified in his application for a confidentiality order or the address last notified by him under such a confidentiality order as the case may be.

(2B) Where the incorporation document or a copy of such delivered under this section includes an address specified in reliance on subsection (2A) there shall be delivered with it or the copy of it a statement in a form approved by the registrar containing particulars of the usual residential address of the member whose address is so specified.]

(3) If a person makes a false statement under subsection (1)(c) which he—

(a) knows to be false, or

(b) does not believe to be true, he commits an offence.

(4) A person guilty of an offence under subsection (3) is liable—

(a) on summary conviction, to imprisonment for a period not exceeding six months or a fine not exceeding the statutory maximum, or to both, or

(b) on conviction on indictment, to imprisonment for a period not exceeding two years or a fine, or to both.

3 Incorporation by registration

(1) When the requirements imposed by paragraphs (b) and (c) of subsection (1) of section 2 have been complied with, the registrar shall retain the incorporation document or copy delivered to him and, unless the requirement imposed by paragraph (a) of that subsection has not been complied with, he shall—

(a) register the incorporation document or copy, and

(b) give a certificate that the limited liability partnership is incorporated by the name specified in the incorporation document.

(2) The registrar may accept the statement delivered under paragraph (c) of subsection (1) of section 2 as sufficient evidence that the requirement imposed by paragraph (a) of that subsection has been complied with.

(3) The certificate shall either be signed by the registrar or be authenticated by his official seal.

(4) The certificate is conclusive evidence that the requirements of section 2 are complied with and that the limited liability partnership is incorporated by the name specified in the incorporation document.

Membership

4 Members

(1) On the incorporation of a limited liability partnership its members are the persons who subscribed their names to the incorporation document (other than any who have died or been dissolved).

(2) Any other person may become a member of a limited liability partnership by and in accordance with an agreement with the existing members.

(3) A person may cease to be a member of a limited liability partnership (as well as by death or dissolution) in accordance with an agreement with the other members or, in the absence of agreement with the other members as to cessation of membership, by giving reasonable notice to the other members.

(4) A member of a limited liability partnership shall not be regarded for any purpose as employed by the limited liability partnership unless, if he and the other

members were partners in a partnership, he would be regarded for that purpose as employed by the partnership.

5 Relationship of members etc

(1) Except as far as otherwise provided by this Act or any other enactment, the mutual rights and duties of the members of a limited liability partnership, and the mutual rights and duties of a limited liability partnership and its members, shall be governed—

(a) by agreement between the members, or between the limited liability partnership and its members, or

(b) in the absence of agreement as to any matter, by any provision made in relation to that matter by regulations under section 15(c).

(2) An agreement made before the incorporation of a limited liability partnership between the persons who subscribe their names to the incorporation document may impose obligations on the limited liability partnership (to take effect at any time after its incorporation).

6 Members as agents

(1) Every member of a limited liability partnership is the agent of the limited liability partnership.

(2) But a limited liability partnership is not bound by anything done by a member in dealing with a person if—

(a) the member in fact has no authority to act for the limited liability partnership by doing that thing, and

(b) the person knows that he has no authority or does not know or believe him to be a member of the limited liability partnership.

(3) Where a person has ceased to be a member of a limited liability partnership, the former member is to be regarded (in relation to any person dealing with the limited liability partnership) as still being a member of the limited liability partnership unless—

(a) the person has notice that the former member has ceased to be a member of the limited liability partnership, or

(b) notice that the former member has ceased to be a member of the limited liability partnership has been delivered to the registrar.

(4) Where a member of a limited liability partnership is liable to any person (other than another member of the limited liability partnership) as a result of a wrongful act or omission of his in the course of the business of the limited liability partnership or with its authority, the limited liability partnership is liable to the same extent as the member.

7 Ex-members

(1) This section applies where a member of a limited liability partnership has either ceased to be a member or—

(a) has died,

(b) has become bankrupt or had his estate sequestrated or has been wound up,

(c) has granted a trust deed for the benefit of his creditors, or

(d) has assigned the whole or any part of his share in the limited liability partnership (absolutely or by way of charge or security).

(2) In such an event the former member or—

(a) his personal representative,

(b) his trustee in bankruptcy or permanent or interim trustee (within the meaning of the Bankruptcy (Scotland) Act 1985) or liquidator,

(c) his trustee under the trust deed for the benefit of his creditors, or

(d) his assignee,

may not interfere in the management or administration of any business or affairs of the limited liability partnership.

(3) But subsection (2) does not affect any right to receive an amount from the limited liability partnership in that event.

8 Designated members

(1) If the incorporation document specifies who are to be designated members—

(a) they are designated members on incorporation, and

(b) any member may become a designated member by and in accordance with an agreement with the other members,

and a member may cease to be a designated member in accordance with an agreement with the other members.

(2) But if there would otherwise be no designated members, or only one, every member is a designated member.

(3) If the incorporation document states that every person who from time to time is a member of the limited liability partnership is a designated member, every member is a designated member.

(4) A limited liability partnership may at any time deliver to the registrar—

(a) notice that specified members are to be designated members, or

(b) notice that every person who from time to time is a member of the limited liability partnership is a designated member,

and, once it is delivered, subsection (1) (apart from paragraph (a)) and subsection (2), or subsection (3), shall have effect as if that were stated in the incorporation document.

(5) A notice delivered under subsection (4)—

(a) shall be in a form approved by the registrar, and

(b) shall be signed by a designated member of the limited liability partnership or authenticated in a manner approved by the registrar.

(6) A person ceases to be a designated member if he ceases to be a member.

9 Registration of membership changes

(1) A limited liability partnership must ensure that—

(a) where a person becomes or ceases to be a member or designated member, notice is delivered to the registrar within fourteen days, and

(b) where there is any change in the name or address of a member, notice is delivered to the registrar within 28 days.

(2) Where all the members from time to time of a limited liability partnership are designated members, subsection (1)(a) does not require notice that a person has become or ceased to be a designated member as well as a member.

(3) A notice delivered under subsection (1)—

(a) shall be in a form approved by the registrar, and

(b) shall be signed by a designated member of the limited liability partnership or authenticated in a manner approved by the registrar,

and, if it relates to a person becoming a member or designated member, shall contain a statement that he consents to becoming a member or designated member signed by him or authenticated in a manner approved by the registrar.

[(3A) Where a confidentiality order under section 723B of the Companies Act 1985 as applied to limited liability partnerships is made in respect of an existing member, the limited liability partnership must ensure that there is delivered within 28 days to the registrar notice in a form approved by the registrar containing the address for the time being notified to it by the member under the Limited Liability Partnerships (Particulars of Usual Residential Address) (Confidentiality Orders) Regulations 2002.

(3B) Where such a confidentiality order is in force in respect of a member the requirement in subsection (1)(b) to notify a change in the address of a member shall be read in relation to that member as a requirement to deliver to the registrar, within 28 days, notice of—

(a) any change in the usual residential address of that member; and

(b)   any change in the address for the time being notified to the limited liability partnership by the member under the Limited Liability Partnerships (Particulars of Usual Residential Address) (Confidentiality Orders) Regulations 2002,

and the registrar may approve different forms for the notification of each kind of address.]

(4)   If a limited liability partnership fails to comply with subsection (1), the partnership and every designated member commits an offence.

(5)   But it is a defence for a designated member charged with an offence under subsection (4) to prove that he took all reasonable steps for securing that subsection (1) was complied with.

(6)   A person guilty of an offence under subsection (4) is liable on summary conviction to a fine not exceeding level 5 on the standard scale.

Taxation

10, 11   [*Amending provisions*]

12   Stamp duty

(1)   Stamp duty shall not be chargeable on an instrument by which property is conveyed or transferred by a person to a limited liability partnership in connection with its incorporation within the period of one year beginning with the date of incorporation if the following two conditions are satisfied.

(2)   The first condition is that at the relevant time the person—

(a)   is a partner in a partnership comprised of all the persons who are or are to be members of the limited liability partnership (and no-one else), or

(b)   holds the property conveyed or transferred as nominee or bare trustee for one or more of the partners in such a partnership.

(3)   The second condition is that—

(a)   the proportions of the property conveyed or transferred to which the persons mentioned in subsection (2)(a) are entitled immediately after the [transfer] are the same as those to which they were entitled at the relevant time, or

(b)   none of the differences in those proportions has arisen as part of a scheme or arrangement of which the main purpose, or one of the main purposes, is avoidance of liability to any duty or tax.

(4)   For the purposes of subsection (2) a person holds property as bare trustee for a partner if the partner has the exclusive right (subject only to satisfying any outstanding charge, lien or other right of the trustee to resort to the property for payment of duty, taxes, costs or other outgoings) to direct how the property shall be dealt with.

(5)   In this section 'the relevant time' means—

(a)   if the person who conveyed or transferred the property to the limited liability partnership acquired the property after its incorporation, immediately after he acquired the property, and

(b)   in any other case, immediately before its incorporation.

(6)   An instrument in respect of which stamp duty is not chargeable by virtue of subsection (1) shall not be taken to be duly stamped unless—

(a)   it has, in accordance with section 12 of the Stamp Act 1891, been stamped with a particular stamp denoting that it is not chargeable with any duty or that it is duly stamped, or

(b)   it is stamped with the duty to which it would be liable apart from that subsection.

13   [*Amending provision*]

Regulations

14   Insolvency and winding up

(1)   Regulations shall make provision about the insolvency and winding up of limited liability partnerships by applying or incorporating, with such modifications as appear appropriate, Parts I to IV, VI and VII of the Insolvency Act 1986.

(2)   Regulations may make other provision about the insolvency and winding up of limited liability partnerships, and provision about the insolvency and winding up of oversea limited liability partnerships, by—

(a)   applying or incorporating, with such modifications as appear appropriate, any law relating to the insolvency or winding up of companies or other corporations which would not otherwise have effect in relation to them, or

(b)   providing for any law relating to the insolvency or winding up of companies or other corporations which would otherwise have effect in relation to them not to apply to them or to apply to them with such modifications as appear appropriate.

(3)   In this Act 'oversea limited liability partnership' means a body incorporated or otherwise established outside Great Britain and having such connection with Great Britain, and such other features, as regulations may prescribe.

15   Application of company law etc

Regulations may make provision about limited liability partnerships and oversea limited liability partnerships (not being provision about insolvency or winding up) by—

(a)   applying or incorporating, with such modifications as appear appropriate, any law relating to companies or other corporations which would not otherwise have effect in relation to them,

(b)   providing for any law relating to companies or other corporations which would otherwise have effect in relation to them not to apply to them or to apply to them with such modifications as appear appropriate, or

(c)   applying or incorporating, with such modifications as appear appropriate, any law relating to partnerships.

16   Consequential amendments

(1)   Regulations may make in any enactment such amendments or repeals as appear appropriate in consequence of this Act or regulations made under it.

(2)   The regulations may, in particular, make amendments and repeals affecting companies or other corporations or partnerships.

17   General

(1)   In this Act 'regulations' means regulations made by the Secretary of State by statutory instrument.

(2)   Regulations under this Act may in particular—

(a)   make provision for dealing with non-compliance with any of the regulations (including the creation of criminal offences),

(b)   impose fees (which shall be paid into the Consolidated Fund), and

(c)   provide for the exercise of functions by persons prescribed by the regulations.

(3)   Regulations under this Act may—

(a)   contain any appropriate consequential, incidental, supplementary or transitional provisions or savings, and

(b)   make different provision for different purposes.

(4)   No regulations to which this subsection applies shall be made unless a draft of the statutory instrument containing the regulations (whether or not together with other provisions) has been laid before, and approved by a resolution of, each House of Parliament.

(5)   Subsection (4) applies to—

(a)   regulations under section 14(2) not consisting entirely of the application or incorporation (with or without modifications) of provisions contained in or made under the Insolvency Act 1986,

    (b)   regulations under section 15 not consisting entirely of the application or incorporation (with or without modifications) of provisions contained in or made under Part I, Chapter VIII of Part V, Part VII, Parts XI to XIII, Parts XVI to XVIII, Part XX or Parts XXIV to XXVI of the Companies Act 1985,

    (c)   regulations under section 14 or 15 making provision about oversea limited liability partnerships, and

    (d)   regulations under section 16.

    (6)   A statutory instrument containing regulations under this Act shall (unless a draft of it has been approved by a resolution of each House of Parliament) be subject to annulment in pursuance of a resolution of either House of Parliament.

Supplementary

18   Interpretation

In this Act—

    'address', in relation to a member of a limited liability partnership, means—

    (a)   if an individual, his usual residential address, and

    (b)   if a corporation or Scottish firm, its registered or principal office,

    'business' includes every trade, profession and occupation,

    'designated member' shall be construed in accordance with section 8,

    'enactment' includes subordinate legislation (within the meaning of the Interpretation Act 1978),

    'incorporation document' shall be construed in accordance with section 2,

    'limited liability partnership' has the meaning given by section 1(2),

    'member' shall be construed in accordance with section 4,

    'modifications' includes additions and omissions,

    'name', in relation to a member of a limited liability partnership, means—

    (a)   if an individual, his forename and surname (or, in the case of a peer or other person usually known by a title, his title instead of or in addition to either or both his forename and surname), and

    (b)   if a corporation or Scottish firm, its corporate or firm name

    'oversea limited liability partnership' has the meaning given by section 14(3),

    'the registrar' means—

    (a)   if the registered office of the limited liability partnership is, or is to be, situated in England and Wales or in Wales, the registrar or other officer performing under the Companies Act 1985 the duty of registration of companies in England and Wales, and

    (b)   if its registered office is, or is to be, situated in Scotland, the registrar or other officer performing under that Act the duty of registration of companies in Scotland, and

    'regulations' has the meaning given by section 17(1).

19   Commencement, extent and short title

    (1)   The preceding provisions of this Act shall come into force on such day as the Secretary of State may by order made by statutory instrument appoint; and different days may be appointed for different purposes.

    (2)   The Secretary of State may by order made by statutory instrument make any transitional provisions and savings which appear appropriate in connection with the coming into force of any provision of this Act.

    (3)   For the purposes of the Scotland Act 1998 this Act shall be taken to be a pre-commencement enactment within the meaning of that Act.

    (4)   Apart from sections 10 to 13 (and this section), this Act does not extend to Northern Ireland.

    (5)   This Act may be cited as the Limited Liability Partnerships Act 2000.

SCHEDULE
NAMES AND REGISTERED OFFICES

PART I
NAMES

Index of names

1   In section 714(1) of the Companies Act 1985 (index of names), after paragraph (d) insert—

'(da) limited liability partnerships incorporated under the Limited Liability Partnerships Act 2000,'.

Name to indicate status

2—(1)   The name of a limited liability partnership must end with—

(a)   the expression 'limited liability partnership', or

(b)   the abbreviation 'llp' or 'LLP'.

(2)   But if the incorporation document for a limited liability partnership states that the registered office is to be situated in Wales, its name must end with—

(a)   one of the expressions 'limited liability partnership' and 'partneriaeth atebolrwydd cyfyngedig', or

(b)   one of the abbreviations 'llp', 'LLP', 'pac' and 'PAC'.

Registration of names

3—(1)   A limited liability partnership shall not be registered by a name—

(a)   which includes, otherwise than at the end of the name, either of the expressions 'limited liability partnership' and 'partneriaeth atebolrwydd cyfyngedig' or any of the abbreviations 'llp', 'LLP', 'pac' and 'PAC',

(b)   which is the same as a name appearing in the index kept under section 714(1) of the Companies Act 1985,

(c)   the use of which by the limited liability partnership would in the opinion of the Secretary of State constitute a criminal offence, or

(d)   which in the opinion of the Secretary of State is offensive.

(2)   Except with the approval of the Secretary of State, a limited liability partnership shall not be registered by a name which—

(a)   in the opinion of the Secretary of State would be likely to give the impression that it is connected in any way with Her Majesty's Government or with any local authority, or

(b)   includes any word or expression for the time being specified in regulations under section 29 of the Companies Act 1985 (names needing approval),

and in paragraph (a) 'local authority' means any local authority within the meaning of the Local Government Act 1972 or the Local Government etc (Scotland) Act 1994, the Common Council of the City of London or the Council of the Isles of Scilly.

Change of name

4—(1)   A limited liability partnership may change its name at any time.

(2)   Where a limited liability partnership has been registered by a name which—

(a)   is the same as or, in the opinion of the Secretary of State, too like a name appearing at the time of registration in the index kept under section 714(1) of the Companies Act 1985, or

(b)   is the same as or, in the opinion of the Secretary of State, too like a name which should have appeared in the index at that time,

the Secretary of State may within twelve months of that time in writing direct the limited liability partnership to change its name within such period as he may specify.

(3)　If it appears to the Secretary of State—

(a)　that misleading information has been given for the purpose of the registration of a limited liability partnership by a particular name, or

(b)　that undertakings or assurances have been given for that purpose and have not been fulfilled,

he may, within five years of the date of its registration by that name, in writing direct the limited liability partnership to change its name within such period as he may specify.

(4)　If in the Secretary of State's opinion the name by which a limited liability partnership is registered gives so misleading an indication of the nature of its activities as to be likely to cause harm to the public, he may in writing direct the limited liability partnership to change its name within such period as he may specify.

(5)　But the limited liability partnership may, within three weeks from the date of the direction apply to the court to set it aside and the court may set the direction aside or confirm it and, if it confirms it, shall specify the period within which it must be complied with.

(6)　In sub-paragraph (5) 'the court' means—

(a)　if the registered office of the limited liability partnership is situated in England and Wales or in Wales, the High Court, and

(b)　if it is situated in Scotland, the Court of Session.

(7)　Where a direction has been given under sub-paragraph (2), (3) or (4) specifying a period within which a limited liability partnership is to change its name, the Secretary of State may at any time before that period ends extend it by a further direction in writing.

(8)　If a limited liability partnership fails to comply with a direction under this paragraph—

(a)　the limited liability partnership, and

(b)　any designated member in default,

commits an offence.

(9)　A person guilty of an offence under sub-paragraph (8) is liable on summary conviction to a fine not exceeding level 3 on the standard scale.

Notification of change of name

5—(1)　Where a limited liability partnership changes its name it shall deliver notice of the change to the registrar.

(2)　A notice delivered under sub-paragraph (1)—

(a)　shall be in a form approved by the registrar, and

(b)　shall be signed by a designated member of the limited liability partnership or authenticated in a manner approved by the registrar.

(3) Where the registrar receives a notice under sub-paragraph (2) he shall (unless the new name is one by which a limited liability partnership may not be registered)—

(a)　enter the new name in the index kept under section 714(1) of the Companies Act 1985, and

(b)　issue a certificate of the change of name.

(4)　The change of name has effect from the date on which the certificate is issued.

Effect of change of name

6　A change of name by a limited liability partnership does not—

(a)　affect any of its rights or duties

(b)　render defective any legal proceedings by or against it

and any legal proceedings that might have been commenced or continued against it by its former name may be commenced or continued against it by its new name.

Improper use of 'limited liability partnership' etc

7—(1)   If any person carries on a business under a name or title which includes as the last words—

(a)   the expression 'limited liability partnership' or 'partneriaeth atebolrwydd cyfyngedig', or

(b)   any contraction or imitation of either of those expressions,

that person, unless a limited liability partnership or oversea limited liability partnership, commits an offence.

(2)   A person guilty of an offence under sub-paragraph (1) is liable on summary conviction to a fine not exceeding level 3 on the standard scale.

Similarity of names

8   In determining for the purposes of this Part whether one name is the same as another there are to be disregarded—

(1)   the definite article as the first word of the name,

(2)   any of the following (or their Welsh equivalents or abbreviations of them or their Welsh equivalents) at the end of the name—

'limited liability partnership',

'company',

'and company',

'company limited',

'and company limited',

'limited',

'unlimited',

'public limited company',

['community interest company',

'community interest public limited company',]

'investment company with variable capital', and

(3)   type and case of letters, accents, spaces between letters and punctuation marks, and 'and' and '&' are to be taken as the same.

PART II
REGISTERED OFFICES

Situation of registered office

9—(1)   A limited liability partnership shall—

(a)   at all times have a registered office situated in England and Wales or in Wales, or

(b)   at all times have a registered office situated in Scotland,

to which communications and notices may be addressed.

(2)   On the incorporation of a limited liability partnership the situation of its registered office shall be that stated in the incorporation document.

(3)   Where the registered office of a limited liability partnership is situated in Wales, but the incorporation document does not state that it is to be situated in Wales (as opposed to England and Wales), the limited liability partnership may deliver notice to the registrar stating that its registered office is to be situated in Wales.

(4)   A notice delivered under sub-paragraph (3)—

(a)   shall be in a form approved by the registrar, and

(b)   shall be signed by a designated member of the limited liability partnership or authenticated in a manner approved by the registrar.

Change of registered office

10—(1)   A limited liability partnership may change its registered office by delivering notice of the change to the registrar.

(2)   A notice delivered under sub-paragraph (1)—

(a)   shall be in a form approved by the registrar, and

(b)   shall be signed by a designated member of the limited liability partnership or authenticated in a manner approved by the registrar.

DEBT ARRANGEMENT AND ATTACHMENT (SCOTLAND) ACT 2002
(2002, asp 17)

PART 1
THE DEBT ARRANGEMENT SCHEME

1   Debt arrangement scheme

This Part of this Act constitutes a scheme (to be known as the 'debt arrangement scheme') under which individuals may arrange for their debts to be paid under debt payment programmes.

2   Debt payment programmes

(1)   A debt payment programme is a programme which provides for the payment of money owed by a debtor.

(2)   The Scottish Ministers may, on an application by a debtor, approve any debt payment programme set out in the application.

(3)   Such an application shall be signed by the debtor and shall—

(a)   specify, to the best of the debtor's knowledge and belief, in relation to each debt which the debtor is proposing to be paid under the debt payment programme—

(i)   the amount outstanding;

(ii)   the creditor to whom the debt is due; and

(iii)   the period for which the debt has been due;

(b)   set out the arrangements under which those debts are, in accordance with the provisions of the programme, to be paid, in particular specifying—

(i)   the amounts which the debtor proposes to pay under the programme;

(ii)   the proposed regularity of those payments;

(iii)   the manner in which those payments are to be made; and

(iv)   the manner in which, and period over which, each of the debts included in the programme is to be paid;

(c)   specify the name and address of the person (the 'payments distributor') who is to—

(i)   receive payments from the debtor; and

(ii)   pay, on behalf of the debtor, the debts included in the programme, in accordance with the provisions of the programme; and

(d)   contain such other information (including information relating to the debtor's financial circumstances), and be in such form, as may be prescribed.

(4)   Such an application shall, subject to any contrary provision in regulations made under section 7(1) below, incorporate the consent, indicated in the prescribed form, of all the debtor's creditors.

(5)   A person's name and address shall not be specified in an application for approval of a debt payment programme as a payments distributor unless that person has been approved by the Scottish Ministers as a person suitable to carry out the functions of a payments distributor.

3   Money advice

(1)   A debtor is not entitled to make an application for the approval, or the variation, of a debt payment programme unless the debtor has obtained the advice of a money adviser in relation to—

(a)   the debtor's financial circumstances;

(b)   the effect of the proposed programme or, as the case may be, the proposed variation of the programme; and

(c)   the preparation of the application.

(2)   Such an application shall—

(a) contain a signed declaration by the money adviser who provided the advice referred to in subsection (1) above that such advice has been given; and

(b) specify the name and address of the money adviser.

4 Effect of debt payment programmes

(1) Where a debt payment programme has been approved or varied, the debts specified in the application for the approval or, as the case may be, the variation shall be paid in accordance with the programme.

(2) It is not competent—

(a) to serve a charge for payment in respect of; or

(b) [other than under subsection (2A),] to commence or execute any diligence to enforce payment of; or

[(c) to commit to prison under section 4 of the Civil Imprisonment (Scotland) Act 1882, other than for the purposes of section 40 of the Child Support Act 1991, in respect of,]

any debt owed by a debtor who has debts which are being paid under an approved debt payment programme.

[(2A) It is competent to—

(a) auction an attached article where—

(i) notice has been given to the debtor under section 27(4) below; or

(ii) an article has been removed, or notice of removal has been given, under section 53 below;

(b) implement a decree of furthcoming;

(c) implement a decree or order for sale of a ship (or a share of it) or cargo; and

(d) sell the effects of a debtor to satisfy a decree obtained in an action for sequestration for rent due by the debtor.]

(3) A creditor is not entitled to found on any debt owed by such a debtor in presenting, or concurring in the presentation of, a petition for the sequestration of the debtor's estate.

(4) There is to be disregarded, for the purposes of the exercise by a creditor of any rights to enforce a debt or remedies to like effect, any period during which the debtor's debts were subject to an approved debt payment programme.

(5) The debts referred to in subsections (2) to (4) above are restricted to—

(a) those to which the debtor's debt payment programme relates; and

(b) any other debts owed to creditors who have been given notice, in the prescribed form, of the approval of the debt payment programme.

5 Variation of debt payment programmes

(1) The Scottish Ministers may, on an application by the debtor or by any creditor, approve the variation of a debt payment programme.

(2) The Scottish Ministers may not consider an application for approval of a variation under subsection (1) above unless—

(a) where the application is made by the debtor, a copy of the application has been given to each creditor who is owed a debt which is being paid under the debt payment programme; or

(b) where the application is made by a creditor, a copy of the application has been given to the debtor and to each other creditor who is owed such a debt.

(3) Such an application may seek the variation of any condition which is attached to the approval of the programme or, as the case may be, a previous variation of the programme.

(4) An application for the variation of a debt payment programme shall—

(a) contain such information, and be in such form, as may be prescribed; and

(b) be signed by the debtor or, as the case may be, the creditor.

6 Deduction from earnings

(1) Where an approved debt payment programme requires sums to be paid to the payments distributor by way of deduction of the debtor's earnings from employment, the debtor shall provide an instruction, in the prescribed form, to the person by whom the debtor is employed to make—

(a) deductions from the debtor's earnings; and

(b) payments of the amounts deducted to the payments distributor, in accordance with the provisions of the debt payment programme.

(2) It is the duty of the employer to comply with any instruction so provided.

7 Debt payment programmes: power to make further provision

(1) The Scottish Ministers may, by regulations, make such further provision as they think fit in connection with—

(a) applications for the approval, or for the variation, of debt payment programmes;

(b) the manner in which such programmes are to operate, including conditions with which debtors, creditors, payments distributors or money advisers must comply;

(c) the effect of such programmes; and

(d) the effect of the failure of an employer to comply with the duty under section 6(2) above.

(2) The regulations may, in particular, make provision about—

(a) the class of person who may or may not make an application for the approval, or the variation, of a debt payment programme;

(b) the class of debt in respect of which such an application may or may not be made;

(c) the matters to which the Scottish Ministers are to have regard in determining whether to approve such an application;

(d) the conditions which may or may not be attached to an approval of such an application;

(e) circumstances in which such an application will not be approved;

(f) appeals against determinations by the Scottish Ministers on such applications;

(g) circumstances in which the consent for the purposes of section 2(4) above of a creditor or creditors generally may be dispensed with;

(h) circumstances in which a creditor may object to—

(i) the dispensation of the creditor's consent; or

(ii) the approval of such an application, and the manner in which such objection may be made;

(i) the remitting of any such application in respect of which a creditor has made an objection to the sheriff for determination;

(j) the manner in which a debt payment programme may be varied;

(k) the priority in which debts are to be paid under a debt payment programme;

(l) the ingathering and sale or other disposal of assets and the distribution to creditors of amounts so realised;

(m) the period for which a debt payment programme is to remain in operation;

(n) circumstances in which, and the procedure under which, any such period can, in relation to a particular debt payment programme, be shortened or extended;

(o) circumstances in which a debt payment programme is to cease to have effect;

(p) subject to section 4 above, the manner in which a debt payment programme affects the rights or remedies of a creditor or other third party;

(q) circumstances in which creditors are to notify debtors of the right to make such an application and the effect of the failure of a creditor to provide that notice;

    (r)   the class of person who may act as a payments distributor;

    (s)   the class of person who may act as a money adviser;

    (t)   the functions of a payments distributor;

    (u)   the functions of a money adviser;

    (v)   the establishment and maintenance by the Scottish Ministers of a register of debt payment programmes and applications for the approval, and variation, of such programmes;

    (w) the information which is to be kept in such a register;

    (x)   the manner in which that information is to be kept and in which it, or any part of it, is to be made available to the public; and

    (y)   the determination, and charging, by the Scottish Ministers of fees in respect of—

       (i)   the consideration of applications for the approval, or the variation, of a debt payment programme; and

       (ii)   the provision of information recorded in the register of debt payment programmes.

    (3)   The regulations may also—

    (a)   make different provision in relation to such different types of debtors, debts or other matters as may be described by the Scottish Ministers;

    (b)   provide that such different provision is to have effect only for such period as is specified by the Scottish Ministers; and

    (c)   provide that, on the expiry of that period, the Scottish Ministers may determine that the different provision to which they relate is to—

       (i)   continue to have effect without limit of time;

       (ii)   continue to have effect for such further period as may be determined by the Scottish Ministers; or

       (iii)   cease to have effect.

    (4)   The regulations may also modify any enactment (including this Act), instrument or document for the purposes of making such further provision as is mentioned in subsection (1) above.

8 Functions of the Scottish Ministers

    (1)   The Scottish Ministers may by order provide that their functions under this Part of this Act may be performed on their behalf by such other person as may be specified in the order.

    (2)   Such an order does not allow regulations under this Part of this Act or any further order under this section to be made by any person other than the Scottish Ministers.

    (3)   Such an order may make different provision for different functions.

9 Interpretation of Part

    (1)   In this Part of this Act—

'money adviser' means any person who has been approved by the Scottish Ministers as a person who may give advice to a debtor for the purposes of section 3(1) above; and

'prescribed' means prescribed by regulations made by the Scottish Ministers.

    (2)   The references in this Part of this Act to a debtor are references to a debtor who is a natural person.

PART 2
ATTACHMENT

Attachment

10   Attachment

(1)   There shall be a form of diligence over corporeal moveable property for recovery of money owed; it is to be known as attachment.

(2)   Attachment is exigible only in execution of a decree or document of debt and only upon property owned (whether alone or in common) by the debtor.

(3)   Attachment is competent only where—

(a)   subject to subsection (4) below, the debtor has been charged to pay, within such period as is specified in the charge, the sum specified in the decree or document of debt, together with any interest accrued on the sum; and

(b)   the creditor has, before taking any steps to execute an attachment, provided the debtor with a debt advice and information package.

(4)   An attachment in pursuance of a summary warrant may be proceeded with in the absence of a charge to pay.

(5)   In this section—

'debt advice and information package' means a document or bundle of documents containing such information (including information regarding the availability of money advice within the debtor's locality), and in such form, as the Scottish Ministers may determine;

'decree' means—

(a)   a decree of the Court of Session, of the High Court of Justiciary or of the sheriff;

(b)   a decree of the Court of Teinds;

(c)   a summary warrant;

(d)   a civil judgment granted outside Scotland by a court, tribunal or arbiter which by virtue of any enactment or rule of law is enforceable in Scotland;

(e)   an order or determination which by virtue of any enactment is enforceable as if it were an extract registered decree arbitral bearing a warrant for execution issued by the sheriff;

(f)   a warrant granted, in criminal proceedings, for enforcement by civil diligence;

(g)   an order under section 114 of the Companies Clauses Consolidation (Scotland) Act 1845 (c 17);

(h)   a determination under section 46 of the Harbours, Docks and Piers Clauses Act 1847 (c 27); or

(i)   a liability order within the meaning of section 33(2) of the Child Support Act 1991 (c 48), being a decree, warrant, judgment, order or determination which, or an extract of which, authorises attachment; and

'document of debt' means—

(a)   a document registered for execution in the Books of Council and Session or the sheriff court books; or

(b)   a document or settlement which by virtue of an Order in Council made under section 13 of the Civil Jurisdiction and Judgments Act 1982 (c 27) is enforceable in Scotland,

being a document, bill or settlement which, or an extract of which, authorises attachment.

(6)   The Scottish Ministers may by order modify the definitions of 'decree' and 'document of debt' in subsection (5) above so as to—

(a)   add or remove types of decree or document to or, as the case may be, from those referred to in that provision; or

(b)   vary any of the descriptions of the types of decree or document there referred to.

(7) In this Act, references to attaching are references to the execution of attachment.

11 Articles exempt from attachment

(1) It is not competent to attach—

(a) any implements, tools of trade, books or other equipment reasonably required for the use of the debtor in the practice of the debtor's profession, trade or business and not exceeding in aggregate value £1,000 or such amount as may be prescribed in regulations made by the Scottish Ministers;

(b) any vehicle, the use of which is so reasonably required by the debtor, not exceeding in value £1,000 or such amount as may be prescribed in regulations made by the Scottish Ministers;

(c) a mobile home which is the debtor's only or principal residence;

(d) any tools or other equipment reasonably required for the purpose of keeping in good order and condition any garden or yard adjacent to, or associated with, a dwellinghouse in which the debtor resides.

(2) The Scottish Ministers may by regulations modify subsection (1) above so as to—

(a) add or remove types of articles to or, as the case may be, from those referred to in that provision; or

(b) vary any of the descriptions of the types of articles there referred to.

12 Times when attachment is not competent

(1) It is not competent to execute an attachment on—

(a) a Sunday;

(b) a day which is a public holiday in the area in which the attachment is to be executed; or

(c) such other day as may be prescribed by Act of Sederunt.

(2) The execution of an attachment shall not—

(a) begin before 8 am or after 8 pm; or

(b) be continued after 8 pm,

unless the officer has obtained prior authority from the sheriff for such commencement or continuation.

13 Presumption of ownership

(1) An officer may, when executing an attachment, proceed on the assumption that the debtor owns, solely or in common with a third party, any article which is in the possession of the debtor.

(2) The officer shall, before attaching any article, make enquiries of any person who is present at the place at which the article is situated as to the ownership of the article (and in particular shall enquire as to whether there is any person who owns the article in common with the debtor).

(3) The officer may not proceed on the assumption mentioned in subsection (1) above where the officer knows or ought to know that the contrary is the case.

(4) The officer is not precluded from relying on that assumption by reason only of one or both of the following circumstances—

(a) that the article belongs to a class which is commonly held under a hire, hire-purchase or conditional sale agreement or on some other limited title of possession;

(b) that an assertion has been made that the article is not owned by the debtor.

Attachment of articles kept outwith dwellinghouses etc

14 Procedure for attachment of articles kept outwith dwellinghouses etc

Sections 15 to 19 below apply only in relation to the attachment of articles which are—

(a) kept outwith a dwellinghouse; or

(b) mobile homes which are not the only or principal residence of the debtor.

15 Power of entry and valuation

(1) An officer may open shut and lockfast places for the purposes of executing an attachment.

(2) When executing an attachment the officer shall, subject to subsection (3) below, value the articles being attached at the price which they are likely to fetch if sold on the open market.

(3) Where the officer considers that an article is such that a valuation by a professional valuer or other suitably skilled person is appropriate, the officer shall arrange for such a valuation and a valuation so arranged shall proceed on the basis set out in subsection (2) above.

16 Attachment of mobile homes

(1) Where a mobile home which is the only or principal residence of a person other than the debtor has been attached—
(a) the officer shall give notice to that other person of that fact; and
(b) the sheriff may, on an application by the debtor or that other person, order that the attachment of the mobile home is to cease to have effect.

(2) The sheriff—
(a) shall consider any application for an order under subsection (1) above which is made before the date which is 14 days after the date on which the mobile home is attached; and
(b) may, on cause shown, consider any such application which is made at any time after that date but before the date on which the attached mobile home is auctioned.

17 Report of attachment

(1) The officer shall, within 14 days of the execution of an attachment (or such longer period as the sheriff on cause shown may allow on application by the officer), make to the sheriff a report of the attachment.

(2) A report made under subsection (1) above shall—
(a) be in the form prescribed by Act of Sederunt; and
(b) be signed by the officer.

(3) Such a report shall specify—
(a) whether any person, in response to enquiries made under section 13(2) above, asserted that any attached article is not owned by the debtor (or is owned in common by the debtor and a third party);
(b) whether any attached article has been redeemed under section 18(1) below.

(4) Such a report need not be made in respect of any article or vehicle which has been sold in pursuance of an order made under section 20(1)(b) or, as the case may be, 22(3) below.

(5) The sheriff may refuse to receive such a report on the ground that it has not been made and signed in accordance with subsections (1) and (2) above.

(6) If the sheriff so refuses—
(a) the attachment to which the report relates is to cease to have effect; and
(b) the sheriff clerk shall intimate the refusal to—
(i) the debtor; and
(ii) if another person is in possession of the attached articles, that person.

18 Redemption

(1) Subject to any order made under section 20(1)(b) below, the debtor is entitled, within 14 days of the date on which an article is attached, to redeem that article.

(2) The amount for which such an article may be redeemed is the value fixed under subsection (2) or (3) of section 15 above.

(3)   The officer shall, on receiving payment from the debtor for the redemption of an attached article, grant a receipt in the form prescribed by Act of Sederunt to the debtor.

(4)   The attachment of the article is, on the grant of such a receipt, to cease to have effect.

(5)   Where an article is redeemed after the officer has made a report under section 17(1) above in respect of the attachment, the officer shall report the redemption as soon as is reasonably practicable to the sheriff.

19   Removal and auction of attached articles

(1)   The officer who attached articles may, after the report of attachment has been received by the sheriff—

(a)   make arrangements for the auction of the attached articles; and

(b)   on the date specified in the notice given under section 27(4) below, remove the attached articles from the place at which they are kept.

(2)   The officer may open shut and lockfast places for the purpose of so removing the attached articles.

(3)   The officer may not remove any vehicle in respect of which an application for an order under subsection (1) or (3) of section 22 below has been made but not disposed of.

(4)   The officer may remove to the place at which the auction is to be held such attached articles as, if sold at their values fixed under subsection (2) or, as the case may be, (3) of section 15 above, would realise in aggregate the sum recoverable at the time of the auction.

(5)   The remaining attached articles will cease to be subject to attachment.

(6)   An attached article shall not, subject to any order made under section 20(1)(b) or 22(3) below, be auctioned before the date which is 7 days after the date on which the article is removed by the officer from the place at which it was attached.

Attachment: further procedure

20   Order for security of articles or sale of articles which are perishable etc

(1)   The sheriff may, on an application by the creditor, the officer or the debtor, at any time after articles have been attached make an order—

(a)   for the security of any of the attached articles;

(b)   in relation to any of the articles which are of a perishable nature or which are likely to deteriorate substantially and rapidly in condition or value, for the creditor or the officer to make arrangements for their immediate sale and for any proceeds of the sale to be consigned in court.

(2)   An application for an order under subsection (1) above—

(a)   by the creditor or the officer, shall be intimated by the creditor or, as the case may be, the officer to the debtor;

(b)   by the debtor, shall be intimated to the creditor and the officer, at the time when it is made.

(3)   A decision of the sheriff to make an order under subsection (1)(b) above shall not be subject to appeal.

(4)   Any sum consigned in court in pursuance of an order made under subsection (1)(b) above shall, where an attachment ceases to have effect before the auction of attached articles is held, be paid to the creditor to the extent necessary to meet the sum recoverable, any surplus thereof being paid to the debtor.

21   Unlawful acts after attachment

(1)   The debtor or person in possession of an attached article shall not move it from the place at which it was attached.

(2)   If an article is so moved—

(a) the debtor or, as the case may be, the person in possession of the attached articles is acting in breach of the attachment; and

(b) the sheriff may, on an application by the creditor or by the officer, by order authorise the attachment of other articles which are owned by the debtor and kept at the place at which the original attachment was executed.

(3) Subsection (1) above does not apply in relation to any vehicle in respect of which an application for an order under subsection (1) or (3) of section 22 below has been made but not disposed of.

(4) The debtor shall not sell, make a gift of or otherwise relinquish ownership of any attached article.

(5) If an attached article is so sold, gifted or otherwise disposed of the debtor is acting in breach of the attachment.

(6) Any person who wilfully damages or destroys any article which that person knows has been attached is acting in breach of the attachment.

(7) Where an attached article is stolen, the debtor shall give notice to the creditor and the officer of that fact and of any related claim which the debtor makes, or intends to make, under a contract of insurance.

(8) Any debtor who fails to give notice as required by subsection (7) above is acting in breach of the attachment.

(9) Any act which is, under subsection (2), (5), (6) or (8) above, a breach of the attachment may be dealt with as a contempt of court.

(10) Where attached articles are damaged, destroyed or stolen the sheriff, on an application by the creditor or by the officer, may by order authorise—

(a) the attachment of other articles which are owned by the debtor and kept at the place at which the original attachment was executed;

(b) the revaluation of any damaged article in accordance with subsection (2) or (3) of section 15 above.

(11) Where the debtor or any third party who knows that an article is attached—

(a) moves it from the place at which the attachment was executed, and it is—

(i) damaged, destroyed, lost or stolen; or

(ii) acquired from or through the debtor or, as the case may be, the third party by another person without knowledge of the attachment and for value; or

(b) wilfully damages or destroys it,

the sheriff may order the debtor or, as the case may be, the third party to consign the sum set out in subsection (12) below in court.

(12) That sum is—

(a) where the article has been damaged but not so damaged as to make it worthless, a sum equal to the difference between the value of the article fixed under subsection (2) or (3) of section 15 above or, as the case may be, under section 51 or 54(1) below and the value of the article so damaged; or

(b) in any other case, a sum equal to the value of the article as fixed under subsection (2) or (3) of section 15 above or, as the case may be, under section 51 or 54(1) below.

(13) For the purposes of subsection (12)(a) above, the officer shall, subject to subsection (14) below, value a damaged article at the price which it is likely to fetch if sold in that condition on the open market.

(14) Where the officer considers that a damaged article is such that a valuation by a professional valuer or other suitably skilled person is appropriate, the officer shall arrange for such a valuation and a valuation so arranged shall proceed on the basis set out in subsection (13) above.

(15) Any sum consigned in court in pursuance of an order made under subsection (11) above shall, where the attachment of a damaged article ceases to have effect before it is auctioned, be paid to the creditor to the extent necessary to meet the sum recoverable, any surplus thereof being paid to the debtor.

22 Release of vehicle from attachment

(1) The sheriff may, on an application by the debtor and on being satisfied that the auction of any vehicle which has been attached would be unduly harsh in the circumstances, make an order—

(a) providing that the attachment of the vehicle is to cease to have effect; and

(b) where the vehicle has been removed by the officer from the place at which it was attached, requiring the officer to return the vehicle to that place.

(2) The sheriff may not make an order under subsection (1) above unless the value of the vehicle (as fixed under subsection (2) or (3) of section 15 above) does not exceed £1,000 or such other amount as may be prescribed in regulations made by the Scottish Ministers.

(3) Where the value (as fixed under subsection (2) or (3) of section 15 above) of an attached vehicle does exceed £1,000 or, as the case may be, such other prescribed amount the sheriff may, on an application by the debtor and on being satisfied that the auction of any vehicle which has been attached would be unduly harsh in the circumstances, make an order requiring the officer to—

(a) make arrangements for the immediate sale of the vehicle;

(b) pay to the debtor from any proceeds of such sale the sum of £1,000 (or such lesser amount as the sheriff may specify); and

(c) consign any surplus remaining in court.

(4) Where the amount realised on the sale of a vehicle in pursuance of an order has been made under subsection (3) above is less than the amount which the officer is required by that order to pay to the debtor, the order shall be deemed to have required the officer to pay the amount realised only.

(5) Where the officer is unable to sell the vehicle in pursuance of an order made under subsection (3) above within 14 days of the date on which the order was made, the attachment of that vehicle is to cease to have effect.

(6) The sheriff may consider an application for an order under subsection (1) or (3) above only where it is made within 14 days of the date on which the vehicle is attached.

23 Appeals against valuation

(1) Where the sheriff is satisfied that the aggregate of the values of attached articles fixed under section 15(2) or (3) above or, as the case may be, section 51 or 54(1) below is substantially below the aggregate of the prices which they are likely to fetch if sold on the open market, the sheriff may, on or before the day which immediately precedes the day on which the articles are to be auctioned, order that the attachment is to cease to have effect.

(2) The sheriff may make an order under subsection (1) above on the application of the debtor or on the sheriff's own accord.

(3) The sheriff shall not make such an order without first giving the debtor and the creditor—

(a) an opportunity to make representations; and

(b) if either party wishes to be heard, an opportunity to be heard.

24 Duration of attachment

(1) An attachment shall, subject to subsections (6), (7) and (8) below, have effect only until—

(a) the earlier of—

(i) the date which is six months after the date on which the article is attached; and

(ii) the date which is 28 days after the date on which the attached article is removed by the officer from the place at which it was attached; or

(b) such other date as may be specified in an order made under subsection (2) or section 29(4)(b) below or in an exceptional attachment order.

(2) Where the sheriff is satisfied—

(a)   that, if the date on which an attachment is to cease to have effect were to be substituted with a later date, the debtor is likely to comply with an agreement between the creditor and the debtor for the payment of the sum recoverable by instalments or otherwise; or

(b)   that the auction of the attached articles cannot take place before the date on which the attachment is to cease to have effect due to circumstances for which the creditor cannot be held responsible and that the attachment ceasing to have effect on that date would prejudice the creditor,

the sheriff may, on an application by the creditor or by the officer, by order provide that the attachment is to remain in effect until such later date as the sheriff considers reasonable in the circumstances.

(3)   Where the period for which an attachment is to have effect is extended by an order made under subsection (2) above, an application may be made for another order under that subsection so as to further extend that period.

(4)   The sheriff may consider an application for an order under subsection (2) above only where it is made during the period in respect of which an extension is being sought.

(5)   A decision of the sheriff on such an application shall be intimated to the debtor by the sheriff clerk.

(6)   Where such an application is made but not disposed of before the date on which the attachment in respect of which it is made would, but for this subsection, cease to have effect, the attachment shall continue to have effect until the application is disposed of.

(7)   Where such an application is—

(a)   made on the ground referred to in paragraph (a) of subsection (2) above; and

(b)   refused by the sheriff within 14 days of the date on which the attachment in respect of which it is made would, but for this subsection, cease to have effect,

the attachment shall continue to have effect until the date which is 14 days after the date of the refusal.

(8)   Where—

(a)   arrangements for an auction of attached articles are, under section 29(1) below, cancelled; and

(b)   the agreement in respect of which the cancellation is made is breached by the debtor,

the period which begins with the date on which the report of agreement was made under section 29(3) below and which ends with the date on which the debtor breaches the agreement is to be disregarded in determining the date on which the attachment is, under subsection (1) above, to cease to have effect.

25 Second attachment at same place

(1)   Subject to—

(a)   section 9(12) (which provides that a debt which remains outstanding on the recall or cessation of a time to pay order may be enforced by certain diligences) of the Debtors (Scotland) Act 1987 (c 18);

(b)   any order made under subsection (2)(b) or (10)(a) of section 21 above; and

(c)   sections 34(3) and 35(4) below,

where articles are attached (or are purported to be attached) at any place, it is not competent to attach other articles kept at that place to enforce the same debt unless those other articles are brought to that place after the execution of the first attachment.

(2)   It is not competent to attach any article in respect of which an attachment has—

(a)   previously been executed in enforcement of the same debt; and

(b) ceased, by virtue of section 16, 18(4), 22(1), 34(1), 35(3), 55(2) or 56(4) of this Act, to have effect.

26 Invalidity and cessation of attachment

(1) Where, at any time before the auction of an article which has been or purports to have been attached, the sheriff is satisfied that—

(a) the attachment has ceased to have effect; or, as the case may be

(b) the purported attachment is invalid (by reason of the attachment being incompetent or otherwise),

the sheriff shall make an order declaring that to be the case and may make such consequential order as appears to the sheriff to be necessary in the circumstances.

(2) An order under subsection (1) above may be made on an application by the debtor or on the sheriff's own initiative.

(3) Where such an order is made on the sheriff's own initiative, the sheriff clerk shall intimate the order to the debtor.

(4) The sheriff shall not make an order under subsection (1) above without first giving the debtor and the creditor—

(a) an opportunity to make representations; and

(b) if either party wishes to be heard, an opportunity to be heard.

(5) Where—

(a) an order is made under subsection (1) above; and

(b) the officer has removed the article from the place at which it was, or purported to be, attached,

the officer shall return the article to the place from which it was removed.

(6) The sheriff shall give reasons for a refusal to grant an order under subsection (1) above.

Auction of attached articles

27 Notice of public auction

(1) The auction of attached articles shall, subject to subsections (2) and (3) below, be by public auction held in an auction room.

(2) If it is impractical to hold the auction of an attached article in an auction room the auction may be held at such other place (other than the debtor's dwellinghouse) as the officer considers appropriate.

(3) The auction of other articles which have been attached together with an article which is to be auctioned at a place other than an auction room may, if the officer considers it appropriate (having had regard, in particular, to the expenses which are likely to be incurred in connection with the auction), also be held at that other place.

(4) The officer authorised to arrange the auction shall give notice to the debtor and to any other person in possession of the attached articles of—

(a) the date on which the auction is to be held;

(b) the location of the auction room or, as the case may be, the other place at which the auction is to be held; and

(c) where sections 15 to 19 above apply in relation to the attached articles, the date arranged for the removal of those attached articles from the place at which they are kept.

(5) The officer shall advertise the auction by public notice.

28 Alteration of arrangements for removal or auction

(1) Subject to subsection (2) below and without prejudice to section 29(4) below, the creditor or the officer is not, after notice has been given under section 27(4) above to the debtor, entitled to arrange—

(a) a new date for the auction; or

(b) where sections 15 to 19 above apply in relation to the attached articles, a new date for the removal of those articles from the place where they are kept.

(2) Where, for any reason for which neither the creditor nor the officer is responsible, it is not possible—

(a)   for the auction to be held on the date specified in the notice given under section 27(4) above; or

(b)   for the attached articles to be removed from the place where they are kept on the date so specified,

the creditor may instruct the officer to arrange a new date for the auction or, as the case may be, a new date for the removal and the officer shall intimate the new date to the debtor and to any other person in possession of the attached articles.

(3) A new date arranged under subsection (2) above shall not in any case be fewer than 7 days after the date of intimation under that subsection.

29   Cancellation of auctions

(1) The officer may, for the purposes of enabling the sum recoverable to be paid in accordance with an agreement between the creditor and the debtor, cancel arrangements for an auction of attached articles.

(2) The officer may not cancel the arrangements for such an auction on more than two occasions.

(3) Where an auction has been cancelled the officer shall—

(a)   make to the sheriff a report of the agreement reached; and

(b)   arrange for the return of any attached articles which have been removed for auction to the place from which they were removed.

(4) The sheriff, if satisfied on an application by the creditor that the debtor is in breach of any agreement which has been reported under subsection (3) above, may by order provide—

(a)   if the arrangements for the auction of the attached articles can still be implemented in accordance with the provisions of this Part and Part 3 of this Act, that the officer may resume making arrangements for the auction in accordance with those provisions;

(b)   if for any reason for which neither the creditor nor the officer is responsible arrangements for the auction cannot be implemented in accordance with those provisions, that the provisions of this Part and Part 3 of this Act which prevent such implementation are not to apply for the purposes of the attachment and auction of those articles.

(5) The sheriff shall not make an order under subsection (4) above without first giving the debtor—

(a)   an opportunity to make representations; and

(b)   if the debtor so wishes, an opportunity to be heard.

30   Auction

(1) The officer shall attend the auction and maintain a record of the attached articles which are sold.

(2) Such a record shall specify the amount for which each attached article is sold.

(3) The officer shall be accompanied at the auction by another person who shall witness the proceedings.

(4) Any attached article exposed for sale in the auction may be purchased by—

(a)   any creditor, including the creditor on whose behalf the article was attached;

(b)   a third party who owns the attached article in common with the debtor.

31   Disposal of proceeds of auction

(1) The officer shall, subject to section 37 (effect of sequestration on diligence) of the Bankruptcy (Scotland) Act 1985 (c 66), dispose of the proceeds of the auction by—

(a)   retaining such amount as necessary to meet the fees and outlays of the officer;

(b)   paying to the creditor the remainder of the proceeds of auction so far as necessary to meet the sum recoverable; and

(c)   paying to the debtor any surplus remaining.

(2)   Where the sum recoverable is not realised by the proceeds of auction and any article remains unsold after being exposed for auction—

(a)   ownership of the article shall, without prejudice to the rights of any third party, pass to the creditor; and

(b)   the value of that article shall be credited against the sum recoverable.

(3)   Where the value of unsold articles exceeds the amount of the sum recoverable which remains outstanding, subsection (2) above shall operate only in relation to such of those articles which have, in aggregate, the value which is nearest to the amount which remains outstanding.

(4)   The references in subsections (2)(b) and (3) above to the value of an article are references to the value of the article as fixed under subsection (2) or (3) of section 15 above or, as the case may be, section 51 or 54(1) below.

(5)   Where the creditor does not uplift an article within 3 working days after the day on which the auction is held the ownership of the article shall revert to the person who owned the article before the operation of subsection (2)(a) above.

(6)   For the purposes of this section—

'proceeds of auction' include any amount—

(a)   consigned in court in pursuance of an order made under section 21(11), 20(1)(b), 22(3) or 50(5) of this Act;

(b)   received by the officer in respect of a transfer, under section 35(2) below, of the debtor's interest in any article owned in common by the debtor and a third party,

but do not include any amount which the officer is required to pay to the debtor in pursuance of an order under section 22(3) above; and

'working day' means a day which is not—

(a)   a Saturday;

(b)   a Sunday;

(c)   New Year's Day;

(d)   2nd January;

(e)   Good Friday;

(f)   Easter Monday;

(g)   Christmas Day;

(h)   Boxing Day; or

(i)   any other day which is a public holiday in the area in which the auction is held.

32   Report of auction

(1)   The officer who arranged the auction shall, within the period of 14 days after the date on which the auction is held, make to the sheriff a report in the form prescribed by Act of Sederunt (a 'report of auction').

(2)   A report of auction shall—

(a)   specify—

(i)   any attached articles which have been sold;

(ii)   the amount for which they have been sold;

(iii)   any attached articles which remain unsold;

(iv)   any chargeable expenses;

(v)   any surplus paid to the debtor; and

(vi)   any balance due by or to the debtor;

(b)   refer to any article in respect of which—

(i)   an attachment has, under section 34(1) below or in pursuance of an order made under section 35(3) below, ceased to have effect;

(ii)   the debtor's interest has, under section 35(2) below, transferred to a third party;

    (c)   contain a declaration by the officer that all the information contained within it is, to the best of the officer's knowledge, true; and

    (d)   be signed by the officer and the witness who attended the auction.

   (3)   If the officer—

    (a)   without reasonable excuse makes a report of auction after the expiry of the period mentioned in subsection (1) above; or

    (b)   wilfully refuses to make, or delays making, a report of auction after the expiry of that period,

the sheriff may make an order providing that the officer is liable for the chargeable expenses, either in whole or in part.

   (4)   An order made under subsection (3) above does not prejudice the right of the sheriff to report the matter to the Court of Session or the sheriff principal under section 79(1)(b) (investigation of alleged misconduct by a messenger-at-arms or sheriff officer) of the Debtors (Scotland) Act 1987 (c 18).

33 Audit of report of auction

   (1)   The sheriff shall remit the report of auction to the auditor of court who shall—

    (a)   tax the chargeable expenses;

    (b)   certify the balance due by or to the debtor following the auction; and

    (c)   make a report to the sheriff.

   (2)   The auditor of court shall not alter the report of auction without first providing all interested persons an opportunity to make representations.

   (3)   The auditor of court shall not charge a fee in respect of the report made under subsection (1)(c) above.

   (4)   On receipt of a report made under subsection (1)(c) above the sheriff shall make an order—

    (a)   declaring the balance due by or to the debtor, as certified by the auditor of court;

    (b)   declaring such a balance after making modifications to the balance so certified; or

    (c)   where the sheriff is satisfied that there has been a substantial irregularity in the execution of the attachment (other than the timing of the report of auction), declaring the attachment and auction to be void.

   (5)   An order made under subsection (4)(c) above may make such consequential provision as the sheriff thinks fit.

   (6)   An order made under subsection (4)(c) above shall not affect the title of a person to any article acquired by that person at the auction, or subsequently, in good faith.

   (7)   The sheriff may not make an order under subsection (4)(b) or (c) above without first providing all interested persons an opportunity to be heard.

   (8)   The sheriff clerk shall intimate the sheriff's order under subsection (4) above to the debtor.

General and miscellaneous provisions

34 Articles belonging to a third party

   (1)   Where at any time before an attached article is auctioned—

    (a)   a third party claims to own the article; and

    (b)   either—

      (i)   the officer is satisfied that the claim is valid and neither the debtor nor any other person in possession of the article disputes the claim; or

      (ii)   the sheriff, on an application by the third party, makes an order stating that the sheriff is so satisfied,

the attachment of that article is to cease to have effect.

   (2)   The making of an application to the sheriff for the purposes of subsection (1)(b)(ii) above does not preclude the third party making the application from

taking any other proceedings for the recovery of an article which is owned by the third party.

(3)   Where the attachment of an article ceases, under subsection (1) above, to have effect, the officer may attach other articles which are owned by the debtor and kept at the place at which the original attachment was executed.

35   Articles in common ownership

(1)   Articles which are owned in common by a debtor and a third party may be attached and disposed of in satisfaction of the debts of the debtor.

(2)   Where at any time before an attached article is auctioned—

    (a)   a third party claims to own the article in common with the debtor;

    (b)   either—

      (i)   the officer is satisfied that the claim is valid; or

      (ii)   the sheriff, on an application by the third party, makes an order stating that the sheriff is so satisfied; and

    (c)   the third party pays to the officer a sum equal to the value of the debtor's interest in the article,

the debtor's interest in the article shall transfer to the third party.

(3)   Where the sheriff is satisfied—

    (a)   that an article which has been removed from the place at which it was attached is owned in common by the debtor and a third party; and

    (b)   that the auction of the article would be unduly harsh to the third party in the circumstances,

the sheriff may, on an application by the third party before the attached article is auctioned, order that the attachment of that article is to cease to have effect.

(4)   Where—

    (a)   the debtor's interest in an article owned in common by the debtor and a third party is, under subsection (2) above, transferred to the third party; or

    (b)   the attachment of an article which is so owned ceases, in pursuance of an order made under subsection (3) above, to have effect,

the officer may attach other articles which are owned by the debtor and kept at the place at which the original attachment was executed.

36   Procedure where articles in common ownership are sold at auction

(1)   This subsection applies where—

    (a)   a third party claimed, before an attached article was auctioned, to own the article in common with the debtor;

    (b)   the debtor's interest in the article has not transferred to the third party under section 35(2) above;

    (c)   the attachment of the article has not, by virtue of an order made under section 35(3) above, ceased to have effect;

    (d)   the third party's interest in the article has, following the auction of the article, been transferred to another person; and

    (e)   either—

      (i)   the third party's claim is, after that transfer of interest, admitted by the creditor and the debtor; or

      (ii)   where the third party's claim is not so admitted, the sheriff, on an application by the third party after that transfer of interest, is satisfied that the claim is valid.

(2)   Where subsection (1) above applies, the creditor shall—

    (a)   where the article has been sold at the auction, pay to the third party the fraction of the proceeds of the sale of the article which corresponded to the third party's interest in the article; or

    (b)   where the ownership of the article has passed to the creditor under section 31(2)(a) above, pay to the third party the fraction of the value of the article which corresponded to the third party's interest in the article.

(3)   The reference in subsection (2)(b) above to the value of an article is a refer-

ence to the value of the article as fixed under subsection (2) or (3) of section 15 above or, as the case may be, section 51 or 54(1) below.

37 Attachment terminated by payment or tender of full amount owing
An attachment is to cease to have effect if the sum recoverable is—
(a) paid to the creditor, the officer or any other person who has authority to receive payment on behalf of the creditor; or
(b) tendered to any of those persons and the tender is not accepted within a reasonable time.

38 Assistance to debtor
The sheriff clerk shall, if requested by the debtor—
(a) provide the debtor with information as to the procedures available to him under any provision of this Part or Part 3 of this Act; and
(b) assist the debtor in the completion of any form required in connection with any proceedings under any provision of this Part or Part 3 of this Act,
but the sheriff clerk shall not be liable for any error or omission by him in performing the duties imposed on him by this section.

39 Expenses chargeable in relation to attachment etc
(1) Schedule 1 to this Act has effect for the purposes of determining the liability, as between the creditor and the debtor, for expenses incurred in serving a charge and in the process of attachment and auction.
(2) The Scottish Ministers may by order modify that schedule so as to—
(a) add or remove types of expenses to or, as the case may be, from those referred to in that schedule; or
(b) vary any of the descriptions of the types of expenses there referred to.

40 Recovery from debtor of expenses of attachment
(1) Subject to subsections (2) and (4) below, any expenses chargeable against the debtor which are incurred in an attachment (including the service of the charge preceding it and the auction following it) are recoverable from the debtor by the attachment concerned but not by any other legal process, and any such expenses which have not been recovered by the time the attachment and auction is completed will cease to be chargeable against the debtor.
(2) The sheriff shall grant decree for payment of—
(a) any expenses awarded by the sheriff against the debtor in favour of the creditor under paragraph 4 or 7 of schedule 1 to this Act; or
(b) any additional sum of expenses awarded by the sheriff against the debtor in favour of the creditor under paragraph 5 of that schedule.
(3) Subsection (4) below applies where an attachment is—
(a) recalled under section 9(2)(a), (d) or (e) (effect of time to pay order on diligence) of the Debtors (Scotland) Act 1987 (c 18) in relation to a time to pay order;
(b) in effect immediately before the date of sequestration (within the meaning of the Bankruptcy (Scotland) Act 1985 (c 66)) of the debtor's estate;
(c) in effect immediately before the presentation of a petition for an administration order under Part II of the Insolvency Act 1986 (c 45);
(d) in effect against property of the debtor immediately before a floating charge attaches to all or part of that property under section 53(7) (attachment on appointment of receiver by holder of charge) or 54(6) (attachment on appointment of receiver by court) of that Act of 1986;
(e) in effect immediately before the commencement of the winding up, under Part IV or V of that Act of 1986, of the debtor; or
(f) rendered unenforceable by virtue of the creditor entering into a composition contract or acceding to a trust deed for creditors or by virtue of the subsistence of a protected trust deed within the meaning of Schedule 5 to the Bankruptcy (Scotland) Act 1985 (c 66).

(4)   Where this subsection applies—

(a)   the expenses of the attachment which were chargeable against the debtor remain so chargeable; and

(b)   if the debtor's obligation to pay the expenses is not discharged under or by virtue of the time to pay order, sequestration, administration order, receivership, winding up, composition contract or trust deed for creditors, those expenses are recoverable by further attachment.

41 Ascription of sums recovered by attachment or while attachment is in effect

(1)   This section applies to any amounts recovered by an attachment or paid to account of the amounts recoverable by the attachment while the attachment is in effect.

(2)   An amount to which this section applies shall be ascribed to the following in the order in which they are mentioned—

(a)   the expenses already incurred in respect of—

(i)   the attachment;

(ii)   any previous diligence the expenses of which are chargeable against and recoverable from the debtor under section 40(4) above or section 93(5) of the Debtors (Scotland) Act 1987 (c 18);

(b)   any interest, due under the decree or other document of debt on which the attachment proceeds, which has accrued at the date of execution of the attachment;

(c)   any sum (including any expenses) due under the decree or other document of debt, other than any expenses or interest mentioned in paragraphs (a) and (b) above.

42 Restriction on fees payable by debtor

No fees shall be payable by a debtor in connection with—

(a)   any application by the debtor;

(b)   objections by the debtor to an application by any other person; or

(c)   a hearing held,

under any provision of this Part or Part 3 of this Act, to any officer of any office or department connected with the Court of Session or the sheriff court the expenses of which are paid wholly or partly out of the Scottish Consolidated Fund.

43, 44   [*Amending provisions*]

45 Interpretation of this Part and Parts 3 and 4

In this Part and in Parts 3 and 4 of this Act—

'chargeable expenses' means expenses chargeable against the debtor in accordance with this Part of this Act;

'dwellinghouse' does not include—

(a)   a garage, even although it forms part of the structure or building which consists of or includes the dwellinghouse; or

(b)   other structures or buildings used in connection with the dwellinghouse, but does include a mobile home or other place used as a dwelling;

'exceptional attachment order' has the meaning given by section 47(1) below;

'mobile home' means a caravan, houseboat or other moveable structure used as a dwelling;

'non-essential assets' has the meaning given by schedule 2 to this Act;

'officer' means the officer of court appointed by a creditor for the purposes of executing an attachment and arranging for the removal and auction of the articles attached;

'sum recoverable' means the debt in respect of which the attachment is executed together with any interest thereon and any chargeable expenses; and

'summary warrant' means a summary warrant granted under, or by virtue of, any enactment.

PART 3
ATTACHMENT OF ARTICLES KEPT IN DWELLINGHOUSES:
SPECIAL PROCEDURE

46 Restriction on attachment of articles kept in dwellinghouses
Articles kept in a dwellinghouse may be attached but only—
    (a)   in pursuance of an exceptional attachment order; and
    (b)   otherwise in accordance with this Part of this Act.

47 Exceptional attachment order
    (1)   The sheriff may, on an application by the creditor and on being satisfied
that there are exceptional circumstances, order that an attachment of non-essential
assets of the debtor's kept in any dwellinghouse specified in the application may
take place; such an order shall be called an 'exceptional attachment order'.
    (2)   An exceptional attachment order shall—
    (a)   authorise the attachment, removal and auction of non-essential assets of
the debtor's which are, at the time when an attachment is executed in pursuance
of the order, kept in any dwellinghouse specified in the application for the
order;
    (b)   specify a period during which the order is to be executed; and
    (c)   empower the officer to open shut and lockfast places for the purpose of
executing the order.
    (3)   In considering whether to make such an order the sheriff shall have regard
to the matters set out in subsection (4) below.
    (4)   Those matters are—
    (a)   the nature of the debt (and, in particular, whether the debt incurred
relates to any tax or duty or to any trade or business carried on by the debtor);
    (b)   whether the debtor resides in the dwellinghouse specified in the
application;
    (c)   whether the debtor carries on a trade or business in that dwellinghouse;
    (d)   whether money advice has been given to the debtor;
    (e)   whether any direction made under section 1 (time to pay directions) of
the Debtors (Scotland) Act 1987 (c 18), or order made under section 5 (time to
pay orders) of that Act, in respect of the debt, or any other debt, has lapsed
under section 4 (lapse of time to pay directions) or, as the case may be, section
11 (lapse of time to pay orders), of that Act of 1987;
    (f)   any agreement between the debtor and creditor for the settlement of the
debt;
    (g)   any declaration or representation made, or document lodged, by or on
behalf of the debtor which relates to—
        (i)   the existence of any non-essential assets owned by the debtor;
        (ii)   where they exist, their value; or
        (iii) the debtor's financial circumstances [; and
    (h)   whether an application by the debtor for approval of a debt payment
programme under Part 1 of this Act has been refused or approved, and if
approved, whether that programme has been varied, or is revoked or
completed.]
    (5)   Before deciding whether to make an exceptional attachment order, the
sheriff may make—
    (a)   an order for a visit to the debtor by a person specified in the order for
the purposes of giving money advice to the debtor; or
    (b)   such other order as the sheriff thinks fit.
    (6)   The Scottish Ministers may by order modify subsection (4) above so as to—
    (a)   add or remove matters to or, as the case may be, from those referred to
in that subsection; or
    (b)   vary any of the descriptions of the matters there referred to.

48   Exceptional circumstances

(1)   The reference in section 47(1) above to the sheriff being satisfied that there are exceptional circumstances is to be regarded as a reference to the sheriff being satisfied—

(a)   that the creditor has taken reasonable steps to negotiate (or seek to negotiate) a settlement of the debt;

(b)   that the creditor has executed, or so far as it is reasonable to do so has attempted to execute—

(i)   an arrestment and action of forthcoming or sale; and

(ii)   an earnings arrestment, in order to secure payment of the debt;

(c)   that there is a reasonable prospect that the sum recovered from an auction of the debtor's non-essential assets would be at least equal to the aggregate of the following—

(i)   a reasonable estimate of any chargeable expenses; and

(ii)   £100 or such other amount as may be specified by order made by the Scottish Ministers; and

(d)   that, having had regard to the matters set out in section 47(4) above and any other matters which the sheriff considers appropriate, it would be reasonable in the circumstances to grant the exceptional attachment order.

(2)   For the purposes of subsection (1)(b) above, a creditor who has not proceeded with the diligences referred to in that subsection on the ground that so proceeding would be unlikely to recover the aggregate of—

(a)   a reasonable estimate of the expenses likely to be incurred by the creditor in exercising the diligences; and

(b)   £100 or such other amount as may be specified by order made by the Scottish Ministers, is to be treated as having attempted to execute those diligences in so far as it is reasonable to do so.

49   Power of entry

(1)   Notwithstanding the authorisation in an exceptional attachment order to open shut and lockfast places, the officer shall not enter a dwellinghouse to execute the order unless the officer—

(a)   at the intended time of entry, is satisfied as to the condition set out in subsection (2) below; or

(b)   has, at least 4 days before the intended date of entry, served notice on the debtor setting out that intention and specifying that date.

(2)   That condition is that there appears to the officer to be a person present who—

(a)   is aged 16 years or over; and

(b)   is not, because of the person's age, knowledge of English, mental illness, mental or physical disability or otherwise, unable to understand the consequences of the procedure being carried out.

(3)   Where the sheriff is satisfied that the requirement of service under subsection (1)(b) above is likely to prejudice the execution of the order the sheriff may, on an application by the officer, dispense with that requirement.

(4)   An application for a dispensation under subsection (3) above need not be intimated to the debtor.

50   Unlawful acts before attachment

(1)   It shall be regarded as a breach of an exceptional attachment order—

(a)   for the debtor or any other person who knows that the order has been made to, without the consent of the sheriff, move any article which forms part of the debtor's non-essential assets from the dwellinghouse in which it is kept; or

(b)   for the debtor, without the consent of the sheriff, to sell, make a gift of or otherwise relinquish ownership of any such article,

before an attachment is executed in pursuance of the order.

(2)   Any person who—

(a)   knows that an exceptional attachment order has been made; and

(b)   before an attachment is executed in pursuance of the order, wilfully damages or destroys any article which forms part of the debtor's non-essential assets,

shall be regarded as acting in breach of the order.

(3)   Where, at any time after an exceptional attachment order has been made, an article which forms part of the debtor's non-essential assets is stolen, the debtor shall give notice to the creditor, the officer and the sheriff who granted the order of that fact and of any related claim which the debtor makes, or intends to make, under a contract of insurance.

(4)   Any failure by the debtor to give notice as required by subsection (3) above is to be regarded as acting in breach of the order.

(5)   Where a debtor or any third party who knows that an exceptional attachment order has been made and that an article forms part of the debtor's non-essential assets—

(a)   moves it from the dwellinghouse in which it is kept before an attachment is executed in pursuance of the order, and it is—

(i)   damaged, destroyed, lost or stolen; or

(ii)   acquired from or through the debtor or, as the case may be, the third party by another person without knowledge of order and for value; or

(b)   wilfully damages or destroys it,

the sheriff may order the debtor or, as the case may be, the third party to consign the sum set out in subsection (6) below in court.

(6)   That sum shall be—

(a)   where the article has been damaged but not so damaged as to make it worthless, a sum equal to the difference between the value of the article before it was damaged and the value of the article so damaged; or

(b)   where the damaged article is worthless, a sum equal to the value of the article before it was so damaged.

(7)   Any reference in subsection (6) above to the value of an article is a reference to the officer's best estimate of the amount which the article is or, as the case may be, was likely to realise on sale by auction.

(8)   Any sum consigned in court in pursuance of an order made under subsection (5) above shall, where that order ceases to have effect before an auction is held in execution of the order, be paid to the creditor to the extent necessary to meet the sum recoverable, any surplus thereof being paid to the debtor.

51   Valuation

When executing an attachment in pursuance of an exceptional attachment order the officer shall value the articles being attached at the price which they are likely to fetch if sold on the open market.

52   Articles with sentimental value

(1)   An officer may not, in executing an exceptional attachment order, attach any articles which the officer considers likely to be of sentimental value to the debtor.

(2)   Subsection (1) above applies only where the aggregate of the values of articles considered likely to be of that type (as fixed by the officer under section 51 above) does not exceed £150 or such other amount as may be prescribed in regulations made by the Scottish Ministers.

53   Removal of articles attached in dwellinghouse

(1)   The officer shall, unless the officer considers it impractical to do so, immediately remove any article which is attached in execution of an exceptional attachment order from the dwellinghouse in which it is attached.

(2)   If an article is not immediately removed from the dwellinghouse in which it is attached, the officer shall give notice to the debtor and to any other person in

possession of the article of the date arranged for the removal of the article from that dwellinghouse.

(3)   The officer may remove from the dwellinghouse only such attached articles as, if sold at their values fixed under section 51 above, would realise in aggregate the sum recoverable.

54   Professional valuation

(1)   The officer may, if the officer considers it appropriate, arrange for an attached article to be valued by a professional valuer or other suitably skilled person.

(2)   Any such valuer or other person shall value an attached article at the price which it is likely to fetch if sold on the open market.

(3)   If such a valuer or other person values an attached article at an amount other than the amount at which that article was valued by the officer when executing the attachment, the officer shall notify the debtor of the value arrived at by the valuer or other person.

55   Release of articles from attachment

(1)   An article attached in execution of an exceptional attachment order shall not, subject to any order made under section 20(1)(b) above, be auctioned before the date which is 7 days after the date on which the article was removed by the officer from the dwellinghouse in which it was attached.

(2)   The sheriff may, on an application by the debtor, make an order—

(a)   providing that the attachment of an article attached in execution of an exceptional attachment order is to cease to have effect; and

(b)   requiring the officer to return the article to the dwellinghouse at which it was attached.

(3)   Where the sheriff is satisfied that—

(a)   the attachment of an article is not competent; or

(b)   the auction of an attached article would be unduly harsh in the circumstances,

the sheriff shall grant an order under subsection (2) above in respect of the article.

(4)   Where the sheriff is satisfied that—

(a)   articles likely to be of sentimental value to the debtor were kept in a dwellinghouse when an exceptional attachment order was executed in the dwellinghouse;

(b)   those articles are likely to realise, on sale by auction, an aggregate amount not exceeding £150 or such other amount as may be prescribed in regulations made under section 52(2) above; and

(c)   an article of that type has been attached in execution of the exceptional attachment order, the sheriff shall grant an order under subsection (2) above in respect of the attached article.

(5)   The sheriff may consider an application for an order under subsection (2) above only where it is made during the period in which the article which is subject of the application may not, by virtue of subsection (1) above, be auctioned.

56   Redemption

(1)   Subject to any order made under section 20(1)(b) above, the debtor is entitled, within 7 days of the date on which an article is attached, to redeem that article.

(2)   The amount for which such an article may be redeemed is the value fixed under section 51 or 54(1) above.

(3)   The officer shall, on receiving payment from the debtor for the redemption of an attached article, grant a receipt in the form prescribed by Act of Sederunt to the debtor.

(4)   The attachment of the article is, on the grant of such a receipt, to cease to have effect.

57 Appeals

(1) An appeal made against any decision of a sheriff made under or for the purposes of this Part or, where the appeal relates to the attachment of articles kept in a dwellinghouse, under or for the purposes of Part 2 of this Act may be made only—

    (a) to the sheriff principal;

    (b) with the leave of the sheriff; and

    (c) on a point of law.

(2) The decision of the sheriff principal on such an appeal is final.

PART 4
ABOLITION OF POINDINGS AND WARRANT SALES

58 Abolition of poindings and warrant sales

(1) It is not, subject to section 59 below, competent to enforce payment of a debt by poinding or warrant sale; and any enactment or rule of law allowing such enforcement shall cease to have effect.

(2) The following provisions of the Debtors (Scotland) Act 1987 (c 18) are repealed—

    (a) Part II;

    (b) section 74(2);

    (c) Schedule 1; and

    (d) Schedule 5.

59 Savings

(1) The provisions set out in subsection (5) below continue to have effect in relation to a poinding in respect of which a warrant sale has been completed before 30 December 2002 as if sections 58(2) above and 61 below had not come into force.

(2) Subject to subsection (3) below, those provisions also continue to have that effect in relation to a poinding executed before that date in respect of which a warrant sale has not been completed before that date.

(3) The saving provided for in subsection (2) above—

    (a) has effect only if the poinding was executed at a place other than a dwellinghouse; and

    (b) continues to have effect after 31 March 2003 only if a warrant sale is completed in respect of the poinding on or before that date.

(4) A summary warrant which, before 30 December 2002, authorised a poinding and sale in accordance with Schedule 5 to the Debtors (Scotland) Act 1987 (c 18) is to be treated on and after that date as authorising an attachment.

(5) The provisions referred to in subsections (1) and (2) above are—

    (a) paragraph 24 of Schedule 7 to the Bankruptcy (Scotland) Act 1985 (c 66);

    (b) the provisions of the Act of 1987 mentioned in section 58(2) above; and

    (c) the provisions of the Act of 2002 mentioned in paragraph 29 of schedule 3 to this Act.

PART 5
MISCELLANEOUS AND GENERAL

60 Application of this Act to sequestration for rent and arrestment

(1) Sections 12, 16, 49 and 55(3) above apply to a landlord's or superior's right of hypothec and its enforcement by a sequestration for rent or feuduty as they apply to an attachment.

(2) It is not competent for such a hypothec to arise in any article—

    (a) of the type described in section 11(1); or

    (b) which is kept in a dwellinghouse and which is not a non-essential asset for the purposes of Part 3 of this Act.

(3) An arrestment (other than an arrestment of a debtor's earnings in the hands

of the debtor's employer) of any article of the type mentioned in paragraph (a) or
(b) of subsection (2) above is incompetent.

(4)   The Scottish Ministers may, by order, modify subsection (1) above by
repealing the words 'or superior's' and 'or feuduty' where they appear in that
subsection.

(5)   Such an order may not have effect before the day appointed by the Scottish
Ministers under section 71 (power to appoint the day on which the feudal system
of land tenure is abolished) of the Abolition of Feudal Tenure etc (Scotland) Act
2000 (asp 5).

61   [*Minor and consequential amendments and repeals*]

62   [*Regulations and orders*]

63   Crown application
This Act binds the Crown acting in its capacity as a creditor or employer.

64   Short title and commencement
(1)   This Act may be cited as the Debt Arrangement and Attachment (Scotland)
Act 2002.

(2)   Subject to subsections (3) and (4) below, this Act (except this section and
sections 43 and 62 above) comes into force on 30 December 2002.

   . . .

SCHEDULES

SCHEDULE 2
NON-ESSENTIAL ASSETS

1   For the purposes of Part 3 of this Act, 'non-essential assets' are, subject to
paragraph 2 below, corporeal moveable property of the debtor's which is kept in a
dwellinghouse.

2   None of the following is a non-essential asset for the purposes of Part 3 of
this Act—
   (a)   an article specified in paragraph 3 below;
   (b)   an article described in paragraph 4 below; and
   (c)   an article the attachment of which is (by virtue of section 11(1) above or
otherwise) incompetent.

3   The articles referred to in paragraph 2(a) above are—
   (a)   clothing reasonably required for the use of the debtor or any member of
the debtor's household;
   (b)   implements, tools of trade, books or other equipment reasonably required
for the use of any member of the debtor's household in the practice of such
member's profession, trade or business, not exceeding in aggregate value £1,000
or such other amount as may be prescribed in regulations made by the Scottish
Ministers;
   (c)   medical aids or medical equipment reasonably required for the use of the
debtor or any member of the debtor's household;
   (d)   books or other articles reasonably required for the education or training
of the debtor or any member of the debtor's household not exceeding in
aggregate value £1,000 or such other amount as may be prescribed in regulations
made by the Scottish Ministers;
   (e)   articles reasonably required for the care or upbringing of a child who is a
member of the debtor's household;
   (f)   toys for the use of any child who is a member of the debtor's household.

4   The articles referred to in paragraph 2(b) above are the following so far as

they are reasonably required, at the time of the attachment, for the use of the debtor or a member of the debtor's household—

    (a)   beds or bedding;

    (b)   household linen;

    (c)   chairs or settees;

    (d)   tables;

    (e)   food;

    (f)   lights or light fittings;

    (g)   heating appliances;

    (h)   curtains;

    (i)   floor coverings;

    (j)   furniture, equipment or utensils used for storing, cooking or eating food;

    (k)   refrigerators;

    (l)   articles used for cleaning, drying, mending, or pressing clothes;

    (m) articles used for cleaning the dwellinghouse;

    (n)   furniture used for storing—

        (i)   clothing, bedding or household linen;

       (ii)   articles used for cleaning the dwellinghouse; or

      (iii)   utensils used for cooking or eating food;

    (o)   articles used for safety in the dwellinghouse;

    (p)   tools used for maintenance or repair of the dwellinghouse or of household articles;

    (q)   computers and accessory equipment;

    (r)   microwave ovens;

    (s)   radios;

    (t)   telephones;

    (u)   televisions.

5   The Scottish Ministers may by regulations modify paragraph 4 above so as to—

    (a)   add or remove types of articles to or, as the case may be, from those referred to in that paragraph; or

    (b)   vary any of the descriptions of the types of articles there referred to.

. . .

ENTERPRISE ACT 2002
(2002, c 40)

PART 1
THE OFFICE OF FAIR TRADING

Establishment of OFT

1 The Office of Fair Trading

(1)   There shall be a body corporate to be known as the Office of Fair Trading (in this Act referred to as 'the OFT').

(2)   The functions of the OFT are carried out on behalf of the Crown.

(3)   Schedule 1 (which makes further provision about the OFT) has effect.

(4)   In managing its affairs the OFT shall have regard, in addition to any relevant general guidance as to the governance of public bodies, to such generally accepted principles of good corporate governance as it is reasonable to regard as applicable to the OFT.

2 The Director General of Fair Trading

(1)   The functions of the Director General of Fair Trading (in this Act referred to as 'the Director'), and his property, rights and liabilities, are transferred to the OFT.

(2)   The office of the Director is abolished.

(3)   Any enactment, instrument or other document passed or made before the commencement of subsection (1) which refers to the Director shall have effect, so far as necessary for the purposes of or in consequence of anything being transferred, as if any reference to the Director were a reference to the OFT.

3   Annual plan

(1)   The OFT shall, before each financial year, publish a document (the 'annual plan') containing a statement of its main objectives and priorities for the year.

(2)   The OFT shall for the purposes of public consultation publish a document containing proposals for its annual plan at least two months before publishing the annual plan for any year.

(3)   The OFT shall lay before Parliament a copy of each document published under subsection (2) and each annual plan.

4   Annual and other reports

(1)   The OFT shall, as soon as practicable after the end of each financial year, make to the Secretary of State a report (the 'annual report') on its activities and performance during that year.

(2)   The annual report for each year shall include-

(a)   a general survey of developments in respect of matters relating to the OFT's functions;

(b)   an assessment of the extent to which the OFT's main objectives and priorities for the year (as set out in the annual plan) have been met;

(c)   a summary of the significant decisions, investigations or other activities made or carried out by the OFT during the year;

(d)   a summary of the allocation of the OFT's financial resources to its various activities during the year; and

(e)   an assessment of the OFT's performance and practices in relation to its enforcement functions.

(3)   The OFT shall lay a copy of each annual report before Parliament and arrange for the report to be published.

(4)   The OFT may—

(a)   prepare other reports in respect of matters relating to any of its functions; and

(b)   arrange for any such report to be published.

General functions of OFT

5   Acquisition of information etc

(1)   The OFT has the function of obtaining, compiling and keeping under review information about matters relating to the carrying out of its functions.

(2)   That function is to be carried out with a view to (among other things) ensuring that the OFT has sufficient information to take informed decisions and to carry out its other functions effectively.

(3)   In carrying out that function the OFT may carry out, commission or support (financially or otherwise) research.

6   Provision of information etc to the public

(1)   The OFT has the function of—

(a)   making the public aware of the ways in which competition may benefit consumers in, and the economy of, the United Kingdom; and

(b)   giving information or advice in respect of matters relating to any of its functions to the public.

(2)   In carrying out those functions the OFT may—

(a)   publish educational materials or carry out other educational activities; or

(b)   support (financially or otherwise) the carrying out by others of such activities or the provision by others of information or advice.

7 Provision of information and advice to Ministers etc

(1) The OFT has the function of—

(a) making proposals, or

(b) giving other information or advice,

on matters relating to any of its functions to any Minister of the Crown or other public authority (including proposals, information or advice as to any aspect of the law or a proposed change in the law).

(2) A Minister of the Crown may request the OFT to make proposals or give other information or advice on any matter relating to any of its functions; and the OFT shall, so far as is reasonably practicable and consistent with its other functions, comply with the request.

8 Promoting good consumer practice

(1) The OFT has the function of promoting good practice in the carrying out of activities which may affect the economic interests of consumers in the United Kingdom.

(2) In carrying out that function the OFT may (without prejudice to the generality of subsection (1)) make arrangements for approving consumer codes and may, in accordance with the arrangements, give its approval to or withdraw its approval from any consumer code.

(3) Any such arrangements must specify the criteria to be applied by the OFT in determining whether to give approval to or withdraw approval from a consumer code.

(4) Any such arrangements may in particular—

(a) specify descriptions of consumer code which may be the subject of an application to the OFT for approval (and any such description may be framed by reference to any feature of a consumer code, including the persons who are, or are to be, subject to the code, the manner in which it is, or is to be, operated and the persons responsible for its operation); and

(b) provide for the use in accordance with the arrangements of an official symbol intended to signify that a consumer code is approved by the OFT.

(5) The OFT shall publish any arrangements under subsection (2) in such manner it considers appropriate.

(6) In this section 'consumer code' means a code of practice or other document (however described) intended, with a view to safeguarding or promoting the interests of consumers, to regulate by any means the conduct of persons engaged in the supply of goods or services to consumers (or the conduct of their employees or representatives).

Miscellaneous

9, 10 [*Amending provisions*]

11 Super-complaints to OFT

(1) This section applies where a designated consumer body makes a complaint to the OFT that any feature, or combination of features, of a market in the United Kingdom for goods or services is or appears to be significantly harming the interests of consumers.

(2) The OFT must, within 90 days after the day on which it receives the complaint, publish a response stating how it proposes to deal with the complaint, and in particular—

(a) whether it has decided to take any action, or to take no action, in response to the complaint, and

(b) if it has decided to take action, what action it proposes to take.

(3) The response must state the OFT's reasons for its proposals.

(4) The Secretary of State may by order amend subsection (2) by substituting any period for the period for the time being specified there.

(5) 'Designated consumer body' means a body designated by the Secretary of State by order.

(6) The Secretary of State—

(a) may designate a body only if it appears to him to represent the interests of consumers of any description, and

(b) must publish (and may from time to time vary) other criteria to be applied by him in determining whether to make or revoke a designation.

(7) The OFT—

(a) must issue guidance as to the presentation by the complainant of a reasoned case for the complaint, and

(b) may issue such other guidance as appears to it to be appropriate for the purposes of this section.

(8) An order under this section—

(a) shall be made by statutory instrument, and

(b) shall be subject to annulment in pursuance of a resolution of either House of Parliament.

(9) In this section—

(a) references to a feature of a market in the United Kingdom for goods or services have the same meaning as if contained in Part 4, and

(b) 'consumer' means an individual who is a consumer within the meaning of that Part.

PART 8
ENFORCEMENT OF CERTAIN CONSUMER LEGISLATION

Introduction

210 Consumers

(1) In this Part references to consumers must be construed in accordance with this section.

(2) In relation to a domestic infringement a consumer is an individual in respect of whom the first and second conditions are satisfied.

(3) The first condition is that—

(a) goods are or are sought to be supplied to the individual (whether by way of sale or otherwise) in the course of a business carried on by the person supplying or seeking to supply them, or

(b) services are or are sought to be supplied to the individual in the course of a business carried on by the person supplying or seeking to supply them.

(4) The second condition is that—

(a) the individual receives or seeks to receive the goods or services otherwise than in the course of a business carried on by him, or

(b) the individual receives or seeks to receive the goods or services with a view to carrying on a business but not in the course of a business carried on by him.

(5) For the purposes of a domestic infringement it is immaterial whether a person supplying goods or services has a place of business in the United Kingdom.

(6) In relation to a Community infringement a consumer is a person who is a consumer for the purposes of—

(a) the Injunctions Directive, and

(b) the listed Directive concerned.

(7) A Directive is a listed Directive—

(a) if it is a Directive of the Council of the European Communities or of the European Parliament and of the Council, and

(b)   if it is specified in Schedule 13 or to the extent that any of its provisions is so specified.

(8)   A business includes—

(a)   a professional practice;

(b)   any other undertaking carried on for gain or reward;

(c)   any undertaking in the course of which goods or services are supplied otherwise than free of charge.

(9)   The Secretary of State may by order modify Schedule 13.

(10)   An order under this section must be made by statutory instrument subject to annulment in pursuance of a resolution of either House of Parliament.

211   Domestic infringements

(1)   In this Part a domestic infringement is an act or omission which—

(a)   is done or made by a person in the course of a business,

(b)   falls within subsection (2), and

(c)   harms the collective interests of consumers in the United Kingdom.

(2)   An act or omission falls within this subsection if it is of a description specified by the Secretary of State by order and consists of any of the following—

(a)   a contravention of an enactment which imposes a duty, prohibition or restriction enforceable by criminal proceedings;

(b)   an act done or omission made in breach of contract;

(c)   an act done or omission made in breach of a non-contractual duty owed to a person by virtue of an enactment or rule of law and enforceable by civil proceedings;

(d)   an act or omission in respect of which an enactment provides for a remedy or sanction enforceable by civil proceedings;

(e)   an act done or omission made by a person supplying or seeking to supply goods or services as a result of which an agreement or security relating to the supply is void or unenforceable to any extent;

(f)   an act or omission by which a person supplying or seeking to supply goods or services purports or attempts to exercise a right or remedy relating to the supply in circumstances where the exercise of the right or remedy is restricted or excluded under or by virtue of an enactment;

(g)   an act or omission by which a person supplying or seeking to supply goods or services purports or attempts to avoid (to any extent) liability relating to the supply in circumstances where such avoidance is restricted or prevented under an enactment.

(3)   But an order under this section may provide that any description of act or omission falling within subsection (2) is not a domestic infringement.

(4)   For the purposes of subsection (2) it is immaterial—

(a)   whether or not any duty, prohibition or restriction exists in relation to consumers as such;

(b)   whether or not any remedy or sanction is provided for the benefit of consumers as such;

(c)   whether or not any proceedings have been brought in relation to the act or omission;

(d)   whether or not any person has been convicted of an offence in respect of the contravention mentioned in subsection (2)(a);

(e)   whether or not there is a waiver in respect of the breach of contract mentioned in subsection (2)(b).

(5)   References to an enactment include references to subordinate legislation (within the meaning of the Interpretation Act 1978 (c 30)).

(6)   The power to make an order under this section must be exercised by statutory instrument.

(7)   But no such order may be made unless a draft of it has been laid before Parliament and approved by a resolution of each House.

212 Community infringements

(1) In this Part a Community infringement is an act or omission which harms the collective interests of consumers and which—

(a) contravenes a listed Directive as given effect by the laws, regulations or administrative provisions of an EEA State, or

(b) contravenes such laws, regulations or administrative provisions which provide additional permitted protections.

(2) The laws, regulations or administrative provisions of an EEA State which give effect to a listed Directive provide additional permitted protections if—

(a) they provide protection for consumers which is in addition to the minimum protection required by the Directive concerned, and

(b) such additional protection is permitted by that Directive.

(3) The Secretary of State may by order specify for the purposes of this section the law in the United Kingdom which—

(a) gives effect to the listed Directives;

(b) provides additional permitted protections.

(4) References to a listed Directive must be construed in accordance with section 210.

(5) An EEA State is a State which is a contracting party to the Agreement on the European Economic Area signed at Oporto on 2nd May 1992 as adjusted by the Protocol signed at Brussels on 17th March 1993.

(6) An order under this section must be made by statutory instrument subject to annulment in pursuance of a resolution of either House of Parliament.

213 Enforcers

(1) Each of the following is a general enforcer—

(a) the OFT;

(b) every local weights and measures authority in Great Britain;

(c) the Department of Enterprise, Trade and Investment in Northern Ireland.

(2) A designated enforcer is any person or body (whether or not incorporated) which the Secretary of State—

(a) thinks has as one of its purposes the protection of the collective interests of consumers, and

(b) designates by order.

(3) The Secretary of State may designate a public body only if he is satisfied that it is independent.

(4) The Secretary of State may designate a person or body which is not a public body only if the person or body (as the case may be) satisfies such criteria as the Secretary of State specifies by order.

(5) A Community enforcer is a qualified entity for the purposes of the Injunctions Directive—

(a) which is for the time being specified in the list published in the Official Journal of the European Communities in pursuance of Article 4.3 of that Directive, but

(b) which is not a general enforcer or a designated enforcer.

(6) An order under this section may designate an enforcer in respect of—

(a) all infringements;

(b) infringements of such descriptions as are specified in the order.

(7) An order under this section may make different provision for different purposes.

(8) The designation of a body by virtue of subsection (3) is conclusive evidence for the purposes of any question arising under this Part that the body is a public body.

(9) An order under this section must be made by statutory instrument subject to annulment in pursuance of a resolution of either House of Parliament.

(10) If requested to do so by a designated enforcer which is designated in

respect of one or more Community infringements the Secretary of State must notify the Commission of the European Communities—

(a) of its name and purpose;

(b) of the Community infringements in respect of which it is designated.

(11) The Secretary of State must also notify the Commission—

(a) of the fact that a person or body in respect of which he has given notice under subsection (10) ceases to be a designated enforcer;

(b) of any change in the name or purpose of a designated enforcer in respect of which he has given such notice;

(c) of any change to the Community infringements in respect of which a designated enforcer is designated.

Enforcement procedure

214 Consultation

(1) An enforcer must not make an application for an enforcement order unless he has engaged in appropriate consultation with—

(a) the person against whom the enforcement order would be made, and

(b) the OFT (if it is not the enforcer).

(2) Appropriate consultation is consultation for the purpose of—

(a) achieving the cessation of the infringement in a case where an infringement is occurring;

(b) ensuring that there will be no repetition of the infringement in a case where the infringement has occurred;

(c) ensuring that there will be no repetition of the infringement in a case where the cessation of the infringement is achieved under paragraph (a);

(d) ensuring that the infringement does not take place in the case of a Community infringement which the enforcer believes is likely to take place.

(3) Subsection (1) does not apply if the OFT thinks that an application for an enforcement order should be made without delay.

(4) Subsection (1) ceases to apply—

(a) for the purposes of an application for an enforcement order at the end of the period of 14 days beginning with the day after the person against whom the enforcement order would be made receives a request for consultation from the enforcer;

(b) for the purposes of an application for an interim enforcement order at the end of the period of seven days beginning with the day after the person against whom the interim enforcement order would be made receives a request for consultation from the enforcer.

(5) The Secretary of State may by order make rules in relation to consultation under this section.

(6) Such an order must be made by statutory instrument subject to annulment in pursuance of a resolution of either House of Parliament.

(7) In this section (except subsection (4)) and in sections 215 and 216 references to an enforcement order include references to an interim enforcement order.

215 Applications

(1) An application for an enforcement order must name the person the enforcer thinks—

(a) has engaged or is engaging in conduct which constitutes a domestic or a Community infringement, or

(b) is likely to engage in conduct which constitutes a Community infringement.

(2) A general enforcer may make an application for an enforcement order in respect of any infringement.

(3) A designated enforcer may make an application for an enforcement order in respect of an infringement to which his designation relates.

(4)   A Community enforcer may make an application for an enforcement order in respect of a Community infringement.

(5)   The following courts have jurisdiction to make an enforcement order—

(a)   the High Court or a county court if the person against whom the order is sought carries on business or has a place of business in England and Wales or Northern Ireland;

(b)   the Court of Session or the sheriff if the person against whom the order is sought carries on business or has a place of business in Scotland.

(6)   If an application for an enforcement order is made by a Community enforcer the court may examine whether the purpose of the enforcer justifies its making the application.

(7)   If the court thinks that the purpose of the Community enforcer does not justify its making the application the court may refuse the application on that ground alone.

(8)   The purpose of a Community enforcer must be construed by reference to the Injunctions Directive.

(9)   An enforcer which is not the OFT must notify the OFT of the result of an application under this section.

216   Applications: directions by OFT

(1)   This section applies if the OFT believes that an enforcer other than the OFT intends to apply for an enforcement order.

(2)   In such a case the OFT may direct that if an application in respect of a particular infringement is to be made it must be made—

(a)   only by the OFT, or

(b)   only by such other enforcer as the OFT directs.

(3)   If the OFT directs that only it may make an application that does not prevent—

(a)   the OFT or any enforcer from accepting an undertaking under section 219, or

(b)   the OFT from taking such other steps it thinks appropriate (apart from making an application) for the purpose of securing that the infringement is not committed, continued or repeated.

(4)   The OFT may vary or withdraw a direction given under this section.

(5)   The OFT must take such steps as it thinks appropriate to bring a direction (or a variation or withdrawal of a direction) to the attention of enforcers it thinks may be affected by it.

(6)   But this section does not prevent an application for an enforcement order being made by a Community enforcer.

217   Enforcement orders

(1)   This section applies if an application for an enforcement order is made under section 215 and the court finds that the person named in the application has engaged in conduct which constitutes the infringement.

(2)   This section also applies if such an application is made in relation to a Community infringement and the court finds that the person named in the application is likely to engage in conduct which constitutes the infringement.

(3)   If this section applies the court may make an enforcement order against the person.

(4)   In considering whether to make an enforcement order the court must have regard to whether the person named in the application—

(a)   has given an undertaking under section 219 in respect of conduct such as is mentioned in subsection (3) of that section;

(b)   has failed to comply with the undertaking.

(5)   An enforcement order must—

(a)   indicate the nature of the conduct to which the finding under subsection (1) or (2) relates, and

(b)   direct the person to comply with subsection (6).
(6)   A person complies with this subsection if he—
(a)   does not continue or repeat the conduct;
(b)   does not engage in such conduct in the course of his business or another business;
(c)   does not consent to or connive in the carrying out of such conduct by a body corporate with which he has a special relationship (within the meaning of section 222(3)).
(7)   But subsection (6)(a) does not apply in the case of a finding under subsection (2).
(8)   An enforcement order may require a person against whom the order is made to publish in such form and manner and to such extent as the court thinks appropriate for the purpose of eliminating any continuing effects of the infringement—
(a)   the order;
(b)   a corrective statement.
(9)   If the court makes a finding under subsection (1) or (2) it may accept an undertaking by the person—
(a)   to comply with subsection (6), or
(b)   to take steps which the court believes will secure that he complies with subsection (6).
(10)   An undertaking under subsection (9) may include a further undertaking by the person to publish in such form and manner and to such extent as the court thinks appropriate for the purpose of eliminating any continuing effects of the infringement—
(a)   the terms of the undertaking;
(b)   a corrective statement.
(11)   If the court—
(a)   makes a finding under subsection (1) or (2), and
(b)   accepts an undertaking under subsection (9),
it must not make an enforcement order in respect of the infringement to which the undertaking relates.
(12)   An enforcement order made by a court in one part of the United Kingdom has effect in any other part of the United Kingdom as if made by a court in that part.

218   Interim enforcement order
(1)   The court may make an interim enforcement order against a person named in the application for the order if it appears to the court—
(a)   that it is alleged that the person is engaged in conduct which constitutes a domestic or Community infringement or is likely to engage in conduct which constitutes a Community infringement,
(b)   that if the application had been an application for an enforcement order it would be likely to be granted,
(c)   that it is expedient that the conduct is prohibited or prevented (as the case may be) immediately, and
(d)   if no notice of the application has been given to the person named in the application that it is appropriate to make an interim enforcement order without notice.
(2)   An interim enforcement order must—
(a)   indicate the nature of the alleged conduct, and
(b)   direct the person to comply with subsection (3).
(3)   A person complies with this subsection if he—
(a)   does not continue or repeat the conduct;
(b)   does not engage in such conduct in the course of his business or another business;

(c)   does not consent to or connive in the carrying out of such conduct by a body corporate with which he has a special relationship (within the meaning of section 222(3)).

(4)   But subsection (3)(a) does not apply in so far as the application is made in respect of an allegation that the person is likely to engage in conduct which constitutes a Community infringement.

(5)   An application for an interim enforcement order against a person may be made at any time before an application for an enforcement order against the person in respect of the same conduct is determined.

(6)   An application for an interim enforcement order must refer to all matters—
    (a)   which are known to the applicant, and
    (b)   which are material to the question whether or not the application is granted.

(7)   If an application for an interim enforcement order is made without notice the application must state why no notice has been given.

(8)   The court may vary or discharge an interim enforcement order on the application of—
    (a)   the enforcer who applied for the order;
    (b)   the person against whom it is made.

(9)   An interim enforcement order against a person is discharged on the determination of an application for an enforcement order made against the person in respect of the same conduct.

(10)   If it appears to the court as mentioned in subsection (1)(a) to (c) the court may instead of making an interim enforcement order accept an undertaking from the person named in the application—
    (a)   to comply with subsection (3), or
    (b)   to take steps which the court believes will secure that he complies with subsection (3).

(11)   An interim enforcement order made by a court in one part of the United Kingdom has effect in any other part of the United Kingdom as if made by a court in that part.

219   Undertakings

(1)   This section applies if an enforcer has power to make an application under section 215.

(2)   In such a case the enforcer may accept from a person to whom subsection (3) applies an undertaking that the person will comply with subsection (4).

(3)   This subsection applies to a person who the enforcer believes—
    (a)   has engaged in conduct which constitutes an infringement;
    (b)   is engaging in such conduct;
    (c)   is likely to engage in conduct which constitutes a Community infringement.

(4)   A person complies with this subsection if he—
    (a)   does not continue or repeat the conduct;
    (b)   does not engage in such conduct in the course of his business or another business;
    (c)   does not consent to or connive in the carrying out of such conduct by a body corporate with which he has a special relationship (within the meaning of section 222(3)).

(5)   But subsection (4)(a) does not apply in the case of an undertaking given by a person in so far as subsection (3) applies to him by virtue of paragraph (c).

(6)   If an enforcer accepts an undertaking under this section it must notify the OFT—
    (a)   of the terms of the undertaking;
    (b)   of the identity of the person who gave it.

220 Further proceedings

(1) This section applies if the court—
  (a) makes an enforcement order under section 217,
  (b) makes an interim enforcement order under section 218, or
  (c) accepts an undertaking under either of those sections.

(2) In such a case the OFT has the same right to apply to the court in respect of a failure to comply with the order or undertaking as the enforcer who made the application for the order.

(3) An application to the court in respect of a failure to comply with an undertaking may include an application for an enforcement order or for an interim enforcement order.

(4) If the court finds that an undertaking is not being complied with it may make an enforcement order or an interim enforcement order (instead of making any other order it has power to make).

(5) In the case of an application for an enforcement order or for an interim enforcement order as mentioned in subsection (3) sections 214 and 216 must be ignored and sections 215 and 217 or 218 (as the case may be) apply subject to the following modifications—
  (a) section 215(1)(b) must be ignored;
  (b) section 215(5) must be ignored and the application must be made to the court which accepted the undertaking;
  (c) section 217(9) to (11) must be ignored;
  (d) section 218(10) must be ignored.

(6) If an enforcer which is not the OFT makes an application in respect of the failure of a person to comply with an enforcement order, an interim enforcement order or an undertaking given under section 217 or 218 the enforcer must notify the OFT—
  (a) of the application;
  (b) of any order made by the court on the application.

221 Community infringements: proceedings

(1) Subsection (2) applies to—
  (a) every general enforcer;
  (b) every designated enforcer which is a public body.

(2) An enforcer to which this subsection applies has power to take proceedings in EEA States other than the United Kingdom for the cessation or prohibition of a Community infringement.

(3) Subsection (4) applies to—
  (a) every general enforcer;
  (b) every designated enforcer.

(4) An enforcer to which this subsection applies may co-operate with a Community enforcer—
  (a) for the purpose of bringing proceedings mentioned in subsection (2);
  (b) in connection with the exercise by the Community enforcer of its functions under this Part.

(5) An EEA State is a State which is a contracting party to the Agreement on the European Economic Area signed at Oporto on 2nd May 1992 as adjusted by the Protocol signed at Brussels on 17th March 1993.

222 Bodies corporate: accessories

(1) This section applies if the person whose conduct constitutes a domestic infringement or a Community infringement is a body corporate.

(2) If the conduct takes place with the consent or connivance of a person (an accessory) who has a special relationship with the body corporate, the consent or connivance is also conduct which constitutes the infringement.

(3) A person has a special relationship with a body corporate if he is—
  (a) a controller of the body corporate, or

(b)   a director, manager, secretary or other similar officer of the body corporate or a person purporting to act in such a capacity.

(4)   A person is a controller of a body corporate if—

(a)   the directors of the body corporate or of another body corporate which is its controller are accustomed to act in accordance with the person's directions or instructions, or

(b)   either alone or with an associate or associates he is entitled to exercise or control the exercise of one third or more of the voting power at any general meeting of the body corporate or of another body corporate which is its controller.

(5)   An enforcement order or an interim enforcement order may be made against an accessory in respect of an infringement whether or not such an order is made against the body corporate.

(6)   The court may accept an undertaking under section 217(9) or 218(10) from an accessory in respect of an infringement whether or not it accepts such an undertaking from the body corporate.

(7)   An enforcer may accept an undertaking under section 219 from an accessory in respect of an infringement whether or not it accepts such an undertaking from the body corporate.

(8)   Subsection (9) applies if—

(a)   an order is made as mentioned in subsection (5), or

(b)   an undertaking is accepted as mentioned in subsection (6) or (7).

(9)   In such a case for subsection (6) of section 217, subsection (3) of section 218 or subsection (4) of section 219 (as the case may be) there is substituted the following subsection—

'( ) A person complies with this subsection if he—

(a)   does not continue or repeat the conduct;

(b)   does not in the course of any business carried on by him engage in conduct such as that which constitutes the infringement committed by the body corporate mentioned in section 222(1);

(c)   does not consent to or connive in the carrying out of such conduct by another body corporate with which he has a special relationship (within the meaning of section 222(3)).'

(10)   A person is an associate of an individual if—

(a)   he is the spouse [or civil partner] of the individual;

(b)   he is a relative of the individual;

(c)   he is a relative of the individual's spouse [or civil partner];

(d)   he is the spouse [or civil partner] of a relative of the individual;

(e)   he is the spouse [or civil partner] of a relative of the individual's spouse;

(f)   he lives in the same household as the individual otherwise than merely because he or the individual is the other's employer, tenant, lodger or boarder;

(g)   he is a relative of a person who is an associate of the individual by virtue of paragraph (f);

(h)   he has at some time in the past fallen within any of paragraphs (a) to (g).

(11)   A person is also an associate of—

(a)   an individual with whom he is in partnership;

(b)   an individual who is an associate of the individual mentioned in paragraph (a);

(c)   a body corporate if he is a controller of it or he is an associate of a person who is a controller of the body corporate.

(12)   A body corporate is an associate of another body corporate if—

(a)   the same person is a controller of both;

(b)   a person is a controller of one and persons who are his associates are controllers of the other;

(c)   a person is a controller of one and he and persons who are his associates are controllers of the other;

(d)   a group of two or more persons is a controller of each company and the groups consist of the same persons;

(e)   a group of two or more persons is a controller of each company and the groups may be regarded as consisting of the same persons by treating (in one or more cases) a member of either group as replaced by a person of whom he is an associate.

(13)   A relative is a brother, sister, uncle, aunt, nephew, niece, lineal ancestor or lineal descendant.

223   Bodies corporate: orders

(1)   This section applies if a court makes an enforcement order or an interim enforcement order against a body corporate and—

(a)   at the time the order is made the body corporate is a member of a group of interconnected bodies corporate,

(b)   at any time when the order is in force the body corporate becomes a member of a group of interconnected bodies corporate, or

(c)   at any time when the order is in force a group of interconnected bodies corporate of which the body corporate is a member is increased by the addition of one or more further members.

(2)   The court may direct that the order is binding upon all of the members of the group as if each of them were the body corporate against which the order is made.

(3)   A group of interconnected bodies corporate is a group consisting of two or more bodies corporate all of whom are interconnected with each other.

(4)   Any two bodies corporate are interconnected—

(a)   if one of them is a subsidiary of the other, or

(b)   if both of them are subsidiaries of the same body corporate.

(5)   'Subsidiary' must be construed in accordance with section 736 of the Companies Act 1985 (c 6).

Information

224   OFT

(1)   The OFT may for any of the purposes mentioned in subsection (2) give notice to any person requiring the person to provide it with the information specified in the notice.

(2)   The purposes are—

(a)   to enable the OFT to exercise or to consider whether to exercise any function it has under this Part;

(b)   to enable a designated enforcer to which section 225 does not apply to consider whether to exercise any function it has under this Part;

(c)   to enable a Community enforcer to consider whether to exercise any function it has under this Part;

(d)   to ascertain whether a person has complied with or is complying with an enforcement order, an interim enforcement order or an undertaking given under section 217(9), 218(10) or 219.

225   Other enforcers

(1)   This section applies to—

(a)   every general enforcer (other than the OFT);

(b)   every designated enforcer which is a public body.

(2)   An enforcer to which this section applies may for any of the purposes mentioned in subsection (3) give notice to any person requiring the person to provide the enforcer with the information specified in the notice.

(3)   The purposes are—

(a)   to enable the enforcer to exercise or to consider whether to exercise any function it has under this Part;

(b)   to ascertain whether a person has complied with or is complying with an enforcement order or an interim enforcement order made on the application of the enforcer or an undertaking given under section 217(9) or 218(10) (as the case may be) following such an application or an undertaking given to the enforcer under section 219.

226   Notices: procedure

(1)   This section applies to a notice given under section 224 or 225.
(2)   The notice must—
   (a)   be in writing;
   (b)   specify the purpose for which the information is required.
(3)   If the purpose is as mentioned in section 224(2)(a), (b) or (c) or 225(3)(a) the notice must specify the function concerned.
(4)   A notice may specify the time within which and manner in which it is to be complied with.
(5)   A notice may require the production of documents or any description of documents.
(6)   An enforcer may take copies of any documents produced in compliance with such a requirement.
(7)   A notice may be varied or revoked by a subsequent notice.
(8)   But a notice must not require a person to provide any information or produce any document which he would be entitled to refuse to provide or produce—
   (a)   in proceedings in the High Court on the grounds of legal professional privilege;
   (b)   in proceedings in the Court of Session on the grounds of confidentiality of communications.

227   Notices: enforcement

(1)   If a person fails to comply with a notice given under section 224 or 225 the enforcer who gave the notice may make an application under this section.
(2)   If it appears to the court that the person to whom the notice was given has failed to comply with the notice the court may make an order under this section.
(3)   An order under this section may require the person to whom the notice was given to do anything the court thinks it is reasonable for him to do for any of the purposes mentioned in section 224 or 225 (as the case may be) to ensure that the notice is complied with.
(4)   An order under this section may require the person to meet all the costs or expenses of the application.
(5)   If the person is a company or association the court in proceeding under subsection (4) may require any officer of the company or association who is responsible for the failure to meet the costs or expenses.
(6)   The court is a court which may make an enforcement order.
(7)   In subsection (5) an officer of a company is a person who is a director, manager, secretary or other similar officer of the company.

Miscellaneous

228   Evidence

(1)   Proceedings under this Part are civil proceedings for the purposes of—
   (a)   section 11 of the Civil Evidence Act 1968 (c 64) (convictions admissible as evidence in civil proceedings);
   (b)   section 10 of the Law Reform (Miscellaneous Provisions) (Scotland) Act 1968 (c 70) (corresponding provision in Scotland);
   (c)   section 7 of the Civil Evidence Act (Northern Ireland) 1971 (c 36 (NI)) (corresponding provision in Northern Ireland).
(2)   In proceedings under this Part any finding by a court in civil proceedings

that an act or omission mentioned in section 211(2)(b), (c) or (d) or 212(1) has occurred—

    (a)   is admissible as evidence that the act or omission occurred;

    (b)   unless the contrary is proved, is sufficient evidence that the act or omission occurred.

(3)   But subsection (2) does not apply to any finding—

    (a)   which has been reversed on appeal;

    (b)   which has been varied on appeal so as to negative it.

229 Advice and information

(1)   As soon as is reasonably practicable after the passing of this Act the OFT must prepare and publish advice and information with a view to—

    (a)   explaining the provisions of this Part to persons who are likely to be affected by them, and

    (b)   indicating how the OFT expects such provisions to operate.

(2)   The OFT may at any time publish revised or new advice or information.

(3)   Advice or information published in pursuance of subsection (1)(b) may include advice or information about the factors which the OFT may take into account in considering how to exercise the functions conferred on it by this Part.

(4)   Advice or information published by the OFT under this section is to be published in such form and in such manner as it considers appropriate.

(5)   In preparing advice or information under this section the OFT must consult such persons as it thinks are representative of persons affected by this Part.

(6)   If any proposed advice or information relates to a matter in respect of which another general enforcer or a designated enforcer may act the persons to be consulted must include that enforcer.

230 Notice to OFT of intended prosecution

(1)   This section applies if a local weights and measures authority in England and Wales intends to start proceedings for an offence under an enactment or subordinate legislation specified by the Secretary of State by order for the purposes of this section.

(2)   The authority must give the OFT—

    (a)   notice of its intention to start the proceedings;

    (b)   a summary of the evidence it intends to lead in respect of the charges.

(3)   The authority must not start the proceedings until whichever is the earlier of the following—

    (a)   the end of the period of 14 days starting with the day on which the authority gives the notice;

    (b)   the day on which it is notified by the OFT that the OFT has received the notice and summary given under subsection (2).

(4)   The authority must also notify the OFT of the outcome of the proceedings after they are finally determined.

(5)   But such proceedings are not invalid by reason only of the failure of the authority to comply with this section.

(6)   Subordinate legislation has the same meaning as in section 21(1) of the Interpretation Act 1978 (c 30).

(7)   An order under this section must be made by statutory instrument subject to annulment in pursuance of a resolution of either House of Parliament.

231 Notice of convictions and judgments to OFT

(1)   This section applies if—

    (a)   a person is convicted of an offence by or before a court in the United Kingdom, or

    (b)   a judgment is given against a person by a court in civil proceedings in the United Kingdom.

(2)   The court may make arrangements to bring the conviction or judgment to the attention of the OFT if it appears to the court—

(a)   having regard to the functions of the OFT under this Part or under the Estate Agents Act 1979 (c 38) that it is expedient for the conviction or judgment to be brought to the attention of the OFT, and

(b)   without such arrangements the conviction or judgment may not be brought to the attention of the OFT.

(3)   For the purposes of subsection (2) it is immaterial that the proceedings have been finally disposed of by the court.

(4)   Judgment includes an order or decree and references to the giving of the judgment must be construed accordingly.

Interpretation

232   Goods and services

(1)   References in this Part to goods and services must be construed in accordance with this section.

(2)   Goods include—

(a)   buildings and other structures;

(b)   ships, aircraft and hovercraft.

(3)   The supply of goods includes—

(a)   supply by way of sale, lease, hire or hire purchase;

(b)   in relation to buildings and other structures, construction of them by one person for another.

(4)   Goods or services which are supplied wholly or partly outside the United Kingdom must be taken to be supplied to or for a person in the United Kingdom if they are supplied in accordance with arrangements falling within subsection (5).

(5)   Arrangements fall within this subsection if they are made by any means and—

(a)   at the time the arrangements are made the person seeking the supply is in the United Kingdom, or

(b)   at the time the goods or services are supplied (or ought to be supplied in accordance with the arrangements) the person responsible under the arrangements for effecting the supply is in or has a place of business in the United Kingdom.

233   Person supplying goods

(1)   This section has effect for the purpose of references in this Part to a person supplying or seeking to supply goods under—

(a)   a hire-purchase agreement;

(b)   a credit-sale agreement;

(c)   a conditional sale agreement.

(2)   The references include references to a person who conducts any antecedent negotiations relating to the agreement.

(3)   The following expressions must be construed in accordance with section 189 of the Consumer Credit Act 1974 (c 39)—

(a)   hire-purchase agreement;

(b)   credit-sale agreement;

(c)   conditional sale agreement;

(d)   antecedent negotiations.

234   Supply of services

(1)   References in this Part to the supply of services must be construed in accordance with this section.

(2)   The supply of services does not include the provision of services under a contract of service or of apprenticeship whether it is express or implied and (if it is express) whether it is oral or in writing.

(3)   The supply of services includes—

(a)   performing for gain or reward any activity other than the supply of goods;

(b)   rendering services to order;

(c)   the provision of services by making them available to potential users.

(4)   The supply of services includes making arrangements for the use of computer software or for granting access to data stored in any form which is not readily accessible.

(5)   The supply of services includes making arrangements by means of a relevant agreement (within the meaning of [paragraph 29 of Schedule 2 to the Telecommunications Act 1984]) for sharing the use of telecommunications apparatus.

(6)   The supply of services includes permitting or making arrangements to permit the use of land in such circumstances as the Secretary of State specifies by order.

(7)   The power to make an order under subsection (6) must be exercised by statutory instrument.

(8)   But no such order may be made unless a draft of it has been laid before Parliament and approved by a resolution of each House.

235   Injunctions Directive
In this Part the Injunctions Directive is Directive 98/27/EC of the European Parliament and of the Council on injunctions for the protection of consumers' interests.

Crown

236   Crown
This Part binds the Crown.

SCHEDULE 13
LISTED DIRECTIVES

Section 210

PART 1
DIRECTIVES

1   Council Directive 84/450/EEC of 10 September 1984 relating to the approximation of the laws, regulations and administrative provisions of the Member States concerning misleading advertising.

2   Council Directive 85/577/EEC of 20 December 1985 to protect the consumer in respect of contracts negotiated away from business premises.

3   Council Directive 87/102/EEC of 22 December 1986 for the approximation of the laws, regulations and administrative provisions of the Member States concerning consumer credit as last amended by Directive 98/7/EC.

4   Council Directive 90/314/EEC of 13 June 1990 on package travel, package holidays and package tours.

5   Council Directive 93/13/EEC of 5 April 1993 on unfair terms in consumer contracts.

6   Directive 94/47/EC of the European Parliament and of the Council of 26 October 1994 on the protection of purchasers in respect of certain aspects of contracts relating to the purchase of the right to use immovable properties on a time-share basis.

7   Directive 97/7/EC of the European Parliament and of the Council of 20 May 1997 on the protection of consumers in respect of distance contracts.

8   Directive 1999/44/EC of the European Parliament and of the Council of 25 May 1999 on certain aspects of the sale of consumer goods and associated guarantees.

9   Directive 2000/31/EC of the European Parliament and of the Council of 8 June 2000 on certain legal aspects of information society services, in particular electronic commerce, in the Internal Market ('Directive on electronic commerce').

[9A   Directive 2002/65/EC of the European Parliament and of the Council of 23 September 2002 concerning the distance marketing of consumer financial services and amending Council Directive 90/619/EEC and Directives 97/7/EC and 98/27/ EC.]

PART 2
PROVISIONS OF DIRECTIVES

10   Articles 10 to 21 of Council Directive 89/552/EEC of 3 October 1989 on the co-ordination of certain provisions laid down by law, regulation or administrative action in Member States concerning the pursuit of television broadcasting activities as amended by Directive 97/36/EC.

[11   Articles 83 to 100 of the Directive 2001/83/EC of the European Parliament and of the Council of 6 November 2001 on the Community Code relating to medicinal products for human use as read with—

    (a)   Directive 2004/24/EC of the European Parliament and of the Council amending, as regards traditional herbal medicinal products, the code, and

    (b)   Directive 2004/27/EC of the European Parliament and of the Council also amending the code.]

PART II
STATUTORY INSTRUMENTS

CONSUMER TRANSACTIONS (RESTRICTIONS ON STATEMENTS) ORDER 1976
(SI 1976/1813)

2—(1)   In this Order—
    'advertisement' includes a catalogue and a circular;
    'consumer' means a person acquiring goods otherwise than in the course of a business but does not include a person who holds himself out as acquiring them in the course of a business;
    'consumer transaction' means—
        [(a)   a consumer sale, that is a sale of goods (other than an excepted sale) by a seller where the goods—
            (i)   are of a type ordinarily bought for private use or consumption, and
            (ii)   are sold to a person who does not buy or hold himself out as buying them in the course of a business.
For the purposes of this paragraph an excepted sale is a sale by auction, a sale by competitive tender and a sale arising by virtue of a contract for the international sale of goods as originally defined in section 62(1) of the Sale of Goods Act 1893 as amended by the Supply of Goods (Implied Terms) Act 1973;
        (b)   a hire-purchase agreement (within the meaning of section 189(1) of the Consumer Credit Act 1974) where the owner makes the agreement in the course of a business and the goods to which the agreement relates—
            (i)   are of a type ordinarily supplied for private use or consumption, and
            (ii)   are hired to a person who does not hire or hold himself out as hiring them in the course of a business;]
        (c)   an agreement for the redemption of trading stamps under a trading stamp scheme within section 10(1) of the Trading Stamps Act 1964 or, as the case may be, within section 9 of the Trading Stamps Act (Northern Ireland) 1965;
    'container' includes any form of packaging of goods whether by way of wholly or partly enclosing the goods or by way of attaching the goods to, or winding the goods round, some other article, and in particular includes a wrapper or confining band;
    'statutory rights' means the rights arising by virtue of sections 13 to 15 of the Sale of Goods Act 1893 as amended by the Act of 1973, sections 9 to 11 of the Act of 1973, or [sections 4, 9, 11D or 11J of the Supply of Goods and Services Act 1982].
(2)   The Interpretation Act 1889 shall apply for the interpretation of this Order as it applies for the interpretation of an Act of Parliament.
3   A person shall not, in the course of a business—
    (a)   display, at any place where consumer transactions are effected (whether wholly or partly), a notice containing a statement which purports to apply, in relation to consumer transactions effected there, a term which would—

[(i)   be void by virtue of section 6 or 20 of the Unfair Contract Terms Act 1977,]

(ii)   be inconsistent with [a term implied by sections 4, 9, 11D or 11J of the Supply of Goods and Services Act 1982],
if applied to some or all such consumer transactions;

(b)   publish or cause to be published any advertisement which is intended to induce persons to enter into consumer transactions and which contains a statement purporting to apply in relation to such consumer transactions such a term as is mentioned in paragraph (a)(i) or (ii), being a term which would be void by virtue of, or as the case may be, inconsistent with, the provisions so mentioned if applied to some or all of those transactions;

(c)   supply to a consumer pursuant to a consumer transaction goods bearing, or goods in a container bearing, a statement which is a term of that consumer transaction and which is void by virtue of, or inconsistent with, the said provisions, or if it were a term of that transaction, would be so void or inconsistent;

(d)   furnish to a consumer in connection with the carrying out of a consumer transaction or to a person likely, as a consumer, to enter into such a transaction, a document which includes a statement which is a term of that transaction and is void or inconsistent as aforesaid, or, if it were a term of that transaction or were to become a term of a prospective transaction, would be so void or inconsistent.

4   A person shall not in the course of a business—

(i)   supply to a consumer pursuant to a consumer transaction goods bearing, or goods in a container bearing, a statement about the rights that the consumer has against that person or about the obligations to the consumer accepted by that person in relation to the goods (whether legally enforceable or not), being rights or obligations that arise if the goods are defective or are not fit for a purpose or do not correspond with a description;

(ii)   furnish to a consumer in connection with the carrying out of a consumer transaction or to a person likely, as a consumer, to enter into such a transaction with him or through his agency a document containing a statement about such rights and obligations,
unless there is in close proximity to any such statement another statement which is clear and conspicuous and to the effect that the first mentioned statement does not or will not affect the statutory rights of a consumer.

5—(1)   This Article applies to goods which are supplied in the course of a business by one person ('the supplier') to another where, at the time of the supply, the goods were intended by the supplier to be, or might reasonably be expected by him to be, the subject of a subsequent consumer transaction.

(2)   A supplier shall not—

(a)   supply goods to which this Article applies if the goods bear, or are in a container bearing, a statement which sets out or describes or limits obligations (whether legally enforceable or not) accepted or to be accepted by him in relation to the goods; or

(b)   furnish a document in relation to the goods which contains such a statement, unless there is in close proximity to any such statement another statement which is clear and conspicuous and to the effect that the first mentioned statement does not or will not affect the statutory rights of a consumer.

(3)   A person does not contravene paragraph (2) above—

(i)   in a case to which sub-paragraph (a) of that paragraph applies, unless the goods have become the subject of a consumer transaction;

(ii)   in a case to which sub-paragraph (b) applies, unless the document has been furnished to a consumer in relation to goods which were the subject of a consumer transaction, or to a person likely to become a consumer pursuant to such a transaction; or

(iii)   by virtue of any statement if before the date on which this Article comes into operation the document containing, or the goods or container bearing, the statement has ceased to be in his possession.

CONSUMER PROTECTION (CANCELLATION OF CONTRACTS CONCLUDED AWAY FROM BUSINESS PREMISES) REGULATIONS 1987 (SI 1987/2117)

2 Interpretation
(1)   In these Regulations—

'business' includes a trade or profession;

'consumer' means a person, other than a body corporate, who, in making a contract to which these Regulations apply, is acting for purposes which can be regarded as outside his business;

['enforcement authority' means, in Great Britain, a weights and measures authority and, in Northern Ireland, the Department of Economic Development;]

'goods' has the meaning given by section 61(1) of the Sale of Goods Act 1979;

'land mortgage' includes any security charged on land and in relation to Scotland includes any heritable security;

'notice of cancellation' has the meaning given by regulation 4(5) below;

'security' in relation to a contract means a mortgage, charge, pledge, bond, debenture, indemnity, guarantee, bill, note or other right provided by the consumer, or at his request (express or implied), to secure the carrying out of his obligations under the contract;

'signed' has the same meaning as in the Consumer Credit Act 1974, and

'trader' means a person who, in making a contract to which these Regulations apply, is acting for the purposes of his business, and anyone acting in the name or on behalf of such a person.

(2)   In Scotland any provision of these Regulations requiring a document to be signed shall be complied with by a body corporate if the document is properly executed in accordance with the law of Scotland.

3 Contracts to which the Regulations apply
(1)   These Regulations apply to a contract, other than an excepted contract, for the supply by a trader of goods or services to a consumer which is made—

(a)   during an unsolicited visit by a trader—

(i)   to the consumer's home or to the home of another person; or

(ii)   to the consumer's place of work;

(b)   during a visit by a trader as mentioned in paragraph (a)(i) or (ii) above at the express request of the consumer where the goods or services to which the contract relates are other than those concerning which the consumer requested the visit of the trader, provided that when the visit was requested the consumer did not know, or could not reasonably have known, that the supply of those other goods or services formed part of the trader's business activities;

(c)   after an offer was made by the consumer in respect of the supply by a trader of the goods or services in the circumstances mentioned in paragraph (a) or (b) above or (d) below; or

(d)   during an excursion organised by the trader away from premises on which he is carrying on any business (whether on a permanent or temporary basis).

(2)   For the purposes of this regulation an excepted contract means;

(a)   any contract—

(i)   for the sale or other disposition of land, or for a lease or land mortgage;

(ii)   to finance the purchase of land;

(iii)   for a bridging loan in connection with the purchase of land; or

(iv)   for the construction or extension of a building or other erection on land:

Provided that these Regulations shall apply to a contract for the supply of goods and their incorporation in any land or a contract for the repair or improvement of a building or other erection on land, where the contract is not financed by a loan secured by a land mortgage;

(b)   any contract for the supply of food, drink or other goods intended for current consumption by use in the household and supplied by regular roundsmen;

(c)   any contract for the supply of goods or services which satisfies all the following conditions, namely—

    (i)   terms of the contract are contained in a trader's catalogue which is readily available to the consumer to read in the absence of the trader or his representative before the conclusion of the contract;

    (ii)   the parties to the contract intend that there shall be maintained continuity of contact between the trader or his representative and the consumer in relation to the transaction in question or any subsequent transaction; and

    (iii)   both the catalogue and the contract contain or are accompanied by a prominent notice indicating that the consumer has a right to return to the trader or his representative goods supplied to him within the period of not less than 7 days from the day on which the goods are received by the consumer and otherwise to cancel the contract within that period without the consumer incurring any liability, other than any liability which may arise from the failure of the consumer to take reasonable care of the goods while they are in his possession;

(d)   contracts of insurance;

[(e)   any agreement the making or performance of which by either party constitutes a relevant regulated activity;]

(f)   any contract not falling within sub-paragraph (g) below under which the total payments to be made by the consumer do not exceed £35; and

(g)   any contract under which credit within the meaning of the Consumer Credit Act 1974 is provided not exceeding £35 other than a hire-purchase or conditional sale agreement.

[(3)   In this regulation 'unsolicited visit' means a visit by a trader, whether or not he is the trader who supplies the goods or services, which does not take place at the express request of the consumer and includes—

(a)   a visit by a trader which takes place after he, or a person acting in his name or on his behalf, telephones the consumer (otherwise than at the consumer's express request) and indicates during the course of the telephone call (either expressly or by implication) that he, or the trader in whose name or on whose behalf he is acting, is willing to visit the consumer; and

(b)   a visit by a trader which takes place after he, or a person acting in his name or on his behalf, visits the consumer (otherwise than at the consumer's express request) and indicates during the course of that visit (either expressly or by implication) that he, or the trader in whose name or on whose behalf he is acting, is willing to make a subsequent visit to the consumer.]

[(4)   For the purposes of paragraph (2)(e)—

(a)   'a relevant regulated activity' means an activity of the following kind, namely—

    (i)   dealing in investments, as principal or as agent,

    (ii)   arranging deals in investments,

    (iii)   managing investments,

    (iv)   safeguarding and administering investments,

    (v)   establishing etc a collective investment scheme; and

(b)   'investment' means—

(i)   shares,
(ii)   instruments creating or acknowledging indebtedness,
(iii)   government and public securities,
(iv)   instruments giving entitlement to investments,
(v)   certificates representing securities,
(vi)   units in a collective investment scheme,
(vii)   options,
(viii)   futures,
(ix)   contracts for differences, and
(x)   rights to or interests in investments.
(5)   Paragraphs (2)(d) and (4) must be read with—
(a)   section 22 of the Financial Services and Markets Act 2000;
(b)   any relevant order under that section; and
(c)   Schedule 2 to that Act,
but any restriction on or exclusion from the meaning of a regulated activity (which is a relevant regulated activity for the purposes of paragraph (2)(e)) which arises from the identity of the person carrying it on is to be disregarded.]

4   Cancellation of contract
(1)   No contract to which these Regulations apply shall be enforceable against the consumer unless the trader has delivered to the consumer notice in writing in accordance with paragraphs (3) and (4) below indicating the right of the consumer to cancel the contract within the period of 7 days mentioned in paragraph (5) below containing both the information set out in Part I of the Schedule to these Regulations and a Cancellation Form in the form set out in Part II of the Schedule and completed in accordance with the footnotes.
(2)   Paragraph (1) above does not apply to a cancellable agreement within the meaning of the Consumer Credit Act 1974 or to an agreement which may be cancelled by the consumer in accordance with terms of the agreement conferring upon him similar rights as if the agreement were such a cancellable agreement.
(3)   The information to be contained in the notice under paragraph (1) above shall be easily legible and if incorporated in the contract or other document shall be afforded no less prominence than that given to any other information in the document apart from the heading to the document and the names of the parties to the contract and any information inserted in handwriting.
(4)   The notice shall be dated and delivered to the consumer—
(a)   in the cases mentioned in regulation 3(1)(a), (b) and (d) above, at the time of the making of the contract; and
(b)   in the case mentioned in regulation 3(1)(c) above, at the time of the making of the offer by the consumer.
(5)   If within the period of 7 days following the making of the contract the consumer serves a notice in writing (a 'notice of cancellation') on the trader or any other person specified in a notice referred to in paragraph (1) above as a person to whom notice of cancellation may be given which, however expressed and whether or not conforming to the cancellation form set out in Part II of the Schedule to these Regulations, indicates the intention of the consumer to cancel the contract, the notice of cancellation shall operate to cancel the contract.
(6)   Except as otherwise provided under these Regulations, a contract cancelled under paragraph (5) above shall be treated as if it had never been entered into by the consumer.
(7)   Notwithstanding anything in section 7 of the Interpretation Act 1978, a notice of cancellation sent by post by a consumer shall be deemed to have been served at the time of posting, whether or not it is actually received.

[4A   Offence relating to the failure to provide notice of cancellation rights
(1)   A trader is guilty of an offence if he enters into a contract to which these Regulations apply (other than an agreement referred to in regulation 4(2) above)

with a consumer but fails (or, in the case mentioned in regulation 3(1)(c) above, has failed) to deliver to the consumer the notice in writing referred to in regulation 4(1) above in accordance with paragraph (2) below.

(2)   A notice is delivered in accordance with this paragraph if it—

(a)   contains what is required by regulation 4(1) above;

(b)   complies with the requirements of regulation 4(3) above; and

(c)   is dated and delivered to the consumer at the time specified in regulation 4(4) above.

(3)   A person who is guilty of an offence under paragraph (1) above shall be liable on summary conviction to a fine not exceeding level 4 on the standard scale.]

[4B   Defence of due diligence

(1)   In proceedings against any person for an offence under regulation 4A above it shall be a defence for that person to show that he took all reasonable steps and exercised all due diligence to avoid committing the offence.

(2)   Where in proceedings against a person for such an offence the defence provided for by paragraph (1) above involves an allegation that the commission of the offence was due—

(a)   to the act or default of another, or

(b)   to reliance on information given by another,

that person shall not, without the leave of the court, be entitled to rely on the defence unless he has served a notice under paragraph (3) below on the person bringing the proceedings not less than seven clear days before the hearing of the proceedings or, in Scotland, the diet of the trial.

(3)   A notice under this paragraph shall give such information identifying or assisting in the identification of the person who committed the act or default or gave the information as is in the possession of the person serving the notice at the time when he serves it.]

[4C   Liability of persons other than the principal offender

(1)   Where the commission by a person of an offence under regulation 4A above is due to the act or default of some other person, that other person is guilty of the offence and may be proceeded against and punished by virtue of this regulation whether or not proceedings are taken against the first-mentioned person.

(2)   Where a body corporate is guilty of an offence under regulation 4A above in respect of any act or default which is shown to have been committed with the consent or connivance of, or to be attributable to any neglect on the part of, any director, manager, secretary or other similar officer of the body corporate or any person who was purporting to act in any such capacity he, as well as the body corporate, shall be guilty of that offence and shall be liable to be proceeded against and punished accordingly.

(3)   Where the affairs of a body corporate are managed by its members, paragraph (2) above shall apply in relation to the acts and defaults of a member in connection with his functions of management as if he were a director of the body corporate.

(4)   Where an offence under regulation 4A above committed in Scotland by a Scottish partnership is proved to have been committed with the consent or connivance of, or to be attributable to neglect on the part of, a partner, he (as well as the partnership) is guilty of the offence and liable to be proceeded against and punished, accordingly.]

[4D   Duty to enforce regulation 4A

(1)   Subject to paragraph (2) below—

(a)   it shall be the duty of every weights and measures authority in Great Britain to enforce regulation 4A above within its area; and

(b)   it shall be the duty of the Department of Economic Development to enforce regulation 4A above in Northern Ireland.

(2)   Nothing in paragraph (1) above shall authorise any weights and measures authority to bring proceedings in Scotland for an offence.]

[4E   Enforcement powers, obstruction of authorised officers and restrictions on disclosure of information
(1)   If a duly authorised officer of an enforcement authority has reasonable grounds for suspecting that an offence has been committed under regulation 4A above, he may—
(a)   require a person carrying on or employed in a business to produce any book, document or record in non-documentary form relating to the business, and take copies of it or any entry in it, or
(b)   require such a person to produce in a visible and legible documentary form any information so relating which is contained in a computer, and take copies of it, for the purposes of ascertaining whether such an offence has been committed.
(2)   If such an officer has reasonable grounds for believing that any books, documents or records may be required as evidence in proceedings for such an offence, he may seize and detain them and shall, if he does so, inform the person from whom they are seized.
(3)   The powers of an officer under this regulation may be exercised by him only at a reasonable hour and on production (if required) of his credentials.
(4)   Nothing in this regulation requires a person to produce, or authorises the taking from a person of, a book, document or record which he could not be compelled to produce in civil proceedings before the High Court or (in Scotland) the Court of Session.]

[4F—(1)   A person who—
(a)   intentionally obstructs an officer of an enforcement authority acting in pursuance of his functions under these Regulations,
(b)   without reasonable cause fails to comply with the requirement made of him by regulation 4E(1) above, or
(c)   without reasonable excuse fails to give an officer of an enforcement authority acting in pursuance of his functions under these Regulations any other assistance or information which the officer has reasonably required of him for the purpose of the performance of the officer's functions under these Regulations,
is guilty of an offence.
(2)   If a person, in giving information to an officer of an enforcement authority who is acting in pursuance of his functions under these Regulations—
(a)   makes a statement which he knows is false in a material particular, or
(b)   recklessly makes a statement which is false in a material particular, he is guilty of an offence.
(3)   A person guilty of an offence under paragraph (1) or (2) above shall be liable on summary conviction to a fine not exceeding level 3 on the standard scale.]

[. . .]

[4H   Nothing in regulations 4E or 4F above requires a person to answer any question or give any information if to do so might incriminate him.]

5   Recovery of money paid by consumer
(1)   Subject to regulation 7(2) below, on the cancellation of a contract under regulation 4 above, any sum paid by or on behalf of the consumer under or in contemplation of the contract shall become repayable.
(2)   If under the terms of the cancelled contract the consumer or any person on his behalf is in possession of any goods, he shall have a lien on them for any sum repayable to him under paragraph (1) above.
(3)   Where any security has been provided in relation to the cancelled contract,

the security, so far as it is so provided, shall be treated as never having had effect and any property lodged with the trader solely for the purposes of the security as so provided shall be returned by him forthwith.

6   Repayment of credit

(1)   Notwithstanding the cancellation of a contract under regulation 4 above under which credit is provided, the contract shall continue in force so far as it relates to repayment of credit and payment of interest.

(2)   If, following the cancellation of the contract, the consumer repays the whole or a portion of the credit—

(a)   before the expiry of one month following service of the notice of cancellation, or

(b)   in the case of a credit repayable by instalments, before the date on which the first instalment is due,

no interest shall be payable on the amount repaid.

(3)   If the whole of a credit repayable by instalments is not repaid on or before the date specified in paragraph (2)(b) above, the consumer shall not be liable to repay any of the credit except on receipt of a request in writing signed by the trader stating the amounts of the remaining instalments (recalculated by the trader as nearly as may be in accordance with the contract and without extending the repayment period), but excluding any sum other than principal and interest.

(4)   Repayment of a credit, or payment of interest, under a cancelled contract shall be treated as duly made if it is made to any person on whom, under regulation 4(5) above, a notice of cancellation could have been served.

(5)   Where any security has been provided in relation to the contract, the duty imposed on the consumer by this regulation shall not be enforceable before the trader has discharged any duty imposed on him by regulation 5(3) above.

(6)   [In this regulation, the following expressions have the meanings hereby assigned to them:—

'cash' includes money in any form;

'credit' means a cash loan and any facility enabling the consumer to overdraw on a current account;

'current account' means an account under which the customer may, by means of cheques or similar orders payable to himself or to any other person, obtain or have the use of money held or made available by the person with whom the account is kept and which records alterations in the financial relationship between the said person and the customer; and

'repayment', in relation to credit, means the repayment of money—

(a)   paid to a consumer before the cancellation of the contract; or

(b)   to the extent that he was overdrawn on his current account before the cancellation.]

7   Return of goods by consumer after cancellation

(1)   Subject to paragraph (2) below, a consumer who has before cancelling a contract under regulation 4 above acquired possession of any goods by virtue of the contract shall be under a duty, subject to any lien, on the cancellation to restore the goods to the trader in accordance with this regulation, and meanwhile to retain possession of the goods and take reasonable care of them.

(2)   The consumer shall not be under a duty to restore—

(i)   perishable goods;

(ii)   goods which by their nature are consumed by use and which, before the cancellation, were so consumed;

(iii)   goods supplied to meet an emergency; or

(iv)   goods which, before the cancellation, had become incorporated in any land or thing not comprised in the cancelled contract,

but he shall be under a duty to pay in accordance with the cancelled contract for the supply of the goods and for the provision of any services in connection with the supply of the goods before the cancellation.

(3)   The consumer shall not be under any duty to deliver the goods except at his own premises and in pursuance of a request in writing signed by the trader and served on the consumer either before, or at the time when, the goods are collected from those premises.

(4)   If the consumer—

(i)   delivers the goods (whether at his own premises or elsewhere) to any person on whom, under regulation 4(5) above, a notice of cancellation could have been served; or

(ii)   sends the goods at his own expense to such a person,

he shall be discharged from any duty to retain possession of the goods or restore them to the trader.

(5)   Where the consumer delivers the goods as mentioned in paragraph (4)(i) above, his obligation to take care of the goods shall cease; and if he sends the goods as mentioned in paragraph (4)(ii) above, he shall be under a duty to take reasonable care to see that they are received by the trader and not damaged in transit, but in other respects his duty to take care of the goods shall cease.

(6)   Where, at any time during the period of 21 days following the cancellation, the consumer receives such a request as is mentioned in paragraph (3) above and unreasonably refuses or unreasonably fails to comply with it, his duty to retain possession and take reasonable care of the goods shall continue until he delivers or sends the goods as mentioned in paragraph (4) above, but if within that period he does not receive such a request his duty to take reasonable care of the goods shall cease at the end of that period.

(7)   Where any security has been provided in relation to the cancelled contract, the duty imposed on the consumer to restore goods by this regulation shall not be enforceable before the trader has discharged any duty imposed on him by regulation 5(3) above.

(8)   Breach of a duty imposed by this regulation on a consumer is actionable as a breach of statutory duty.

8   Goods given in part-exchange

(1)   This regulation applies on the cancellation of a contract under regulation 4 above where the trader agreed to take goods in part-exchange (the 'part-exchange goods') and those goods have been delivered to him.

(2)   Unless, before the end of the period of ten days beginning with the date of cancellation, the part-exchange goods are returned to the consumer in a condition substantially as good as when they were delivered to the trader, the consumer shall be entitled to recover from the trader a sum equal to the part-exchange allowance.

(3)   During the period of ten days beginning with the date of cancellation, the consumer, if he is in possession of goods to which the cancelled contract relates, shall have a lien on them for—

(a)   delivery of the part-exchange goods in a condition substantially as good as when they were delivered to the trader; or

(b)   a sum equal to the part-exchange allowance;

and if the lien continues to the end of that period it shall thereafter subsist only as a lien for a sum equal to the part-exchange allowance.

(4)   In this regulation the part-exchange allowance means the sum agreed as such in the cancelled contract, or if no such sum was agreed, such sum as it would have been reasonable to allow in respect of the part-exchange goods if no notice of cancellation had been served.

10   No contracting-out

(1)   A term contained in a contract to which these Regulations apply is void if,

and to the extent that, it is inconsistent with a provision for the protection of the consumer contained in these Regulations.

(2)   Where a provision of these Regulations specifies the duty or liability of the consumer in certain circumstances a term contained in a contract to which these Regulations apply is inconsistent with that provision if it purports to impose, directly or indirectly, an additional duty or liability on him in those circumstances.

11   Service of documents

(1)   A document to be served under these Regulations on a person may be so served—

(a)   by delivering it to him, or by sending it by post to him, or by leaving it with him, at his proper address addressed to him by name;

(b)   if the person is a body corporate, by serving it in accordance with paragraph (a) above on the secretary or clerk of that body; or

(c)   if the person is a partnership, by serving it in accordance with paragraph (a) above on a partner or on a person having the control or management of the partnership business.

(2)   For the purposes of these Regulations, a document sent by post to, or left at, the address last known to the server of the document as the address of a person shall be treated as sent by post to, or left at, his proper address.

SCHEDULE
Regulation 4(i)
PART I
INFORMATION TO BE CONTAINED IN NOTICE OF CANCELLATION RIGHTS

1   The name of the trader.

2   The trader's reference number, code or other details to enable the contract or offer to be identified.

3   A statement that the consumer has a right to cancel the contract if he wishes and that this right can be exercised by sending or taking a written notice of cancellation to the person mentioned in paragraph 4 within the period of 7 days following the making of the contract.

4   The name and address of a person to whom notice of cancellation may be given.

5   A statement that the consumer can use the cancellation form provided if he wishes.

PART II
CANCELLATION FORM TO BE INCLUDED IN NOTICE OF CANCELLATION RIGHTS

(Complete, detach and return this form ONLY IF YOU WISH TO CANCEL THE CONTRACT)

To: 1

I/We* hereby give notice that I/We* wish to cancel my/our* contract   2

Signed

Date

*Delete as appropriate

Notes:

1   Trader to insert name and address of person to whom notice may be given.

2   Trader to insert reference number, code or other details to enable the contract or offer to be identified. He may also insert the name and address of the consumer.

CONTROL OF MISLEADING ADVERTISEMENTS REGULATIONS 1988
(SI 1988/915)
(as amended by the Control of Misleading Advertisements (Amendment) Regulations 2003 (SI 2003/3183))

2 Interpretation
(1) In these Regulations—
'advertisement' means any form of representation which is made in connection with a trade, business, craft or profession in order to promote the supply or transfer of goods or services, immovable property, rights or obligations;
[. . .]
'court', in relation to England and Wales and Northern Ireland, means the High Court, and, in relation to Scotland, the Court of Session;
'Director' means the Director General of Fair Trading;*
[. . .]
['licensed service' means a service in respect of which a licence has been granted under Part I or II of the Broadcasting Act 1996.]
['OFCOM' means the Office of Communications established by section 1(1) of the Office of Communications Act 2002;]
'products with designation of origin' are those products to which Council Regulation (EEC) No 2081/92 of 14 July 1992 applies;]
'publication' in relation to an advertisement means the dissemination of that advertisement whether to an individual person or a number of persons and whether orally or in writing or in any other way whatsoever, and 'publish' shall be construed accordingly;
['S4C' and 'S4C Digital' have the same meaning as in Part 3 of the Communications Act 2002;]
(2) For the purposes of these Regulations an advertisement is misleading if in any way, including its presentation, it deceives or is likely to deceive the persons to whom it is addressed or whom it reaches and if, by reason of its deceptive nature, it is likely to affect their economic behaviour or, for those reasons, injures or is likely to injure a competitor of the person whose interests the advertisement seeks to promote.
[(2A) For the purposes of these Regulations an advertisement is comparative if in any way, either explicitly or by implication, it identifies a competitor or goods or services offered by a competitor.]
(3) In the application of these Regulations to Scotland for references to an injunction or an [interim injunction] there shall be substituted references to an interdict or an interim interdict respectively.

[. . .]

4 Complaints to the Director
(1) Subject to paragraphs (2) and (3) below, it shall be the duty of the Director to consider any complaint made to him that an advertisement is misleading [, or is a comparative advertisement and is not permitted under regulation 4A below], unless the complaint appears to the Director to be frivolous or vexatious.
(2) The Director shall not consider any complaint which these Regulations require or would require, leaving aside any question as to the frivolous or vexatious nature of the complaint, [OFCOM] to consider.
(3) Before considering any complaint under paragraph (1) above the Director may require the person making the complaint to satisfy him that—
(a) there have been invoked in relation to the same or substantially the same

---
*All references to 'the Director' have effect as if they were references to 'the OFT': Enterprise Act 2002, s 2.

complaint about the advertisement in question such established means of dealing with such complaints as the Director may consider appropriate, having regard to all the circumstances of the particular case;

(b) a reasonable opportunity has been allowed for those means to deal with the complaint in question; and

(c) those means have not dealt with the complaint adequately.

(4) In exercising the powers conferred on him by these Regulations the Director shall have regard to—

(a) all the interests involved and in particular the public interest; and

(b) the desirability of encouraging the control, by self-regulatory bodies, of advertisements.

[4A Comparative advertisements

(1) A comparative advertisement shall, as far as the comparison is concerned, be permitted only when the following conditions are met:

(a) it is not misleading;

(b) it compares goods or services meeting the same needs or intended for the same purpose;

(c) it objectively compares one or more material, relevant, verifiable and representative features of those goods and services, which may include price;

(d) it does not create confusion in the market place between the advertiser and a competitor or between the advertiser's trade marks, trade names, other distinguishing marks, goods or services and those of a competitor;

(e) it does not discredit or denigrate the trade marks, trade names, other distinguishing marks, goods, services, activities, or circumstances of a competitor;

(f) for products with designation of origin, it relates in each case to products with the same designation;

(g) it does not take unfair advantage of the reputation of a trade mark, trade name or other distinguishing marks of a competitor or of the designation of origin of competing products;

(h) it does not present goods or services as imitations or replicas of goods or services bearing a protected trade mark or trade name.

(2) In the case of a comparative advertisement referring to a special offer, such an advertisement is not permitted unless it indicates in a clear and unequivocal way the date on which the offer ends or, where appropriate, that the special offer is subject to the availability of the goods and services, and, where the special offer has not yet begun, the date of the start of the period during which the special price or other specific conditions shall apply.

(3) The provisions of this regulation shall not be construed as—

(a) conferring a right of action in any civil proceedings in respect of any contravention of this regulation (save as provided for in these Regulations); or

(b) derogating from any right of action or other remedy (whether civil or criminal) in proceedings instituted otherwise than by virtue of these Regulations.]

5 Applications to the court by the Director

(1) If, having considered a complaint about an advertisement pursuant to regulation 4(1) above, he considers that the advertisement is misleading [, or is a comparative advertisement and is not permitted under regulation 4A], the Director may, if he thinks it appropriate to do so, bring proceedings for an injunction (in which proceedings he may also apply for an [interim injunction]) against any person appearing to him to be concerned or likely to be concerned with the publication of the advertisement.

(2) The Director shall give reasons for his decision to apply or not to apply, as the case may be, for an injunction in relation to any complaint which these Regulations require him to consider.

6 Functions of the court

(1) The court on an application by the Director may grant an injunction on such terms as it may think fit but (except where it grants an [interim injunction]) only if the court is satisfied that the advertisement to which the application relates is misleading [or is a comparative advertisement and is not permitted under regulation 4A]. Before granting an injunction the court shall have regard to all the interests involved and in particular the public interest.

(2) An injunction may relate not only to a particular advertisement but to any advertisement in similar terms or likely to convey a similar impression.

(3) In considering an application for an injunction the court may, whether or not on the application of any party to the proceedings, require any person appearing to the court to be responsible for the publication of the advertisement to which the application relates to furnish the court with evidence of the accuracy of any factual claim made in the advertisement. The court shall not make such a requirement unless it appears to the court to be appropriate in the circumstances of the particular case, having regard to the legitimate interests of the person who would be the subject of or affected by the requirement and of any other person concerned with the advertisement.

(4) If such evidence is not furnished to it following a requirement made by it under paragraph (3) above or if it considers such evidence inadequate, the court may decline to consider the factual claim mentioned in that paragraph accurate.

(5) The court shall not refuse to grant an injunction for lack of evidence that—

(a) the publication of the advertisement in question has given rise to loss or damage to any person; or

(b) the person responsible for the advertisement intended it to be misleading or failed to exercise proper care to prevent its being misleading; [or

(c) the person responsible for the comparative advertisement intended to breach the conditions in regulation 4A(1) and (2) or failed to exercise proper care to meet the conditions in regulation 4A(1) and (2).]

(6) An injunction may prohibit the publication or the continued or further publication of an advertisement.

7 Powers of the Director to obtain and disclose information and disclosure of information generally

(1) For the purpose of facilitating the exercise by him of any functions conferred on him by these Regulations, the Director may, by notice in writing signed by him or on his behalf, require any person to furnish to him such information as may be specified or described in the notice or to produce to him any documents so specified or described.

(2) A notice under paragraph (1) above may—

(a) specify the way in which and the time within which it is to be complied with; and

(b) be varied or revoked by a subsequent notice.

(3) Nothing in this regulation compels the production or furnishing by any person of a document or of information which he would in an action in a court be entitled to refuse to produce or furnish on grounds of legal professional privilege or, in Scotland, on the grounds of confidentiality as between client and professional legal adviser.

(4) If a person makes default in complying with a notice under paragraph (1) above the court may, on the application of the Director, make such order as the court thinks fit for requiring the default to be made good, and any such order may provide that all the costs or expenses of and incidental to the application shall be borne by the person in default or by any officers of a company or other association who are responsible for its default.

(5) Subject to any provision to the contrary made by or under any enactment, where the Director considers it appropriate to do so for the purpose of controlling

misleading advertisements [or comparative advertisements which do not comply with regulation 4A], he may refer to any person any complaint (including any related documentation) about an advertisement or disclose to any person any information (whether or not obtained by means of the exercise of the power conferred by paragraph (1) above).

(6)   [*Amends assorted statutes.*]

[. . .]

(8)   The Director may arrange for the dissemination in such form and manner as he considers appropriate of such information and advice concerning the operation of these Regulations as may appear to him to be expedient to give to the public and to all persons likely to be affected by these Regulations.

[8   Complaints to [OFCOM]

[(1)   It shall be the duty of OFCOM to consider any complaint made to them that any advertisement included or proposed to be included in a licensed service is misleading or is a comparative advertisement and is not permitted under regulation 4A, unless the complaint appears to OFCOM to be frivolous or vexatious.]

[. . .]

(3)   [OFCOM shall give reasons for their decisions.]

(4)   In exercising the powers [conferred on them] by these Regulations [OFCOM] shall have regard to all the interests involved and in particular the public interest.

9   Control by [OFCOM] of misleading advertisements and comparative advertisements

[(1)   If, having considered a complaint about an advertisement pursuant to regulation 8(1) above, they consider that the advertisement is misleading, or is a comparative advertisement and is not permitted under regulation 4A, OFCOM may, if they think it appropriate to do so, exercise in relation to the advertisement any power conferred on them by virtue of a condition included in a licence in accordance with section 325(4) of the Communications Act 2003.]

(2)   [OFCOM may] require any person [appearing to them] to be responsible for an advertisement which [OFCOM] believe may be misleading[, or may be a comparative advertisement which is not permitted under regulation 4A, to furnish them] with evidence as to the accuracy of any factual claim made in the advertisement. In deciding whether or not to make such a requirement [OFCOM shall have regard] to the legitimate interests of any person who would be the subject of or affected by the requirement.

(3)   If such evidence is not [furnished to them following a requirement made by them] under paragraph (2) above [within a time specified by OFCOM] or if [they] consider such evidence inadequate, [OFCOM] may consider the factual claim inaccurate.

10   Complaints about advertisements on S4C and S4C Digital

[(1)   It shall be the duty of OFCOM to consider any complaint made to them that any advertisement broadcast or proposed to be broadcast on S4C or S4C Digital is misleading, or is a comparative advertisement and is not permitted under regulation 4A, unless the complaint appears to OFCOM to be frivolous or vexatious.]

[. . .]

[(3) OFCOM shall give reasons for their decisions.]

(4)   In exercising the powers conferred on them by these Regulations the Welsh Authority shall have regard to all the interests involved and in particular the public interest.

11   [Control of misleading advertisements and comparative advertisements on S4C and S4C Digital]

[(1)   If, having considered a complaint about an advertisement pursuant to regulation 10(1) above, they consider that the advertisement is misleading, or is a comparative advertisement and is not permitted under regulation 4A, OFCOM may, if they think it appropriate to do so, exercise in relation to the advertisement, the power conferred by paragraph 14 of Schedule 12 to the Communications Act 2003.]

(2) [OFCOM] may require any person appearing to them to be responsible for an advertisement which [OFCOM] believe may be misleading [, or may be a comparative advertisement which is not permitted under regulation 4A,] to furnish them with evidence as to the accuracy of any factual claim made in the advertisement. In deciding whether or not to make such a requirement the Authority shall have regard to the legitimate interests of any person who would be the subject of or affected by the requirement.

(3) If such evidence is not furnished to them following a requirement made by them under paragraph (2) above [within a time specified by OFCOM] or if they consider such evidence inadequate, OFCOM may consider the factual claim inaccurate.]

COMMERCIAL AGENTS (COUNCIL DIRECTIVE) REGULATIONS 1993
(SI 1993/3053)
(as amended by the Commercial Agents (Council Directive) (Amendment) Regulations 1993 (SI 1993/3173) and 1998 (SI 1998/2868).)

PART I
GENERAL

1 Citation, commencement and applicable law

(1) These Regulations may be cited as the Commercial Agents (Council Directive) Regulations 1993 and shall come into force on 1st January 1994.

(2) These Regulations govern the relations between commercial agents and their principals and, subject to paragraph (3), apply in relation to the activities of commercial agents in Great Britain.

[(3) A court or tribunal shall:

(a) apply the law of the other member State concerned in place of regulations 3 to 22 where the parties have agreed that the agency contract is to be governed by the law of that member State;

(b) (whether or not it would otherwise be required to do so) apply these Regulations where the law of another member State corresponding to these Regulations enables the parties to agree that the agency contract is to be governed by the law of a different member State and the parties have agreed that it is to be governed by the law of England and Wales or Scotland.]

2 Interpretation, application and extent

(1) In these Regulations—

'commercial agent' means a self-employed intermediary who has continuing authority to negotiate the sale or purchase of goods on behalf of another person (the 'principal'), or to negotiate and conclude the sale or purchase of goods on behalf of and in the name of that principal; but shall be understood as not including in particular:

(i) a person who, in his capacity as an officer of a company or association, is empowered to enter into commitments binding on that company or association;

(ii) a partner who is lawfully authorised to enter into commitments binding on his partners;

(iii) a person who acts as an insolvency practitioner (as that expression is defined in section 388 of the Insolvency Act 1986) or the equivalent in any other jurisdiction;

'commission' means any part of the remuneration of a commercial agent which varies with the number or value of business transactions;

['EEA Agreement' means the Agreement on the European Economic Area signed at Oporto on 2nd May 1992 as adjusted by the Protocol signed at Brussels on 17th March 1993;

'member State' includes a State which is a contracting party to the EEA Agreement;]

'restraint of trade clause' means an agreement restricting the business activities of a commercial agent following termination of the agency contract.

(2)   These Regulations do not apply to—

(a)   commercial agents whose activities are unpaid;

(b)   commercial agents when they operate on commodity exchanges or in the commodity market;

(c)   the Crown Agents for Overseas Governments and Administrations, as set up under the Crown Agents Act 1979, or its subsidiaries.

(3)   The provisions of the Schedule to these Regulations have effect for the purpose of determining the persons whose activities as commercial agents are to be considered secondary.

(4)   These Regulations shall not apply to the persons referred to in paragraph (3) above.

(5)   These Regulations do not extend to Northern Ireland.

PART II
RIGHTS AND OBLIGATIONS

3   Duties of a commercial agent to his principal

(1)   In performing his activities a commercial agent must look after the interests of his principal and act dutifully and in good faith.

(2)   In particular, a commercial agent must—

(a)   make proper efforts to negotiate and, where appropriate, conclude the transactions he is instructed to take care of;

(b)   communicate to his principal all the necessary information available to him;

(c)   comply with reasonable instructions given by his principal.

4   Duties of a principal to his commercial agent

(1)   In his relations with his commercial agent a principal must act dutifully and in good faith.

(2)   In particular, a principal must—

(a)   provide his commercial agent with the necessary documentation relating to the goods concerned;

(b)   obtain for his commercial agent the information necessary for the performance of the agency contract, and in particular notify his commercial agent within a reasonable period once he anticipates that the volume of commercial transactions will be significantly lower than that which the commercial agent could normally have expected.

(3)   A principal shall, in addition, inform his commercial agent within a reasonable period of his acceptance or refusal of, and of any non-execution by him of, a commercial transaction which the commercial agent has procured for him.

5   Prohibition on derogation from regulations 3 and 4 and consequence of breach

(1)   The parties may not derogate from regulations 3 and 4 above.

(2)   The law applicable to the contract shall govern the consequence of breach of the rights and obligations under regulations 3 and 4 above.

PART III
REMUNERATION

6   Form and amount of remuneration in absence of agreement

(1)   In the absence of any agreement as to remuneration between the parties, a commercial agent shall be entitled to the remuneration that commercial agents appointed for the goods forming the subject of his agency contract are customarily allowed in the place where he carries on his activities and, if there is no such customary practice, a commercial agent shall be entitled to reasonable remuneration taking into account all the aspects of the transaction.

(2)   This regulation is without prejudice to the application of any enactment or rule of law concerning the level of remuneration.

(3)   Where a commercial agent is not remunerated (wholly or in part) by commission, regulations 7 to 12 below shall not apply.

7   Entitlement to commission on transactions concluded during agency contract

(1)   A commercial agent shall be entitled to commission on commercial transactions concluded during the period covered by the agency contract—

(a)   where the transaction has been concluded as a result of his action; or

(b)   where the transaction is concluded with a third party whom he has previously acquired as a customer for transactions of the same kind.

(2)   A commercial agent shall also be entitled to commission on transactions concluded during the period covered by the agency contract where he has an exclusive right to a specific geographical area or to a specific group of customers and where the transaction has been entered into with a customer belonging to that area or group.

8   Entitlement to commission on transactions concluded after agency contract has terminated

Subject to regulation 9 below, a commercial agent shall be entitled to commission on commercial transactions concluded after the agency contract has terminated if—

(a)   the transaction is mainly attributable to his efforts during the period covered by the agency contract and if the transaction was entered into within a reasonable period after that contract terminated; or

(b)   in accordance with the conditions mentioned in regulation 7 above, the order of the third party reached the principal or the commercial agent before the agency contract terminated.

9   Apportionment of commission between new and previous commercial agents

(1)   A commercial agent shall not be entitled to the commission referred to in regulation 7 above if that commission is payable, by virtue of regulation 8 above, to the previous commercial agent, unless it is equitable because of the circumstances for the commission to be shared between the commercial agents.

(2)   The principal shall be liable for any sum due under paragraph (1) above to the person entitled to it in accordance with that paragraph, and any sum which the other commercial agent receives to which he is not entitled shall be refunded to the principal.

10   When commission due and date for payment

(1)   Commission shall become due as soon as, and to the extent that, one of the following circumstances occurs:

(a)   the principal has executed the transaction; or

(b)   the principal should, according to his agreement with the third party, have executed the transaction; or

(c)   the third party has executed the transaction.

(2)　Commission shall become due at the latest when the third party has executed his part of the transaction or should have done so if the principal had executed his part of the transaction, as he should have.

(3)　The commission shall be paid not later than on the last day of the month following the quarter in which it became due, and, for the purposes of these Regulations, unless otherwise agreed between the parties, the first quarter period shall run from the date the agency contract takes effect, and subsequent periods shall run from that date in the third month thereafter or the beginning of the fourth month, whichever is the sooner.

(4)　Any agreement to derogate from paragraphs (2) and (3) above to the detriment of the commercial agent shall be void.

11　Extinction of right to commission

(1)　The right to commission can be extinguished only if and to the extent that—

　(a)　it is established that the contract between the third party and the principal will not be executed; and

　(b)　that fact is due to a reason for which the principal is not to blame.

(2)　Any commission which the commercial agent has already received shall be refunded if the right to it is extinguished.

(3)　any agreement to derogate from paragraph (1) above to the detriment of the commercial agent shall be void.

12　Periodic supply of information as to commission due and right of inspection of principal's books

(1)　The principal shall supply his commercial agent with a statement of the commission due, not later than the last day of the month following the quarter in which the commission has become due, and such statement shall set out the main components used in calculating the amount of the commission.

(2)　A commercial agent shall be entitled to demand that he be provided with all the information (and in particular an extract from the books) which is available to his principal and which he needs in order to check the amount of the commission due to him.

(3)　Any agreement to derogate from paragraphs (1) and (2) above shall be void.

(4)　Nothing in this regulation shall remove or restrict the effect of, or prevent reliance upon, any enactment or rule of law which recognises the right of an agent to inspect the books of a principal.

PART IV
CONCLUSION AND TERMINATION OF THE AGENCY CONTRACT

13　Right to signed written statement of terms of agency contract

(1)　The commercial agent and principal shall each be entitled to receive from the other, on request, a signed written document setting out the terms of the agency contract including any terms subsequently agreed.

(2)　Any purported waiver of the right referred to in paragraph (1) above shall be void.

14　Conversion of agency contract after expiry of fixed period

An agency contract for a fixed period which continues to be performed by both parties after that period has expired shall be deemed to be converted into an agency contract for an indefinite period.

15　Minimum periods of notice for termination of agency contract

(1)　Where an agency contract is concluded for an indefinite period either party may terminate it by notice.

(2)　The period of notice shall be—

   (a)   1 month for the first year of the contract;
   (b)   2 months for the second year commenced;
   (c)   3 months for the third year commenced and for the subsequent years;
and the parties may not agree on any shorter periods of notice.
   (3)   If the parties agree on longer periods than those laid down in paragraph (2) above, the period of notice to be observed by the principal must not be shorter than that to be observed by the commercial agent.
   (4)   Unless otherwise agreed by the parties, the end of the period of notice must coincide with the end of a calendar month.
   (5)   The provisions of this regulation shall also apply to an agency contract for a fixed period where it is converted under regulation 14 above into an agency contract for an indefinite period subject to the proviso that the earlier fixed period must be taken into account in the calculation of the period of notice.

16   Savings with regard to immediate termination
These Regulations shall not affect the application of any enactment or rule of law which provides for the immediate termination of the agency contract—
   (a)   because of the failure of one party to carry out all or part of his obligations under that contract; or
   (b)   where exceptional circumstances arise.

17   Entitlement of commercial agent to indemnity or compensation on termination of agency contract
   (1)   This regulation has effect for the purpose of ensuring that the commercial agent is, after termination of the agency contract, indemnified in accordance with paragraphs (3) to (5) below or compensated for damage in accordance with paragraphs (6) and (7) below.
   (2)   Except where the agency [contract] otherwise provides, the commercial agent shall be entitled to be compensated rather than indemnified.
   (3)   Subject to paragraph (9) and to regulation 18 below, the commercial agent shall be entitled to an indemnity if and to the extent that—
   (a)   he has brought the principal new customers or has significantly increased the volume of business with existing customers and the principal continues to derive substantial benefits from the business with such customers; and
   (b)   the payment of this indemnity is equitable having regard to all the circumstances and, in particular, the commission lost by the commercial agent on the business transacted with such customers.
   (4)   The amount of the indemnity shall not exceed a figure equivalent to an indemnity for one year calculated from the commercial agent's average annual remuneration over the preceding five years and if the contract goes back less than five years the indemnity shall be calculated on the average for the period in question.
   (5)   The grant of an indemnity as mentioned above shall not prevent the commercial agent from seeking damages.
   (6)   Subject to paragraph (9) and to regulation 18 below, the commercial agent shall be entitled to compensation for the damage he suffers as a result of the termination of his relations with his principal.
   (7)   For the purpose of these Regulations such damage shall be deemed to occur particularly when the termination takes place in either or both of the following circumstances, namely circumstances which—
   (a)   deprive the commercial agent of the commission which proper performance of the agency contract would have procured for him whilst providing his principal with substantial benefits linked to the activities of the commercial agent; or
   (b)   have not enabled the commercial agent to amortize the costs and expenses that he had incurred in the performance of the agency contract on the advice of his principal.

(8) Entitlement to the indemnity or compensation for damage as provided for under paragraphs (2) to (7) above shall also arise where the agency contract is terminated as a result of the death of the commercial agent.

(9) The commercial agent shall lose his entitlement to the indemnity or compensation for damage in the instances provided for in paragraphs (2) to (8) above if within one year following termination of his agency contract he has not notified his principal that he intends pursuing his entitlement.

18 Grounds for excluding payment of indemnity or compensation under regulation 17

The [indemnity or] compensation referred to in regulation 17 above shall not be payable to the commercial agent where—

(a) the principal has terminated the agency contract because of default attributable to the commercial agent which would justify immediate termination of the agency contract pursuant to regulation 16 above; or

(b) the commercial agent has himself terminated the agency contract, unless such termination is justified—

(i) by circumstances attributable to the principal, or

(ii) on grounds of the age, infirmity or illness of the commercial agent in consequence of which he cannot reasonably be required to continue his activities; or

(c) the commercial agent, with the agreement of his principal, assigns his rights and duties under the agency contract to another person.

19 Prohibition on derogation from regulations 17 and 18

The parties may not derogate from regulations 17 and 18 to the detriment of the commercial agent before the agency contract expires.

20 Restraint of trade clauses

(1) A restraint of trade clause shall be valid only if and to the extent that—

(a) it is concluded in writing; and

(b) it relates to the geographical area or the group of customers and the geographical area entrusted to the commercial agent and to the kind of goods covered by his agency under the contract.

(2) A restraint of trade clause shall be valid for not more than two years after termination of the agency contract.

(3) Nothing in this regulation shall affect any enactment or rule of law which imposes other restrictions on the validity or enforceability of restraint of trade clauses or which enables a court to reduce the obligations on the parties resulting from such clauses.

PART V
MISCELLANEOUS AND SUPPLEMENTAL

21 Disclosure of information

Nothing in these Regulations shall require information to be given where such disclosure would be contrary to public policy.

22 Service of notice etc

(1) Any notice, statement or other document to be given or supplied to a commercial agent or to be given or supplied to the principal under these Regulations may be so given or supplied:

(a) by delivering it to him;

(b) by leaving it at his proper address addressed to him by name;

(c) by sending it by post to him addressed either to his registered address or to the address of his registered or principal office;

or by any other means provided for in the agency contract.

(2) Any such notice, statement or document may—

(a)   in the case of a body corporate, be given or served on the secretary or clerk of that body;

(b)   in the case of a partnership, be given to or served on any partner or on any person having the control or management of the partnership business.

23   Transitional provisions

(1)   Notwithstanding any provision in an agency contract made before 1st January 1994, these Regulations shall apply to that contract after that date and, accordingly any provision which is inconsistent with these Regulations shall have effect subject to them.

(2)   Nothing in these Regulations shall affect the rights and liabilities of a commercial agent or a principal which have accrued before 1st January 1994.

Regulation 2(3)   THE SCHEDULE

1   The activities of a person as a commercial agent are to be considered secondary where it may reasonably be taken that the primary purpose of the arrangement with his principal is other than as set out in paragraph 2 below.

2   An arrangement falls within this paragraph if—

(a)   the business of the principal is the sale, or as the case may be purchase, of goods of a particular kind; and

(b)   the goods concerned are such that—

(i)   transactions are normally individually negotiated and concluded on a commercial basis, and

(ii)   procuring a transaction on one occasion is likely to lead to further transactions in those goods with that customer on future occasions, or to transactions in those goods with other customers in the same geographical area or among the same group of customers, and

that accordingly it is in the commercial interests of the principal in developing the market in those goods to appoint a representative to such customers with a view to the representative devoting effort, skill and expenditure from his own resources to that end.

3   The following are indications that an arrangement falls within paragraph 2 above, and the absence of any of them is an indication to the contrary—

(a)   the principal is the manufacturer, importer or distributor of the goods;

(b)   the goods are specifically identified with the principal in the market in question rather than, or to a greater extent than, with any other person;

(c)   the agent devotes substantially the whole of his time to representative activities (whether for one principal or for a number of principals whose interests are not conflicting);

(d)   the goods are not normally available in the market in question other than by means of the agent;

(e)   the arrangement is described as one of commercial agency.

4   The following are indications that an arrangement does not fall within paragraph 2 above—

(a)   promotional material is supplied direct to potential customers;

(b)   persons are granted agencies without reference to existing agents in a particular area or in relation to a particular group;

(c)   customers normally select the goods for themselves and merely place their orders through the agent.

5   The activities of the following categories of persons are presumed, unless the contrary is established, not to fall within paragraph 2 above—

Mail order catalogue agents for consumer goods.

Consumer credit agents.

UNFAIR TERMS IN CONSUMER CONTRACTS REGULATIONS 1999
(SI 1999/2083)

3 Interpretation
(1) In these Regulations—

'the Community' means the European Community;

'consumer' means any natural person who, in contracts covered by these Regulations, is acting for purposes which are outside his trade, business or profession;

'court' in relation to England and Wales and Northern Ireland means a county court or the High Court, and in relation to Scotland, the Sheriff or the Court of Session;

'Director' means the Director General of Fair Trading;*

'EEA Agreement' means the Agreement on the European Economic Area signed at Oporto on 2nd May 1992 as adjusted by the protocol signed at Brussels on 17th March 1993;

'Member State' means a State which is a contracting party to the EEA Agreement;

'notified' means notified in writing;

'qualifying body' means a person specified in Schedule 1;

'seller or supplier' means any natural or legal person who, in contracts covered by these Regulations, is acting for purposes relating to his trade, business or profession, whether publicly owned or privately owned;

'unfair terms' means the contractual terms referred to in regulation 5.

[(1A) The references—
    (a) in regulation 4(1) to a seller or a supplier, and
    (b) in regulation 8(1) to a seller or supplier,
include references to a distance supplier and to an intermediary.

(1B) In paragraph (1A) and regulation 5(6)—

'distance supplier' means—
    (a) a supplier under a distance contract within the meaning of the Financial Services (Distance Marketing) Regulations 2004, or
    (b) a supplier of unsolicited financial services within regulation 15 of those Regulations; and

'intermediary' has the same meaning as in those Regulations.]

(2) In the application of these Regulations to Scotland for references to an 'injunction' or an 'interim injunction' there shall be substituted references to an 'interdict' or 'interim interdict' respectively.

4 Terms to which these Regulations apply
(1) These Regulations apply in relation to unfair terms in contracts concluded between a seller or a supplier and a consumer.

(2) These Regulations do not apply to contractual terms which reflect—
    (a) mandatory statutory or regulatory provisions (including such provisions under the law of any Member State or in Community legislation having effect in the United Kingdom without further enactment);
    (b) the provisions or principles of international conventions to which the Member States or the Community are party.

5 Unfair terms
(1) A contractual term which has not been individually negotiated shall be regarded as unfair if, contrary to the requirement of good faith, it causes a significant imbalance in the parties' rights and obligations arising under the contract, to the detriment of the consumer.

(2) A term shall always be regarded as not having been individually negotiated

---

* All references to 'the Director' have effect as if they were references to 'the OFT': Enterprise Act 2002, s 2.

where it has been drafted in advance and the consumer has therefore not been able to influence the substance of the term.

(3)   Notwithstanding that a specific term or certain aspects of it in a contract has been individually negotiated, these Regulations shall apply to the rest of a contract if an overall assessment of it indicates that it is a pre-formulated standard contract.

(4)   It shall be for any seller or supplier who claims that a term was individually negotiated to show that it was.

(5)   Schedule 2 to these Regulations contains an indicative and non-exhaustive list of the terms which may be regarded as unfair.

[(6)   Any contractual term providing that the consumer bears the burden of proof in respect of showing that the supplier complied with any or all of the obligations upon him resulting from the Directive and any rule or enactment implementing it shall always be regarded as unfair.

(7)   In paragraph (6)—

'the Directive' means Directive 2002/65/EC of the European Parliament and of the Council of 23 September 2002 concerning the distance marketing of consumer financial services and amending Council Directive 90/619/EEC and Directive 97/7/EC and 98/27/EC; and

'rule' means a rule made by the Financial Services Authority under the Financial Services and Markets Act 2000 or by a designated professional body within the meaning of section 326(2) of that Act.]

6   Assessment of unfair terms

(1)   Without prejudice to regulation 12, the unfairness of a contractual term shall be assessed, taking into account the nature of the goods or services for which the contract was concluded and by referring, at the time of conclusion of the contract, to all the circumstances attending the conclusion of the contract and to all the other terms of the contract or of another contract on which it is dependent.

(2)   In so far as it is in plain intelligible language, the assessment of fairness of a term shall not relate—

(a)   to the definition of the main subject matter of the contract, or

(b)   to the adequacy of the price or remuneration, as against the goods or services supplied in exchange.

7   Written contracts

(1)   A seller or supplier shall ensure that any written term of a contract is expressed in plain, intelligible language.

(2)   If there is doubt about the meaning of a written term, the interpretation which is most favourable to the consumer shall prevail but this rule shall not apply in proceedings brought under regulation 12.

8   Effect of unfair term

(1)   An unfair term in a contract concluded with a consumer by a seller or supplier shall not be binding on the consumer.

(2)   The contract shall continue to bind the parties if it is capable of continuing in existence without the unfair term.

9   Choice of law clauses

These Regulations shall apply notwithstanding any contract term which applies or purports to apply the law of a non-Member State, if the contract has a close connection with the territory of the Member States.

10   Complaints—consideration by Director

(1)   It shall be the duty of the Director to consider any complaint made to him that any contract term drawn up for general use is unfair, unless—

(a)   the complaint appears to the Director to be frivolous or vexatious; or

(b)   a qualifying body has notified the Director that it agrees to consider the complaint.

(2)   The Director shall give reasons for his decision to apply or not to apply, as the case may be, for an injunction under regulation 12 in relation to any complaint which these Regulations require him to consider.

(3)   In deciding whether or not to apply for an injunction in respect of a term which the Director considers to be unfair, he may, if he considers it appropriate to do so, have regard to any undertakings given to him by or on behalf of any person as to the continued use of such a term in contracts concluded with consumers.

11   Complaints—consideration by qualifying bodies

(1)   If a qualifying body specified in Part One of Schedule I notifies the Director that it agrees to consider a complaint that any contract term drawn up for general use is unfair, it shall be under a duty to consider that complaint.

(2)   Regulation 10(2) and (3) shall apply to a qualifying body which is under a duty to consider a complaint as they apply to the Director.

12   Injunctions to prevent continued use of unfair terms

(1)   The Director or, subject to paragraph (2), any qualifying body may apply for an injunction (including an interim injunction) against any person appearing to the Director or that body to be using, or recommending use of, an unfair term drawn up for general use in contracts concluded with consumers.

(2)   A qualifying body may apply for an injunction only where—

(a)   it has notified the Director of its intention to apply at least fourteen days before the date on which the application is made, beginning with the date on which the notification was given; or

(b)   the Director consents to the application being made within a shorter period.

(3)   The court on an application under this regulation may grant an injunction on such terms as it thinks fit.

(4)   An injunction may relate not only to use of a particular contract term drawn up for general use but to any similar term, or a term having like effect, used or recommended for use by any person.

13   Powers of the Director and qualifying bodies to obtain documents and information

(1)   The Director may exercise the power conferred by this regulation for the purpose of—

(a)   facilitating his consideration of a complaint that a contract term drawn up for general use is unfair; or

(b)   ascertaining whether a person has complied with an undertaking or court order as to the continued use, or recommendation for use, of a term in contracts concluded with consumers.

(2)   A qualifying body specified in Part One of Schedule 1 may exercise the power conferred by this regulation for the purpose of—

(a)   facilitating its consideration of a complaint that a contract term drawn up for general use is unfair; or

(b)   ascertaining whether a person has complied with—

(i)   an undertaking given to it or to the court following an application by that body, or

(ii)   a court order made on an application by that body,

as to the continued use, or recommendation for use, of a term in contracts concluded with consumers.

(3)   The Director may require any person to supply to him, and a qualifying body specified in Part One of Schedule 1 may require any person to supply to it—

(a)   a copy of any document which that person has used or recommended for use, at the time the notice referred to in paragraph (4) below is given, as a pre-formulated standard contract in dealings with consumers;

(b)   information about the use, or recommendation for use, by that person of that document or any other such document in dealings with consumers.

(4)   The power conferred by this regulation is to be exercised by a notice in writing which may—

(a)   specify the way in which and the time within which it is to be complied with; and

(b)   be varied or revoked by a subsequent notice.

(5)   Nothing in this regulation compels a person to supply any document or information which he would be entitled to refuse to produce or give in civil proceedings before the court.

(6)   If a person makes default in complying with a notice under this regulation, the court may, on the application of the Director or of the qualifying body, make such order as the court thinks fit for requiring the default to be made good, and any such order may provide that all the costs or expenses of and incidental to the application shall be borne by the person in default or by any officers of a company or other association who are responsible for its default.

14   Notification of undertakings and orders to Director
A qualifying body shall notify the Director—

(a)   of any undertaking given to it by or on behalf of any person as to the continued use of a term which that body considers to be unfair in contracts concluded with consumers,

(b)   of the outcome of any application made by it under regulation 12, and of the terms of any undertaking given to, or order made by, the court;

(c)   of the outcome of any application made by it to enforce a previous order of the court.

15   Publication, information and advice
(1)   The Director shall arrange for the publication in such form and manner as he considers appropriate, of—

(a)   details of any undertaking or order notified to him under regulation 14;

(b)   details of any undertaking given to him by or on behalf of any persons to the continued use of a term which the Director considers to be unfair in contracts concluded with consumers;

(c)   details of any application made by him under regulation 12, and of the terms of any undertaking given to, or order made by, the court;

(d)   details of any application made by the Director to enforce a previous order of the court.

(2)   The Director shall inform any person on request whether a particular term to which these Regulations apply has been—

(a)   the subject of an undertaking given to the Director or notified to him by a qualifying body; or

(b)   the subject of an order of the court made upon application by him or notified to him by a qualifying body;

and shall give that person details of the undertaking or a copy of the order, as the case may be, together with a copy of any amendments which the person giving the undertaking has agreed to make to the term in question.

(3)   The Director may arrange for the dissemination in such form and manner as he considers appropriate of such information and advice concerning the operation of these Regulations as may appear to him to be expedient to give to the public and to all persons likely to be affected by these Regulations.

[16   The functions of the Financial Services Authority
The functions of the Financial Services Authority under these Regulations shall be

treated as functions of the Financial Services Authority under the [Financial Services and Markets Act 2000.]

Regulation 3	SCHEDULE 1
	QUALIFYING BODIES

PART ONE

[1   The Information Commissioner.
2   The Gas and Electricity Markets Authority.
3   The Director General of Electricity Supply for Northern Ireland.
4   The Director General of Gas for Northern Ireland.
5   [The Office of Communications.]
6   [The Water Services Authority.]
7   The Rail Regulator.
8   Every weights and measures authority in Great Britain.
9   The Department of Enterprise, Trade and Investment in Northern Ireland.
10   The Financial Services Authority.

PART TWO

11   Consumers' Association.]

Regulation 5(5)	SCHEDULE 2
	INDICATIVE AND NON-EXHAUSTIVE LIST OF TERMS WHICH MAY BE REGARDED AS UNFAIR

1   Terms which have the object or effect of—

(a)   excluding or limiting the legal liability of a seller or supplier in the event of the death of a consumer or personal injury to the latter resulting from an act or omission of that seller or supplier;

(b)   inappropriately excluding or limiting the legal rights of the consumer vis-à-vis the seller or supplier or another party in the event of total or partial non-performance or inadequate performance by the seller or supplier of any of the contractual obligations, including the option of offsetting a debt owed to the seller or supplier against any claim which the consumer may have against him;

(c)   making an agreement binding on the consumer whereas provision of services by the seller or supplier is subject to a condition whose realisation depends on his own will alone;

(d)   permitting the seller or supplier to retain sums paid by the consumer where the latter decides not to conclude or perform the contract, without providing for the consumer to receive compensation of an equivalent amount from the seller or supplier where the latter is the party cancelling the contract;

(e)   requiring any consumer who fails to fulfil his obligation to pay a disproportionately high sum in compensation;

(f)   authorising the seller or supplier to dissolve the contract on a discretionary basis where the same facility is not granted to the consumer, or permitting the seller or supplier to retain the sums paid for services not yet supplied by him where it is the seller or supplier himself who dissolves the contract;

(g)   enabling the seller or supplier to terminate a contract of indeterminate duration without reasonable notice except where there are serious grounds for doing so;

(h)   automatically extending a contract of fixed duration where the consumer does not indicate otherwise, when the deadline fixed for the consumer to express his desire not to extend the contract is unreasonably early;

(i)   irrevocably binding the consumer to terms with which he had no real opportunity of becoming acquainted before the conclusion of the contract;

(j)   enabling the seller or supplier to alter the terms of the contract unilaterally without a valid reason which is specified in the contract;

(k)   enabling the seller or supplier to alter unilaterally without a valid reason any characteristics of the product or service to be provided;

(l)   providing for the price of goods to be determined at the time of delivery or allowing a seller of goods or supplier of services to increase their price without in both cases giving the consumer the corresponding right to cancel the contract if the final price is too high in relation to the price agreed when the contract was concluded;

(m)   giving the seller or supplier the right to determine whether the goods or services supplied are in conformity with the contract, or giving him the exclusive right to interpret any term of the contract;

(n)   limiting the seller's or supplier's obligation to respect commitments under-taken by his agents or making his commitments subject to compliance with a parti-cular formality;

(o)   obliging the consumer to fulfil all his obligations where the seller or sup-plier does not perform his;

(p)   giving the seller or supplier the possibility of transferring his rights and obligations under the contract, where this may serve to reduce the guarantees for the consumer, without the latter's agreement,

(q)   excluding or hindering the consumer's right to take legal action or exercise any other legal remedy, particularly by requiring the consumer to take disputes exclusively to arbitration not covered by legal provisions, unduly restricting the evidence available to him or imposing on him a burden of proof which, according to the applicable law, should lie with another party to the contract.

2   Scope of paragraphs 1(g), (j) and (1)—

(a)   Paragraph 1(g) is without hindrance to terms by which a supplier of finan-cial services reserves the right to terminate unilaterally a contract of indeterminate duration without notice where there is a valid reason provided that the supplier is required to inform the other contracting party or parties thereof immediately.

(b)   Paragraph 1(j) is without hindrance to terms under which a supplier of financial services reserves the right to alter the rate of interest payable by the con-sumer or due to the latter, or the amount of other charges for financial services without notice where there is a valid reason, provided that the supplier is required to inform the other contracting party or parties thereof at the earliest opportunity and that the latter are free to dissolve the contract immediately.

Paragraph 1(j) is also without hindrance to terms under which a seller or sup-plier reserves the right to alter unilaterally the conditions of a contract of inde-terminate duration, provided that he is required to inform the consumer with reasonable notice and that the consumer is free to dissolve the contract.

(c)   Paragraphs 1(g), (j) and (l) do not apply to:

—transactions in transferable securities, financial instruments and other pro-ducts or services where the price is linked to fluctuations in a stock exchange quotation or index or a financial market rate that the seller or supplier does not control;

—contracts for the purchase or sale of foreign currency, traveller's cheques or international money orders denominated in foreign currency;

(d)   Paragraph 1(1) is without hindrance to price indexation clauses, where lawful, provided that the method by which prices vary is explicitly described.

CONSUMER PROTECTION (DISTANCE SELLING) REGULATIONS 2000
(SI 2000/2334)
(as amended by the Consumer Protection (Distance Selling) (Amendment) Regulations 2005 (SI 2005/689))

3 Interpretation
(1) In these Regulations—

['the 2000 Act' means the Financial Services and Markets Act 2000;

'appointed representative' has the same meaning as in section 39(2) of the 2000 Act;

'authorised person' has the same meaning as in section 31(2) of the 2000 Act;]

'breach' means contravention by a supplier of a prohibition in, or failure to comply with a requirement of, these Regulations;

'business' includes a trade or profession;

'consumer' means any natural person who, in contracts to which these Regulations apply, is acting for purposes which are outside his business;

'court' in relation to England and Wales and Northern Ireland means a county court or the High Court, and in relation to Scotland means the Sheriff Court or the Court of Session;

'credit' includes a cash loan and any other form of financial accommodation, and for this purpose 'cash' includes money in any form;

'Director' means the Director General of Fair Trading;*

'distance contract' means any contract concerning goods or services concluded between a supplier and a consumer under an organised distance sales or service provision scheme run by the supplier who, for the purpose of the contract, makes exclusive use of one or more means of distance communication up to and including the moment at which the contract is concluded;

'EEA Agreement' means the Agreement on the European Economic Area signed at Oporto on 2 May 1992 as adjusted by the Protocol signed at Brussels on 17 March 1993;

'enactment' includes an enactment comprised in, or in an instrument made under, an Act of the Scottish Parliament;

'enforcement authority' means the Director, every weights and measures authority in Great Britain, and the Department of Enterprise, Trade and Investment in Northern Ireland;

'excepted contract' means a contract such as is mentioned in regulation 5(1);

['financial service' means any service of a banking, credit, insurance, personal pension, investment or payment nature;]

'means of distance communication' means any means which, without the simultaneous physical presence of the supplier and the consumer, may be used for the conclusion of a contract between those parties; and an indicative list of such means is contained in Schedule 1;

'Member State' means a State which is a contracting party to the EEA Agreement;

'operator of a means of communication' means any public or private person whose business involves making one or more means of distance communication available to suppliers;

'period for performance' has the meaning given by regulation 19(2);

'personal credit agreement' has the meaning given by regulation 14(8);

['regulated activity' means an activity which is a regulated activity within the meaning of section 22 of the 2000 Act, read with any relevant order under that section and Schedule 2 to that Act;]

---

* All references to 'the Director' have effect as if they were references to 'the OFT': Enterprise Act 2002, s 2.

'related credit agreement' has the meaning given by regulation 15(5);

'supplier' means any person who, in contracts to which these Regulations apply, is acting in his commercial or professional capacity; and

'working days' means all days other than Saturdays, Sundays and public holidays.

(2)   In the application of these Regulations to Scotland, for references to an 'injunction' or an 'interim injunction' there shall be substituted references to an 'interdict' or an 'interim interdict' respectively.

4   Contracts to which these Regulations apply

These Regulations apply, subject to regulation 6, to distance contracts other than excepted contracts.

5   Excepted contracts

(1)   The following are excepted contracts, namely any contract—

(a)   for the sale or other disposition of an interest in land except for a rental agreement;

(b)   for the construction of a building where the contract also provides for a sale or other disposition of an interest in land on which the building is constructed, except for a rental agreement;

(c)   relating to financial services; [. . .]

(d)   concluded by means of an automated vending machine or automated commercial premises;

(e)   concluded with a telecommunications operator through the use of a public pay-phone;

(f)   concluded at an auction.

(2)   References in paragraph (1) to a rental agreement—

(a)   if the land is situated in England and Wales, are references to any agreement which does not have to be made in writing (whether or not in fact made in writing) because of section 2(5)(a) of the Law of Property (Miscellaneous Provisions) Act 1989;

(b)   if the land is situated in Scotland, are references to any agreement for the creation, transfer, variation or extinction of an interest in land, which does not have to be made in writing (whether or not in fact made in writing) as provided for in section 1(2) and (7) of the Requirements of Writing (Scotland) Act 1995; and

(c)   if the land is situated in Northern Ireland, are references to any agreement which is not one to which section II of the Statute of Frauds, (Ireland) 1695 applies.

(3)   Paragraph (2) shall not be taken to mean that a rental agreement in respect of land situated outside the United Kingdom is not capable of being a distance contract to which these Regulations apply.

[(4)   Regulations 7 to 14, 17 to 20, and 22 to 29 shall not apply to any contract which is made by an authorised person, the making or performance of which constitutes or is part of a regulated activity carried on by him.

(5)   Regulations 7 to 9, 17 to 20, and 22 to 29 shall not apply to any contract which is made by an appointed representative, the making or performance of which constitutes or is part of a regulated activity carried on by him.]

6   Contracts to which only part of these Regulations apply

(1)   Regulations 7 to 20 shall not apply to a contract which is a 'timeshare agreement' within the meaning of the Timeshare Act 1992 and to which that Act applies.

(2)   Regulations 7 to 19(1) shall not apply to—

(a)   contracts for the supply of food, beverages or other goods intended for everyday consumption supplied to the consumer's residence or to his workplace by regular roundsmen; or

(b)   contracts for the provision of accommodation, transport, catering or leisure services, where the supplier undertakes, when the contract is concluded, to provide these services on a specific date or within a specific period.

(3)   Regulations 19(2) to (8) and 20 do not apply to a contract for a 'package' within the meaning of the Package Travel, Package Holidays and Package Tours Regulations 1992 which is sold or offered for sale in the territory of the Member States.

[(4)   Regulations 7 to 14, 17 to 20 and 25 do not apply to any contract which is made, and regulation 24 does not apply to any unsolicited services which are supplied, by an unauthorised person where the making or performance of that contract or the supply of those services, as the case may be, constitutes or is part of a regulated activity carried on by him.

(5)   Regulations 7 to 9, 17 to 20 and 25 do not apply to any contract which is made, and regulation 24 does not apply to any unsolicited services which are supplied, by an appointed representative where the making or performance of that contract or the supply of those services, as the case may be, constitutes or is part of a regulated activity carried on by him.]

7   Information required prior to the conclusion of the contract

(1)   Subject to paragraph (4), in good time prior to the conclusion of the contract the supplier shall—

(a)   provide to the consumer the following information—

(i)   the identity of the supplier and, where the contract requires payment in advance, the supplier's address;

(ii)   a description of the main characteristics of the goods or services;

(iii)   the price of the goods or services including all taxes;

(iv)   delivery costs where appropriate;

(v)   the arrangements for payment, delivery or performance;

(vi)   the existence of a right of cancellation except in the cases referred to in regulation 13;

(vii)   the cost of using the means of distance communication where it is calculated other than at the basic rate;

(viii)   the period for which the offer or the price remains valid; and

(ix)   where appropriate, the minimum duration of the contract, in the case of contracts for the supply of goods or services to be performed permanently or recurrently;

(b)   inform the consumer if he proposes, in the event of the goods or services ordered by the consumer being unavailable, to provide substitute goods or services (as the case may be) of equivalent quality and price; and

(c)   inform the consumer that the cost of returning any such substitute goods to the supplier in the event of cancellation by the consumer would be met by the supplier.

(2)   The supplier shall ensure that the information required by paragraph (1) is provided in a clear and comprehensible manner appropriate to the means of distance communication used, with due regard in particular to the principles of good faith in commercial transactions and the principles governing the protection of those who are unable to give their consent such as minors.

(3)   Subject to paragraph (4), the supplier shall ensure that his commercial purpose is made clear when providing the information required by paragraph (1).

(4)   In the case of a telephone communication, the identity of the supplier and the commercial purpose of the call shall be made clear at the beginning of the conversation with the consumer.

8   Written and additional information

(1)   Subject to regulation 9, the supplier shall provide to the consumer in writing, or in another durable medium which is available and accessible to the consumer, the information referred to in paragraph (2), either—

(a)   prior to the conclusion of the contract, or

(b)   thereafter, in good time and in any event—

(i)   during the performance of the contract, in the case of services;

(ii)   at the latest at the time of delivery where goods not for delivery to third parties are concerned;

[(iii)   in the case of a contract for the supply of services, information as to how the right to cancel may be affected by the consumer agreeing to performance of the services beginning before the end of the seven working day period referred to in regulation 12.]

(2)   The information required to be provided by paragraph (1) is—

(a)   the information set out in paragraphs (i) to (vi) of regulation 7(1)(a);

(b)   information about the conditions and procedures for exercising the right to cancel under regulation 10, including—

(i)   where a term of the contract requires (or the supplier intends that it will require) that the consumer shall return the goods to the supplier in the event of cancellation, notification of that requirement;

(ii)   information as to whether the consumer or the supplier would be responsible under these Regulations for the cost of returning any goods to the supplier, or the cost of his recovering them, if the consumer cancels the contract under regulation 10;

[(iii)   in the case of a contract for the supply of services, information as to how the right to cancel may be affected by the consumer agreeing to performance of the services beginning before the end of the seven working day period referred to in regulation 12;]

(c)   the geographical address of the place of business of the supplier to which the consumer may address any complaints;

(d)   information about any after-sales services and guarantees; and

(e)   the conditions for exercising any contractual right to cancel the contract, where the contract is of an unspecified duration or a duration exceeding one year.

[. . .]

9   Services performed through the use of a means of distance communication

(1)   Regulation 8 shall not apply to a contract for the supply of services which are performed through the use of a means of distance communication, where those services are supplied on only one occasion and are invoiced by the operator of the means of distance communication.

(2)   But the supplier shall take all necessary steps to ensure that a consumer who is a party to a contract to which paragraph (1) applies is able to obtain the supplier's geographical address and the place of business to which the consumer may address any complaints.

10   Right to cancel

(1)   Subject to regulation 13, if within the cancellation period set out in regulations 11 and 12, the consumer gives a notice of cancellation to the supplier, or any other person previously notified by the supplier to the consumer as a person to whom notice of cancellation may be given, the notice of cancellation shall operate to cancel the contract.

(2)   Except as otherwise provided by these Regulations, the effect of a notice of cancellation is that the contract shall be treated as if it had not been made.

(3)   For the purposes of these Regulations, a notice of cancellation is a notice in writing or in another durable medium available and accessible to the supplier (or to the other person to whom it is given) which, however expressed, indicates the intention of the consumer to cancel the contract.

(4)   A notice of cancellation given under this regulation by a consumer to a supplier or other person is to be treated as having been properly given if the consumer—

(a)   leaves it at the address last known to the consumer and addressed to the supplier or other person by name (in which case it is to be taken to have been given on the day on which it was left);

(b)   sends it by post to the address last known to the consumer and addressed to the supplier or other person by name (in which case, it is to be taken to have been given on the day on which it was posted);

(c)   sends it by facsimile to the business facsimile number last known to the consumer (in which case it is to be taken to have been given on the day on which it is sent); or

(d)   sends it by electronic mail, to the business electronic mail address last known to the consumer (in which case it is to be taken to have been given on the day on which it is sent).

(5)   Where a consumer gives a notice in accordance with paragraph (4)(a) or (b) to a supplier who is a body corporate or a partnership, the notice is to be treated as having been properly given if—

(a)   in the case of a body corporate, it is left at the address of, or sent to, the secretary or clerk of that body; or

(b)   in the case of a partnership, it is left with or sent to a partner or a person having control or management of the partnership business.

11   Cancellation period in the case of contracts for the supply of goods

(1)   For the purposes of regulation 10, the cancellation period in the case of contracts for the supply of goods begins with the day on which the contract is concluded and ends as provided in paragraphs (2) to (5).

(2)   Where the supplier complies with regulation 8, the cancellation period ends on the expiry of the period of seven working days beginning with the day after the day on which the consumer receives the goods.

(3)   Where a supplier who has not complied with regulation 8 provides to the consumer the information referred to in regulation 8(2), and does so in writing or in another durable medium available and accessible to the consumer, within the period of three months beginning with the day after the day on which the consumer receives the goods, the cancellation period ends on the expiry of the period of seven working days beginning with the day after the day on which the consumer receives the information.

(4)   Where neither paragraph (2) nor (3) applies, the cancellation period ends on the expiry of the period of three months and seven working days beginning with the day after the day on which the consumer receives the goods.

(5)   In the case of contracts for goods for delivery to third parties, paragraphs (2) to (4) shall apply as if the consumer had received the goods on the day on which they were received by the third party.

12   Cancellation period in the case of contracts for the supply of services

(1)   For the purposes of regulation 10, the cancellation period in the case of contracts for the supply of services begins with the day on which the contract is concluded and ends as provided in paragraphs (2) to (4).

(2)   Where the supplier complies with regulation 8 on or before the day on which the contract is concluded, the cancellation period ends on the expiry of the period of seven working days beginning with the day after the day on which the contract is concluded.

(3)   [Subject to paragraph (3A)] where a supplier who has not complied with regulation 8 on or before the day on which the contract is concluded provides to the consumer the information referred to in regulation 8(2) [. . .], and does so in writing or in another durable medium available and accessible to the consumer, within the period of three months beginning with the day after the day on which the contract is concluded, the cancellation period ends on the expiry of the period of seven working days beginning with the day after the day on which the consumer receives the information.

[(3A)   Where the performance of the contract has begun with the consumer's agreement before the expiry of the period of seven working days beginning with the day after the day on which the contract was concluded and the supplier has not complied with regulation 8 on or before the day on which performance began, but provides to the consumer the information referred to in regulation 8(2) in good time during the performance of the contract, the cancellation period ends—

(a)   on the expiry of the period of seven working days beginning with the day after the day on which the consumer receives the information; or

(b)   if the performance of the contract is completed before the expiry of the period referred to in sub-paragraph (a), on the day when the performance of the contract is completed.]

(4)   Where [none of paragraphs (2) to (3A) applies], the cancellation period ends on the expiry of the period of three months and seven working days beginning with the day after the day on which the contract is concluded.

13   Exceptions to the right to cancel

(1)   Unless the parties have agreed otherwise, the consumer will not have the right to cancel the contract by giving notice of cancellation pursuant to regulation 10 in respect of contracts—

[(a)   for the supply of services if the performance of the contract has begun with the consumer's agreement—

(i)   before the end of the cancellation period applicable under regulation 12(2); and

(ii)   after the supplier has provided the information referred to in regulation 8(2).]

(b)   for the supply of goods or services the price of which is dependent on fluctuations in the financial market which cannot be controlled by the supplier;

(c)   for the supply of goods made to the consumer's specifications or clearly personalised or which by reason of their nature cannot be returned or are liable to deteriorate or expire rapidly;

(d)   for the supply of audio or video recordings or computer software if they are unsealed by the consumer;

(e)   for the supply of newspapers, periodicals or magazines; or

(f)   for gaming, betting or lottery services.

14   Recovery of sums paid by or on behalf of the consumer on cancellation, and return of security

(1)   On the cancellation of a contract under regulation 10, the supplier shall reimburse any sum paid by or on behalf of the consumer under or in relation to the contract to the person by whom it was made free of any charge, less any charge made in accordance with paragraph (5).

(2)   The reference in paragraph (1) to any sum paid on behalf of the consumer includes any sum paid by a creditor who is not the same person as the supplier under a personal credit agreement with the consumer.

(3)   The supplier shall make the reimbursement referred to in paragraph (1) as soon as possible and in any case within a period not exceeding 30 days beginning with the day on which the notice of cancellation was given.

(4)   Where any security has been provided in relation to the contract, the security (so far as it is so provided) shall, on cancellation under regulation 10, be treated as never having had effect and any property lodged with the supplier solely for the purposes of the security as so provided shall be returned by him forthwith.

(5)   Subject to paragraphs (6) and (7), the supplier may make a charge, not exceeding the direct costs of recovering any goods supplied under the contract, where a term of the contract provides that the consumer must return any goods supplied if he cancels the contract under regulation 10 but the consumer does not comply with this provision or returns the goods at the expense of the supplier.

(6)   Paragraph (5) shall not apply where—

(a)   the consumer cancels in circumstances where he has the right to reject the goods under a term of the contract, including a term implied by virtue of any enactment, or

(b)   the term requiring the consumer to return any goods supplied if he cancels the contract is an 'unfair term' within the meaning of the Unfair Terms in Consumer Contracts Regulations 1999.

(7)   Paragraph (5) shall not apply to the cost of recovering any goods which were supplied as substitutes for the goods ordered by the consumer.

(8)   For the purposes of these Regulations, a personal credit agreement is an agreement between the consumer and any other person ('the creditor') by which the creditor provides the consumer with credit of any amount.

15   Automatic cancellation of a related credit agreement

(1)   Where a notice of cancellation is given under regulation 10 which has the effect of cancelling the contract, the giving of the notice shall also have the effect of cancelling any related credit agreement.

(2)   Where a related credit agreement is cancelled by virtue of paragraph (1), the supplier shall, if he is not the same person as the creditor under that agreement, forthwith on receipt of the notice of cancellation inform the creditor that the notice has been given.

(3)   Where a related credit agreement is cancelled by virtue of paragraph (1)—

(a)   any sum paid by or on behalf of the consumer under, or in relation to, the credit agreement which the supplier is not obliged to reimburse under regulation 14(1) shall be reimbursed, except for any sum which, if it had not already been paid, would have to be paid under sub-paragraph (b);

(b)   the agreement shall continue in force so far as it relates to repayment of the credit and payment of interest, subject to regulation 16; and

(c)   subject to sub-paragraph (b), the agreement shall cease to be enforceable.

(4)   Where any security has been provided under a related credit agreement, the security, so far as it is so provided, shall be treated as never having had effect and any property lodged with the creditor solely for the purposes of the security as so provided shall be returned by him forthwith.

(5)   For the purposes of this regulation and regulation 16, a 'related credit agreement' means an agreement under which fixed sum credit which fully or partly covers the price under a contract cancelled under regulation 10 is granted—

(a)   by the supplier, or

(b)   by another person, under an arrangement between that person and the supplier.

(6)   For the purposes of this regulation and regulation 16—

(a)   'creditor' is a person who grants credit under a related credit agreement;

(b)   'fixed sum credit' has the same meaning as in section 10 of the Consumer Credit Act 1974;

(c)   'repayment' in relation to credit means repayment of money received by the consumer, and cognate expressions shall be construed accordingly; and

(d)   'interest' means interest on money so received.

16   Repayment of credit and interest after cancellation of a related credit agreement

(1)   This regulation applies following the cancellation of a related credit agreement by virtue of regulation 15(1).

(2)   If the consumer repays the whole or a portion of the credit—

(a)   before the expiry of one month following the cancellation of the credit agreement, or

(b)   in the case of a credit repayable by instalments, before the date on which the first instalment is due,

no interest shall be payable on the amount repaid.

(3)   If the whole of a credit repayable by instalments is not repaid on or before the date referred to in paragraph (2)(b), the consumer shall not be liable to repay any of the credit except on receipt of a request in writing, signed by the creditor, stating the amounts of the remaining instalments (recalculated by the creditor as nearly as may be in accordance with the agreement and without extending the repayment period), but excluding any sum other than principal and interest.

(4)   Where any security has been provided under a related credit agreement the duty imposed on the consumer to repay credit and to pay interest shall not be enforceable before the creditor has discharged any duty imposed on him by regulation 15(4) to return any property lodged with him as security on cancellation.

17   Restoration of goods by consumer after cancellation

(1)   This regulation applies where a contract is cancelled under regulation 10 after the consumer has acquired possession of any goods under the contract other than any goods mentioned in regulation 13(1)(b) to (e).

(2)   The consumer shall be treated as having been under a duty throughout the period prior to cancellation—
  (a)   to retain possession of the goods, and
  (b)   to take reasonable care of them.

(3)   On cancellation, the consumer shall be under a duty to restore the goods to the supplier in accordance with this regulation, and in the meanwhile to retain possession of the goods and take reasonable care of them.

(4)   The consumer shall not be under any duty to deliver the goods except at his own premises and in pursuance of a request in writing, or in another durable medium available and accessible to the consumer, from the supplier and given to the consumer either before, or at the time when, the goods are collected from those premises.

(5)   If the consumer—
  (a)   delivers the goods (whether at his own premises or elsewhere) to any person to whom, under regulation 10(1), a notice of cancellation could have been given; or
  (b)   sends the goods at his own expense to such a person,
he shall be discharged from any duty to retain possession of the goods or restore them to the supplier.

(6)   Where the consumer delivers the goods in accordance with paragraph (5)(a), his obligation to take care of the goods shall cease; and if he sends the goods in accordance with paragraph (5)(b), he shall be under a duty to take reasonable care to see that they are received by the supplier and not damaged in transit, but in other respects his duty to take care of the goods shall cease when he sends them.

(7)   Where, at any time during the period of 21 days beginning with the day notice of cancellation was given, the consumer receives such a request as is mentioned in paragraph (4), and unreasonably refuses or unreasonably fails to comply with it, his duty to retain possession and take reasonable care of the goods shall continue until he delivers or sends the goods as mentioned in paragraph (5), but if within that period he does not receive such a request his duty to take reasonable care of the goods shall cease at the end of that period.

(8)   Where—
  (a)   a term of the contract provides that if the consumer cancels the contract, he must return the goods to the supplier, and
  (b)   the consumer is not otherwise entitled to reject the goods under the terms of the contract or by virtue of any enactment,
paragraph (7) shall apply as if for the period of 21 days there were substituted the period of 6 months.

(9)   Where any security has been provided in relation to the cancelled contract, the duty to restore goods imposed on the consumer by this regulation shall not be

enforceable before the supplier has discharged any duty imposed on him by regulation 14(4) to return any property lodged with him as security on cancellation.

(10)　Breach of a duty imposed by this regulation on a consumer is actionable as a breach of statutory duty.

18　Goods given in part-exchange

(1)　This regulation applies on the cancellation of a contract under regulation 10 where the supplier agreed to take goods in part-exchange (the 'part-exchange goods') and those goods have been delivered to him.

(2)　Unless, before the end of the period of 10 days beginning with the date of cancellation, the part-exchange goods are returned to the consumer in a condition substantially as good as when they were delivered to the supplier, the consumer shall be entitled to recover from the supplier a sum equal to the part-exchange allowance.

(3)　In this regulation the part-exchange allowance means the sum agreed as such in the cancelled contract, or if no such sum was agreed, such sum as it would have been reasonable to allow in respect of the part-exchange goods if no notice of cancellation had been served.

(4)　Where the consumer recovers from the supplier a sum equal to the part-exchange allowance, the title of the consumer to the part-exchange goods shall vest in the supplier (if it has not already done so) on recovery of that sum.

19　Performance

(1)　Unless the parties agree otherwise, the supplier shall perform the contract within a maximum of 30 days beginning with the day after the day the consumer sent his order to the supplier.

(2)　Subject to paragraphs (7) and (8), where the supplier is unable to perform the contract because the goods or services ordered are not available, within the period for performance referred to in paragraph (1) or such other period as the parties agree ('the period for performance'), he shall—

    (a)　inform the consumer; and

    (b)　reimburse any sum paid by or on behalf of the consumer under or in relation to the contract to the person by whom it was made.

(3)　The reference in paragraph (2)(b) to any sum paid on behalf of the consumer includes any sum paid by a creditor who is not the same person as the supplier under a personal credit agreement with the consumer.

(4)　The supplier shall make the reimbursement referred to in paragraph (2)(b) as soon as possible and in any event within a period of 30 days beginning with the day after the day on which the period for performance expired.

(5)　A contract which has not been performed within the period for performance shall be treated as if it had not been made, save for any rights or remedies which the consumer has under it as a result of the non-performance.

(6)　Where any security has been provided in relation to the contract, the security (so far as it is so provided) shall, where the supplier is unable to perform the contract within the period for performance, be treated as never having had any effect and any property lodged with the supplier solely for the purposes of the security as so provided shall be returned by him forthwith.

(7)　Where the supplier is unable to supply the goods or services ordered by the consumer, the supplier may perform the contract for the purposes of these Regulations by providing substitute goods or services (as the case may be) of equivalent quality and price provided that—

    (a)　this possibility was provided for in the contract;

    (b)　prior to the conclusion of the contract the supplier gave the consumer the information required by regulation 7(1)(b) and (c) in the manner required by regulation 7(2).

(8)　In the case of outdoor leisure events which by their nature cannot be rescheduled, paragraph 2(b) shall not apply where the consumer and the supplier so agree.

20 Effect of non-performance on related credit agreement

Where a supplier is unable to perform the contract within the period for performance—

(a) regulations 15 and 16 shall apply to any related credit agreement as if the consumer had given a valid notice of cancellation under regulation 10 on the expiry of the period for performance; and

(b) the reference in regulation 15(3)(a) to regulation 14(1) shall be read, for the purposes of this regulation, as a reference to regulation 19(2).

21 Payment by card

(1) Subject to paragraph (4), the consumer shall be entitled to cancel a payment where fraudulent use has been made of his payment card in connection with a contract to which this regulation applies by another person not acting, or to be treated as acting, as his agent.

(2) Subject to paragraph (4), the consumer shall be entitled to be recredited, or to have all sums returned by the card issuer, in the event of fraudulent use of his payment card in connection with a contract to which this regulation applies by another person not acting, or to be treated as acting, as the consumer's agent.

(3) Where paragraphs (1) and (2) apply, in any proceedings if the consumer alleges that any use made of the payment card was not authorised by him it is for the card issuer to prove that the use was so authorised.

(4) Paragraphs (1) and (2) shall not apply to an agreement to which section 83(1) of the Consumer Credit Act 1974 applies.

(5) [amends Consumer Credit Act 1974].

(6) For the purposes of this regulation—

'card issuer' means the owner of the card; and

'payment card' includes credit cards, charge cards, debit cards and store cards.

22, 23 [Amending provisions]

24 Inertia selling

(1) Paragraphs (2) and (3) apply if—

(a) unsolicited goods are sent to a person ('the recipient') with a view to his acquiring them;

(b) the recipient has no reasonable cause to believe that they were sent with a view to their being acquired for the purposes of a business; and

(c) the recipient has neither agreed to acquire nor agreed to return them.

(2) The recipient may, as between himself and the sender, use, deal with or dispose of the goods as if they were an unconditional gift to him.

(3) The rights of the sender to the goods are extinguished.

(4) A person who, not having reasonable cause to believe there is a right to payment, in the course of any business makes a demand for payment, or asserts a present or prospective right to payment, for what he knows are—

(a) unsolicited goods sent to another person with a view to his acquiring them for purposes other than those of his business, or

(b) unsolicited services supplied to another person for purposes other than those of his business,

is guilty of an offence and liable, on summary conviction, to a fine not exceeding level 4 on the standard scale.

(5) A person who, not having reasonable cause to believe there is a right to payment, in the course of any business and with a view to obtaining payment for what he knows are unsolicited goods sent or services supplied as mentioned in paragraph (4)—

(a) threatens to bring any legal proceedings, or

(b)   places or causes to be placed the name of any person on a list of defaulters or debtors or threatens to do so, or

(c)   invokes or causes to be invoked any other collection procedure or threatens to do so,

is guilty of an offence and liable, on summary conviction, to a fine not exceeding level 5 on the standard scale.

(6)   In this regulation—

'acquire' includes hire;

'send' includes deliver;

'sender', in relation to any goods, includes—

(a)   any person on whose behalf or with whose consent the goods are sent;

(b)   any other person claiming through or under the sender or any person mentioned in paragraph (a); and

(c)   any person who delivers the goods; and

'unsolicited' means, in relation to goods sent or services supplied to any person, that they are sent or supplied without any prior request made by or on behalf of the recipient.

(7)   For the purposes of this regulation, an invoice or similar document which—

(a)   states the amount of a payment, and

(b)   fails to comply with the [conditions set out in Part 2 of the Schedule to the Regulatory Reform (Unsolicited Goods and Services Act 1971) (Directory Entries and Demands for Payment) Order 2005] or, as the case may be, [the requirements of regulations made under] Article 6 of the Unsolicited Goods and Services (Northern Ireland) Order 1976 applicable to it,

is to be regarded as asserting a right to the payment.

(8)   Section 3A of the Unsolicited Goods and Services Act 1971 applies for the purposes of this regulation in its application to England, Wales and Scotland as it applies for the purposes of that Act.

(9)   Article 6 of the Unsolicited Goods and Services (Northern Ireland) Order 1976 applies for the purposes of this regulation in its application to Northern Ireland as it applies for the purposes of that Order.

(10)   This regulation applies only to goods sent and services supplied after the date on which it comes into force.

25   No contracting-out

(1)   A term contained in any contract to which these Regulations apply is void if, and to the extent that, it is inconsistent with a provision for the protection of the consumer contained in these Regulations.

(2)   Where a provision of these Regulations specifies a duty or liability of the consumer in certain circumstances, a term contained in a contract to which these Regulations apply, other than a term to which paragraph (3) applies, is inconsistent with that provision if it purports to impose, directly or indirectly, an additional duty or liability on him in those circumstances.

(3)   This paragraph applies to a term which requires the consumer to return any goods supplied to him under the contract if he cancels it under regulation 10.

(4)   A term to which paragraph (3) applies shall, in the event of cancellation by the consumer under regulation 10, have effect only for the purposes of regulations 14(5) and 17(8).

(5)   These Regulations shall apply notwithstanding any contract term which applies or purports to apply the law of a non-Member State if the contract has a close connection with the territory of a Member State.

26   Consideration of complaints

(1)   It shall be the duty of an enforcement authority to consider any complaint made to it about a breach unless—

(a)   the complaint appears to the authority to be frivolous or vexatious; or

(b)   another enforcement authority has notified the Director that it agrees to consider the complaint.

(2)   If an enforcement authority notifies the Director that it agrees to consider a complaint made to another enforcement authority, the first mentioned authority shall be under a duty to consider the complaint.

(3)   An enforcement authority which is under a duty to consider a complaint shall give reasons for its decision to apply or not to apply, as the case may be, for an injunction under regulation 27.

(4)   In deciding whether or not to apply for an injunction in respect of a breach an enforcement authority may, if it considers it appropriate to do so, have regard to any undertaking given to it or another enforcement authority by or on behalf of any person as to compliance with these Regulations.

27   Injunctions to secure compliance with these Regulations

(1)   The Director or, subject to paragraph (2), any other enforcement authority may apply for an injunction (including an interim injunction) against any person who appears to the Director or that authority to be responsible for a breach.

(2)   An enforcement authority other than the Director may apply for an injunction only where—

(a)   it has notified the Director of its intention to apply at least fourteen days before the date on which the application is to be made, beginning with the date on which the notification was given; or

(b)   the Director consents to the application being made within a shorter period.

(3)   The court on an application under this regulation may grant an injunction on such terms as it thinks fit to secure compliance with these Regulations.

28   Notification of undertakings and orders to the Director

An enforcement authority other than the Director shall notify the Director—

(a)   of any undertaking given to it by or on behalf of any person who appears to it to be responsible for a breach;

(b)   of the outcome of any application made by it under regulation 27 and of the terms of any undertaking given to or order made by the court;

(c)   of the outcome of any application made by it to enforce a previous order of the court.

29   Publication, information and advice

(1)   The Director shall arrange for the publication in such form and manner as he considers appropriate of—

(a)   details of any undertaking or order notified to him under regulation 28;

(b)   details of any undertaking given to him by or on behalf of any person as to compliance with these Regulations;

(c)   details of any application made by him under regulation 27, and of the terms of any undertaking given to, or order made by, the court;

(d)   details of any application made by the Director to enforce a previous order of the court.

(2)   The Director may arrange for the dissemination in such form and manner as he considers appropriate of such information and advice concerning the operation of these Regulations as it may appear to him to be expedient to give to the public and to all persons likely to be affected by these Regulations.

Regulation 3   SCHEDULE 1
            INDICATIVE LIST OF MEANS OF DISTANCE COMMUNICATION

1   Unaddressed printed matter.
2   Addressed printed matter.
3   Letter.

4   Press advertising with order form.
5   Catalogue.
6   Telephone with human intervention.
7   Telephone without human intervention (automatic calling machine, audio-text).
8   Radio.
9   Videophone (telephone with screen).
10 Videotext (microcomputer and television screen) with keyboard or touch screen.
11 Electronic mail.
12 Facsimile machine (fax).
13 Television (teleshopping).

LIMITED LIABILITY PARTNERSHIPS REGULATIONS 2001
(SI 2001/1090)

PART VI
DEFAULT PROVISION

7   Default provision for limited liability partnerships
The mutual rights and duties of the members and the mutual rights and duties of the limited liability partnership and the members shall be determined, subject to the provisions of the general law and to the terms of any limited liability partnership agreement, by the following rules:
(1)   All the members of a limited liability partnership are entitled to share equally in the capital and profits of the limited liability partnership.
(2)   The limited liability partnership must indemnify each member in respect of payments made and personal liabilities incurred by him—
(a)   in the ordinary and proper conduct of the business of the limited liability partnership; or
(b)   in or about anything necessarily done for the preservation of the business or property of the limited liability partnership.
(3)   Every member may take part in the management of the limited liability partnership.
(4)   No member shall be entitled to remuneration for acting in the business or management of the limited liability partnership.
(5)   No person may be introduced as a member or voluntarily assign an interest in a limited liability partnership without the consent of all existing members.
(6)   Any difference arising as to ordinary matters connected with the business of the limited liability partnership may be decided by a majority of the members, but no change may be made in the nature of the business of the limited liability partnership without the consent of all the members.
(7)   The books and records of the limited liability partnership are to be made available for inspection at the registered office of the limited liability partnership or at such other place as the members think fit and every member of the limited liability partnership may when he thinks fit have access to and inspect and copy any of them.
(8)   Each member shall render true accounts and full information of all things affecting the limited liability partnership to any member or his legal representatives.
(9)   If a member, without the consent of the limited liability partnership, carries on any business of the same nature as and competing with the limited liability partnership, he must account for and pay over to the limited liability partnership all profits made by him in that business.
(10)   Every member must account to the limited liability partnership for any benefit derived by him without the consent of the limited liability partnership

from any transaction concerning the limited liability partnership, or from any use by him of the property of the limited liability partnership, name or business connection.

8 Expulsion
No majority of the members can expel any member unless a power to do so has been conferred by express agreement between the members.

ELECTRONIC COMMERCE (EC DIRECTIVE) REGULATIONS 2002
(SI 2002/2013)

2 Interpretation
(1) In these Regulations and in the Schedule—
'commercial communication' means a communication, in any form, designed to promote, directly or indirectly, the goods, services or image of any person pursuing a commercial, industrial or craft activity or exercising a regulated profession, other than a communication—
(a) consisting only of information allowing direct access to the activity of that person including a geographic address, a domain name or an electronic mail address; or
(b) relating to the goods, services or image of that person provided that the communication has been prepared independently of the person making it (and for this purpose, a communication prepared without financial consideration is to be taken to have been prepared independently unless the contrary is shown);
'the Commission' means the Commission of the European Communities;
'consumer' means any natural person who is acting for purposes other than those of his trade, business or profession;
'coordinated field' means requirements applicable to information society service providers or information society services, regardless of whether they are of a general nature or specifically designed for them, and covers requirements with which the service provider has to comply in respect of—
(a) the taking up of the activity of an information society service, such as requirements concerning qualifications, authorisation or notification, and
(b) the pursuit of the activity of an information society service, such as requirements concerning the behaviour of the service provider, requirements regarding the quality or content of the service including those applicable to advertising and contracts, or requirements concerning the liability of the service provider,
but does not cover requirements such as those applicable to goods as such, to the delivery of goods or to services not provided by electronic means;
'the Directive' means Directive 2000/31/EC of the European Parliament and of the Council of 8 June 2000 on certain legal aspects of information society services, in particular electronic commerce, in the Internal Market (Directive on electronic commerce);
'EEA Agreement' means the Agreement on the European Economic Area signed at Oporto on 2 May 1992 as adjusted by the Protocol signed at Brussels on 17 March 1993;
'enactment' includes an enactment comprised in Northern Ireland legislation and comprised in, or an instrument made under, an Act of the Scottish Parliament;
'enforcement action' means any form of enforcement action including, in particular—
(a) in relation to any legal requirement imposed by or under any enactment, any action taken with a view to or in connection with imposing any sanction (whether criminal or otherwise) for failure to observe or comply with it; and
(b) in relation to a permission or authorisation, anything done with a view to removing or restricting that permission or authorisation;

'enforcement authority' does not include courts but, subject to that, means any person who is authorised, whether by or under an enactment or otherwise, to take enforcement action;

'established service provider' means a service provider who is a national of a member State or a company or firm as mentioned in Article 48 of the Treaty and who effectively pursues an economic activity by virtue of which he is a service provider using a fixed establishment in a member State for an indefinite period, but the presence and use of the technical means and technologies required to provide the information society service do not, in themselves, constitute an establishment of the provider; in cases where it cannot be determined from which of a number of places of establishment a given service is provided, that service is to be regarded as provided from the place of establishment where the provider has the centre of his activities relating to that service; references to a service provider being established or to the establishment of a service provider shall be construed accordingly;

'information society services' (which is summarised in recital 17 of the Directive as covering 'any service normally provided for remuneration, at a distance, by means of electronic equipment for the processing (including digital compression) and storage of data, and at the individual request of a recipient of a service') has the meaning set out in Article 2(a) of the Directive, (which refers to Article 1(2) of Directive 98/34/EC of the European Parliament and of the Council of 22 June 1998 laying down a procedure for the provision of information in the field of technical standards and regulations, as amended by Directive 98/48/EC of 20 July 1998);

'member State' includes a State which is a contracting party to the EEA Agreement;

'recipient of the service' means any person who, for professional ends or otherwise, uses an information society service, in particular for the purposes of seeking information or making it accessible;

'regulated profession' means any profession within the meaning of either Article 1(d) of Council Directive 89/48/EEC of 21 December 1988 on a general system for the recognition of higher-education diplomas awarded on completion of professional education and training of at least three years' duration or of Article 1(f) of Council Directive 92/51/EEC of 18 June 1992 on a second general system for the recognition of professional education and training to supplement Directive 89/48/EEC;

'service provider' means any person providing an information society service;

'the Treaty' means the treaty establishing the European Community.

(2) In regulation 4 and 5, 'requirement' means any legal requirement under the law of the United Kingdom, or any part of it, imposed by or under any enactment or otherwise.

(3) Terms used in the Directive other than those in paragraph (1) above shall have the same meaning as in the Directive.

3 Exclusions
(1) Nothing in these Regulations shall apply in respect of—
(a) the field of taxation;
(b) questions relating to information society services covered by the Data Protection Directive and the Telecommunications Data Protection Directive and Directive 2002/58/EC of the European Parliament and of the Council of 12th July 2002 concerning the processing of personal data and the protection of privacy in the electronic communications sector (Directive on privacy and electronic communications);
(c) questions relating to agreements or practices governed by cartel law; and
(d) the following activities of information society services—
(i) the activities of a public notary or equivalent professions to the extent

that they involve a direct and specific connection with the exercise of public authority,

    (ii) the representation of a client and defence of his interests before the courts, and

    (iii) betting, gaming or lotteries which involve wagering a stake with monetary value.

(2) These Regulations shall not apply in relation to any Act passed on or after the date these Regulations are made or in exercise of a power to legislate after that date.

(3) In this regulation—

'cartel law' means so much of the law relating to agreements between undertakings, decisions by associations of undertakings or concerted practices as relates to agreements to divide the market or fix prices;

'Data Protection Directive' means Directive 95/46/EC of the European Parliament and of the Council of 24 October 1995 on the protection of individuals with regard to the processing of personal data and on the free movement of such data; and

'Telecommunications Data Protection Directive' means Directive 97/66/EC of the European Parliament and of the Council of 15 December 1997 concerning the processing of personal data and the protection of privacy in the telecommunications sector.

4 Internal market

(1) Subject to paragraph (4) below, any requirement which falls within the coordinated field shall apply to the provision of an information society service by a service provider established in the United Kingdom irrespective of whether that information society service is provided in the United Kingdom or another member State.

(2) Subject to paragraph (4) below, an enforcement authority with responsibility in relation to any requirement in paragraph (1) shall ensure that the provision of an information society service by a service provider established in the United Kingdom complies with that requirement irrespective of whether that service is provided in the United Kingdom or another member State and any power, remedy or procedure for taking enforcement action shall be available to secure compliance.

(3) Subject to paragraphs (4), (5) and (6) below, any requirement shall not be applied to the provision of an information society service by a service provider established in a member State other than the United Kingdom for reasons which fall within the coordinated field where its application would restrict the freedom to provide information society services to a person in the United Kingdom from that member State.

(4) Paragraphs (1), (2) and (3) shall not apply to those fields in the annex to the Directive set out in the Schedule.

(5) The reference to any requirements the application of which would restrict the freedom to provide information society services from another member State in paragraph (3) above does not include any requirement maintaining the level of protection for public health and consumer interests established by Community acts.

(6) To the extent that anything in these Regulations creates any new criminal offence, it shall not be punishable with imprisonment for more than two years or punishable on summary conviction with imprisonment for more than three months or with a fine of more than level 5 on the standard scale (if not calculated on a daily basis) or with a fine of more than £100 a day.

5 Derogations from regulation 4

(1) Notwithstanding regulation 4(3), an enforcement authority may take

measures, including applying any requirement which would otherwise not apply by virtue of regulation 4(3) in respect of a given information society service, where those measures are necessary for reasons of—

(a)   public policy, in particular the prevention, investigation, detection and prosecution of criminal offences, including the protection of minors and the fight against any incitement to hatred on grounds of race, sex, religion or nationality, and violations of human dignity concerning individual persons;

(b)   the protection of public health;

(c)   public security, including the safeguarding of national security and defence, or

(d)   the protection of consumers, including investors,

and proportionate to those objectives.

(2)   Notwithstanding regulation 4(3), in any case where an enforcement authority with responsibility in relation to the requirement in question is not party to the proceedings, a court may, on the application of any person or of its own motion, apply any requirement which would otherwise not apply by virtue of regulation 4(3) in respect of a given information society service, if the application of that enactment or requirement is necessary for and proportionate to any of the objectives set out in paragraph (1) above.

(3)   Paragraphs (1) and (2) shall only apply where the information society service prejudices or presents a serious and grave risk of prejudice to an objective in paragraph (1)(a) to (d).

(4)   Subject to paragraphs (5) and (6), an enforcement authority shall not take the measures in paragraph (1) above, unless it—

(a)   asks the member State in which the service provider is established to take measures and the member State does not take such measures or they are inadequate; and

(b)   notifies the Commission and the member State in which the service provider is established of its intention to take such measures.

(5)   Paragraph (4) shall not apply to court proceedings, including preliminary proceedings and acts carried out in the course of a criminal investigation.

(6)   If it appears to the enforcement authority that the matter is one of urgency, it may take the measures under paragraph (1) without first asking the member State in which the service provider is established to take measures and notifying the Commission and the member State in derogation from paragraph (4).

(7)   In a case where a measure is taken pursuant to paragraph (6) above, the enforcement authority shall notify the measures taken to the Commission and to the member State concerned in the shortest possible time thereafter and indicate the reasons for urgency.

(8)   In paragraph (2), 'court' means any court or tribunal.

6   General information to be provided by a person providing an information society service

(1)   A person providing an information society service shall make available to the recipient of the service and any relevant enforcement authority, in a form and manner which is easily, directly and permanently accessible, the following information—

(a)   the name of the service provider;

(b)   the geographic address at which the service provider is established;

(c)   the details of the service provider, including his electronic mail address, which make it possible to contact him rapidly and communicate with him in a direct and effective manner;

(d)   where the service provider is registered in a trade or similar register available to the public, details of the register in which the service provider is entered and his registration number, or equivalent means of identification in that register;

(e)   where the provision of the service is subject to an authorisation scheme, the particulars of the relevant supervisory authority;

(f)   where the service provider exercises a regulated profession—

(i)   the details of any professional body or similar institution with which the service provider is registered;

(ii) his professional title and the member State where that title has been granted;

(iii) a reference to the professional rules applicable to the service provider in the member State of establishment and the means to access them; and

(g)   where the service provider undertakes an activity that is subject to value added tax, the identification number referred to in Article 22(1) of the sixth Council Directive 77/388/EEC of 17 May 1977 on the harmonisation of the laws of the member States relating to turnover taxes—Common system of value added tax: uniform basis of assessment.

(2)   Where a person providing an information society service refers to prices, these shall be indicated clearly and unambiguously and, in particular, shall indicate whether they are inclusive of tax and delivery costs.

7   Commercial communications

A service provider shall ensure that any commercial communication provided by him and which constitutes or forms part of an information society service shall—

(a)   be clearly identifiable as a commercial communication;

(b)   clearly identify the person on whose behalf the commercial communication is made;

(c)   clearly identify as such any promotional offer (including any discount, premium or gift) and ensure that any conditions which must be met to qualify for it are easily accessible, and presented clearly and unambiguously; and

(d)   clearly identify as such any promotional competition or game and ensure that any conditions for participation are easily accessible and presented clearly and unambiguously.

8   Unsolicited commercial communications

A service provider shall ensure that any unsolicited commercial communication sent by him by electronic mail is clearly and unambiguously identifiable as such as soon as it is received.

9   Information to be provided where contracts are concluded by electronic means

(1)   Unless parties who are not consumers have agreed otherwise, where a contract is to be concluded by electronic means a service provider shall, prior to an order being placed by the recipient of a service, provide to that recipient in a clear, comprehensible and unambiguous manner the information set out in (a) to (d) below—

(a)   the different technical steps to follow to conclude the contract;

(b)   whether or not the concluded contract will be filed by the service provider and whether it will be accessible;

(c)   the technical means for identifying and correcting input errors prior to the placing of the order; and

(d)   the languages offered for the conclusion of the contract.

(2)   Unless parties who are not consumers have agreed otherwise, a service provider shall indicate which relevant codes of conduct he subscribes to and give information on how those codes can be consulted electronically.

(3)   Where the service provider provides terms and conditions applicable to the contract to the recipient, the service provider shall make them available to him in a way that allows him to store and reproduce them.

(4)   The requirements of paragraphs (1) and (2) above shall not apply to

contracts concluded exclusively by exchange of electronic mail or by equivalent individual communications.

10 Other information requirements
Regulations 6, 7, 8 and 9(1) have effect in addition to any other information requirements in legislation giving effect to Community law.

11 Placing of the order
(1) Unless parties who are not consumers have agreed otherwise, where the recipient of the service places his order through technological means, a service provider shall—

(a) acknowledge receipt of the order to the recipient of the service without undue delay and by electronic means; and

(b) make available to the recipient of the service appropriate, effective and accessible technical means allowing him to identify and correct input errors prior to the placing of the order.

(2) For the purposes of paragraph (1)(a) above—

(a) the order and the acknowledgement of receipt will be deemed to be received when the parties to whom they are addressed are able to access them; and

(b) the acknowledgement of receipt may take the form of the provision of the service paid for where that service is an information society service.

(3) The requirements of paragraph (1) above shall not apply to contracts concluded exclusively by exchange of electronic mail or by equivalent individual communications.

12 Meaning of the term 'order'
Except in relation to regulation 9(11)(c) and regulation 11(1)(b) where 'order' shall be the contractual offer, 'order' may be but need not be the contractual offer for the purposes of regulations 9 and 11.

13 Liability of the service provider
The duties imposed by regulations 6, 7, 8, 9(1) and 11(1)(a) shall be enforceable, at the suit of any recipient of a service, by an action against the service provider for damages for breach of statutory duty.

14 Compliance with regulation 9(3)
Where on request a service provider has failed to comply with the requirement in regulation 9(3), the recipient may seek an order from any court having jurisdiction in relation to the contract requiring that service provider to comply with that requirement.

15 Right to rescind contract
Where a person—

(a) has entered into a contract to which these Regulations apply, and

(b) the service provider has not made available means of allowing him to identify and correct input errors in compliance with regulation 11(1)(b),

he shall be entitled to rescind the contract unless any court having jurisdiction in relation to the contract in question orders otherwise on the application of the service provider.

SCHEDULE
Regulation 4(4)

1   Copyright, neighbouring rights, rights referred to in Directive 87/54/EEC and Directive 96/9/EC and industrial property rights.

2   The freedom of the parties to a contract to choose the applicable law.

3   Contractual obligations concerning consumer contracts.

4   Formal validity of contracts creating or transferring rights in real estate where such contracts are subject to mandatory formal requirements of the law of the member State where the real estate is situated.

5   The permissibility of unsolicited commercial communications by electronic mail.

PRICE MARKING ORDER 2004
(SI 2004/102)

1   Citation, commencement and interpretation

(1)   This Order may be cited as the Price Marking Order 2004 and shall come into force on 22nd July 2004.

(2)   In this Order—

'advertisement' means any form of advertisement which is made in order to promote the sale of a product but does not include any advertisement by means of which the trader intends to encourage a consumer to enter into a distance contract, a catalogue, a price list, a container or a label;

'consumer' means any individual who buys a product for purposes that do not fall within the sphere of his commercial or professional activity;

'cosmetic products' means any substance or preparation intended to be placed in contact with an external part of the human body, or with the teeth, inside of the mouth or throat with a view exclusively or mainly to one or more of the following purposes: cleaning, perfuming, changing the appearance of, protecting, and keeping in good condition it or them or correcting body odour;

'distance contract' means any contract concerning products concluded between a trader and a consumer, by any means, without the simultaneous physical presence of the trader and the consumer;

'itinerant trader' means any trader who, as a pedestrian, or from a train, aircraft, vessel, vehicle, stall, barrow, or other mobile sales unit, offers products to consumers other than by means of pre-printed material;

'liquid medium' has the meaning given for the purposes of paragraph 4 of Article 8 of Directive 2000/13/EC of the European Parliament and of the Council on the approximation of the laws of the Member States relating to the labelling, presentation and advertising of foodstuffs;

'make-up products' means cosmetic products solely intended temporarily to change the appearance of the face or nails, including (but not limited to) lipsticks, mascaras, eye shadows, blushers and concealers;

'net drained weight' means the weight of a solid food product when it is presented in a liquid medium;

'precious metal' means gold, silver or platinum, or any other metal to which by an order under section 17 of the Hallmarking Act 1973 the provisions of that Act are applied;

'products sold from bulk' means products which are not pre-packaged and are weighed or measured at the request of the consumer;

'relevant floor area' in relation to a shop means the internal floor area of the shop excluding any area not used for the retail sale of products or for the display of such products for retail sale;

'selling price' means the final price for a unit of a product, or a given quantity of a product, including VAT and all other taxes;

'shop' includes a store, kiosk and a franchise or concession within a shop;

'small shop' means any shop which has a 'relevant floor area' not exceeding 280 square metres;

'standard of fineness' means any one of the standards of fineness specified in column (2) of paragraph 2 of Schedule 2 to the Hallmarking Act 1973;

'trader' means any person who sells or offers or exposes for sale products which fall within his commercial or professional activity;

'unit price' means the final price, including VAT and all other taxes, for one kilogram, one litre, one metre, one square metre or one cubic metre of a product, except (i) in respect of the products specified in Schedule 1, where unit price means the final price including VAT and all other taxes for the corresponding units of quantity set out in that Schedule; and (ii) in respect of products sold by number, where unit price means the final price including VAT and all other taxes for an individual item of the product.

2 Revocation
The Price Marking Order 1999 is hereby revoked.

3 Scope of application of the Order
(1) This Order shall not apply:
(a) to products which are supplied in the course of the provision of a service; or
(b) to sales by auction or sales of works of art or antiques.
(2) The Electronic Commerce (EC Directive) Regulations 2002 shall apply to this Order notwithstanding Regulation 3(2) of those Regulations.

4 Obligation to indicate selling price
(1) Subject to paragraph (2) and articles 9 and 10, where a trader indicates that any product is or may be for sale to a consumer, he shall indicate the selling price of that product in accordance with the provisions of this Order.
(2) The requirement in paragraph (1) above shall not apply in respect of:
(a) products sold from bulk; or
(b) an advertisement for a product.

5 Obligation to indicate unit price
(1) Subject to paragraph (2), (3) and (4) and article 9, where a trader indicates that any product is or may be for sale to a consumer, he shall indicate the unit price of that product in accordance with the provisions of this Order.
(2) The requirement in paragraph (1) only applies in respect of products sold from bulk or required by or under Parts IV or V of the Weights and Measures Act 1985 to be:
(a) marked with an indication of quantity; or
(b) made up in a quantity prescribed by or under that Act.
(3) The requirement in paragraph (1) shall not apply in relation to:
(a) any product which falls within Schedule 2;
(b) any product the unit price of which is identical to its selling price;
(c) bread made up in a prescribed quantity which is or may be for sale in a small shop, by an itinerant trader or from a vending machine; or
(d) any product which is pre-packaged in a constant quantity which is or may be for sale in a small shop, by an itinerant trader or from a vending machine.
(4) The requirement in paragraph (1) applies in relation to an advertisement for a product only where the selling price of the product is indicated in the advertisement.

Manner of indication of selling price and unit price
6—(1) The indication of selling price and unit price shall be in sterling.
(2) If a trader indicates his willingness to accept foreign currency in payment for a product, he shall, in addition to the required price indications in sterling:
(a) give an indication of the selling price and any unit price required for the product in the foreign currency in question together with any commission to be charged; or
(b) clearly identify the conversion rate on the basis of which the foreign currency price will be calculated together with any commission to be charged; and indicate that such selling price, unit price or conversion rate as the case may

be does not apply to transactions via a payment card to be applied to accounts denominated in currencies other than sterling, the conversion rate for which will be that applied by the relevant payment scheme which processes the transaction.

7—(1)   An indication of selling price, unit price, commission, conversion rate or a change in the rate or coverage of value added tax given in accordance with article 11 shall be—

(a)   unambiguous, easily identifiable and clearly legible;

(b)   subject to paragraph 2, given in proximity to:

(i)   the product; or

(ii)   in the case of distance contracts and advertisements, a visual or written description of the product; and

(c)   so placed as to be available to consumers without the need for them to seek assistance from the trader or someone on his behalf in order to ascertain it.

(2)   Paragraph (1)(b)(i) does not apply to an indication given in relation to any item of jewellery, item of precious metal, or watch displayed in a window of the premises where it is or may be for sale and the selling price of which is in excess of £3,000.

(3)   The indication of any charges for postage, package or delivery of a product shall be unambiguous, easily identifiable and clearly legible.

(4)   Where, in addition to a unit price, a price per quantity is indicated in relation to a supplementary indication of quantity the unit price shall predominate and the price per supplementary indication of quantity shall be expressed in characters no larger than the unit price.

(5)   In paragraph (4) 'supplementary indication of quantity' refers to an indication of quantity expressed in a unit of measurement other than a metric unit as authorised by section 8(5A) of the Weights and Measures Act 1985.

8   In the case of a pre-packaged solid food product presented in a liquid medium, the unit price shall refer to the net drained weight of the product. Where a unit price is also given with reference to the net weight of the product, it shall be clearly indicated which unit price relates to net drained weight and which to net weight.

9   Special provisions relating to general reductions

Where a trader proposes to sell products to which this Order applies at less than the selling price or the unit price previously applicable and indicated in accordance with article 7(1), he may comply with the obligations specified in articles 4(1) (to indicate the selling price) and 5(1) (to indicate the unit price) by indicating by a general notice or any other visible means that the products are or may be for sale at a reduction, provided that the details of the reduction are prominently displayed, unambiguous, easily identifiable and clearly legible.

10   Special provisions relating to precious metals

In the case of products the selling price of which varies from day to day according to the price of the precious metals contained in them the obligation to indicate the selling price referred to in article 4(1) may be complied with by indicating in a manner which is unambiguous, easily identifiable and clearly legible:

(a)   the weight, type and standard of fineness of each precious metal contained in the product; and

(b)   any element of the selling price which is not referable to weight, accompanied by a clearly legible and prominent notice stating the price per unit of weight for the type and standard of fineness of each precious metal contained in the product.

11   Change in Value Added Tax etc

Where there is a change in the rate or coverage of VAT or any other tax, a trader who adjusts his prices in consequence may comply with the provisions of this Order—

(a) by means of a general notice or notices for a period of 14 days from the date any such change takes effect, indicating that any products subject to that change are not for sale at the price indicated and that such price will be adjusted to take account of the change; and

(b) if he continues to distribute any catalogue or sales literature printed or ordered to be printed before a change is announced and there is firmly attached to it a label which prominently states that some or all of the prices printed in it are to be adjusted to reflect the change, and:

(i) the label includes sufficient information to enable consumers to establish the adjusted price of any product listed, or

(ii) the label refers to and is accompanied by a supplement which enables them to do so.

Decimal places and rounding of unit prices

12 Where the unit price of a product falls below £1 it shall be expressed to the nearest 0.1p. Where the figure denoting one hundredths of one penny in the unit price is 5 or higher, it shall be rounded up and where it is 4 or lower it shall be rounded down.

13 Where the unit price of a product falls above £1 it may be expressed to the nearest:

(a) 1p, in which case where the figure denoting tenths of one penny in the unit price is 5 or higher, it shall be rounded up and where it is 4 or lower it shall be rounded down; or

(b) 0.1p, in which case where the figure denoting one hundredths of one penny in the unit price is 5 or higher it shall be rounded up and where it is 4 or lower it shall be rounded down.

14 Units of quantity

For the purposes of Schedule 1, the figure denoting the relevant units of quantity in the second column of the table for the corresponding product in the first column of the table refers, as indicated by or under the Weights and Measures Act 1985, and unless specified otherwise to:

(a) grams where the product is sold by weight;

(b) millilitres where the product is sold by volume; and

(c) either grams or millilitres, as indicated by the manufacturer of the product, where the product is permitted to be sold by either weight or volume.

15 Enforcement

For the purpose of ascertaining whether any trader enjoys exemption from unit pricing under article 5(3)(c) or (d) in respect of a small shop, a local weights and measures authority may require that trader to produce such documentary evidence relating to the shop in question as it considers necessary.

SCHEDULE 2
PRODUCTS IN RESPECT OF WHICH A TRADER IS EXEMPT FROM THE REQUIREMENT TO UNIT PRICE

Article 5(3)

1 Any product which is offered by traders to consumers by means of an advertisement which is:

(a) purely aural;

(b) broadcast on television;

(c) shown at a cinema; or

(d) inside a small shop.

2 Any product the price of which has been reduced from the usual price at which it is sold, on account of:
   (a)   its damaged condition; or
   (b)   the danger of its deterioration.
3 Any product which comprises an assortment of different items sold in a single package.
4 Any product the unit price of which is 0.0p as a result of article 12 (Decimal places and rounding of unit prices) of this Order.

GENERAL PRODUCT SAFETY REGULATIONS 2005
(SI 2005/1803)

PART 1
GENERAL

2 Interpretation
In these Regulations—
'the 1987 Act' means the Consumer Protection Act 1987;
'Community law' includes a law in any part of the United Kingdom which implements a Community obligation;
'contravention' includes a failure to comply and cognate expressions shall be construed accordingly;
'dangerous product' means a product other than a safe product;
'distributor' means a professional in the supply chain whose activity does not affect the safety properties of a product;
'enforcement authority' means the Secretary of State, any other Minister of the Crown in charge of a government department, any such department and any authority or council mentioned in regulation 10;
'general safety requirement' means the requirement that only safe products should be placed on the market;
'the GPS Directive' means Directive 2001/95/EC of the European Parliament and of the Council of 3 December 2001 on general product safety;
'magistrates' court' in relation to Northern Ireland, means a court of summary jurisdiction;
'Member State' means a Member State, Norway, Iceland or Liechtenstein;
'notice' means a notice in writing;
'officer', in relation to an enforcement authority, means a person authorised in writing to assist the authority in carrying out its functions under or for the purposes of the enforcement of these Regulations and safety notices, except in relation to an enforcement authority which is a government department where it means an officer of that department;
'producer' means—
   (a)   the manufacturer of a product, when he is established in a Member State and any other person presenting himself as the manufacturer by affixing to the product his name, trade mark or other distinctive mark, or the person who reconditions the product;
   (b)   when the manufacturer is not established in a Member State—
      (i)   if he has a representative established in a Member State, the representative,
      (ii)   in any other case, the importer of the product from a state that is not a Member State into a Member State;
   (c)   other professionals in the supply chain, insofar as their activities may affect the safety properties of a product;
'product' means a product which is intended for consumers or likely, under reasonably foreseeable conditions, to be used by consumers even if not intended for them and which is supplied or made available, whether for consideration or

not, in the course of a commercial activity and whether it is new, used or reconditioned and includes a product that is supplied or made available to consumers for their own use in the context of providing a service. 'Product' does not include equipment used by service providers themselves to supply a service to consumers, in particular equipment on which consumers ride or travel which is operated by a service provider;

'recall' means any measure aimed at achieving the return of a dangerous product that has already been supplied or made available to consumers;

'recall notice' means a notice under regulation 15;

'record' includes any book or document and any record in any form;

'requirement to mark' means a notice under regulation 12;

'requirement to warn' means a notice under regulation 13;

'safe product' means a product which, under normal or reasonably foreseeable conditions of use including duration and, where applicable, putting into service, installation and maintenance requirements, does not present any risk or only the minimum risks compatible with the product's use, considered to be acceptable and consistent with a high level of protection for the safety and health of persons. In determining the foregoing, the following shall be taken into account in particular—

(a)   the characteristics of the product, including its composition, packaging, instructions for assembly and, where applicable, instructions for installation and maintenance,

(b)   the effect of the product on other products, where it is reasonably foreseeable that it will be used with other products,

(c)   the presentation of the product, the labelling, any warnings and instructions for its use and disposal and any other indication or information regarding the product, and

(d)   the categories of consumers at risk when using the product, in particular children and the elderly.

The feasibility of obtaining higher levels of safety or the availability of other products presenting a lesser degree of risk shall not constitute grounds for considering a product to be a dangerous product;

'safety notice' means a suspension notice, a requirement to mark, a requirement to warn, a withdrawal notice or a recall notice;

'serious risk' means a serious risk, including one the effects of which are not immediate, requiring rapid intervention;

'supply' in relation to a product includes making it available, in the context of providing a service, for use by consumers;

'suspension notice' means a notice under regulation 11;

'withdrawal' means any measure aimed at preventing the distribution, display or offer of a dangerous product to a consumer;

'withdrawal notice' means a notice under regulation 14.

3   Application

(1)   Each provision of these Regulations applies to a product in so far as there are no specific provisions with the same objective in rules of Community law governing the safety of the product other than the GPS Directive.

(2)   Where a product is subject to specific safety requirements imposed by rules of Community law other than the GPS Directive, these Regulations shall apply only to the aspects and risks or category of risks not covered by those requirements. This means that:

(a)   the definition of 'safe product' and 'dangerous product' in regulation 2 and regulations 5 and 6 shall not apply to such a product in so far as concerns the risks or category of risks covered by the specific rules, and

(b)   the remainder of these Regulations shall apply except where there are specific provisions governing the aspects covered by those regulations with the same objective.

4 These Regulations do not apply to a second-hand product supplied as a product to be repaired or reconditioned prior to being used, provided the supplier clearly informs the person to whom he supplies the product to that effect.

PART 2
OBLIGATIONS OF PRODUCERS AND DISTRIBUTORS

5 General safety requirement
(1) No producer shall place a product on the market unless the product is a safe product.

(2) No producer shall offer or agree to place a product on the market or expose or possess a product for placing on the market unless the product is a safe product.

(3) No producer shall offer or agree to supply a product or expose or possess a product for supply unless the product is a safe product.

(4) No producer shall supply a product unless the product is a safe product.

6 Presumption of conformity
(1) Where, in the absence of specific provisions in rules of Community law governing the safety of a product, the product conforms to the specific rules of the law of part of the United Kingdom laying down the health and safety require-ments which the product must satisfy in order to be marketed in the United King-dom, the product shall be deemed safe so far as concerns the aspects covered by such rules.

(2) Where a product conforms to a voluntary national standard of the United Kingdom giving effect to a European standard the reference of which has been published in the Official Journal of the European Union in accordance with Article 4 of the GPS Directive, the product shall be presumed to be a safe product so far as concerns the risks and categories of risk covered by that national standard. The Secretary of State shall publish the reference number of such national standards in such manner as he considers appropriate.

(3) In circumstances other than those referred to in paragraphs (1) and (2), the conformity of a product to the general safety requirement shall be assessed taking into account—

    (a) any voluntary national standard of the United Kingdom giving effect to a European standard, other than one referred to in paragraph (2),

    (b) other national standards drawn up in the United Kingdom,

    (c) recommendations of the European Commission setting guidelines on product safety assessment,

    (d) product safety codes of good practice in the sector concerned,

    (e) the state of the art and technology, and

    (f) reasonable consumer expectations concerning safety.

(4) Conformity of a product with the criteria designed to ensure the general safety requirement is complied with, in particular the provisions mentioned in paragraphs (1) to (3), shall not bar an enforcement authority from exercising its powers under these Regulations in relation to that product where there is evidence that, despite such conformity, it is dangerous.

7 Other obligations of producers
(1) Within the limits of his activities, a producer shall provide consumers with the relevant information to enable them—

    (a) to assess the risks inherent in a product throughout the normal or reasonably foreseeable period of its use, where such risks are not immediately obvious without adequate warnings, and

    (b) to take precautions against those risks.

(2)   The presence of warnings does not exempt any person from compliance with the other requirements of these Regulations.

(3)   Within the limits of his activities, a producer shall adopt measures commensurate with the characteristics of the products which he supplies to enable him to—

(a)   be informed of the risks which the products might pose, and

(b)   take appropriate action including, where necessary to avoid such risks, withdrawal, adequately and effectively warning consumers as to the risks or, as a last resort, recall.

(4)   The measures referred to in paragraph (3) include—

(a)   except where it is not reasonable to do so, an indication by means of the product or its packaging of—

(i)   the name and address of the producer, and

(ii)   the product reference or where applicable the batch of products to which it belongs; and

(b)   where and to the extent that it is reasonable to do so—

(i)   sample testing of marketed products,

(ii)   investigating and if necessary keeping a register of complaints concerning the safety of the product, and

(iii)   keeping distributors informed of the results of such monitoring where a product presents a risk or may present a risk.

8   Obligations of distributors

(1)   A distributor shall act with due care in order to help ensure compliance with the applicable safety requirements and in particular he—

(a)   shall not expose or possess for supply or offer or agree to supply, or supply, a product to any person which he knows or should have presumed, on the basis of the information in his possession and as a professional, is a dangerous product; and

(b)   shall, within the limits of his activities, participate in monitoring the safety of a product placed on the market, in particular by—

(i)   passing on information on the risks posed by the product,

(ii)   keeping the documentation necessary for tracing the origin of the product,

(iii)   producing the documentation necessary for tracing the origin of the product, and (iv) cooperating in action taken by a producer or an enforcement authority to avoid the risks.

(2)   Within the limits of his activities, a distributor shall take measures enabling him to co-operate efficiently in the action referred to in paragraph (1)(b)(iii).

9   Obligations of producers and distributors

(1)   Subject to paragraph (2), where a producer or a distributor knows that a product he has placed on the market or supplied poses risks to the consumer that are incompatible with the general safety requirement, he shall forthwith notify an enforcement authority in writing of that information and—

(a)   the action taken to prevent risk to the consumer; and

(b)   where the product is being or has been marketed or otherwise supplied to consumers outside the United Kingdom, of the identity of each Member State in which, to the best of his knowledge, it is being or has been so marketed or supplied.

(2)   Paragraph (1) shall not apply—

(a)   in the case of a second-hand product supplied as an antique or as a product to be repaired or reconditioned prior to being used, provided the supplier clearly informed the person to whom he supplied the product to that effect,

(b)   in conditions concerning isolated circumstances or products.

(3) In the event of a serious risk the notification under paragraph (1) shall include the following—

(a) information enabling a precise identification of the product or batch of products in question,

(b) a full description of the risks that the product presents,

(c) all available information relevant for tracing the product, and

(d) a description of the action undertaken to prevent risks to the consumer.

(4) Within the limits of his activities, a person who is a producer or a distributor shall co-operate with an enforcement authority (at the enforcement authority's request) in action taken to avoid the risks posed by a product which he supplies or has supplied. Every enforcement authority shall maintain procedures for such co-operation, including procedures for dialogue with the producers and distributors concerned on issues related to product safety.

PART 3
ENFORCEMENT

10 Enforcement

(1) It shall be the duty of every authority to which paragraph (4) applies to enforce within its area these Regulations and safety notices.

(2) An authority in England or Wales to which paragraph (4) applies shall have the power to investigate and prosecute for an alleged contravention of any provision imposed by or under these Regulations which was committed outside its area in any part of England and Wales.

(3) A district council in Northern Ireland shall have the power to investigate and prosecute for an alleged contravention of any provision imposed by or under these Regulations which was committed outside its area in any part of Northern Ireland.

(4) The authorities to which this paragraph applies are:

(a) in England, a county council, district council, London Borough Council, the Common Council of the City of London in its capacity as a local authority and the Council of the Isles of Scilly,

(b) in Wales, a county council or a county borough council,

(c) in Scotland, a council constituted under section 2 of the Local Government etc (Scotland) Act 1994,

(d) in Northern Ireland any district council.

(5) An enforcement authority shall in enforcing these Regulations act in a manner proportionate to the seriousness of the risk and shall take due account of the precautionary principle. In this context, it shall encourage and promote voluntary action by producers and distributors. Notwithstanding the foregoing, an enforcement authority may take any action under these Regulations urgently and without first encouraging and promoting voluntary action if a product poses a serious risk.

11 Suspension notices

(1) Where an enforcement authority has reasonable grounds for suspecting that a requirement of these Regulations has been contravened in relation to a product, the authority may, for the period needed to organise appropriate safety evaluations, checks and controls, serve a notice ('a suspension notice') prohibiting the person on whom it is served from doing any of the following things without the consent of the authority, that is to say—

(a) placing the product on the market, offering to place it on the market, agreeing to place it on the market or exposing it for placing on the market, or

(b) supplying the product, offering to supply it, agreeing to supply it or exposing it for supply.

(2) A suspension notice served by an enforcement authority in relation to a

product may require the person on whom it is served to keep the authority informed of the whereabouts of any such product in which he has an interest.

(3) A consent given by the enforcement authority for the purposes of paragraph (1) may impose such conditions on the doing of anything for which the consent is required as the authority considers appropriate.

12 Requirements to mark

(1) Where an enforcement authority has reasonable grounds for believing that a product is a dangerous product in that it could pose risks in certain conditions, the authority may serve a notice ('a requirement to mark') requiring the person on whom the notice is served at his own expense to undertake either or both of the following, as specified in the notice—

(a) to ensure that the product is marked in accordance with requirements specified in the notice with warnings as to the risks it may present,

(b) to make the marketing of the product subject to prior conditions as specified in the notice so as to ensure the product is a safe product.

(2) The requirements referred to in paragraph (1)(a) shall be such as to ensure that the product is marked with a warning which is suitable, clearly worded and easily comprehensible.

13 Requirements to warn

Where an enforcement authority has reasonable grounds for believing that a product is a dangerous product in that it could pose risks for certain persons, the authority may serve a notice ('a requirement to warn') requiring the person on whom the notice is served at his own expense to undertake one or more of the following, as specified in the notice—

(a) where and to the extent it is practicable to do so, to ensure that any person who could be subject to such risks and who has been supplied with the product be given warning of the risks in good time and in a form specified in the notice,

(b) to publish a warning of the risks in such form and manner as is likely to bring those risks to the attention of any such person,

(c) to ensure that the product carries a warning of the risks in a form specified in the notice.

14 Withdrawal notices

(1) Where an enforcement authority has reasonable grounds for believing that a product is a dangerous product, the authority may serve a notice ('a withdrawal notice') prohibiting the person on whom it is served from doing any of the following things without the consent of the authority, that is to say—

(a) placing the product on the market, offering to place it on the market, agreeing to place it on the market or exposing it for placing on the market, or

(b) supplying the product, offering to supply it, agreeing to supply it or exposing it for supply.

(2) A withdrawal notice may require the person on whom it is served to take action to alert consumers to the risks that the product presents.

(3) In relation to a product that is already on the market, a withdrawal notice may only be served by an enforcement authority where the action being undertaken by the producer or the distributor concerned in fulfilment of his obligations under these Regulations is unsatisfactory or insufficient to prevent the risks concerned to the health and safety of persons.

(4) Paragraph (3) shall not apply in the case of a product posing a serious risk requiring, in the view of the enforcement authority, urgent action.

(5) A withdrawal notice served by an enforcement authority in relation to a product may require the person on whom it is served to keep the authority informed of the whereabouts of any such product in which he has an interest.

(6) A consent given by the enforcement authority for the purposes of para-

graph (1) may impose such conditions on the doing of anything for which the consent is required as the authority considers appropriate.

15 Recall notices

(1) Subject to paragraph (4), where an enforcement authority has reasonable grounds for believing that a product is a dangerous product and that it has already been supplied or made available to consumers, the authority may serve a notice ('a recall notice') requiring the person on whom it is served to use his reasonable endeavours to organise the return of the product from consumers to that person or to such other person as is specified in the notice.

(2) A recall notice may require—

    (a) the recall to be effected in accordance with a code of practice applicable to the product concerned, or

    (b) the recipient of the recall notice to—

        (i) contact consumers who have purchased the product in order to inform them of the recall, where and to the extent it is practicable to do so,

        (ii) publish a notice in such form and such manner as is likely to bring to the attention of purchasers of the product the risk the product poses and the fact of the recall, or

        (iii) make arrangements for the collection or return of the product from consumers who have purchased it or for its disposal,

and may impose such additional requirements on the recipient of the notice as are reasonable and practicable with a view to achieving the return of the product from consumers to the person specified in the notice or its disposal.

(3) In determining what requirements to include in a recall notice, the enforcement authority shall take into consideration the need to encourage distributors, users and consumers to contribute to its implementation.

(4) A recall notice may only be issued by an enforcement authority where—

    (a) other action which it may require under these Regulations would not suffice to prevent the risks concerned to the health and safety of persons,

    (b) the action being undertaken by the producer or the distributor concerned in fulfilment of his obligations under these Regulations is unsatisfactory or insufficient to prevent the risks concerned to the health and safety of persons, and

    (c) the authority has given not less than seven days' notice to the person on whom the recall notice is to be served of its intention to serve such a notice and where that person has before the expiry of that period by notice required the authority to seek the advice of such person as the Institute determines on the questions of—

        (i) whether the product is a dangerous product,

        (ii) whether the issue of a recall notice is proportionate to the seriousness of the risk,

and the authority has taken account of such advice.

(5) Paragraphs (4)(b) and (c) shall not apply in the case of a product posing a serious risk requiring, in the view of the enforcement authority, urgent action.

(6) Where a person requires an enforcement authority to seek advice as referred to in paragraph (4)(c), that person shall be responsible for the fees, costs and expenses of the Institute and of the person appointed by the Institute to advise the authority.

(7) In paragraphs 4(c) and (6) 'the Institute' means the charitable organisation with registered number 803725 and known as the Chartered Institute of Arbitrators.

(8) A recall notice served by an enforcement authority in relation to a product may require the person on whom it is served to keep the authority informed of the whereabouts of any such product to which the recall notice relates, so far as he is able to do so.

(9)   Where the conditions in paragraph (1) for serving a recall notice are satisfied and either the enforcement authority has been unable to identify any person on whom to serve a recall notice, or the person on whom such a notice has been served has failed to comply with it, then the authority may itself take such action as could have been required by a recall notice.

(10)   Where—

(a)   an authority has complied with the requirements of paragraph (4); and

(b)   the authority has exercised its powers under paragraph (9) to take action following the failure of the person on whom the recall notice has been served to comply with that notice,

then the authority may recover from the person on whom the notice was served summarily as a civil debt, any costs or expenses reasonably incurred by it in undertaking the action referred to in sub-paragraph (b).

(11)   A civil debt recoverable under the preceding paragraph may be recovered—

(a)   in England and Wales by way of complaint (as mentioned in section 58 of the Magistrates' Courts Act 1980,

(b)   in Northern Ireland in proceedings under Article 62 of the Magistrates' Courts (Northern Ireland) Order 1981.

16   Supplementary provisions relating to safety notices

(1)   Whenever feasible, prior to serving a safety notice the authority shall give an opportunity to the person on whom the notice is to be served to submit his views to the authority. Where, due to the urgency of the situation, this is not feasible the person shall be given an opportunity to submit his views to the authority after service of the notice.

(2)   A safety notice served by an enforcement authority in respect of a product shall—

(a)   describe the product in a manner sufficient to identify it;

(b)   state the reasons on which the notice is based;

(c)   indicate the rights available to the recipient of the notice under these Regulations and (where applicable) the time limits applying to their exercise; and

(d)   in the case of a suspension notice, state the period of time for which it applies.

(3)   A safety notice shall have effect throughout the United Kingdom.

(4)   Where an enforcement authority serves a suspension notice in respect of a product, the authority shall be liable to pay compensation to a person having an interest in the product in respect of any loss or damage suffered by reason of the notice if—

(a)   there has been no contravention of any requirement of these Regulations in relation to the product; and

(b)   the exercise by the authority of the power to serve the suspension notice was not attributable to any neglect or default by that person.

(5)   Where an enforcement authority serves a withdrawal notice in respect of a product, the authority shall be liable to pay compensation to a person having an interest in the product in respect of any loss or damage suffered by reason of the notice if—

(a)   the product was not a dangerous product; and

(b)   the exercise by the authority of the power to serve the withdrawal notice was not attributable to any neglect or default by that person.

(6)   Where an enforcement authority serves a recall notice in respect of a product, the authority shall be liable to pay compensation to the person on whom the notice was served in respect of any loss or damage suffered by reason of the notice if—

(a)   the product was not a dangerous product; and

(b)   the exercise by the authority of the power to serve the recall notice was not attributable to any neglect or default by that person.

(7)   An enforcement authority may vary or revoke a safety notice which it has served provided that the notice is not made more restrictive for the person on whom it is served or more onerous for that person to comply with.

(8)   Wherever feasible prior to varying a safety notice the authority shall give an opportunity to the person on whom the original notice was served to submit his views to the authority.

17   Appeals against safety notices

(1)   A person on whom a safety notice has been served and a person having an interest in a product in respect of which a safety notice (other than a recall notice) has been served may, before the end of the period of 21 days beginning with the day on which the notice was served, apply for an order to vary or set aside the terms of the notice.

(2)   On an application under paragraph (1) the court or the sheriff, as the case may be, shall make an order setting aside the notice only if satisfied that—

(a)   in the case of a suspension notice, there has been no contravention in relation to the product of any requirement of these Regulations,

(b)   in the case of a requirement to mark or a requirement to warn, the product is not a dangerous product,

(c)   in the case of a withdrawal notice—

(i)   the product is not a dangerous product, or

(ii)   where applicable, regulation 14(3) has not been complied with by the enforcement authority concerned,

(d)   in the case of a recall notice—

(i)   the product is not a dangerous product, or

(ii)   regulation 15(4) has not been complied with,

(e)   in any case, the serving of the safety notice concerned was not proportionate to the seriousness of the risk.

(3)   On an application concerning the period of time specified in a suspension notice as the period for which it applies, the court or the sheriff, as the case may be, may reduce the period to such period as it considers sufficient for organising appropriate safety evaluations, checks and controls.

(4)   On an application to vary the terms of a notice, the court or the sheriff, as the case may be, may vary the requirements specified in the notice as it considers appropriate.

(5)   A person on whom a recall notice has been served and who proposes to make an application under paragraph (1) in relation to the notice may, before the end of the period of seven days beginning with the day on which the notice was served, apply to the court or the sheriff for an order suspending the effect of the notice and the court or the sheriff may, in any case where it considers it appropriate to do so, make an order suspending the effect of the notice.

(6)   If the court or the sheriff makes an order suspending the effect of a recall notice under paragraph (5) in the absence of the enforcement authority, the enforcement authority may apply for the revocation of such order.

(7)   An order under paragraph (5) shall take effect from the time it is made until—

(a)   it is revoked under paragraph (6),

(b)   where no application is made under paragraph (1) in respect of the recall notice within the time specified in that paragraph, the expiration of that time,

(c)   where such an application is made but is withdrawn or dismissed for want of prosecution, the date of dismissal or withdrawal of the application, or

(d)   where such an application is made and is not withdrawn or dismissed for want of prosecution, the determination of the application.

(8)   Subject to paragraph (6), in Scotland the sheriff's decision under paragraph (5) shall be final.

(9)   An application under this regulation may be made—

(a)   by way of complaint to any magistrates' court in which proceedings have been brought in England and Wales or Northern Ireland—

(i)   in respect of a contravention in relation to the product of a requirement imposed by or under these Regulations; or

(ii)   for the forfeiture of the product under regulation 18;

(b)   where no such proceedings have been brought, by way of complaint to any magistrates' court; or

(c)   in Scotland, by summary application to the sheriff.

(10)   A person aggrieved by an order made pursuant to an application under paragraph (1) by a magistrates' court in England, Wales or Northern Ireland, or by a decision of such a court not to make such an order, may appeal against that order or decision—

(a)   in England and Wales, to the Crown Court;

(b)   in Northern Ireland, to the county court.

18   [*Does not apply to Scotland*]

19   Forfeiture: Scotland

(1)   In Scotland a sheriff may make an order for forfeiture of a product on the grounds that the product is a dangerous product—

(a)   on an application by a procurator-fiscal made in the manner specified in section 134 of the Criminal Procedure (Scotland) Act 1995, or

(b)   where a person is convicted of any offence in respect of a contravention in relation to the product of a requirement imposed by or under these Regulations, in addition to any other penalty which the sheriff may impose.

(2)   The procurator-fiscal making an application under paragraph (1)(a) shall serve on any person appearing to him to be the owner of, or otherwise to have an interest in, the product to which the application relates a copy of the application, together with a notice giving him the opportunity to appear at the hearing of the application to show cause why the product should not be forfeited.

(3)   Service under paragraph (2) shall be carried out, and such service may be proved, in the manner specified for citation of an accused in summary proceedings under the Criminal Procedure (Scotland) Act 1995.

(4)   A person upon whom notice is served under paragraph (2) and any other person claiming to be the owner of, or otherwise to have an interest in, the product to which the application relates shall be entitled to appear at the hearing of the application to show cause why the product should not be forfeited.

(5)   The sheriff shall not make an order following an application under paragraph (1)(a)—

(a)   if any person on whom notice is served under paragraph (2) does not appear, unless service of the notice on that person is proved; or

(b)   if no notice under paragraph (2) has been served, unless the sheriff is satisfied that in the circumstances it was reasonable not to serve notice on any person.

(6)   The sheriff may make an order under this regulation only if he is satisfied that the product is a dangerous product.

(7)   Where an order for the forfeiture of a product is made following an application by the procurator-fiscal under paragraph (1)(a), any person who appeared, or was entitled to appear to show cause why the product should not be forfeited may, within twenty-one days of the making of the order, appeal to the High Court by Bill of Suspension on the ground of an alleged miscarriage of justice; and section 182(5)(a) to (e) of the Criminal Procedure (Scotland) Act 1995 shall apply to an appeal under this paragraph as it applies to a stated case under Part X of that Act.

(8) An order following an application under paragraph (1)(a) shall not take effect—

(a) until the end of the period of twenty-one days beginning with the day after the day on which the order is made; or

(b) if an appeal is made under paragraph (7) within that period, until the appeal is determined or abandoned.

(9) An order under paragraph (1)(b) shall not take effect—

(a) until the end of the period within which an appeal against the order could be brought under the Criminal Procedure (Scotland) Act 1995; or

(b) if an appeal is made within that period, until the appeal is determined or abandoned.

(10) Subject to paragraph (11), a product forfeited under this regulation shall be destroyed in accordance with such directions as the sheriff may give.

(11) If he thinks fit, the sheriff may direct that the product be released to such person as he may specify, on condition that that person does not supply the product to any other person otherwise than as mentioned in paragraph (11) of regulation 18.

20 Offences

(1) A person who contravenes regulations 5 or 8(1)(a) shall be guilty of an offence and liable on conviction on indictment to imprisonment for a term not exceeding 12 months or to a fine not exceeding £20,000 or to both, or on summary conviction to imprisonment for a term not exceeding three months or to a fine not exceeding the statutory maximum or to both.

(2) A person who contravenes regulation 7(1), 7(3) (by failing to take any of the measures specified in regulation 7(4)), 8(1)(b)(i), (ii) or (iii) or 9(1) shall be guilty of an offence and liable on summary conviction to imprisonment for a term not exceeding three months or to a fine not exceeding level 5 on the standard scale or to both.

(3) A producer or distributor who does not give notice to an enforcement authority under regulation 9(1) in respect of a product he has placed on the market or supplied commits an offence where it is proved that he ought to have known that the product poses risks to consumers that are incompatible with the general safety requirement and he shall be liable on summary conviction to imprisonment for a term not exceeding three months or to a fine not exceeding level 5 on the standard scale or to both.

(4) A person who contravenes a safety notice shall be guilty of an offence and liable on conviction on indictment to imprisonment for a term not exceeding 12 months or to a fine not exceeding £20,000 or to both, or on summary conviction to imprisonment for a term not exceeding three months or to a fine not exceeding the statutory maximum or to both.

21 Test purchases

(1) An enforcement authority shall have power to organise appropriate checks on the safety properties of a product, on an adequate scale, up to the final stage of use or consumption and for that purpose may make a purchase of a product or authorise an officer of the authority to make a purchase of a product.

(2) Where a product purchased under paragraph (1) is submitted to a test and the test leads to—

(a) the bringing of proceedings for an offence in respect of a contravention in relation to the product of any requirement imposed by or under these Regulations or for the forfeiture of the product under regulation 18 or 19, or

(b) the serving of a safety notice in respect of the product, and

(c) the authority is requested to do so and it is practicable for the authority to comply with the request,

then the authority shall allow the person from whom the product was purchased, a person who is a party to the proceedings, on whom the notice was served or who has an interest in the product to which the notice relates, to have the product tested.

22 Powers of entry and search etc

(1)   An officer of an enforcement authority may at any reasonable hour and on production, if required, of his credentials exercise any of the powers conferred by the following provisions of this regulation.

(2)   The officer may, for the purposes of ascertaining whether there has been a contravention of a requirement imposed by or under these Regulations, enter any premises other than premises occupied only as a person's residence and inspect any record or product.

(3)   The officer may, for the purpose of ascertaining whether there has been a contravention of a requirement imposed by or under these Regulations, examine any procedure (including any arrangements for carrying out a test) connected with the production of a product.

(4)   If the officer has reasonable grounds for suspecting that the product has not been placed on the market or supplied in the United Kingdom since it was manufactured or imported he may for the purpose of ascertaining whether there has been a contravention in relation to the product of a requirement imposed by or under these Regulations—

(a)   require a person carrying on a commercial activity, or employed in connection with a commercial activity, to supply all necessary information relating to the activity, including by the production of records,

(b)   require any record which is stored in an electronic form and is accessible from the premises to be produced in a form —

(i)   in which it can be taken away, and

(ii)   in which it is visible and legible.

(c)   for the purpose of ascertaining (by testing or otherwise) whether there has been any such contravention, seize and detain samples of the product,

(d)   take copies of, or of an entry in, any records produced by virtue of sub-paragraph (a).

(5)   If the officer has reasonable grounds for suspecting that there has been a contravention in relation to a product of a requirement imposed by or under these Regulations, he may—

(a)   for the purpose of ascertaining whether there has been any such contravention, require a person carrying on a commercial activity, or employed in connection with a commercial activity, to supply all necessary information relating to the activity, including by the production of records,

(b)   for the purpose of ascertaining whether there has been any such contravention, require any record which is stored in an electronic form and is accessible from the premises to be produced in a form—

(i)   in which it can be taken away, and

(ii)   in which it is visible and legible,

(c)   for the purpose of ascertaining (by testing or otherwise) whether there has been any such contravention, seize and detain samples of the product,

(d)   take copies of, or of an entry in, any records produced by virtue of sub-paragraph (a).

(6)   The officer may seize and detain any products or records which he has reasonable grounds for believing may be required as evidence in proceedings for an offence in respect of a contravention of any requirement imposed by or under these Regulations.

(7)   If and to the extent that it is reasonably necessary to do so to prevent a contravention of any requirement imposed by or under these Regulations, the officer may, for the purpose of exercising his power under paragraphs (4) to (6) to seize products or records—

(a) require any person having authority to do so to open any container or to open any vending machine; and

(b) himself open or break open any such container or machine where a requirement made under sub-paragraph (a) in relation to the container or machine has not been complied with.

23 Provisions supplemental to regulation 22 and search warrants etc

(1) An officer seizing any products or records shall, before he leaves the premises, provide to the person from whom they were seized a written notice—

(a) specifying the products (including the quantity thereof) and records seized,

(b) stating the reasons for their seizure, and

(c) explaining the right of appeal under regulation 25.

(2) References in paragraph (1) and regulation 25 to the person from whom something has been seized, in relation to a case in which the power of seizure was exercisable by reason of the product having been found on any premises, are references to the occupier of the premises at the time of the seizure.

(3) If a justice of the peace—

(a) is satisfied by written information on oath that there are reasonable grounds for believing either—

(i) that any products or records which an officer has power to inspect under regulation 22 are on any premises and that their inspection is likely to disclose evidence that there has been a contravention of any requirement imposed by or under these Regulations, or

(ii) that such a contravention has taken place, is taking place or is about to take place on any premises, and

(b) is also satisfied by such information either—

(i) that admission to the premises has been or is likely to be refused and that notice of the intention to apply for a warrant under this paragraph has been given to the occupier, or

(ii) that an application for admission, or the giving of such a notice, would defeat the object of the entry or that the premises are unoccupied or that the occupier is temporarily absent and it might defeat the object of the entry to await his return,

the justice may by warrant under his hand, which shall continue in force for a period of one month, authorise any officer of an enforcement authority to enter the premises, if need be by force.

(4) An officer entering premises by virtue of regulation 22 or a warrant under paragraph (3) may take with him such other persons and equipment as may appear to him necessary.

(5) On leaving any premises which a person is authorised to enter by a warrant under paragraph (3), that person shall, if the premises are unoccupied or the occupier is temporarily absent—

(a) leave the premises as effectively secured against trespassers as he found them,

(b) attach a notice such as is mentioned in paragraph (1) in a prominent place at the premises.

(6) Where a product seized by an officer of an enforcement authority under regulation 22 or 23 is submitted to a test, the authority shall inform the person mentioned in paragraph (1) of the result of the test and, if—

(a) proceedings are brought for an offence in respect of a contravention in relation to the product of any requirement imposed by or under these Regulations or for the forfeiture of the product under regulation 18 or 19; or

(b) a safety notice is served in respect of the product; and

(c) the authority is requested to do so and it is practicable for him to comply with the request, then the authority shall allow a person who is a party to the proceedings or on whom the notice was served or who has an interest in the product to which the notice relates to have the product tested.

(7) If a person who is not an officer of an enforcement authority purports to act as such under regulation 22 or under this regulation he shall be guilty of an offence and liable on summary conviction to a fine not exceeding level 5 on the standard scale.

(8) In the application of this section to Scotland, the reference in paragraph (3) to a justice of the peace shall include a reference to a sheriff and the reference to written information on oath shall be construed as a reference to evidence on oath.

(9) In the application of this section to Northern Ireland, the reference in paragraph (3) to a justice of the peace shall include a reference to a lay magistrate and the references to an information on oath shall be construed as a reference to a complaint on oath.

24 Obstruction of officers

(1) A person who—

(a) intentionally obstructs an officer of an enforcement authority who is acting in pursuance of any provision of regulation 22 or 23; or

(b) intentionally fails to comply with a requirement made of him by an officer of an enforcement authority under any provision of those regulations; or

(c) without reasonable cause fails to give an officer of an enforcement authority who is so acting any other assistance or information which the officer may reasonably require of him for the purposes of the exercise of the officer's functions under any provision of those regulations,

shall be guilty of an offence and liable on summary conviction to a fine not exceeding level 5 on the standard scale.

(2) A person shall be guilty of an offence if, in giving any information which is required by him by virtue of paragraph (1)(c)—

(a) he makes a statement which he knows is false in a material particular; or

(b) he recklessly makes a statement which is false in a material particular.

(3) A person guilty of an offence under paragraph (2) shall be liable—

(a) on conviction on indictment, to a fine;

(b) on summary conviction, to a fine not exceeding the statutory maximum.

25 Appeals against detention of products and records

(1) A person referred to in regulation 23(1) may apply for an order requiring any product or record which is for the time being detained under regulation 22 or 23 by an enforcement authority or by an officer of such an authority to be released to him or to another person.

(2) An application under the preceding paragraph may be made—

(a) to any magistrates' court in which proceedings have been brought in England and Wales or Northern Ireland—

(i) for an offence in respect of a contravention in relation to the product of a requirement imposed by or under these Regulations, or

(ii) for the forfeiture of the product under regulation 18,

(b) where no such proceedings have been brought, by way of complaint to a magistrates' court;

(c) in Scotland, by summary application to the sheriff.

(3) On an application under paragraph (1) to a magistrates' court or to the sheriff, the court or the sheriff may make an order requiring a product or record to be released only if the court or sheriff is satisfied—

(a) that proceedings—

(i) for an offence in respect of any contravention in relation to the product or, in the case of a record, the product to which the record relates, of any requirement imposed by or under these Regulations; or

    (ii) for the forfeiture of the product or, in the case of a record, the product to which the record relates, under regulation 18 or 19,
have not been brought or, having been brought, have been concluded without the product being forfeited; and

(b) where no such proceedings have been brought, that more than six months have elapsed since the product or records was seized.

(4) In determining whether to make an order under this regulation requiring the release of a product or record the court or sheriff shall take all the circumstances into account including the results of any tests on the product which have been carried out by or on behalf of the enforcement authority and any statement made by the enforcement authority to the court or sheriff as to its intention to bring proceedings for an offence in respect of a contravention in relation to the product of any requirement imposed by or under these Regulations.

(5) Where—

(a) more than 12 months have elapsed since a product or records were seized and the enforcement authority has not commenced proceedings for an offence in respect of a contravention in relation to the product (or, in the case of records, the product to which the records relate) of any requirement imposed by or under these Regulations or for the forfeiture of the product under regulation 18 or 19, or

(b) an enforcement authority has brought proceedings for an offence as mentioned in sub-paragraph (a) and the proceedings were dismissed and all rights of appeal have been exercised or the time for appealing has expired,
the authority shall be under a duty to return the product or records detained under regulation 22 or 23 to the person from whom they were seized.

(6) Where the authority is satisfied that some other person has a better right to a product or record than the person from whom it was seized, the authority shall, instead of the duty in paragraph (5), be under a duty to return it to that other person or, as the case may be, to the person appearing to the authority to have the best right to the product or record in question.

(7) Where different persons claim to be entitled to the return of a product or record that is required to be returned under paragraph (5), then it may be retained for as long as is reasonably necessary for the determination in accordance with paragraph (6) of the person to whom it must be returned.

(8) A person aggrieved by an order made under this regulation by a magistrates' court in England and Wales or Northern Ireland, or by a decision of such a court not to make such an order, may appeal against that order or decision—

(a) in England and Wales, to the Crown Court;

(b) in Northern Ireland, to the county court;
and an order so made may contain such provision as appears to the court to be appropriate for delaying the coming into force of the order pending the making and determination of any appeal (including any application under section 111 of the Magistrates' Courts Act 1980 or article 146 of the Magistrates' Courts (Northern Ireland) Order 1981 (statement of case)).

26 Compensation for seizure and detention

Where an officer of an enforcement authority exercises any power under regulation 22 or 23 to seize and detain a product, the enforcement authority shall be liable to pay compensation to any person having an interest in the product in respect of any loss or damage caused by reason of the exercise of the power if—

(a) there has been no contravention in relation to the product of any requirement imposed by or under these Regulations, and

(b) the exercise of the power is not attributable to any neglect or default by that person.

27 Recovery of expenses of enforcement

(1) This regulation shall apply where a court—

(a)   convicts a person of an offence in respect of a contravention in relation to a product of any requirement imposed by or under these Regulations, or

(b)   makes an order under regulation 18 or 19 for the forfeiture of a product.

(2)   The court may (in addition to any other order it may make as to costs or expenses) order the person convicted or, as the case may be, any person having an interest in the product to reimburse an enforcement authority for any expenditure which has been or may be incurred by that authority—

(a)   in connection with any seizure or detention of the product by or on behalf of the authority, or

(b)   in connection with any compliance by the authority with directions given by the court for the purposes of any order for the forfeiture of the product.

28   Power of Secretary of State to obtain information

(1)   If the Secretary of State considers that, for the purposes of deciding whether to serve a safety notice, or to vary or revoke a safety notice which he has already served, he requires information or a sample of a product he may serve on a person a notice requiring him—

(a)   to furnish to the Secretary of State, within a period specified in the notice, such information as is specified;

(b)   to produce such records as are specified in the notice at a time and place so specified (and to produce any such records which are stored in any electronic form in a form in which they are visible and legible) and to permit a person appointed by the Secretary of State for that purpose to take copies of the records at that time and place;

(c)   to produce such samples of a product as are specified in the notice at a time and place so specified.

(2)   A person shall be guilty of an offence if he—

(a)   fails, without reasonable cause, to comply with a notice served on him under paragraph (1); or

(b)   in purporting to comply with a requirement which by virtue of paragraph (1)(a) or (b) is contained in such a notice—

(i)   furnishes information or records which he knows are false in a material particular, or

(ii)   recklessly furnishes information or records which are false in a material particular.

(3)   A person guilty of an offence under paragraph (2) shall—

(a)   in the case of an offence under sub-paragraph (a) of that paragraph, be liable on summary conviction to a fine not exceeding level 5 on the standard scale; and

(b)   in the case of an offence under sub-paragraph (b) of that paragraph, be liable—

(i)   on conviction on indictment, to a fine;

(ii)   on summary conviction, to a fine not exceeding the statutory maximum.

29   Defence of due diligence

(1)   Subject to the following provisions of this regulation, in proceedings against a person for an offence under these Regulations it shall be a defence for that person to show that he took all reasonable steps and exercised all due diligence to avoid committing the offence.

(2)   Where in any proceedings against any person for such an offence the defence provided by paragraph (1) involves an allegation that the commission of the offence was due—

(a)   to the act or default of another, or

(b)   to reliance on information given by another,

that person shall not, without the leave of the court, be entitled to rely on the defence unless, not less than seven clear days before, in England, Wales and

Northern Ireland, the hearing of the proceedings or, in Scotland, the trial diet, he
has served a notice under paragraph (3) on the person bringing the proceedings.

(3)   A notice under this paragraph shall give such information identifying or
assisting in the identification of the person who—

(a)   committed the act or default, or

(b)   gave the information,

as is in the possession of the person serving the notice at the time he serves it.

(4)   A person may not rely on the defence provided by paragraph (1) by reason
of his reliance on information supplied by another, unless he shows that it was
reasonable in all the circumstances to have relied on the information, having regard in particular—

(a)   to the steps which he took, and those which might reasonably have been
taken, for the purpose of verifying the information; and

(b)   to whether he had any reason to disbelieve the information.

30   Defence in relation to antiques

(1)   This regulation shall apply in proceedings against any person for an offence
under regulation 20(1) in respect of the supply, offer or agreement to supply or
exposure or possession for supply of second hand products supplied as antiques.

(2)   It shall be a defence for that person to show that the terms on which he
supplied the product or agreed or offered to supply the product or, in the case of a
product which he exposed or possessed for supply, the terms on which he intended to supply the product, contemplated the acquisition of an interest in the
product by the person supplied or to be supplied.

(3)   Paragraph (2) applies only if the producer or distributor clearly informed
the person to whom he supplied the product, or offered or agreed to supply the
product or, in the case of a product which he exposed or possessed for supply, he
intended to so inform that person, that the product is an antique.

31   Liability of person other than principal offender

(1)   Where the commission by a person of an offence under these Regulations is
due to an act or default committed by some other person in the course of a commercial activity of his, the other person shall be guilty of the offence and may be
proceeded against and punished by virtue of this paragraph whether or not proceedings are taken against the first-mentioned person.

(2)   Where a body corporate is guilty of an offence under these Regulations
(including where it is so guilty by virtue of paragraph (1)) in respect of any act or
default which is shown to have been committed with the consent or connivance of,
or to be attributable to any neglect on the part of, any director, manager, secretary
or other similar officer of the body corporate or any person who was purporting to
act in any such capacity he, as well as the body corporate, shall be guilty of that
offence and shall be liable to be proceeded against and punished accordingly.

(3)   Where the affairs of a body corporate are managed by its members, paragraph (2) shall apply in relation to the acts and defaults of a member in connection
with his functions of management as if he were a director of the body corporate.

(4)   Where a Scottish partnership is guilty of an offence under these Regulations
(including where it is so guilty by virtue of paragraph (1)) in respect of any act or
default which is shown to have been committed with the consent or connivance of,
or to be attributable to any neglect on the part of, a partner in the partnership, he,
as well as the partnership, shall be guilty of that offence and shall be liable to be
proceeded against and punished accordingly.

PART 4

MISCELLANEOUS

32   Reports

(1)   It shall be the duty of the Secretary of State to lay before each House of

Parliament a report on the exercise during the period to which the report relates of the functions which are exercisable by enforcement authorities under these Regulations.

(2)   The first such report shall relate to the period beginning on the day on which these Regulations come into force and ending on 31 March 2008 and subsequent reports shall relate to a period of not more than five years beginning on the day after the day on which the period to which the previous report relates ends.

(3)   The Secretary of State may from time to time prepare and lay before each House of Parliament such other reports on the exercise of those functions as he considers appropriate.

(4)   The Secretary of State may direct an enforcement authority to report at such intervals as he may specify in the direction on the discharge by that authority of the functions exercisable by it under these Regulations.

(5)   A report under paragraph (4) shall be in such form and shall contain such particulars as are specified in the direction of the Secretary of State.

33   Duty to notify Secretary of State and Commission
(1)   An enforcement authority which has received a notification under regulation 9(1) shall immediately pass the same on to the Secretary of State, who shall immediately pass it on to the competent authorities appointed for the purpose in the Member States where the product in question is or has been marketed or otherwise supplied to consumers.

(2)   Where an enforcement authority takes a measure which restricts the placing on the market of a product, or requires its withdrawal or recall, it shall immediately notify the Secretary of State, specifying its reasons for taking the action. It shall also immediately notify the Secretary of State of any modification or lifting of such a measure.

(3)   On receiving a notification under paragraph (2), or if he takes a measure which restricts the placing on the market of a product, or requires its withdrawal or recall, the Secretary of State shall (to the extent that such notification is not required under article 12 of the GPS Directive or any other Community legislation) immediately notify the European Commission of the measure taken, specifying the reasons for taking it. The Secretary of State shall also immediately notify the European Commission of any modification or lifting of such a measure. If the Secretary of State considers that the effects of the risk do not or cannot go beyond the territory of the United Kingdom, he shall notify the European Commission of the measure concerned insofar as it involves information likely to be of interest to Member States from the product safety standpoint, and in particular if it is in response to a new risk which has not yet been reported in other notifications.

(4)   Where an enforcement authority adopts or decides to adopt, recommend or agree with producers and distributors, whether on a compulsory or voluntary basis, a measure or action to prevent, restrict or impose specific conditions on the possible marketing or use of a product (other than a pharmaceutical product) by reason of a serious risk, it shall immediately notify the Secretary of State. It shall also immediately notify the Secretary of State of any modification or withdrawal of any such measure or action.

(5)   On receiving a notification under paragraph (4), or if he adopts or decides to adopt, recommend or agree with producers and distributors, whether on a compulsory or voluntary basis, a measure or action to prevent, restrict or impose specific conditions on the possible marketing or use of a product (other than a pharmaceutical product) by reason of a serious risk, the Secretary of State shall immediately notify the European Commission of it through the Community Rapid Information System, known as RAPEX. The Secretary of State shall also inform the European Commission without delay of any modification or withdrawal of any such measure or action.

(6)   If the Secretary of State considers that the effects of the risk do not or cannot go beyond the territory of the United Kingdom, he shall notify the European Commission of the measures or action concerned insofar as they involve information likely to be of interest to Member States of the European Union from the product safety standpoint, and in particular if they are in response to a new risk which has not been reported in other notifications.

(7)   Before deciding to adopt such a measure or take such an action as is referred to in paragraph (5), the Secretary of State may pass on to the European Commission any information in his possession regarding the existence of a serious risk. Where he does so, he must inform the European Commission, within 45 days of the day of passing the information to it, whether he confirms or modifies that information.

(8)   Upon receipt of a notification from the European Commission under article 12(2) of the GPS Directive, the Secretary of State shall notify the Commission of the following—

(a)   whether the product the subject of the notification has been marketed in the United Kingdom;

(b)   what measure concerning the product the enforcement authorities in the United Kingdom may be adopting, stating the reasons, including any differing assessment of risk or any other special circumstance justifying the decision as to the measure, in particular lack of action or follow-up; and

(c)   any relevant supplementary information he has obtained on the risk involved, including the results of any test or analysis carried out.

(9)   The Secretary of State shall notify the European Commission without delay of any modification or withdrawal of any measures notified to it under paragraph (8)(b).

(10)   In this regulation—

(a)   references to a product excludes a second hand product supplied as an antique or as a product to be repaired or reconditioned prior to being used, provided the supplier clearly informs the person to whom he supplies the product to that effect;

(b)   'pharmaceutical product' means a product falling within Council Directive 2001/83/EC of the European Parliament and of the Council on the Community code relating to medicinal products for human use.

34   Provisions supplemental to regulation 33

(1)   A notification under regulation 33(2) to (6), (8) or (9) to the Secretary of State or the Commission shall be in writing and shall provide all available details and at least the following information—

(a)   information enabling the product to be identified,

(b)   a description of the risk involved, including a summary of the results of any test or analysis and of their conclusions which are relevant to assessing the level of risk,

(c)   the nature and the duration of the measures or action taken or decided on, if applicable,

(d)   information on supply chains and distribution of the product, in particular on destination countries.

(2)   Where a measure notified to the Commission under regulation 33 seeks to limit the marketing or use of a chemical substance or preparation, the Secretary of State shall provide to the Commission as soon as possible either a summary or the references of the relevant data relating to the substance or preparation considered and to known and available substitutes, where such information is available. The Secretary of State shall also notify the Commission of the anticipated effects of the measure on consumer health and safety together with the assessment of the risk carried out in accordance with the general principles for the risk evaluation of chemical substances as referred to in article 10(4) of Council Regulation (EEC) No

793/93 of 23 March 1993 on the evaluation and control of the risks of existing sub-stances, in the case of an existing substance, or in article 3(2) of Council Directive 67/548/EEC on the approximation of laws, regulations and administrative pro-visions relating to the classification, packaging and labelling of dangerous substances in the case of a new substance.

(3)   Where the Commission carries out an investigation under paragraph 5 of Annex II to the GPS Directive, the Secretary of State shall supply the Commission with such information as it requests, to the best of his ability.

35   Implementation of Commission decisions

(1)   This regulation applies where the Commission adopts a decision pursuant to article 13 of the GPS Directive.

(2)   The Secretary of State shall—

(a)   take such action under these Regulations, or

(b)   direct another enforcement authority to take such action under these Regulations, as is necessary to comply with the decision.

(3)   Where an enforcement authority serves a safety notice pursuant to para-graph (2), the following provisions of these Regulations shall not apply in relation to that notice, namely regulations 14(3), 15(4) to (6) and 16(1), 16(2)(c) and (d), 16(5) to (7) and 17.

(4)   Unless the Commission's decision provides otherwise, export from the Community of a dangerous product which is the subject of such a decision is pro-hibited with effect from the date the decision comes into force.

(5)   The enforcement of the prohibition in paragraph (4) shall be treated as an assigned matter within the meaning of section 1(1) of the Customs and Excise Management Act 1979.

(6)   The measures necessary to implement the decision shall be taken within 20 days, unless the decision specifies a different period.

(7)   The Secretary of State or, where the Secretary of State has directed another enforcement authority to take action under paragraph (2)(b), that enforcement authority shall, within one month, give the parties concerned an opportunity to submit their views and shall inform the Commission accordingly.

36   Market surveillance

In order to ensure a high level of consumer health and safety protection, enforce-ment authorities shall within the limits of their responsibility and to the extent of their ability undertake market surveillance of products employing appropriate means and procedures and co-operating with other enforcement authorities and competent authorities of other Member States which may include:

(a)   establishment, periodical updating and implementation of sectoral surveillance programmes by categories of products or risks and the monitoring of surveillance activities, findings and results,

(b)   follow-up and updating of scientific and technical knowledge concerning the safety of products,

(c)   the periodical review and assessment of the functioning of the control activities and their effectiveness and, if necessary, revision of the surveillance approach and organisation put in place.

37   Complaints procedures

An enforcement authority shall maintain and publish a procedure by which com-plaints may be submitted by any person on product safety and on surveillance and control activities, which complaints shall be followed up as appropriate.

38   Co-operation between enforcement authorities

(1)   It shall be the duty of an enforcement authority to co-operate with other enforcement authorities in carrying out the functions conferred on them by these Regulations. In particular—

(a)   enforcement authorities shall share their expertise and best practices with each other;

(b)   enforcement authorities shall undertake collaborative working where they have a shared interest.

(2)   The Secretary of State shall inform the European Commission as to the arrangements for the enforcement of these Regulations, including which bodies are enforcement authorities.

39   Information

(1)   An enforcement authority shall in general make available to the public such information as is available to it on the following matters relating to the risks to consumer health and safety posed by a product—

(a)   the nature of the risk,

(b)   the product identification,

and the measures taken in respect of the risk, without prejudice to the need not to disclose information for effective monitoring and investigation activities.

(2)   Paragraph (1) shall not apply to any information obtained by an enforcement authority for the purposes of these Regulations which, by its nature, is covered by professional secrecy, unless the circumstances require such information to be made public in order to protect the health and safety of consumers.

(3)   [*Amending provision*]

40   Service of documents

(1)   A document required or authorised by virtue of these Regulations to be served on a person may be so served—

(a)   on an individual by delivering it to him or by leaving it at his proper address or by sending it by post to him at that address;

(b)   on a body corporate other than a limited liability partnership, by serving it in accordance with sub-paragraph (a) on the secretary of the body;

(c)   on a limited liability partnership, by serving it in accordance with sub-paragraph (a) on a member of the partnership; or

(d)   on a partnership, by serving it in accordance with sub-paragraph (a) on a partner or a person having the control or management of the partnership business;

(e)   on any other person by leaving it at his proper address or by sending it by post to him at that address.

(2)   For the purposes of paragraph (1), and for the purposes of section 7 of the Interpretation Act 1978 (which relates to the service of documents by post) in its application to that paragraph, the proper address of a person on whom a document is to be served by virtue of these Regulations shall be his last known address except that—

(a)   in the case of a body corporate (other than a limited liability partnership) or its secretary, it shall be the address of the registered or principal office of the body;

(b)   in the case of a limited liability partnership or a member of the partnership, it shall be the address of the registered or principal office of the partnership;

(c)   in the case of a partnership or a partner or a person having the control or management of a partnership business, it shall be the address of the principal office of the partnership,

and for the purposes of this paragraph the principal officer of a company constituted under the law of a country or territory outside the United Kingdom or of a partnership carrying on business outside the United Kingdom is its principal office within the United Kingdom.

(3)   A document required or authorised by virtue of these Regulations to be served on a person may also be served by transmitting the request by any means of electronic communication to an electronic address (which includes a fax number and

an e-mail address) being an address which the person has held out as an address at which he or it can be contacted for the purposes of receiving such documents.

(4) A document transmitted by any means of electronic communication in accordance with the preceding paragraph is, unless the contrary is proved, deemed to be received on the business day after the notice was transmitted over a public electronic communications network.

41 Extension of time for bringing summary proceedings

(1) Notwithstanding section 127 of the Magistrates' Courts Act 1980 or article 19 of the Magistrates' Courts (Northern Ireland) Order 1981, in England, Wales and Northern Ireland a magistrates' court may try an information (in the case of England and Wales) or a complaint (in the case of Northern Ireland) in respect of an offence under these Regulations if (in the case of England and Wales) the information is laid or (in the case of Northern Ireland) the complaint is made within three years from the date of the offence or within one year from the discovery of the offence by the prosecutor whichever is the earlier.

(2) Notwithstanding section 136 of the Criminal Procedure (Scotland) Act 1995, in Scotland summary proceedings for an offence under these Regulations may be commenced within three years from the date of the offence or within one year from the discovery of the offence by the prosecutor whichever is the earlier.

(3) For the purposes of paragraph (2), section 136(3) of the Criminal Procedure (Scotland) Act 1995 shall apply as it applies for the purposes of that section.

42 Civil proceedings

These Regulations shall not be construed as conferring any right of action in civil proceedings in respect of any loss or damage suffered in consequence of a contravention of these Regulations.

43 Privileged information

(1) Nothing in these Regulations shall be taken as requiring a person to produce any records if he would be entitled to refuse to produce those records in any proceedings in any court on the grounds that they are the subject of legal professional privilege or, in Scotland, that they contain a confidential communication made by or to an advocate or solicitor in that capacity, or as authorising a person to take possession of any records which are in the possession of a person who would be so entitled.

(2) Nothing in these Regulations shall be construed as requiring a person to answer any question or give any information if to do so would incriminate that person or that person's spouse or civil partner.

44 Evidence in proceedings for offence relating to regulation 9(1)

(1) This regulation applies where a person has given a notification to an enforcement authority pursuant to regulation 9(1).

(2) No evidence relating to that statement may be adduced and no question relating to it may be asked by the prosecution in any criminal proceedings (other than proceedings in which that person is charged with an offence under regulation 20 for a contravention of regulation 9(1)), unless evidence relating to it is adduced, or a question relating to it is asked, in the proceedings by or on behalf of that person.

45 Transitional provisions

Where, in relation to a product, a suspension notice (within the meaning of the 1987 Act) has (by virtue of regulation 11(b) of the General Product Safety Regulations 1994) been served under section 14 of the 1987 Act and is in force immediately prior to the coming into force of these Regulations, it shall continue in force notwithstanding the revocation of the General Product Safety Regulations 1994 by these Regulations, and those Regulations shall continue to apply accordingly.

46–47 *[Amendment provisions]*

PART III

EC MATERIALS

**DIRECTIVE OF THE EUROPEAN PARLIAMENT AND OF THE COUNCIL
OF 11 MAY 2005
('Unfair Commercial Practices Directive')**

(Directive 2005/29/EC: Text with EEA relevance)

THE EUROPEAN PARLIAMENT AND THE COUNCIL OF THE EUROPEAN
UNION,

Having regard to the Treaty establishing the European Community, and in particular Article 95 thereof,

Having regard to the proposal from the Commission,

Having regard to the opinion of the European Economic and Social Committee,

Acting in accordance with the procedure laid down in Article 251 of the Treaty,

Whereas:

(1) Article 153(1) and (3)(a) of the Treaty provides that the Community is to contribute to the attainment of a high level of consumer protection by the measures it adopts pursuant to Article 95 thereof.

(2) In accordance with Article 14(2) of the Treaty, the internal market comprises an area without internal frontiers in which the free movement of goods and services and freedom of establishment are ensured. The development of fair commercial practices within the area without internal frontiers is vital for the promotion of the development of crossborder activities.

(3) The laws of the Member States relating to unfair commercial practices show marked differences which can generate appreciable distortions of competition and obstacles to the smooth functioning of the internal market. In the field of advertising, Council Directive 84/450/EEC of 10 September 1984 concerning misleading and comparative advertising establishes minimum criteria for harmonizing legislation on misleading advertising, but does not prevent the Member States from retaining or adopting measures which provide more extensive protection for consumers. As a result, Member States' provisions on misleading advertising diverge significantly.

(4) These disparities cause uncertainty as to which national rules apply to unfair commercial practices harming consumers' economic interests and create many barriers affecting business and consumers. These barriers increase the cost to business of exercising internal market freedoms, in particular when businesses wish to engage in cross border marketing, advertising campaigns and sales promotions. Such barriers also make consumers uncertain of their rights and undermine their confidence in the internal market.

(5) In the absence of uniform rules at Community level, obstacles to the free movement of services and goods across borders or the freedom of establishment could be justified in the light of the case-law of the Court of Justice of the European Communities as long as they seek to protect recognised public interest objectives and are proportionate to those objectives. In view of the Community's

objectives, as set out in the provisions of the Treaty and in secondary Community law relating to freedom of movement, and in accordance with the Commission's policy on commercial communications as indicated in the Communication from the Commission entitled 'The follow-up to the Green Paper on Commercial Communications in the Internal Market', such obstacles should be eliminated. These obstacles can only be eliminated by establishing uniform rules at Community level which establish a high level of consumer protection and by clarifying certain legal concepts at Community level to the extent necessary for the proper functioning of the internal market and to meet the requirement of legal certainty.

(6)   This Directive therefore approximates the laws of the Member States on unfair commercial practices, including unfair advertising, which directly harm consumers' economic interests and thereby indirectly harm the economic interests of legitimate competitors. In line with the principle of proportionality, this Directive protects consumers from the consequences of such unfair commercial practices where they are material but recognises that in some cases the impact on consumers may be negligible. It neither covers nor affects the national laws on unfair commercial practices which harm only competitors' economic interests or which relate to a transaction between traders; taking full account of the principle of subsidiarity, Member States will continue to be able to regulate such practices, in conformity with Community law, if they choose to do so. Nor does this Directive cover or affect the provisions of Directive 84/450/EEC on advertising which misleads business but which is not misleading for consumers and on comparative advertising. Further, this Directive does not affect accepted advertising and marketing practices, such as legitimate product placement, brand differentiation or the offering of incentives which may legitimately affect consumers' perceptions of products and influence their behaviour without impairing the consumer's ability to make an informed decision.

(7)   This Directive addresses commercial practices directly related to influencing consumers' transactional decisions in relation to products. It does not address commercial practices carried out primarily for other purposes, including for example commercial communication aimed at investors, such as annual reports and corporate promotional literature. It does not address legal requirements related to taste and decency which vary widely among the Member States. Commercial practices such as, for example, commercial solicitation in the streets, may be undesirable in Member States for cultural reasons. Member States should accordingly be able to continue to ban commercial practices in their territory, in conformity with Community law, for reasons of taste and decency even where such practices do not limit consumers' freedom of choice. Full account should be taken of the context of the individual case concerned in applying this Directive, in particular the general clauses thereof.

(8)   This Directive directly protects consumer economic interests from unfair business-to-consumer commercial practices. Thereby, it also indirectly protects legitimate businesses from their competitors who do not play by the rules in this Directive and thus guarantees fair competition in fields coordinated by it. It is understood that there are other commercial practices which, although not harming consumers, may hurt competitors and business customers. The Commission should carefully examine the need for Community action in the field of unfair competition beyond the remit of this Directive and, if necessary, make a legislative proposal to cover these other aspects of unfair competition.

(9)   This Directive is without prejudice to individual actions brought by those who have been harmed by an unfair commercial practice. It is also without prejudice to Community and national rules on contract law, on intellectual property rights, on the health and safety aspects of products, on conditions of establishment and authorization regimes, including those rules which, in conformity with Community law, relate to gambling activities, and to Community competition rules and the national provisions implementing them. The Member States will thus be able

to retain or introduce restrictions and prohibitions of commercial practices on grounds of the protection of the health and safety of consumers in their territory wherever the trader is based, for example in relation to alcohol, tobacco or pharmaceuticals. Financial services and immovable property, by reason of their complexity and inherent serious risks, necessitate detailed requirements, including positive obligations on traders. For this reason, in the field of financial services and immovable property, this Directive is without prejudice to the right of Member States to go beyond its provisions to protect the economic interests of consumers. It is not appropriate to regulate here the certification and indication of the standard of fineness of articles of precious metal.

(10) It is necessary to ensure that the relationship between this Directive and existing Community law is coherent, particularly where detailed provisions on unfair commercial practices apply to specific sectors. This Directive therefore amends Directive 84/450/EEC, Directive 97/7/EC of the European Parliament and of the Council of 20 May 1997 on the protection of consumers in respect of distance contracts, Directive 98/27/EC of the European Parliament and of the Council of 19 May 1998 on injunctions for the protection of consumers' interests and Directive 2002/65/EC of the European Parliament and of the Council of 23 September 2002 concerning the distance marketing of consumer financial services. This Directive accordingly applies only in so far as there are no specific aspects of unfair commercial practices, such as information requirements and rules on the way the information is presented to the consumer. It provides protection for consumers where there is no specific sectoral legislation at Community level and prohibits traders from creating a false impression of the nature of products. This is particularly important for complex products with high levels of risk to consumers, such as certain financial services products. This Directive consequently complements the Community *acquis*, which is applicable to commercial practices harming consumers' economic interests.

(11) The high level of convergence achieved by the approximation of national provisions through this Directive creates a high common level of consumer protection. This Directive establishes a single general prohibition of those unfair commercial practices distorting consumers' economic behaviour. It also sets rules on aggressive commercial practices, which are currently not regulated at Community level.

(12) Harmonization will considerably increase legal certainty for both consumers and business. Both consumers and business will be able to rely on a single regulatory framework based on clearly defined legal concepts regulating all aspects of unfair commercial practices across the EU. The effect will be to eliminate the barriers stemming from the fragmentation of the rules on unfair commercial practices harming consumer economic interests and to enable the internal market to be achieved in this area.

(13) In order to achieve the Community's objectives through the removal of internal market barriers, it is necessary to replace Member States' existing, divergent general clauses and legal principles. The single, common general prohibition established by this Directive therefore covers unfair commercial practices distorting consumers' economic behaviour. In order to support consumer confidence the general prohibition should apply equally to unfair commercial practices which occur outside any contractual relationship between a trader and a consumer or following the conclusion of a contract and during its execution. The general prohibition is elaborated by rules on the two types of commercial practices which are by far the most common, namely misleading commercial practices and aggressive commercial practices.

(14) It is desirable that misleading commercial practices cover those practices, including misleading advertising, which by deceiving the consumer prevent him from making an informed and thus efficient choice. In conformity with the laws and practices of Member States on misleading advertising, this Directive classifies

misleading practices into misleading actions and misleading omissions. In respect of omissions, this Directive sets out a limited number of key items of information which the consumer needs to make an informed transactional decision. Such information will not have to be disclosed in all advertisements, but only where the trader makes an invitation to purchase, which is a concept clearly defined in this Directive. The full harmonization approach adopted in this Directive does not preclude the Member States from specifying in national law the main characteristics of particular products such as, for example, collectors' items or electrical goods, the omission of which would be material when an invitation to purchase is made. It is not the intention of this Directive to reduce consumer choice by prohibiting the promotion of products which look similar to other products unless this similarity confuses consumers as to the commercial origin of the product and is therefore misleading. This Directive should be without prejudice to existing Community law which expressly affords Member States the choice between several regulatory options for the protection of consumers in the field of commercial practices. In particular, this Directive should be without prejudice to Article 13(3) of Directive 2002/58/EC of the European Parliament and of the Council of 12 July 2002 concerning the processing of personal data and the protection of privacy in the electronic communications sector.

(15) Where Community law sets out information requirements in relation to commercial communication, advertising and marketing that information is considered as material under this Directive. Member States will be able to retain or add information requirements relating to contract law and having contract law consequences where this is allowed by the minimum clauses in the existing Community law instruments. A non-exhaustive list of such information requirements in the *acquis* is contained in Annex II. Given the full harmonization introduced by this Directive only the information required in Community law is considered as material for the purpose of Article 7(5) thereof. Where Member States have introduced information requirements over and above what is specified in Community law, on the basis of minimum clauses, the omission of that extra information will not constitute a misleading omission under this Directive. By contrast Member States will be able, when allowed by the minimum clauses in Community law, to maintain or introduce more stringent provisions in conformity with Community law so as to ensure a higher level of protection of consumers' individual contractual rights.

(16) The provisions on aggressive commercial practices should cover those practices which significantly impair the consumer's freedom of choice. Those are practices using harassment, coercion, including the use of physical force, and undue influence.

(17) It is desirable that those commercial practices which are in all circumstances unfair be identified to provide greater legal certainty. Annex I therefore contains the full list of all such practices. These are the only commercial practices which can be deemed to be unfair without a case-by-case assessment against the provisions of Articles 5 to 9. The list may only be modified by revision of the Directive.

(18) It is appropriate to protect all consumers from unfair commercial practices; however the Court of Justice has found it necessary in adjudicating on advertising cases since the enactment of Directive 84/450/EEC to examine the effect on a notional, typical consumer. In line with the principle of proportionality, and to permit the effective application of the protections contained in it, this Directive takes as a benchmark the average consumer, who is reasonably well informed and reasonably observant and circumspect, taking into account social, cultural and linguistic factors, as interpreted by the Court of Justice, but also contains provisions aimed at preventing the exploitation of consumers whose characteristics make them particularly vulnerable to unfair commercial practices. Where a commercial practice is specifically aimed at a particular group of consumers, such as

children, it is desirable that the impact of the commercial practice be assessed from the perspective of the average member of that group. It is therefore appropriate to include in the list of practices which are in all circumstances unfair a provision which, without imposing an outright ban on advertising directed at children, protects them from direct exhortations to purchase. The average consumer test is not a statistical test. National courts and authorities will have to exercise their own faculty of judgement, having regard to the case-law of the Court of Justice, to determine the typical reaction of the average consumer in a given case.

(19)   Where certain characteristics such as age, physical or mental infirmity or credulity make consumers particularly susceptible to a commercial practice or to the underlying product and the economic behaviour only of such consumers is likely to be distorted by the practice in a way that the trader can reasonably foresee, it is appropriate to ensure that they are adequately protected by assessing the practice from the perspective of the average member of that group.

(20)   It is appropriate to provide a role for codes of conduct, which enable traders to apply the principles of this Directive effectively in specific economic fields. In sectors where there are specific mandatory requirements regulating the behaviour of traders, it is appropriate that these will also provide evidence as to the requirements of professional diligence in that sector. The control exercised by code owners at national or Community level to eliminate unfair commercial practices may avoid the need for recourse to administrative or judicial action and should therefore be encouraged. With the aim of pursuing a high level of consumer protection, consumers' organisations could be informed and involved in the drafting of codes of conduct.

(21)   Persons or organisations regarded under national law as having a legitimate interest in the matter must have legal remedies for initiating proceedings against unfair commercial practices, either before a court or before an administrative authority which is competent to decide upon complaints or to initiate appropriate legal proceedings. While it is for national law to determine the burden of proof, it is appropriate to enable courts and administrative authorities to require traders to produce evidence as to the accuracy of factual claims they have made.

(22)   It is necessary that Member States lay down penalties for infringements of the provisions of this Directive and they must ensure that these are enforced. The penalties must be effective, proportionate and dissuasive.

(23)   Since the objectives of this Directive, namely to eliminate the barriers to the functioning of the internal market represented by national laws on unfair commercial practices and to provide a high common level of consumer protection, by approximating the laws, regulations and administrative provisions of the Member States on unfair commercial practices, cannot be sufficiently achieved by the Member States and can therefore be better achieved at Community level, the Community may adopt measures, in accordance with the principle of subsidiarity as set out in Article 5 of the Treaty. In accordance with the principle of proportionality, as set out in that Article, this Directive does not go beyond what is necessary in order to eliminate the internal market barriers and achieve a high common level of consumer protection.

(24)   It is appropriate to review this Directive to ensure that barriers to the internal market have been addressed and a high level of consumer protection achieved. The review could lead to a Commission proposal to amend this Directive, which may include a limited extension to the derogation in 11.6.2005 EN Official Journal of the European Union L 149/25 Article 3(5), and/or amendments to other consumer protection legislation reflecting the Commission's Consumer Policy Strategy commitment to review the existing *acquis* in order to achieve a high, common level of consumer protection.

(25)   This Directive respects the fundamental rights and observes the principles recognised in particular by the Charter of Fundamental Rights of the European Union, HAVE ADOPTED THIS DIRECTIVE:

CHAPTER 1
GENERAL PROVISIONS

Article 1: Purpose
The purpose of this Directive is to contribute to the proper functioning of the internal market and achieve a high level of consumer protection by approximating the laws, regulations and administrative provisions of the Member States on unfair commercial practices harming consumers' economic interests.

Article 2: Definitions
For the purposes of this Directive:
   (a) 'consumer' means any natural person who, in commercial practices covered by this Directive, is acting for purposes which are outside his trade, business, craft or profession;
   (b) 'trader' means any natural or legal person who, in commercial practices covered by this Directive, is acting for purposes relating to his trade, business, craft or profession and anyone acting in the name of or on behalf of a trader;
   (c) 'product' means any goods or service including immovable property, rights and obligations;
   (d) 'business-to-consumer commercial practices' (hereinafter also referred to as commercial practices) means any act, omission, course of conduct or representation, commercial communication including advertising and marketing, by a trader, directly connected with the promotion, sale or supply of a product to consumers;
   (e) 'to materially distort the economic behaviour of consumers' means using a commercial practice to appreciably impair the consumer's ability to make an informed decision, thereby causing the consumer to take a transactional decision that he would not have taken otherwise;
   (f) 'code of conduct' means an agreement or set of rules not imposed by law, regulation or administrative provision of a Member State which defines the behaviour of traders who undertake to be bound by the code in relation to one or more particular commercial practices or business sectors;
   (g) 'code owner' means any entity, including a trader or group of traders, which is responsible for the formulation and revision of a code of conduct and/or for monitoring compliance with the code by those who have undertaken to be bound by it;
   (h) 'professional diligence' means the standard of special skill and care which a trader may reasonably be expected to exercise towards consumers, commensurate with honest market practice and/or the general principle of good faith in the trader's field of activity;
   (i) 'invitation to purchase' means a commercial communication which indicates characteristics of the product and the price in a way appropriate to the means of the commercial communication used and thereby enables the consumer to make a purchase;
   (j) 'undue influence' means exploiting a position of power in relation to the consumer so as to apply pressure, even without using or threatening to use physical force, in a way which significantly limits the consumer's ability to make an informed decision;
   (k) 'transactional decision' means any decision taken by a consumer concerning whether, how and on what terms to purchase, make payment in whole or in part for, retain or dispose of a product or to exercise a contractual right in relation to the product, whether the consumer decides to act or to refrain from acting;
   (l) 'regulated profession' means a professional activity or a group of professional activities, access to which or the pursuit of which, or one of the modes of pursuing which, is conditional, directly or indirectly, upon possession of specific professional qualifications, pursuant to laws, regulations or administrative provisions.

Article 3: Scope

1   This Directive shall apply to unfair business-to-consumer commercial practices, as laid down in Article 5, before, during and after a commercial transaction in relation to a product.

2   This Directive is without prejudice to contract law and, in particular, to the rules on the validity, formation or effect of a contract.

3   This Directive is without prejudice to Community or national rules relating to the health and safety aspects of products.

4   In the case of conflict between the provisions of this Directive and other Community rules regulating specific aspects of unfair commercial practices, the latter shall prevail and apply to those specific aspects.

5   For a period of six years from 12 June 2007, Member States shall be able to continue to apply national provisions within the field approximated by this Directive which are more restrictive or prescriptive than this Directive and which implement directives containing minimum harmonisation clauses. These measures must be essential to ensure that consumers are adequately protected against unfair commercial practices and must be proportionate to the attainment of this objective. The review referred to in Article 18 may, if considered appropriate, include a proposal to prolong this derogation for a further limited period.

6   Member States shall notify the Commission without delay of any national provisions applied on the basis of paragraph 5.

7   This Directive is without prejudice to the rules determining the jurisdiction of the courts.

8   This Directive is without prejudice to any conditions of establishment or of authorisation regimes, or to the deontological codes of conduct or other specific rules governing regulated professions in order to uphold high standards of integrity on the part of the professional, which Member States may, in conformity with Community law, impose on professionals.

9   In relation to 'financial services', as defined in Directive 2002/65/EC, and immovable property, Member States may impose requirements which are more restrictive or prescriptive than this Directive in the field which it approximates.

10   This Directive shall not apply to the application of the laws, regulations and administrative provisions of Member States relating to the certification and indication of the standard of fineness of articles of precious metal.

Article 4: Internal market

Member States shall neither restrict the freedom to provide services nor restrict the free movement of goods for reasons falling within the field approximated by this Directive.

CHAPTER 2
UNFAIR COMMERCIAL PRACTICES

Article 5: Prohibition of unfair commercial practices

1   Unfair commercial practices shall be prohibited.

2   A commercial practice shall be unfair if:

(a)   it is contrary to the requirements of professional diligence, and

(b)   it materially distorts or is likely to materially distort the economic behaviour with regard to the product of the average consumer whom it reaches or to whom it is addressed, or of the average member of the group when a commercial practice is directed to a particular group of consumers.

3   Commercial practices which are likely to materially distort the economic behaviour only of a clearly identifiable group of consumers who are particularly vulnerable to the practice or the underlying product because of their mental or physical infirmity, age or credulity in a way which the trader could reasonably be expected to foresee, shall be assessed from the perspective of the average member of that group. This is without prejudice to the common and legitimate advertising

practice of making exaggerated statements or statements which are not meant to be taken literally.

4   In particular, commercial practices shall be unfair which:
   (a)   are misleading as set out in Articles 6 and 7, or
   (b)   are aggressive as set out in Articles 8 and 9.

5   Annex I contains the list of those commercial practices which shall in all circumstances be regarded as unfair. The same single list shall apply in all Member States and may only be modified by revision of this Directive.

Section 1   Misleading commercial practices

Article 6: Misleading actions

1   A commercial practice shall be regarded as misleading if it contains false information and is therefore untruthful or in any way, including overall presentation, deceives or is likely to deceive the average consumer, even if the information is factually correct, in relation to one or more of the following elements, and in either case causes or is likely to cause him to take a transactional decision that he would not have taken otherwise:
   (a)   the existence or nature of the product;
   (b)   the main characteristics of the product, such as its availability, benefits, risks, execution, composition, accessories, aftersale customer assistance and complaint handling, method and date of manufacture or provision, delivery, fitness for purpose, usage, quantity, specification, geographical or commercial origin or the results to be expected from its use, or the results and material features of tests or checks carried out on the product;
   (c)   the extent of the trader's commitments, the motives for the commercial practice and the nature of the sales process, any statement or symbol in relation to direct or indirect sponsorship or approval of the trader or the product;
   (d)   the price or the manner in which the price is calculated, or the existence of a specific price advantage;
   (e)   the need for a service, part, replacement or repair;
   (f)   the nature, attributes and rights of the trader or his agent, such as his identity and assets, his qualifications, status, approval, affiliation or connection and ownership of industrial, commercial or intellectual property rights or his awards and distinctions;
   (g)   the consumer's rights, including the right to replacement or reimbursement under Directive 1999/44/EC of the European Parliament and of the Council of 25 May 1999 on certain aspects of the sale of consumer goods and associated guarantees, or the risks he may face.

2   A commercial practice shall also be regarded as misleading if, in its factual context, taking account of all its features and circumstances, it causes or is likely to cause the average consumer to take a transactional decision that he would not have taken otherwise, and it involves:
   (a)   any marketing of a product, including comparative advertising, which creates confusion with any products, trade marks, trade names or other distinguishing marks of a competitor;
   (b)   non-compliance by the trader with commitments contained in codes of conduct by which the trader has undertaken to be bound, where:
      (i)   the commitment is not aspirational but is firm and is capable of being verified, and
      (ii)   the trader indicates in a commercial practice that he is bound by the code.

Article 7: Misleading omissions

1   A commercial practice shall be regarded as misleading if, in its factual context, taking account of all its features and circumstances and the limitations of the communication medium, it omits material information that the average consumer

needs, according to the context, to take an informed transactional decision and thereby causes or is likely to cause the average consumer to take a transactional decision that he would not have take otherwise.

2   It shall also be regarded as a misleading omission when, taking account of the matters described in paragraph 1, a trader hides or provides in an unclear, unintelligible, ambiguous or untimely manner such material information as referred to in that paragraph or fails to identify the commercial intent of the commercial practice if not already apparent from the context, and where, in either case, this causes or is likely to cause the average consumer to take a transactional decision that he would not have taken otherwise.

3   Where the medium used to communicate the commercial practice imposes limitations of space or time, these limitations and any measures taken by the trader to make the information available to consumers by other means shall be taken into account in deciding whether information has been omitted.

4   In the case of an invitation to purchase, the following information shall be regarded as material, if not already apparent from the context:

(a)   the main characteristics of the product, to an extent appropriate to the medium and the product;

(b)   the geographical address and the identity of the trader, such as his trading name and, where applicable, the geographical address and the identity of the trader on whose behalf he is acting;

(c)   the price inclusive of taxes, or where the nature of the product means that the price cannot reasonably be calculated in advance, the manner in which the price is calculated, as well as, where appropriate, all additional freight, delivery or postal charges or, where these charges cannot reasonably be calculated in advance, the fact that such additional charges may be payable;

(d)   the arrangements for payment, delivery, performance and the complaint handling policy, if they depart from the requirements of professional diligence;

(e)   for products and transactions involving a right of withdrawal or cancellation, the existence of such a right.

5   Information requirements established by Community law in relation to commercial communication including advertising or marketing, a non-exhaustive list of which is contained in Annex II, shall be regarded as material.

Section 2. Aggressive commercial practices

Article 8: Aggressive commercial practices
A commercial practice shall be regarded as aggressive if, in its factual context, taking account of all its features and circumstances, by harassment, coercion, including the use of physical force, or undue influence, it significantly impairs or is likely to significantly impair the average consumer's freedom of choice or conduct with regard to the product and thereby causes him or is likely to cause him to take a transactional decision that he would not have taken otherwise.

Article 9: Use of harassment, coercion and undue influence
In determining whether a commercial practice uses harassment, coercion, including the use of physical force, or undue influence, account shall be taken of:

(a)   its timing, location, nature or persistence;

(b)   the use of threatening or abusive language or behaviour;

(c)   the exploitation by the trader of any specific misfortune or circumstance of such gravity as to impair the consumer's judgement, of which the trader is aware, to influence the consumer's decision with regard to the product;

(d)   any onerous or disproportionate non-contractual barriers imposed by the trader where a consumer wishes to exercise rights under the contract, including rights to terminate a contract or to switch to another product or another trader;

(e)   any threat to take any action that cannot legally be taken.

CHAPTER 3
CODES OF CONDUCT

Article 10: Codes of conduct
This Directive does not exclude the control, which Member States may encourage, of unfair commercial practices by code owners and recourse to such bodies by the persons or organizations referred to in Article 11 if proceedings before such bodies are in addition to the court or administrative proceedings referred to in that Article.

Recourse to such control bodies shall never be deemed the equivalent of foregoing a means of judicial or administrative recourse as provided for in Article 11.

CHAPTER 4
FINAL PROVISIONS

Article 11: Enforcement
1   Member States shall ensure that adequate and effective means exist to combat unfair commercial practices in order to enforce compliance with the provisions of this Directive in the interest of consumers.

Such means shall include legal provisions under which persons or organisations regarded under national law as having a legitimate interest in combating unfair commercial practices, including competitors, may:

(a)   take legal action against such unfair commercial practices; and/or

(b)   bring such unfair commercial practices before an administrative authority competent either to decide on complaints or to initiate appropriate legal proceedings.

It shall be for each Member State to decide which of these facilities shall be available and whether to enable the courts or administrative authorities to require prior recourse to other established means of dealing with complaints, including those referred to in Article 10. These facilities shall be available regardless of whether the consumers affected are in the territory of the Member State where the trader is located or in another Member State.

It shall be for each Member State to decide:

(a)   whether these legal facilities may be directed separately or jointly against a number of traders from the same economic sector; and

(b)   whether these legal facilities may be directed against a code owner where the relevant code promotes non-compliance with legal requirements.

2   Under the legal provisions referred to in paragraph 1, Member States shall confer upon the courts or administrative authorities powers enabling them, in cases where they deem such measures to be necessary taking into account all the interests involved and in particular the public interest:

(a)   to order the cessation of, or to institute appropriate legal proceedings for an order for the cessation of, unfair commercial practices; or

(b)   if the unfair commercial practice has not yet been carried out but is imminent, to order the prohibition of the practice, or to institute appropriate legal proceedings for an order for the prohibition of the practice,

even without proof of actual loss or damage or of intention or negligence on the part of the trader.

Member States shall also make provision for the measures referred to in the first subparagraph to be taken under an accelerated procedure:

—either with interim effect, or

—with definitive effect,

on the understanding that it is for each Member State to decide which of the two options to select.

Furthermore, Member States may confer upon the courts or administrative authorities powers enabling them, with a view to eliminating the continuing effects of unfair commercial practices the cessation of which has been ordered by a final decision:

(a)   to require publication of that decision in full or in part and in such form as they deem adequate;

(b)   to require in addition the publication of a corrective statement.

3   The administrative authorities referred to in paragraph 1 must:

(a)   be composed so as not to cast doubt on their impartiality;

(b)   have adequate powers, where they decide on complaints, to monitor and enforce the observance of their decisions effectively;

(c)   normally give reasons for their decisions.

Where the powers referred to in paragraph 2 are exercised exclusively by an administrative authority, reasons for its decisions shall always be given. Furthermore, in this case, provision must be made for procedures whereby improper or unreasonable exercise of its powers by the administrative authority or improper or unreasonable failure to exercise the said powers can be the subject of judicial review.

Article 12: Courts and administrative authorities: substantiation of claims

Member States shall confer upon the courts or administrative authorities powers enabling them in the civil or administrative proceedings provided for in Article 11:

(a)   to require the trader to furnish evidence as to the accuracy of factual claims in relation to a commercial practice if, taking into account the legitimate interest of the trader and any other party to the proceedings, such a requirement appears appropriate on the basis of the circumstances of the particular case; and

(b)   to consider factual claims as inaccurate if the evidence demanded in accordance with (a) is not furnished or is deemed insufficient by the court or administrative authority.

Article 13: Penalties

Member States shall lay down penalties for infringements of national provisions adopted in application of this Directive and shall take all necessary measures to ensure that these are enforced.

These penalties must be effective, proportionate and dissuasive.

[*Articles 14–16 are amending provisions*]

Article 17: Information

Member States shall take appropriate measures to inform consumers of the national law transposing this Directive and shall, where appropriate, encourage traders and code owners to inform consumers of their codes of conduct.

Article 18: Review

1   By 12 June 2011 the Commission shall submit to the European Parliament and the Council a comprehensive report on the application of this Directive, in particular of Articles 3(9) and 4 and Annex I, on the scope for further harmonisation and simplification of Community law relating to consumer protection, and, having regard to Article 3(5), on any measures that need to be taken at Community level to ensure that appropriate levels of consumer protection are maintained. The report shall be accompanied, if necessary, by a proposal to revise this Directive or other relevant parts of Community law.

2   The European Parliament and the Council shall endeavour to act, in accordance with the Treaty, within two years of the presentation by the Commission of any proposal submitted under paragraph 1.

Article 19: Transposition

Member States shall adopt and publish the laws, regulations and administrative provisions necessary to comply with this Directive by 12 June 2007. They shall forthwith inform the Commission thereof and inform the Commission of any subsequent amendments without delay.

They shall apply those measures by 12 December 2007. When Member States adopt those measures, they shall contain a reference to this Directive or be accompanied by such a reference on the occasion of their official publication. Member States shall determine how such reference is to be made.

Article 20: Entry into force
This Directive shall enter into force on the day following its publication in the *Official Journal of the European Union*.

Article 21: Addressees
This Directive is addressed to the Member States.

ANNEX I
COMMERCIAL PRACTICES WHICH ARE IN ALL CIRCUMSTANCES
CONSIDERED UNFAIR

Misleading commercial practices
   1   Claiming to be a signatory to a code of conduct when the trader is not.
   2   Displaying a trust mark, quality mark or equivalent without having obtained the necessary authorisation.
   3   Claiming that a code of conduct has an endorsement from a public or other body which it does not have.
   4   Claiming that a trader (including his commercial practices) or a product has been approved, endorsed or authorised by a public or private body when he/it has not or making such a claim without complying with the terms of the approval, endorsement or authorisation.
   5   Making an invitation to purchase products at a specified price without disclosing the existence of any reasonable grounds the trader may have for believing that he will not be able to offer for supply or to procure another trader to supply, those products or equivalent products at that price for a period that is, and in quantities that are, reasonable having regard to the product, the scale of advertising of the product and the price offered (bait advertising).
   6   Making an invitation to purchase products at a specified price and then:
       (a)   refusing to show the advertised item to consumers; or
       (b)   refusing to take orders for it or deliver it within a reasonable time; or
       (c)   demonstrating a defective sample of it,
with the intention of promoting a different product (bait and switch)
   7   Falsely stating that a product will only be available for a very limited time, or that it will only be available on particular terms for a very limited time, in order to elicit an immediate decision and deprive consumers of sufficient opportunity or time to make an informed choice.
   8   Undertaking to provide after-sales service to consumers with whom the trader has communicated prior to a transaction in a language which is not an official language of the Member State where the trader is located and then making such service available only in another language without clearly disclosing this to the consumer before the consumer is committed to the transaction.
   9   Stating or otherwise creating the impression that a product can legally be sold when it cannot.
   10   Presenting rights given to consumers in law as a distinctive feature of the trader's offer.
   11   Using editorial content in the media to promote a product where a trader has paid for the promotion without making that clear in the content or by images or sounds clearly identifiable by the consumer (advertorial). This is without prejudice to Council Directive 89/552/EEC.
   12   Making a materially inaccurate claim concerning the nature and extent of the risk to the personal security of the consumer or his family if the consumer does not purchase the product.

13 Promoting a product similar to a product made by a particular manufacturer in such a manner as deliberately to mislead the consumer into believing that the product is made by that same manufacturer when it is not.

14 Establishing, operating or promoting a pyramid promotional scheme where a consumer gives consideration for the opportunity to receive compensation that is derived primarily from the introduction of other consumers into the scheme rather than from the sale or consumption of products.

15 Claiming that the trader is about to cease trading or move premises when he is not.

16 Claiming that products are able to facilitate winning in games of chance.

17 Falsely claiming that a product is able to cure illnesses, dysfunction or malformations.

18 Passing on materially inaccurate information on market conditions or on the possibility of finding the product with the intention of inducing the consumer to acquire the product at conditions less favourable than normal market conditions.

19 Claiming in a commercial practice to offer a competition or prize promotion without awarding the prizes described or a reasonable equivalent.

20 Describing a product as 'gratis', 'free', 'without charge' or similar if the consumer has to pay anything other than the unavoidable cost of responding to the commercial practice and collecting or paying for delivery of the item.

21 Including in marketing material an invoice or similar document seeking payment which gives the consumer the impression that he has already ordered the marketed product when he has not.

22 Falsely claiming or creating the impression that the trader is not acting for purposes relating to his trade, business, craft or profession, or falsely representing oneself as a consumer.

23 Creating the false impression that after-sales service in relation to a product is available in a Member State other than the one in which the product is sold.

Aggressive commercial practices

24 Creating the impression that the consumer cannot leave the premises until a contract is formed.

25 Conducting personal visits to the consumer's home ignoring the consumer's request to leave or not to return except in circumstances and to the extent justified, under national law, to enforce a contractual obligation.

26 Making persistent and unwanted solicitations by telephone, fax, e-mail or other remote media except in circumstances and to the extent justified under national law to enforce a contractual obligation. This is without prejudice to Article 10 of Directive 97/7/EC and Directives 95/46/EC and 2002/58/EC.

27 Requiring a consumer who wishes to claim on an insurance policy to produce documents which could not reasonably be considered relevant as to whether the claim was valid, or failing systematically to respond to pertinent correspondence, in order to dissuade a consumer from exercising his contractual rights.

28 Including in an advertisement a direct exhortation to children to buy advertised products or persuade their parents or other adults to buy advertised products for them. This provision is without prejudice to Article 16 of Directive 89/552/EEC on television broadcasting.

29 Demanding immediate or deferred payment for or the return or safekeeping of products supplied by the trader, but not solicited by the consumer except where the product is a substitute supplied in conformity with Article 7(3) of Directive 97/7/EC (inertia selling).

30 Explicitly informing a consumer that if he does not buy the product or service, the trader's job or livelihood will be in jeopardy.

31 Creating the false impression that the consumer has already won, will win, or will on doing a particular act win, a prize or other equivalent benefit, when in fact either:

—there is no prize or other equivalent benefit, or
—taking any action in relation to claiming the prize or other equivalent benefit is subject to the consumer paying money or incurring a cost.

ANNEX II
COMMUNITY LAW PROVISIONS SETTING OUT RULES FOR ADVERTISING AND COMMERCIAL COMMUNICATION

Articles 4 and 5 of Directive 97/7/EC

Article 3 of Council Directive 90/314/EEC of 13 June 1990 on package travel, package holidays and package tours

Article 3(3) of Directive 94/47/EC of the European Parliament and of the Council of 26 October 1994 on the protection of purchasers in respect of certain aspects of contracts relating to the purchase of a right to use immovable properties on a timeshare basis

Article 3(4) of Directive 98/6/EC of the European Parliament and of the Council of 16 February 1998 on consumer protection in the indication of the prices of products offered to consumers

Articles 86 to 100 of Directive 2001/83/EC of the European Parliament and of the Council of 6 November 2001 on the Community code relating to medicinal products for human use

Articles 5 and 6 of Directive 2000/31/EC of the European Parliament and of the Council of 8 June 2000 on certain legal aspects of information society services, in particular electronic commerce, in the Internal Market (Directive on electronic commerce)

Article 1(d) of Directive 98/7/EC of the European Parliament and of the Council of 16 February 1998 amending Council Directive 87/102/EEC for the approximation of the laws, regulations and administrative provisions of the Member States concerning consumer credit

Articles 3 and 4 of Directive 2002/65/EC

Article 1(9) of Directive 2001/107/EC of the European Parliament and of the Council of 21 January 2002 amending Council Directive 85/611/EEC on the coordination of laws, regulations and administrative provisions relating to undertakings for collective investment in transferable securities (UCITS) with a view to regulating management companies and simplified prospectuses

Articles 12 and 13 of Directive 2002/92/EC of the European Parliament and of the Council of 9 December 2002 on insurance mediation

Article 36 of Directive 2002/83/EC of the European Parliament and of the Council of 5 November 2002 concerning life assurance

Article 19 of Directive 2004/39/EC of the European Parliament and of the Council of 21 April 2004 on markets in financial instruments

Articles 31 and 43 of Council Directive 92/49/EEC of 18 June 1992 on the coordination of laws, regulations and administrative provisions relating to direct insurance other than life assurance (third non-life insurance Directive)

Articles 5, 7 and 8 of Directive 2003/71/EC of the European Parliament and of the Council of 4 November 2003 on the prospectus to be published when securities are offered to the public or admitted to trading

INDEX

Accountant in Bankruptcy
accounting for intromissions, 257–58
appointment, 234
directions to, 236
discharge, 289–90
duty, 297
fees, 296
performance of functions, 235–36
supervisory functions, 234–35
Applicable law
1996 Accession Convention, 358–59
Conventions, the—
  force of law, 345
  interpretation, 345–46
  meaning, 345
  revision, 346
Brussels Protocol, 355–57
Funchal Convention, 357–58
Luxembourg Convention, 354–55
Rome Convention, 347–54
Attachment
appeals against valuation, 386
articles belonging to third party, 391–92
articles in common ownership, 392–93
articles kept in dwellinghouse—
  appeals, 399
  exceptional attachment order, 395
  exceptional circumstances, 396
  power of entry, 396
  redemption, 398
  release from attachment, 398
  removal of attached articles, 397–98
  restrictions on attachment, 395
  sentimental value, 397
  unlawful acts, 396–97
  valuation, 397
articles outwith dwellinghouse—
  mobile homes, 382–83
  power of entry and valuation, 383
  procedure, 382–83
  redemption, 383–84
  removal and auction, 384
  report of attachment, 383
ascription of sums recovered, 394
auction of attached articles—
  alteration of arrangements, 388–89
  cancellation, 389
  disposal of proceeds, 389–90
  notice of auction, 388
  outwith dwellinghouse, 384
  procedure, 389
  report of, 390–91
competent, when not, 382
duration, 386–87
exempt articles, 382
expenses, 393
fees payable, 394
invalidity and cessation, 388

Attachment—contd
meaning, 381–82
non-essential assets, 400–01
perishable articles, 384
presumption of ownership, 382
recovery of expenses, 393–94
second attachment, 387–88
sequestration for rent, 399–400
termination, 393
unlawful acts, 384–85
vehicle, release of, 386

Bankruptcy
Accountant in Bankruptcy, *see Accountant in Bankruptcy*
administration by permanent trustee—
  contractual powers, 278
  debtor's family home, 276–77
  management and realisation of estate, 274–75
  money received by, 278
  protection of rights—
    civil partner, of, 277–78
    spouse, of, 277
  taking possession of estate, 274
adjudication of claims, 281–82
apparent insolvency, 240–41
arbitration and compromise, 294
arrestments and poindings, 314–15
'associate', meaning, 300
commissioners, 260–61
composition, discharge on, 288, 307–11
co-obligants, liabilities and rights, 291
co-operation between debtor and
  permanent trustee, 293–94
creditor's claim—
  aliment and periodical allowance, 301–02
  amount generally, 301
  debts depending on contingency, 302
  debts due under composition contracts, 302
  partnership debts, 303
  secured debts, 302–03
creditor's entitlement to vote, 282–83
creditor's oath, 244
debtor's discharge, 286–88
distribution of estate—
  accounting periods, 284–85
  intromissions with, 285–86
  order of priority, 283–84
Edinburgh Gazette, 297
examination of debtor—
  ancillary provisions, 279
  conduct of, 280
  private examination, 278
  public examination, 279
extortionate credit transactions, 292

INDEX OF STATUTORY MATERIALS